Microsoft®

Visual Basic 2008

for Windows, Mobile, Web, Office, and Database Applications
Comprehensive

Gary B. Shelly

Corinne Hoisington
Central Virginia Community College

Shelly Cashman Series®
An imprint of Course Technology, Cengage Learning

COURSE TECHNOLOGY
CENGAGE Learning™

Australia • Brazil • Japan • Korea • Mexico • Singapore • Spain • United Kingdom • United States

COURSE TECHNOLOGY
CENGAGE Learning

Microsoft® Visual Basic 2008 for Windows, Mobile, Web, Office, and Database Applications: Comprehensive
Gary B. Shelly
Corinne Hoisington

Vice President, Publisher: Nicole Pinard

Senior Product Manager: Reed Curry

Developmental Editor: Lisa Ruffolo

Product Manager: Klenda Martinez

Associate Product Manager: Jon Farnham

Editorial Assistant: Lauren Brody

Director of Marketing: Cheryl Costantini

Marketing Manager: Tristen Kendall

Marketing Coordinator: Julie Schuster

Production Director: Patty Stephan

Content Project Manager: Heather Furrow

Art Director: Marissa Falco

Cover designer: Joel Sadagursky

Cover photo: Jon Chomitz

Text designer: Pre-Press PMG

Manufacturing Coordinator: Julio Esperas

Copyeditor: Gary Spahl

Proofreader: Harold Johnson

Compositor: Pre-Press PMG

For product information and technology assistance, contact us at
Cengage Learning Customer & Sales Support, 1-800-354-9706
For permission to use material from this text or product,
submit all requests online at **cengage.com/permissions**
Further permissions questions can be emailed to
permissionrequest@cengage.com

ISBN-13: 978-1-4239-2716-7

ISBN-10: 1-4239-2716-8

Course Technology
25 Thomson Place
Boston, MA 02210
USA

Cengage Learning is a leading provider of customized learning solutions with office locations around the globe, including Singapore, the United Kingdom, Australia, Mexico, Brazil, and Japan. Locate your local office at:
international.cengage.com/region

Cengage Learning products are represented in Canada by Nelson Education, Ltd.

For your lifelong learning solutions, visit **course.cengage.com**
Purchase any of our products at your local college store or at our preferred online store **www.ichapters.com**

Printed in the United States of America
1 2 3 4 5 6 7 12 11 10 09 08

CONTENTS

CHAPTER 4   # Variables and Arithmetic Operations

CHAPTER 5 Mobile Applications Using Decision Structures

CHAPTER 6   Loop Structures

CHAPTER 7   Creating Web Applications

CHAPTER 8

Using Procedures and Exception Handling

CHAPTER 9   Using Arrays and File Handling

CHAPTER 10   Incorporating Databases with ADO.NET

CHAPTER 11   Multiple Classes and Inheritance

CHAPTER 12   Cell Phone Applications and Web Services

ENRICHMENT CHAPTER Visual Studio Tools for Office

PREFACE

The Shelly Cashman Series® offers the finest textbooks in computer education. This *Microsoft Visual Basic 2008* book utilizes an innovative step-by-step pedagogy, which integrates demonstrations of professional-quality programs with in-depth discussions of programming concepts and techniques and opportunities for hands-on practice and reinforcement. The popular **Guided Program Development** section supports students as they work independently to create useful, realistic, and appealing applications, building their confidence and skills while guiding them to select appropriate Visual Basic 2008 programming methods. Online Reinforcement boxes direct students to online videos that show how to perform a series of steps. Other marginal elements, such as In the Real World boxes, provide expert tips to add interest and depth to topics. A robust and varied collection of exercises, including a series of practical case-based programming projects, ensures students gain the knowledge and expertise they need to succeed when developing professional programs.

Visual Basic 2008 builds on the features of Visual Basic 2005, which was the most significant upgrade of this programming language since the introduction of Visual Basic. Some of the major enhancements to Visual Basic 2008 include rapid application development tools, new compiler features, improved IntelliSense features to increase productivity, and a more helpful debugging experience. Using Visual Basic 2008, you can design, create, and deploy Windows, Mobile, Web, Database, and Office applications. Visual Studio 2008 includes several productivity enhancements including IntelliSense tools, new and updated project types, improved ClickOnce deployment, greater XML integration, expanded sample applications, and more.

Objectives of this Textbook

Microsoft Visual Basic 2008 for Windows, Mobile, Web, Office, and Database Applications: Comprehensive is intended for a year-long course that instructs students in the correct ways to design and write programs using Visual Basic 2008. The goal of this text is to provide a rigorous and comprehensive course in computer programming for students with little or no previous programming experience. The objectives of this book are:

► To teach the fundamentals of the Microsoft Visual Basic 2008 programming language
► To understand and apply graphical user interface design principles
► To emphasize the development cycle when creating applications, which mirrors the same approach that professional developers use
► To illustrate well-written and readable programs using a disciplined coding style, including documentation and indentation standards
► To create Visual Basic applications that deploy on multiple platforms such as hand-held computers, cell phones, Web pages, Windows, and Office environments

- ▶ To demonstrate how to implement logic involving sequence, selection, and repetition using Visual Basic 2008
- ▶ To write useful, well-designed programs for personal computers and handheld computers that solve practical business problems
- ▶ To create appealing, interactive Web applications that can be delivered and executed on the Internet
- ▶ To organize complex programs by using procedures and to anticipate and prevent errors by managing exceptions
- ▶ To produce sophisticated, professional programs by using arrays and files that handle data and to make programs more robust by defining classes and using the power of inheritance
- ▶ To encourage independent study and help those who are working on their own in a distance education environment

The Shelly Cashman Approach

Features of this *Microsoft Visual Basic 2008* book include:

- ▶ **Realistic, Up-to-Date Applications** Each programming chapter focuses on building a sample project, a complete, useful application that showcases Visual Basic 2008 features and the latest technology, including mobile computing devices.

- ▶ **Guided Steps to Encourage Independence** After observing how a professional developer would build the chapter project and exploring related programming concepts and Visual Basic 2008 techniques, students create the sample application on their own in the Guided Program Development section. This step-by-step section provides enough guidance for students to work independently, with Hint Screens that verify students are performing the tasks correctly.

- ▶ **More Than Step-By-Step** Each chapter offers clear, thorough discussions of the programming concepts students need to understand to build the sample application. Important Visual Basic 2008 design and programming features are also highlighted, including time-saving techniques such as using IntelliSense, code snippets, and the Toolbox. As appropriate, students design and prepare for applications the way professional developers do — by creating or analyzing requirements documents, use case definitions, and event planning documents.

- ▶ **Online Reinforcement Boxes** The Online Reinforcement boxes send students to the Online Companion at scsite.com/vb2008 to watch videos illustrating each step in the chapter project. Students can refer to the Online Reinforcement boxes when they work through or review the chapter, watching videos as they prepare to create the chapter application on their own.

- ▶ **Heads Up Boxes** Heads Up boxes appear in the margin to give advice for following best programming practices and tips about alternative ways of completing the same task.

▶ **In the Real World Boxes** This marginal feature provides insight into how developers use Visual Basic tools or programming techniques to save time or enhance professional development projects.

▶ **Watch Out For Boxes** These boxes explain how to avoid common pitfalls when using a particular command, programming structure, or technique.

Organization of this Textbook

Microsoft Visual Basic 2008 for Windows, Mobile, Web, Office, and Database Applications: Comprehensive provides detailed instructions on how to use Visual Basic 2008 to build authentic, effective, and appealing applications for Microsoft Windows personal computers and mobile devices. The material is divided into thirteen chapters and five appendices as follows:

Chapter 1 — Introduction to Visual Basic 2008 Programming Chapter 1 provides an overview of programming with Visual Basic 2008. The chapter defines a computer program, describes the role of a developer in creating computer programs, and discusses event-driven programs that have a graphical user interface (GUI). The chapter also explains the roles of input, processing, output, and data when running a program on a computer; examines the basic arithmetic and logical operations a program can perform; and explores the use of databases and computer programming languages in general. Finally, the chapter introduces Visual Studio 2008 and the .NET 3.5 Framework, including the .NET class libraries and related features, and surveys the types of Visual Basic 2008 applications.

Chapter 2 — Program and Graphical User Interface Design Chapter 2 introduces students to the major elements of the Visual Studio 2008 integrated development environment (IDE) while designing a graphical user interface mock-up. Topics include opening Visual Studio 2008, creating a Windows Forms Application project, adding objects to a Windows form, assigning properties to objects, aligning objects on the Windows form, and saving Visual Basic projects. The chapter also discusses how to apply GUI design principles and examines the first two phases of the program development life cycle (PDLC).

Chapter 3 — Program Design and Coding Chapter 3 provides students with the skills and knowledge necessary to complete phases 2, 3, and 4 of the PDLC by enhancing a GUI mock-up, designing program processing objects, and coding a program. Topics include using IntelliSense when writing code and enhancing a Visual Basic 2008 form by changing the BackColor property of an object and displaying images. This chapter also explains how to enter Visual Basic 2008 code, correct errors, and run a completed program. Finally, the chapter discusses the value of creating an event planning document.

Chapter 4 — Variables and Arithmetic Operations Chapter 4 introduces variables and arithmetic operations used in the coding of a Visual Basic application. The chapter provides in-depth coverage of declaring variables, gathering input for an application, differentiating data types, performing mathematical calculations, and understanding the proper scope of variables. The chapter also shows how to use various types of TextBox objects.

Chapter 5 — Mobile Applications Using Decision Structures

Chapter 5 begins by exploring handheld computers and programs written for these devices to manage personal information and perform sophisticated business tasks. It then explains how to create a Visual Basic 2008 mobile application to run on a handheld computer. This mobile application uses decision structures to take different actions depending on the user's input. Topics include using If...Then statements, If...Then...Else statements, nested If statements, logical operators, and Case statements. The chapter also explores how to use the Panel object, place RadioButton objects, display a message box, insert code snippets, and test input to ensure it is valid.

Chapter 6 — Loop Structures

Chapter 6 presents another type of fundamental programming structure — the repetition structure, including Do While, Do Until, For...Next, For Each...Next, and While...End While loops. Topics include repeating a process using the For...Next and Do loops; priming a loop; creating a nested loop; selecting the best type of loop; avoiding infinite loops; validating data; and understanding compound operators, counters, and accumulators. The chapter also shows how to insert a MenuStrip object, use the InputBox function, display data using the ListBox object, debug programs using DataTips at breakpoints, and publish a finished application using ClickOnce technology.

Chapter 7 — Creating Web Applications

Chapter 7 explains how to create a Web application by building an interactive Web form, a page displayed in a browser that requests data from users. The chapter examines ASP.NET 3.5 technology and explores tools that help to create appealing, useful Web applications, including Web form properties, CheckBox, DropDownList, and Calendar objects, and custom tables. The chapter also explains how to validate data on Web forms and format text using the HTML <br> tag and the string manipulation properties and procedures in the Visual Basic String class. Because the layout from Expression Studio is now integrated in Visual Studio 2008, you can open a Web application in either Visual Basic 2008 or in Expression Web.

Chapter 8 — Using Procedures and Exception Handling

Chapter 8 focuses on using procedures to organize complex programs and handling exceptions to prevent errors. The chapter begins by demonstrating how to create a splash screen that is displayed as a program loads. It then explores how to organize long, complex programs into procedures, including Sub and Function procedures, and shows how to pass an argument to a procedure by value and by reference, how to code a Function procedure to return a value, and how to create a class-level variable. The chapter concludes by discussing exception handling and using Try-Catch blocks to detect errors and take corrective actions.

Chapter 9 — Using Arrays and File Handling

Chapter 9 explains how to develop applications that maintain data for later processing, including sorting, calculating, and displaying the data. The chapter project demonstrates an application that reads data from a file, displays the data in a ComboBox object, and then uses the data in calculations. This chapter also shows how to create a Windows application that uses more than one form.

Chapter 10 — Incorporating Databases with ADO.NET

Chapter 10 examines databases and explores the ADO.NET 3.5 technology. The chapter discusses how to take advantage of the data access technology of ADO.NET 3.5 to connect to databases and update, add, and delete data and retrieve database information for viewing and decision making. The chapter project demonstrates how to create a professional application that connects to a Microsoft Office Access database, temporarily stores data from the database, and lets users add, select, and delete records.

Chapter 11 — Multiple Classes and Inheritance

Chapter 11 explores the advanced topics of defining classes, using inheritance, and designing a three-tier structure for a program. The chapter begins by introducing the three-tier program structure and thoroughly defining classes and the object-oriented programming concepts related to classes. The chapter project shows how to create a class, instantiate an object, write a class constructor, call a procedure in a separate class, and use inheritance to code a base class and a subclass. Other topics include calling procedures in a base and subclass, writing overridable and overrides procedures, and creating and writing a comma-delimited text file.

Chapter 12 — Cell Phone Applications and Web Services

Chapter 12 explains how to create programs for Windows-based cell phones called smartphones, and how to include Web services in Windows applications. The chapter includes two projects, one that demonstrates creating a Smartphone application and the other introducing Web services, software available on the Internet that uses WSDL operations to share information. Finally, the chapter discusses how to use the new Microsoft Reports feature, a component of Visual Studio 2008, to create business reports.

Enrichment Chapter — Visual Studio Tools for Office

The Enrichment Chapter explains how to create applications that run in Microsoft Office 2007 documents by using Visual Studio Tools for Office (VSTO). The chapter introduces VSTO and shows how to use its tools to develop an Office template. The chapter also explains how to add a DateTimePicker object and ActionsPane object to a VSTO application, format text and pictures using a Word table, and use the PMT function and Math class to perform calculations.

Appendices

This book concludes with five appendices. Appendix A explains the purpose of Unicode and provides a table listing Unicode characters and their equivalents. Appendix B examines the My namespace element of Visual Basic 2008 in detail. Appendix C describes how to use the Help feature in Visual Basic 2008. Appendix D lists the common data types used in Visual Basic 2008, including the recommended naming convention for the three-character prefix preceding variable names. Appendix E explains how to use Language Integrated Query (LINQ), a new feature provided with Visual Basic 2008 and .NET Framework 3.5 that lets you query SQL databases from a Visual Basic application.

End-of-Chapter Activities

A notable strength of this *Microsoft Visual Basic 2008* book is the extensive student activities at the end of each chapter. Well-structured student activities can make the difference between students merely participating in a class and retaining the information they learn. These end-of-chapter activities include the following:

▶ **Learn It Online** The Learn It Online section directs students to Web-based exercises, which are fun, interactive activities that include chapter reinforcement (true/false, multiple choice, and short answer questions), practice tests, and a crossword puzzle challenge to augment concepts, key terms, techniques, and other material in the chapter.

▶ **Knowledge Check** The Knowledge Check section includes short exercises and review questions that reinforce concepts and provide opportunities to practice skills.

▶ **Debugging Exercises** In these exercises, students examine short code samples to identify errors and solve programming problems.

▶ **Program Analysis** The Program Analysis exercises let students apply their knowledge of Visual Basic 2008 and programming techniques. In some exercises, students write programming statements that meet a practical goal or solve a problem. In other exercises, students analyze code samples and identify the output.

▶ **Case Programming Assignments** Nine programming assignments for each chapter challenge students to create applications using the skills learned in the chapter. Each assignment presents a realistic business scenario and requires students to create programs of varying difficulty.

• Easiest: The first three assignments provide most of the program design information, such as a requirements document and use case definition, for a business application. Students design an application, create an event planning document, and write the code for the application.

•• Intermediate: The next three assignments provide some of the program design information, such as a requirements document. Students create other design documents, such as a use case definition and event planning document, and then build the user interface and code the application.

••• Challenging: The final three assignments provide only a description of a business problem, and students create all the design documents, design the user interface, and code the application.

To the Instructor

Each chapter in this book focuses on a realistic, appealing Visual Basic 2008 application. A chapter begins with a completed application, which you can run to demonstrate how it works, the tasks it performs, and the problems it solves. The chapter introduction also identifies the application's users and their requirements, such as running the program on a handheld computer or validating input data.

The steps in the next section of a chapter show how to create the user interface for the application. You can perform these steps in class — each step clearly explains an action, describes the results, and includes a figure showing the results, with call-outs directing your attention to key elements on the screen. Some marginal features, such as the Heads Up boxes, provide additional tips for completing the steps. The Online Reinforcement boxes direct students to videos that replay the steps, which is especially helpful for review and for distance learning students.

This section also explains the Visual Basic 2008 tools and properties needed to understand and create the user interface. For example, while placing a text box in an application, the chapter describes the purpose of a text box and why you should set its maximum and minimum size. You can discuss these ideas and strategies, and then continue your demonstration to show students how to apply them to the chapter application.

After completing the user interface, the chapter explores the programming concepts students should understand to create the application, such as proper syntax, variables, data types, conditional statements, and loops. This section uses the same types of steps, figures, and marginal features to demonstrate how to enter code to complete and test the application.

To prepare students for building the application on their own, the chapter next considers the program design and logic by examining planning documents:

▶ *Requirements document* — The requirements document identifies the purpose, procedures, and calculations of the program, and specifies details such as the application title, restrictions, and comments that help to explain the program.
▶ *Use case definition* — The use case definition describes what the user does and how the program responds to each action.
▶ *Event planning document* — The event planning document lists each object in the user interface that causes an event, the action the user takes to trigger the event, and the event processing that must occur.

You can discuss these documents in class and encourage students to review them as they create a program, reinforcing how professional developers create applications in the modern workplace.

In the innovative Guided Program Development section students work on their own to create the chapter application. They complete the tasks within each numbered step, referring to Hint Screens when they need a reminder about how to perform a step or which method to use. Many tasks reference figures shown earlier in the chapter. Students can refer to these figures for further help — they show exactly how to use a particular technique for completing a task. Steps end with a results figure, which illustrates how the application should look if students performed the tasks correctly. To reinforce how students learned the chapter material, the Guided Program Development section also focuses first on designing the user interface and then on coding the application. A complete program listing appears at the end of this section, which students can use to check their work.

At the end of each chapter, you'll find plenty of activities that provide review, practice, and challenge for your students, including a summary table that lists skills and corresponding figures and videos, descriptions of online learning opportunities, and exercises ranging from short, focused review questions to assignments requiring complete programs and related planning documents. You can assign the Learn It Online, Knowledge Check, Debugging Exercises, and Program Analysis activities as necessary to reinforce and assess learning. Depending on the expertise of your class, you can assign the Case Programming Assignments as independent projects, selecting one from each level of difficulty (easiest, intermediate, and challenging) or concentrating on the level that is most appropriate for your class.

SHELLY CASHMAN SERIES INSTRUCTOR RESOURCES

The Shelly Cashman Series is dedicated to providing you with all of the tools you need to make your class a success. Information on all supplementary materials is available through your Course Technology representative or by calling one of the following telephone numbers: Colleges, Universities, Continuing Education Departments, Post-Secondary Vocational Schools, Career Colleges, Business, Industry, Government, Trade, Retailer, Wholesaler, Library and Resellers, 800-648-7450; K-12 Schools, Secondary Vocational Schools, Adult Education and School Districts, 800-824-5179; Canada, 800-268-2222.

Instructor Resources

The Instructor Resources disc (ISBN 1-4239-2717-6) includes teaching and testing aids, including the following resources:

► **Instructor's Manual** The Instructor's Manual consists of Microsoft Word files, which include chapter objectives, lecture notes, teaching tips, classroom activities, lab activities, quick quizzes, figures and boxed elements summarized in the chapters, and a glossary page. The new format of the Instructor's Manual will allow you to map through every chapter easily.

► **Syllabus** Sample syllabi, which can be customized easily to a course, cover policies, class and lab assignments, exams, and procedural information.

► **Figure Files** Illustrations for every figure in the textbook are available in electronic form. Use this ancillary to present a slide show in lecture or to print transparencies for use in lecture with an overhead projector. If you have a personal computer and LCD device, this ancillary can be an effective tool for presenting lectures.

► **PowerPoint Presentation** PowerPoint Presentations is a multimedia lecture presentation system that provides slides for each chapter. Presentations are based on chapter objectives. Use this presentation system to present well-organized lectures that are both interesting and knowledge based. PowerPoint Presentations provides consistent coverage at schools that use multiple lecturers.

► **Solutions to Exercises** Solutions are included for the Knowledge Check, Chapter Reinforcement, Debugging Exercises, Program Analysis, and for the Easiest and Intermediate Case Programming Assignments.

► **Test Bank & Test Engine** In the ExamView test bank, you will find a variety of question types (40 multiple-choice, 25 true/false, 20 completion, 5 modified multiple-choice, 5 modified true/false and 10 matching), including Critical Thinking questions (3 essays and 2 cases with 2 questions each). Each test bank contains 112 questions for every chapter with page number references, and when appropriate, figure references. A version of the test bank you can print also is included. The test bank comes with a copy of the test engine, ExamView, the ultimate tool for your objective-based testing needs. ExamView is a state-of-the-art test builder that is easy to use. ExamView enables you to create paper-, LAN-, or Web-based tests from test banks designed specifically for your Course Technology textbook Utilize the ultra-efficient QuickTest Wizard to create tests in less than five minutes by taking advantage of Course Technology's question banks, or customize your own exams from scratch.

▶ **Printed Test Bank** A version of the test bank you can print also is included.

▶ **Data Files for Students** All the files that are required by students to complete the exercises and programs are included. You can distribute the files on the Instructor Resources disc to your students over a network, or you can have them follow the instructions on the inside back cover of this book to obtain a copy of the data files.

▶ **Additional Activities for Students** These additional activities consist of Chapter Reinforcement Exercises, which are true/false, multiple-choice, and short answer questions that help students gain confidence in the material learned.

Software Bundling Opportunities

Microsoft Visual Basic 2008 texts can be bundled with Microsoft® Visual Studio 2008 Professional Edition, 90-day trial. This DVD of Visual Studio 2008 Professional Edition is a comprehensive set of tools that accelerates the process of turning the developer's vision into reality. Visual Studio 2008 Professional Edition was engineered to support development project that target the Web (including ASP.NET AJAX), Windows Vista, Windows Server 2008, the 2007 Microsoft Office system, SQL Server 2008, and Windows Mobile devices.

About Our Covers

Learning styles of students have changed, but the Shelly Cashman Series' dedication to their success has remained steadfast for over 30 years. We are committed to continually updating our approach and content to reflect the way today's students learn and experience new technology.

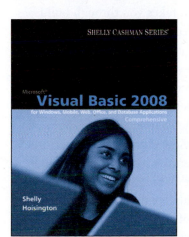

This focus on the user is reflected in our bold cover design, which features photographs of real students using the Shelly Cashman Series in their courses. Each book features a different user, reflecting the many ages, experiences, and backgrounds of all of the students learning with our books. When you use the Shelly Cashman Series, you can be assured that you are learning computer skills using the most effective courseware available.

We would like to thank the administration and faculty at the participating schools for their help in making our vision a reality. Most of all, we'd like to thank the wonderful students from all over the world who learn from our text and appear on our covers.

To the Student

GETTING THE MOST OUT OF YOUR BOOK

Welcome to *Microsoft Visual Basic 2008 for Windows, Mobile, Web, Office, and Database Applications: Comprehensive*. To save yourself time and gain a better understanding of the elements in this text, spend a few minutes reviewing the descriptions and figures in this section.

Introduction and Initial Chapter Figures   Each chapter presents a programming project and shows the solution in the first figure of the chapter. The introduction and initial chapter figure let you see first-hand how your finished product will look and illustrate your programming goals.

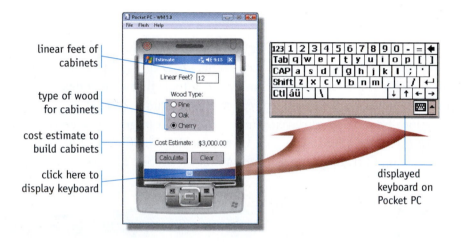

linear feet of cabinets

type of wood for cabinets

cost estimate to build cabinets

click here to display keyboard

displayed keyboard on Pocket PC

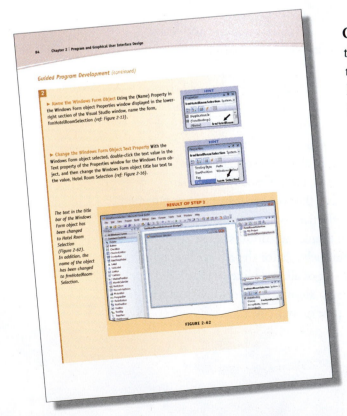

Guided Program Development   After reading through the chapter and observing how to create the chapter application, the Guided Program Development section takes you through building the chapter project step by step. As you perform each task, you can refer to Hint Screens that remind you how to complete a step or use a particular technique. If you need further help, some steps include references to figures shown earlier in the chapter — you can revisit these figures to review exactly how to perform a task. Each step ends with a results figure, so you can make sure your application is on the right track. A complete program listing also appears at the end of the Guided Program Development section, which you can use to check your work.

Visual Basic 2008 Online Reinforcement Videos   The first of their kind, the Shelly Cashman Online Companion provides video reenactments of every new Visual Basic process that is introduced in each chapter. These animated tutorials provide a Web-based visual instruction on how to complete a Visual Basic task. You can watch these videos to learn how to perform the steps shown in the book or to review the steps and techniques.

To access the Online Reinforcement videos, you need only a computer with an Internet connection. Use your Web browser to visit *www.scsite.com/vb2008*, click the link to the appropriate chapter, and then click the link to a figure to play a video.

Marginal Boxes   Marginal elements include Heads Up boxes, which offer tips and programming advice, In the Real World boxes, which indicate how professional developers use Visual Basic 2008 tools, and Watch Out For boxes, which identify common errors and explain how to avoid them.

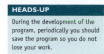

HEADS-UP
During the development of the program, periodically you should save the program so you do not lose your work.

IN THE REAL WORLD
Program names can contain spaces and some special characters, but by convention most developers use a name with no spaces and capital letters at the beginning of each word in the name.

WATCH OUT FOR
You should give a name to every object but each name must be unique. You cannot use the same name for two different objects in the same program.

Learn It Online   Reinforcing what you're learning is a snap with the Chapter Reinforcement exercises, Practice Test, and other learning games on the Learn It Online page of the Online Companion. Visit scsite.com/vb2008 to access these fun, interactive exercises.

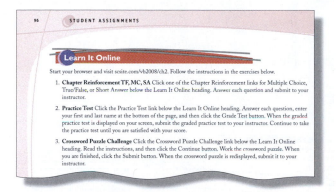

Knowledge Check   To verify you've learned the essential information in the chapter, you can work through the Knowledge Check exercises. Use these short exercises to test your knowledge of concepts and tools and to prepare for longer programming assignments.

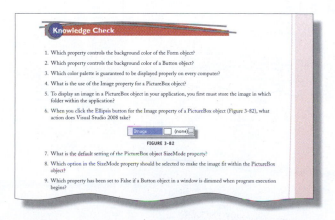

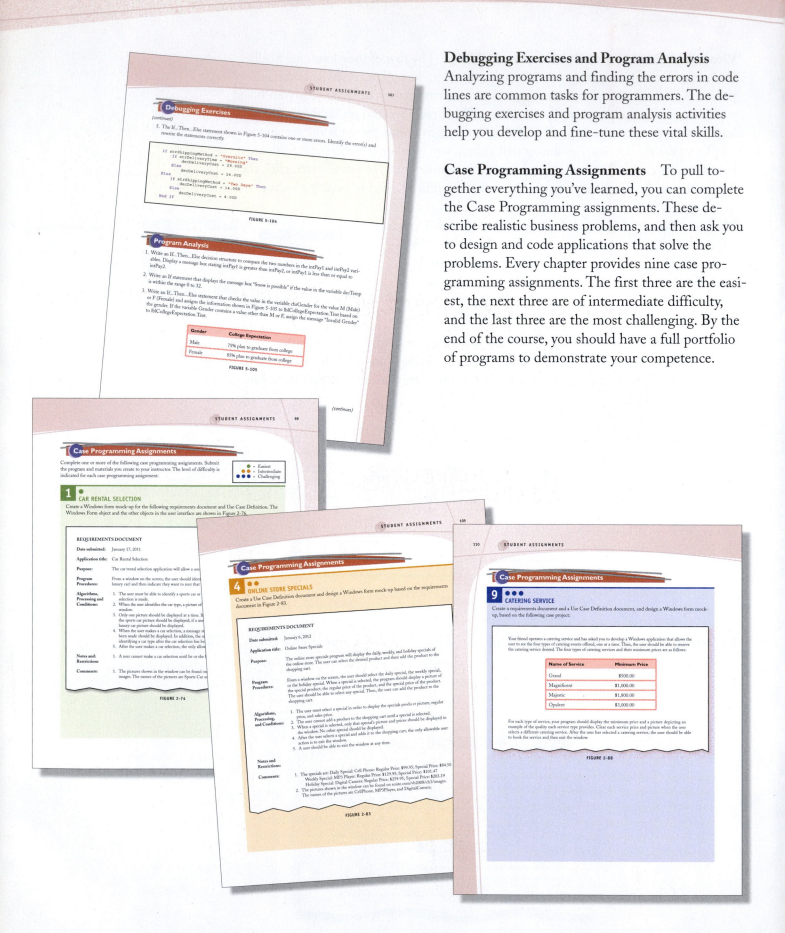

Debugging Exercises and Program Analysis
Analyzing programs and finding the errors in code lines are common tasks for programmers. The debugging exercises and program analysis activities help you develop and fine-tune these vital skills.

Case Programming Assignments   To pull together everything you've learned, you can complete the Case Programming assignments. These describe realistic business problems, and then ask you to design and code applications that solve the problems. Every chapter provides nine case programming assignments. The first three are the easiest, the next three are of intermediate difficulty, and the last three are the most challenging. By the end of the course, you should have a full portfolio of programs to demonstrate your competence.

CHAPTER ONE

Introduction to Visual Basic 2008 Programming

OBJECTIVES

You will have mastered the material in this chapter when you can:

- Understand software and computer programs

- State the role of a developer in creating computer programs

- Specify the use of a graphical user interface and describe an event-driven program

- Specify the roles of input, processing, output, and data when running a program on a computer

- Describe the arithmetic operations a computer program can perform

- Explain the logical operations a computer program can perform

- Define and describe the use of a database

- Identify the use of a computer programming language in general, and Visual Basic 2008 in particular

- Explain the use of Visual Studio 2008 when developing Visual Basic 2008 programs

- Specify the programming languages available for use with Visual Studio 2008

- Explain the .NET 3.5 Framework

- Explain RAD

- Describe classes, objects, and the .NET Framework 3.5 class libraries

- Explain ADO.NET 3.5, ASP.NET 3.5, MSIL, and CLR

- Specify the types of Visual Basic 2008 applications

Introduction

A computer is an electronic device that completes tasks, under the direction of a sequence of instructions, to produce useful results for people. The set of instructions that directs a computer to perform tasks is called **computer software**, or a **computer program**.

When controlled by programs, computers can accomplish a wide variety of activities. For example, computers can interpret and display a page from the World Wide Web, compute and write payroll checks for millions of employees, display video and play audio from the Web or from digital video discs (DVDs), create messages on mobile phones and personal digital assistants (PDAs), and be used to write a book (Figure 1-1).

Two vital components of a computer must interact with one another regardless of the activity performed. These components are computer hardware and computer software. **Computer hardware** is the physical equipment associated with a computer.

FIGURE 1-1

FIGURE 1-2

This includes the keyboard, mouse, monitor, central processing unit, random access memory (RAM), hard disk, DVD drive, printer, and other devices (Figure 1-2).

Computer software, or a computer program, is a set of electronic instructions that directs the computer hardware to perform tasks such as displaying a character on the monitor when a key on the keyboard is pressed, adding an employee's regular time pay and overtime pay to calculate the total pay for that employee, or displaying a picture from an attached digital camera on the monitor. Computer hardware cannot perform any activity unless an instruction directs that hardware to act. In most cases, the instruction is part of a computer program a developer has created to carry out the desired activity.

A third component required by most computer programs is data. **Data** includes words, numbers, videos, graphics, and sound that programs manipulate, display, and otherwise process. The basic function of many programs is to accept some form of data (sometimes called **input data**), manipulate the data in some manner (sometimes called **processing**), and create some form of data usable by people or other computers (sometimes called **output data**, or **information**) (Figure 1-3). In short, many computer programs perform the following general steps: accept input data, process the data, and create output data. The data that acts as input to a program, the processing that occurs, and the output that is created varies with the requirements of the program.

FIGURE 1-3

In order for the computer to execute a program, or carry out the instructions in the program, both the program and the data must be placed in the computer's **random access memory (RAM)** (Figure 1-4). Once the program is stored in RAM, the **central processing unit (CPU)** of the computer can access the instructions in the program and the data in RAM to perform activities as directed by the program.

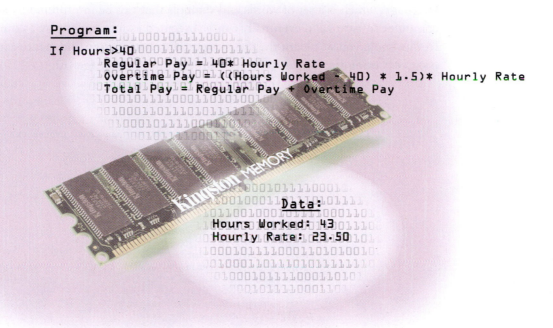

```
Program:
If Hours>40
        Regular Pay = 40* Hourly Rate
        Overtime Pay = ((Hours Worked - 40) * 1.5)* Hourly Rate
        Total Pay = Regular Pay + Overtime Pay
```

```
Data:
Hours Worked: 43
Hourly Rate: 23.50
```

FIGURE 1-4

One other activity that the hardware and software typically carry out is saving both the data and the software. **Saving**, or **storing**, data refers to placing the data or software electronically on a storage medium such as hard disk or Universal Serial Bus (USB) drive. The software and data are stored so they can be accessed and retrieved at a later time. Stored data is said to be **persistent** because it remains available even after the computer power is turned off.

COMPUTER PROGRAMMERS AND DEVELOPERS

A computer program is designed and developed by people known as **computer programmers**, or developers. **Developers** are people skilled in designing computer programs and creating them using programming languages. Some computer programs are small and relatively simple, but often a problem to be solved on a computer requires more than one program. Thus, you will find that developers speak of developing an **application**, which can mean several computer programs working together to solve a problem.

When designing a program, developers analyze the problem and determine how to solve it. Once a computer program or an application is designed, the developer must create it so it can be executed on a computer. In most cases, the developer creates the program by writing the code for the program(s) using a **programming language**, which is a set of words and symbols that can be interpreted by special computer software and eventually can be executed as instructions by a computer. In this book, you will learn the skills required to both design and create computer programs using the Visual Basic 2008 programming language (Figure 1-5).

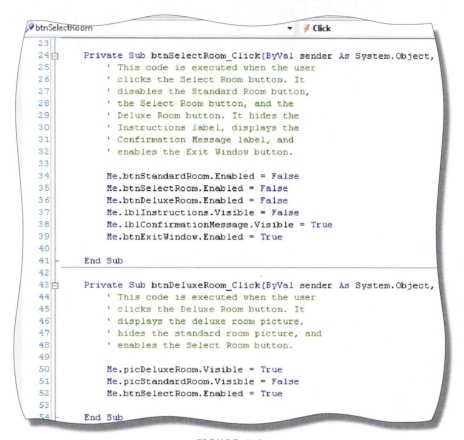

```
btnSelectRoom                                          ▼    ⚡ Click
23
24      Private Sub btnSelectRoom_Click(ByVal sender As System.Object,
25          ' This code is executed when the user
26          ' clicks the Select Room button. It
27          ' disables the Standard Room button,
28          ' the Select Room button, and the
29          ' Deluxe Room button. It hides the
30          ' Instructions label, displays the
31          ' Confirmation Message label, and
32          ' enables the Exit Window button.
33
34          Me.btnStandardRoom.Enabled = False
35          Me.btnSelectRoom.Enabled = False
36          Me.btnDeluxeRoom.Enabled = False
37          Me.lblInstructions.Visible = False
38          Me.lblConfirmationMessage.Visible = True
39          Me.btnExitWindow.Enabled = True
40
41      End Sub
42
43      Private Sub btnDeluxeRoom_Click(ByVal sender As System.Object,
44          ' This code is executed when the user
45          ' clicks the Deluxe Room button. It
46          ' displays the deluxe room picture,
47          ' hides the standard room picture, and
48          ' enables the Select Room button.
49
50          Me.picDeluxeRoom.Visible = True
51          Me.picStandardRoom.Visible = False
52          Me.btnSelectRoom.Enabled = True
53
54      End Sub
```

FIGURE 1-5

EVENT-DRIVEN COMPUTER PROGRAMS WITH A GRAPHICAL USER INTERFACE

Most Visual Basic 2008 programs are **event-driven programs** that communicate with the user through a **graphical user interface (GUI)**. The GUI usually consists of a window, containing a variety of objects, that can be displayed on various devices such as a computer monitor, a PDA screen, or a mobile phone screen. Users employ the GUI objects to select options, enter data, and cause events to occur. An **event** means the user has initiated an action that causes the program to perform the type of processing called for by the user's action. For example, a user might enter data into the program, and then click a button. Clicking the button triggers an event, resulting in the program performing the processing called for by clicking the button.

To illustrate the process of entering data when using a graphical user interface and then triggering an event, consider the window shown in Figure 1-6.

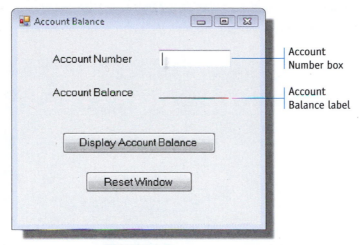

FIGURE 1-6

This window is part of a banking application. When it is displayed, the teller at the bank or a user over the World Wide Web can enter an account number. Then the user can click the Display Account Balance button (that is, trigger an event) and the program displays the account balance. The following steps illustrate the dynamics of the interaction with the program:

STEP 1   The user enters the account number in the Account Number box.

The account number the user entered is displayed in the Account Number text box (Figure 1-7). The Account Balance label displays no information.

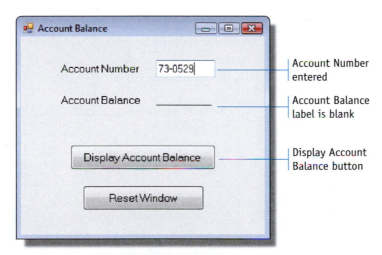

FIGURE 1-7

STEP 2   The user clicks the Display Account Balance button.

The account balance is displayed in the Account Balance label (Figure 1-8). Clicking the Display Account Balance button triggered the event that caused the program to determine and display the account balance based on data that the program accessed.

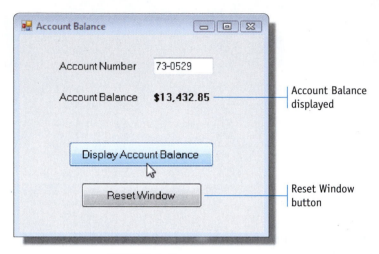

FIGURE 1-8

STEP 3   The user clicks the Reset Window button to clear the text box and the label and prepare the user interface for the next account number.

Clicking the Reset Window button triggers another event. The text box and the label are cleared and the insertion point is placed in the Account Number text box (Figure 1-9). The user now can enter a new account number to determine the account balance.

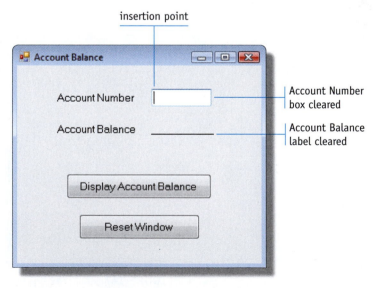

FIGURE 1-9

The events in the previous example consist of clicking the Display Account Balance button and clicking the Reset Window button. The program reacts to the events by performing specific actions (showing the account balance and resetting the text box and label). This is an example of an event-driven program. The Visual Basic developer designs the user interface and writes the program code that performs these event-triggered actions.

Basic Program Operations

All programs, regardless of their size and complexity, execute only a few fundamental operations: input, output, basic arithmetic operations, and logical operations. These operations can be combined in millions of different ways to accomplish the tasks required of the program. The following pages describe these basic program operations.

INPUT OPERATION

As noted previously, a fundamental operation in most computer programs is the user entering data. For instance, in Figure 1-7 on page 7, the user entered the account number. The steps that occurred when the user typed the account number are shown in Figure 1-10.

Step 1:
User types the account number on the keyboard.

Step 2:
The data is stored in RAM.

Step 3:
Data is displayed on the computer screen.

FIGURE 1-10

In Figure 1-10, the banking computer program that processes the user's request is stored in RAM. The data entered by the user also is stored in RAM. Depending on the input device, data entered might also be displayed on the computer screen. The input device used to enter data depends on the application. In Figure 1-10, the user typed the account number on a keyboard. Other applications might allow data to be entered with a scanner, digital camera, video camera, mouse, or other device. In each instance, the data is stored in the computer's RAM. When the data is in RAM, instructions in the program can operate on the data.

OUTPUT OPERATION

The second basic program operation is creating output, or information. As you learned previously, a major goal of most computer programs is to create output data, or information, that is useful to people. In Figure 1-8 on page 8, the information requested of the program is the account balance. The process of creating output is shown in Figure 1-11.

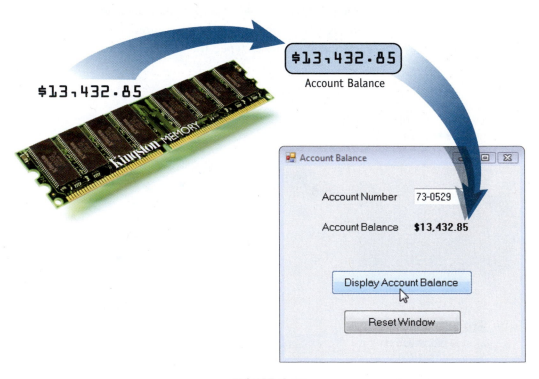

FIGURE 1-11

As always, the program must be stored in RAM to control the operations of the computer. In the example, the program sets the text of the Account Balance label equal to the account balance, and then displays it on the screen.

As with input operations, a variety of devices can present output. Common devices, in addition to computer monitors, include printers, PDA screens, and Smartphone screens (Figure 1-12).

smartphone

PDA

printer

FIGURE 1-12

Input and output operations are basic to all computers and most computer programs. It is the ability to enter data, process it in some manner, and create output in the form of useful information that makes a computer valuable. Understanding the input/output operations is mandatory because they provide the foundation for many of the programs you will write in this text.

BASIC ARITHMETIC OPERATIONS

Once data is stored in main computer memory as a result of the input operation, the program can process it in some manner. In many programs, arithmetic operations (addition, subtraction, multiplication, and division) are performed on numeric data to produce useful output.

Prior to performing arithmetic operations, the numeric data used in calculations must be stored in RAM. Then, program instructions that also are stored in RAM can direct the computer to add, subtract, multiply, or divide the numbers. The answers from arithmetic operations can be used in additional calculations and processing, stored for future use, and used as output from the program.

The example in Figure 1-13 illustrates the steps an application performs to calculate an average test score. The average test score is calculated from the three test scores a user enters.

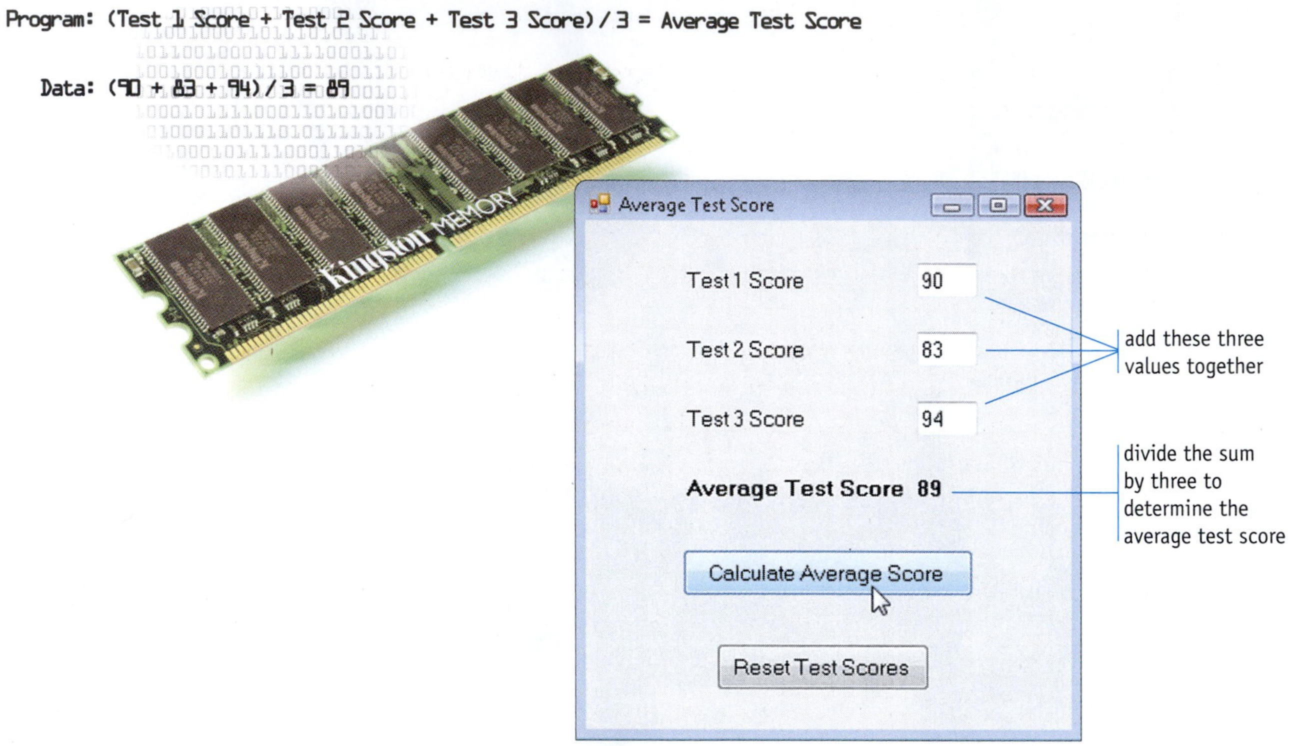

Program: (Test 1 Score + Test 2 Score + Test 3 Score) / 3 = Average Test Score

Data: (90 + 83 + 94) / 3 = 89

Test 1 Score   90
Test 2 Score   83   } add these three values together
Test 3 Score   94

Average Test Score 89   — divide the sum by three to determine the average test score

Calculate Average Score

Reset Test Scores

FIGURE 1-13

In the example in Figure 1-13, the program adds the three test scores the user enters, and then divides the total by 3 to obtain the average score. As always, both the program and the data required to calculate the average test score must be stored in the computer's RAM. As you can see, when the user enters data in a text box, the data is stored in RAM and is available for arithmetic operations and other operations.

This example demonstrates the three fundamental operations of input (entering the three test scores), processing (calculating the average test score), and output (displaying the average test score). Although most applications are more complex than the one illustrated, the input, process, and output operations often are used; and arithmetic operations commonly are part of the processing step.

LOGICAL OPERATIONS

It is the ability of a computer to perform logical operations that separates it from other types of calculating devices. Computers, through the use of computer programs, can compare numbers, letters of the alphabet, and special characters. Based on the result of the comparison, the program can perform one processing task if the condition tested for is true and another processing task if the condition is not true. Using a program to compare data and perform alternative operations allows the computer to complete sophisticated tasks such as predicting weather, formatting and altering digital photographs, editing digital video, and running high-speed games.

A program can perform the following types of logical operations:

▶ Comparing to determine if two values are equal.
▶ Comparing to determine if one value is greater than another value.
▶ Comparing to determine if one value is less than another value.

Based on the results of these comparisons, the program can direct the computer to take alternative actions.

Comparing — Equal Condition

A program can compare two values stored in RAM to determine whether they are equal. If the values are equal, one set of instructions will be executed; if they are not equal, another set of instructions will be executed.

Comparing to determine if two values are equal requires comparing one value to another. In an application for calculating student tuition, different rates might apply based on the student's residence. If the school is located in Texas, and the student resides in Texas, the tuition per unit is one value; if the student does not reside in Texas, the tuition per unit is another value (Figure 1-14).

BEFORE:

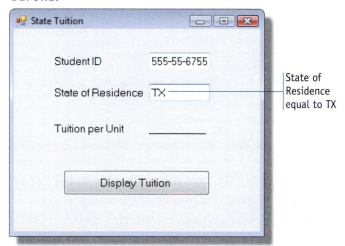

AFTER:

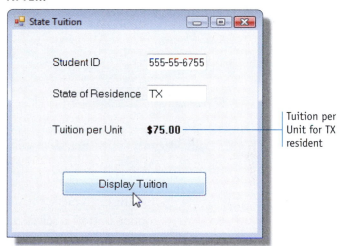

BEFORE:

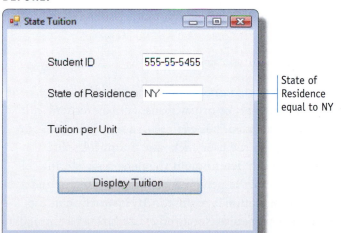

AFTER:

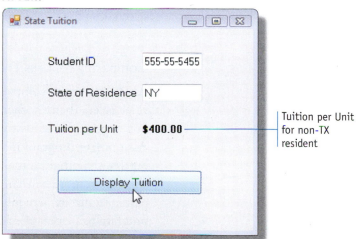

FIGURE 1-14

When the Display Tuition button is clicked and the state is equal to TX, the program displays the in-state tuition per unit. If the state is not equal to TX, the program displays the out-of-state tuition per unit.

Comparing also can be used to determine if a condition is selected. For example, in Figure 1-15, the Campus Parking Fees window contains a Student Name text box that provides space for the student name; and the On-Campus Housing and Off-Campus Housing option buttons, or radio buttons, that allow the user to select either on-campus housing or off-campus housing. When the user clicks the Calculate Parking Fees button, the program displays the appropriate parking fee.

EXAMPLE 1:

On-Campus Housing selected

Parking fee for On-Campus Housing

EXAMPLE 2:

Off-Campus Housing selected

Parking fee for Off-Campus Housing

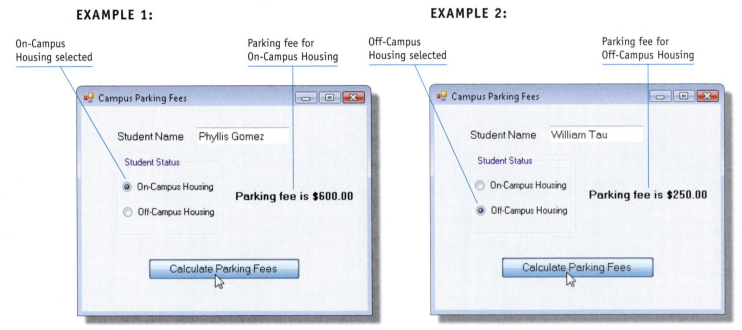

FIGURE 1-15

In Example 1, the user name is Phyllis Gomez and the On-Campus Housing option button is selected. When the user clicks the Calculate Parking Fees button, by comparing the program determines that the On-Campus Housing button is checked. Because it is checked, the result in the comparison is true and the program displays the parking fee for on-campus housing. In Example 2, the Off-Campus Housing button is selected, so the program displays the parking fee for off-campus housing.

Comparing — Less Than Condition

A second type of comparison a computer program can perform is to determine if one value is less than another value. If it is, one set of instructions will be executed; if it is not, another set of instructions will be executed. For example, in the Student Dorm Assignment program in Figure 1-16, when the user clicks the Submit Application button, the program makes a comparison to determine if the person registering for a dorm room is less than 18 years old. If so, the person is considered a minor and a parent signature is required. If not, no signature is required. An instruction in the program to place a check in the Parent Signature Required check box is performed if the age is less than 18, and the instruction is not executed if the age is 18 or more.

BEFORE:

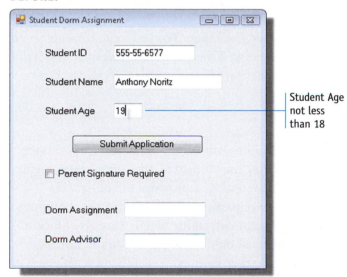

AFTER:

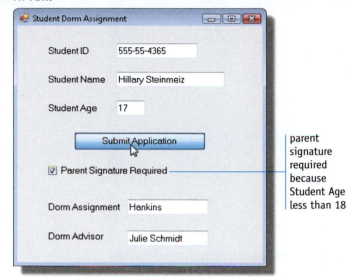

BEFORE:

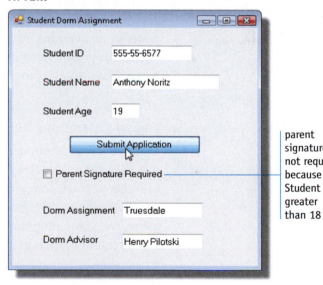

AFTER:

FIGURE 1-16

Comparing — Greater Than Condition

The other condition a computer program can determine is whether one value is greater than another value. For example, in a payroll application, the hours worked by an employee can be compared to the value, 40. If the hours worked are greater than 40, then overtime pay (1.5 times the hourly rate) is calculated for the hours over 40 worked by the employee. If the employee worked 40 hours or less, no overtime pay is calculated. This comparing operation is shown in Figure 1-17 on page 16.

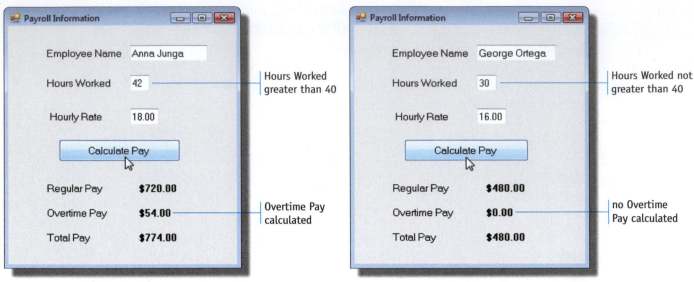

FIGURE 1-17a

FIGURE 1-17b

In Figure 1-17a, the Hours Worked box contains 42, so the program calculates overtime pay for employee Anna Junga. In Figure 1-17b, George Ortega worked 30 hours so no overtime pay is calculated. When the Hours Worked value is greater than 40, the program executes one set of instructions; if the Hours Worked value is not greater than 40, the program executes another set of instructions.

Logical Operations Summary

While the logical operations shown in the previous examples might seem simple, it is the ability of a computer running under the control of a program to perform millions of these comparisons in a single second that provides the processing power of a computer. For example, if you are participating in a road race computer game, the game program uses comparisons to determine where your car is located on the screen, which graphic road elements should be displayed on the screen, where the car you are racing is located, whether your car has collided with your competitor, and so on. All of the many decisions that are required to display your game on the screen and respond to your actions as you participate in the game are made based on comparisons to determine if one value is equal to, greater than, or less than another value. As you can imagine, millions of these decisions must be made every second in order for your high-speed road race game to provide you with an enjoyable experience.

SAVING SOFTWARE AND DATA

When you develop and write a program, the code you write and the other features of the program you create, such as the graphical user interface, must be saved on disk. Then, when you want the program to run, you can cause the program to load into RAM and execute. By saving the program on disk, you can execute the same program many times without rewriting it each time you want to run it.

The program you write, however, also can save data. This data, which can be generated from the processing in the program, can be saved on disk for future use. For example, in a banking application, a customer might open an account. The computer program that is used to open the account saves the customer's information, such as name, address, account number, and account balance, on disk. Later, when the customer makes a deposit or withdrawal, the customer information will be retrieved and modified to reflect the deposit or withdrawal.

In most cases, data such as a customer's name and address is saved in a database. A **database** is a collection of data organized in a manner that allows access, retrieval, and use of that data. Once the data is saved in the database, any programs with permission can reference the data. You will learn more about databases and their use when programming using Visual Basic 2008 later in this textbook.

Visual Basic 2008 and Visual Studio 2008

To write a computer program, a developer uses a programming language. As you learned previously, a programming language is a set of written words, symbols, and codes, with a strict set of usage rules called the language syntax, that a developer uses to communicate instructions to a computer. An example of code statements in the Visual Basic 2008 programming language is shown in Figure 1-18.

```
27          If IsNumeric(Me.txtLinearFeet.Text) Then
28              decLinearFeet = Convert.ToDecimal(Me.txtLinearFeet.Text)
29              ' Is Linear Feet greater than zero
30              If decLinearFeet > 0 Then
31                  ' The radio button selected determines the cost of wood
32                  If Me.radPine.Checked Then
33                      decCostPerFoot = decPineCost
34                  ElseIf Me.radOak.Checked Then
35                      decCostPerFoot = decOakCost
36                  ElseIf Me.radCherry.Checked Then
37                      decCostPerFoot = decCherryCost
38                  End If
39                  ' Calculate and display cost estimate
40                  decCostEstimate = decLinearFeet * decCostPerFoot
41                  Me.lblCostEstimate.Text = decCostEstimate.ToString("C")
42              Else
43                  ' Display MessageBox if a negative value is entered
44                  MessageBox.Show("You entered " & decLinearFeet.ToString() & _
45                      ". Enter a Number Greater Than Zero.", "Input Error")
46                  Me.txtLinearFeet.Text = ""
47                  Me.txtLinearFeet.Focus()
48              End If
49          Else
50              ' Display MessageBox if the value entered is non-numeric
51              MessageBox.Show("Enter the Linear Feet of the Cabinets.", _
52                  "Input Error")
53              Me.txtLinearFeet.Text = ""
54              Me.txtLinearFeet.Focus()
55          End If
56      End Sub
57
```

FIGURE 1-18

HEADS UP

Various versions of Visual Studio 2008 are available, including Visual Studio Standard Edition, Visual Studio Professional Edition, Visual Studio Express Edition, and Visual Studio Team System 2008 Team Foundation Server and Team Suite. The MSDN Academic Alliance allows students to get a free copy of Microsoft Visual Studio Professional 2008 if the school is part of the Academic Alliance. For more information, see the MSDN link at http://msdn2. microsoft.com/en-us/academic/ bb676724.aspx.

Each program statement causes the computer to perform one or more operations. When written, these instructions must conform to the rules of the Visual Basic 2008 language. Coding a program is a precise skill. The developer must follow the **programming rules**, or **syntax**, of the programming language precisely. Even a single coding error can cause a program to execute improperly. Therefore, the developer must pay strict attention to coding an error-free program.

When writing Visual Basic 2008 programs, most developers use a tool called Visual Studio 2008. **Visual Studio 2008** is a software application that allows you, as the developer, to create Visual Basic 2008 programs using code you write, code prewritten by others that can be incorporated into your program, and sophisticated tools that speed up the programming process significantly while resulting in better executing and more reliable programs. In this book, you will be using Visual Studio 2008 to write Visual Basic 2008 programs.

Visual Studio 2008 is a type of **integrated development environment (IDE)**, which provides services and tools that enable a developer to code, test, and implement a single program, or sometimes the series of programs that comprise an application. Visual Studio 2008, which was developed by Microsoft Corporation, works specifically with Visual Basic 2008 as well as other programming languages to develop program code.

After you start the Visual Studio 2008 application, the Visual Studio 2008 window is displayed. In this window, you can develop and write your Visual Basic 2008 program, as shown in Figure 1-19.

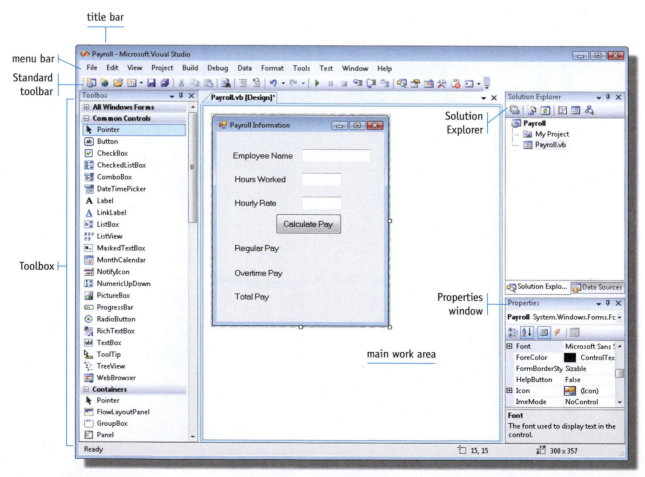

FIGURE 1-19

The following are general guidelines to use this window. In subsequent chapters you will learn to use each of the elements found in the Visual Studio 2008 window.

Title Bar: The title bar identifies the window and the application open in the window. In Figure 1-19, the open application is Payroll.

Menu Bar: The menu bar displays the Visual Studio 2008 menu names, each representing a list of commands that allow you to create, edit, save, print, test, and run a Visual Basic program, as well as perform other functions that are critical to the development of Visual Basic programs.

Standard Toolbar: The Standard toolbar contains buttons that execute frequently used commands such as Open New Project, Save, Cut, Copy, Paste, and Undo.

Toolbox: The Toolbox contains **.NET components** that you can use to develop the graphical user interface for the program. For example, through the use of the Toolbox, you can place buttons, picture boxes, labels, radio buttons, and other Windows GUI objects in the window you develop for your program.

Main Work Area: The main work area is used to contain the item on which you are working. In Figure 1-19, it contains the Payroll Information window, which has been developed in the Payroll program.

Solution Explorer: The Solution Explorer window displays the elements of the **Visual Basic solution**, which is the name given to the Visual Basic program and other items that are generated by Visual Studio so the program will execute properly. You will learn about these items and how to use the Solution Explorer window throughout this book.

Properties Window: An item that is a visible part of a graphical user interface, such as the Calculate Pay button in Figure 1-19, is called an **object**, or **control**. Each object in a Visual Basic program has a set of characteristics called the **properties** of the object. These properties, such as the size of the button and the text that displays within the button, can be set in the Properties window within Visual Studio. You will learn about the properties of many objects throughout this book.

To code a Visual Basic program, the developer starts the Visual Studio program, identifies the kind of program to be developed, and then uses the tools and features of Visual Studio to actually create the program.

Programming Languages

Several thousand programming languages exist today. Each language has its own rules and syntax for writing instructions. Languages often are designed for specific purposes, such as scientific applications, business solutions, or Web page development.

Visual Studio can be used to write programs in three languages: Visual Basic, Visual C++ (pronounced Cee Plus Plus), and Visual C# (pronounced Cee Sharp). Each of these languages is described in the following sections.

VISUAL BASIC

Visual Basic 2008 is a programming language that allows developers to easily build complex Windows and Web programs, as well as other software tools. Visual Basic 2008 is based on the Visual Basic programming language that Microsoft developed in the early 1990s. Visual Basic, in turn, was based on the BASIC (Beginner's All-purpose Symbolic Instructional Code) language, which was developed in the 1960s.

Visual Basic's popularity evolved from the wide range of productivity features that enabled developers to quickly generate high-quality software applications for Windows. Today, Visual Basic is the most widely used programming language in the world because it is English-like and is considered one of the easier enterprise-level programming languages to learn. Visual Basic is the only language in Visual Studio that is not case sensitive, which makes it easy for entry-level programmers. It is as powerful as the other programming languages in the Visual Studio suite such as C++ or C#. An example of Visual Basic 2008 code is shown in Figure 1-18 on page 17.

In this book, you will learn to become a proficient Visual Basic developer.

C++

C++ is a derivative of the programming language, C, which originally was developed at Bell Labs in the 1970s. It gives developers exacting control of their applications through optimized code and access to system-provided services. It contains powerful language constructs, though at the price of added complexity. C++ provides unrivaled performance and precision for applications that require a high degree of control.

VISUAL C#

Introduced in 2001 by Microsoft, Visual C# offers a synthesis of the elegance and syntax of C++ with many of the productivity benefits enjoyed in Visual Basic. Visual C# can be used to create both Windows and Web applications, as well as other types of software tools. Microsoft designed Visual C# to augment some of the limitations of C++ while still providing the depth of control C++ developers demand. The C# language includes aspects of several other programming languages such as C++, Java, and Delphi with a strong emphasis on code simplification.

.NET Framework 3.5

In the year 2000, Microsoft announced a set of software technologies and products under the umbrella name of .NET. The .NET technologies and products were designed to work together to allow businesses to connect information, people, systems, and devices through software. Much of this connection occurs over the Internet.

The software environment in which programs and applications can be developed for .NET is called the **.NET Framework**, which provides tools and processes developers can use to produce and run programs. The most recent version is called **.NET Framework 3.5**. Visual Studio 2008 provides the development environment for the developer to have access to the .NET Framework 3.5 tools and processes. This version of the .NET Framework provides better computer performance, faster application startup, and smoother animations.

Four major features of .NET Framework 3.5 are the .NET class library, ADO.NET 3.5 (provides the ability to read and write data in databases), ASP.NET 3.5 (provides the ability to develop Web applications), and the Common Language Runtime (allows programs to run on different computers under different operating systems). Each of these features is explained in the following sections.

.NET CLASS LIBRARY

As you have learned, most programs written using Visual Basic 2008 are event-driven programs where a user performs an action, such as clicking a button, and the program executes the appropriate instructions. The instructions a program executes when a user clicks a button normally are written by the Visual Basic developer and are unique to the processing required by the program. For example, when a user clicks a button in one program, the overtime pay for an employee is calculated, whereas in another program parking fees are calculated. Each program responds to the events triggered by users with unique processing based on the requirements of the program.

In many programs, however, much of the programming that must be developed is common for all the programs. For example, in all the programs you have seen in this chapter, a button was used to trigger an event in the program. The button appears in a window on a screen and senses when it has been clicked through the use of program instructions.

When certain programming is common to multiple programs, the best approach is to write the programming one time and then reuse the programming wherever its use is appropriate. For example, whenever a button is required in the graphical user interface of a program, it is more efficient to use common programming code that can place the button in the user interface rather than requiring a developer to write all the code for a button each time one is required. When a common task must be performed or a unique object such as a button is required, a developer can write the code one time and save it as a class that then can be referenced by all other programs when the task or object is required.

In short, the coding required for a button can be placed in a class. A **class** is a named group of program code. Once the class is coded, it can be stored in a **class library**, which makes the class available to all developers who need to use it. For example, when you as a developer need to place a button in the user interface, you can use the Button class stored in a class library to create the button without writing all the programming associated with the button (Figure 1-20).

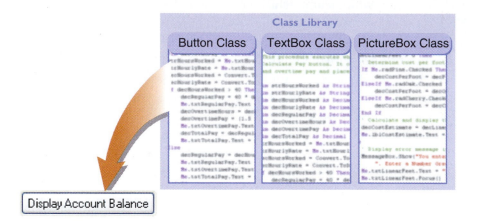

FIGURE 1-20

A button created from a class is called an **object**, or sometimes an **instance** of a class. In programming terminology, the process of creating a Button object from the Button class is called **instantiation**. As you can see, a class acts as a general template and an object is a specific item generated based on the class template. Thus, all buttons can be generated, or instantiated, from the Button class. The Display Account Balance button in Figure 1-20 is a specific Button object instantiated from the Button class.

In Visual Studio 2008, to create a Button object from the Button class, all you must do is drag the Button .NET component from the Toolbox to a Windows Form object, as you will learn in Chapter 2.

A button in a graphical user interface is only a single example of using classes and class libraries. The .NET Framework 3.5 class library contains thousands of classes and many class libraries that can be used by Visual Basic developers who use Visual Studio to create programs.

With so many classes available in .NET Framework 3.5, developers use a method of program development called rapid application development. **Rapid application development (RAD)** refers to the process of using prebuilt classes to make application development faster, easier, and more reliable. Throughout this book you will gain a further understanding of classes and their use in modern computer programming, and will see how the classes in the .NET Framework 3.5 class libraries can be used for rapid application development.

ADO.NET 3.5

Often, programs you write must access data stored in a database. A set of prewritten classes called ADO.NET 3.5 (ActiveX Data Objects) provides the functionality for a program to perform the four primary tasks required when working with a database: get the data, examine the data, edit the data, and update the data.

Getting the data refers to retrieving the data from the database and making it available to the program. Once the data is retrieved from the database, ADO.NET 3.5 provides the tools for the program to examine the data and determine how to use it. For example, a program might retrieve data from a database to create a printed report. The program can examine the data to determine its use for the report.

In other applications, the program might examine the data to determine if it is appropriate data to display for a user. Thus, in a banking application such as in Figure 1-21, the program might require the user enter a special value, such as the mother's maiden name, to verify the identity of the person requesting the information. The program, using ADO.NET 3.5 classes, can compare the special value to the data retrieved from the database to determine if the user may access the data.

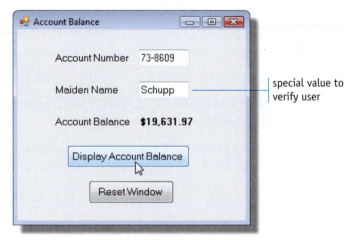

FIGURE 1-21

A third facility provided by ADO.NET 3.5 is the ability to edit the data, which means make changes to the data. For example, if you change your address or telephone number, those values in your account database information should be changed. ADO.NET 3.5 supports the ability to make those changes.

Finally, once changes to data have been made, ADO.NET 3.5 enables a program to update the database with the new information by writing the data into the database.

ADO.NET 3.5 is a powerful and necessary part of the .NET Framework 3.5. The developer uses Visual Studio 2008 to access the ADO.NET 3.5 classes.

ASP.NET 3.5

The Internet and the World Wide Web are integral technological resources. Modern Web sites provide services ranging from purchasing products to referencing the latest medical research on any known disease. The development and maintenance of these Web sites is a constant requirement and consumes many developer hours.

With recognition of the importance of the Web, Microsoft included in .NET Framework 3.5 a programming framework called ASP.NET 3.5 that developers, through Visual Studio 2008, can use to build powerful, sophisticated Web applications on a Web server. Using ASP.NET 3.5 classes, the Visual Basic 2008 programmer can create Web sites that are able to perform any function available on the Web today.

ASP.NET 3.5 offers several advantages for developers. First, almost all the objects available in the .NET framework, such as buttons, text boxes, and picture boxes, are available in ASP.NET 3.5. So, developers can use the same techniques to create a Web application that they use to create Windows applications such as those shown in this chapter. In addition, deploying the Web application on a Web server almost is automatic. Visual Studio 2008 now incorporates a new Web designer interface into ASP.NET 3.5 that uses the design engine of a popular Web page designing program named Microsoft Expression Web. This design engine greatly improves moving between HTML (Hypertext Markup Language) source code, cascading style sheets that assist in layout, and Visual Basic code.

Important Web requirements such as performance and security are enhanced and maximized through the use of the tools offered with ASP.NET 3.5. In short, ASP.NET 3.5 offers a complete solution for developing modern Web applications.

MICROSOFT INTERMEDIATE LANGUAGE (MSIL) AND COMMON LANGUAGE RUNTIME (CLR)

After a developer writes a program in a programming language such as Visual Basic 2008 using Visual Studio 2008, the programming statements must be translated into a collection of instructions that eventually can be understood by the electronics of the computer. These electronic instructions then are executed by the computer to carry out the tasks of the program. This process of translation is called **program compilation**.

Program compilation for a Visual Basic 2008 program creates a set of electronic code expressed in an intermediate language called the **Microsoft Intermediate Language (MSIL)**. When the program is executed, a portion of .NET 3.5 called the **Common Language Runtime (CLR)** reads the MSIL and causes the actual instructions within the program to be executed (Figure 1-22).

In Figure 1-22, the Visual Basic program written by a developer is compiled, which translates the human-readable statements in Visual Basic into MSIL, which is the set of electronic code that forms the input to CLR. Then, when the program is ready for execution, the CLR reads the MSIL and places the MSIL in RAM in a form that allows the electronics of the computer to actually execute the instructions in the program.

The use of MSIL and CLR offers multiple benefits that provide speed and flexibility for both the development and execution environments of a program. Utmost in these benefits is the fact that a program written using Visual Studio 2008 and compiled into MSIL can be executed on any computer using any operating system so long as .NET Framework 3.5 is available on the computer. So, with no changes to a program you write, the program could be executed on a Dell computer running Windows Vista and on an IBM computer using the Linux operating system. This flexibility in being able to execute programs on different computers running different operating systems is a primary benefit of using .NET Framework 3.5.

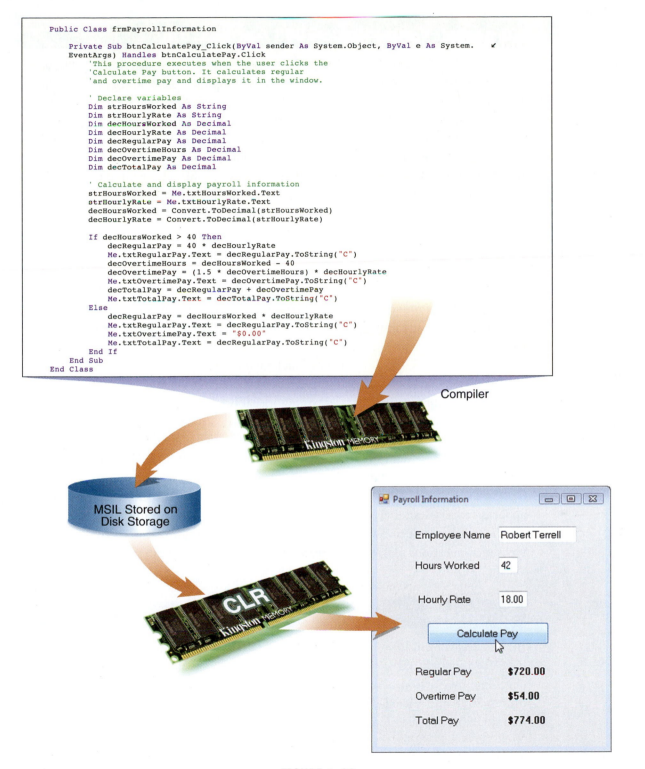

```
Public Class frmPayrollInformation

    Private Sub btnCalculatePay_Click(ByVal sender As System.Object, ByVal e As System.  ↵
    EventArgs) Handles btnCalculatePay.Click
        'This procedure executes when the user clicks the
        'Calculate Pay button. It calculates regular
        'and overtime pay and displays it in the window.

        ' Declare variables
        Dim strHoursWorked As String
        Dim strHourlyRate As String
        Dim decHoursWorked As Decimal
        Dim decHourlyRate As Decimal
        Dim decRegularPay As Decimal
        Dim decOvertimeHours As Decimal
        Dim decOvertimePay As Decimal
        Dim decTotalPay As Decimal

        ' Calculate and display payroll information
        strHoursWorked = Me.txtHoursWorked.Text
        strHourlyRate = Me.txtHourlyRate.Text
        decHoursWorked = Convert.ToDecimal(strHoursWorked)
        decHourlyRate = Convert.ToDecimal(strHourlyRate)

        If decHoursWorked > 40 Then
            decRegularPay = 40 * decHourlyRate
            Me.txtRegularPay.Text = decRegularPay.ToString("C")
            decOvertimeHours = decHoursWorked - 40
            decOvertimePay = (1.5 * decOvertimeHours) * decHourlyRate
            Me.txtOvertimePay.Text = decOvertimePay.ToString("C")
            decTotalPay = decRegularPay + decOvertimePay
            Me.txtTotalPay.Text = decTotalPay.ToString("C")
        Else
            decRegularPay = decHoursWorked * decHourlyRate
            Me.txtRegularPay.Text = decRegularPay.ToString("C")
            Me.txtOvertimePay.Text = "$0.00"
            Me.txtTotalPay.Text = decRegularPay.ToString("C")
        End If
    End Sub
End Class
```

Compiler

MSIL Stored on
Disk Storage

CLR
Kingston MEMORY

Payroll Information

Employee Name   Robert Terrell

Hours Worked   42

Hourly Rate   18.00

Calculate Pay

Regular Pay $720.00

Overtime Pay $54.00

Total Pay $774.00

FIGURE 1-22

Types of Visual Basic 2008 Applications

When you begin creating a new Visual Basic 2008 program in Visual Studio 2008, you must choose the type of application you will be developing. Based on your choice, Visual Studio 2008 provides the classes, tools, and features required for that type of application.

Five major types of applications are: Windows applications, mobile applications, Web site applications, Office applications, and database applications. A **Windows application** means the program will run on a computer or other device that supports the Windows graphical user interface. A Windows graphical user interface includes objects such as buttons, text boxes, radio buttons, and so on. You can run a Windows application on a variety of computers.

You can create **mobile applications** that are designed to run on mobile devices such as Smartphones, Pocket PCs, and computers running the Windows CE operating system.

You create a **Web site application** using ASP.NET 3.5. The application runs on a Web server. It produces Hypertext Markup Language (HTML) code that is downloaded to the client computer where the browser on the client computer interprets the HTML and displays the contents of a Web page. In a Web application created with ASP.NET 3.5, the developer can include items such as security and forms processing to provide all the services required of a modern Web site.

An **Office application** includes writing Visual Basic 2008 code to automate and manipulate documents created using both Microsoft Office 2003 and Microsoft Office 2007.

A **database application** is written using ADO.NET 3.5 to reference, access, display, and update data stored in a database. The Visual Basic 2008 developer writes the code to process the data.

Other types of applications Visual Basic 2008 developers can create include console applications, classes for class libraries, certain controls to use in Windows applications, Web services, and device-specific applications. For more information regarding the types of applications that you can create, visit msdn.microsoft.com/vbasic.

Summary

In this chapter you have learned the fundamentals of computer programming and have been introduced to the Visual Studio 2008 and Visual Basic 2008 program development environments. In subsequent chapters you will learn to use Visual Studio 2008 and Visual Basic 2008 to create Windows applications, mobile applications, database applications, Web applications, and Office 2007 applications.

Knowledge Check

1. Explain the differences between computer hardware and computer software.

2. The basic functions of many programs are: a) _____; b) _____; c) _____.

3. Match the following terms and their definitions:

a) Developer	1. A collection of classes that are available for use in programs
b) Persistent data	2. Someone skilled in designing computer programs and implementing them in programming languages
c) Programming language	3. A window with a variety of objects that can be displayed on a variety of devices
d) Graphical user interface	4. Data that is stored on a storage medium
e) Database	5. The process of using prebuilt classes to make application development faster, easier, and more reliable
f) Class library	6. A collection of data organized in a manner that allows access, retrieval, and use of that data
g) Rapid application development (RAD)	7. A set of words and symbols that can be interpreted by special computer software and eventually can be executed as instructions by a computer

4. Explain what an event is in the context of event-driven programs. Give two examples.

5. Give examples of the differences between an input operation and an output operation.

6. What are the four primary arithmetic operations a computer program can perform? Give an example of each.

7. In the following examples, identify the condition a program would detect (the first exercise is solved for you):

a. 4 is _____ 3	a. greater than
b. 8 is _____ 8	b. _____
c. 17 is _____ 17.8	c. _____
d. 75 is _____ 85	d. _____
e. "Developer" is _____ "Developer"	e. _____

(continues)

Knowledge Check

(continued)

8. Describe three different databases where you think information about yourself might be stored.

9. What is programming language syntax? Why is it important?

10. Visual Studio 2008 is a type of _____ developed by _____.

11. What is a Toolbox in Visual Studio 2008? Why is it valuable?

12. Name two properties that a Button object can possess.

13. What are the three programming languages you can use with Visual Studio 2008?

14. State three reasons that Visual Basic is the most widely used programming language in the world.

15. What are four major features of .NET Framework 3.5?

16. Why is a class developed? How are classes organized and stored?

17. Differentiate between a class and an object. Give three examples of a class and an object.

18. What is the primary use of ADO.NET 3.5?

19. What is the process of translating statements written by a developer called? What is the result of this process?

20. What are five types of applications you can create in Visual Basic 2008?

CHAPTER TWO

Program and Graphical User Interface Design

OBJECTIVES

You will have mastered the material in this chapter when you can:

- ▶ Open and close Visual Studio 2008

- ▶ Create a Visual Basic 2008 Windows Application project

- ▶ Name and set the title bar text in a Windows Form object; resize a Windows Form object

- ▶ Add a Label object to a Windows Form object; name the Label object; set the text in the Label object; change the Font properties of the text in the Label object

- ▶ Add a PictureBox object to the Windows Form object; name the PictureBox object; resize the PictureBox object

- ▶ Add a Button object to the Windows Form object; name the Button object; set the text in the Button object; change the Button object size

- ▶ Align objects on the Windows Form object

- ▶ Save and open Visual Basic projects

- ▶ Understand and implement graphical user interface design principles

- ▶ Understand and implement the first two phases of the program development life cycle

Introduction

Before a program actually can be coded using Visual Basic 2008, it must be designed. Designing a program can be compared to constructing a building. Before cement slabs are poured, steel beams are put in place, and walls are built, architects and engineers must design a building to ensure it will perform as required and be safe and reliable. The same holds true for a computer program. Once the program is designed, it can be implemented through the use of the Visual Basic 2008 programming language to perform the functions for which it was designed.

To illustrate the process of designing and implementing a computer program in the Visual Basic 2008 programming language using **Visual Studio 2008** as the integrated development environment, the application shown in Figure 2-1 will be designed and implemented in this chapter and in Chapter 3.

Hotel Room Selection window

Select Room button

Standard Room button

instructions

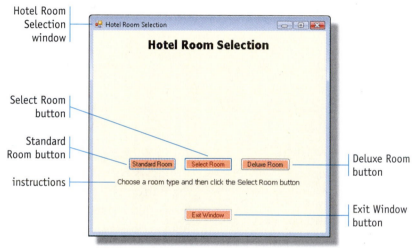

Deluxe Room button

Exit Window button

FIGURE 2-1a

picture of standard room

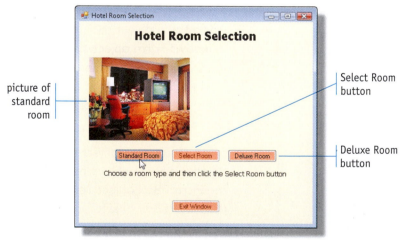

Select Room button

Deluxe Room button

FIGURE 2-1b

The application in Figure 2-1 could be part of a larger computer application that is used to make hotel reservations. The program that creates the window in Figure 2-1 will run on a personal computer using the Windows operating system and will allow a reservation clerk or a customer to select the room type for a hotel reservation.

In Figure 2-1a, the program begins by displaying the Hotel Room Selection window on a PC monitor. The program provides instructions that tell the user to choose the room type (by clicking the Standard Room or Deluxe Room button), and then click the Select Room button to make a room selection. If the user clicks the Standard Room button, a picture of a standard room is displayed (Figure 2-1b). If the user clicks the Deluxe Room button, a picture of a deluxe room is displayed (Figure 2-1c). After choosing a room type, the user can click the Select Room button and the program informs the user the room selection has been completed (Figure 2-1d). To close the window and exit the program, the user can click the Exit Window button after making a room selection.

By the end of Chapter 3, you will have completed the design and implementation of this program.

ONLINE REINFORCEMENT

To view a video of the program execution shown in Figure 2-1, visit scsite.com/vb2008/ch2 and then click Figure 2-1.

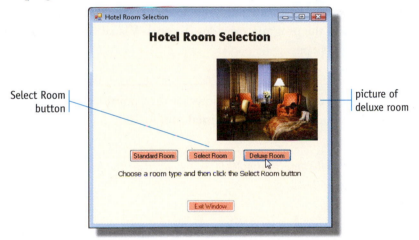

Select Room button — picture of deluxe room

FIGURE 2-1c

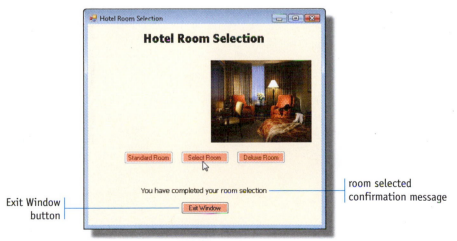

Exit Window button — You have completed your room selection — room selected confirmation message

FIGURE 2-1d

Using Visual Studio 2008

When designing an event-driven program that uses a graphical user interface (GUI), such as the program in this chapter, one of the first steps is to design the user interface itself. Recall that the user interface is the window that is displayed on the screen when the program is running, together with the variety of objects such as buttons that are displayed in the window. Before beginning to design the user interface, however, the developer should know how to use certain Visual Studio and Visual Basic **rapid application development (RAD)** tools because these tools are used in the design process. For example, you use the Visual Studio tools to place a button on the window. So, before starting the design of the user interface for the program in this chapter, you should know how to accomplish the Visual Studio tasks described in the following pages.

OPEN VISUAL STUDIO 2008

To design a user interface using Visual Studio, the developer must open Visual Studio 2008 and then use the tools the program provides. To open Visual Studio 2008, you can complete the following steps:

STEP 1 Click the Start button on the Windows taskbar, point to All Programs on the Start menu, and then point to Microsoft Visual Studio 2008 on the All Programs submenu.

The program name, Microsoft Visual Studio 2008, is displayed on the Microsoft Visual Studio 2008 submenu (Figure 2–2).

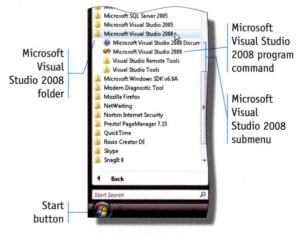

FIGURE 2-2

STEP 2 Click Microsoft Visual Studio 2008 on the submenu.

For a short time, a Visual Studio splash screen appears, and then Microsoft Visual Studio 2008 opens (Figure 2–3). The title of the window is Microsoft Visual Studio. The menu bar and the Standard toolbar are displayed at the top of the window. The Start Page contains information regarding Visual Basic. To close the Start Page, click the Close button on the Start Page title bar. You will learn the other elements of this window as you progress through this book.

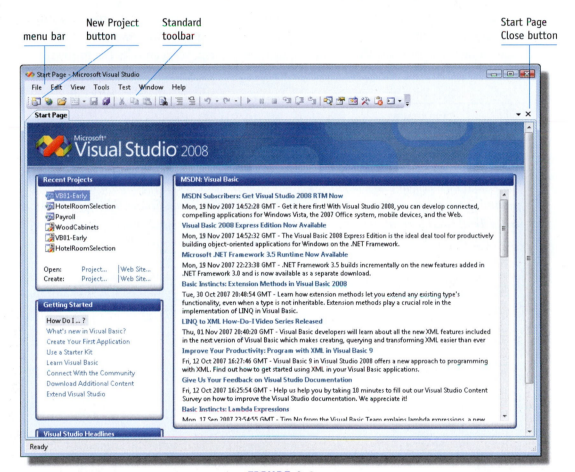

FIGURE 2-3

ONLINE REINFORCEMENT

To view a video of the process in the previous steps, visit scsite.com/vb2008/ch2 and then click Figure 2-2.

CREATE A NEW VISUAL BASIC 2008 WINDOWS APPLICATION PROJECT

A **project** is equivalent to a single program created using Visual Studio. A **Windows Application project** is a program that will include, as the user interface, a window on the screen of a computer using the Windows operating system. When the program is executed, the user will interact with the program by using the window and its components (the user interface).

To create a new project using Visual Studio, you must specify the programming language you want to use and the type of program, or application, you will create. To create a new Visual Basic Windows Application project, you can take the following steps:

STEP 1   Click the New Project button on the Standard toolbar.

Visual Studio opens the New Project window (Figure 2–4). The New Project window on your computer might be displayed differently, depending on selections made at the time Visual Studio was installed on your computer. The left pane (titled Project types) contains the programming languages and other types of projects available in Visual Studio. The right pane (titled Templates) contains the types of applications you can create within each programming language. At this time, you want to create a Windows Application using Visual Basic.

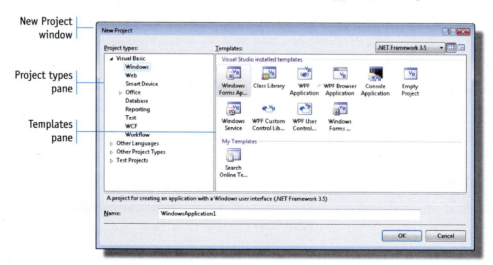

FIGURE 2-4

STEP 2 If necessary, in the Project types pane (left pane), click Visual Basic so it is selected.

Visual Basic is highlighted in the Project types pane and the types of projects you can create using Visual Basic are listed in the Templates pane (right pane) (Figure 2-5).

Visual Basic selected   Windows Forms Application

FIGURE 2-5

STEP 3 If necessary, click Windows Forms Application in the Templates pane.

Windows Forms Application is selected in the Templates pane (Figure 2-6). By making this selection, you have specified you want to create a program that will run under the Windows operating system using the Windows graphical user interface.

Windows Forms
Application selected

Name
text box

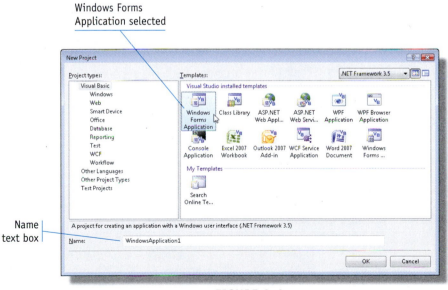

FIGURE 2-6

STEP 4 Double-click the text, WindowsApplication1, in the Name text box to select the text. Type the project name. For this example, you could type `HotelRoomSelection` as the name.

The project name appears in the Name text box (Figure 2-7).

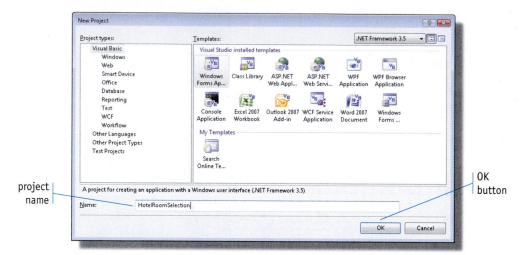

project name

OK button

FIGURE 2-7

STEP 5 Click the OK button in the New Project window.

Visual Studio creates a new project (Figure 2-8). The project name is displayed in the title bar of the window.

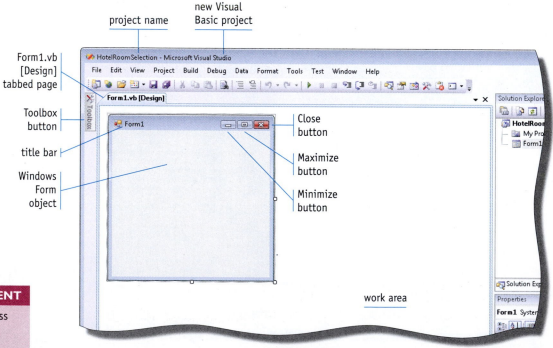

project name

new Visual Basic project

Form1.vb [Design] tabbed page

Toolbox button

title bar

Windows Form object

Close button

Maximize button

Minimize button

work area

FIGURE 2-8

The Visual Studio window contains several important features of which you should be aware. First, in the portion of the window known as the **work area**, a tabbed page named Form1.vb [Design] contains a Windows Form object called Form1. A **Windows Form object** is the window you will use to build the program and is the window that will be displayed on your screen when you execute the program. The Windows Form object is the fundamental object in the graphical user interface you will create using Visual Studio tools. Notice in Figure 2-8 that the Windows Form object contains a blue title bar, a window title (Form1), a Minimize button, a Maximize button, and a Close button.

A second important element is displayed on the left of the window. Depending on the settings within Visual Studio, the left portion of the window will appear as shown in Figure 2-8 or as shown in Figure 2-9. In Figure 2-8, the left margin contains the Toolbox button. The Toolbox button also appears on the Standard toolbar.

DISPLAY THE TOOLBOX

You can use the **Toolbox button** to display the Toolbox. The **Toolbox** is the primary tool you will use to place objects such as buttons on the Windows Form object. To display the Toolbox, you can take the following steps:

STEP 1   If the window does not already display the Toolbox, point to the Toolbox button in the left margin of the window.

When you point to the Toolbox button, the Toolbox is displayed on the window (Figure 2-9). Notice that the Toolbox hides part of the Form1 Windows Form object.

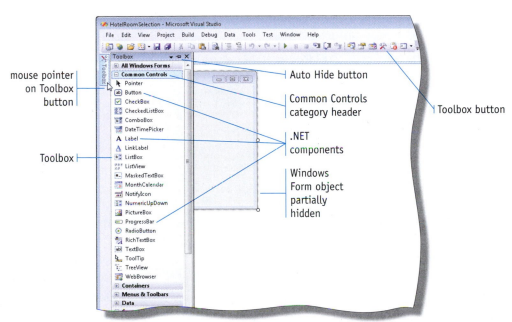

FIGURE 2-9

WATCH OUT FOR

In Figure 2-9 the Common Controls category of tools is open and all the tools in the category are visible. If the Common Category is not open, a Plus sign is placed to the left of the category header (Common Controls). To open the category, click the Plus sign.

ONLINE REINFORCEMENT

To view a video of the process in the previous step, visit scsite.com/vb2008/ch2 and then click Figure 2-9.

The Toolbox contains, among other things, many graphical elements called **.NET components** that you can place on the Windows Form object as graphical user interface objects. For example, it contains buttons that can be placed on the Windows Form object. You will learn how to perform this activity in the next section of this chapter.

PERMANENTLY DISPLAY THE TOOLBOX

As long as the mouse pointer is within the Toolbox, the Toolbox is displayed. If, however, you move the mouse pointer off the Toolbox, it no longer is displayed.

When you are designing the graphical user interface, normally it is advantageous to display the Toolbox at all times. To keep the Toolbox on the window at all times, you can complete the following step:

STEP 1 If necessary, point to the Toolbox button in the left margin of the window to display the Toolbox. Then, click the **Auto Hide button** on the Toolbox title bar.

When you click the Auto Hide button, the Pushpin icon on the Auto Hide button on the Toolbox title bar changes from being horizontal, which indicates Auto Hide, to vertical, which indicates the Toolbox has been "pinned" to the window and will remain there (Figure 2-10). Form1 is moved to the right so you can see both the Toolbox and all of Form1.

Pushpin icon on the Auto Hide button is vertical

Toolbox diplayed at all times

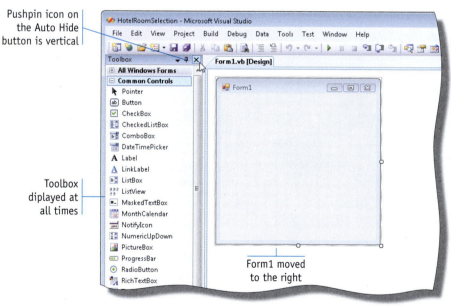

Form1 moved to the right

FIGURE 2-10

When the Pushpin icon is vertical, the Toolbox is said to be in Dockable mode, which means it can be dragged around and placed anywhere within the Visual Studio window. In most applications, it should remain on the left of the window as shown in Figure 2-10. Later, you can change the Toolbox back to Auto Hide mode by clicking the Auto Hide button again.

VIEW OBJECT PROPERTIES

Every object you create in the user interface, including the Windows Form object, has properties. **Properties** can describe a multitude of elements about the object, including its color, size, name, and position on the screen. You will learn about the properties of all the objects you create using the Toolbox.

To view the properties for an object in Visual Studio, you use the Properties window. By default, the Properties window is displayed in the lower-right section of the Visual Studio window (Figure 2-11).

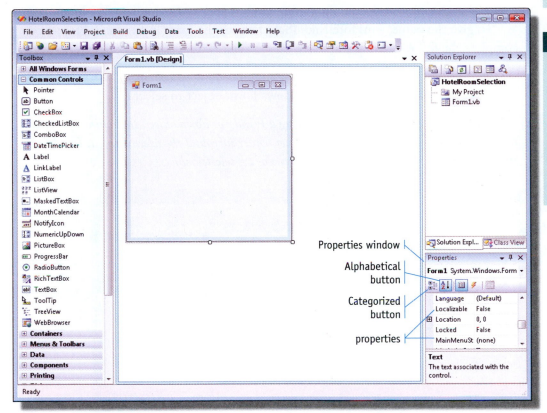

FIGURE 2-11

In the **Properties window** shown in Figure 2-11, the property names in the left list appear in Alphabetical view. Many developers find the Alphabetical view the easiest to use when searching for properties. Some developers, however, prefer the Categorized view, where properties are organized according to type. You can change the order of the properties into Categorized if you click the Categorized button on the Properties window toolbar (see Figure 2-11). In this book, the properties are shown in Alphabetical view, which is achieved by clicking the Alphabetical button on the Properties window toolbar.

NAME THE WINDOWS FORM OBJECT

Visual Studio gives every object in a Visual Basic graphical user interface a default name. For example, the name for the first Windows Form object in a project is Form1. In virtually every instance, a developer should assign a meaningful name to an object so the program can reference it if required. The name for an object should reflect the object's use. For example, a good name for the Hotel Room Selection window might be HotelRoomSelection. Notice in the name that each word is capitalized and the remaining letters are lowercase. You should always follow this naming method when naming objects.

No spaces or other special characters are allowed in the object name. Also, by convention, each object name should begin with a prefix that identifies the type of object. For Windows Form objects, the prefix is frm. Therefore, the complete name for the Windows Form object would be frmHotelRoomSelection. The form name should be changed in two places—in the Properties window and in the Solution Explorer.

To give the name, frmHotelRoomSelection, to the form in Figure 2-11, you can complete the following steps:

STEP 1   Click anywhere in the Windows Form object to select it.

When you click within any object, including a Windows Form object, that object is selected (Figure 2-12). Sizing handles and a heavier border surround the selected object. In addition, the Properties window displays the properties of the selected object.

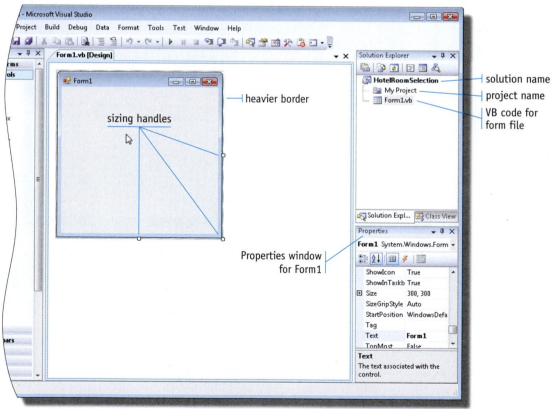

FIGURE 2-12

STEP 2   Scroll in the Properties window until you find the (Name) property in the Properties window (it is near the top of the list). Then, double-click in the right column for the (Name) property. Type the new name, `frmHotelRoomSelection` on your keyboard, and then press the ENTER key.

The name, Form1, is selected in the right column for the (Name) property, as shown by the blue background. When you select a property in the Properties window, you can change that property. The Windows Form object is given the new name, frmHotelRoomSelection, because the Name property is changed when you enter the new name (Figure 2-13).

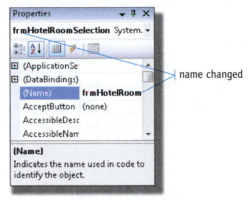

FIGURE 2-13

STEP 3 In the Solution Explorer window, right-click the Form1.vb form file and then click Rename. Type `frmHotelRoomSelection.vb` and press the ENTER key.

The shortcut menu for the name Form1.vb appears. Rename is selected (Figure 2-14a). The Form1.vb form file is given the new name frmHotelRoomSelection.vb in the Solution Explorer window (Figure 2-14b).

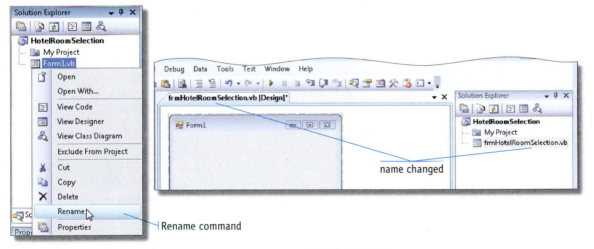

FIGURE 2-14a   **FIGURE 2-14b**

SET THE TITLE BAR TEXT IN A WINDOWS FORM OBJECT

After you name the Windows Form object, often the next step in the graphical user interface design is to change the title bar text so it reflects the function of the program. In this example, the name used is Hotel Room Selection. The **Text property** in the Windows Form object Properties window contains the value that is displayed in the title bar of the window. You can set the Text property using the following steps:

STEP 1 With the Windows Form object selected, scroll in the Properties window until you find the Text property. (Remember: The properties are in alphabetic order.) Then, double-click in the right column for the Text property.

The text, Form1, is selected in the Properties window (Figure 2-15). Form1 is the default text value for the first Windows Form object created in a project. Whenever a property is selected, you can change the property.

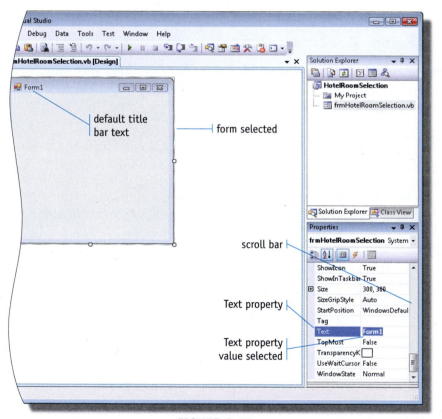

FIGURE 2-15

STEP 2   Type Hotel Room Selection and then press the ENTER key.

The value, Hotel Room Selection, is displayed for the Text property in the Properties window and also is displayed in the title bar of the Windows Form object (Figure 2–16). You can enter any value you like for the Text property of the Windows Form object.

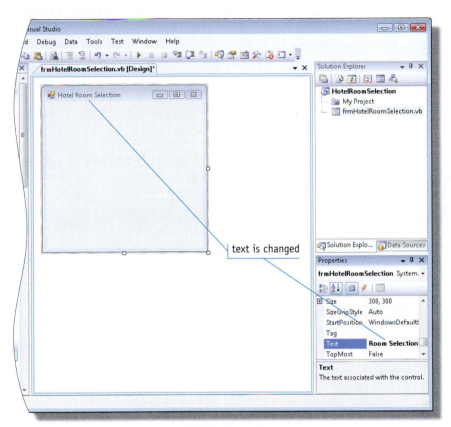

FIGURE 2-16

ONLINE REINFORCEMENT

To view a video of the process in the previous steps, visit scsite.com/vb2008/ch2 and then click Figure 2-15.

You can change many of the properties for any object in the graphical user interface using the techniques just illustrated.

RESIZE A FORM

To resize a Windows Form object, you can change the **Size property** in the Properties window to the exact number of horizontal and vertical pixels you desire. You also can change the Windows Form object size by dragging the vertical border to change the width of the window or the horizontal border to change the height. Another way to change the size is to drag a corner sizing handle, which allows you to change both the width and the height at the same time.

The following steps illustrate using the sizing handles to change the size of the Windows Form object shown in Figure 2-17:

> **STEP 1**   Place the mouse pointer over the sizing handle in the lower-right corner of the Windows Form object.

When the mouse pointer is over the sizing handle, it changes to a two-headed arrow that indicates you can drag to change the size of the Windows Form object (Figure 2-17).

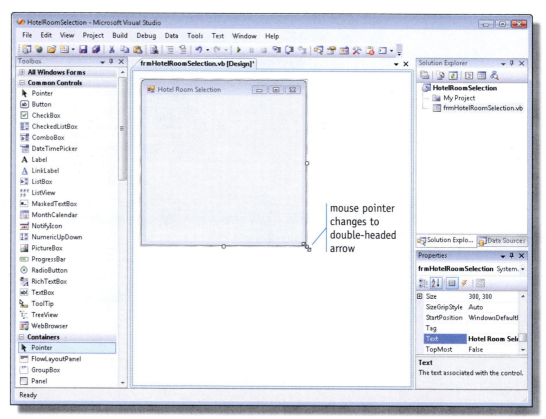

FIGURE 2-17

STEP 2   Drag the sizing handle to the right and down until the window is the size you want. Then, release the left mouse button.

The Windows Form object has been resized (Figure 2-18). The exact size of the Windows Form object is shown on the Status bar as (number of horizontal pixels, number of vertical pixels). In Figure 2-18, the size of the Windows Form object is 437 pixels horizontally by 402 pixels vertically.

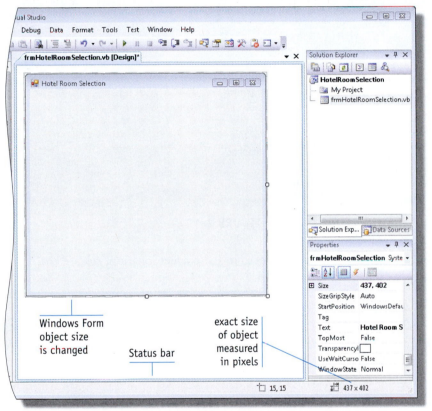

FIGURE 2-18

ONLINE REINFORCEMENT

To view a video of the process in the previous steps, visit scsite.com/vb2008/ch2 and then click Figure 2-17.

ADD A LABEL OBJECT

After sizing the Windows Form object, you can use the Toolbox to add other GUI objects as required. For example, a graphical user interface often displays a message or labels an item in the window. To accomplish this, you can use the **Label .NET component** in the Toolbox to place a **Label object** on the Windows Form object. To add a Label object to a Windows Form object, you can complete the steps on the next page.

STEP 1   Drag the Label .NET component button from the Common Controls category in the Toolbox over the Windows Form object to the approximate location where you want to place the Label object.

The mouse pointer changes to a crosshair and small rectangle when you place it over the Windows Form object (Figure 2-19). The Label object will be placed on the form at the location of the small rectangle in the mouse pointer.

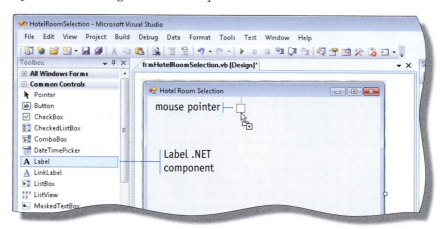

FIGURE 2-19

STEP 2   When the mouse pointer is in the correct location, release the left mouse button.

The Label object is placed on the Windows Form object at the location you selected (Figure 2-20). The label is selected, as identified by the dotted border surrounding it. The default text within the label is Label1. In virtually all cases, you must change the label text to reflect the needs of the interface.

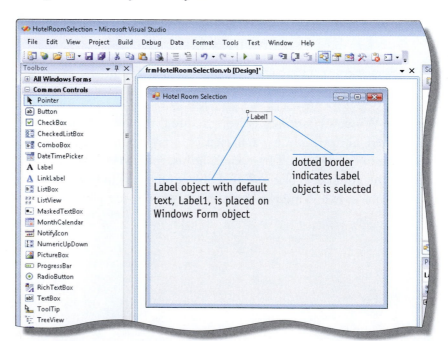

FIGURE 2-20

NAME THE LABEL OBJECT

As with most objects you place on the Windows Form object, the first step after creating the object should be to name the object. To give the Label object the name, Heading, together with the Label prefix, lbl, complete the following steps:

STEP 1   With the Label object selected, scroll in the Properties window until you find the (Name) property. Then double-click in the right column for the (Name) property.

The default name, Label1, is selected (Figure 2-21). When a property is selected, you can change the property.

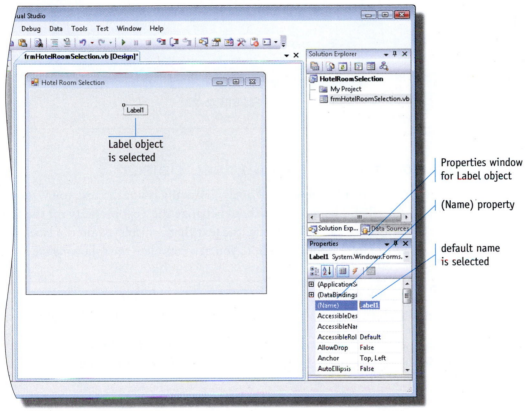

FIGURE 2-21

STEP 2 Type the new name, `lblHeading` and then press the ENTER key.

The name you entered is displayed in the Name property in the Properties window (Figure 2-22). You now can reference the Label object by its name in other parts of the program.

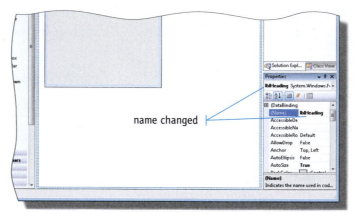

FIGURE 2-22

CHANGE THE TEXT IN A LABEL OBJECT

The default text in a Label object, Label1, normally is not the text you want to display in the label. Therefore, you should change the Text property for the Label object to the desired value. To change the text that is displayed on the label in Figure 2-22 to Hotel Room Selection, you can complete the following steps:

STEP 1 With the Label object selected, scroll in the Properties dialog box until you find the Text property. Then, double-click the Text value in the right column.

The text value in the right column of the Text property, which is the text that is displayed in the label, is selected (Figure 2-23). When the Text value is selected, you can change it.

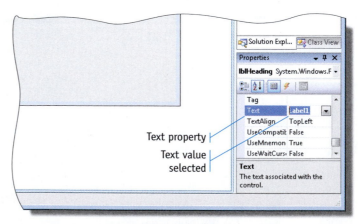

FIGURE 2-23

STEP 2   Type `Hotel Room Selection` for the Text property.

The text you typed, Hotel Room Selection, is displayed in the Text property for the Label object (Figure 2-24).

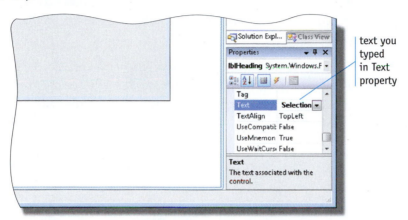

FIGURE 2-24

STEP 3   To enter the Text property, press the ENTER key.

The text you entered, Hotel Room Selection, is displayed in the Text property and also in the label itself (Figure 2-25). The text is, by default, 8 point in size. The Label object automatically expanded horizontally to accommodate the text you typed. By default, Label objects will change size so they are just the right size for the text in the Text property.

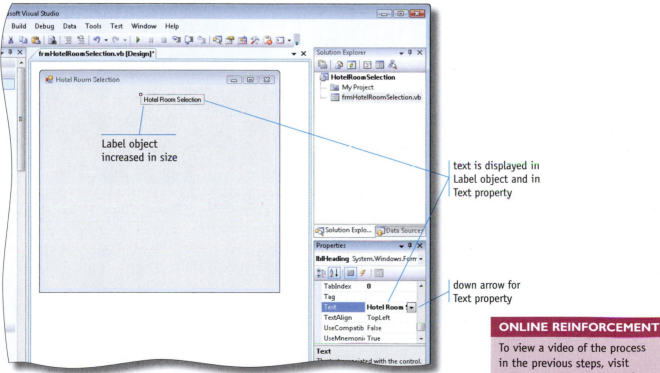

FIGURE 2-25

ONLINE REINFORCEMENT

To view a video of the process in the previous steps, visit scsite.com/vb2008/ch2 and then click Figure 2-23.

The text in a Label object can be multiple lines. To enter multiple lines for a Label object, you can complete the following steps:

STEP 1 With the Label object selected, click the Text property name in the left column of the Properties window. Then, click the down arrow in the right column of the Text property.

A box opens in which you can enter multiple lines (Figure 2-26). As you type, you can move the insertion point to the next line by pressing the ENTER key. To accept the text for the label, press CTRL + ENTER (this nomenclature means you hold down the CTRL key, press the ENTER key, and then release both keys).

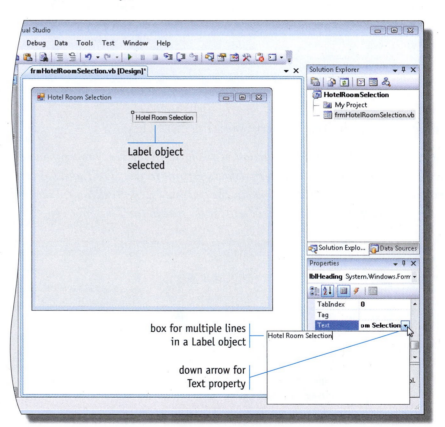

FIGURE 2-26

ONLINE REINFORCEMENT

To view a video of the process in the previous step, visit scsite.com/vb2008/ch2 and then click Figure 2-26.

CHANGE LABEL FONT, FONT STYLE, AND FONT SIZE

Many times, the default font, font style, and font size of the text in a Label object must be changed to reflect the purpose of the label. For example, in a label that is used as a heading for a window, the text should be larger than the default 8-point font used for Label objects, and should be bold so it stands out as a heading. To change the font, font style, and font size of a label, you can select the label and then use the **Font property** to make the change. To change the text that appears in the lblHeading label to Tahoma font, make the font bold, and increase the font size to 16 point, you can complete the following steps:

STEP 1 Click the Label object to select it. Scroll until you find the Font property in the Properties window. Click the Font property in the left column of the Label property window.

The Label object is selected as shown by the dotted border surrounding it (Figure 2-27). When you click the Font property in the Properties window, an ellipsis button (a button with three dots) is displayed in the right column. In the Properties window, an ellipsis button indicates multiple choices for the property will be made available when you click the button.

WATCH OUT FOR

When you click an object to select it, you might double-click it accidentally. If you do, a tabbed page with programming code opens. To return to the form and continue developing the user interface, click the [Design] tab for your form, such as the frmHotelRoomSelection.vb [Design] tab.

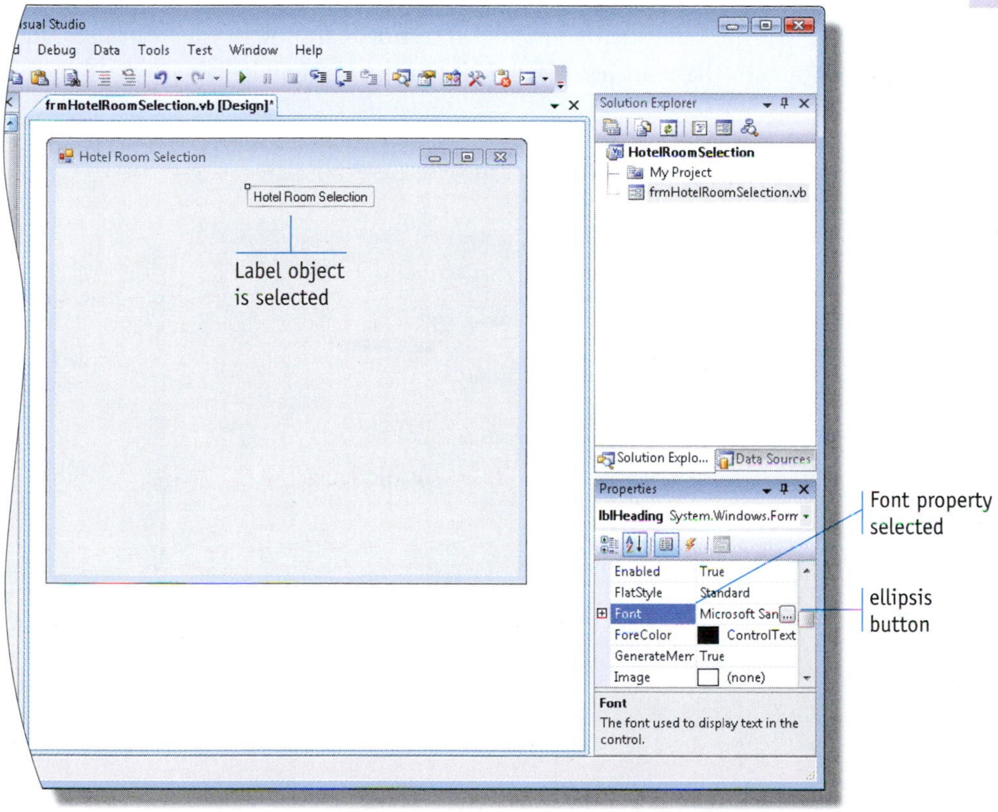

FIGURE 2-27

STEP 2 Click the ellipsis button for the Font property.

The Font dialog box is displayed (Figure 2-28). Using the Font dialog box, you can change the Font, Font style, and Size of the text in the Label object.

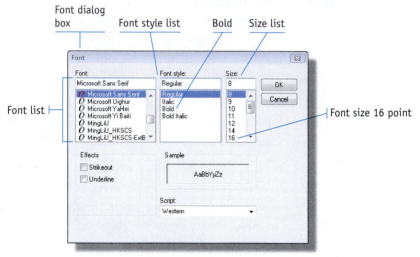

FIGURE 2-28

STEP 3 In the Font dialog box, scroll to find Tahoma in the Font list and then click Tahoma in the Font list. Click Bold in the Font style list. Click 16 in the Size list.

The selections are highlighted in the Font dialog box (Figure 2-29).

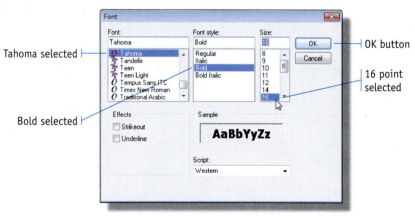

FIGURE 2-29

STEP 4   Click the OK button.

The font, font style, and font size in the Label object are changed as specified in the Font dialog box (Figure 2-30). The Label object automatically expands to accommodate the changed font. The changes also are made for the Font property in the Properties window.

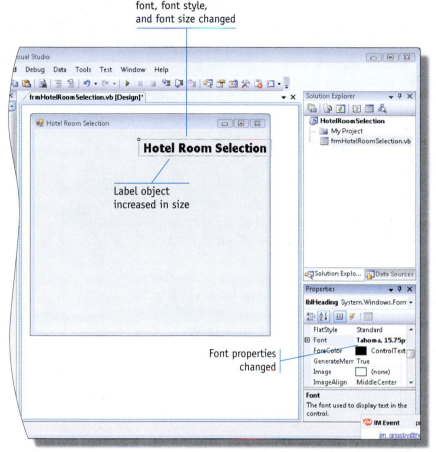

FIGURE 2-30

ONLINE REINFORCEMENT

To view a video of the process in the previous steps, visit scsite.com/vb2008/ch2 and then click Figure 2-27.

CENTER A LABEL OBJECT IN THE WINDOWS FORM OBJECT

When you place an object on the Windows Form object, the object you place may not be located in precisely the correct position. So, you must align the object in the window. A single label often is centered horizontally in the window; that is, the distance from the left frame of the window to the beginning of the text should be the same as the distance from the end of the text to the right frame of the window. To horizontally center the label containing the heading, you can complete the following steps:

STEP 1 With the Label object selected, click Format on the menu bar and then point to Center in Form on the Format menu.

The Format menu is displayed and the mouse pointer is located on the Center in Form command (Figure 2-31). The Center in Form submenu also is displayed. The two choices on the Center in Form submenu are Horizontally and Vertically. Horizontally means the label will be centered between the left and right edges of the window. Vertically means the label will be centered between the top edge and the bottom edge of the window.

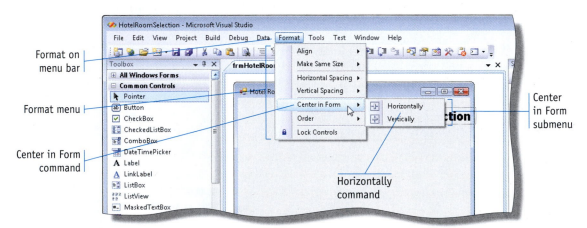

Format on menu bar

Format menu

Center in Form command

Center in Form submenu

Horizontally command

FIGURE 2-31

STEP 2 Click Horizontally on the Center in Form submenu.

The label is centered horizontally in the window (Figure 2-32).

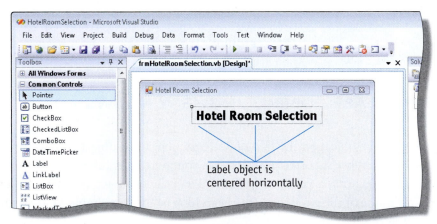

Label object is centered horizontally

FIGURE 2-32

ONLINE REINFORCEMENT

To view a video of the process in the previous steps, visit scsite.com/vb2008/ch2 and then click Figure 2-31.

Object alignment is an important aspect of user interface design because carefully aligned objects in an interface make them and the interface easy to use. Centering within the Windows Form object is the first of several alignment requirements you will encounter in this chapter.

DELETE GUI OBJECTS

In some instances, you might find that you add an object to the Windows Form object and later discover you do not want or need the object in the user interface. When this occurs, you should delete the object from the Windows Form object. Visual Studio provides two primary ways to delete an object from the Windows Form object: the keyboard and a shortcut menu. To delete an object using the keyboard, perform the following steps:

STEP 1   Select the object to be deleted by clicking it.

When you click an object, such as the label in Figure 2–33, the object is selected. When a label is selected, it is surrounded by a dotted border. As you saw with the Windows Form object (Figure 2–12), other objects are surrounded by a heavier border and sizing handles.

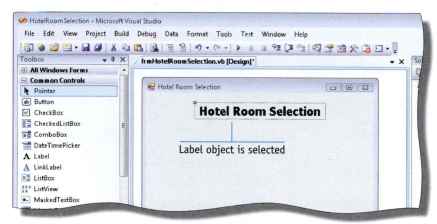

FIGURE 2-33

STEP 2   Press the DELETE key on the keyboard.

When you press the DELETE key, Visual Studio removes the object from the screen (Figure 2–34).

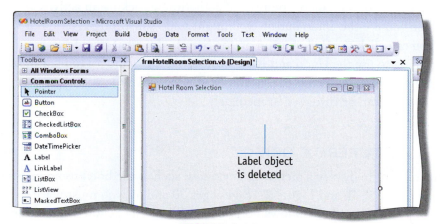

FIGURE 2-34

ONLINE REINFORCEMENT

To view a video of the process in the previous steps, visit scsite.com/vb2008/ch2 and then click Figure 2-33.

A second way to delete an object is to use a shortcut menu. To use a shortcut menu, right-click the object to be deleted and then select Delete on the shortcut menu.

USE THE UNDO BUTTON ON THE STANDARD TOOLBAR

As you work in Visual Studio to create a graphical user interface, you might delete an object or perform another activity that you realize was an error. You can undo an action you just performed by clicking the Undo button on the Standard toolbar. To undo the action of deleting the heading label, you can perform the following step:

STEP 1 Click the Undo button on the Standard toolbar.

When you click the Undo button, the last action performed in Visual Studio is "undone." In Figure 2-35, the action that deleted the label (Figure 2-34) is undone and the Label object now appears on the Windows Form object again.

FIGURE 2-35

You can use the Undo button to undo more than just the last action performed. If you click the Undo button arrow (Figure 2-35), many of the previous activities are shown in a list. You can undo a number of activities by clicking an activity in the list.

When you use the Undo button, you might undo something you do not want to undo. You can click the Redo button on the Standard toolbar to redo an action.

Learning to use the Undo and Redo buttons on the Standard toolbar means you can add or delete items in the graphical user interface with the assurance that any error you make can be corrected immediately.

ADD A PICTUREBOX OBJECT

When you want to display a picture in a window, such as the hotel room pictures shown in Figure 2-1b and Figure 2-1c on pages 30 and 31, you must place a PictureBox object on the Windows Form object. Then, the picture is placed in the PictureBox object. In this section, you will learn to add a PictureBox object to the Windows Form object. In Chapter 3, you will learn how to place a picture in the PictureBox object.

A **PictureBox** is an object much like a label. To add a PictureBox object to the window, you can use the Toolbox, as shown in the following steps:

STEP 1   With the Toolbox visible, drag the PictureBox .NET component on the Toolbox over the Windows Form object to the approximate location where you want the PictureBox object to be displayed.

The mouse pointer changes when you place it over the Windows Form object (Figure 2-36). The upper-left corner of the PictureBox object will be placed on the form at the location of the small square in the mouse pointer.

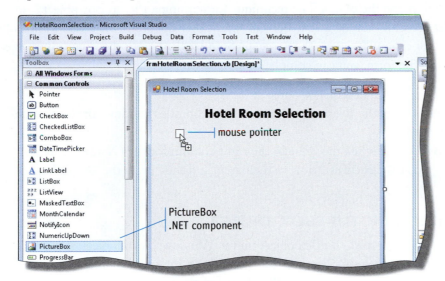

FIGURE 2-36

STEP 2   When the mouse pointer is in the correct location, release the left mouse button.

A PictureBox object is placed on the Windows Form object in the default size (Figure 2-37). The PictureBox object is selected as indicated by the sizing handles and the heavier border. Notice that when the mouse pointer is inside the PictureBox object, it changes to a crosshair with four arrowheads. This indicates you can drag the PictureBox object anywhere on the Windows Form object.

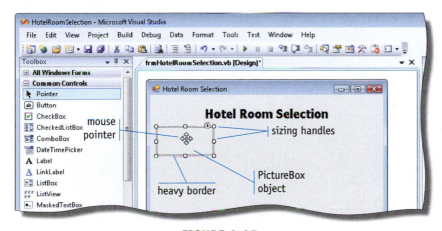

FIGURE 2-37

ONLINE REINFORCEMENT

To view a video of the process in the previous steps, visit scsite.com/vb2008/ch2 and then click Figure 2-36.

As you can see, placing a PictureBox object on the Windows Form object is similar to placing a Label object on the Windows Form object. You will find you can use the same technique for most objects within the Toolbox.

NAME A PICTUREBOX OBJECT

When you add an object to the Windows Form object, the first action you should take is to name the object. The technique for naming a PictureBox object is identical to that used for naming a Label object except that the prefix for a PictureBox object is pic. For example, to give the name, picStandardRoom, to the PictureBox object just added to the form, you can complete the following steps:

1. Select the PictureBox object.
2. Locate the (Name) property in the Properties window for the PictureBox object.
3. Double-click the value in the right column for the (Name) property, type `picStandardRoom` as the name, and then press the ENTER key.

RESIZE A PICTUREBOX OBJECT

When you place a PictureBox object on the Windows Form object, it often is not the size required for the application. You can resize a PictureBox object using the same technique you used to resize the Windows Form object. The step on the next page will resize the Picture Box object:

STEP 1   Place the mouse pointer over the sizing handle at the lower-right corner of the PictureBox object, and then drag the handle to the size required.

When you drag the sizing handle, both the width and the height of the PictureBox object can be changed. In Figure 2-38, the width and the height of the PictureBox object are increased. The actual size of the PictureBox object in pixels (horizontal pixels, vertical pixels) is shown on the Status bar.

HEADS UP

The Size property will change to the new size in the Properties dialog box. If you know an exact size, you can also enter that size directly in the Size property for that object.

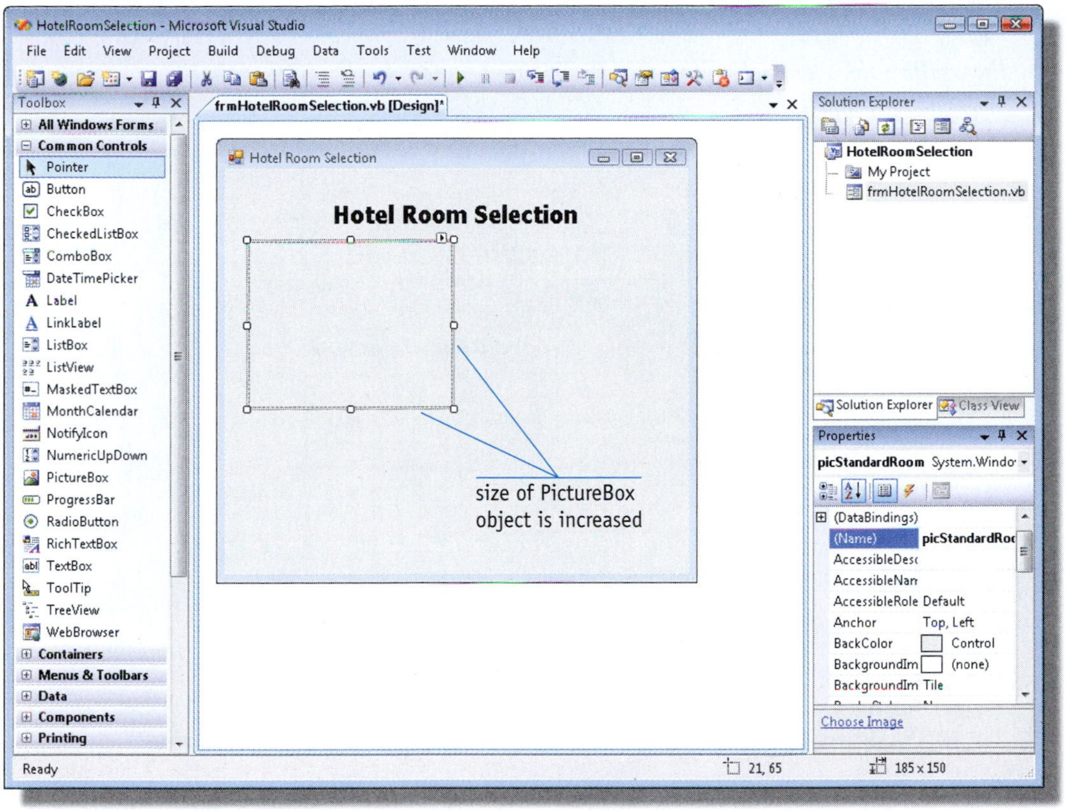

FIGURE 2-38

ONLINE REINFORCEMENT

To view a video of the process in the previous step, visit scsite.com/vb2008/ch2 and then click Figure 2-38.

ADD A SECOND PICTUREBOX OBJECT

You can add a second PictureBox object to the Windows Form object by performing the same technique you have seen previously, as in the following step:

STEP 1 Drag the PictureBox .NET component in the Toolbox to any location in the Windows Form object, and then release the left mouse button.

The PictureBox object is placed on the Windows Form object (Figure 2-39). Notice that the PictureBox objects in Figure 2-39 are different sizes. If you see a blue line as you drag the PictureBox object onto the Windows Form object, ignore it. You will learn about these lines later in this chapter.

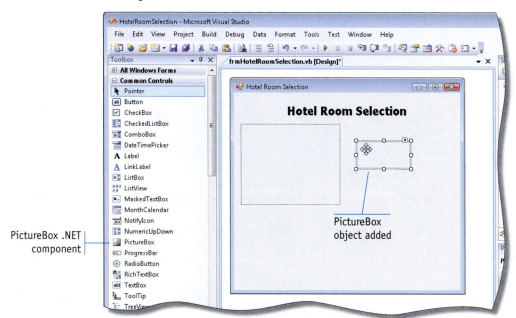

FIGURE 2-39

ONLINE REINFORCEMENT

To view a video of the process in the previous step, visit scsite.com/vb2008/ch2 and then click Figure 2-39.

As with all objects added to the Windows Form object, you should name the PictureBox object immediately after adding it. A good name for the second PictureBox object is picDeluxeRoom.

MAKE OBJECTS THE SAME SIZE

Often you will want Picture Boxes and other GUI elements in your user interface to be the same size. You can use the Format menu to make GUI objects the same size, as shown in the steps on the next page:

STEP 1   Select the object whose size you want to duplicate (in this example, the left PictureBox object in the window), and then hold down the CTRL key and click the object you want to resize (the right PictureBox object in the window).

Both the left PictureBox object and the right PictureBox object are selected (Figure 2-40). The left PictureBox object is surrounded by white sizing handles and the right PictureBox object is surrounded by black sizing handles, which indicates the left PictureBox object is the "controlling" object when sizing or alignment commands are executed. The first object selected always is the controlling object.

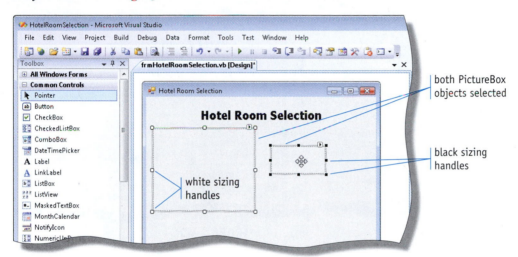

FIGURE 2-40

STEP 2   Click Format on the menu bar and then point to the Make Same Size command on the Format menu.

The Format menu and the Make Same Size submenu are displayed (Figure 2-41). The Make Same Size submenu provides commands to make the width, the height, or both dimensions the same as the controlling object.

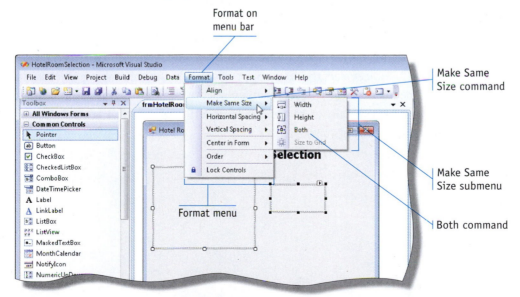

FIGURE 2-41

STEP 3 Click Both on the Make Same Size submenu.

Visual Studio changes the size of the right PictureBox object to match the size of the left PictureBox object (Figure 2–42). Both the width and the height of the right PictureBox object are changed.

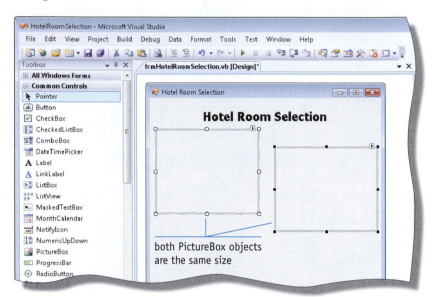

FIGURE 2-42

ALIGN THE PICTUREBOX OBJECTS

Notice in Figure 2-42 that the left PictureBox object is higher in the form than the right PictureBox object. When designing a graphical user interface, you should consider aligning the elements to create a clean, uncluttered look for the user. **Alignment** means one element in the GUI is lined up horizontally (left and right) or vertically (up and down) with another element in the window. For example, in Figure 2-42 the GUI would be better if the PictureBox objects were aligned horizontally so their tops and bottoms were even across the window.

When you want to align objects already on the Windows Form object, select the objects to align, and then specify the alignment you want. As you have seen when changing the object size, the first object selected is the controlling object; when aligning, this means the other objects that are selected will be aligned on the first object selected. To horizontally align the two PictureBox objects in Figure 2-42, you can perform the following steps:

STEP 1   With the left and right PictureBox objects selected as shown in Figure 2–42, click Format on the menu bar and then point to Align on the Format menu.

The Format menu and the Align submenu are displayed (Figure 2–43). The left PictureBox object is the "controlling" object as indicated by the white sizing handles, so the right PictureBox object will be aligned horizontally with the left PictureBox object.

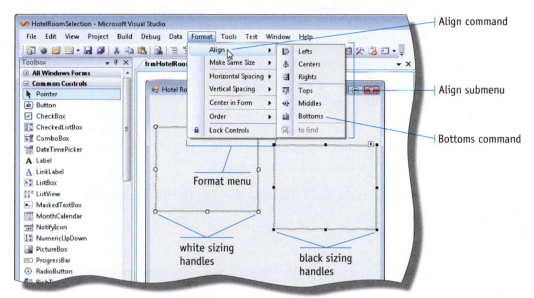

FIGURE 2-43

STEP 2   Click Bottoms on the Align submenu.

The bottom of the right PictureBox object is aligned horizontally with the bottom of the left PictureBox object (Figure 2–44). In addition, because the PictureBox objects are the same size, the tops also are aligned.

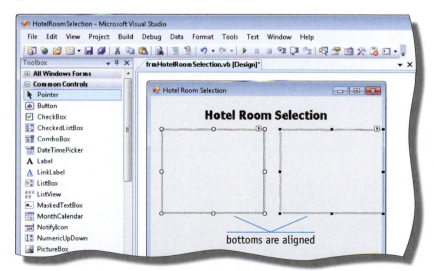

FIGURE 2-44

ONLINE REINFORCEMENT

To view a video of the process in the previous steps, visit scsite.com/vb2008/ch2 and then click Figure 2-43.

Notice on the Align submenu in Figure 2–43 that Visual Studio offers seven choices for alignment. When you are aligning objects horizontally, you should choose from the Tops, Middles, and Bottoms group. When you are aligning objects vertically, you should choose from the Lefts, Centers, and Rights group. Aligning to a grid will be covered later in this book.

CENTER MULTIPLE OBJECTS HORIZONTALLY IN THE WINDOW

From Figure 2-44 on page 63 you can see that the PictureBox objects are not centered horizontally in the Windows Form object. As you learned, you can center one or more objects horizontally within the Windows Form object by using a command from the Format menu. To center the two PictureBox objects as a unit, you can complete the following steps:

STEP 1   With both PictureBox objects selected, click Format on the menu bar and then point to the Center in Form command.

The Format menu is displayed (Figure 2-45). The Center in Form submenu also is displayed.

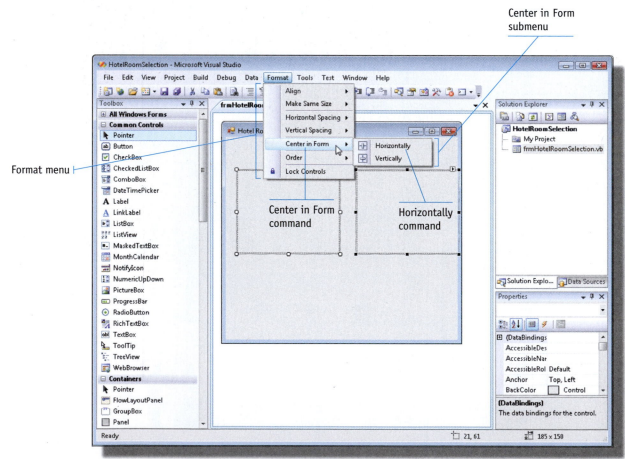

FIGURE 2-45

STEP 2   Click Horizontally on the Center in Form submenu.

The two PictureBox objects, as a unit, are centered horizontally in the Windows Form object (Figure 2–46). The left border for the left PictureBox object is the same distance from the window frame as the right border for the right PictureBox object.

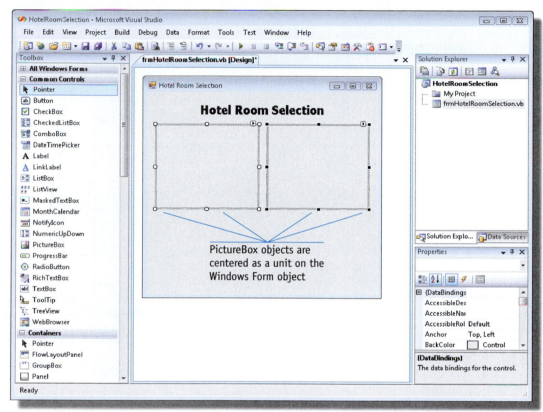

FIGURE 2-46

Adding an object, naming it, sizing it, and aligning it are basic to all graphical user interface design.

ADD A BUTTON OBJECT

A **Button object** is a commonly used object in a graphical user interface. For example, you probably are familiar with the OK button that is used in many applications. Generally, when the program is executing, buttons are used to cause an event to occur. To place a Button object on the Windows Form object, you use the Toolbox. To create a Button object, you can complete the steps on the next page:

ONLINE REINFORCEMENT

To view a video of the process in the previous steps, visit scsite.com/vb2008/ch2 and then click Figure 2-45.

STEP 1 With the Toolbox displayed in the Visual Studio window, drag the Button .NET component in the Toolbox over the Windows Form object to the position where you want to place the button.

When you drag the button over the Windows Form object, the mouse pointer changes (Figure 2–47). The upper-left corner of the Button object will be placed where the upper-left corner of the rectangle is located.

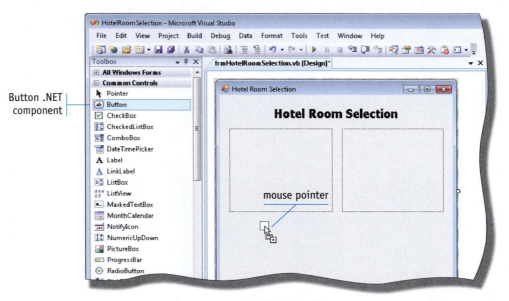

Button .NET component

mouse pointer

FIGURE 2-47

STEP 2 When the mouse pointer is positioned properly, release the left mouse button.

A standard-sized Button object is added to the Windows Form object (Figure 2–48). The text on the button is the default, Button1. In addition, the button is selected as indicated by the heavier border and sizing handles.

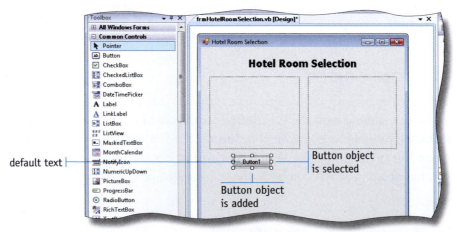

default text

Button object is selected

Button object is added

FIGURE 2-48

NAME AND SET TEXT FOR A BUTTON OBJECT

As with other objects added to the Windows Form object, the first step after adding the Button object is to name it. A Button object name should contain the prefix, btn. For example, the name for the button you just added could be, btnStandardRoom.

In most cases, you also will change the text that appears on the Button object. To change the text on the btnStandardRoom button, you can do the following:

STEP 1   With the Button object selected, scroll in the Properties dialog box until you find the Text property. Double-click the Text value in the right column, type `Standard Room` and then press the ENTER key.

The text for the Standard Room button is changed both on the button and in the Properties window (Figure 2-49). The button is not large enough to contain the words, Standard Room, so only the word, Standard, is displayed. In the next set of steps, you will learn how to enlarge the size of the Button object.

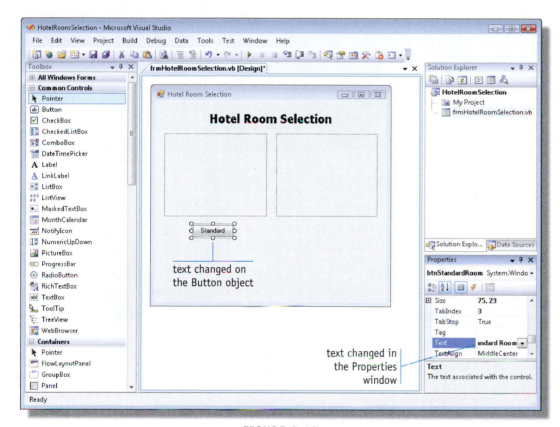

FIGURE 2-49

CHANGE BUTTON OBJECT SIZE

Sometimes, the button size may not be big enough to display the button text (see Figure 2-49 on the previous page). To change a Button object size to accommodate the text, you can perform the following steps:

STEP 1   Place the mouse pointer over the right edge of the Button object until the pointer changes to a double-headed arrow.

The mouse pointer changes to a double-headed arrow, which indicates you can drag the border of the button to increase or decrease its size (Figure 2-50).

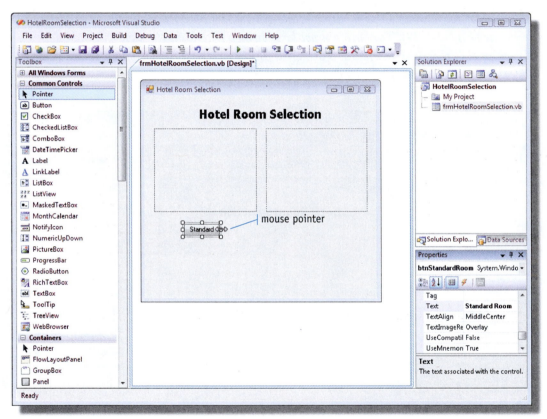

FIGURE 2-50

STEP 2 Drag the mouse pointer to the right until the Button object is just big enough to display the text, Standard Room, and then release the left mouse button.

As you drag the mouse pointer to the right, the button is made bigger (Figure 2-51). When the button is big enough to display the text, it is the right size.

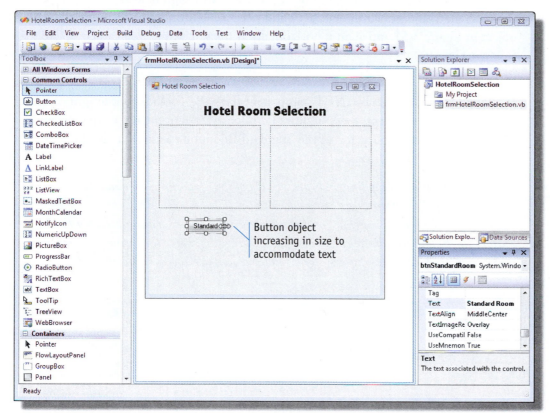

FIGURE 2-51

You can move a Button object by placing the mouse pointer on the button (the mouse pointer changes to a crosshair with four arrowheads) and then dragging the button to any location on the Windows Form object. You can move other objects on the Windows Form object using the same technique.

ONLINE REINFORCEMENT

To view a video of the process in the previous steps, visit scsite.com/vb2008/ch2 and then click Figure 2-50.

IN THE REAL WORLD

Some developers use the AutoSize property for a Button object to ensure the button always is large enough for text. By setting the AutoSize property for a Button object to True in the Properties window, the Button object will expand or contract when you change the text so the text fits precisely fits in the button.

ADD AND ALIGN A SECOND BUTTON

Often, a window requires more than one button. When a second button is added to the window, a normal requirement is that the buttons be aligned. As with PictureBox objects, you can align Button objects horizontally or vertically.

With the PictureBox objects, you saw that you can align objects after they have been placed on the Windows Form object. You also can align objects when you place them on the Windows Form object. To add a second button to the Windows Form object in Figure 2-51 and align it horizontally at the same time, you can complete the following steps:

STEP 1 Drag the Button .NET component from the Toolbox to the right of the Standard Room button on the Windows Form object. Align the top of the rectangle in the mouse pointer to the top of the Standard Room button until a blue line displays along the tops of the buttons.

*The blue line, called a **snap line**, indicates the top of the Standard Room button is aligned with the top of the Button object being added to the Windows Form object (Figure 2-52). You can drag the Button object left or right to obtain the desired spacing between the buttons. If the blue line disappears while you are dragging, move the mouse pointer up or down until the blue line reappears, signaling the objects are horizontally aligned.*

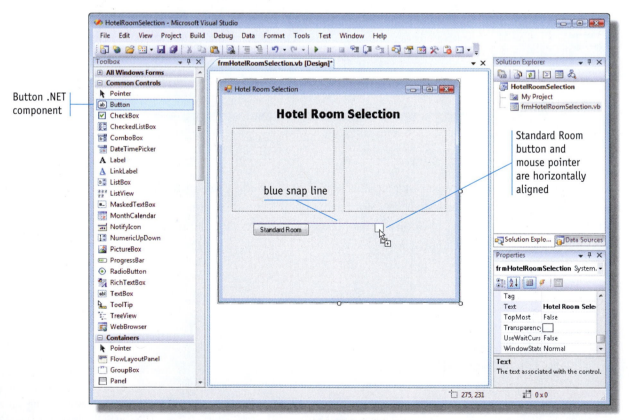

FIGURE 2-52

STEP 2   When the buttons are aligned and spaced as you like, release the left mouse button.

The Button1 object is aligned horizontally with the Standard Room button (Figure 2-53). Their tops are on the same line and, because they are the same vertical size, their bottoms are aligned as well.

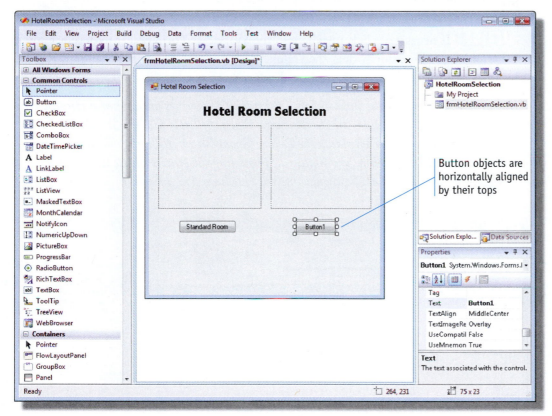

FIGURE 2-53

ONLINE REINFORCEMENT

To view a video of the process in the previous steps, visit scsite.com/vb2008/ch2 and then click Figure 2-52.

After adding the second Button object, you should name it, change the text as needed, and size the Button object if necessary. For the second Button object, assume you have named it btnDeluxeRoom, have changed the button text to Deluxe Room, and have made the two buttons the same size. You will recall that you can make the Deluxe Room button the same size as the Standard Room button by completing the following steps:

Step 1: Click the Standard Room button and then, while holding down the CTRL key, click the Deluxe Room button.
Step 2: Click Format on the menu bar, point to Make Same Size on the Format menu, and then click Both on the Make Same Size submenu.
Step 3: To unselect the Button objects, click anywhere on the Windows Form object except on another object.

ALIGN OBJECTS VERTICALLY

The buttons in Figure 2-53 are aligned horizontally. They also can be aligned vertically. To illustrate this and to show how to align objects already on the Windows Form object using snap lines, assume that the Standard Room button and the Deluxe Room button should be vertically aligned on the left side of the Windows Form object with the Standard Room button above the Deluxe Room button. To vertically align the Button objects, you can complete the following steps:

STEP 1 If necessary, click anywhere in the Windows Form object to deselect any other objects. Then, slowly drag the Deluxe Room button below the Standard Room button until vertical blue snap lines are displayed.

*As you drag, **blue snap lines** indicate when the sides of the objects are aligned vertically. In Figure 2-54, since the buttons are the same size, when the left side of the Standard Room button is aligned with the left side of the Deluxe Room button, the right sides are aligned as well, so two blue vertical lines are displayed. If you drag the button a little further to the left or right, the buttons will not be aligned and the blue lines will disappear.*

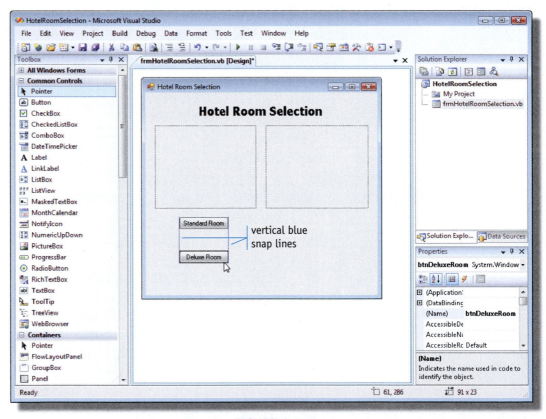

FIGURE 2-54

STEP 2   When the blue lines appear, indicating the buttons are aligned vertically, drag the Standard Room button up or down to create the proper spacing between the buttons, and then release the left mouse button.

The vertical distance between the buttons is a judgment call, based on the needs of the application, the size of the Windows Form object, and the number of other elements within the window (Figure 2-55). As with many aspects of GUI design, the eye of the developer will be critical in determining the actual placement of objects in the window.

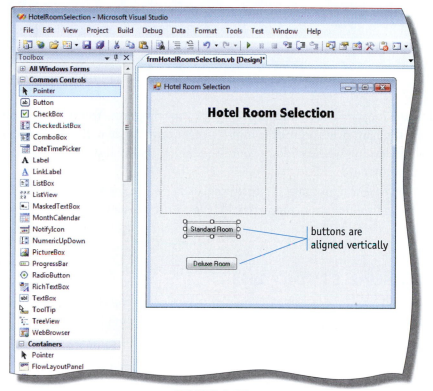

FIGURE 2-55

ONLINE REINFORCEMENT

To view a video of the process in the previous steps, visit scsite.com/vb2008/ch2 and then click Figure 2-54.

In the previous examples, you have seen the use of blue snap lines. As you drag objects, you also might see red snap lines flash on the screen. A **red snap line** indicates text within an object is aligned. For example, if you drag a button and the text in the button you are dragging aligns horizontally with the text in another button, a red snap line will be displayed. The use of red and blue snap lines allows you to align objects on the Windows Form object by dragging instead of selecting the objects and using the Format menu.

Visual Studio offers a variety of tools to create and align elements in the graphical user interface, and to make the user interface as effective and useful as possible.

SAVE A VISUAL BASIC PROJECT

As you are working on a Visual Basic project, a mandatory practice is to save your work on a regular basis. Some developers save every 10-15 minutes while others might wait for a natural break to save their work. Regardless, it is important to develop the habit of regularly saving your work.

To save the work you have completed, you can click the Save All button on the Standard toolbar. The first time you save a project, the Save Project dialog box shown in Figure 2-56 is displayed.

location for
saving project

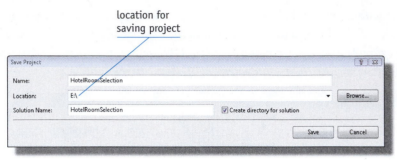

FIGURE 2-56

Select the location where you want to store your program. You might use an USB drive, the hard drive on your computer, or a network drive. If you have any questions concerning where to store your program, check with your instructor or network administrator.

After you save the program the first time, each time you click the Save All button on the Standard toolbar, your program will be saved in the same location with the same name.

CLOSE VISUAL STUDIO 2008

To close Visual Studio, you can click the Close button on the right of the Visual Studio window title bar. If, when you close Visual Studio, you have never saved your program, Visual Studio will display the Close Project dialog box (Figure 2-57).

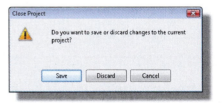

FIGURE 2-57

You can choose to save your program or to discard your program. If you click the Save button, the Save Project dialog box will be displayed (Figure 2-56) and you can save your program. If you click the Discard button, your program will be discarded and not saved.

If, when you close Visual Studio, you have accomplished work since you last saved your project, Visual Studio will ask if you want to save the elements of the project that have changed since you last saved the project. In most cases, you should choose Yes.

OPEN A VISUAL BASIC PROJECT

After you save a project and close Visual Studio, you often will want to open the project and work on it again. To open a saved project, you can follow one of several methods:

Method 1: Double-click the solution file in the folder in which it is stored. This method will open the solution and allow you to continue your work.

Method 2: With Visual Studio open, click the Open File button on the Standard toolbar, locate the solution file, and open it in the same manner you use for most programs running under the Windows operating system.

Method 3: With Visual Studio open, click File on the menu bar and then point to Recent Projects on the File menu. A list of the projects most recently worked on is displayed. Click the name of the project you want to open. This method might not work well if you are using a computer that is not your own because other persons' projects might be listed.

After using one of these methods, you can continue the work on your project.

> **WATCH OUT FOR**
>
> Sometimes when you open a Visual Basic project, the Form1.vb[Design] tabbed page is not displayed. (This page is renamed as frmHotelRoomSelection.vb in your project.) To display it, double-click Form1 or the new name in this project, frmHotelRoomSelection.vb, in the Solution Explorer window at the upper-right section of the Visual Studio window.

Program Development Life Cycle

Now that you have learned the Visual Studio and Visual Basic skills necessary to design a user interface, you are ready to learn about the program development life cycle. The **program development life cycle** is a set of phases and steps that are followed by developers to design, create, and maintain a computer program. The phases of the program development life cycle are:

1. **Gather and Analyze the Program Requirements** — The developer must obtain the information that identifies the program requirements and then document these requirements.
2. **Design the User Interface** — After the developer understands the program requirements, the next step is to design the user interface. The user interface provides the framework for the processing that will occur within the program.
3. **Design the Program Processing Objects** — A computer program consists of one or more processing objects that perform the tasks required within the program. The developer must determine what processing objects are required, and then determine the requirements of each object.
4. **Code the Program** — After the processing object has been designed, the object must be implemented in program code. **Program code** consists of the instructions written using a programming language such as Visual Basic 2008 that ultimately can be executed by a computer.
5. **Test the Program** — As the program is being coded, and after the coding is completed, the developer should test the program code to ensure it is executing properly. The testing process is ongoing, and includes a variety of stages.
6. **Document the Program/System** — As a program is being designed and coded, and after that process is completed, the developer should be documenting the program. **Documenting a program** means writing down in

a prescribed manner the instructions for using the program, the way in which a program performs its tasks, and other items that users, other developers, and management might require.

7. **Maintain the Program/System** — After a program is put into use, the program likely will have to be changed, or modified, some time in the future. For example, in the hotel room selection program, if a third type of room, such as a suite, is added to the rooms available in the hotel, the program must be changed to reflect the new room type. The process of changing and updating programs is called **program and system maintenance**.

The program development life cycle rarely is accomplished in a linear fashion, with one phase complete before the next phase starts. Rather, programs are developed iteratively, which means phases and steps within phases might have to be repeated a number of times before the program is completed. For example, the requirements for a program might be changed after the developer has begun coding the program. If this occurs, the developer must return to Phase 1 and gather and document the new requirements. Then, changes might have to be made to the user interface or other parts of the program to accommodate the updated requirements. This process of moving back and forth within the program development cycle is normal when developing a computer program.

The next sections in this chapter explain in detail Phase 1 and Phase 2 of the program development life cycle. The remaining phases are explained in Chapter 3.

PHASE 1: GATHER AND ANALYZE THE PROGRAM REQUIREMENTS

An old programming adage states, "If you don't understand the problem to be solved, you will never develop a solution." While this seems self-evident, too often a program does not perform in the desired manner is because the designer did not understand the problem to be solved. Therefore, it is mandatory that, before beginning the user interface design, the developer understand the problem to be solved.

In many programming projects in industry, the developer is responsible for gathering the program requirements by interviewing users, reviewing current procedures, and completing other fact-gathering tasks. The emphasis in this book is on learning to program using the Visual Basic 2008 language, so the process of gathering program requirements is beyond the scope of the book. You will be given the program requirements for each program in this book.

When the requirements have been determined, they must be documented so the developers can proceed to design and implement the program. The exact form of the requirements documentation can vary significantly. The format and amount of documentation might be dictated by the application itself, or by the documentation standards of the organization for which the program is being developed. For Windows applications in this book, two types of requirements documentation will be provided for you. The first is the requirements document.

A **requirements document** identifies the purpose of the program being developed, the application title, the procedures to be followed when using the program, any equations and calculations required in the program, any conditions within the program that must be tested, notes and restrictions that must be followed by the program, and any other comments that would be helpful to understanding the problem.

Recall that the program to be developed in this chapter and in Chapter 3 is the Hotel Room Selection program (see Figure 2-1 on pages 30 and 31). The requirements document for the Hotel Room Selection program is shown in Figure 2-58.

The requirements document contains all the information that should be needed by a developer to design the program. In an event-driven program such as the Hotel Room Selection program, however, one additional document often is developed in

---

REQUIREMENTS DOCUMENT

Date submitted: January 23, 2011

Application title: Hotel Room Selection

Purpose: The hotel room selection program will allow a user to view different room types and make a room selection.

Program Procedures: From a window on the screen, the user should choose the room type and then make a room selection.

Algorithms, Processing, and Conditions:
1. The user must be able to view a standard room and a deluxe room until he or she makes a room selection.
2. When the user chooses a room type, a picture of that room type should appear in the window.
3. Only one picture should be displayed at a time, so if a user chooses a standard room, only the standard room picture should be displayed; if a user then chooses a deluxe room, the deluxe room picture should be displayed and the standard room picture should not be displayed.
4. When the user makes a room selection, a confirming message should be displayed. In addition, the user should be prevented from identifying a room type after the room selection is made.
5. After the user makes a room selection, the only allowable action is to exit the window.

Notes and Restrictions:
1. The user should not be able to make a room selection until he or she has chosen a room type.

Comments:
1. The pictures shown in the window should be selected from the pictures available on the Web.

FIGURE 2-58

order to clarify for the developer exactly what should occur in the program. The document is the Use Case Definition.

A **use case** is a sequence of actions a user will perform when using the program. The **Use Case Definition** specifies each of these sequences of actions by describing what the user will do and how the program will respond. The Use Case Definition for the Hotel Room Selection program is shown in Figure 2-59.

USE CASE DEFINITION

1. User clicks Standard Room or Deluxe Room button.
2. Program displays a picture of the room chosen by the user and enables the room selection button.
3. User clicks room buttons to view rooms if desired. Program displays the picture of the chosen room.
4. User clicks the Select Room button.
5. Program displays a room selection confirmation message, and disables both room buttons and the Select Room button. The Exit Window button becomes active.
6. User terminates the program by clicking the Exit Window button.

FIGURE 2-59

As you can see, the Use Case Definition specifies the actions performed by the user and the actions the program is to take in response.

The Use Case Definition is an important part of the requirements documentation for two reasons: 1) It defines for the developer exactly what is to occur as the user uses the program; 2) It allows the users to review the requirements documentation to ensure the specifications are correct before the developer actually begins designing the program.

When gathering and documenting the program requirements, it is critical that the users be involved. After all, the program is being developed for their use. When the users concur that the program requirements documentation is correct, the developer can move forward into the design phases for the program with the most confidence possible that the program will fulfill the needs of the users.

For the programs you will design in this book, the program requirements, including the requirements document and the Use Case Definition, will be provided to you. You should be aware, however, that in many cases in industry, an experienced developer must gather the requirements as well as implement them in a program.

PHASE 2: DESIGN THE USER INTERFACE

Virtually all programs developed for a graphical user interface are driven by the user's actions when using the interface. It is these actions that dictate the processing the program should execute. Therefore, by designing the user interface, the developer will obtain a foundation for designing the rest of the program. In addition, by designing the user interface early in the design process, the developer can interact with users and ensure that the interface will fulfill the user requirements.

Expert program developers recognize the importance of the graphical user interface. These developers spend 25% to 40% of the program design time on the user interface, which sometimes is called the **presentation layer** of the program, because it is so critical to the program's success.

In the past, developers would draw the user interface on paper and present the drawings to users for their approval. When using Visual Studio 2008, however, with the rapid application development tools you have learned, the developer should use Visual Studio to create the user interface. The interface is created with no functionality; that is, none of the buttons or other GUI elements will cause processing to occur. Often, these interface designs are called **mock-ups** because they are provided for approval of the design only. When the users or others approve the interface design, the developer can design the program elements required to implement the functionality of the program.

An additional benefit when using Visual Studio to design the user interface is that when you have completed the design, you can use it in the actual program and you do not have to recreate it using other software.

Principles of User Interface Design

Because the presentation layer of the program is so important, a number of principles, or guidelines, have been developed over the years for user interface design. While the intent of this book is not to create expert user interface design specialists, nonetheless you should understand some of the principles so you can develop programs that are useful and usable. The following are some **design principles** you should incorporate into your user interface designs:

1. The most important principle to remember is that the user's ability to use the program effectively depends to a large extent on the design of the interface. If the GUI is easy to use and follow, the user will have a productive and enjoyable experience. If, on the other hand, the user must struggle to figure out how to enter data or which button to click, the user interface design is defeating the purpose of the program.
2. If the user interface is not easy to use, the user will not be satisfied with the application regardless of how well it does its work.
3. The user interface includes the windows, graphics, and text shown on the screen, as well as the methods used to interact with your program and cause operations to occur. Three primary means of interacting in a user interface are the keyboard, a pointing device such as a mouse, and voice input. The correct use of these tools significantly increases the probability of success for a user interface.
4. Use of the interface should feel natural and normal. This principle means the developer must be aware of who the user is and the manner in which the user is accustomed to working. For example, the interface for a banking program where a teller is entering account information will be different from that of a graphic arts program that allows manipulation of graphics and photographs. Each must reflect the needs of the user.

5. Visual Studio contains a wide variety of objects for use in the GUI, many of which can be used for similar purposes. A good user interface provides the most appropriate object for each requirement. You will learn about all these objects and their correct use throughout this text.

6. Once an object is used for a particular purpose in the user interface, such as a button being used to cause a particular action, then that object should be used for the same purpose throughout the program interface.

7. The objects in the interface must be arranged in the sequence in which they are used so the user can move from item to item on the screen in a logical, straightforward manner. Following this principle creates a clean and easy to use interface. It once again requires the developer to understand the needs of the user. When this principle is not followed, a confusing interface can result.

8. The interface should be kept a simple as possible, while containing all the functionality required for the program. Generally, the simpler the interface, the more effective it will be.

9. When implemented, the user interface should be intuitive, which means the user should be able to use it with little or no instruction. In fact, the user should feel that no other interface could have been designed because the one they are using is the most "natural."

By following these principles, you will create user interfaces that assist the user. The success of your program can depend on the user interface you design.

Sample Program

As you learned earlier, the Hotel Room Selection program is the sample program for this chapter and for Chapter 3 (see Figure 2-1 on page pages 30 and 31). The requirements document for this program is shown in Figure 2-58 on page 77 and the Use Case Definition is in Figure 2-59 on page 78. With these documents in hand, the first phase of the program development cycle is complete.

SAMPLE PROGRAM — PHASE 2: USER INTERFACE DESIGN

When beginning the design of the user interface, the primary source of reference is the requirements document and the Use Case Definition for the program. Using these documents, the developer must analyze the program requirements and determine the elements required in the user interface.

On a line-for-line basis, the analysis of the requirements document in Figure 2-58 could proceed as follows:

1. The application will be presented in a window on the screen, so a Windows Forms Application using a Windows Form object is the appropriate means for creating the program.

2. The user will choose either a standard room or a deluxe room and then will make a room selection. In addition, when the room is chosen, a picture of the room should be displayed. While Visual Studio provides a variety of user interface tools for a user to make selections, a commonly used tool and one that is easily understood by users is the Button object. That is, when a user clicks a button, the user has made a choice and the program responds appropriately. In this application, a good design decision is to use buttons for the user to make a choice of rooms and make a room selection. When the user clicks the Standard Room button, a picture of the standard room will be displayed. When the user clicks the Deluxe Room button, a picture of the deluxe room will be displayed. When the user clicks the Select Room button, a room selection is made.

3. Two different pictures must be displayed in the user interface — a standard room picture and a deluxe room picture. While two different pictures can be displayed in a single PictureBox object, depending on the choice of the user, a simpler and more easily understood user interface can be developed if a PictureBox object and a button work together; that is, when the Standard Room button is clicked, the standard room picture is displayed in the standard room PictureBox object; and when the Deluxe Room button is clicked, the deluxe room picture is displayed in the deluxe room PictureBox object. In this way, the user can associate a button with a picture box location and the user interface is intuitive and easy to use.

4. When the user makes a room selection by clicking the Select Room button, a message must be displayed confirming the room selection. Therefore, a Label object must be included for the confirmation message.

5. After the user makes a room selection, the only action then available to the user is to exit the window, so an Exit Window button is required.

6. In addition to the exact requirements in the program requirements document, standard procedure usually dictates that a heading should appear in the program window. Also, it is common practice to include simple instructions in the window for the user so no confusion can result from using the interface. The heading and instructions can be included as Label objects.

7. As a result of this analysis, the user interface should include the following items: a Windows Form object that will contain all the other objects; two PictureBox objects to contain the pictures of the standard room and the deluxe room; four Button objects (Standard Room button, Deluxe Room button, Select Room button, and Exit Window button); and three Label objects (Heading, Instructions, and Room Selection Confirmation).

After the developer has determined the elements required for the user interface, Visual Studio 2008 can be used to create a mock-up of the user interface. The exact placement of objects in the window is a creative process, guided by the principles of user interface design you have learned. Usually, no "right answer" exists because each developer will see the solution to the problem a little differently, but you must adhere to good user interface design principles. Figure 2-60 shows the mock-up that was created for the Hotel Room Selection program.

FIGURE 2-60

Guided Program Development

This guided program development takes you step-by-step through the process of creating the sample program in this chapter. To create the mock-up shown in Figure 2-60, complete the steps on the following pages:

Guided Program Development

1

▶ **Open Visual Studio 2008**
Open Visual Studio using the Start button on the Windows taskbar and the All Programs submenu *(ref: Figure 2-2)*. If necessary, maximize the Visual Studio window. If necessary, close the Start page.

HINT

Microsoft Visual Studio 2008
Microsoft Visual Studio 2008 Docum
Microsoft Visual Studio 2008
Visual Studio Remote Tools
Visual Studio Tools

◀ **Back**

Start Search

HEADS UP

During the development of the program, periodically you should save the program so you do not lose your work.

▶ **Create a new Visual Basic Windows Application**
Create a new Visual Basic Windows Forms Application project by clicking the New Project button, selecting Visual Basic in the left pane, selecting Windows Forms Application in the right pane, naming the project, and then clicking the OK button in the New Project dialog box *(ref: Figure 2-4)*.

HINT

Start Page - Microsoft Visual
File Edit View Tools Te
Start Page
New Project
Microsoft®

▶ **Keep the Toolbox Visible** If necessary, click the Auto Hide button to keep the Toolbox visible *(ref: Figure 2-10)*.

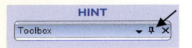

HINT

Toolbox

RESULT OF STEP 1

The Visual Studio application opens and a new project is displayed in the window (Figure 2-61). The Toolbox remains visible regardless of the location of the mouse pointer.

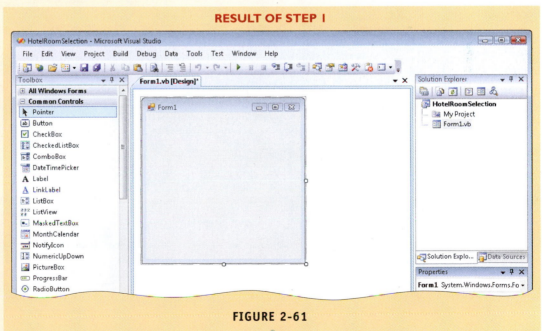

FIGURE 2-61

(continues)

Guided Program Development (continued)

2

▶ **Name the Windows Form Object** Using the (Name) Property in the Windows Form object Properties window displayed in the lower-right section of the Visual Studio window, name the form, frmHotelRoomSelection *(ref: Figure 2-13)*.

▶ **Change the Windows Form Object Text Property** With the Windows Form object selected, double-click the text value in the Text property of the Properties window for the Windows Form object, and then change the Windows Form object title bar text to the value, Hotel Room Selection *(ref: Figure 2-16)*.

The text in the title bar of the Windows Form object has been changed to Hotel Room Selection (Figure 2-62). In addition, the name of the object has been changed to frmHotelRoom-Selection.

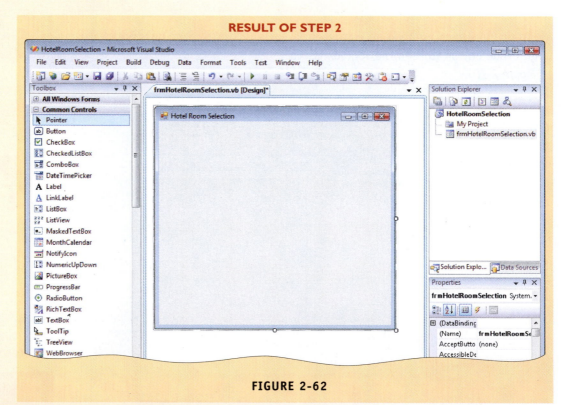

FIGURE 2-62

Guided Program Development (continued)

3

▶ **Resize the Windows Form Object** Resize the Windows Form object to the approximate size shown in Figure 2-60 (437,402) by dragging the sizing handle in the lower-right corner of the Windows Form object *(ref: Figure 2-17)*.

4

▶ **Add a Label Object** Add a Label object by dragging the Label .NET component from the Toolbox to the Windows Form object. Place the label near the center and top of the Windows Form object *(ref: Figure 2-19)*.

▶ **Name the Label Object** Change the name of the Label object to lblHeading by using the (Name) property in the Properties window for the Label object *(ref: Figure 2-21)*.

▶ **Change the Label Object Text Property** Double-click the text value in the Text property in the Properties window for the Label object, and then change the Text property of the lblHeading Label object to Hotel Room Selection *(ref: Figure 2-23)*.

▶ **Open the Font Dialog Box** Click the Font property in the Properties window for the Label object and then click the ellipsis button (...) for the Font property *(ref: Figure 2-27)*.

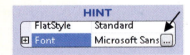

▶ **Change the Font for the Label Object** In the Font list of the Font dialog box, change the font in the lblHeading Label object to Tahoma *(ref: Figure 2-29)*.

▶ **Change the Font Style for the Label Object** Using the Font style list in the Font dialog box, change the Font style in the lblHeading Label object to Bold *(ref: Figure 2-29)*.

(continues)

Guided Program Development (continued)

▶ **Change the Size for the Label Object** Using the Size list in the Font dialog box, change the font size in the lblHeading Label object to 16 point (ref: Figure 2-29).

HINT

Size:

16

8
9
10
11
12
14
16

▶ **Center the Heading Horizontally** If necessary, select the lblHeading Label object. Then, using the Center in Form command on the Format menu, click the Horizontally command on the Center in Form submenu to center the lblHeading Label object horizontally on the Windows Form object (ref: Figure 2-31).

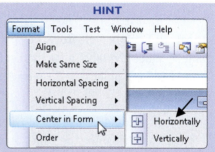

HINT

Format	Tools	Test	Window	Help

Align
Make Same Size
Horizontal Spacing
Vertical Spacing
Center in Form ▶   ⊞ Horizontally   ⊞ Vertically
Order

The Heading Label object text has been changed and the Label object is centered horizontally on the Windows Form object (Figure 2-63). The vertical placement of the label, that is, the distance from the top of the window frame, is dependent on the eye of the developer, the size of the Windows Form object, and the other objects that are part of the graphical user interface. While you may have placed the label in your window a little higher or a little lower, your window should closely resemble the one in Figure 2-63.

RESULT OF STEPS 3 AND 4

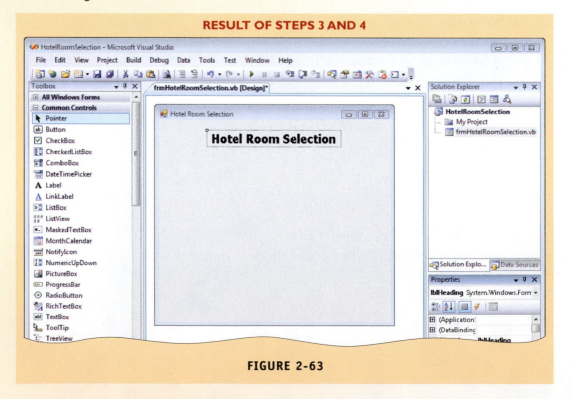

FIGURE 2-63

Guided Program Development *(continued)*

5

▶ **Add a PictureBox Object** Add a PictureBox object to the Windows Form object by dragging a PictureBox .NET component from the Toolbox to the Windows Form object. Place the PictureBox object below and to the left of the heading label in a location similar to that shown in Figure 2-64 *(ref: Figure 2-36)*.

▶ **Name the PictureBox Object** Using the (Name) property in the PictureBox Properties Window, name the PictureBox object, picStandardRoom.

▶ **Resize the PictureBox Object** Resize the PictureBox object to the approximate size of the PictureBox object in Figure 2-64 (185,150) by dragging the sizing handle in the lower-right corner of the PictureBox object *(ref: Figure 2-38)*.

HINT

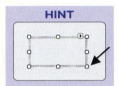

HINT

A properly sized PictureBox object is displayed in the Windows Form object (Figure 2-64). This PictureBox object will be used to display a picture of a standard room when the program is completed in Chapter 3.

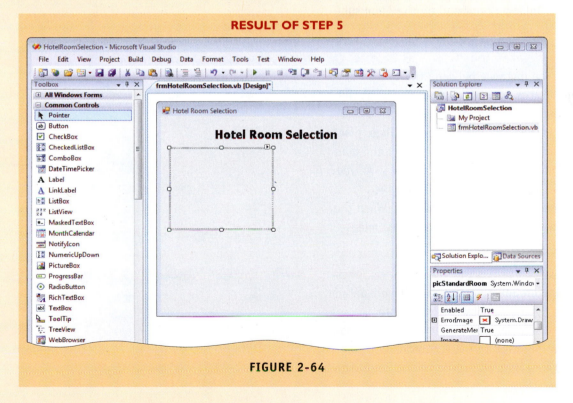

FIGURE 2-64

(continues)

Guided Program Development *(continued)*

6

▶ **Add a PictureBox Object** Add a second PictureBox object to the Windows Form object by dragging a PictureBox .NET component from the Toolbox to the Windows Form object. Place it to the right of the PictureBox object already in the Windows Form object *(ref: Figure 2-39)*.

▶ **Name the PictureBox Object** Using the (Name) property in the PictureBox Properties window, name the PictureBox object, picDeluxeRoom.

▶ **Size the PictureBox Object** Make the second PictureBox object on the right of the Windows Form object the same size as the PictureBox object on the left of the Windows Form object by using the Both command on the Make Same Size submenu of the Format menu *(ref: Figure 2-41)*.

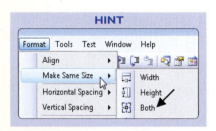

▶ **Align the PictureBox Objects Horizontally** Align the two PictureBox objects so their bottoms are horizontally aligned by using the Bottoms command on the Align submenu of the Format menu *(ref: Figure 2-43)*.

▶ **Set the Distance Between the PictureBox Objects** If necessary, adjust the distance between the two PictureBox objects so it is approximately the same as the distance in Figure 2-65. To do so, click the Windows Form object to unselect the two PictureBox objects. Then, place the mouse pointer in the right PictureBox object and drag the object left or right to set the correct distance. As you drag, blue snap lines should appear to indicate the PictureBox objects still are horizontally aligned. When the PictureBox objects are the correct distance apart, release the left mouse button.

▶ **Center the PictureBox Objects in the Windows Form Object** Center the PictureBox objects as a unit horizontally within the Windows Form object by selecting both PictureBox objects, displaying the Center in Form command on the Format menu, pointing to the Center in Form command, and then clicking Horizontally on the Center in Form submenu *(ref: Figure 2-45)*.

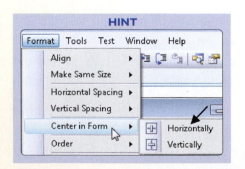

Guided Program Development *(continued)*

The PictureBox objects are sized and located properly within the Windows Form object (Figure 2-65).

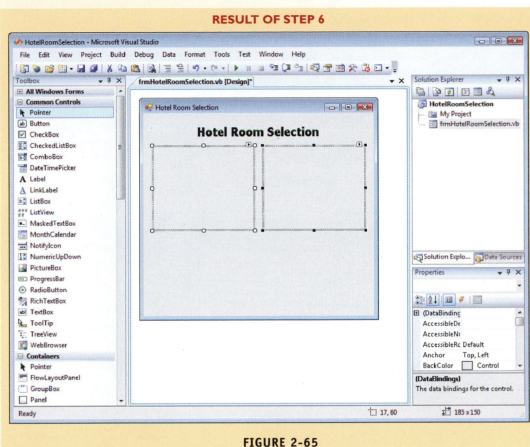

FIGURE 2-65

▶ **Add Three Button Objects to the Windows Form Object** Add three Button objects to the Windows Form object by dragging three Button .NET components onto the Windows Form object. They should be horizontally aligned below the PictureBox objects at about the same locations as shown in Figure 2-60 on page 82. Use blue snap lines to horizontally align the buttons on the Windows Form object as you drag them onto the form *(ref: Figure 2-47, Figure 2-52).*

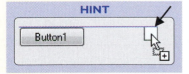

HINT

(continues)

Guided Program Development (continued)

▶ **Name the Three Button Objects** By using the (Name) property in the Properties window, name the leftmost Button object, btnStandardRoom; the center Button object, btnSelectRoom; and the rightmost Button object, btnDeluxeRoom.

▶ **Change the Text Property for Three Button Objects** By using the Text property in the Properties window, change the text for each of the Button objects to the text shown in Figure 2-66 on the next page *(ref: Figure 2-49)*.

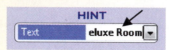

HINT

▶ **Change the Button Object Size** Change the size of the Standard Room button to accommodate the text, Standard Room *(ref: Figure 2-50)*.

HINT

▶ **Resize the Button Objects** Using the same technique you used for sizing the PictureBox objects, make all three Button objects the same size as the Standard Room Button object.

▶ **Align the btnStandardRoom Button Object** Center the Standard Room Button object under the standard room PictureBox object by: (a) selecting the standard room PictureBox first and then selecting the Standard Room Button object through the use of the CTRL key and clicking *(ref: Figure 2-40)*; (b) With the standard room PictureBox object as the controlling object, use the Centers command on the Align submenu of the Format menu to align the PictureBox object and the Standard Room Button object *(ref: Figure 2-43)*.

HINT

▶ **Align the btnDeluxeRoom Button Object** Using the same technique, center the Deluxe Room Button object beneath the deluxe room PictureBox object.

▶ **Center the btnSelectRoom Button Object** Center the Select Room Button object horizontally within the Windows Form object by selecting the Select Room Button object and then using the Horizontally command on the Center in Form submenu of the Format menu *(ref: Figure 2-31)*.

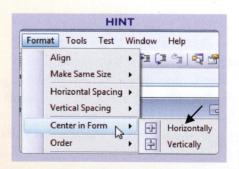

HINT

Guided Program Development *(continued)*

The Button objects are sized and placed properly within the Windows Form object (Figure 2-66). All three buttons are the same size. The Standard Room and Deluxe Room buttons are centered under their respective PictureBox objects, while the Select Room button is centered in the Windows Form object.

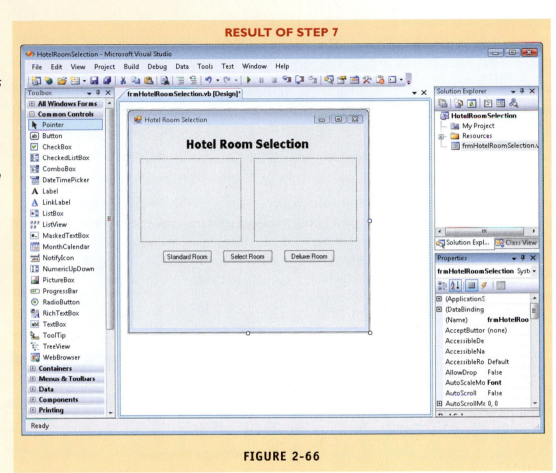

RESULT OF STEP 7

FIGURE 2-66

8

▶ **Add a Label Object** Add the instructions Label object to the Windows Form object by dragging a Label .NET object from the Toolbox to the Windows Form object. Place it below the Button objects at the approximate location shown in Figure 2-60 on page 82 *(ref: Figure 2-19)*.

▶ **Name a Label Object** Using the techniques you have learned, give the Label object the name, lblInstructions.

HINT

(continues)

Guided Program Development *(continued)*

▶ **Change the Label Object Text Property** Using the techniques you have learned, change the text in the lblInstructions Label object to, Choose a room type and then click the Select Room button.

▶ **Change the Label Object Font** Using the techniques you have learned, change the font for the lblInstructions Label object to Tahoma, change the Font style to Regular, and change the Size to 10 point.

▶ **Center the Label Object** Using the techniques you have learned, center the lblInstructions Label object horizontally within the Windows Form object.

▶ **Add a Label Object** Using the techniques you have learned, add the final message Label object whose text should read, You have completed your room selection, to the Windows Form object. Place the Label object in the location shown in Figure 2-67. Give it the name, lblConfirmationMessage. Change the font to Tahoma, the Font style to Regular, and the Size to 10 point. Center the Label object within the Windows Form object.

The two Label objects contain the correct text and are centered horizontally in the Windows Form object (Figure 2-67).

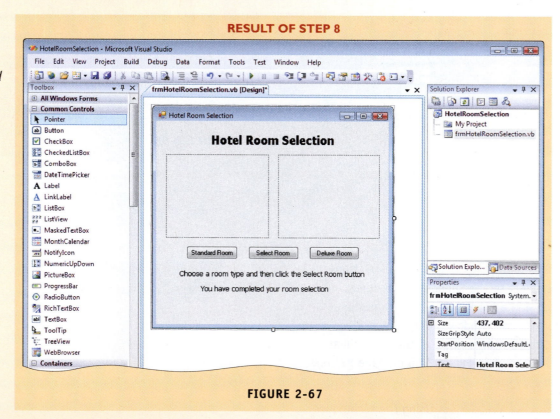

FIGURE 2-67

Guided Program Development *(continued)*

9

Add a Button Object Add the Exit Window Button object by dragging a Button .NET component onto the Windows Form object. Place it in the approximate location shown in Figure 2-68. Then, using techniques you have learned, give the name, btnExitWindow to the Button object; change its text to, Exit Window; make the Exit Window Button object the same size as the other Button objects in the window; and center the Exit Window Button object horizontally in the window.

The user interface mock-up now is complete (Figure 2-68).

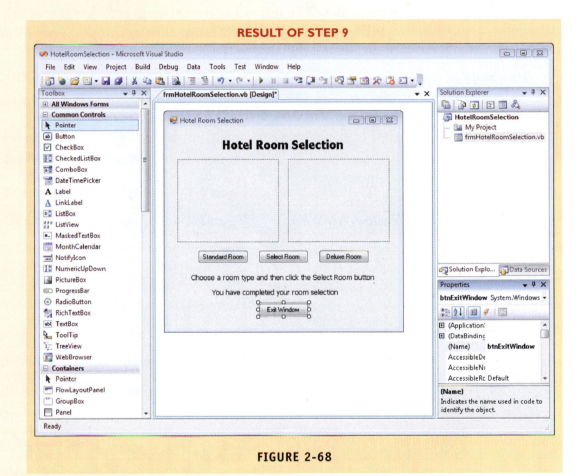

FIGURE 2-68

After completing the user interface mock-up, the designers would distribute the design to the users and others for their approval. In many cases, the developers must implement requested changes. They then will resubmit the design for approval.

Summary

You have completed the steps to create the graphical user interface mock-up for the Hotel Room Selection program. As you can see, many of the steps required are somewhat repetitive; that is, the same technique is used repeatedly to accomplish similar tasks. When you master these techniques, together with the principles of user interface design, you will be able to design user interfaces for a variety of different programs.

The items listed in the following table include all the new Visual Studio and Visual Basic skills you have learned in this chapter.

VISUAL BASIC SKILLS		
Skill	Figure Number	Web Address for Video
Open Visual Studio 2008	Figure 2-2	scsite.com/vb2008/ch2/figure2-2
Create a New Visual Basic 2008 Windows Application	Figure 2-4	scsite.com/vb2008/ch2/figure2-4
Display the Toolbox	Figure 2-9	scsite.com/vb2008/ch2/figure2-9
Permanently Display the Toolbox	Figure 2-10	scsite.com/vb2008/ch2/figure2-10
Name an Object	Figure 2-12	scsite.com/vb2008/ch2/figure2-12
Set Title Bar Text in Windows Form Object	Figure 2-15	scsite.com/vb2008/ch2/figure2-15
Resize a Form	Figure 2-17	scsite.com/vb2008/ch2/figure2-17
Add a Label Object	Figure 2-19	scsite.com/vb2008/ch2/figure2-19
Name a Label Object	Figure 2-21	scsite.com/vb2008/ch2/figure2-21
Change the Text in a Label Object	Figure 2-23	scsite.com/vb2008/ch2/figure2-23
Enter Multiple Lines for a Label Object	Figure 2-26	scsite.com/vb2008/ch2/figure2-26
Change Label Font, Font Style, and Font Size	Figure 2-27	scsite.com/vb2008/ch2/figure2-27
Center a Label Object in the Windows Form Object	Figure 2-31	scsite.com/vb2008/ch2/figure2-31
Delete GUI Objects	Figure 2-33	scsite.com/vb2008/ch2/figure2-33
Use the Undo Button on the Standard Toolbar	Figure 2-35	scsite.com/vb2008/ch2/figure2-35
Add a PictureBox Object	Figure 2-36	scsite.com/vb2008/ch2/figure2-36
Resize a PictureBox Object	Figure 2-38	scsite.com/vb2008/ch2/figure2-38

VISUAL BASIC SKILLS (continued)		
Skill	**Figure Number**	**Web Address for Video**
Add a Second PictureBox Object	Figure 2-39	scsite.com/vb2008/ch2/figure2-39
Make Objects the Same Size	Figure 2-40	scsite.com/vb2008/ch2/figure2-40
Align PictureBox Objects	Figure 2-43	scsite.com/vb2008/ch2/figure2-43
Center Multiple Objects Horizontally	Figure 2-45	scsite.com/vb2008/ch2/figure2-45
Add a Button Object	Figure 2-47	scsite.com/vb2008/ch2/figure2-47
Name a Button Object	Page 67	
Change the Button Object Text	Figure 2-49	scsite.com/vb2008/ch2/figure2-49
Change Button Object Size	Figure 2-50	scsite.com/vb2008/ch2/figure2-50
Add a Button with Alignment (Use Snap Lines)	Figure 2-52	scsite.com/vb2008/ch2/figure2-52
Align Objects Vertically	Figure 2-54	scsite.com/vb2008/ch2/figure2-54
Save and Close a Visual Basic Project	Figure 2-56, 2-57	
Open a Visual Basic project	Page 75	

FIGURE 2-69

Learn It Online

Start your browser and visit scsite.com/vb2008/ch2. Follow the instructions in the exercises below.

1. **Chapter Reinforcement TF, MC, SA** Click one of the Chapter Reinforcement links for Multiple Choice, True/False, or Short Answer below the Learn It Online heading. Answer each question and submit to your instructor.

2. **Practice Test** Click the Practice Test link below the Learn It Online heading. Answer each question, enter your first and last name at the bottom of the page, and then click the Grade Test button. When the graded practice test is displayed on your screen, submit the graded practice test to your instructor. Continue to take the practice test until you are satisfied with your score.

3. **Crossword Puzzle Challenge** Click the Crossword Puzzle Challenge link below the Learn It Online heading. Read the instructions, and then click the Continue button. Work the crossword puzzle. When you are finished, click the Submit button. When the crossword puzzle is redisplayed, submit it to your instructor.

Knowledge Check

1–5. Label the following parts of the window:

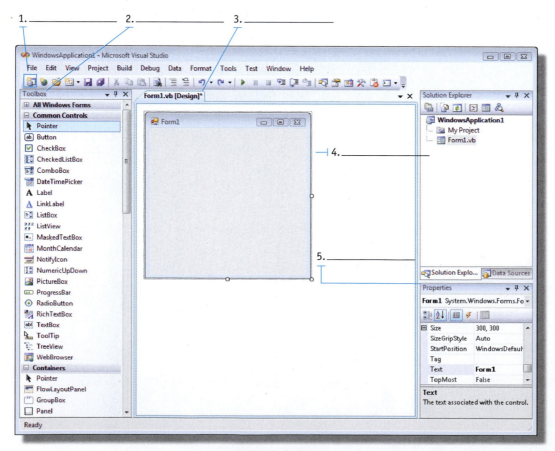

FIGURE 2-70

Knowledge Check

(continued)

6. What does RAD stand for?

7. What is the purpose of the Auto Hide button on the Toolbox title bar?

8. What is the difference between red and blue snap lines?

9. Which Windows Form object property was changed to display the words "Welcome Screen" on the title bar in Figure 2-71?

10. A Button, a Label, and a PictureBox are all _____.

11. How do you select three Button objects on the Windows Form object at the same time for formatting purposes?

FIGURE 2-71

12. What is the purpose of a mock-up?

13. What are the first two phases of the program development life cycle?

14. Write the Label object name, Title, together with the correct prefix.

15. Write the Button object name, Submit, together with the correct prefix.

16. Write the PictureBox object name, Computer, together with the correct prefix.

17. Which property of the Label object do you use to change the name of the label from Label1 to a new name?

18. What is the name of the button you can click to sort the property names in the Properties window from A to Z?

19. How do you save the project you have created for the user interface mock-up?

20. Name the four objects you learned in Chapter 2 together with the purpose of each object.

Debugging Exercises

1. List the steps required to change the poorly aligned buttons on the left to the properly aligned buttons on the right.

BEFORE

FIGURE 2-72a

AFTER

FIGURE 2-72b

(continues)

Debugging Exercises

(continued)

2. Change the order of the following Use Case Definition steps to correspond to the following problem definition: A college provides every incoming freshman with either a laptop or desktop PC. The student should select the type of computer she or he wants. A program opens a window that displays each computer type when the student clicks the corresponding button, one picture at a time. When a student makes a decision about the type of computer, the student should click the Select PC button. After the student selects the type of computer, the student should exit the application.

USE CASE DEFINITION

1. User clicks the Select PC button.
2. User clicks the Laptop or Desktop button.
3. User terminates the program by clicking the Exit Window button.
4. Program displays a PC confirmation message and disables both computer type buttons. The Exit Window button becomes active.
5. Program displays a picture of the type of PC clicked by the user and will enable the Select PC button.
6. Program displays a picture of the type of PC clicked by the user.

Program Analysis

1. After you have placed objects on the Windows Form object (Figure 2-73), list the steps you would follow to change the font for the On Line Auction label to Tahoma font, bold, 18 point.

2. List the steps you would perform to center horizontally the On Line Auction label.

3. List the steps you would perform to center horizontally the PictureBox object on the Windows Form object in Figure 2-73.

4. List the steps you would perform to change the font for the Click to Bid label in Figure 2-73 to Tahoma, 12 point; and then center the label horizontally.

FIGURE 2-73

5. List the steps you would perform to align the two Button objects horizontally by the tops of the buttons on the Windows Form object in Figure 2-73.

6. List the steps you would perform to center both the Bid Now button and the Cancel button horizontally on the Windows Form object in Figure 2-73.

7. In the real world, why is it important to get a user interface mock-up approved before proceeding with the rest of the project?

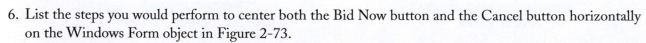

Case Programming Assignments

Complete one or more of the following case programming assignments. Submit the program and materials you create to your instructor. The level of difficulty is indicated for each case programming assignment.

● = Easiest
●● = Intermediate
●●● = Challenging

1 ●
CAR RENTAL SELECTION

Create a Windows form mock-up for the following requirements document and Use Case Definition. The Windows Form object and the other objects in the user interface are shown in Figure 2-76.

REQUIREMENTS DOCUMENT

Date submitted: January 17, 2011

Application title: Car Rental Selection

Purpose: The car rental selection application will allow a user to select a sports car or luxury car.

Program Procedures: From a window on the screen, the user should identify a rental car type (sports car or luxury car) and then indicate they want to rent that car.

Algorithms, Processing and Conditions:
1. The user must be able to identify a sports car or luxury car, back and forth until the selection is made.
2. When the user identifies the car type, a picture of that car type should appear in the window.
3. Only one picture should be displayed at a time. If a user identifies the sports car, only the sports car picture should be displayed; if a user identifies the luxury car, only the luxury car picture should be displayed.
4. When the user makes a car selection, a message stating that the selection of a car has been made should be displayed. In addition, the user should be stopped from identifying a car type after the car selection has been made.
5. After the user makes a car selection, the only allowable action is to exit the window.

Notes and Restrictions
1. A user cannot make a car selection until he or she has identified a car type.

Comments:
1. The pictures shown in the window can be found on scsite.com/vb2008/ch3/ images. The names of the pictures are Sports Car and Luxury Car.

FIGURE 2-74

(continues)

Case Programming Assignments

Car Rental Selection (continued)

USE CASE DEFINITION

1. User clicks Sports Car button or Luxury Car button.
2. Program displays a picture of the car identified by the user and enables the car selection button.
3. User clicks car buttons to view cars if desired. Program displays the picture of the identified car.
4. User clicks the Select Car button.
5. Program displays a car selection confirmation message, and disables both car buttons and the Select Car button. The Exit Window button becomes active.
6. User terminates the program by clicking the Exit Window button.

FIGURE 2-75

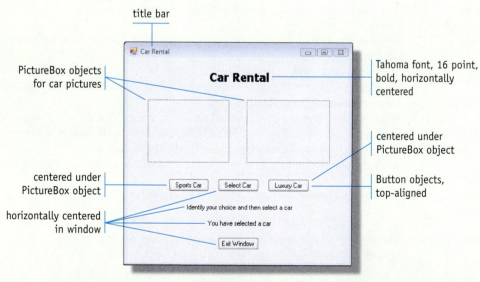

FIGURE 2-76

Case Programming Assignments

2 • BANKING

Create a Windows form mock-up for the following requirements document and Use Case Definition. The Windows Form object and the other objects in the user interface are shown in Figure 2-79.

REQUIREMENTS DOCUMENT

Date submitted: January 14, 2011

Application title: Bank Welcome Screen with Banking Hours

Purpose: This application displays a welcome screen for the First Corner National Bank. The user can choose an option to view the hours of the bank.

Program Procedures: From a window on the screen, the user makes a request to see the bank's open hours.

Algorithms, Processing and Conditions:
1. The user first views a welcome screen that displays the bank's name (First Corner National Bank), bank picture, and a phrase that states the bank is FDIC insured.
2. When the user opts to view the bank hours, the following hours are displayed:
   Monday–Thursday   9:00am–5:00pm
   Friday   9:00am–8:00pm
   Saturday   9:00am–1:00 pm
3. After the user views the hours, the only allowable action is to exit the window.

Notes and Restrictions:

Comments:
1. The picture shown in the window can be found on scsite.com/vb2008/ch3/ images. The name of the picture is Bank Building.

FIGURE 2-77

(continues)

Case Programming Assignments

Banking (continued)

USE CASE DEFINITION

1. The window opens, displaying the title of the bank, the bank's picture, and a message that the bank is FDIC insured. All buttons are enabled.
2. User clicks the View Banking Hours button.
3. Program displays the banking hours above the buttons. The View Banking Hours button is disabled.
4. User clicks the Exit Window button to terminate the application.

FIGURE 2-78

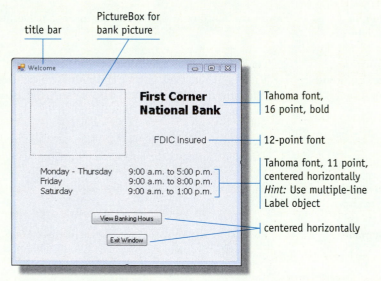

FIGURE 2-79

Case Programming Assignments

3
VISUAL BASIC 2008 TERMS

Create a Windows form mock-up for the following requirements document and Use Case Definition. The Windows Form object and the other objects in the user interface are shown in Figure 2-82.

REQUIREMENTS DOCUMENT

Date submitted: August 16, 2011

Application title: Visual Basic 2008 Terms

Purpose: This application displays the definitions of common Visual Basic terms. When the user chooses to view a definition, the term's definition is displayed.

Program Procedures: From a window on the screen, the user makes a request to see one of three VB definitions.

Algorithms, Processing, and Conditions:
1. The user first views a screen that displays three VB terms.
2. An image of a computer is displayed at the top of the window throughout the running of the application.
3. The user can select any of the three terms displayed on the buttons, and the definition appears after each selection is made.
4. The user can click any of the term buttons and the definition will appear. Any previous definitions will disappear.
5. An exit button is available at all times, allowing the user to end the application.

Notes and Restrictions:
1. Only one definition should be displayed at a time, so if a user selects a second term, the second definition only should be displayed.

Comments:
1. The computer picture shown in the window can be found on scsite.com/vb2008/ch3/images. The name of the picture is Computer.

FIGURE 2-80

(continues)

Case Programming Assignments

Visual Basic 2008 Terms (continued)

USE CASE DEFINITION

1. The window opens and displays a computer image, the title (Visual Basic 2008 Terms), three buttons labeled with VB terms, and an Exit Window button. All buttons are enabled.
2. User clicks each of the term buttons to review the definitions.
3. Program displays the definitions to the right of the buttons.
4. Only one definition shows at a time.
5. User clicks the Exit Window button to terminate the application.

FIGURE 2-81

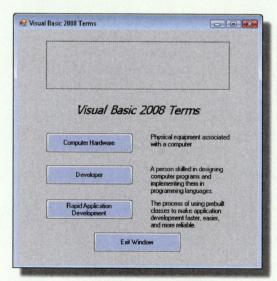

FIGURE 2-82

Case Programming Assignments

4 ●● ONLINE STORE SPECIALS

Create a Use Case Definition document and design a Windows form mock-up based on the requirements document in Figure 2-83.

REQUIREMENTS DOCUMENT

Date submitted:	January 6, 2012
Application title:	Online Store Specials

Purpose: The online store specials program will display the daily, weekly, and holiday specials of the online store. The user can select the desired product and then add the product to the shopping cart.

Program Procedures: From a window on the screen, the user should select the daily special, the weekly special, or the holiday special. When a special is selected, the program should display a picture of the special product, the regular price of the product, and the special price of the product. The user should be able to select any special. Then, the user can add the product to the shopping cart.

Algorithms, Processing, and Conditions:
1. The user must select a special in order to display the special's product picture, regular price, and sales price.
2. The user cannot add a product to the shopping cart until a special is selected.
3. When a special is selected, only that special's picture and prices should be displayed in the window. No other special should be displayed.
4. After the user selects a special and adds it to the shopping cart, the only allowable user action is to exit the window.
5. A user should be able to exit the window at any time.

Notes and Restrictions:

Comments:
1. The specials are: Daily Special: Cell Phone: Regular Price: $99.95; Special Price: $84.50
   Weekly Special: MP3 Player: Regular Price: $129.95; Special Price: $101.47
   Holiday Special: Digital Camera: Regular Price: $259.95; Special Price: $203.19
2. The pictures shown in the window can be found on scsite.com/vb2008/ch3/images. The names of the pictures are CellPhone, MP3Player, and DigitalCamera.

FIGURE 2-83

Case Programming Assignments

5 ●●
CHILDREN GIFT SELECTION

Create a Use Case Definition document and design a Windows form mock-up based on the requirements document in Figure 2-84.

REQUIREMENTS DOCUMENT

Date submitted: March 21, 2011

Application title: Children Gift Selection

Purpose: Your city has started a program that provides gifts for disadvantaged children over the December holidays. Each child can choose one of three toys. So they can choose, the program must display each of the toys upon request of the child. The child then can make the choice of the toy he or she would like to receive.

Program Procedures: From a window on the screen, the user selects one of three toys. A picture of the toy is displayed in the window. The user then can choose the toy he or she wants to receive.

Algorithms, Processing, and Conditions:
1. The user selects a toy. Then, a picture of the toy is displayed in the window.
2. The user can select any of the three toys. Only the picture for the selected toy should be displayed.
3. The user can select toys back and forth to see the pictures for the toys.
4. After the user finds a toy he or she wants, the user chooses that toy for delivery in the December holidays.
5. After the user chooses a toy, a message stating that a toy has been chosen should be displayed.
6. After the user chooses a toy, the only allowable action is to exit the window.

Notes and Restrictions:
1. The user should not be able to choose a toy until they have viewed the picture of at least one toy.

Comments:
1. The toys available are a ball, a doll, and a toy airplane.
2. The pictures shown in the window can be found on scsite.com/vb2008/ch3/ images. The names of the pictures are Ball, Doll, and Airplane.

FIGURE 2-84

Case Programming Assignments

6 ● ● ●
#1 SONG VOTING

Create a Use Case Definition document and design a Windows form mock-up based on the requirements document in Figure 2-85.

REQUIREMENTS DOCUMENT

Date submitted:	February 22, 2011
Application title:	#1 Song Voting
Purpose:	In your mall, a music store named "Millennium Music" wants a program that shows the #1 song in each of three music genres, and allows the user to vote for his or her overall favorite. The user should be able to select one of three music genres and then be able to vote for that song/genre as the user's overall favorite.
Program Procedures:	From a window on the screen, the user selects one of three music genres. The name of the #1 song in the selected genre is displayed together with a picture of the artist or band for the song. Then, the user can vote for that song/genre as his or her overall favorite.
Algorithms, Processing, and Conditions:	1. The user selects a music genre. Then, the #1 song title in the genre and picture of the artist or band is displayed in the window.
	2. The user can select any of the three music genres. Only the name of the song and the picture for the selected genre should be displayed.
	3. The user can select music genres back and forth to see the #1 song for each genre and the associated artist or band.
	4. After the user selects a genre, the user should be able to vote for that genre/song as the favorite. The user cannot vote until the user has selected a genre.
	5. After the user votes, a message stating that voting has occurred should be displayed.
	6. After the user votes, the only allowable action is to exit the window.
Notes and Restrictions:	1. The user should not be able to vote until he or she has selected a music genre.
Comments:	1. You (the developer) should select the three music genres and the #1 song for each of the genres.
	2. The pictures of the artist or the band will depend on your selection of both the music genres and the #1 song in each of the genres. You should download a picture of the artist or band from the World Wide Web. You can search anywhere on the Web for the pictures. You will find that www.google.com/images is a good source.

FIGURE 2-85

Case Programming Assignments

7 •••
ENGLISH-TO-SPANISH TRANSLATOR

Create a requirements document and a Use Case Definition document, and design a Windows form mock-up, based on the following case project:

The Bonita Travel Agency would like to create an English-to-Spanish translator of the most commonly used Spanish words for those booking a Spanish-speaking destination. Develop a Windows application for the Bonita Travel Spanish Translator. The English phrase should be displayed in a window. When the user selects an English phrase, the corresponding Spanish translation is displayed. Only one Spanish translation should be displayed at any given time. The user should be able to exit the window at any time.

English	Spanish Translation
Good morning	Buenos dias
Thank you	Gracias
Goodbye	Adios
Money	Dinero

FIGURE 2-86

Case Programming Assignments

8 ●●● TRAVEL SPECIALS

Create a requirements document and a Use Case Definition document, and design a Windows form mock-up, based on the following case project:

Your local travel agent would like a computer application to advertise the travel specials of the week from your city. This week's flight specials are:

Destination	Price
Orlando	$129 round trip
Las Vegas	$219 round trip
New Orleans	$189 round trip
Aruba	$419 round trip
Hawaii	$728 round trip

Write an application that will allow the user to select any of the five vacation destinations. When the user selects a vacation destination, the corresponding flight price and a picture of the destination should be displayed. Clear each prior price and picture when the user selects a different vacation destination. In addition to a picture of the destination, include a Web page address that features the location selected. After the user has selected a destination, the user should be able to book the flight and then exit the window.

FIGURE 2-87

Case Programming Assignments

9 •••
CATERING SERVICE

Create a requirements document and a Use Case Definition document, and design a Windows form mock-up, based on the following case project:

Your friend operates a catering service and has asked you to develop a Windows application that allows the user to see the four types of catering events offered, one at a time. Then, the user should be able to reserve the catering service desired. The four types of catering services and their minimum prices are as follows:

Name of Service	Minimum Price
Grand	$500.00
Magnificent	$1,000.00
Majestic	$1,800.00
Opulent	$3,000.00

For each type of service, your program should display the minimum price and a picture depicting an example of the quality each service type provides. Clear each service price and picture when the user selects a different catering service. After the user has selected a catering service, the user should be able to book the service and then exit the window.

FIGURE 2-88

CHAPTER THREE

Program Design and Coding

OBJECTIVES

You will have mastered the material in this chapter when you can:

- ► Change the BackColor property of an object
- ► Add images to a PictureBox object
- ► Locate and save an image from the World Wide Web
- ► Import an image into the Program Resources folder
- ► Size an image
- ► Set the Visible property in the Properties window
- ► Set the Enabled property in the Properties window
- ► Run a Visual Basic 2008 program
- ► Enter Visual Basic 2008 code
- ► Understand Visual Basic 2008 code statement formats

- ► Use IntelliSense to enter Visual Basic 2008 code statements
- ► Using code, set the Visible property of an object
- ► Using code, set the Enabled property of an object
- ► Enter comments in Visual Basic 2008 code
- ► Correct errors in Visual Basic 2008 code
- ► Write code to use the Close() procedure
- ► Print code
- ► Prepare an Event Planning Document

Introduction

In Chapter 2 you completed the design of the graphical user interface (GUI) mock-up. While users and others can approve the mock-up as being functional, the developer normally must make a variety of changes to the GUI to prepare it for the actual production version of the program. Among these changes are:

1. Adding color to the interface to make it more visually appealing.
2. Acquiring and including images that are required for the program.
3. Setting interface object properties in accordance with the needs of the program.

Once these tasks have been completed, Phase 2 of the program development life cycle (PDLC) has been completed.

The next two phases of the PDLC are:

Phase 3: Design the program processing objects
Phase 4: Code the program

This chapter will provide the skills and knowledge necessary first to complete phase 2 of the PDLC and then complete phases 3 and 4.

Sample Program

You will recall that the sample program for Chapter 2 and this chapter is the Hotel Room Selection program. Windows for the program are shown in Figure 3-1.

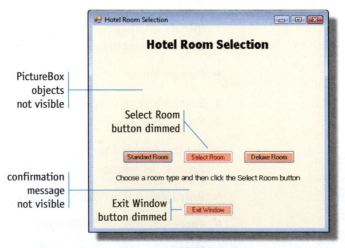

FIGURE 3-1a

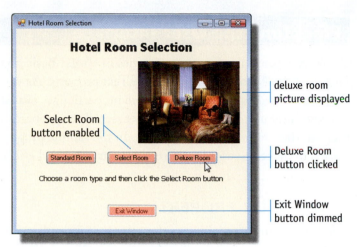

FIGURE 3-1b

deluxe room
picture displayed

Select Room
button enabled

Deluxe Room
button clicked

Exit Window
button dimmed

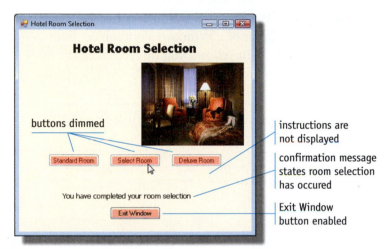

FIGURE 3-1c

buttons dimmed

instructions are
not displayed

confirmation message
states room selection
has occured

Exit Window
button enabled

In the opening window (Figure 3-1a), you can see that no images appear in the PictureBox objects that are included in the window, and that the Select Room button and the Exit Window button are dimmed, which means they are disabled when the program begins. In Figure 3-1b, the user clicked the Deluxe Room button, so the picture is displayed. In addition, the Select Room button is enabled. The Exit Window button still is dimmed. In Figure 3-1c, the user has selected a room, so the room selection confirmation message is displayed; the Standard Room, Select Room, and Deluxe Room buttons are dimmed; and the Exit Window button is enabled. Each of these changes occurs through the use of code you enter into the program, as you will discover later in this chapter.

Fine-Tune the User Interface

You have learned about some properties of Visual Basic objects in Chapter 2, including the Name property and the Text property. As you probably noted in the Properties window in Chapter 2, more properties are available for each of the objects in a graphical user interface. In many cases, these properties are used to fine-tune the user interface to make it more usable. In the sample program, the BackColor property is used to make the user interface more attractive and effective.

BACKCOLOR PROPERTY

The **BackColor** of an object is the color that is displayed in its background. For example, in Figure 3-1 the BackColor of the Windows Form object is a light yellow, while the BackColor of the Button objects is an orange shade. You can select the BackColor of an object through the use of the **BackColor property** in the Properties window. For example, to change the BackColor of a Windows Form object from its default color of Control (gray) to Cornsilk (light yellow), you can complete the following steps:

STEP 1   Click the Windows Form object to select it. (Do not click any of the objects on the Windows Form object.)

The Windows Form object is selected, as indicated by the thick border and the sizing handles (Figure 3-2).

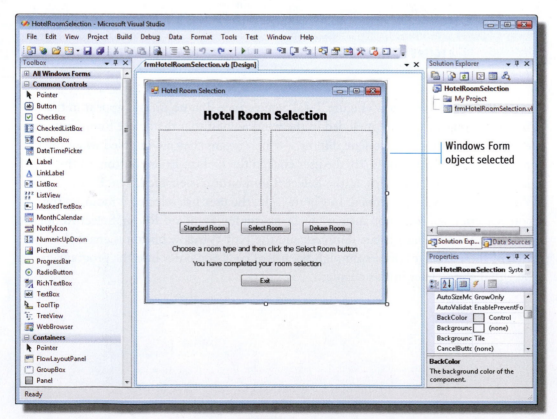

FIGURE 3-2

STEP 2 If necessary, scroll in the Properties window until the BackColor property is displayed, and then click the right column of the BackColor property.

The BackColor property is selected, and the BackColor arrow is displayed (Figure 3-3).

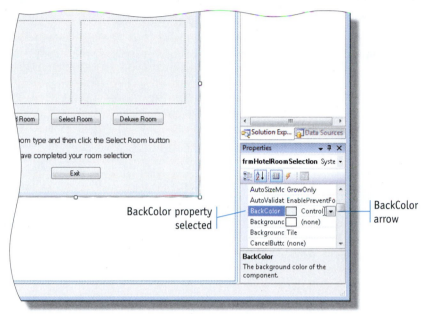

BackColor property selected

BackColor arrow

FIGURE 3-3

STEP 3 Click the BackColor arrow. Then, if necessary, click the Web tab to display the Web tabbed page.

The color window within the Properties window opens (Figure 3-4). The Web tabbed page contains more than 100 named colors you can select to display as the BackColor for the selected object, which in this case is the Windows Form object.

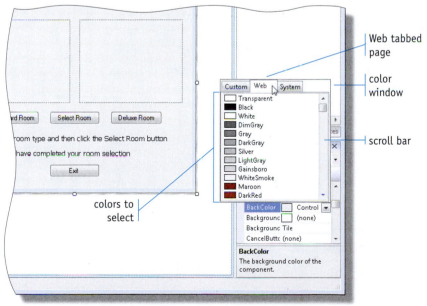

Web tabbed page

color window

scroll bar

colors to select

FIGURE 3-4

STEP 4 Scroll until the Cornsilk color is displayed in the list of colors.

The name and a sample of the Cornsilk color are displayed (Figure 3-5).

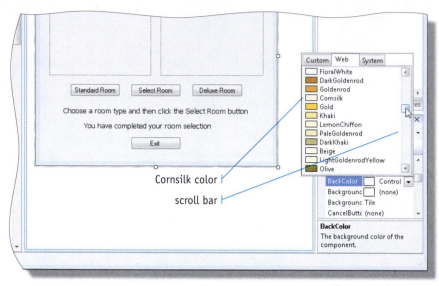

FIGURE 3-5

STEP 5 Click Cornsilk on the color list.

The background color in the Windows Form object is changed to Cornsilk (Figure 3-6).

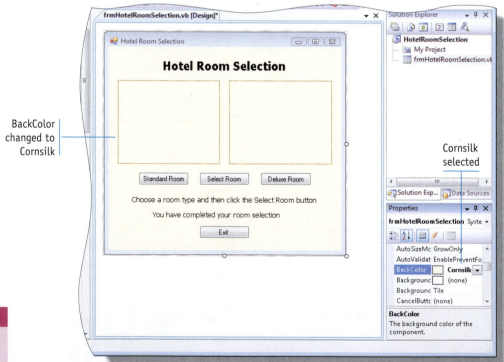

FIGURE 3-6

You can use the same technique to change the BackColor on any object that contains the BackColor property, including Button and Label objects.

ADDING IMAGES TO A PICTUREBOX OBJECT

PictureBox objects are used to display a graphic image. In the sample program, a picture of both a standard room and a deluxe room are displayed. You must specify the image that will be displayed in a particular PictureBox object. Before specifying the image, however, you must locate the image and then place it in the Resources folder that is linked to the application. The steps for displaying an image in a PictureBox object are:

1. Locate the image to be displayed in the PictureBox object. You might locate this image on the Web, in which case you must then store the image in a folder on your computer; or it might already be stored on your computer or a local network.
2. Import the image into the **Resources folder**. This step makes the image available for display within the PictureBox object. Multiple images can be placed in the Resources folder.
3. Specify the image to be displayed within the PictureBox object.

Each of these steps will be shown on the following pages.

Locate and Save an Image from the World Wide Web

Images are available from a multitude of sources, ranging from your own digital camera to millions of publicly available images on the Web. If you work for a company, the company might have photos and graphic images that can be used in company applications.

For purposes of the images used in this book, you can use the scsite.com/vb2008 Web site to retrieve an image. For example, to retrieve the standard room image from this site, you could complete the steps beginning on page 118:

HEADS UP

While many Web sites offer images you can select, three sites are particularly useful. These sites are: www.google.com/images, www.webshots.com, and www.corbis.com. When you visit sites, not all images are available for free download. In some cases, the images are copyrighted and you must acquire rights to use the image. In addition, some sites require a fee to be paid before the image can be used. Therefore, you should download only those images for which you have paid, or acquired the rights to use or those images that are free of copyright and can be used by anyone.

STEP 1   Open your Internet browser (in this example, Internet Explorer is used. Steps for other browsers might vary slightly). Then, enter `scsite.com/vb2008/ch3/images` in the Address box and press the ENTER key.

The browser window is open and the scsite.com/vb2008/ch3/images Web page is displayed (Figure 3-7). The names and thumbnails of the images used in this chapter are displayed on the Web page.

FIGURE 3-7

STEP 2   Locate the StandardRoom.jpg image and then right-click the image.

The shortcut menu is displayed (Figure 3-8).

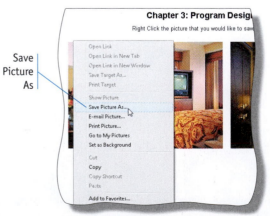

FIGURE 3-8

STEP 3   Click Save Picture As on the shortcut menu.

The Save Picture dialog box opens (Figure 3-9). You must identify the drive and folder in which you want to store the image. Each of these items will be unique for your computer and drives. In all sample programs in this book, images are stored on a USB drive that is designated as drive E. You also must enter a file name under which the image will be stored.

Save Picture
dialog box

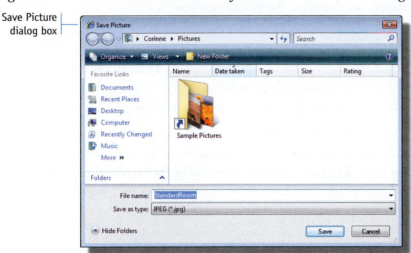

FIGURE 3-9

STEP 4   Identify the drive and folder where the image will be stored. Enter the image file name, StandardRoom, in the File name text box.

The information required to store the image is entered in the Save Picture dialog box (Figure 3-10). You must remember where you save the images because later you must locate them when you import them into the Resources folder for use within the program. Image file names should not contain spaces.

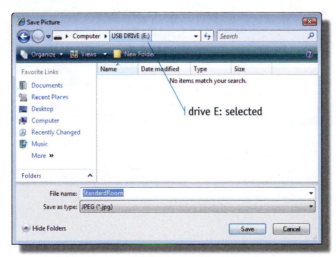

drive E: selected

FIGURE 3-10

STEP 5   Click the Save button in the Save Picture dialog box to save the image in the selected location.

ONLINE REINFORCEMENT

To view a video of the process in the previous steps, visit scsite.com/vb2008/ch3 and then select Figure 3-7.

IMPORT THE IMAGE INTO THE PROGRAM RESOURCES FOLDER

After you have saved an image on a storage device available to your computer, you should import the image into the Resources folder of the program so the image is available for use by the program. To import the Standard Room image into the Resources folder, you can complete the following steps:

STEP 1   With Visual Studio 2008 and the Hotel Room Selection Visual Basic program open, select the picStandardRoom PictureBox object by clicking it. Scroll in the PictureBox Properties window until the Image property is visible. Click the Image property name in the left list in the Properties window.

*With the PictureBox object selected, the Properties window displays all the properties of the object (Figure 3–11). The **Image property** specifies the image that should be displayed in the selected PictureBox object. The Image property is selected in the Properties window. The Image property Ellipsis button is displayed in the right column of the Image property.*

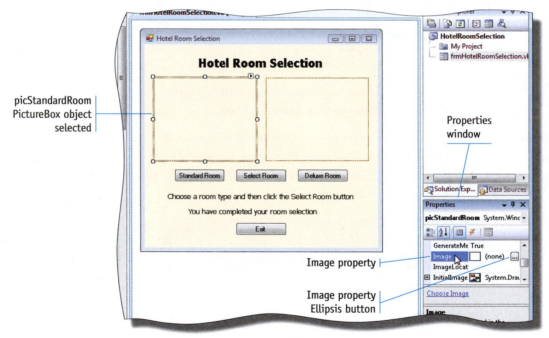

FIGURE 3-11

STEP 2   Click the Ellipsis button in the right column of the Image property.

*The **Select Resource dialog box** opens (Figure 3-12), and displays the resources that have been imported for the program. In Figure 3-12, no resources have been imported.*

Select Resource | dialog box
no resources | imported
Import button |

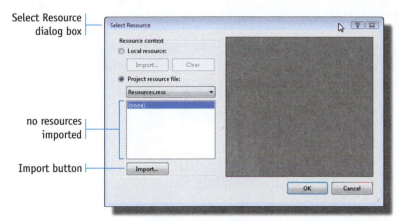

FIGURE 3-12

STEP 3   Click the Import button in the Select Resource dialog box. Then, using the features of the Open dialog box, locate the file you want to import into the program. In this case, the file is the StandardRoom.jpg file that is stored on drive E, which is a USB drive.

The Open dialog box opens when you click the Import button (Figure 3-13). The location of the StandardRoom.jpg file is on drive E.

Open dialog | box

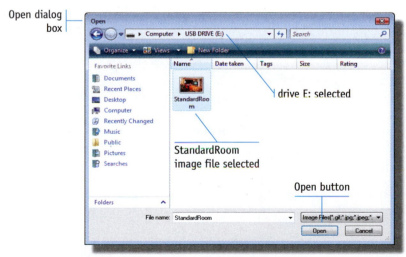

FIGURE 3-13

STEP 4 Click the Open button in the Open dialog box.

The Select Resource dialog box is displayed again, but now the StandardRoom image is identified in the Project resource file list (Figure 3-14). The image appears in the preview window. This means the image has been made a part of the resources for the program. It no longer is necessary to locate the image on the USB drive in order to include the image in a PictureBox object.

Select Resource dialog box

StandardRoom image in preview window

StandardRoom image included

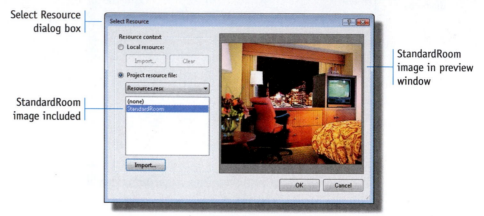

FIGURE 3-14

STEP 5 With the StandardRoom file name selected in the Project resource file list, click the OK button in the Select Resource dialog box.

The StandardRoom image becomes the image displayed in the picStandardRoom PictureBox object (Figure 3-15). In addition, the Resources folder is added to the Solution Explorer window, indicating the Resources folder now is part of the program.

StandardRoom image in picStandardRoom PictureBox object

Resources folder

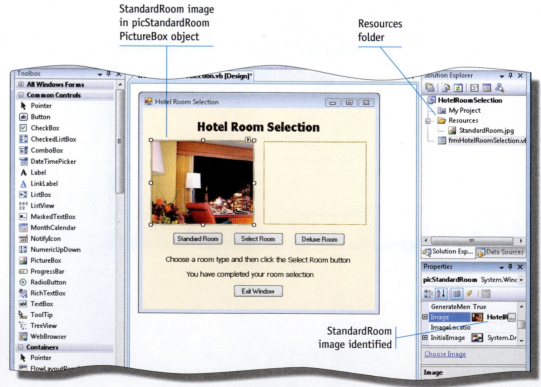

StandardRoom image identified

FIGURE 3-15

ONLINE REINFORCEMENT

To view a video of the process in the previous steps, visit scsite.com/vb2008/ch3 and then select Figure 3-11.

SIZE AN IMAGE

In most cases, when you import an image into a program, the image will not fit in the PictureBox object perfectly. This occurs for two reasons: the image is a different size from the PictureBox object, and/or the image has a dimension different than the PictureBox object. In all cases, the developer must adjust the size of the image to fit in the PictureBox object, or adjust the size of the PictureBox object to accommodate the image.

In Figure 3-15, you can see that the image is larger than the PictureBox object (compare the image in Figure 3-14 to the image in Figure 3-15). Because the PictureBox object must remain its current size, the image must be adjusted using the **SizeMode property**. To adjust an image size to fit in a PictureBox object, you can complete the following steps:

STEP 1   With the PictureBox object containing the StandardRoom image selected, scroll in the picStandardRoom Properties window until you see the SizeMode property. Click the SizeMode property name in the left column and then click the SizeMode arrow in the right column of the SizeMode property.

The SizeMode property list is displayed (Figure 3-16). The list contains five choices you can use to change either the size of the image or the size of the PictureBox object. Normal is selected because it is the default value.

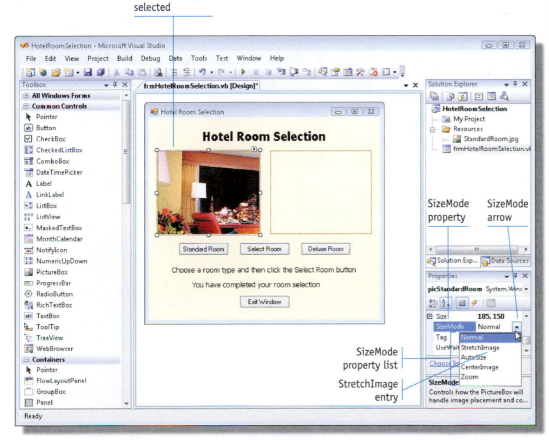

FIGURE 3-16

STEP 2   Click StretchImage in the SizeMode list.

The SizeMode list is closed and the image is resized to fit within the picStandardRoom PictureBox object (Figure 3-17). When you use the **StretchImage option***, some distortion of the image might occur in order to make the image fit within the PictureBox object. This is why it is important to select an image that has the same approximate dimensions (or at least the same aspect ratio) as the PictureBox object in which the image will be placed.*

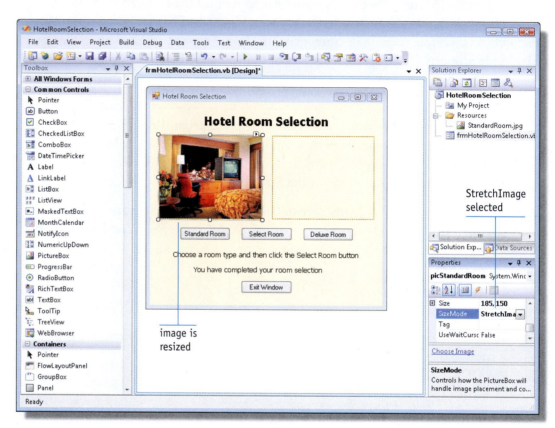

FIGURE 3-17

VISIBLE PROPERTY

As you have learned, when the Hotel Room Selection program begins execution, neither the standard room picture nor the deluxe room picture is displayed in the window. When the user clicks the Standard Room button, the program displays the standard room picture in the Standard Room PictureBox object; and when the user clicks the Deluxe Room button, the program displays the deluxe room picture in the Deluxe Room PictureBox object.

The property that controls whether an object is displayed on the Windows Form object is the **Visible property**. By default, the Visible property is set to True so that any object you place on the Windows Form object will be displayed when the program runs. To cause the object not to display, you must set the Visible property to False. To set the Visible property for the picStandardRoom PictureBox object to False, you can complete the following steps:

STEP 1   If necessary, select the picStandardRoom PictureBox object. Scroll in the Properties window until the Visible property is displayed. Click the Visible property name in the left column, and then click the Visible arrow in the right column of the Visible property.

When you click the Visible arrow, the list displays the words True and False (Figure 3-18). To make the object visible when the program starts running, select True. To make the object not visible when the program starts running, select False.

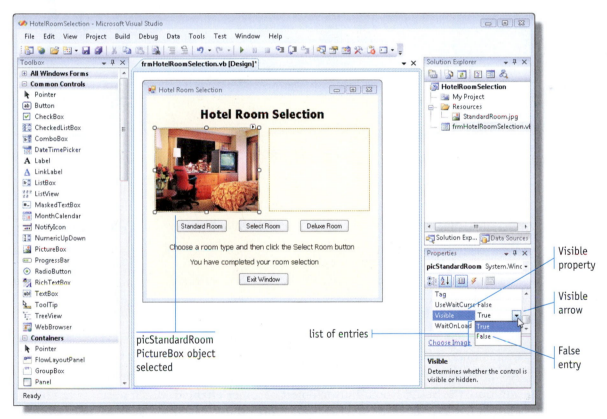

FIGURE 3-18

STEP 2 Click False on the Visible property list.

The Visible property is set to False (Figure 3-19). When the program begins running, the picStandardRoom object will not be displayed on the Windows Form object. Note that the image and object are displayed on the frmHotelRoomSelection.vb [Design] tabbed page regardless of the Visible property setting.

FIGURE 3-19

Once you have set the Visible property for an object to False, the only way to display the object on the Windows Form object while the program is running is to set the Visible property to True during program execution. You can do this by writing code, as you will see later in this chapter.

ENABLED PROPERTY

In an event-driven program, objects such as Button objects can be used to cause events to occur. For example, in the sample program, when you click the Standard Room button, a picture of a standard room is displayed in the PictureBox object. In addition, the Select Room Button object becomes **enabled**, which means it can be clicked to cause an event to occur. When the program begins execution, however, the Select Room button is **disabled**, which means nothing will happen when you click the button. A disabled button is displayed as a dimmed button (see Figure 3-1a) on page 112).

The **Enabled property** controls when a Button object is enabled, which means clicking the button can cause an event to occur; and when a Button object is not enabled, which means clicking the button causes no action to occur. The default for the Enabled property is True, which means the associated Button object is enabled. To set the Enabled property to False for the Select Room button, you can complete the steps on the next page:

STEP 1 Select the btnSelectRoom object. Scroll in the Properties window until the Enabled property is displayed. Click the Enabled property name in the left column, and then click the Enabled arrow in the right column of the Enabled property.

The list displayed when you click the Enabled arrow contains the words, True and False (Figure 3-20). To make the object enabled when the program starts running, select True. To make the object not enabled when the program starts running, select False.

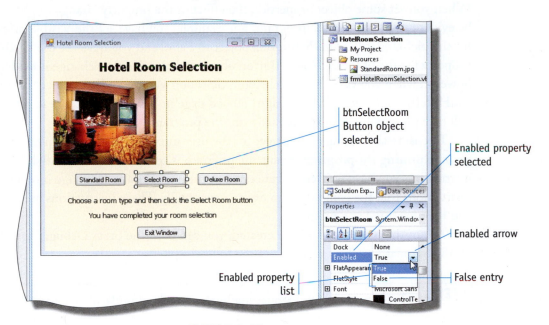

FIGURE 3-20

STEP 2 Click False on the Enabled property list.

The Enabled property is set to False (Figure 3-21). When the program begins running, the btnSelectRoom Button object will not be enabled on the Windows Form object.

FIGURE 3-21

ONLINE REINFORCEMENT

To view a video of the process in the previous steps, visit scsite.com/vb2008/ch3 and then select Figure 3-20.

Once you have set the Enabled property to False, the only way to cause a Button object to be enabled on the Windows Form object while the program is running is to set the Enabled property to True. You can do this by writing code, as you will see later in this chapter.

RUNNING A PROGRAM

When you set some object properties, the effect of the property change might not be evident until you run the program. For example, you have set the Visible property for the picStandardRoom PictureBox object to False, and you have set the Enabled property for the btnSelectRoom Button object to False. Neither change is evident, however, when you view the Hotel Room Selection Windows Form object on the frmHotelRoomSelection.vb [Design] tabbed page in Visual Studio. These settings will take place only when you actually run the program.

To ensure the settings are correct for the user interface, you must run the program. **Running the program** means the program is compiled, or translated, from the instructions you have written or generated in the Visual Basic language into a form of instructions that the computer can execute eventually. These instructions are saved and then executed as a program.

To run the program you have created, you can click the Start Debugging button on the Standard toolbar, as shown in the following steps:

STEP 1 Point to the Start Debugging button on the Standard toolbar.

The pointer points to the Start Debugging button (Figure 3–22).

Start Debugging button

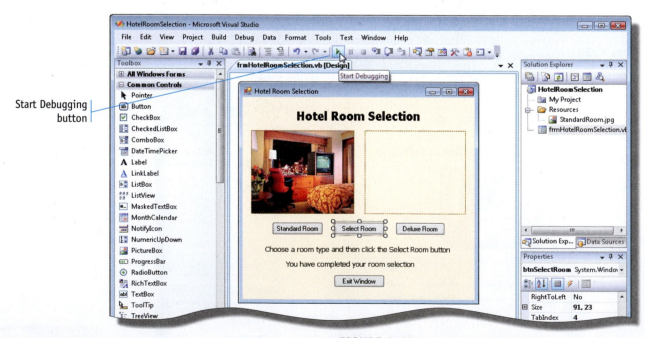

FIGURE 3-22

STEP 2   Click the Start Debugging button on the Standard toolbar.

The program is compiled and saved, and then is run on the computer. When the program runs, the Hotel Room Selection window is displayed on the screen (Figure 3-23). Notice that the Standard Room image is not displayed in the window because the Visible property for the picStandardRoom PictureBox object was set to False (see Figure 3-19 on page 126). Notice also that the Select Room button is dimmed, which indicates its Enabled property is set to False.

Hotel Room
Selection window

Close button

StandardRoom
image not displayed

Select Room
button dimmed

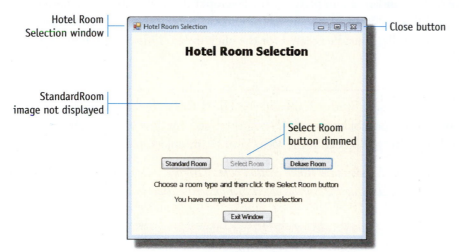

FIGURE 3-23

Once you have started running the program, it will continue to run until you close it. To close a program, click the Close button on the right of the window title bar (see Figure 3-23).

Once you have set all the properties for the objects in the user interface, the design of the user interface is complete. You now are ready to move to the next phase of the program development life cycle — design the program processing objects.

Visual Basic Program Coding

Prior to beginning the design of the program processing objects, the developer must understand certain program coding principles and techniques so he or she can apply this knowledge to the program design. **Program code** is the set of instructions written by the developer that direct the program to carry out the processing required in the program. The following sections explain the Visual Basic 2008 code required for the Hotel Room Selection program.

ENTERING VISUAL BASIC CODE FOR EVENT HANDLING

As you have learned, most program processing in an event-driven program occurs when the user triggers an event. For example, when a user clicks a button on the graphical user interface, this activity can trigger an event and the program performs the required processing. The developer writes program code to carry out the processing. This code is placed in a section of the program called an **event handler** — so-called because it "handles" the event that the user action triggers by executing code that performs the required processing.

To write the code for an event handler, the developer first must identify the GUI object that will be used to trigger the event. For example, in the sample program, you have learned that when the Standard Room button is clicked, the standard room picture should appear in the picStandardRoom PictureBox object. To write the code that will display the standard room picture, the developer must inform Visual Studio that the Standard Room button is the object for which the code is to be written, and that an event handler must be created for the click event. This can be done using the following steps:

STEP 1   With Visual Studio 2008 and the Hotel Room Selection program open and the frmHotelRoomSelection.vb [Design] tabbed window visible, point to the Standard Room Button object in the Windows Form object.

The pointer points to the Standard Room Button object (Figure 3-24). The four-headed arrow pointer indicates you can drag the Button object to another location in the window if desired.

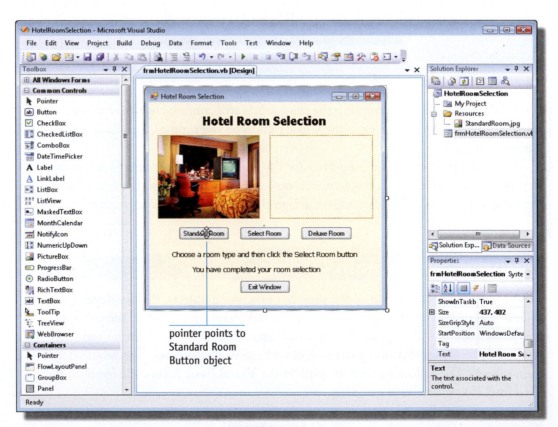

FIGURE 3-24

STEP 2   Double-click the Standard Room Button object.

The code window is displayed on the frmHotelRoomSelection.vb* tabbed page (Figure 3-25). The code in the window is generated by Visual Studio. This code identifies an event handler, which is the code that executes when an event is triggered. In this case, when the Standard Room button is clicked, the code in this event handler will be executed by the program. The list box at the upper-left of the tabbed page identifies the object for which the event hander will execute — in this case, the btnStandardRoom object. The list box at the upper-right of the tabbed page identifies the event that must occur in order to execute the code in the event handler. The event identified in Figure 3-25 is Click. So, when the user clicks the Standard Room button, the program will execute the code between the Private Sub statement and the End Sub statement. In Figure 3-25, no code other than the event handler identification code generated by Visual Studio has been entered. The insertion point is located where the developer should begin entering the code that executes when the user clicks the btnStandardRoom Button object.

frmHotelRoomSelection.vb* tabbed page   object for which event handler will execute

event handler identification code generated by Visual Studio

line numbers

insertion point   event that must occur for this code to be executed

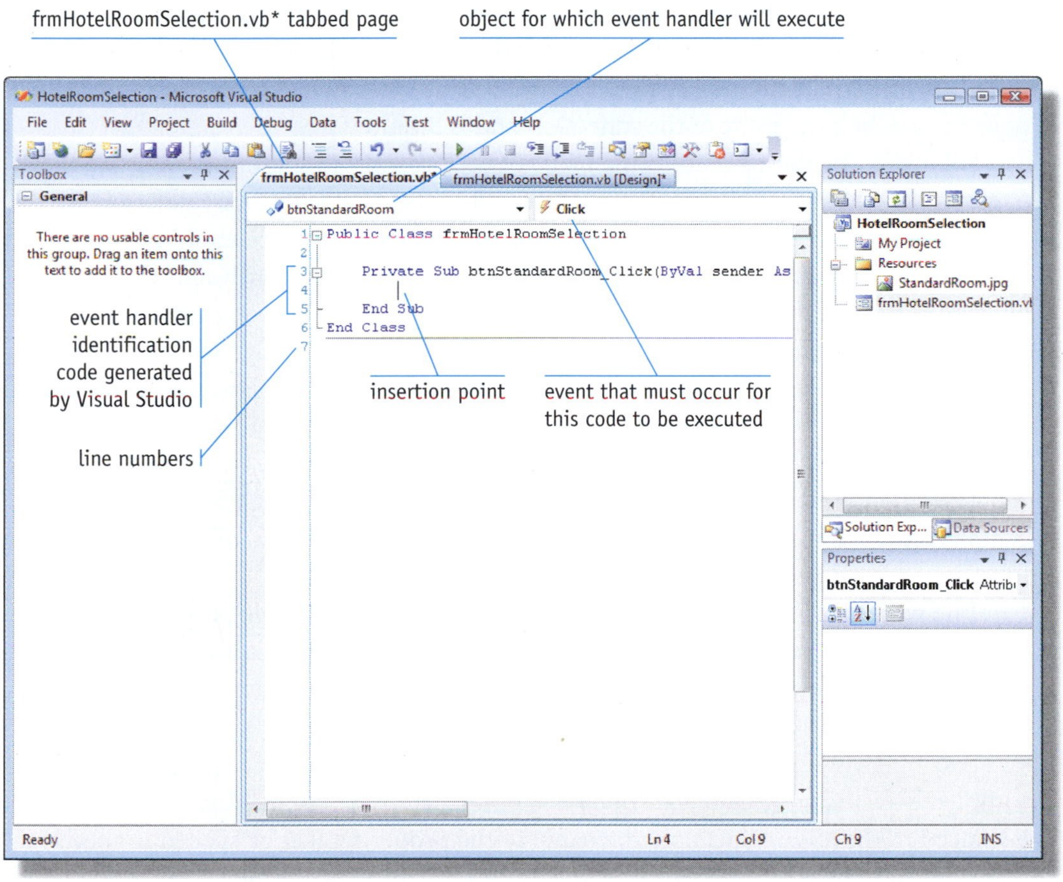

FIGURE 3-25

HEADS UP

In the left column of the coding window in Figure 3-25, line numbers appear. These line numbers help identify each line of code in the coding window. They do not appear by default, however, so you must instruct Visual Studio to display the line numbers. If line numbers do not appear in the coding window on a computer you are using, you can display them by completing the following steps: 1) Click Tools on the menu bar; 2) Click Options on the Tools menu; 3) If necessary, click the triangle next to Text Editor in the Options dialog box; 4) If necessary, click the triangle next to Basic in the list below Text Editor; 5) Click Editor in the list below Basic; 6) Place a check mark in the Line numbers check box; 7) Click the OK button in the Options dialog box.

ONLINE REINFORCEMENT

To view a video of the process in the previous steps, visit scsite.com/vb2008/ch3 and then select Figure 3-24.

VISUAL BASIC 2008 CODING STATEMENTS

A Visual Basic 2008 coding statement contains instruction(s) that the computer eventually executes. Visual Basic has a set of rules, or **syntax**, that specifies how each statement must be written.

In the Hotel Room Selection program, you will recall that when the user clicks the Standard Room Button while the program is running, the standard room image should be displayed in the picStandardRoom PictureBox object. Figure 3-26 shows a Visual Basic coding statement that sets the Visible property for the picStandardRoom PictureBox object to True so the image is displayed in the picture box after the statement is executed.

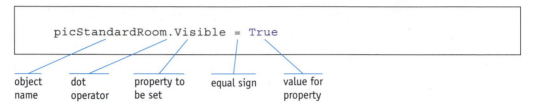

FIGURE 3-26

The first part of the statement, picStandardRoom, identifies the object containing the property to set. The name of the object is followed by the dot operator (period) with no intervening spaces. The dot operator separates the name of the object from the next entry in the statement and is required.

Following the dot operator is the name of the property to set. In Figure 3-26, the name of the property is Visible. You will recall that the Visible property determines whether an image is displayed in the PictureBox object when the program is running. In Figure 3-19 on page 126, the Visible property for the picStandardRoom PictureBox object was set to False so the image would not be displayed when the program was started. This statement sets the Visible property to True so the image will be displayed.

The property name is followed by a space and then an equal sign. The space is not required, but good coding practice dictates that elements within a statement should be separated by a space so the statement is easier to read. One or more spaces can be used, but most developers use only one space. The equal sign is required because it indicates that the value to be used for setting the property follows. A space follows the equal sign for ease of readability.

The word True follows the space. The value True in the Visible property indicates that the image in the PictureBox object should be displayed. When the program is running, as soon as the Visible property is set to True, the image appears in the picture box.

Each entry within the program statement must be correct or the program will not compile. This means the object name must be spelled properly, the dot operator must be placed in the correct location, the name of the property must be spelled properly, the equal sign must be present, and a valid entry for the property must follow the equal sign. For the Visible property, the only valid entries are True and False, so the word True or the word False must follow the equal sign.

GENERAL FORMAT OF A VISUAL BASIC STATEMENT

The general format of the Visual Basic statement shown in Figure 3-26 appears in Figure 3-27.

General Format: Property Value Assignment Statement
`objectname.property = propertyvalue`

EXAMPLE	RESULT
picStandardRoom.Visible = True	Picture is visible
btnSelectRoom.Enabled = False	Button is dimmed

FIGURE 3-27

In the general format, the object name always is the first item in the Visual Basic statement. The object name is the name you specified in the (Name) property in the Properties window. In Figure 3-26, the object name is picStandardRoom because that is the name given to the standard room PictureBox object.

The dot operator (period) is required. It follows the object name with no space between them. Immediately following the dot operator is the name of the property that will be set by the statement. The property name must be spelled correctly and must be a valid property for the object named in the statement. Valid properties that can be specified in the statement are identified in the Properties window associated with the object.

The equal sign must follow zero or more spaces in the statement. Visual Basic statements do not require spaces nor is there is a limit on how many spaces can be contained between elements in the statement. The equal sign identifies the statement as an **assignment statement**, which means the value on the right side of the equal sign is assigned to the element on the left side of the equal sign. When setting properties, it means the value on the right side of the equal sign is assigned to the property identified on the left side of the equal sign.

The property value specified in the assignment statement must be a valid value for the property identified on the left side of the equal sign. You can see the valid values for a given property by looking in the Properties window for the object whose property you are setting.

After you have entered the property value, the Visual Basic statement is complete. Because correct programming protocol states that only one statement should appear on a line, the next step is to press the ENTER key to move the insertion point to the next line in the coding window.

The general statement format shown in Figure 3-27 is used for all statements in which the code sets the value of an object property.

INTELLISENSE

In Figure 3-25 on page 131, the insertion point is located in the coding window. To enter the statement in Figure 3-26 into the actual program in the coding window, you can type the entire statement. Visual Studio, however, provides help when entering a statement so that you will be less prone to make an error when entering the statement. This help is called IntelliSense.

IntelliSense displays all allowable entries you can make in a Visual Basic statement each time a dot (period), equal sign, or other special character required for the statement is typed. To take full advantage of the use of IntelliSense, however, you must make one additional entry in a Visual Basic statement. That additional entry is the word Me, followed by a dot before the name of the object. Therefore, when using IntelliSense, the complete Visual Basic statement would be as shown in Figure 3-28:

```
Me.picStandardRoom.Visible = True
```

FIGURE 3-28

When you type me followed by a period, IntelliSense displays a list of all the entries, including all the objects, that can be specified in the statement.

ENTER A VISUAL BASIC STATEMENT

To enter the Visual Basic statement in Figure 3-28 using IntelliSense, you can complete the following steps:

STEP 1 With the code editing window open and the insertion point positioned as shown in Figure 3-25 on page 131, type me followed by a period. Notice that the letter m in me is automatically capitalized.

The characters Me. are displayed in the code window (Figure 3-29). IntelliSense displays a list of all the entries that can follow the period in the statement. Sometimes the entry selected in the list is the correct entry for the statement you are entering, but often it is not the correct entry. Therefore, you must identify the correct statement in the list before entering it.

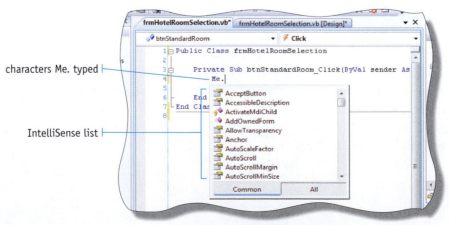

characters Me. typed

IntelliSense list

FIGURE 3-29

STEP 2   To identify the correct entry, type the first letters of the entry until the entry is selected. In this case, type `pics` on your keyboard.

When you type characters, IntelliSense highlights in the list an entry that begins with the letters you type (Figure 3–30). When you enter pics, IntelliSense highlights the only term in the list that begins with pics, which is picStandardRoom. This is the object name you want to enter into the Visual Basic statement.

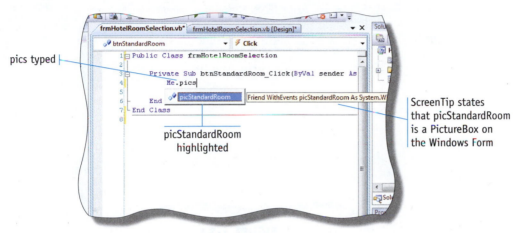

pics typed

picStandardRoom highlighted

ScreenTip states that picStandardRoom is a PictureBox on the Windows Form

FIGURE 3-30

STEP 3   When IntelliSense highlights the correct object name, press the key on the keyboard corresponding to the entry that is to follow the object name. In this case, press the PERIOD key.

IntelliSense automatically enters the entire object name into the Visual Basic statement and the period (the character you typed) following the object name (Figure 3-31). In addition, because IntelliSense realizes that the dot you entered means more information is required in the statement, a list of the allowable entries following the dot is displayed.

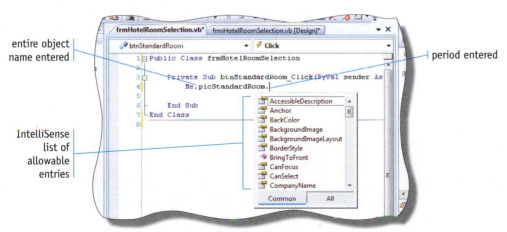

entire object name entered

period entered

IntelliSense list of allowable entries

FIGURE 3-31

STEP 4 As with the object name in step 2, the next step is to enter one or more characters until IntelliSense highlights the desired property in the list. Type the letter v on your keyboard.

IntelliSense highlights the only property in the list that begins with the letter v (Visible) (Figure 3-32). Because the Visible property is the one required for the statement, no further action is required to select the Visible property.

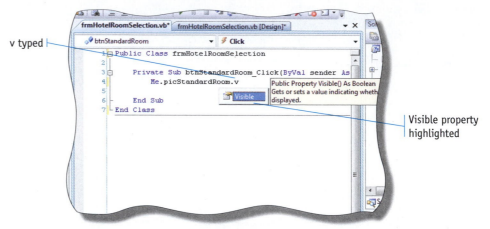

FIGURE 3-32

When you enter a statement using IntelliSense, by default IntelliSense will format the statement after you press the ENTER key. So, if you did not enter spaces in the statement before and after the equal sign, IntelliSense automatically would insert the spaces when you press the ENTER key. You can choose whether to enter spaces as you enter the statement, or let IntelliSense insert the spaces when you press the ENTER key.

STEP 5 Press the key for the character that is to follow the property name. In this case, press the SPACEBAR on the keyboard.

IntelliSense enters the highlighted property name (Visible) followed by the character you typed (space) (Figure 3-33). The space indicates to Visual Basic that the object name and property name entry is complete. Notice also that the IntelliSense tip specifies what the statement will be able to do. In Figure 3-33, it states that the statement "gets or sets a value indicating whether the control is displayed." This means the Visible property indicates whether the picStandardRoom PictureBox object is displayed.

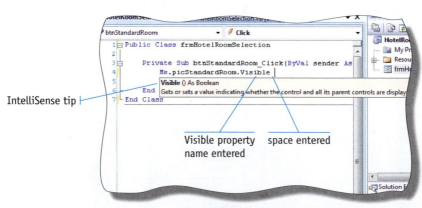

FIGURE 3-33

STEP 6   Press the EQUAL SIGN key on the keyboard and then press the SPACEBAR.

The equal sign and a space are displayed and then IntelliSense displays a list containing the entries you can make (Figure 3–34). For the Visible property, the only possible entries following the equal sign are False (which indicates the PictureBox object should not be visible) and True (which indicates the PictureBox object should be visible).

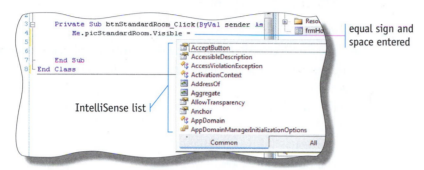

FIGURE 3-34

STEP 7   Type t on the keyboard.

IntelliSense highlights the True entry (Figure 3–35).

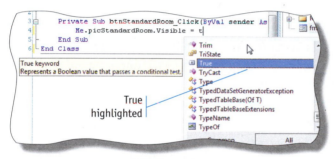

FIGURE 3-35

STEP 8   Press the key for the character that is to follow the True entry. In this case, press the ENTER key.

Because you pressed the ENTER key, IntelliSense enters True into the statement and then Visual Studio moves the indented insertion point to the next line (Figure 3–36). The Visual Basic statement now is completely entered. Note that IntelliSense capitalizes the word Me, when the statement is entered.

FIGURE 3-36

Visual Studio and IntelliSense automatically create the indentations in the program statements in Figure 3-36 because the indentations make the statements easier to read and understand. As programs become more complex, proper indentation of program statements can be an important factor in developing error-free programs.

The following steps summarize the procedure for using IntelliSense to enter a Visual Basic statement that sets a property:

1. Type me .
2. Type the first letter(s) of the name of the object whose property will be set until the object name is selected in the IntelliSense list.
3. Press the PERIOD key.
4. Type the first letter(s) of the name of the property to be set until the name is highlighted in the IntelliSense list.
5. Press the SPACEBAR to complete the first portion of the statement.
6. Press the EQUAL SIGN key.
7. Press the SPACEBAR.
8. Press the first letter(s) of the entry you want to select in the list until the entry is highlighted; or if IntelliSense does not display a list, type the value for the property.
9. Press the ENTER key.

Using IntelliSense to enter a Visual Basic statement provides two significant advantages: 1) It is faster to enter a statement using IntelliSense than it is to enter a statement by typing it; 2) Using IntelliSense reduces the number of errors committed when entering a statement to almost zero. By using only the entries contained on the IntelliSense lists, the developer seldom will make a mistake by entering an invalid entry. In addition, because the entry is chosen from a list, it is not possible for the entry to be misspelled or mistyped.

Entering a programming statement is a fundamental skill of a Visual Basic programmer. You should understand thoroughly how to enter a programming statement using IntelliSense.

SET VISIBLE PROPERTY TO FALSE

In Figure 3-36 on page 137, the programming statement set the Visible property for the picStandardRoom PictureBox object to True, which will cause the image in the picture box to be displayed when the statement is executed. The statement will be executed when the user clicks the Standard Room button because the statement is within the btnStandardRoom_Click event handler.

Another setting that must take place when the user clicks the Standard Room button is to set the Visible property for the picDeluxeRoom PictureBox to False so the deluxe room picture is not displayed when the standard room picture is displayed. To set the Visible property for the picDeluxeRoom PictureBox object to False, you could complete the steps on the next page:

STEP 1   With the insertion point on the second line of the code editing window for the click event of the Standard Room button, type me. on your keyboard.

The letters you typed are displayed in the code editing window and the IntelliSense list shows the valid entries you can choose (Figure 3-37). The entry, picStandardRoom is high-lighted because it is the last entry that was selected from this list.

me. typed

IntelliSense list

picStandardRoom highlighted

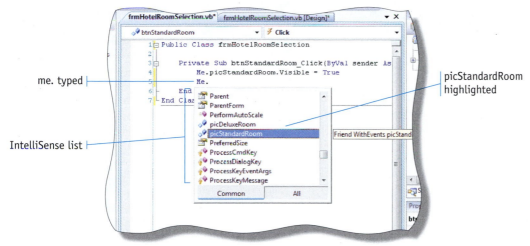

FIGURE 3-37

STEP 2   Type picd to highlight the picDeluxeRoom entry in the IntelliSense list. (You also could press the UP ARROW key one time to highlight the picDeluxeRoom entry.)

IntelliSense highlights picDeluxeRoom in the list because this is the only entry that starts with the characters, picd (Figure 3-38).

picd typed

picDeluxeRoom highlighted

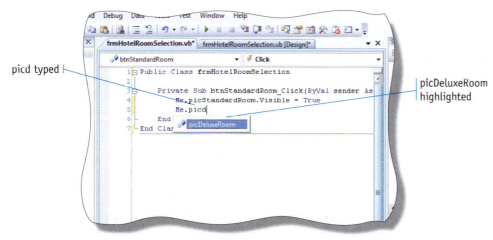

FIGURE 3-38

STEP 3   Press the key on the keyboard for the character that is to follow the object name. In this case, press the PERIOD key.

The picDeluxeRoom entry is placed in the statement followed by the dot operator (period) you typed (Figure 3–39). In addition, IntelliSense displays the list of allowable entries.

Visible is highlighted in the list because it was the entry selected the last time the list was used. If Visible was not highlighted, you could type the letter to highlight Visible in the list. A ScreenTip is displayed to the left of the Visible property explaining that the property has a Boolean setting, which means that the value of Visible can be set to True or False.

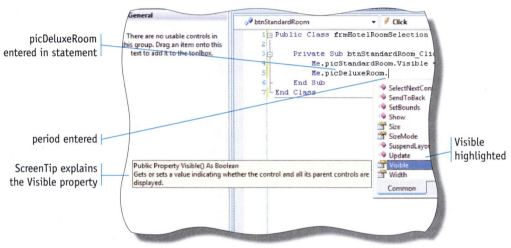

picDeluxeRoom entered in statement

period entered

ScreenTip explains the Visible property

Visible highlighted

FIGURE 3-39

STEP 4   Press the SPACEBAR, press the EQUAL SIGN key, and then press the SPACEBAR.

IntelliSense places the Visible entry in the statement (Figure 3–40). Next, the space you typed appears, followed by the equal sign and the space you typed. When you typed the equal sign, IntelliSense displayed the list of allowable entries following the equal sign.

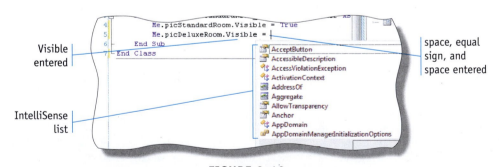

Visible entered

IntelliSense list

space, equal sign, and space entered

FIGURE 3-40

STEP 5   Type f and then press the ENTER key.

When you type the letter f, IntelliSense highlights False in the list. When you press the ENTER key, IntelliSense inserts False (Figure 3-41).

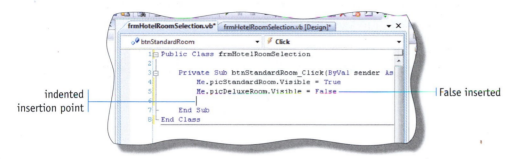

FIGURE 3-41

Once again, using IntelliSense to enter a Visual Basic programming statement results in a correct statement in minimum time with reduced chance of error.

ENABLED PROPERTY

You learned earlier that if the Enabled property for a Button object is True, the click event code for the button will be executed when the user clicks the button. If the Enabled property for a Button object is False, the event code for the button will not be executed. In Figure 3-21 on page 127, the Enabled property for the Select Room button was set to False so that the button is not active when the program begins execution. When a picture button such as the Standard Room button is clicked, however, the Enabled property must be set to True so the Select button is active. To set the Enabled property to True, a coding statement to set the Enabled property for the btnSelectRoom Button object is required. To enter the coding statement into the btnStandardRoom_Click event handler, you can complete the following steps:

STEP 1   Type me. (including the period) to display the IntelliSense list (Figure 3-42).

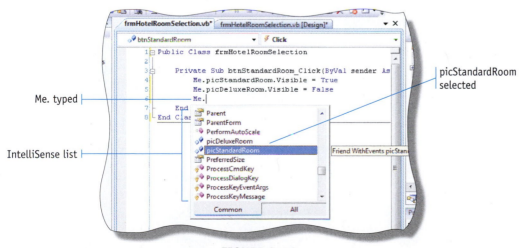

FIGURE 3-42

STEP 2   Type btnse (or fewer characters if necessary) until IntelliSense highlights the btnSelectRoom entry in the list.

IntelliSense highlights btnSelectRoom, the only entry that starts with the characters, btnse (Figure 3-43). Sometimes, the correct entry will be highlighted before you type all the distinguishing characters. If so, you need not type any more characters.

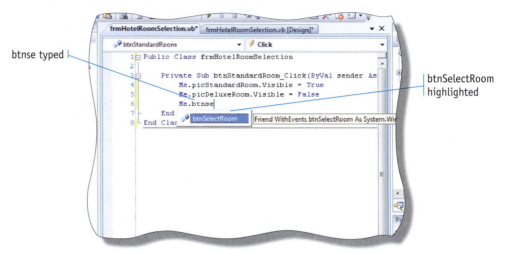

FIGURE 3-43

STEP 3   Type a period, type e, press the SPACEBAR, press the EQUAL SIGN key, press the SPACEBAR again, and then type t to select True in the IntelliSense list.

IntelliSense places the highlighted entry (btnSelectRoom) into the statement and displays a list of the next allowable entries. When you typed e, Enabled was selected in the list. Pressing the SPACEBAR caused IntelliSense to place the entry, Enabled, and then the space into the statement. When you typed the equal sign and space, IntelliSense inserted the equal sign and space, and displayed the list of entries that can follow the equal sign (Figure 3-44). When you typed the letter t, IntelliSense highlighted True in the list.

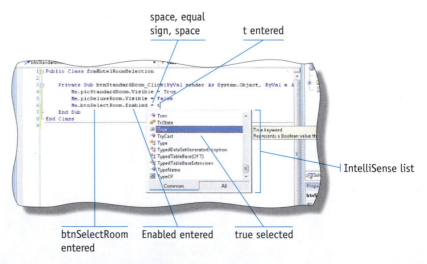

FIGURE 3-44

STEP 4 Press the ENTER key to enter the completed statement and place the insertion point on the next line.

IntelliSense enters the entry, True, into the statement (Figure 3-45). Pressing the ENTER key completes the statement and moves the indented insertion point to the next line.

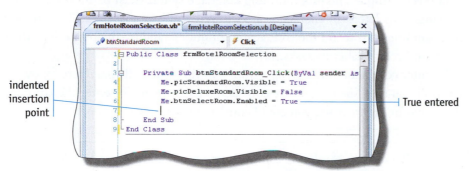

FIGURE 3-45

ONLINE REINFORCEMENT

To view a video of the process in the previous steps, visit scsite.com/vb2008/ch3 and then select Figure 3-42.

Learning the process of entering program statements through the use of IntelliSense is fundamental to writing programs using the Visual Basic 2008 language.

COMMENTS IN PROGRAM STATEMENTS

A well-written Visual Basic 2008 program normally contains **comment statements** within the code itself to document what the code is doing. An example of comment statements in code is shown in Figure 3-46.

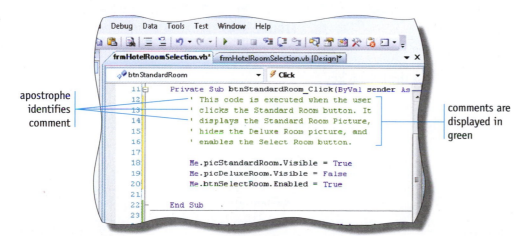

FIGURE 3-46

A comment is preceded by an apostrophe. Whenever the Visual Basic compiler encounters an apostrophe in the code, it ignores the remaining characters on the line. To the compiler, it's as if the comments do not exist.

The comments in the code, which are displayed in green text, describe the processing that will occur in the code that follows. Because comments are ignored by the Visual Basic compiler, no programming language syntax must be followed within the comments. Any letters or characters are allowed within comments. The general reason for comments is to aid the code reader in understanding the purpose of the code and how it accomplishes its tasks.

To enter comments, type an apostrophe in the code. All characters following the apostrophe on that line of code are considered a comment. To enter the comment code shown in Figure 3-46, you could complete the following steps:

STEP 1   To insert a blank line following the event code generated by Visual Studio that begins with the word Private, click anywhere in that line and then press the END key on your keyboard.

Visual Studio positions the insertion point at the end of the line that you clicked (Figure 3–47).

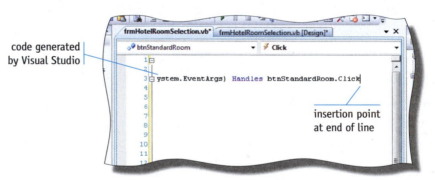

code generated by Visual Studio

insertion point at end of line

FIGURE 3-47

STEP 2   Press the ENTER key.

Visual Studio inserts a blank line in the code and then moves the insertion point to the blank line (Figure 3–48). The comments can be inserted on the blank line.

insertion point moved to next line

Visual Studio inserted blank line

FIGURE 3-48

STEP 3 Type the first line of the comments, beginning with an apostrophe, as shown in Figure 3-46 on page 143, and then press the ENTER key.

The apostrophe as the first character typed identifies the rest of the line as a comment (Figure 3–49). The comment line is displayed in green text. When you press the ENTER key, Visual Studio creates a new blank line and places the indented insertion point on that line.

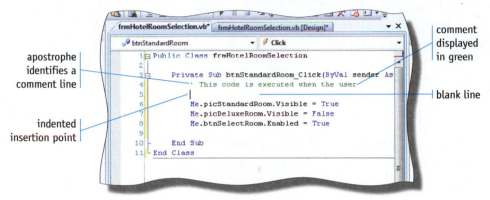

FIGURE 3-49

You can continue to enter lines of comments by typing an apostrophe and the comment, and then pressing the ENTER key until all comments are completed.

Same Line Comments

Because the Visual Basic compiler treats all characters following an apostrophe as comments, it is possible to place a comment on the same line as executable code. In Figure 3-50, a comment is shown on the same line as the statement that sets the btnSelectRoom Enabled property to True.

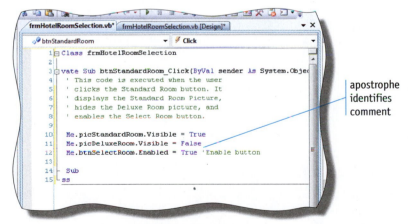

FIGURE 3-50

In Figure 3-50, the apostrophe specifies that all characters remaining on the line are to be treated as comments. Therefore, the text, Enable button, is displayed in green and is treated as a comment. To enter a comment on any line, enter an apostrophe and then type the comment. Remember that all characters following an apostrophe on a line of code are treated as comments.

Introductory Comments

Every program should begin with comments that state the name of the program, the developer's name, the date, and the purpose of the program. These comments should precede any other statements in the program (Figure 3-51).

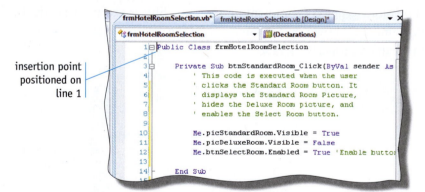

introductory comments

FIGURE 3-51

Notice that the introductory comments precede all code in the program — even the code generated by Visual Studio. To enter introductory comments, you can complete the following steps:

STEP 1   Click to the left of the word Public on line 1 in the program to place the insertion point on that line.

The insertion point is positioned at the beginning of line 1 in the code (Figure 3-52).

insertion point positioned on line 1

FIGURE 3-52

STEP 2   Press the ENTER key one time, and then press the UP ARROW key
one time.

*When you press the ENTER key, Visual Studio inserts a blank line on line 1 of the code and
moves the line that begins with the words, Public Class, down to line 2 (Figure 3-53). Visual
Studio also moves the insertion point to line 2 when you press the ENTER key. When you press
the UP ARROW key, the insertion point moves to the first line, which is blank.*

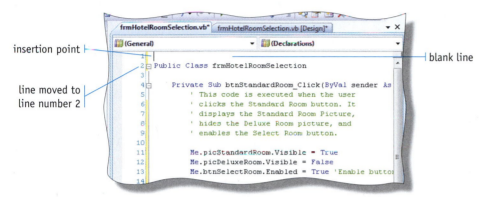

FIGURE 3-53

STEP 3   Type an apostrophe, a space, the text, `Program Name:` and then press
the TAB key one time.

*The apostrophe identifies all characters and words that follow as comments, so the characters are
displayed in green (Figure 3-54). The first line of introductory comments normally specifies the
name of the program. Pressing the TAB key moves the insertion point to the right.*

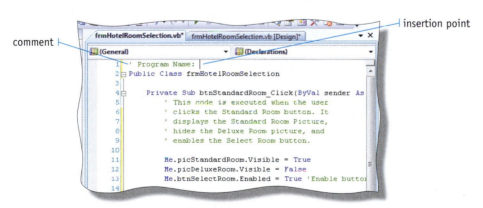

FIGURE 3-54

STEP 4 Type Hotel Room Selection as the name of the program. Then, press the ENTER key.

The program name appears in the first line of comments and the insertion point is moved to line 2 (Figure 3-55).

FIGURE 3-55

You can enter the remaining comments using the same techniques. Press the TAB key one or more times to align vertically the paragraphs on the right so they appear as shown in Figure 3-51 on page 146.

CORRECTING ERRORS IN CODE

Using IntelliSense to assist you when entering code reduces the likelihood of coding errors considerably. Nevertheless, because you could create one or more errors when entering code, you should understand what to do when a coding error occurs.

One possible error you could commit would be to forget an apostrophe in a comment statement. In Figure 3-56, a comment was entered without a leading apostrophe.

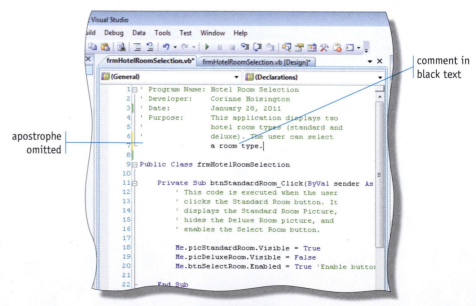

FIGURE 3-56

In Figure 3-56, the comment words are displayed in black text, which is a clue that this is an error because comment characters normally are displayed in green text. Nonetheless, Visual Studio gives no other indication that an error has occurred.

From this point where the error occurred, the developer might take any course of action. For example, she might immediately run the program. Or, she might click anywhere in the window to move the insertion point, or press the ENTER key to insert a blank line. If the program in Figure 3-56 is executed immediately by clicking the Start Debugging button on the Standard toolbar, the window shown in Figure 3-57 will be displayed.

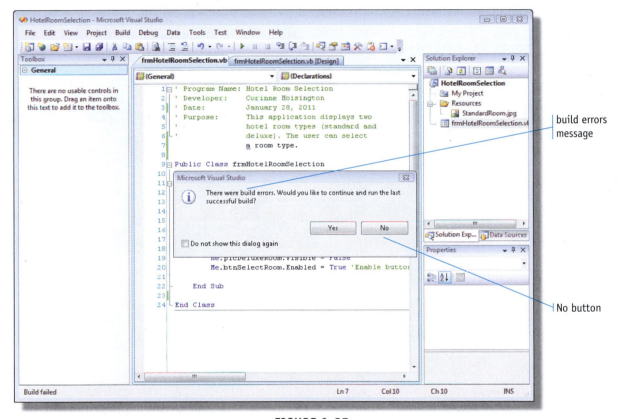

FIGURE 3-57

The **build errors message** means the Visual Basic compiler detected a coding error in the program. An absolute requirement when programming Visual Basic programs is that when you see the build errors message, you *always click the No button*. Under no circumstances should you click the Yes button in the dialog box. When you click the No button, you can perform the steps on the next page to make corrections in your program:

STEP 1 Click the No button in the Microsoft Visual Studio dialog box that informs you of a build error (see Figure 3-57).

*When you click the No button, Visual Studio displays the program code and the Error List window (Figure 3-58). The **Error List window** identifies the number of errors that occurred and displays a description of the error detected. The description, Declaration expected, in Figure 3-58 means Visual Studio expected to find a different type of statement than it found. In addition, the window contains the file in which the error occurred (frmHotelRoomSelection.vb), the line number of the statement in error (7), and the vertical column within the statement where the error was detected (17). In the code editing window, the location of the error is noted by a blue squiggly line.*

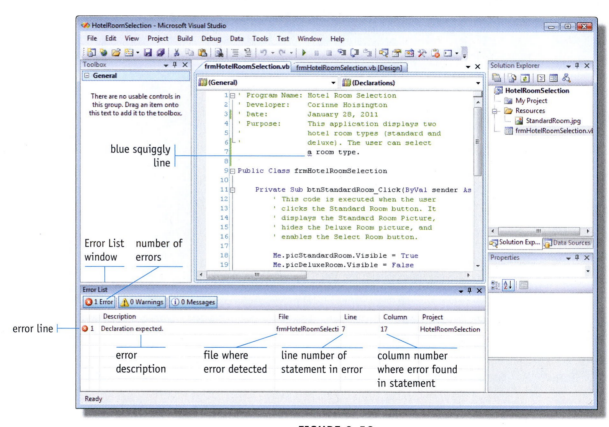

FIGURE 3-58

STEP 2   Double-click anywhere on the error line.

Visual Studio highlights the error in blue so the developer, if desired, can type and replace the highlighted text with the correct code (Figure 3-59). With the error highlighted, the developer must examine the statement to determine the error. By looking at line 7, column 17, where the letter a is highlighted, it is clear that a line intended to be a comment was not treated as a comment by Visual Studio. Further examination reveals the required apostrophe is missing.

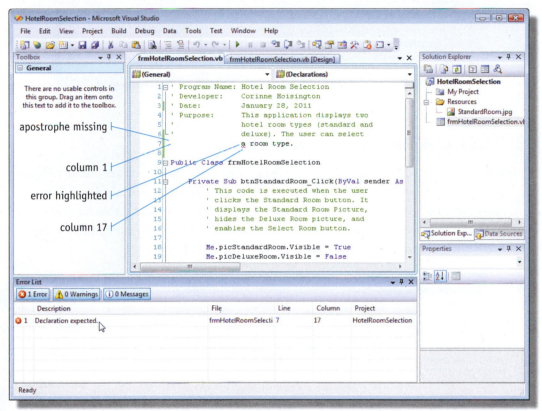

FIGURE 3-59

STEP 3   Click in the leftmost column on line 7 to place the insertion point at that location.

The insertion point is located in the leftmost column on line 7 of the program (Figure 3-60).

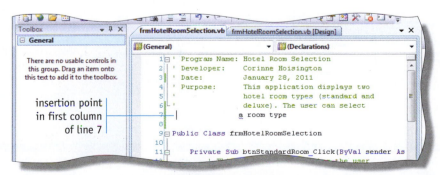

FIGURE 3-60

STEP 4 Type an apostrophe.

The apostrophe is located in the first column on line 7 of the program (Figure 3-61).

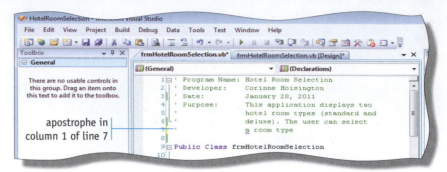

FIGURE 3-61

STEP 5 Click anywhere in the code editing window.

When you click anywhere in the window, the insertion point moves to that location (Figure 3-62). If the statement has been corrected, the error line is removed from the Error List window, and the number of errors is reduced by one. In Figure 3-62, the number of errors is zero because only one error was found in the program. It is possible to have multiple errors detected when the program is compiled.

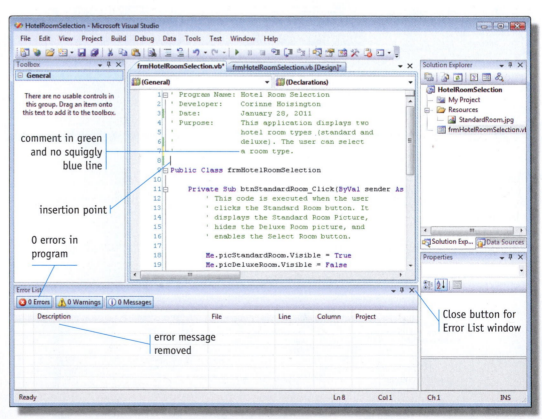

FIGURE 3-62

ONLINE REINFORCEMENT

To view a video of the process in the previous steps, visit scsite.com/vb2008/ch3 and then select Figure 3-58.

You can close the Error List window by clicking the Close button for the window (see Figure 3-62).

In Figure 3-57 on page 149, it was assumed the developer, after making the error, immediately ran the program. If, before running the program, the developer moved the insertion point to any other part of the program, or clicked any other element in the window, then Visual Studio would provide a visual cue that an error was made by displaying a blue squiggly line under the error. The line shown in Figure 3-58 is the type of line that Visual Studio would display. If you see a blue squiggly line in your code, it means you have made an error entering the code. You do not have to run the program to find coding errors. If a blue squiggly line appears in your code, an error has been made and you must correct it.

ADDITIONAL CLICK EVENTS

In the sample program in this chapter, multiple buttons can trigger events. For example, when the user clicks the Exit Window button, the program window should close and the program should terminate. To indicate that clicking the Exit Window button will trigger an event, and to prepare to write the code for the event, complete the same steps for the Exit Window button that you learned for the Standard Room button, as shown in the following figure:

STEP 1 On the frmHotelRoomSelection.vb [Design] tabbed page, double-click the Exit Window Button object.

Visual Studio opens the code editing window and displays the frmHotelRoomSelection.vb tabbed page (Figure 3-63). Visual Studio also inserts the event handler code for the click event on the btnExitWindow object. Two horizontal lines separate the event handler code for the btnExitWindow object from code for other event handlers that might be in the program. The developer must write the code that will be executed when the click event occurs. The insertion point is located in the proper place to begin writing code.

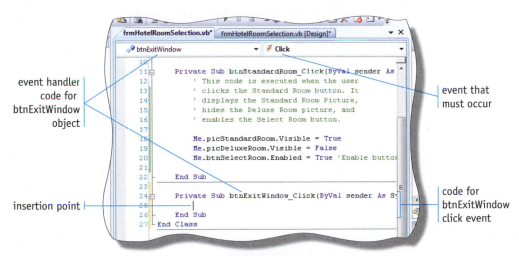

FIGURE 3-63

ENTERING CODE

As you have seen, you can enter code in the code window using the IntelliSense tools you have learned. The first code written for an event, however, should be comment code that indicates what the event is and what processing will occur. The comment code for the Exit Window event handler is shown in Figure 3-64.

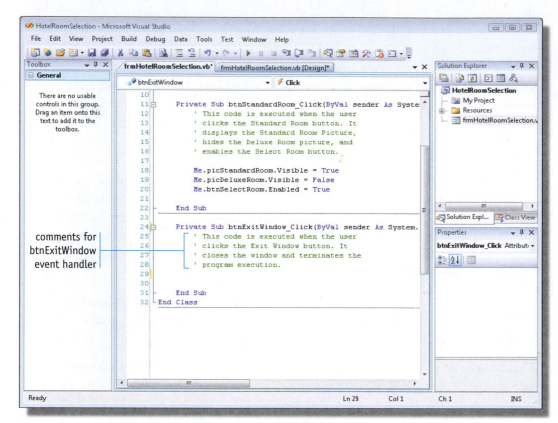

FIGURE 3-64

CLOSE PROCEDURE

The Visual Basic statement to close the window and terminate the program calls a procedure that performs the actual processing. A **procedure** is a set of prewritten code that can be called by a statement in the Visual Basic program. When the procedure is called, it performs its processing. The procedure used to close a window and terminate a program is the Close procedure.

You can use the statement in Figure 3-65 to call the Close procedure:

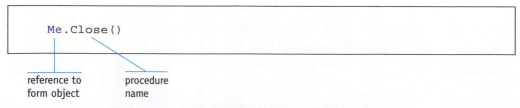

FIGURE 3-65

In Figure 3-65, the entry, me. references the Windows Form object and is required in the statement. The dot separates the reference to the Windows Form object from the name of the procedure being called. The word Close specifies the name of the procedure to be called. The left and right parentheses immediately following the name of the procedure identifies the Visual Basic statement as a **procedure call statement**.

When the statement in Figure 3-65 is executed, the Close procedure will be called and control will be given to the prewritten programming statements in the Close procedure. These statements will close the window and terminate the application.

To enter the Close statement into the program, you can type me. and then select Close in the IntelliSense list, as shown in the following steps.

STEP 1 With the insertion point positioned as shown in Figure 3-64 on page 154, type me. to display the IntelliSense list. Type cl to highlight Close in the IntelliSense list.

IntelliSense displays the list when you type the period (Figure 3-66). When you type the letters cl, IntelliSense highlights the word Close in the IntelliSense list.

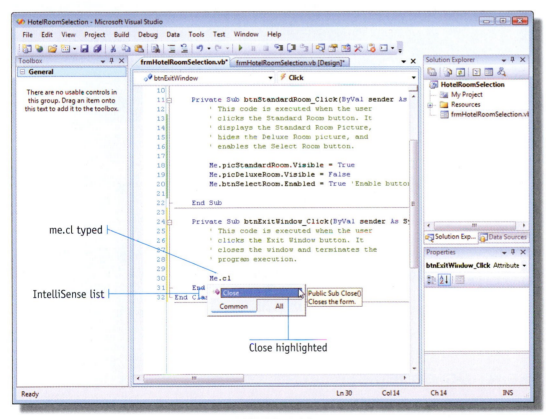

FIGURE 3-66

STEP 2 Press the ENTER key.

IntelliSense enters Close in the statement and, because it knows Close is a procedure call, automatically appends the open and closed parentheses to the statement (Figure 3-67). Then, Visual Studio returns the insertion point to the next line.

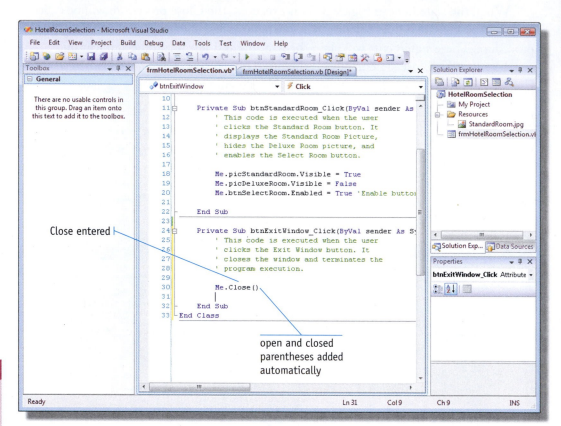

FIGURE 3-67

Prewritten procedures available to Visual Basic developers through Visual Studio are an important element when using rapid application development because the developer is not required to write the procedure code. The developer merely writes a single statement to call the procedure. You will use many procedures in this book for a variety of reasons.

PRINTING CODE

In some instances, you will find the need to print the code in the program. Sometimes as you review the code, you might find it easier to read and understand the code on a printed page rather than on your computer screen. In other cases, you might want to share the code with another developer and the printed page often is a better tool for this than a monitor screen. To print the code in a program, you can complete the following steps:

1. Click File on the menu bar to display the File menu.
2. Click Print on the File menu to display the Print dialog box.

3. Ensure that a check mark appears in the Include line numbers check box if you want line numbers on your printout. Most developers prefer line numbers on printouts.
4. Make any other selections you find necessary in the Print dialog box.
5. Click the OK button in the Print dialog box to print the code.

If you have a color printer, the code will be printed with correct color. Otherwise, shades of gray will represent the colors shown in the code editing window. If a line of code extends beyond one printed line, an arrow will appear at the end of the first printed line to indicate it continues to the next printed line.

CODING SUMMARY

Writing code is the essence of programming in Visual Basic 2008. Much of the emphasis in this book will be on writing the code required to implement applications of all kinds.

Once you understand coding and the statements shown in this chapter, you are ready to continue the process of designing and implementing the Hotel Room Selection program.

Phase 3 — Design the Program Processing Objects

The next phase in the program development life cycle requires determining the processing objects for the program and creating the event planning document. In the Hotel Room Selection program and in programs of similar complexity, the designer need not be concerned about determining the processing objects. The only processing object required for the program is the Windows Form object. In later, more complex programs, this task will become important.

So, for the Hotel Room Selection program, the next task is to design the event planning document.

EVENT PLANNING DOCUMENT

As you have learned, programs written using a graphical user interface normally are event-driven programs. An **event** means the user has initiated an action that causes the program to perform the type of processing called for by the user's action. Once the mock-up for the user interface has been created, the developer must document the events that can occur based on the user interface.

The **event planning document** consists of a table that specifies an object in the user interface that will cause an event, the action taken by the user to trigger the event, and the event processing that must occur. The event planning document for the Hotel Room Selection program is shown in Figure 3-68 on the next page.

EVENT PLANNING DOCUMENT

Program Name: Hotel Room Selection	Developer: Corinne Hoisington	Object: frmHotelRoomSelection	Date: January 28, 2011
OBJECT	**EVENT TRIGGER**	**EVENT PROCESSING**	
btnStandardRoom	Click	Display the standard room picture Hide the deluxe room picture Enable the Select Room button	
btnSelectRoom	Click	Disable the Standard Room button Disable the Select Room button Disable the Deluxe Room button Hide the Instructions label Display the Confirmation Message label Enable the Exit Window button	
btnDeluxeRoom	Click	Display the deluxe room picture Hide the standard room picture Enable the Select Room button	
btnExitWindow	Click	Close the window and terminate the program	

FIGURE 3-68

The leftmost column on the event planning document identifies the object in the graphical user interface that can be used to trigger an event. In the Hotel Room Selection program, the four Button objects each can be used to trigger an event, so each of the Button objects must be included in the event planning document. Notice each of the Button objects is identified by its name. Using this technique ensures that the documentation is precise, and provides little room for error when the developer creates the code to implement these events.

The middle column identifies the event trigger, which is the action a user takes to cause the event to occur. In all four event cases in Figure 3-68, clicking the button triggers the event. As you will learn in this book, a variety of acts by a user can trigger an event. For example, a user might point to an object, right-click the object, or double-click the object. Each of these event triggers could trigger a different event.

The rightmost column on the event planning document specifies the event processing that the program must accomplish when the event occurs. This list of tasks for each event is a critical element in the program design. It must be precise and accurate. No processing step that must occur should be left out of the event processing column. The tasks should be in the same sequence as they will be accomplished in the program.

For example, the first task for the btnStandardRoom_Click event is to display the standard room picture. This is the primary task for the Standard Room button. In addition, however, several other tasks must be completed. When the program begins, the deluxe room picture is not visible, but if the user clicks the Deluxe Room button, then the picture will be visible. When the user clicks the Standard Room button, however, the deluxe room picture should not be visible. Therefore, each time the user clicks the Standard Room button, the processing must hide the deluxe room picture.

You also will recall that when program execution begins, the Select Room button is dimmed (disabled) and, after the user clicks a room button, it should be enabled. Therefore, each time the user clicks the Standard Room button, the Select Room button must be enabled because it might be the first time the user clicked the Standard Room button.

As you review the event planning document in Figure 3-68 on page 158, be sure you understand the processing that must occur for each event.

You should note that the event processing tasks in the right column identify *what* processing must be done when the event occurs. The manner in which these tasks will be accomplished is not identified specifically, although the information in the event planning document must be precise enough that the developer easily can write the code to implement the tasks specified.

Phase 4 — Code the Program

After the events and tasks within the events have been identified, the developer is ready to code the program. As you have learned in this chapter, coding the program means entering Visual Basic statements to accomplish the tasks specified on the event planning document. As the developer enters the code, she also will implement the logic to carry out the required processing.

Guided Program Development

To fine-tune the user interface in the Hotel Room Selection program and enter the code required to process each event in the program, complete the following steps to create the program shown in Figure 3-1 on pages 112 and 113.

NOTE TO THE LEARNER

In the following activity, you should complete the tasks within the specified steps. Each of the tasks is accompanied by a Hint Screen. The purpose of the Hint Screen is to indicate where in the Visual Studio window you should perform the activity; it also serves as a reminder of the method that you should use to create the user interface or enter code. If you need further help completing the step, refer to the figure number identified by the term ref: in the step.

Guided Program Development

1

▶ **Open the Mock-Up File** Open Visual Studio and then open the mock-up file for the user interface you created in Chapter 2. (If you did not create a mock-up file in Chapter 2, consult with your instructor to obtain the file).

▶ **Show the Windows Form Object BackColor Property** To finish the user interface, the back color of the Windows Form object must be specified. Select the frmHotelRoomSelection Windows Form object. In the Properties window, scroll until the BackColor property is visible, click the BackColor property name in the left column, and then click the BackColor arrow in the right column. If necessary, click the Web tab (*ref: Figure 3-3*).

▶ **Choose the Windows Form Object BackColor** Scroll in the Web tabbed page until Cornsilk is visible and then click Cornsilk in the list (*ref: Figure 3-5*).

▶ **Select the Buttons** Next, you must specify the BackColor for the Button objects. Select the four buttons in the window using techniques you have learned previously.

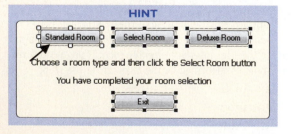

Guided Program Development *(continued)*

► **Choose the BackColor for the Buttons**

Scroll in the Properties window until the BackColor property is visible. Click the BackColor property name in the left column, click the BackColor arrow in the right column, if necessary click the Web tab, scroll until the LightSalmon color is visible, and then click LightSalmon in the Web list. Click anywhere in the window to deselect the buttons *(ref: Figure 3-4)*.

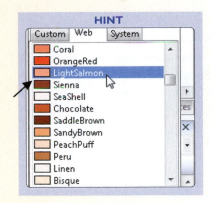

The BackColor for the Windows Form object is changed to Cornsilk and the BackColor for the buttons in the window is changed to LightSalmon (Figure 3-69).

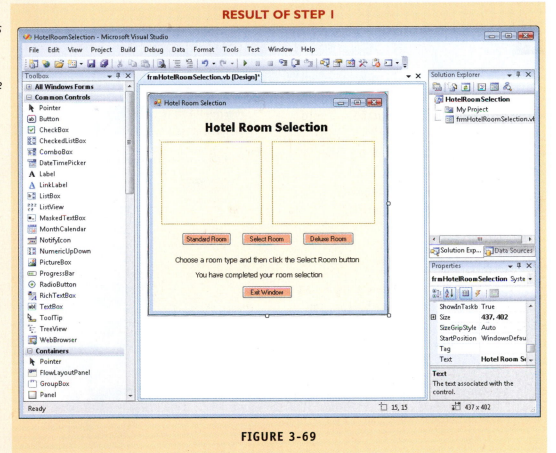

FIGURE 3-69

(continues)

Guided Program Development *(continued)*

2

▶ **Download the StandardRoom Image** To display
the pictures in the PictureBox object, you must
download the pictures from the Web and store them
on your computer. Download the StandardRoom
image from scsite.com/vb2008/ch3/images. Save
the StandardRoom image on a USB drive or other
storage media you have available on your computer
(ref: Figure 3-7).

▶ **Download the DeluxeRoom Image** Download
the DeluxeRoom image from scsite.com/vb2008/
ch3/images. Save the DeluxeRoom image on a USB
drive or other storage media you have available on
your computer *(ref: Figure 3-7)*.

3

▶ **Display the Select Resource Dialog Box** After
acquiring the pictures, you must import them into
the Resources Folder and specify the PictureBox
object where they will be displayed. Select the
picStandardRoom PictureBox object. In the
Properties window, click Image and then click
the Ellipsis button in the right column *(ref:
Figure 3-11)*.

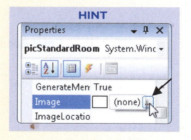

▶ **Import the StandardRoom Image** In the Select
Resource dialog box, click the Import button, import the StandardRoom image from where you saved
it in Step 2, and then click the OK button *(ref:
Figure 3-14)*.

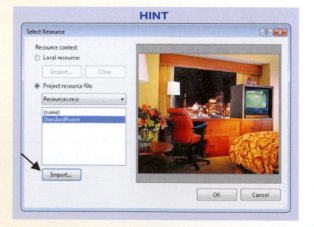

Guided Program Development (continued)

▶ **Import the DeluxeRoom Image** Using the
Properties window and the same techniques, specify
the DeluxeRoom image as the image for the
picDeluxeRoom PictureBox object.

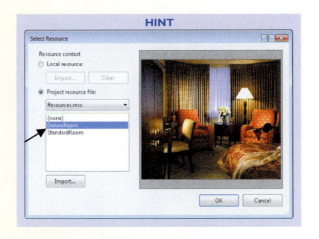

▶ **Set the SizeMode Property for the
StandardRoom Image to StretchImage** When you
import a picture, normally you must resize either
the picture or the PictureBox object so the picture
is displayed properly. To resize the StandardRoom
image, select the picStandardRoom PictureBox
object. In the Properties window for the
picStandardRoom PictureBox object, click the
SizeMode property name, click the SizeMode arrow,
and then set the property to StretchImage *(ref:
Figure 3-16)*.

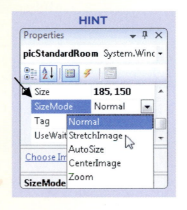

▶ **Set the SizeMode Property for the DeluxeRoom
Image to StretchImage** Using the same technique,
set the SizeMode property for the picDeluxeRoom
PictureBox object to StretchImage.

(continues)

Guided Program Development *(continued)*

The images are displayed in the correct PictureBox objects (Figure 3-70).

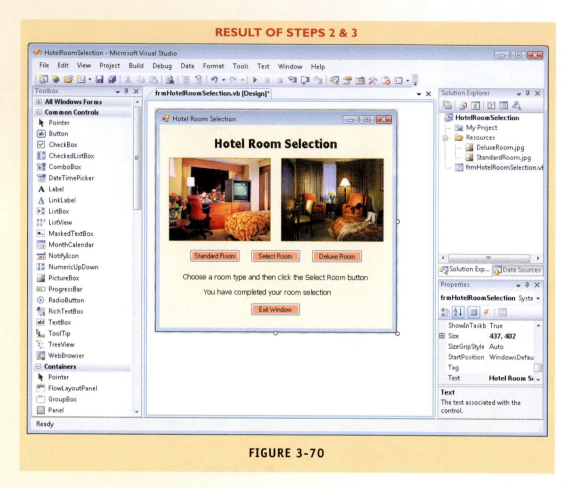

RESULT OF STEPS 2 & 3

FIGURE 3-70

4

▶ **Set the Visible Property for the StandardRoom Image to False** When program execution begins, the pictures are not displayed in the window, so their Visible property must be set to False. In the Properties window for the picStandardRoom PictureBox object, click the Visible property name in the left column, click the Visible arrow for the Visible property, and then set the Visible property for the picStandardRoom PictureBox object to False *(ref: Figure 3-18)*.

Guided Program Development *(continued)*

▶ **Set the Visible Property for the DeluxeRoom Image to False** Using the same technique, in the Properties window set the Visible property for the picDeluxeRoom PictureBox object to False *(ref: Figure 3-18)*.

▶ **Set the Visible Property for the Confirmation Message to False** The confirmation message is not displayed when program execution begins. Therefore, using the same technique, in the Properties window set the Visible property for the lblConfirmationMessage Label object to False *(ref: Figure 3-18)*.

▶ **Run the Program** After you have made changes to a program, you should run it to ensure your changes work properly. Run the program to ensure the changes you have made are correct *(ref: Figure 3-22)*.

In Figure 3-71, the room pictures are not displayed. In addition, the confirmation message is not displayed.

FIGURE 3-71

(continues)

Guided Program Development *(continued)*

5

▶ **Set the Select Room Button Enabled Property to False** Initially, the Select Room button and the Exit Window button must be dimmed. In the Properties window for the btnSelectRoom object, click the Enabled property name, click the Enabled arrow, and then set the Enabled property for the btnSelectRoom Button object to False *(ref: Figure 3-20)*.

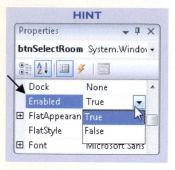

HINT

▶ **Set the Exit Window Button Enabled Property to False** Using the same technique, set the Enabled property for the btnExitWindow Button object to False *(ref: Figure 3-20)*.

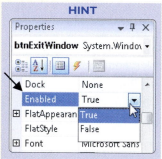

HINT

▶ **Run the Program** Once again, after you make changes always ensure the changes are correct. Run the program.

Both the Select Room button and the Exit Window button are dimmed, indicating the Enabled property for both buttons is False (Figure 3-72).

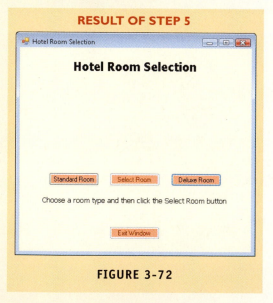

RESULT OF STEP 5

Hotel Room Selection

Hotel Room Selection

Standard Room   Select Room   Deluxe Room

Choose a room type and then click the Select Room button

Exit Window

FIGURE 3-72

6

▶ **Open the Code Editing Window for the btnStandardRoom Event Handler** The user interface now is complete, so you should begin writing the code for the program. To write code, you must open the code editing window. Double-click the Standard Room button to open the code editing window for the btnStandardRoom_Click event *(ref: Figure 3-24)*.

HINT

Guided Program Development *(continued)*

▶ **Position the Insertion Point** When you begin writing the code for a program, the first step is to write the introductory comments. Click in the leftmost position of the first coding line (Public Class) *(ref: Figure 3-52)*.

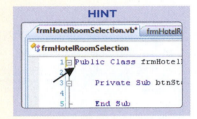

▶ **Create a Blank Line and Position the Insertion Point** Press the ENTER key and then press the UP ARROW key *(ref: Figure 3-53)*.

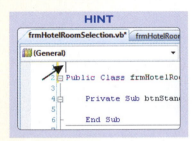

▶ **Enter the First Line of the Introductory Comments** The introductory comments provide the code reader with important information regarding the program. The first line normally specifies the name of the program. Type an apostrophe, press the SPACEBAR one time, type `Program Name:` on your keyboard, press the TAB key one time, type `Hotel Room Selection` and then press the ENTER key *(ref: Figure 3-54)*.

▶ **Enter the Developer Identification Comment Line** Type an apostrophe, press the SPACEBAR one time, type `Developer:` on your keyboard, press the TAB key one time, type your name and then press the ENTER key.

▶ **Enter the Date Comment Line** Type an apostrophe, press the SPACEBAR one time, type `Date:` on your keyboard, press the TAB key three times, enter the current date, and then press the ENTER key.

▶ **Enter the First Program Purpose Comment Line** Type an apostrophe, press the SPACEBAR one time, type Purpose: on your keyboard, press the TAB key two times, enter the first line of your own comments about the program, and then press the ENTER key.

▶ **Enter the Remaining Program Purpose Comment Lines** Insert additional lines of comments concerning the purpose of the program as you see fit.

(continues)

Guided Program Development (continued)

The comments appear at the top of the program (Figure 3-73).

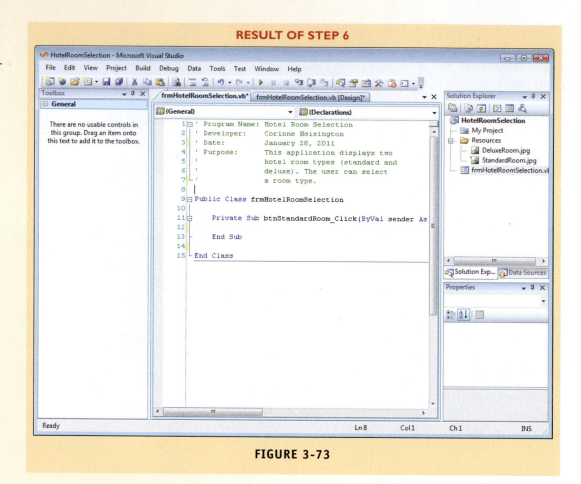

RESULT OF STEP 6

FIGURE 3-73

7

▶ **Position the Insertion Point Inside the Click Event Handler**
With the insertion point located on the line above the line of
code that begins with Public Class (see Figure 3-73), press the
DOWN ARROW key four times and then press the TAB key two times to
position the insertion point *(ref: Figure 3-48)*.

▶ **Enter the First Line of the Event Handler Comments** Each
event handler should begin with comments describing what
the event handler accomplishes. Type an apostrophe, press the
SPACEBAR one time, and then enter the first line of comments
for the btnStandardRoom_Click event handler. Press the ENTER
key *(ref: Figure 3-49)*.

Guided Program Development *(continued)*

▶ **Enter the Remaining Event Handler Comments** Enter the remaining comments for the btnStandardRoom_Click event handler.

HINT

```
 9 ⊟ Public Class frmHotelRoomSelection
10
11 ⊟     Private Sub btnStandardRoom_Click(ByVal sender
12              ' This code is executed when the user
13              ' clicks the Standard Room button. It
14              ' displays the Standard Room Picture,
15              ' hides the Deluxe Room picture, and
16              ' enables the Select Room button.
17
18
19 └       End Sub
```

▶ **Make the StandardRoom PictureBox Object Visible** The first executable line of code in the Standard Room Button object click event handler must make the StandardRoom PictureBox object visible. Using IntelliSense, enter the Visual Basic code statement to set the Visible property for the picStandardRoom PictureBox object to True *(ref: Figure 3-29)*.

HINT

```
Me.picStandardRoom.
    End Sub
End Class
```
SelectNextControl
SendToBack
SetBounds
Show
Size
SizeMode
SuspendLayout
Update
Visible
Width

ontrol and all its parent controls are

Common   All

▶ **Make the DeluxeRoom Picture Box Object Not Visible** As documented in the event planning document, the next task is to make the Deluxe Room picture not visible in the window. Using IntelliSense, enter the Visual Basic code statement to set the Visible property for the picDeluxeRoom PictureBox object to False *(ref: Figure 3-37)*.

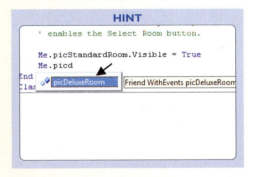

HINT

```
    ' enables the Select Room button.

    Me.picStandardRoom.Visible = True
    Me.picd
End
Clas    picDeluxeRoom        Friend WithEvents picDeluxeRoom
```

▶ **Enable the Select Room Button Object** The last task for the Standard Room button click event is to enable the Select Room button. Using IntelliSense, enter the Visual Basic code statement to set the Enabled property for the btnSelectRoom Button object to True *(ref: Figure 3-44)*.

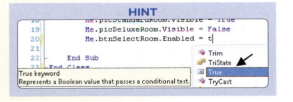

HINT

```
18          Me.picStandardRoom.Visible = True
19          Me.picDeluxeRoom.Visible = False
20          Me.btnSelectRoom.Enabled = t
21
22      End Sub
23  End Class
```
Trim
TriState
True
TryCast

True keyword
Represents a Boolean value that passes a conditional test.

(continues)

Guided Program Development *(continued)*

The lines of code are entered in the Standard Room Button object click event handler (Figure 3-74). The code will set the Visible property for the picStandardRoom PictureBox object to True, set the Visible property for the picDeluxeRoom PictureBox object to False, and set the Enabled property for the btnSelectRoom Button object to True.

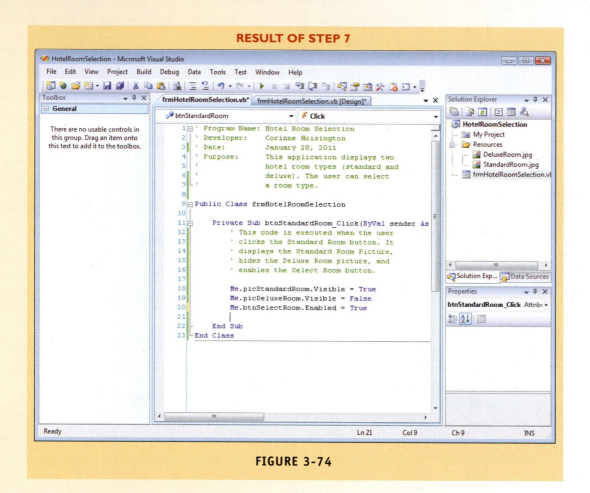

FIGURE 3-74

8

▶ **Run the Program** When the code for an event handler is complete, good practice dictates that you should run the program to ensure the event handler code works properly. Run the program. Click the Standard Room button.

Guided Program Development *(continued)*

When you click the Standard Room button, the Standard Room picture is displayed, the Deluxe Room picture is not displayed, and the Select Room button is enabled (Figure 3-75). These are the correct results. Note that if you click any of the other buttons in the window nothing happens. This is because you have not yet written the event handler code for these objects.

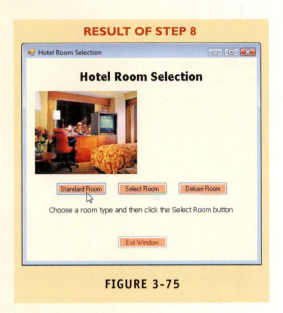

RESULT OF STEP 8

FIGURE 3-75

9

▶ **Display the Design Window** When the code for an event handler is completed, the next task is to write the code for another event handler. To do so, you must indicate the object for which the code will be written. You can do this on the Design tabbed page. Click the frmHotelRoomSelection.vb [Design] tab to return to the Design tabbed page.

HINT

▶ **Open the Code Editing Window for the btnSelectRoom Event Handler** You must open the code editing window for the btnSelectRoom Button object to enter code for the event handler. Double-click the Select Room button to open the code editing window for the btnSelectRoom_Click event *(ref: Figure 3-24)*.

HINT

▶ **Enter Event Handler Comments** When beginning the code for an event handler, the first step is to enter the event handler comments. Enter the comments that describe the processing in the btnSelectRoom_Click event handler.

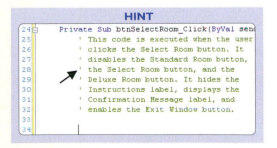
HINT

(continues)

Guided Program Development (continued)

▶ **Disable the btnStandardRoom Button Object** Referencing the event planning document (Figure 3-68 on page 158) the first task is to disable the Standard Room button. Using IntelliSense, enter the Visual Basic code statement to set the Enabled property for the btnStandardRoom Button object to False *(ref: Figure 3-42)*.

HINT

```
34          Me.btnStandardRoom.Enabled = False
35
36    End Sub
```

▶ **Disable the btnSelectRoom Button Object** The next task is to disable the Select Room button. Using IntelliSense, enter the Visual Basic code statement to set the Enabled property for the btnSelectRoom Button object to False *(ref: Figure 3-42)*.

HINT

```
34          Me.btnStandardRoom.Enabled = False
35          Me.btnSelectRoom.Enabled = False
36
```

▶ **Disable the btnDeluxeRoom Button Object** Using IntelliSense, enter the Visual Basic code statement to set the Enabled property for the btnDeluxeRoom Button object to False *(ref: Figure 3-42)*.

▶ **Hide the Instructions Label Object** When the Select Room button is clicked, the instructions should not be displayed. Using IntelliSense, enter the Visual Basic code statement to set the Visible property for the lblInstructions Label object to False *(ref: Figure 3-29)*.

HINT

```
28          ' the Select Room button, and the
29          ' Deluxe Room button. It hides the
30          ' Instructions label, displays the
31          ' Confirmation Message label, and
32          ' enables the Exit Window button.
33
34          Me.btnStandardRoom.Enabled = False
35          Me.btnSelectRoom.Enabled = False
36          Me.btnDeluxeRoom.Enabled = False
37          Me.lblInstructions.v|    Public Property Visibl
38    End Sub                        Gets or sets a value in
39                        Visible    displayed.
```

▶ **Display the Confirmation Message** The confirmation message must be displayed when the user clicks the Select Room button. Using IntelliSense, enter the Visual Basic code statement to set the Visible property for the lblConfirmationMessage Label object to True *(ref: Figure 3-29)*.

HINT

```
35          Me.btnSelectRoom.Enabled = False
36          Me.btnDeluxeRoom.Enabled = False
37          Me.lblInstructions.Visible = False
38  ➤       Me.lblConfirmationMessage.Visible = t
39    End Sub                              ● Trim
40                                         ⚙ TriState
41                                         ▣ True
```

▶ **Enable the Exit Window Button** After the user clicks the Select Room button, the only allowable action is to click the Exit Window button and close the application. Therefore, the Exit Window button must be enabled. Using IntelliSense, enter the Visual Basic code statement to set the Enabled property for the btnExitWindow Button object to True *(ref: Figure 3-42)*.

HINT

```
36          Me.btnDeluxeRoom.Enabled = False
37          Me.lblInstructions.Visible = False
38          Me.lblConfirmationMessage.Visible = True
39  ➤       Me.btnExitWindow.Enabled = True
40
```

Guided Program Development (continued)

▶ **Run the Program** Run the program to ensure that it works correctly. Click the Standard Room button and then click the Select Room button.

After clicking the two buttons, the standard room picture is displayed; the Standard Room, Select Room, and Deluxe Room buttons are disabled; the Instructions label is not displayed; the Confirmation Message label is displayed; and the Exit Window button is enabled (Figure 3-76).

RESULT OF STEP 9

FIGURE 3-76

10

▶ **Display the Design Window** The next task is to write the code for the btnDeluxeRoom event handler. To return to the Design tabbed page so you can select the Deluxe Room button, click the frmHotelRoomSelection.vb [Design] tab.

▶ **Open the Code Editing Window for the btnDeluxeRoom Event Handler** Double-click the Deluxe Room button to open the code editing window for the btnDeluxeRoom_Click event (ref: Figure 3-24).

▶ **Enter the Event Handler Comments** Using the techniques you have learned, enter the comments that describe the processing in the btnDeluxeRoom_Click event handler.

▶ **Make the DeluxeRoom PictureBox Object Visible** By referencing the event planning document, you can see the first task is to make the Deluxe Room picture visible. Using IntelliSense, enter the Visual Basic code statement to set the Visible property for the picDeluxeRoom PictureBox object to True (ref: Figure 3-29).

HINT

HINT

(continues)

Guided Program Development (continued)

▶ **Make the Standard Room Picture Not Visible** Using IntelliSense, enter the Visual Basic code statement to set the Visible property for the picStandardRoom PictureBox object to False (ref: Figure 3-29).

▶ **Enable the Select Room Button** Using IntelliSense, enter the Visual Basic code statement to set the Enabled property for the btnSelectRoom Button object to True (ref: Figure 3-42).

▶ **Run the Program** Run the program and then click the Deluxe Room button to ensure your code works correctly.

The completed code for the Select Room button event handler and the Deluxe Room button event handler is shown in Figure 3-77.

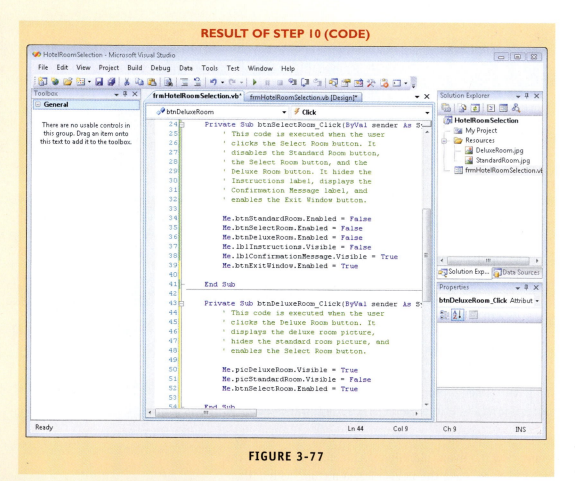

FIGURE 3-77

Guided Program Development (continued)

When you click
the Deluxe Room
button, the Deluxe
Room picture is
displayed, the
Standard Room
picture is not
displayed, and the
Select Room button
is enabled (Figure
3-78). The program
is working properly.

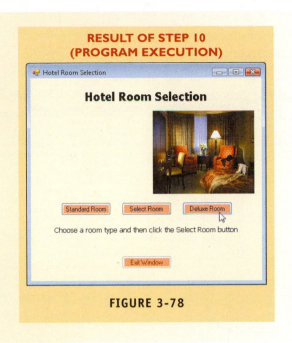

**RESULT OF STEP 10
(PROGRAM EXECUTION)**

FIGURE 3-78

11

▶ **Display the Design Window** Click the
frmHotelRoomSelection.vb [Design] tab to return
to the Design tabbed page.

▶ **Open the Code Editing Window for the
btnExitWindow Event Handler** Double-click the Exit
Window button to open the code editing window for the
btnExitWindow_Click event *(ref: Figure 3-24)*.

▶ **Enter the Event Handler Comments** Using the techniques you have learned, enter the comments that describe the processing in the btnExitWindow_Click event
handler.

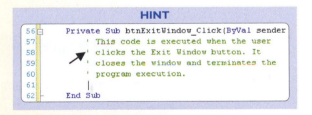

▶ **Enter the Close() Procedure Call** Using IntelliSense,
enter the Visual Basic code statement to close the window and terminate the program *(ref: Figure 3-66)*.

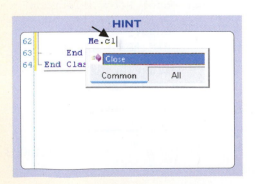

(continues)

Guided Program Development (continued)

The Close()
procedure call
statement is
entered (Figure
3-79). When the
procedure call is
executed, the appli-
cation will be
closed.

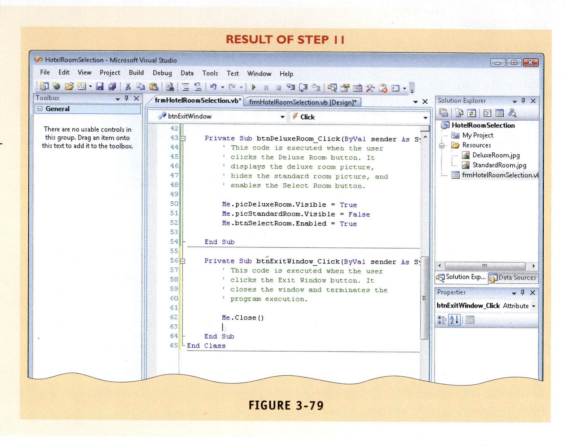

FIGURE 3-79

12

▶ **Run the Program** Run the program to ensure that it works correctly: 1. Click the Standard Room button; 2. Click the
Deluxe Room button; 3. Click the Standard Room button; 4. Click the Select Room button; 5. Click the Exit Window button.

Code Listing

The complete code for the sample program is shown in Figure 3-80.

```
1 ' Program Name: Hotel Room Selection
2 ' Developer:    Corinne Hoisington
3 ' Date:         January 28, 2011
4 ' Purpose:      This application displays two
5 '               hotel room types (standard and
6 '               deluxe). The user can select
7 '               a room type.
8
9 Public Class frmHotelRoomSelection
10
```

FIGURE 3-80 (continues)

```
11      Private Sub btnStandardRoom_Click(ByVal sender As System.Object, ByVal e As System.↙
        EventArgs) Handles btnStandardRoom.Click
12              ' This code is executed when the user
13              ' clicks the Standard Room button. It
14              ' displays the Standard Room Picture,
15              ' hides the Deluxe Room picture, and
16              ' enables the Select Room button.
17
18              Me.picStandardRoom.Visible = True
19              Me.picDeluxeRoom.Visible = False
20              Me.btnSelectRoom.Enabled = True
21
22      End Sub
23
24      Private Sub btnSelectRoom_Click(ByVal sender As System.Object, ByVal e As System.  ↙
        EventArgs) Handles btnSelectRoom.Click
25              ' This code is executed when the user
26              ' clicks the Select Room button. It
27              ' disables the Standard Room button,
28              ' the Select Room button, and the
29              ' Deluxe Room button. It hides the
30              ' Instructions label, displays the
31              ' Confirmation Message label, and
32              ' enables the Exit Window button.
33
34              Me.btnStandardRoom.Enabled = False
35              Me.btnSelectRoom.Enabled = False
36              Me.btnDeluxeRoom.Enabled = False
37              Me.lblInstructions.Visible = False
38              Me.lblConfirmationMessage.Visible = True
39              Me.btnExitWindow.Enabled = True
40
41      End Sub
42
43      Private Sub btnDeluxeRoom_Click(ByVal sender As System.Object, ByVal e As System.  ↙
        EventArgs) Handles btnDeluxeRoom.Click
44              ' This code is executed when the user
45              ' clicks the Deluxe Room button. It
46              ' displays the deluxe room picture,
47              ' hides the standard room picture, and
48              ' enables the Select Room button.
49
50              Me.picDeluxeRoom.Visible = True
51              Me.picStandardRoom.Visible = False
52              Me.btnSelectRoom.Enabled = True
53
54      End Sub
55
56      Private Sub btnExitWindow_Click(ByVal sender As System.Object, ByVal e As System.  ↙
        EventArgs) Handles btnExitWindow.Click
57              ' This code is executed when the user
58              ' clicks the Exit Window button. It
59              ' closes the window and terminates the
60              ' program execution.
61
62              Me.Close()
63
64      End Sub
65 End Class
```

FIGURE 3-80 (continued)

Summary

In this chapter you have learned to fine-tune a graphical user interface to maximize its usefulness and to enter code for object event handlers.

The items listed in the table in Figure 3-81 include all the new Visual Studio and Visual Basic skills you have learned in this chapter.

VISUAL BASIC SKILLS		
Skill	**Figure Number**	**Web Address for Video**
Set the BackColor property	Figure 3-2	scsite.com/vb2008/ch3/figure3-2
Locate and Save an Image from the World Wide Web	Figure 3-7	scsite.com/vb2008/ch3/figure3-7
Import an Image into the Program Resources Folder	Figure 3-11	scsite.com/vb2008/ch3/figure3-11
Size an Image	Figure 3-16	scsite.com/vb2008/ch3/figure3-16
Set the Visible Property in the Properties Window	Figure 3-18	scsite.com/vb2008/ch3/figure3-18
Set the Enabled Property in the Properties Window	Figure 3-20	scsite.com/vb2008/ch3/figure3-20
Run a Visual Basic 2008 Program	Figure 3-22	scsite.com/vb2008/ch3/figure3-22
Enter Visual Basic 2008 Code for Event Handling	Figure 3-24	scsite.com/vb2008/ch3/figure3-24
Enter a Visual Basic 2008 Statement using IntelliSense	Figure 3-29	scsite.com/vb2008/ch3/figure3-29
Enter a Visual Basic 2008 Statement to Set the Visible Property to True	Figure 3-29	scsite.com/vb2008/ch3/figure3-29
Enter a Visual Basic 2008 Statement to Set the Visible Property to False	Figure 3-37	scsite.com/vb2008/ch3/figure3-37
Enter a Visual Basic 2008 Statement to Set the Enabled Property to True	Figure 3-42	scsite.com/vb2008/ch3/figure3-42
Enter Comments in Visual Basic 2008 Code	Figure 3-47	scsite.com/vb2008/ch3/figure3-47
Enter Introductory Comments in Visual Basic 2008 Code	Figure 3-52	scsite.com/vb2008/ch3/figure3-52
Correct Errors in a Visual Basic 2008 Program	Figure 3-58	scsite.com/vb2008/ch3/figure3-58
Enter a Close() Statement into Visual Basic 2008 Code	Figure 3-66	scsite.com/vb2008/ch3/figure3-66
Print Code	Pages 156–157	

FIGURE 3-81

Learn It Online

Start your browser and visit scsite.com/vb2008/ch3. Follow the instructions in the exercises below.

1. **Chapter Reinforcement TF, MC, SA** Click one of the Chapter Reinforcement links for Multiple Choice, True/False, or Short Answer below the Learn It Online heading. Answer each question and submit to your instructor.

2. **Practice Test** Click the Practice Test link. Answer each question, enter your first and last name at the bottom of the page, and then click the Grade Test button. When the graded practice test is displayed on your screen, submit the graded practice test to your instructor. Continue to take the practice test until you are satisfied with your score.

3. **Crossword Puzzle Challenge** Click the Crossword Puzzle Challenge link below the Learn It Online heading. Read the instructions, and then click the Continue button. Work the crossword puzzle. When you are finished, click the Submit button. When the crossword puzzle is redisplayed, submit it to your instructor.

Knowledge Check

1. Which property controls the background color of the Form object?

2. Which property controls the background color of a Button object?

3. Which color palette is guaranteed to be displayed properly on every computer?

4. What is the use of the Image property for a PictureBox object?

5. To display an image in a PictureBox object in your application, you first must store the image in which folder within the application?

6. When you click the Ellipsis button for the Image property of a PictureBox object (Figure 3-82), what action does Visual Studio 2008 take?

FIGURE 3-82

7. What is the default setting of the PictureBox object SizeMode property?

8. Which option in the SizeMode property should be selected to make the image fit within the PictureBox object?

9. Which property has been set to False if a Button object in a window is dimmed when program execution begins?

(continues)

Knowledge Check

(continued)

10. Which property has been set to False if a PictureBox object is not displayed when you run the application?

11. What two options can you select for the Visible property in the Properties window?

12. Write a line of code that would set the Visible property for a PictureBox object named picHomeTown to False. (Use the Me command in your answer.)

13. Write a line of code that would set the Enabled property for a Button object named btnStart to True. (Use the Me command in your answer.)

14. Write a line of code that would set the Visible property for a Label object named lblDisplayTuition to True. (Use the Me command in your answer.)

15. Write a comment line of code that states, "The following code displays the image".

16. What color text is used to display comments in the code editing window of Visual Basic 2008?

17. Write a line of code that will close an application window and terminate the application. (Use the Me command in your answer.)

18. What does a blue squiggly line mean in the code editing window?

19. Why is it best that you use IntelliSense when you enter code in the code editing window? List two reasons.

20. Which symbol is associated with the assignment statement?

Debugging Exercises

1. Fix the following line of code to set the Visible property for the picCompanyLogo PictureBox object to True.

   ```
   Me.picCompanyLogo.Visible.True
   ```

2. Fix the following line of code to disable the btnExitProgram Button object.

   ```
   Me.btnExitProgram.Enabled = No
   ```

3. Fix the following line of code to set the Visible property for the lblDirections Label object to False.

   ```
   Me.lblDirections.Visible = ' False
   ```

Debugging Exercises

(continued)

4. Fix the following comment line of code.

```
The ' following line of code makes the college logo visible
```

5. Fix the following line of code.

```
Me.Close
```

6. Examine the code window and the Error List window in Figure 3-83. Then, write a line of code to replace the line of code in error.

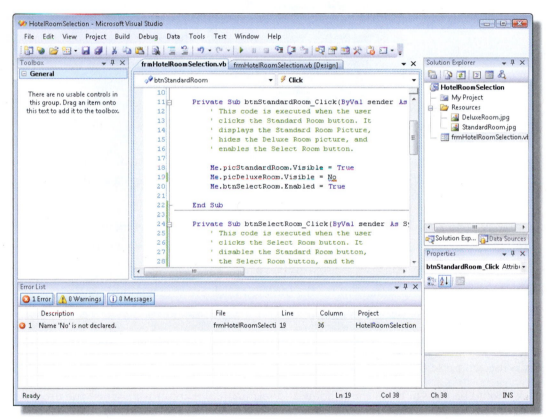

FIGURE 3-83

Program Analysis

1. For a bakery application shown in Figure 3-84, write the Visual Basic 2008 coding statement to view the cake picture when the user clicks the btnView button, assuming the Visible property for the picCake PictureBox object had been set to False in the Properties window.

FIGURE 3-84

2. Which property in the Properties window controls whether the btnPlaceOrder button is dimmed when the program begins execution? Which option for the property would you select to cause the button to be dimmed when the program begins execution?

3. When you import the picture of the cake into the Resources folder and select the image for use in the picCake PictureBox object, which SizeMode property option would you select to view the complete picture?

4. Write the Visual Basic 2008 coding statement for the btnView click event that would cause the btnPlaceOrder button to be active (not dimmed).

5. To make the window background color Orchid as shown in Figure 3-84, what property should you modify?

6. What property is used to cause the text, Birthday Cake Order Form, to be displayed in the window title bar?

7. What procedure should be used to close the window and terminate the application when the user clicks the Place Order button?

Case Programming Assignments

Complete one or more of the following case programming assignments. Submit the program and materials you create to your instructor. The level of difficulty is indicated for each case programming assignment.

● = Easiest
●● = Intermediate
●●● = Challenging

1 ●
CAR RENTAL SELECTION

Based on the Windows form mock-up you created in Chapter 2, complete the Car Rental Selection program by changing the window background color, downloading and adding the images, and writing the code that will execute according to the program requirements. Before writing the code, create an event planning document for each event in the program. The completed Windows Form object and the other objects in the user interface are shown in Figure 3-87a, Figure 3-87b, and Figure 3-87c.

REQUIREMENTS DOCUMENT

Date submitted: January 17, 2011

Application title: Car Rental Selection

Purpose: The car rental selection application will allow a user to select a sports car or luxury car.

Program Procedures: From a window on the screen, the user should identify a rental car type (sports car or luxury car) and then indicate he or she wants to rent that car.

Algorithms, Processing, and Conditions:
1. The user must be able to view a sports car or luxury car, back and forth until the selection is made.
2. When the user identifies the car type, a picture of that car type should appear in the window.
3. Only one picture should be displayed at a time. If a user identifies the sports car, only the sports car picture should be displayed; if a user identifies the luxury car, only the luxury car picture should be displayed.
4. When the user makes a car selection, a message stating that the selection of a car has been made should be displayed. In addition, the user should be stopped from identifying a car type after the car selection has been made.
5. After the user makes a car selection, the only allowable action is to exit the window.

Notes and Restrictions
1. A user cannot make a car selection until he or she has identified a car type.

Comments:
1. The pictures shown in the window can be found on scsite.com/vb2008/ch3/images. The names of the pictures are Sports Car and Luxury Car.

FIGURE 3-85

(continues)

Case Programming Assignments

Car Rental Selection (continued)

USE CASE DEFINITION

1. User clicks Sports Car button or Luxury Car button.
2. Program displays a picture of the car identified by the user and enables the car selection button.
3. User clicks car buttons to view cars if desired. Program displays the picture of the identified car.
4. User clicks the Select Car button.
5. Program displays a car selection confirmation message, and disables both car buttons and the Select Car button. The Exit Window button becomes active.
6. User terminates the program by clicking the Exit Window button.

FIGURE 3-86

In Figure 3-87a, no button has been clicked. In Figure 3-87b, the user has clicked the Luxury Car button. In Figure 3-87c, the user has clicked the Select Car button.

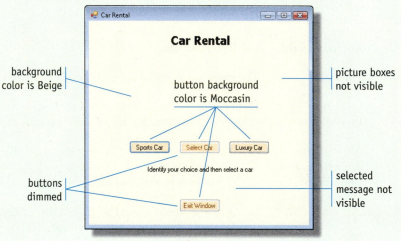

FIGURE 3-87a

FIGURE 3-87b

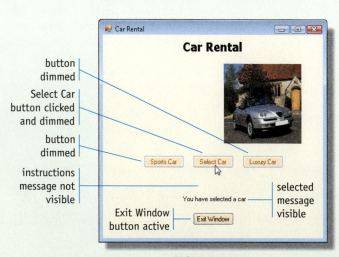

FIGURE 3-87c

Case Programming Assignments

2 ● BANKING

Based on the Windows form mock-up you created in Chapter 2, complete the Banking program by changing the window background color, downloading and adding the image, and writing the code that will execute according to the program requirements. Before writing the code, create an event planning document for each event in the program. The completed Windows Form object and the other objects in the user interface are shown in Figure 3-90a and Figure 3-90b.

REQUIREMENTS DOCUMENT

Date submitted: January 14, 2011

Application title: Bank Welcome Screen with Banking Hours

Purpose: This application displays a welcome screen for the First Corner National Bank. The user can choose an option to view the hours of the bank.

Program Procedures: From a window on the screen, the user makes a request to see the bank's open hours.

Algorithms, Processing, and Conditions:
1. The user first views a welcome screen that displays the bank's name (First Corner National Bank), bank picture, and a phrase that states the bank is FDIC insured.
2. When the user opts to view the bank hours, the following hours are displayed:

Monday–Thursday	9:00am–5:00pm
Friday	9:00am–8:00pm
Saturday	9:00am–1:00 pm

3. After the user views the hours, the only allowable action is to exit the window.

Notes and Restrictions:

Comments:
1. The picture shown in the window can be found on scsite.com/vb2008/ch3/images. The name of the picture is Bank Building.

FIGURE 3-88

(continues)

Case Programming Assignments

Banking (continued)

USE CASE DEFINITION

1. The window opens, displaying the title of the bank, the bank's picture, and a message that the bank is FDIC insured. The View Banking Hours button and the Exit Window button are enabled.
2. User clicks View Banking Hours button.
3. Program displays the banking hours above the buttons. The View Banking Hours button is disabled.
4. User clicks the Exit Window button to terminate the application.

FIGURE 3-89

In Figure 3-90a, no button has been clicked. In Figure 3-90b, the user has clicked the View Banking Hours button.

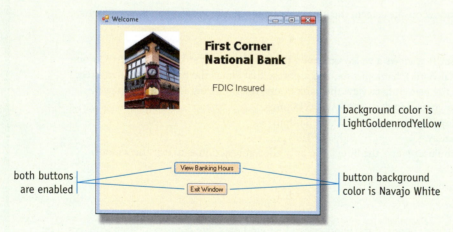

FIGURE 3-90a

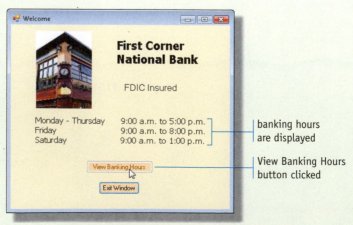

FIGURE 3-90b

Case Programming Assignments

3 ● VISUAL BASIC 2008 TERMS

Based on the Windows form mock-up you created in Chapter 2, complete the Visual Basic 2008 Terms program by changing the window background color, downloading and adding the image, and writing the code that will execute according to the program requirements. Before writing the code, create an event planning document for each event in the program. The completed Windows Form object and the other objects in the user interface are shown in Figure 3-93a and Figure 3-93b.

REQUIREMENTS DOCUMENT

Date submitted: August 16, 2011

Application title: Visual Basic 2008 Terms

Purpose: This application displays the definitions of common Visual Basic terms. When the user chooses to view the definition, the term's definition is displayed.

Program Procedures: From a window on the screen, the user makes a request to see one of three VB definitions.

Algorithms, Processing, and Conditions:
1. The user first views a screen that displays three VB terms.
2. An image of a computer is displayed at the top of the window throughout the running of the application.
3. The user can select any of the three terms displayed on the buttons, and the definition appears after each selection is made.
4. The user can click any of the terminology buttons and the definition will appear. Any previous definitions will disappear.
5. An exit button is available at all times allowing the user to end the application.

Notes and Restrictions:
1. Only one definition should be displayed at a time, so if a user selects a second term, the second definition only should be displayed.

Comments:
1. The computer picture shown in the window can be found on scsite.com/vb2008/ch3/images. The name of the picture is Computer.

FIGURE 3-91

(continues)

Case Programming Assignments

Visual Basic 2008 Terms (continued)

USE CASE DEFINITION

1. The window opens and displays a computer image, the title (Visual Basic 2008 Terms), three buttons labeled with VB terms, and an Exit Window button. The Exit Window button is enabled.
2. User clicks each of the terminology buttons to review the definitions.
3. Program displays the definitions to the right of the buttons.
4. Only one definition shows at a time.
5. User clicks the Exit Window button to terminate the application.

FIGURE 3-92

In Figure 3-93a, no button has been clicked. In Figure 3-93b, the user has clicked the Developer button.

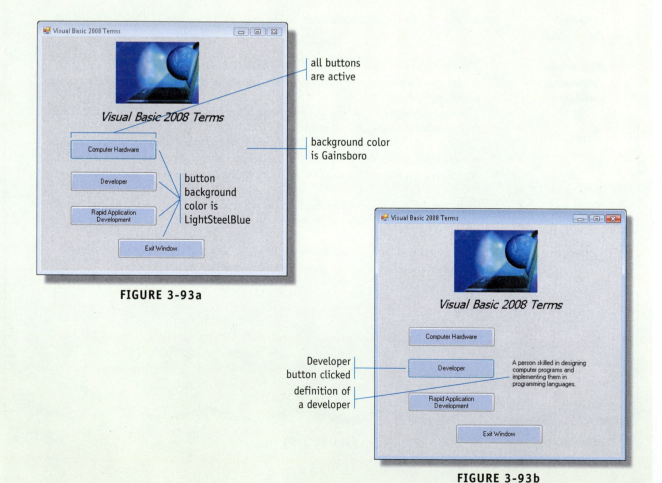

FIGURE 3-93a

FIGURE 3-93b

Case Programming Assignments

4 ●● ONLINE STORE SPECIALS

Based on the Windows form mock-up you created in Chapter 2, complete the Online Store Specials program by finishing the user interface, downloading and adding the images, and writing the code that will execute according to the program requirements. Before writing the code, create an event planning document for each event in the program.

REQUIREMENTS DOCUMENT

Date submitted: January 6, 2012

Application title: Online Store Specials

Purpose: The online store specials program will display the daily, weekly, and holiday specials of the online store. The user can select the desired product and then add the product to the shopping cart.

Program Procedures: From a window on the screen, the user should select the daily special, the weekly special, or the holiday special. When a special is selected, the program should display a picture of the special product, the regular price of the product, and the special price of the product. The user should be able to select any special. Then, the user can add the product to the shopping cart.

Algorithms, Processing, and Conditions:

1. The user must select a special in order to display the special's product picture, regular price, and sales price.
2. The user cannot add a product to the shopping cart until a special is selected.
3. When a special is selected, only that special's picture and prices should be displayed in the window. No other special should be displayed.
4. After the user selects a special and adds it to the shopping cart, the only allowable user action is to exit the window.
5. A user should be able to exit the window at any time.

Notes and Restrictions:

Comments:

1. The specials are: Daily Special: Cell Phone: Regular Price: $99.95; Special Price: $84.50
   Weekly Special: MP3 Player: Regular Price: $129.95; Special Price: $101.47
   Holiday Special: Digital Camera: Regular Price: $259.95; Special Price: $203.19
2. The pictures shown in the window can be found on scsite.com/vb2008/images. The names of the pictures are Cell Phone, MP3 Player, and Digital Camera.

FIGURE 3-94

Case Programming Assignments

5 ●● CHILDREN GIFT SELECTION

Based on the Windows form mock-up you created in Chapter 2, complete the Children Gift Selection program by finishing the user interface, downloading and adding the images, and writing the code that will execute according to the program requirements. Before writing the code, create an event planning document for each event in the program.

REQUIREMENTS DOCUMENT

Date submitted: March 21, 2011

Application title: Children Gift Selection

Purpose: Your city has started a program that provides gifts for disadvantaged children over the December holidays. Each child can choose one of three toys. So they can choose, the program must display each of the toys upon request of the child. The child then can make the choice of the toy he or she would like to receive.

Program Procedures: From a window on the screen, the user selects one of three toys. A picture of the toy is displayed in the window. The user then can choose the toy he or she wants to receive.

Algorithms, Processing, and Conditions:
1. The user selects a toy. Then, a picture of the toy is displayed in the window.
2. The user can select any of the three toys. Only the picture for the selected toy should be displayed.
3. The user can select toys back and forth to see the pictures for the toys.
4. After the user finds a toy he or she wants, the user chooses that toy for delivery in the December holidays.
5. After the user chooses a toy, a message stating that a toy has been chosen should be displayed.
6. After the user chooses a toy, the only allowable action is to exit the window.

Notes and Restrictions:
1. The user should not be able to choose a toy until he or she has viewed the picture of at least one toy.

Comments:
1. The toys available are a ball, a doll, and a toy airplane.
2. The pictures shown in the window can be found on scsite.com/vb2008/ch3/images. The names of the pictures are Ball, Doll, and Airplane.

FIGURE 3-95

Case Programming Assignments

6 ●●
#1 SONG VOTING

Based on the Windows form mock-up you created in Chapter 2, complete the #1 Song Voting program by finishing the user interface, downloading and adding the images, and writing the code that will execute according to the program requirements. Before writing the code, create an event planning document for each event in the program.

REQUIREMENTS DOCUMENT

Date submitted: February 22, 2011

Application title: #1 Song Voting

Purpose: In your mall, a music store named "Millennium Music" wants a program that shows the #1 song in each of three music genres and allows the user to vote for his or her overall favorite. The user should be able to select one of three genres and then be able to vote for that song/genre as the user's overall favorite.

Program Procedures: From a window on the screen, the user selects one of three music genres. The name of the #1 song in the selected genre is displayed together with a picture of the artist or band for the song. Then, the user can vote for that song/genre as their overall favorite.

Algorithms, Processing, and Conditions:
1. The user selects a music genre. Then, the #1 song title in the genre and picture of the artist or band is displayed in the window.
2. The user can select any of the three music genres. Only the name of the song and the picture for the selected genre should be displayed.
3. The user can select music genres back and forth to see the #1 song for each genre and the associated artist or band.
4. After the user selects a genre, the user should be able to vote for that genre/song as the favorite. The user cannot vote until the user has selected a genre.
5. After the user votes, a message stating that voting has occurred should be displayed.
6. After the user votes, the only allowable action is to exit the window.

Notes and Restrictions:
1. The user should not be able to vote until he or she has selected a music genre.

Comments:
1. You (the developer) should select the three music genres and the #1 song for each of the genres.
2. The pictures of the artist or the band will depend on your selection of both the music genres and the #1 song in each of the genres. You should download a picture of the artist or band from the World Wide Web. You can search anywhere on the Web for the pictures. You will find that www.google.com/images is a good source.

FIGURE 3-96

Case Programming Assignments

7 ●●●
ENGLISH-TO-SPANISH TRANSLATOR

Based on the problem definition (Figure 3-97) and the Windows form mock-up you created in Chapter 2, complete the English-to-Spanish translator program by finishing the user interface, downloading and adding any required images, and writing the code that will execute according to the program requirements. Before writing the code, create an event planning document for each event in the program.

The Bonita Travel Agency would like to create an English-to-Spanish translator of the most commonly used Spanish words for those booking a trip to a Spanish-speaking destination. Develop a Windows application for the Bonita Travel Spanish Translator. The English phrase should be displayed in the window. When the user selects an English phrase, the corresponding Spanish translation is displayed. Only one Spanish translation should be displayed at any given time. The user should be able to exit the window at any time.

English	Spanish Translation
Good morning	Buenos dias
Thank you	Gracias
Goodbye	Adios
Money	Dinero

FIGURE 3-97

Case Programming Assignments

8 ●●●
TRAVEL SPECIALS

Based on the problem definition (Figure 3-98) and the Windows form mock-up you created in Chapter 2, complete the Travel Specials program by finishing the user interface, downloading and adding any required images, and writing the code that will execute according to the program requirements. Before writing the code, create an event planning document for each event in the program.

Your local travel agent would like a computer application to advertise the travel specials of the week from your city. This week's flight specials are:

Destination	Price
Orlando	$129 round trip
Las Vegas	$219 round trip
New Orleans	$189 round trip
Aruba	$419 round trip
Hawaii	$728 round trip

Write an application that will allow the user to select any of the five vacation destinations. When the user selects a vacation destination, the corresponding price and a picture of the destination should be displayed. Clear each prior price and picture when the user selects a different vacation destination. In addition to a picture of the destination, include a Web page address that features the selected location. After the user has selected a destination, the user should be able to book the vacation and then exit the window.

FIGURE 3-98

Case Programming Assignments

9 ●●●
CATERING SERVICE

Based on the problem definition (Figure 3-99) and the Windows form mock-up you created in Chapter 2, complete the Catering Service program by finishing the user interface, downloading and adding any required images, and writing the code that will execute according to the program requirements. Before writing the code, create an event planning document for each event in the program.

Your friend operates a catering service and has asked you to develop a Windows application that allows the user to see the four types of catering events offered, one at a time. Then, the user should be able to reserve the catering service desired. The four types of catering services and their minimum prices are as follows:

Name of Service	Minimum Price
Grand	$500.00
Magnificent	$1,000.00
Majestic	$1,800.00
Opulent	$3,000.00

For each type of service, your program should display the minimum price and a picture depicting an example of the quality each service type provides. Clear each service price and picture when the user selects a different catering service. After the user has selected a catering service, the user should be able to book the service and then exit the window.

FIGURE 3-99

CHAPTER FOUR

Variables and Arithmetic Operations

OBJECTIVES

You will have mastered the material in this chapter when you can:

- ▶ Create, modify, and program a TextBox object
- ▶ Use code to place data in the Text property of a Label object
- ▶ Use the AcceptButton and CancelButton properties
- ▶ Understand and declare String and Numeric variables
- ▶ Use assignments statements to place data in variables
- ▶ Use literals and constants in coding statements

- ▶ Understand scope rules for variables
- ▶ Convert string and numeric data
- ▶ Understand and use arithmetic operators and arithmetic operations
- ▶ Format and display numeric data as a string
- ▶ Create a form load event
- ▶ Create a concatenated string
- ▶ Debug a program

Introduction

In the Hotel Room Selection program developed in Chapter 2 and Chapter 3, when the user clicked buttons in the user interface, events were triggered; but the user did not enter data. In many applications, users must enter data and then the program uses the data in its processing.

When processing data entered by a user, a common requirement is to perform arithmetic operations on the data in order to generate useful output information. Arithmetic operations include adding, subtracting, multiplying, and dividing numeric data.

To illustrate the use of user data input and arithmetic operations, the application in this chapter allows the user to enter the number of songs to be downloaded from the World Wide Web. The application then calculates the total cost of the downloads. The user interface for the program is shown in Figure 4-1.

FIGURE 4-1

ONLINE REINFORCEMENT

To view a video of program execution, visit scsite.com/vb2008/ch4 and then select Figure 4-1.

In Figure 4-1, the user entered 5 as the number of songs to download. When the user clicked the Calculate Cost button, the program multiplied 5 times the cost per song (99 cents) and then displayed the result as the total cost of downloads. When the user clicks the Clear button, the values for the number of song downloads and the total cost of downloads are cleared so the next user can enter a value. Clicking the Exit button closes the window and terminates the program.

To create this application, the developer must understand how to perform the following processes, among others:

1. Define a text box for data entry.
2. Define a label to hold the results of arithmetic operations.
3. Convert data in a text box to data that can be used for arithmetic operations.
4. Perform arithmetic operations on data a user enters.

The following pages describe the tools and techniques required to create the program shown in Figure 4-1.

User Interface

As you have learned in Chapter 2 and Chapter 3, after the program requirements document for an application has been completed, the first step is to define the graphical user interface. In this chapter, three new elements are introduced:

1. TextBox object
2. Labels intended for variable text property values.
3. Setting focus within the user interface.

Each of these elements is described in the following paragraphs:

TEXTBOX OBJECTS

A **TextBox object** allows users to enter data into a program. In Figure 4-2, the user can enter a value into the text box.

FIGURE 4-2

In Figure 4-2, the TextBox object is placed on the Windows Form object. A TextBox object automatically allows the user to enter data into the text box. To place a TextBox object on the Windows Form object, you can complete the steps on the following pages. (Note: The examples in this chapter illustrate new objects in the user interface. Portions of the user interface have already been completed. You should not expect to "click along" with these examples unless you create these elements or unless you follow the steps using an unformatted user interface.)

STEP 1   With Visual Studio open and the frmDigitalDownloads.vb [Design] tabbed page visible, point to the TextBox .NET component in the Toolbox.

The TextBox .NET component is highlighted in the Toolbox (Figure 4-3).

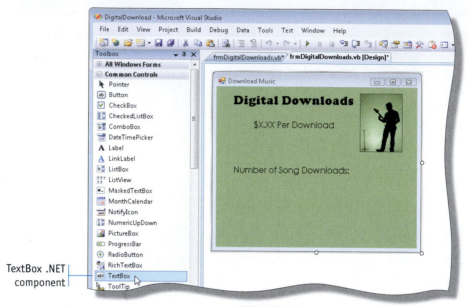

TextBox .NET component

FIGURE 4-3

STEP 2   Drag the TextBox .NET component onto the Windows Form object at the desired location.

While you drag, the mouse pointer changes to indicate a TextBox object will be placed on the Windows Form object (Figure 4-4). Snap lines indicate where the TextBox object aligns with other objects on the Windows Form object. In Figure 4-4, the top of the TextBox object aligns with the top of the Label object. When adding a TextBox object to the Windows Form object, top alignment often provides a good beginning position.

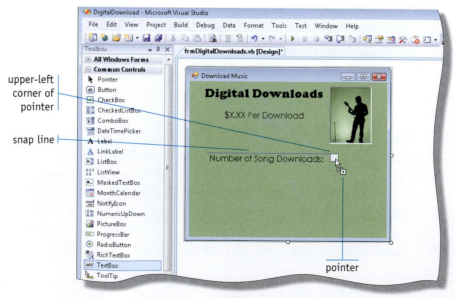

upper-left corner of pointer

snap line

pointer

FIGURE 4-4

STEP 3   When the upper-left corner of the pointer is located where you want the
TextBox object's upper-left corner, release the left mouse button.

*Visual Studio places the TextBox object at the location identified by the mouse pointer
(Figure 4-5). The default size of the TextBox object is 100 pixels wide by 20 pixels high.
Notice that by default the TextBox object contains no text. You can change that by entering
text in the Text property of the TextBox object.*

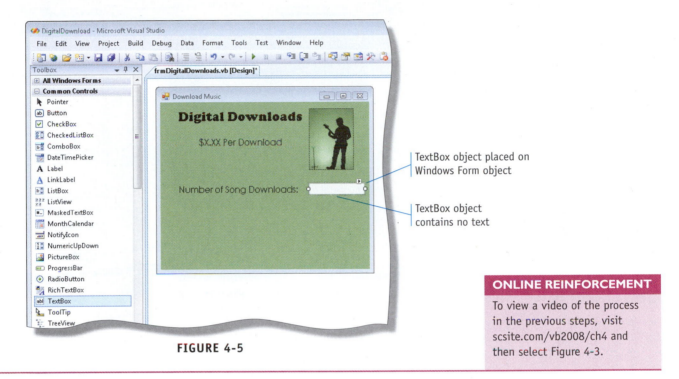

FIGURE 4-5

As you have learned, whenever you place an object on the Windows Form
object, you must name the object. When naming a TextBox object, the prefix
should be txt. Therefore, the name of the TextBox object in Figure 4-5 could be
txtNumberOfDownloads.

Sizing and Positioning a TextBox Object

To properly place a TextBox object on the Windows Form object, you need to know
the minimum and maximum size of the text box. The minimum size of the text box
normally is determined by the maximum number of characters the user will enter into
the text box. For example, if in the sample program the maximum number of downloads the user should order is 999, the minimum size of the text box must be large
enough to display three numbers. Although it can be larger, it should not be smaller.

The maximum size of the text box often is determined by the design of the user
interface; that is, the size should look and feel good in the user interface. To determine the minimum size of the text box, you can use the technique on the following
pages:

STEP 1   Select the TextBox object. Scroll in the Properties window until the Text property is visible and then click the right column for the Text property.

The TextBox object is selected, as shown by the thick border and sizing handles (Figure 4-6). The Text property for the TextBox object is highlighted and the insertion point indicates you can enter text for the Text property.

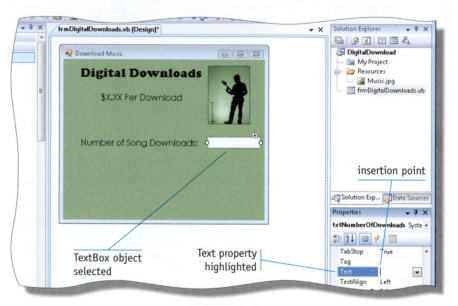

FIGURE 4-6

STEP 2   Type the maximum number of characters the user normally will enter into the text box and then press the ENTER key. When entering numbers, the digit 8 often is entered because it is wider than other digits. In this example, the value 888 is entered because three digits is the maximum number of digits the user normally will enter.

When the value is entered in the Text property of the TextBox object, the value is displayed in the TextBox object (Figure 4-7).

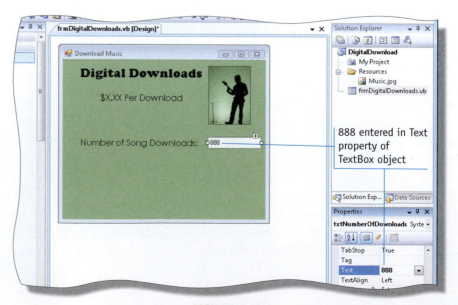

FIGURE 4-7

STEP 3 Using the Font property in the Properties window, change the Font property to the correct font and font size. For this application, change the font to Century Gothic and change the font size to 12. Then, drag the right edge of the TextBox object to resize the TextBox object so it is slightly wider than the 888 entry.

As you drag, the size of the TextBox object changes (Figure 4–8). When you release the left mouse button, the text box will be resized. When the font size is changed, the horizontal alignment of the text will change.

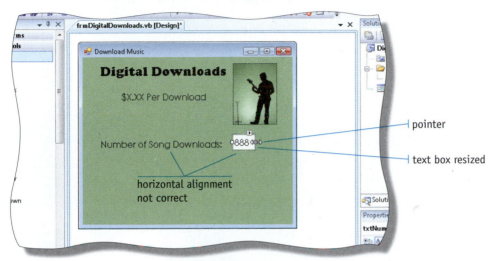

FIGURE 4-8

STEP 4 To horizontally align the text in the label and the text in the text box, drag the text box up until a red snap line indicates the bottoms of the text are aligned (Figure 4-9). Then, release the left mouse button.

When you drag the TextBox object, the red snap line indicates when the bottoms of the text are aligned (Figure 4-9). When you release the left mouse button, the TextBox object will be placed so the bottoms of the text are aligned.

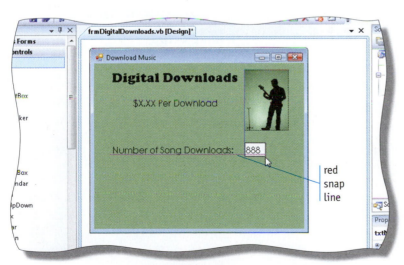

FIGURE 4-9

Aligning Text in a TextBox Object

In Figure 4-9, the numbers are left-aligned in the text box. Often, the user interface will be more useful if the value the user enters is centered in the text box. To align the text in a TextBox object, you can use the following method:

STEP 1   Select the TextBox object. In the Properties window, scroll until the TextAlign property is visible, click the TextAlign property in the left column, and then click the list arrow in the right column of the TextAlign property.

The TextAlign property list contains the values Left, Right, and Center (Figure 4-10).

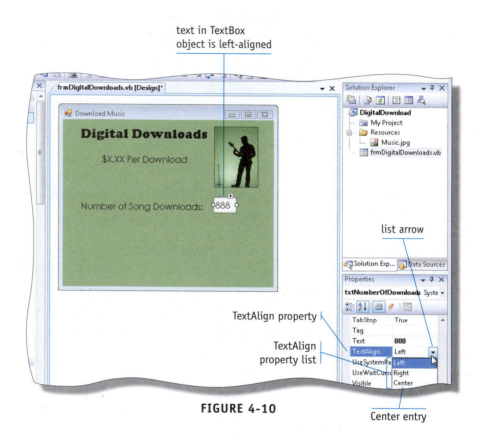

FIGURE 4-10

STEP 2   Click Center in the TextAlign property list.

The text in the TextBox object is centered (Figure 4-11). When a user enters data into the text box, the text also will be centered.

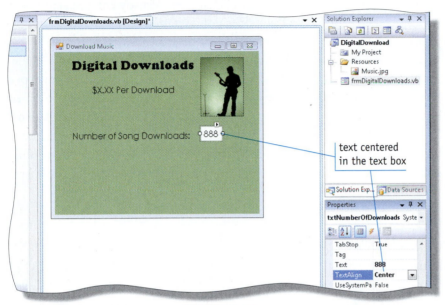

FIGURE 4-11

STEP 3   Because the TextBox object is sized properly, remove the digits in the TextBox object. Select the characters 888 in the Text property, press the DELETE key on your keyboard, and then press the ENTER key.

The TextBox object contains no text and is ready for use in the user interface (Figure 4-12).

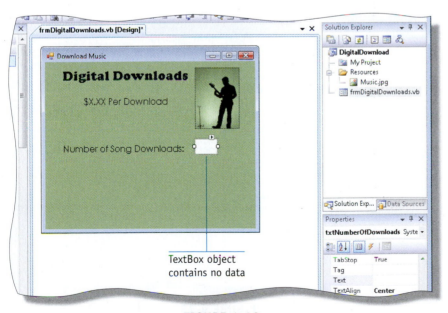

FIGURE 4-12

ONLINE REINFORCEMENT

To view a video of the process in the previous steps, visit scsite.com/vb2008/ch4 and then select Figure 4-10.

Entering Data in a TextBox Object

When the program is executed, the user can enter data in the text box. Users can enter both numbers and characters. In a text box, the user can enter many characters even though the program expects to find only a few. If the user enters more characters than can be displayed in the text box, the characters already entered scroll to the left and no longer are visible. A text box does not contain a scroll bar, so if a user enters more characters than can be visible in the text box, the user must move the insertion point left or right with the arrow keys on the keyboard to view the data in the text box. In most situations, a user should not enter more characters than are expected, and the text box should be designed to display all the characters that are expected.

In a default text box, only a single line of text can be entered regardless of the number of characters entered. A special option for a text box can be selected to allow the user to enter multiple lines of text. Additionally, the MaskedTextBox object can be used to control the format of the data a user enters. These types of text boxes are explained in the following sections.

Creating a MultiLine Text Box

A MultiLine text box allows the user to enter multiple lines in the text box. The TextBox object must be resized vertically to display the multiple lines. To create a TextBox object that can accept multiple lines, you can complete the following step:

STEP 1　Select the TextBox object, click the Action tag, and point to the MultiLine check box.

The TextBox Tasks list is displayed with the MultiLine check box (Figure 4–13). When you click the MultiLine check box, the TextBox object will be able to accept multiple lines.

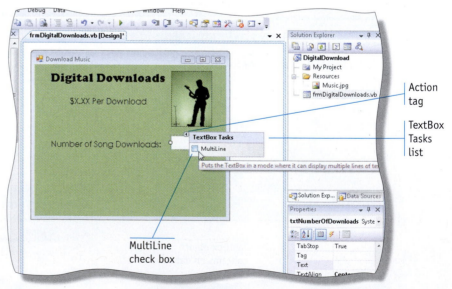

FIGURE 4-13

STEP 2 Click the MultiLine check box.

The text box is enabled to accept multiple lines.

ONLINE REINFORCEMENT

To view a video of the process in the previous steps, visit scsite.com/vb2008/ch4 and then select Figure 4-13.

In addition to enabling multiple lines, you should increase the vertical size of the TextBox object so the multiple lines will be visible when the user enters them.

Creating a MaskedTextBox Object

The MaskedTextBox object allows you to specify the data format of the value typed into the text box. Using the MaskedTextBox object removes confusion concerning what format should be used for the data the user enters. The term, mask, refers to a predefined layout for the data a user must enter. Figure 4-14 shows three examples of the use of the MaskedTextBox for the Short date input mask, the Phone number input mask, and the Social Security number input mask.

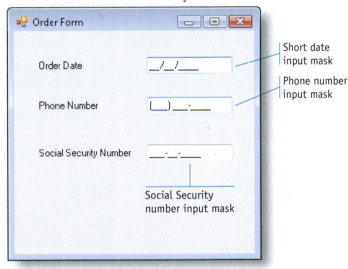

Prior to Data Entry

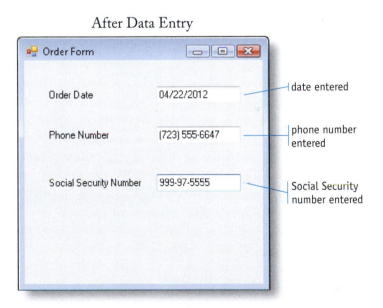

After Data Entry

FIGURE 4-14

In Figure 4-14, before the user enters data the mask demonstrates to the user the format of the data to be entered. To enter data, the user merely selects the text box and then types data into the text box. The user need not enter any punctuation or any spacing. Therefore, to enter the date in the Order Date text box, the user typed 04222012, with no spaces, punctuation, or other keystrokes. Similarly, for the phone number, the user typed 7235556647, again with no spaces or other keystrokes. For the Social Security number, the user typed 999975555.

ONLINE REINFORCEMENT

To view a video of the process in the previous figure, visit scsite.com/vb2008/ch4 and then select Figure 4-14.

To place a MaskedTextBox object on the Windows Form object, you can complete the following steps:

STEP 1 Drag a MaskedTextBox .NET component from the Toolbox to the Windows Form object. Then, click the Action tag on the TextBox object and point to the Set Mask command.

The MaskedTextBox object is placed on the Windows Form object (Figure 4-15). When the Action button is clicked, the MaskedTextBoxTasks list is displayed. The Set Mask command is the only command in the list.

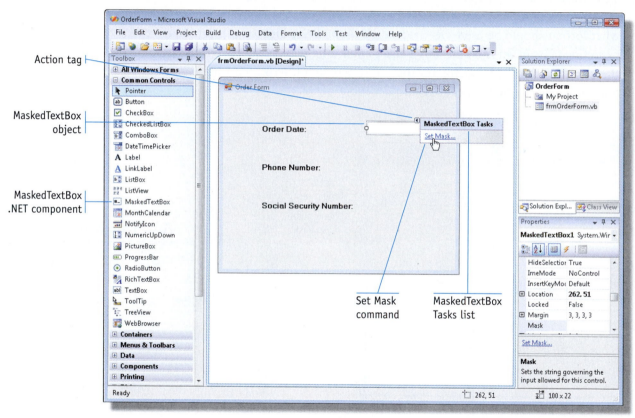

FIGURE 4-15

STEP 2   Click Set Mask on the MaskedTextBox Tasks list and then click the Short date mask description in the Input Mask dialog box.

Visual Studio displays the Input Mask dialog box (Figure 4-16). The Mask Description column contains all the masks that can be used for the MaskedTextBox object. The Short date mask description is highlighted. In the Preview box, you can type data to see how the mask will perform when it is used in the MaskedTextBox object. The Use Validating Type check box is selected so the object will verify the user entered valid numeric data.

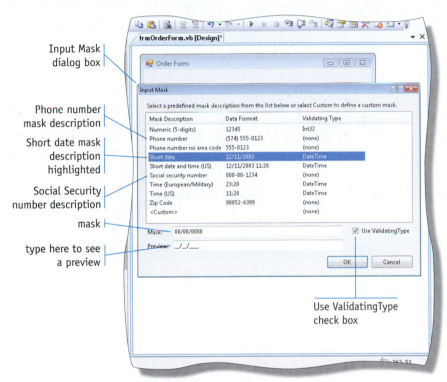

Input Mask dialog box

Phone number mask description

Short date mask description highlighted

Social Security number description

mask

type here to see a preview

Use ValidatingType check box

FIGURE 4-16

STEP 3 Click the OK button in the Input Mask dialog box and then click anywhere in the Windows Form object.

The mask is placed in the MaskedTextBox object (Figure 4-17).

Short date mask in
MaskedTextBox
object

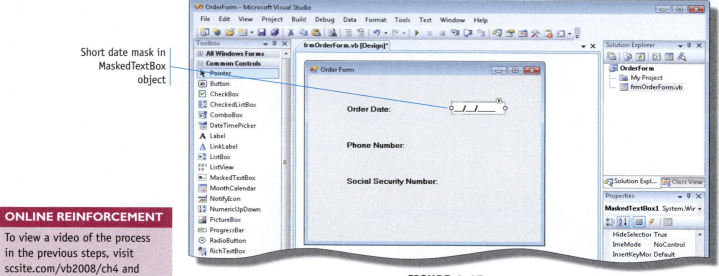

FIGURE 4-17

You can use the same technique to place the Phone number and Social Security number in the MaskedTextBox.

LABEL OBJECTS

In the sample program, a Label object is used to display the total cost of downloads (see Figure 4-1 on page 196). The developer must accomplish two tasks to prepare the label for this purpose: a) Place the label on the Windows Form object at the correct location; b) Ensure that when the Label object contains its maximum value, its location on the Windows Form object will work within the user interface design.

To accomplish these two tasks, you can complete the steps on the following page:

STEP 1 Drag a Label object onto the Windows Form object to the correct location. Name the label lblTotalCostOfDownloads. Change the label to the appropriate font size (Century Gothic, 12 point). In the Text property for the Label object, enter the maximum number of characters ($888.88) that will appear in the label during execution of the program.

The properly sized characters appear in the label (Figure 4–18). The label is aligned vertically, but should be moved up to align horizontally with the Total Cost of Downloads label.

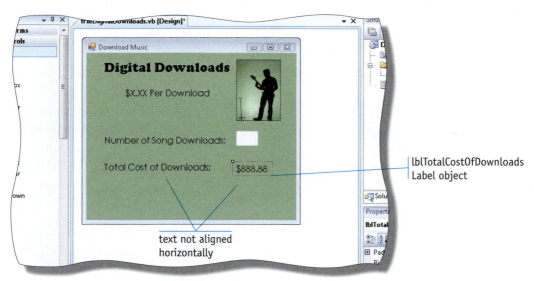

FIGURE 4-18

STEP 2 Drag the Label object up until the red snap line appears (Figure 4-19). Then release the left mouse button.

The label is aligned (Figure 4-19).

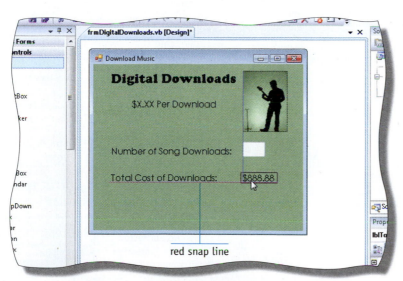

FIGURE 4-19

ONLINE REINFORCEMENT

To view a video of the process in the previous steps, visit scsite.com/vb2008/ch4 and then select Figure 4-18.

When program execution begins (see Figure 4-1 on page 196), the label that will contain the total cost of downloads should be blank. In Figure 4-19, however, it contains the value in the Text property of the Label object ($888.88). If the Text property in a Label object is set to no content, the Label object will not be displayed in the Windows Form object during design time, which makes the Label object difficult to work with in Design mode. Therefore, most designers place a value in the Text property of the Label object and leave it there during user interface design. Then, when program execution begins, the Label Text property will be set to blank. You will learn to do this later in this chapter.

ACCEPT BUTTON IN FORM PROPERTIES

Computer users often press the ENTER key to enter data into a text box and cause processing to occur. For example, in the sample program for this chapter, instead of typing the number of downloads and clicking the Calculate Cost button, users might prefer to have the option of typing the number of downloads and pressing the ENTER key.

You can assign a button in the user interface to be an Accept button, which means the program will carry out the event handler processing associated with the button if the user clicks the button or if the user presses the ENTER key. To assign the Calculate Cost button as the Accept button, you can complete the following steps:

STEP 1   Click a blank area in the Windows Form object to select it. Scroll in the Properties window until the AcceptButton property is visible. Click the AcceptButton property name in the left column and then click the AcceptButton property list arrow in the right column.

The AcceptButton property list displays the names of the Button objects on the selected Windows Form object (Figure 4–20). Any of these buttons can be chosen as the Accept button.

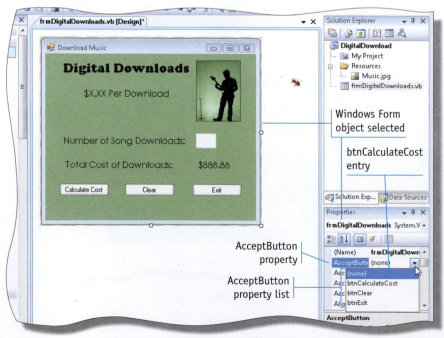

FIGURE 4-20

STEP 2   Click btnCalculateCost in the AcceptButton property list.

The btnCalculateCost Button object is designated as the Accept button. When the program is running, the user can press the ENTER key after entering data and the event handler processing for the Calculate Cost button will be executed.

ONLINE REINFORCEMENT

To view a video of the process in the previous steps, visit scsite.com/vb2008/ch4 and then select Figure 4-20.

CANCEL BUTTON IN FORM PROPERTIES

In the same manner as the Accept button, you can designate a Cancel button for the Windows Form object. When the user presses the ESC key, the event handler processing for the button identified as the Cancel button will be executed. In the sample program, the Cancel button will be used to clear the text box and the total cost of downloads, and place the insertion point in the text box. Thus, it performs the same activity as if the user clicks the Clear button. To specify the Cancel button for the sample program, you can complete the following steps.

Step 1:   Click a blank area in the Windows Form object to select it.
Step 2:   Click the CancelButton property name in the left column in the Properties window for the Windows Form object, and then click the CancelButton list arrow.
Step 3:   Click the button name (btnClear) in the CancelButton property list.

When the program is executed, the user can press the ESC key to perform the same processing as when the Clear button is clicked.

VISUAL STUDIO PREPARATION FOR CODE ENTRY

When designing and creating the user interface, the Toolbox in Visual Studio 2008 provides the objects that you can place in the interface. When writing the code in the code editing window, however, the Toolbox is of little use. Therefore, many developers close the Toolbox when writing code in order to increase the space used for coding. To close the Toolbox, you can complete the step on the following page:

STEP 1 With the Toolbox visible (see Figure 4-21), click the Toolbox Close button. The Toolbox closes and the work area expands in size. To reshow the Toolbox after it has been closed, click the Toolbox button on the Standard toolbar.

Figure 4-21 illustrates the screen before the Toolbox is closed. The Toolbox Close button is visible. When the Toolbox is closed, clicking the Toolbox button on the Standard toolbar will open the Toolbox.

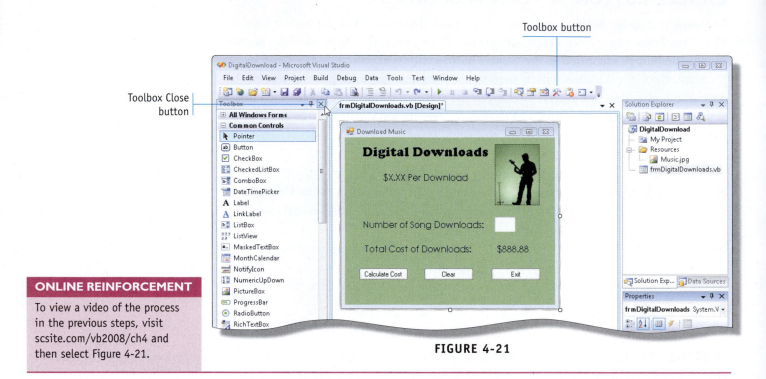

Toolbox button

Toolbox Close button

FIGURE 4-21

In the following sections, the Toolbox has been closed in the windows that show code.

Introduction to Data Entry and Data Types

As you have seen, the user can enter data into the program through the use of the TextBox object. When the user enters the data, the data becomes the value stored in the Text property of the object. For example, if the user enters the value 15 as the number of downloads, the Text property for the txtNumberOfDownloads TextBox object will contain the value 15.

STRING DATA TYPE

Whenever data is stored in RAM, it is stored as a particular data type. Each data type allows data to be used in a specific manner. For example, to add two values together, the values must be stored in one of the numeric data types. The data type for the value the user enters in a TextBox object and that is stored in the Text property of the TextBox object is string. A **String** data type allows every character available on the computer to be stored in it.

When the user enters data into a TextBox object, often it is good programming style to copy the value entered from the Text property of the TextBox object to a String variable. A **variable** is a named location in RAM where data is stored. A **String variable** is a named location in RAM that can store a string value. Thus, a person's name, a dollar amount, a telephone number, or the number of song downloads can be stored in a String variable.

A variable is defined in the coding of the program. The statement in Figure 4-22 defines a string

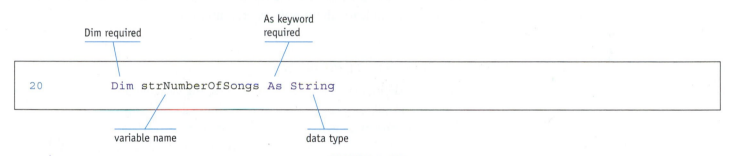

FIGURE 4-22

To begin the statement, the keyword Dim is required. This keyword stands for variable dimension. It indicates to the Visual Basic compiler that the entries that follow it are defining a variable.

The next entry is the variable name. Every variable must have a name so it can be referenced in other statements within the program. By convention, every String variable name begins with the letters, str, followed by a descriptive name. The name in Figure 4-22 (strNumberOfSongs) indicates the variable is a String variable that will contain the number of songs entered by the user.

The keyword As must follow the name of the variable as shown in Figure 4-22. If it is not included, a compilation error will occur. Following the word As is the declaration for the data type of variable being defined. In Figure 4-22, the data type is specified as String.

As a result of the statement in Figure 4-22, when the program is compiled the Visual Basic compiler will allocate an area in RAM that is reserved to contain the value in the string.

VARIABLE NAME RULES

Variable names used in Visual Basic must follow a few simple rules: 1) The name must begin with a letter or an underline symbol (_); 2) The name can contain letters, numbers, and the underline symbol. It cannot contain spaces or other special characters; 3) No Visual Basic reserved words (words that appear in blue in the code editing window) can be used for variable names.

The general format to define any variable is shown in Figure 4-23.

General Format: Define a Variable
Dim VariableName As DataType

EXAMPLE	RESULT
Dim strNumberOfSongs As String	String variable
Dim intNumberOfSongs As Integer	Integer variable
Dim decFinalCosts As Decimal	Decimal variable

FIGURE 4-23

The Integer and Decimal variables defined as examples in Figure 4-23 are numeric variables. You will learn about numeric variables shortly.

ASSIGNMENT STATEMENTS

When a variable is defined as shown in Figure 4-22, the variable does not contain any data. One method to place data in the variable is to use an **assignment statement**. The assignment statement shown in Figure 4-24 will copy the data from the Text property of the txtNumberOfDownloads TextBox object into the strNumberOfSongs String variable.

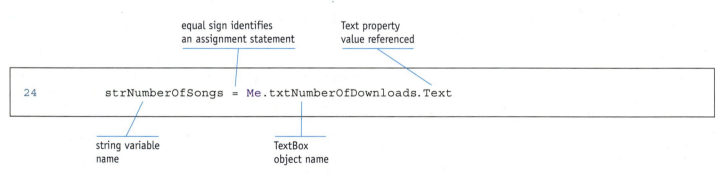

```
24        strNumberOfSongs = Me.txtNumberOfDownloads.Text
```

equal sign identifies an assignment statement

Text property value referenced

string variable name

TextBox object name

FIGURE 4-24

The variable name on the left of the assignment statement (strNumberOfSongs) identifies the variable to which a value will be copied. The equal sign indicates to the Visual Basic compiler that the statement is an assignment statement. It is required.

The value on the right of the equal sign is the value that will be copied to the variable on the left of the equal sign. In Figure 4-24, the value in the Text property of the txtNumberOfDownloads TextBox object will be copied to the strNumberOfSongs variable.

To enter the definition of the strNumberOfSongs variable and then enter the assignment statement in Figure 4-24 using IntelliSense, you can complete the following steps:

STEP 1 With Visual Studio displaying the code editing window and the insertion point located in the desired column, type Dim followed by a space. Then, type the name of the String variable you want to define, strNumberOfSongs on your keyboard.

The Dim keyword and the string name you typed are displayed in the code window (Figure 4-25). Notice the word, Dim, is blue to indicate it is a keyword.

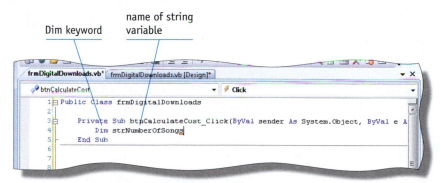

FIGURE 4-25

STEP 2 Press the SPACEBAR, type the word As and then press the SPACEBAR again.

The letters you typed are entered and when you typed the space following the word As, IntelliSense displayed a list (Figure 4-26). The IntelliSense list contains all the allowable entries that can follow the As keyword. To define a String variable, the entry should be String.

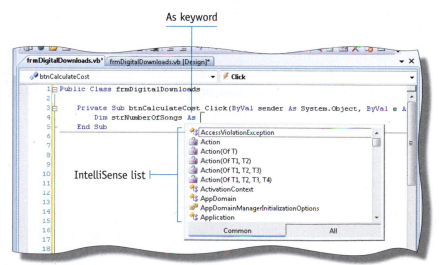

FIGURE 4-26

STEP 3 Because the entry should be String, type `str` on your keyboard.

IntelliSense highlights String in the IntelliSense list (Figure 4-27).

str typed ⊢
String highlighted ⊢

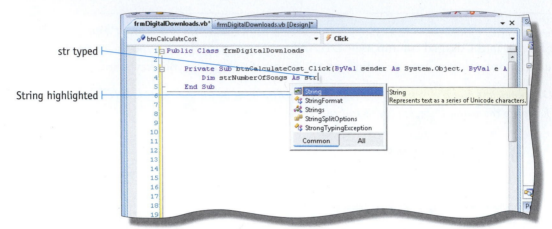

FIGURE 4-27

STEP 4 Press the ENTER key.

The Dim statement is entered (Figure 4-28). The green squiggly underline indicates the variable is not referenced within the program. Visual Studio will remove the line when the variable is used in an assignment statement or other statement.

variable not   Dim statement
referenced   complete

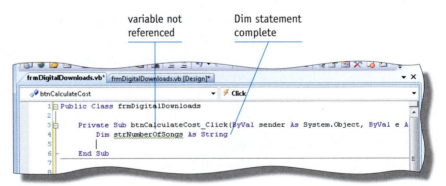

FIGURE 4-28

STEP 5 To begin the assignment statement, type `strn`. IntelliSense displays the only variable name that starts with the letter strn, the String variable strNumberOfDownloads.

IntelliSense displays a list of the entries that can be made in the statement (Figure 4-29). This is similar to typing me. when referencing objects in the program. Whenever you want to reference a variable name in a statement, you can begin to type the first few letters of the variable name to have IntelliSense display a list of the allowable entries. The variable name strNumberOfSongs is highlighted because you typed strn.

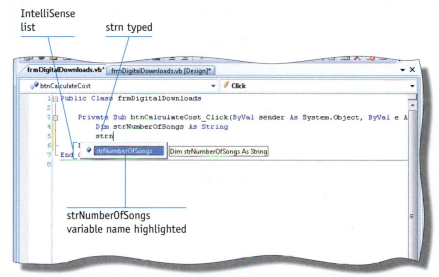

IntelliSense list   strn typed

strNumberOfSongs
variable name highlighted

FIGURE 4-29

STEP 6 Press the SPACEBAR, press the EQUAL SIGN key, and then press the SPACEBAR.

IntelliSense enters the highlighted variable name, the spaces, and the equal sign you typed (Figure 4-30). The spaces are not required in Visual Basic but should be included in the statement for ease of reading. An IntelliSense listing automatically appears displaying the possible valid entries.

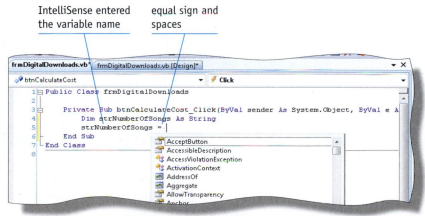

IntelliSense entered   equal sign and
the variable name   spaces

FIGURE 4-30

STEP 7   Type me. to display the IntelliSense list of the Form objects, and then type txt to identify the txtNumberOfDownloads TextBox object in the IntelliSense list.

The IntelliSense list contains the valid entries for the statement; in this case only one object has the prefix of txt. Visual Basic changes me. to Me. The TextBox object txtNumberOfDownloads is highlighted in the list (Figure 4-31).

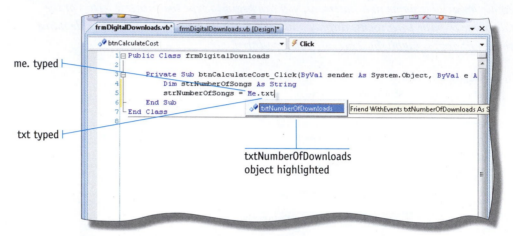

FIGURE 4-31

STEP 8   Press the PERIOD key and then, if necessary, type te to highlight the Text entry in the IntelliSense list.

After the dot operator (period) and the strNumberOfSongs object name are entered, Visual Studio displays the IntelliSense list (Figure 4-32). When you typed te, the Text entry was highlighted in the IntelliSense list.

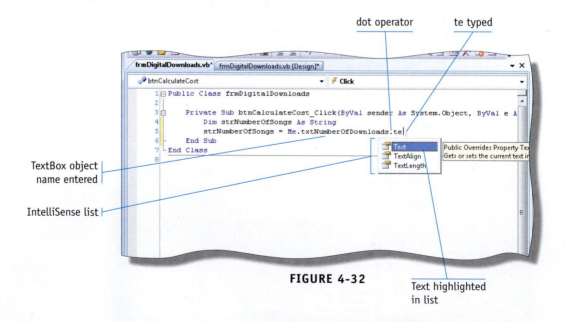

FIGURE 4-32

STEP 9 Press the ENTER key.

The assignment statement is entered (Figure 4-33). When the statement is executed, the value in the Text property of the txtNumberOfDownloads TextBox object will be copied to the location in memory identified by the strNumberOfSongs variable name. Notice also that the green squiggly lines in the Dim statement are removed because the variable now is referenced in a statement.

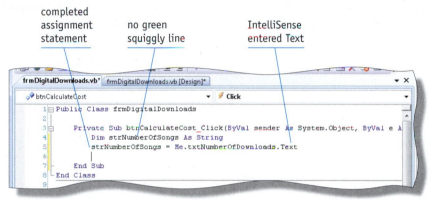

FIGURE 4-33

ONLINE REINFORCEMENT

To view a video of the process in the previous steps, visit scsite.com/vb2008/ch4 and then select Figure 4-25.

You can use the method shown in the previous steps to declare a variable name and include it in assignment statements for all the variables you might define within a program. IntelliSense works the same with each variable name, regardless of the variable type.

HEADS UP

The rule for using IntelliSense to enter object names and variable names into a Visual Basic statement is: 1) To enter the name of an object that has been defined in the user interface, type me.; 2) To enter a variable name you have declared in the program, type the first few letters of the variable name to display an IntelliSense listing of possible names. In each case, IntelliSense will display a list of the allowable entries.

NUMERIC DATA TYPES

As you will recall, the String data type can contain any character that can be entered or stored on a computer. String data types, however, cannot be used in arithmetic operations. A **numeric data type** must be used in arithmetic operations. So, in order to multiply two values, the values must be stored in one of the numeric data types.

Visual Basic allows a variety of numeric data types, depending on the need of the application. Each numeric data type requires a different amount of RAM in which the numeric value is stored, can contain a different type of numeric data, and can contain a different maximum range of values. The table in Figure 4-34 illustrates three widely used numeric data types. The data types are explained in the following sections.

Data Type	Sample Value	Memory Allocation	Range of Values
Integer	48	4 bytes	−2,147,483,648 to 2,147,483,647
Decimal	3.14519	16 bytes	Decimal values that may have up to 28 significant digits
Double	5.3452307 or 673.6529	8 bytes	−1.79769313486232e308 to +1.79769313486232e308

FIGURE 4-34

HEADS UP

Visual Basic 2008 now allows you to omit the data type without error. For example, entering Dim intValue = 1 does not produce an error because the compiler infers that the value of intValue is an Integer data type. This is called type inference. While you are learning beginning programming, it is best to use the data types to understand the changes as you convert one data type to another.

Integer Data Type

An **Integer data type** holds a nondecimal whole number in Visual Basic. As you can see from Figure 4-34, an Integer data type can store a value greater or less than 2 billion. Examples of an integer would be the number of songs to download, the number of credit hours you are taking in a semester, and the number of points your favorite football team scored. Notice that each of these examples is a whole number.

Normally, an Integer data type is stored in an Integer variable. An **Integer variable** identifies a location in RAM where an integer value is stored. To define an Integer variable and place a value in the variable through the use of an assignment statement, you can use the Dim statement and the assignment statement, as shown in Figure 4-35.

```
        Dim intNumberOfSongs As Integer
        intNumberOfSongs = 34
```

FIGURE 4-35

The Dim statement in Figure 4-35 is the similar to the Dim statement used to define the String variable (Figure 4-28 on page 216) except that the variable name begins with the prefix int; and the word Integer follows the word As. Four bytes of RAM will be reserved for any value that is stored in the intNumberOfSongs Integer variable as a result of the Dim statement in Figure 4-35.

The definition in Figure 4-35 will not place a value in the intNumberOfSongs variable. To place a value in the variable, you can use an assignment statement. The variable into which the value is to be placed (intNumberOfSongs) is entered on the left side of the equal sign, and the value to be placed in the variable (34) is entered on the right side of the equal sign. When the statement is executed, the value 34 will be copied to the RAM location identified by the variable name intNumberOfSongs.

You also can place an initial value in the variable. For example, to define an Integer variable to hold the number of credit hours you are taking, and to place the value 12 in that variable, you could write the Dim statement in Figure 4-36.

value placed in
intCreditHours
Integer variable

```
        Dim intCreditHours As Integer = 12
```

FIGURE 4-36

The statement in Figure 4-36 defines the Integer variable named intCreditHours. The equal sign following the word Integer indicates to the Visual Basic compiler that the value to its right should be placed in the variable. As a result, the value 12 will be placed in the intCreditHours Integer variable when the program is compiled.

Decimal Data Type

A **Decimal data type** can represent accurately large or very precise decimal numbers. It is ideal for use in the accounting and scientific fields to ensure numbers keep their precision and are not subject to rounding errors. The Decimal data type can be accurate to 28 significant digits. Often, Decimal data types are used to store dollar amounts. For example, to define the cost of downloads Decimal variable for the sample program in this chapter, the statement in Figure 4-37 can be used.

```
22          Dim decTotalCostOfDownloads As Decimal
```

FIGURE 4-37

The Dim statement is used to define the Decimal variable. The dec prefix is used for all Decimal variable names. When the compiler processes the statement in Figure 4-37, 16 bytes of RAM will be reserved for a value to be placed in the decTotalCostOfDownloads variable. Initially, no value will be present in the variable unless you specify a value, as shown in Figure 4-36. You can use an assignment statement to place data into the decTotalCostOfDownloads variable.

Double Data Type

A **Double data type** can represent huge positive and very small negative numbers that can include values to the right of the decimal point. Sometimes, a Double data type is said to represent floating-point numbers, which means the decimal point can be anywhere within the number. The Dim statement in Figure 4-38 declares a Double variable that could be used in a tax application.

> **HEADS UP**
>
> A Double data type represents numbers in such a way that the number might not be precisely correct. For example, the value 0.07875 might be represented in the Double data type as 0.078749999999. Therefore, when exact precision is required, the Decimal data type is preferred over the Double data type. The advantages of the Double data type are that it can store a much larger and a much smaller number than the Decimal data type, and it requires only 8 bytes of memory for each Double variable versus 16 bytes for each Decimal variable.

```
13          Dim dblTaxRate As Double
14          dblTaxRate = 0.07875
```

FIGURE 4-38

In Figure 4-38, the dblTaxRate Double variable is declared and then the assignment statement places the value 0.07875 in the memory location identified by the variable name. Note that a Double variable begins with the dbl prefix.

OTHER DATA TYPES

Visual Basic supports a number of other data types that are used for more specialized situations. The two most widely used other types are the Char data type and the Boolean data type. These data types are summarized in the table in Figure 4-39.

Data Type	Sample Value	Memory Allocation	Range of Values
Char	A single character such as ? or M	2 bytes	Any single character
Boolean	True or False	2 bytes	True or False

FIGURE 4-39

Char Data Type

The **Char data type** represents a single keystroke such as a letter of the alphabet, punctuation, or a symbol. The prefix for a Char variable name is chr. When you assign a value to a Char variable, you must place quotation marks around the value. This is shown in Figure 4-40, where the value A is assigned to the chrTopGrade Char variable.

```
16        Dim chrTopGrade As Char
17        chrTopGrade = "A"
```

FIGURE 4-40

The value A in the assignment statement has quotation marks around it. In addition, Visual Studio displays the letter and the quotation marks in red text, indicating they are not Visual Basic keywords nor are they variable or object names. In fact, the value is called a literal. You will learn more about literals in a few pages.

Visual Studio allows 65,534 different characters in a program. These characters consist of numbers, letters, and punctuation symbols. In addition, a wide variety of technical characters, mathematical symbols, and worldwide textual characters are available, allowing developers to work in almost every known language, such as the Korean shown in Figure 4-41. These characters are represented by a coding system called Unicode. To learn more about Unicode, visit www.unicode.org.

유니코드에 대해 ?

어떤 플랫폼,
어떤 프로그램,
어떤 언어에도 상관없이
유니코드는 모든 문자에 대해 고유 번호를 제공합니다.

FIGURE 4-41

Even though you can assign a number to a char variable, a Char variable cannot be used in arithmetic operations. A number to be used in an arithmetic operation must be assigned to a numeric variable.

Boolean Data Type

A Boolean data variable, whose name begins with the bln prefix, can contain a value that Visual Basic interprets as either True or False. If a variable in your program is intended to represent whether a condition is true or a condition is not true, then the variable should be a Boolean variable. In Figure 4-42, a Boolean variable called blnFullTimeStudent is declared and then the assignment statement sets the Boolean variable to True.

```
19        Dim blnFullTimeStudent As Boolean
20        blnFullTimeStudent = True
```

FIGURE 4-42

In Figure 4-42, the Dim statement is used to declare the blnFullTimeStudent Boolean variable. The assignment sets the Boolean variable to True. This variable can be checked in the program to determine if it is true or false, and appropriate processing can occur based on the finding.

Miscellaneous Data Types

Visual Basic also has a number of other data types that are used less often than the ones you have seen. These data types are summarized in the table in Figure 4-43.

Data Type	Sample Value	Memory Allocation	Range of Values
Byte	A whole number such as 7	1 bytes	0 to 255
Date	April 22, 2008	8 bytes	Dates and times
Long	A whole number such as 342,534,538	8 bytes	$-9,223,372,036,854,775,808$ through $+9,223,372,036,854,775,807$
Object	Holds a reference	4 bytes	A memory address
Short	A whole number such as 16,546	2 bytes	$-32,786$ through 32,767
Single	A number such as 312,672.3274	4 bytes	$-3.4028235E+38$ through $1.401298E-45$ for negative values; and from $1.401298E-45$ through $3.4028235E+38$ for positive values

FIGURE 4-43

As a review, the prefixes for each of the data type variable names are shown in Figure 4-44.

Data Type	Prefix
String	str
Integer	int
Decimal	dec
Double	dbl
Char	chr
Boolean	bln
Byte	byt
Date	dtm
Long	lng
Short	shr
Single	sng

FIGURE 4-44

LITERALS

When you include a value in an assignment statement, such as in Figure 4-38 on page 221 and Figure 4-40 on page 222, this value is called a **literal** because the value being used in the assignment statement is literally the value that is required. It is not a variable. The Visual Basic compiler determines the data type of the value you have used for a literal based on the value itself. For example, if you type "Chicago," the compiler treats the literal as a String data type, while if you type 49.327, the compiler treats the literal as a Double data type. The table in Figure 4-45 displays the default literal types as determined by the Visual Basic compiler.

Standard Literal Form	Default Data Type	Example
Numeric, no fractional part	Integer	104
Numeric, no fractional part, too large for Integer data type	Long	3987925494
Numeric, fractional part	Double	0.99 8.625
Enclosed within double quotes	String	"Brittany"
Enclosed within number signs	Date	#3/17/1990 3:30 PM#

FIGURE 4-45

FORCED LITERAL TYPES

Sometimes you might want a literal to be a different data type than the Visual Basic default. For example, you may want to assign the number 0.99 to a Decimal data variable to take advantage of the precision characteristics of the Decimal data type. As you can see in Figure 4-45, Visual Basic will, by default, consider the value 0.99 to be a Double data type. To define the literal as a Decimal literal, you must use special literal-type characters to force the literal to assume a data type other than the one Visual Basic uses as the default. You do this by placing the literal-type character at the end of the literal value. The table in Figure 4-46 shows the available literal-type characters, together with examples of their usage.

Literal-Type Character	Data Type	Example
S	Short	Dim shoAge As Short shoAge = 40S
I	Integer	Dim intHeight as Integer intHeight = 76I
D	Decimal	Dim decPricePerSong As Decimal decPricePerSong = 0.99D
R	Double	Dim dblWeight As Double dblWeight = 8491R
C	Char	Dim chrNumberOfDays As Char chrNumberOfDays = "7"C

FIGURE 4-46

In the first example, the value 40 will be processed by Visual Basic as a Short data type literal even though the value would by default be considered a Integer value. In the second example, the literal-type character confirms the value should be treated as an Integer data type. In the third example, the value 0.99 will be processed as a Decimal data type even though it would by default be considered a Double data type. In the fourth example, the value 8491 would, by default, be considered an Integer data value but because the R literal-type character is used, Visual Basic will treat it as a Double data type. In example 5, the value 7 will be treated as a Char data type.

CONSTANTS

Recall that a variable identifies a location in memory where a value can be stored. By its nature, the value in a variable can be changed by statements within the program. For example, in the sample program in this chapter, if one user requested 5 downloads and another user requested 12 downloads, the value in the strNumberOfSongs variable would be changed based on the needs of the user. In some instances, however, you might not want the value to be changed. For example, the price per download in the sample program is $0.99 per song. This value will not change, regardless of how many songs the user wants to download.

When a value in a program will remain the same throughout the execution of the program, a special variable called a constant should be used. A **constant** variable will contain one permanent value throughout the execution of the program. It cannot be changed by any statement within the program. To define a constant variable, you can use the code in Figure 4-47.

```
12      Const cdecPricePerDownload As Decimal = 0.99D
```

FIGURE 4-47

The following rules apply to a constant:

1. The declaration of a constant variable begins with the letters Const, not the letters Dim.
2. You must assign the value to be contained in the constant on the same line as the definition of the constant. In Figure 4-47, the value 0.99D is assigned to the constant variable on the same line as the Const definition of the constant.
3. You cannot attempt to change the value in the constant variable anywhere in the program. If you attempt this, you will produce a compiler error.
4. The letter c often is placed before the prefix of the constant variable name to identify throughout the program that it is a constant variable and cannot be changed.
5. Other than the letter c constant variable names are formed using the same rules and techniques as nonconstant names.

Using a named constant variable instead of a literal provides several significant advantages and should be done whenever a constant value is required in a program. These advantages include:

1. The program becomes easier to read because the value is identified through the use of the name. For example, instead of using the value 0.99D in a literal, it is used in a constant called cdecPricePerDownload. This variable name describes the use of the value 0.99D and makes the program easier to read.
2. If the constant is used in more than one place in the program and it must be changed in the code, it is much easier and more reliable to change the value one time in the constant as opposed to changing every occurrence of the value in a literal.

REFERENCING A VARIABLE

You learned earlier that when a variable is declared, it will be underlined with a green squiggly line until it is referenced in a statement. This feature of Visual Basic is intended to ensure that you do not declare a variable and then forget to use it. It also helps ensure you do not waste memory by declaring an unnecessary variable.

It is mandatory when using a variable in a program that the variable is defined prior to using the variable name in a statement. For example, the code in the statements in Figure 4-48 *will cause an error* because the variable is used in an assignment statement before it is declared.

```
25          strNumberOfSongs = Me.txtNumberOfDownloads.Text
26          Dim strNumberOfSongs As String
```

FIGURE 4-48

In the code in Figure 4-48, the variable strNumberOfSongs is referenced in an assignment statement (line 25) before it is defined (line 26). This creates a compile error as indicated by the blue squiggly line beneath the variable name strNumberOfSongs on line 25. If you attempt to compile the statements on lines 25 and 26, you will receive a build error. Always define a variable before it is used in a statement.

SCOPE OF VARIABLES

When you declare a variable in Visual Basic, you not only declare the data type of the variable, you also, implicitly, define the scope of the variable. The **scope of a variable** specifies where within the program the variable can be referenced in a Visual Basic statement. In larger programs, with multiple classes and multiple forms, scope becomes critical, but it is important that you understand the concept at this point.

You declare a variable in a region within a program. For example, in the sample program in this chapter, you can declare a variable in the click event handler for the Calculate Cost button. You could declare another variable in the click event handler for the Clear button. Scope determines where each of these variables can be referenced and used in the Visual Basic program. **The rule is: A variable can be referenced only within the region of the program where it is defined.** A region in the programs you have seen thus far in the book is the code between the Sub statement and the End Sub statement in the event handlers. The code between the Sub statement and the End Sub statement is a **procedure**.

Therefore, if you declare a variable within the click event handler for the Calculate Cost button, that variable cannot be referenced in the click event handler for the Clear button, and vice versa. A variable that can only be referenced within the region of the program where it is defined is called a **local variable**. This means the value in a variable defined in one region of the program cannot be changed by a statement in another region of the program.

In addition, when a variable is defined in a procedure and the procedure ends, the values in the local variables defined in the procedure are destroyed. Thus, local variables have a certain **lifetime** in the program. They are only "alive" from the time the procedure begins executing until the procedure ends. If the procedure is executed again, whatever value the variable once contained no longer is present. One execution of the procedure is a variable's lifetime. Therefore, if a user clicks the Calculate Cost button, the values in the variables are valid until the click event execution is completed. When the user clicks the Calculate Cost button again, all values from the first click are gone.

It is possible in a Visual Basic program to define variables that can be used in multiple regions of a program. These variables are called **global variables**. In most programs, local variables should be used because they minimize the errors than can be generated when using global variables.

Understanding the scope of a variable is important when developing a program. You will learn more about the scope of variables later in this chapter and throughout this book.

CONVERTING VARIABLE DATA

Variables used in arithmetic statements in a Visual Basic program must be numeric variables. String variables cannot be used in arithmetic statements. If you attempt to do so, you will create a compilation error.

A user often enters data in a text box. Data in the Text property of a TextBox object is treated as String data. Because String data cannot be used in an arithmetic statement, the String data entered by a user must be converted to numeric data before it can be used in an arithmetic statement.

For example, in the sample program in this chapter, before the number of songs to download a user enters can be used in an arithmetic statement to determine the total cost of the downloads, that value must be converted to an Integer data type.

Visual Basic includes several procedures that allow you to convert one data type to another data type. You will recall that a **procedure** is a prewritten set of code that can be called by a statement in the Visual Basic program. When the procedure is called, it performs a particular task. In this case, the task is to convert the String value the user entered into an Integer data type that can be used in an arithmetic operation. A procedure to convert a String data type to an Integer data type is named ToInt32. The number 32 in the procedure name identifies that the representation of the integer will require 32 bits or 4 bytes, which is the memory required for the Integer data type. The procedure is found in the Convert class, which is available in a Visual Studio 2008 class library.

Using a Procedure

When you require the use of a procedure to accomplish a task in your program, you need to understand what the procedure does and how to code the procedure call in a program statement. A procedure can operate in one of two ways: it can perform its task and return a value, or it can perform its task and not return a value. You will recall in the Chapter 3 program that the Close() procedure closed the window and terminated the program. This is an example of a procedure that performs its task but does not return a value. A procedure of this type is called a **Sub procedure**.

In the Song Download program in this chapter, the requirement is to convert the number of songs String value the user enters into an Integer data type. Then, it can be used in an arithmetic operation. Therefore the procedure must return a value (the Integer value for the number of songs). A procedure that returns a value is called a **Function procedure**, or a **function**.

In addition, a procedure might require data to be passed to it when it is called in order to carry out its processing. In the sample program in this chapter, the Function procedure to convert a String variable to an Integer variable must be able to access the String variable in order to convert it. Therefore, in the statement that calls the Function procedure, the variable name for the String variable to be converted must be passed to the procedure. A value is passed to a procedure through the use of an argument.

An **argument** identifies a value required by a procedure. It is passed to the procedure by including its name within parentheses following the name of the procedure in the calling statement. For example, to pass the value stored in the strNumberOfSongs variable to the ToInt32 procedure, the statement in Figure 4-49 could be used.

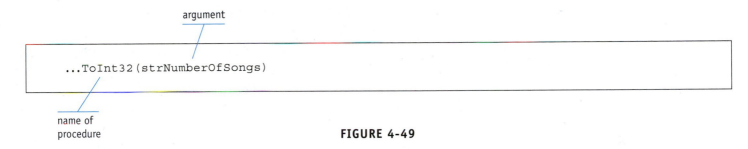

FIGURE 4-49

The name of the procedure is ToInt32. The argument is strNumberOfSongs, which is the String variable that contains the value to be converted to an Integer data type by the ToInt32 procedure. Notice that the argument is enclosed within parentheses.

Every procedure is a part of a class in Visual Basic. You will recall from Chapter 1 that a **class** is a named grouping of program code. When the calling statement must call a procedure, it first must identify the class that contains the procedure. Thus, in Figure 4-49 the calling statement is incomplete because the class name is not included in the statement. The class containing the ToInt32 procedure is the Convert class. To complete the procedure call statement, the class must be added, as shown in Figure 4-50.

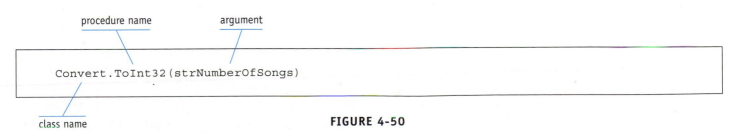

FIGURE 4-50

In Figure 4-50, the class name Convert begins the procedure call. A dot operator separates the class name from the procedure name (ToInt32). The argument (strNumberOfSongs) within the parentheses completes the procedure call.

When a Function procedure returns a value, such as the ToInt32 procedure that returns an Integer value, in effect the returned value replaces the procedure call in the assignment statement containing the Function procedure call. So, in Figure 4-51, you can see that when the processing within the Function procedure is completed, the Integer value is substituted for the procedure call in the assignment statement.

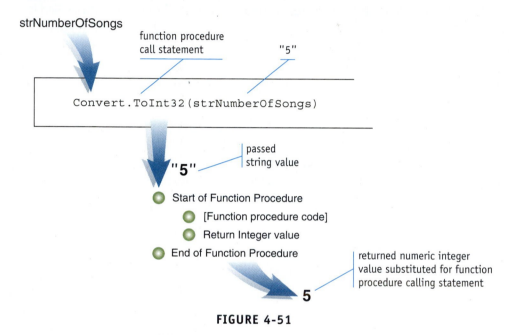

FIGURE 4-51

The complete assignment statement to convert the String data type in the strNumberOfSongs variable to an Integer data type and place it in the intNumberOfSongs variable is shown in Figure 4-52.

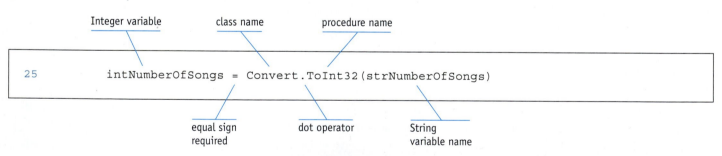

FIGURE 4-52

The intNumberOfSongs variable name on the left of the equal sign identifies the Integer variable where the converted value will be copied. The equal sign in the assignment statement is required. As a result of the assignment statement in Figure 4-52, the ToInt32 Function procedure found in the Convert class will convert the value in the strNumberOfSongs String variable to an integer value. The assignment statement will place that integer value in the intNumberOfSongs variable.

The use of Function procedures, and arguments with the procedure calls, is common when programming in Visual Basic. You will encounter many examples of Function procedure calls throughout this book.

OPTION STRICT ON

In the previous section, you saw an example of explicitly changing a value from one data type to another. Visual Basic will, by default, automatically convert data types if the data type on the right side of the equal sign in an assignment statement is different from the data type on the left side of the equal sign. Quite often, however, the automatic conversion can introduce errors and produce an incorrect converted value. Therefore, allowing automatic conversion normally is not good programming style.

To prevent automatic conversion of values, the developer must insert the Option Strict On statement in the program prior to any event handler code in the program. In Figure 4-53, the Option Strict On statement is shown just following the introductory comments in the sample program for this chapter.

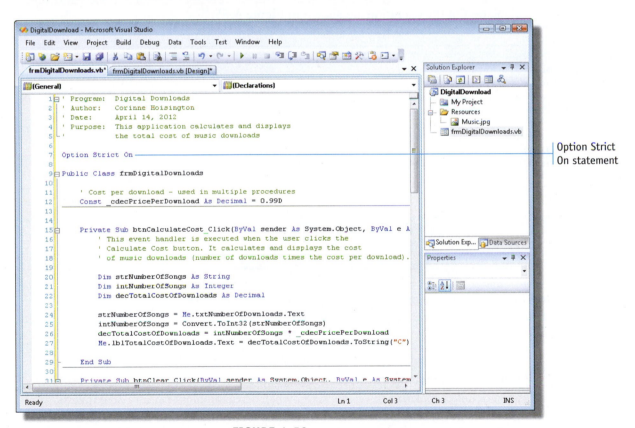

FIGURE 4-53

The Option Strict On statement explicitly disallows any default data type conversions in which data loss would occur and any conversion between numeric types and strings. Therefore, you must write explicit conversion statements in order to convert from one data type to another. This approach minimizes potential errors that can occur from data conversion.

Arithmetic Operations

The ability to perform arithmetic operations on numeric data is fundamental to computer programs. Many programs require arithmetic operations to add, subtract, multiply, and divide numeric data. For example, in the Digital Downloads program in this chapter, the price per song downloaded must be multiplied by the number of songs to be downloaded in order to calculate the total cost of downloads. The formula is shown in Figure 4-54.

Total Cost of Downloads = Number of Song Downloads times Price per Download

FIGURE 4-54

An assignment statement is used in Visual Basic 2008 to perform the arithmetic operation shown in Figure 4-54. The statements used in the sample program and a depiction of the operation are shown in Figure 4-55.

```
20          Dim strNumberOfSongs As String
21          Dim intNumberOfSongs As Integer
22          Dim decTotalCostOfDownloads As Decimal
23          Const cdecPricePerDownload As Decimal = 0.99D
24
25          strNumberOfSongs = Me.txtNumberOfDownloads.Text
26          intNumberOfSongs = Convert.ToInt32(strNumberOfSongs)
27          decTotalCostOfDownloads = intNumberOfSongs * cdecPricePerDownload
```

decTotalCostOfDownloads = intNumberOfSongs * cdecPricePerDownload

FIGURE 4-55

In the code in Figure 4-55, the variable strNumberOfSongs is assigned the value the user entered by the assignment statement on line 25 (see Figure 4-24 for a detailed explanation of this statement). The statement on line 26 converts the value in the strNumberOfSongs variable to an Integer and copies it to the intNumberOfSongs variable (see Figure 4-52 for an explanation of this statement).

The statement on line 27 multiplies the Integer value in the intNumberOfSongs variable times the constant value in the cdecPricePerDownload variable, and then copies the result to the decTotalCostOfDownloads variable. For example, if the user enters the value 5 as the number of downloads, as depicted in the diagram, the value 5 is multiplied by the value .99 (the value in the cdecPricePerDownload variable), and the result (4.95) is copied to the decTotalCostOfDownloads variable.

ARITHMETIC OPERATORS

An important element on the right side of the equal sign in the assignment statement on line 27 is the multiply **arithmetic operator**, which is an asterisk (*). Whenever the compiler encounters the multiply arithmetic operator, the value on the left of the operator is multiplied by the value on the right of the operator and these values are replaced in the assignment statement by the product of the two numbers. Thus, in Figure 4-55 the arithmetic expression intNumberOfSongs * cdecPricePerDownload is replaced by the value 4.95. Then, the assignment statement places the value 4.95 in the decTotalCostOfDownloads variable.

The multiply arithmetic operator is only one of the arithmetic operators available in Visual Basic 2008. The table in Figure 4-56 lists the Visual Basic 2008 arithmetic operators, their use, and an example of an arithmetic expression showing their use.

Arithmetic Operator	Use	Assignment Statement Showing Their Use
+	Addition	decTotal = decPrice + decTax
−	Subtraction	decCost = decRegularPrice − decDiscount
*	Multiplication	decTax = decItemPrice * decTaxRate
/	Division	decClassAverage = decTotalScores / intNumberOfStudents
^	Exponentiation	intSquareArea = intSquareSide ^ 2
\	Integer Division	intResult = 13 \ 5
Mod	Modulus Arithmetic (remainder)	intRemainder = 13 Mod 5

FIGURE 4-56

The arithmetic operators shown in Figure 4-56 are explained in the following paragraphs.

Addition

The **addition arithmetic operator** (+) causes the numeric values immediately to the left and immediately to the right of the operator to be added together and to replace the arithmetic expression in the assignment statement. For example, in Figure 4-57, the value in the decPrice variable is added to the value in the decTax variable.

arithmetic expression

```
40          decTotal = decPrice + decTax
```

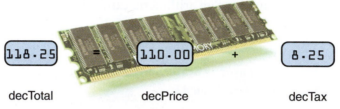

decTotal   decPrice   decTax

FIGURE 4-57

In Figure 4-57, the arithmetic expression (decPrice + decTax) is evaluated by adding the value in the decPrice variable to the value in the decTax variable. Then, the assignment statement copies the sum to the decTotal variable in RAM.

An arithmetic expression that uses the addition operator can contain more than two numeric values to be added. For example, in Figure 4-58, three variables are used in the arithmetic expression.

```
47          decTotalPay = decRegularPay + decOvertimePay + decBonusPay
```

FIGURE 4-58

In Figure 4-58, the value in decRegularPay is added to the value in decOvertimePay. The result then is added to decBonusPay. That sum is copied to the decTotalPay variable. Visual Basic imposes no limit on the number of variables that can be used in an arithmetic expression.

In addition to variables, arithmetic expressions can contain literals. The assignment statement in Figure 4-59 uses a literal.

```
53          decTicketCost = decInternetTicketCost + 10.25
```

FIGURE 4-59

In Figure 4-59, the value 10.25 is added to the value in the decInternetTicketCost variable and that sum is placed in the decTicketCost variable. Generally, literals should not be used in arithmetic expressions unless it is known that the value will not change. For example, if the extra cost for the ticket could change in the future, good program design would dictate that the value be placed in a variable (perhaps even a constant).

Subtraction

In order to subtract one value from another in an assignment statement, the **subtraction arithmetic operator** (−) is used, as shown in Figure 4-60.

```
59          decNetProfit = decRevenue - decCosts
```

FIGURE 4-60

In Figure 4-60, the value in the decCosts variable is subtracted from the value in the decRevenue variable. The result then is copied into the decNetProfit variable. If the value in decCosts is greater than the value in decRevenue, the value placed in the decNetProfit variable will be negative.

Using Arithmetic Results

After an arithmetic operation has been performed using an assignment statement, the values used in the arithmetic operation together with the answer obtained can be used in subsequent arithmetic operations or for other purposes within the program. For example, the result of one operation can be used in a subsequent calculation (Figure 4-61).

```
67          decComputerCost = decMonitorCost + decSystemUnitCost
68          decNetComputerCost = decComputerCost - decSystemDiscount
```

FIGURE 4-61

In Figure 4-61, the statement on line 67 determines the computer cost by adding the cost of the monitor and the cost of the system unit. The statement on line 68 calculates the net computer cost by subtracting the system discount from the computer cost that is calculated on line 67. Whenever a value is stored in a variable, it can be used in other statements within the program.

Multiplication

Multiplication is accomplished through the use of an assignment statement and the multiplication operator (*), as shown in Figure 4-62.

```
74          intLandPlotArea = intLandPlotLength * intLandPlotWidth
```

FIGURE 4-62

In Figure 4-62, the value in the intLandPlotLength variable is multiplied by the value in the intLandPlotWidth variable. The product of the multiplication is placed in the intLandPlotArea variable.

When multiplication takes place, the signs of the numbers are considered. If two positive numbers are multiplied, the answer is positive. If two negative numbers are multiplied, the answer is positive. If one positive number and one negative number are multiplied, the answer is negative.

When two numbers are multiplied, you must be aware of the size of the result. The largest number of digits that can appear in the product of two numbers is the sum of the number of digits in each of the values being multiplied. If the product is greater than the value that can be stored in the variable on the left of the assignment statement, an overflow error can occur and the program will be terminated.

Division

Visual Basic 2008 provides three arithmetic operators for division and related calculations. These operators are the slash (/), the backslash (\), and the entry MOD.

You use the slash for normal division. For example, in Figure 4-63, the value in the decTestScores variable is divided by 3 in order to obtain the average test score.

```
79          decAverageTestScore = decTestScores / 3
```

WATCH OUT FOR

Be sure that the divisor (the number on the right of the division operator) is not zero. If you attempt to divide by zero, your program will be terminated with an error.

FIGURE 4-63

You use the backslash (\) for integer division. With integer division, the quotient returned from the division operation is an integer. If the division operation produces a quotient with a remainder, the remainder is dropped, or truncated. The examples in Figure 4-64 illustrate the use of the integer division arithmetic operator.

Division Operation	Result
12\5	2
25\4	6
30\7	4

FIGURE 4-64

Notice in each example in Figure 4-64 that the result is a whole number with the remainder truncated.

The MOD operator divides the number on the left of the operator by the number on the right of the operator and returns an integer value that is the remainder of division operation. Integer division and the MOD operator often are used together, as shown in Figure 4-65.

```
86          intHours = intTotalNumberOfMinutes \ 60
87          intMinutes = intTotalNumberOfMinutes Mod 60
```

FIGURE 4-65

In Figure 4-65, the operation on line 86 will return only the integer value of the division. For example, if the intTotalNumberOfMinutes variable contains 150, a result of 2 (2 = 150\60) will be placed in the intHours variable. The operation on line 87 will place the remainder in the intMinutes variable. The remainder in the example is 30 (150 divided by 60 is 2, with a remainder of 30).

Exponentiation

Exponentiation means raising a number to a power. Exponentiation is accomplished by using the exponentiation arithmetic operator (^), as shown in Figure 4-66.

exponentiation
arithmetic operator

```
92          intCubeArea = intLengthOfCubeSide ^ 3
```

FIGURE 4-66

In Figure 4-66, the arithmetic expression is the same as intLengthOfCubeSide * intLengthOfCubeSide * intLengthOfCubeSide. So the value is cubed and copied to the intCubeArea variable.

The exponent used in the exponentiation operation can be a fraction. If the exponent is a fraction, the root is taken (Figure 4-67).

```
94          intLengthOfCubeSide = intCubeArea ^ (1 / 3)
```

FIGURE 4-67

In Figure 4-67, the cube root of the value in the intCubeArea variable is calculated and the result is copied to the intLengthOfCubeSide variable. Thus, if the area of the cube is 64, the value calculated for the length of the cube side would be 4 (4 * 4 * 4 = 64). The fractional exponent can never be negative, and it must be placed within parentheses.

Multiple Operations

A single assignment statement can contain multiple arithmetic operations. In Figure 4-68, the addition and subtraction operators are used to calculate the new balance in a savings account by adding the deposits to the old balance and subtracting withdrawals.

```
101         decNewBalance = decOldBalance + decDeposits - decWithdrawals
```

FIGURE 4-68

When the assignment statement in Figure 4-68 is executed, the value in the decOldBalance variable is added to the value in the decDeposits variable. Then, the value in the decWithdrawals variable is subtracted from that sum and the result is copied to the decNewBalance variable.

Notice in Figure 4-68 that the calculations proceed from the left to the right through the arithmetic expression.

Hierarchy of Operations

When multiple operations are included in a single assignment statement, the sequence of performing the calculations is determined by the following rules:

1. Exponentiation (^) is performed first.
2. Multiplication (*) and division (/) are performed next.
3. Integer division (\) is next.
4. MOD then occurs.
5. Addition (+) and subtraction (−) are performed last.
6. Within these five steps, calculations are performed left to right.

As a result of this predetermined sequence, an arithmetic expression such as decBonus + decHours * decHourlyRate would result in the product of decHours * decHourlyRate being added to decBonus.

An arithmetic expression such as intGrade1 + intGrade2 / 2 would result in the value in the intGrade2 variable being divided by 2, and then the quotient being added to the value in intGrade1 because division is performed before addition. It is likely that this is not the intended calculation to be performed. Instead, the intent was to add the value in intGrade1 to the value in intGrade2 and then divide the sum by 2. To force certain operations to be performed before others, you can use parentheses. Any arithmetic expression within parentheses is evaluated before expressions outside the parentheses, as shown in Figure 4-69.

```
108          decAverageGrade = (decGrade1 + decGrade2) / 2
```

FIGURE 4-69

In Figure 4-69, because it is inside the parentheses, the addition operation will be completed before the division operation. Therefore, the result of the arithmetic expression is that the value in decGrade1 is added to the value in decGrade2. That sum then is divided by the value 2 and the quotient is copied to the decAverageGrade variable.

It is advisable to use parentheses around multiple arithmetic operations in an arithmetic expression even if the predetermined sequence of operations will produce the correct answer because then the sequence of operations is explicitly clear.

DISPLAYING NUMERIC OUTPUT DATA

As you have learned, the result of an arithmetic expression is a numeric value that normally is stored in a numeric variable. In most cases, to display the numeric data as information in a graphical user interface, the numeric data must be placed in the Text property of a Label object or a TextBox object. The Text property of these objects, however, requires that this data be a String data type. Therefore, to display a numeric value in a label or a text box, the numeric data must be converted to a String data type.

Each of the numeric data types provides a function called the ToString function that converts data from the numeric data type to the String data type. The general format of the function call for a Decimal numeric variable is shown in Figure 4-70.

General Format: ToString Function

```
decimalvariable.ToString()
```

FIGURE 4-70

IN THE REAL WORLD

You know that a procedure is a group of code that a program can call to perform a particular function, such as converting data stored in a numeric data type to data stored as a String data type. In some programming languages, a procedure is called a method. Therefore, in Visual Studio Help, as you search the index or other areas, you might find the word method used. Just remember that the terms method and procedure (both a Sub procedure and a function) are virtually synonymous.

The statement shown in Figure 4-70 consists of the name of the decimal variable containing data to be converted, the dot operator (.), and the name of the function (ToString). Notice that the function name is followed immediately by closed parentheses, which indicates to the Visual Basic compiler that ToString is a procedure name. When the function call is executed, the value returned by the ToString function replaces the call.

The function call normally is contained within an assignment statement to assign the returned string value to the Text property of a Label or TextBox object. The example in Figure 4-71 shows the assignment statement to convert the numeric value in the decTemperature variable to a String value that then is placed in the Text property of the lblTemperature Label object.

```
                                        ToString
        name of decimal variable        function call

118         lblTemperature.Text = decTemperature.ToString()
```

FIGURE 4-71

In Figure 4-71, the name of the decimal variable (decTemperature) is followed by the dot operator and then the name of the function (ToString) with the required parentheses. When the statement on line 118 is executed, the ToString function is called. It converts the numeric value in the decTemperature variable to a String data type and returns the String data. The assignment statement then copies the returned String data to the Text property of the Temperature Label object.

Format Specifications for the ToString Function

In the example in Figure 4-71, the conversion from numeric value to String value is a straight conversion, which means the value is returned but it is not formatted in any manner. For example, if the numeric value in the Decimal variable was 47.235, then this same value was returned as a String value.

The ToString function, however, can convert numeric data to String data using a specified format. For example, the value 2317.49 could be returned as $2,317.49. Notice that the returned value is in the form of dollars and cents, or currency. To identify the format for the numeric data to be returned by the ToString function, the **format specifier** must be included as an argument in the parentheses following the ToString function name. The table in Figure 4-72 identifies the commonly used format specifiers (assume the value in the numeric field is 8976.43561).

HEADS UP

An important consideration when determining the formatting of a number is rounding. When using the ToString function, all values are rounded based on the digit following the last digit to be displayed. For example, if the value being converted to a Currency string from a numeric format is 729.837, the returned result will be rounded up ($729.84). If the value to be converted is 575.371, the returned result will be rounded down ($575.37). This feature is true when the precision specifier is used as well.

Format Specifier	Format	Description	Output from the Function
General(G)	ToString("G")	Displays the numbers as is	8976.43561
Currency(C)	ToString("C")	Displays the number with a dollar sign, a thousands separator (comma), two digits to the right of the decimal and negative numbers in parentheses	$8,976.44
Fixed(F)	ToString("F")	Displays the number with 2 digits to the right of the decimal and a minus sign for negative numbers	8976.44
Number(N)	ToString("N")	Displays a number with a thousands separator, 2 digits to the right of the decimal and a minus sign for negative numbers	8,976.44
Percent(P)	ToString("P")	Displays the number multiplied by 100 with a % sign, a thousands separator, 2 digits to the right of the decimal and a minus sign for negative numbers	897,643.56%
Scientific(E)	ToString("E")	Displays the number in E-notation and a minus sign for negative numbers	8.976436E+03

FIGURE 4-72

In Figure 4-72, each format specifier is used as an argument within parentheses. The argument must be included in the quotation marks (" ") on each side of the format specifier, as shown. The letter for the format specifier can either be uppercase or lowercase.

Precision Specifier

Each format specifier has a default number of digits to the right of the decimal point that will be returned. You can use a precision specifier, however, to override the default number of positions to the right of the decimal point. The **precision specifier** is a number that is included within the quotation marks in the function call to identify the number of positions to the right of the decimal point that should be returned. The examples in Figure 4-73 illustrate the use of the precision specifier (assume the value in the decNumericValue variable is 8976.43561):

Statement	Copied to Text Property of lblOutput Label Object
lblOutput = decNumericValue.ToString("C2")	$8,976.44
lblOutput = decNumericValue.ToString("C3")	$8,976.436
lblOutput = decNumericValue.ToString("F1")	8976.4
lblOutput = decNumericValue.ToString("N4")	8,976.4356
lblOutput = decNumericValue.ToString("P0")	897,644%

FIGURE 4-73

As you can see, the precision specifier identifies the number of digits to the right of the decimal point that should be displayed in the string returned from the ToString function. Notice that if the precision specifier is 0, no digits to the right of the decimal point are returned.

As with all conversions, when the number of positions to the right of the decimal point in the returned string is less than the number of digits to the right of the decimal point in the numeric value being converted, the returned value is rounded to the specified number of decimal places.

CLEARING THE FORM — CLEAR PROCEDURE AND FOCUS PROCEDURE

You will recall from the explanation of the Digital Downloads program in this chapter that when the user clicks the Clear button (see Figure 4-1 on page 196), the event handler for the Clear button must clear the results from window, allowing the user to enter the next value for the number of downloads. To perform this task, the Clear button event handler must complete the following tasks: 1) Clear the Text property of the TextBox object; 2) Clear the Text property of the Label object that displays the total cost of the downloads; 3) Set the focus on the TextBox object, which means place the insertion point in the text box. You will learn to accomplish these tasks in the following sections.

Clear Procedure

The Clear procedure clears any data currently placed in the Text property of a TextBox object. The general format of the Clear procedure is shown in Figure 4-74.

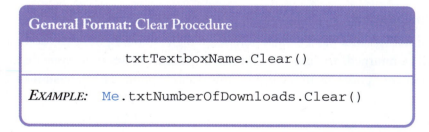

General Format: Clear Procedure

```
txtTextboxName.Clear()
```

EXAMPLE: Me.txtNumberOfDownloads.Clear()

FIGURE 4-74

When the Clear procedure is executed, the Text property is cleared of any data. As with every procedure call, the name of the procedure must be followed by parentheses.

Clear the Text Property of a Label

The Clear procedure cannot be used with a Label object. Instead, to clear the Text property of a Label object, you must write an assignment statement that assigns a null length string to the Text property of a Label object. A null length string is a string with no length, which means no characters. A null length string is represented by two quotation marks with no character between them (" "). To assign a null length string to the Text property, you can use the statement shown in Figure 4-75.

```
39          Me.lblTotalCostOfDownloads.Text = ""
```

FIGURE 4-75

In Figure 4-75, the null length string represented by the two quotation marks with no character between them is assigned to the Text property of the lblTotalCostOfDownloads Label object. As a result of the assignment statement, the Text property of the Label object is cleared.

Set the Focus

When the focus is on a TextBox object, the insertion point is located in the text box (Figure 4-76).

FIGURE 4-76

When the user clicks a button or any other item in the graphical user interface, the focus shifts to that item. Therefore, to place the focus on a text box, the user can click the text box. To place the focus on a text box without requiring to user to click it first, and thus making it easier for the user to enter data in the text box, the Focus procedure is used (Figure 4-77).

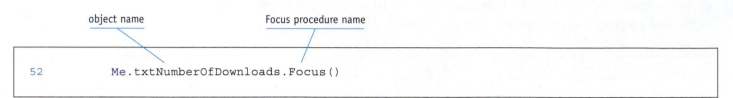

```
52          Me.txtNumberOfDownloads.Focus()
```

FIGURE 4-77

As with most procedure calls, the name of the object is stated first in the statement, followed immediately by the dot operator (period). The name of the procedure (Focus) follows the dot operator. When the statement on line 52 is executed, the focus is placed on the txtNumberOfDownloads TextBox object, which means the insertion point is placed in the text box.

FORM LOAD EVENT

In the program in Chapter 3 and in the program in this chapter, you have seen that an event can occur when the user clicks a button. The code in the event handler for the button click is executed when the user clicks the button. For example, in the Digital Downloads program in this chapter, when the user clicks the Calculate Cost button, the event handler code multiplies the number of songs times the price per song and displays the result (see Figure 4-1 on page 196).

Clicking a button is not the only action that can trigger an event. For example, a form load event occurs each time a program is started and the Windows Form object is loaded into computer memory. For the program in this chapter, a form load event occurs when the program starts and the Digital Downloads form is loaded. In some programs, an event handler is not written for this particular event and no processing occurs. In the Digital Downloads program, however, a form loading event handler is required. This event handler completes the following tasks:

1. Display the cost per download heading.
2. Clear the placeholder from the lblTotalCostOfDownloads Text property.
3. Set the focus on the txtNumberOfDownloads text box.

Concatenation

In the Digital Downloads program, the lblCostHeading Label object displays the cost per download (see Figure 4-1). In the user interface design, the lblCostHeading Label contains words for the placement of the label, but does not contain the actual cost per download (Figure 4-78).

lblCostHeading label does not contain actual cost per download

FIGURE 4-78

In Figure 4-78, the label contains placeholder information for the actual cost per download. The reason the actual cost is not placed in the label at design time is twofold: 1) In the original implementation of the program, the cost per download is 99 cents. In the future, however, the cost might change. Generally, data that might change should be placed in the Text property of a Label object during execution time, not at design time. Therefore, the cost should be placed in the label when the form opens (in the form load event handler); 2) The cost per download is used in two places in the program — in the label and when the actual calculation to determine total cost is performed (see Figure 4-55 on page 232). When a value is to be used more than one time, it should be declared one time in a variable and then used wherever necessary. If the value must be changed in the future, it must be changed only one time. For example, if the cost per download changed to 85 cents, the cost can be changed in the cost per download variable and it then will be correct for all uses of the variable. To illustrate, the variable for the cost per download is shown in Figure 4-79.

```
12      Const cdecPricePerDownload As Decimal = 0.99D
```

FIGURE 4-79

HEADS UP

In some instances, it is advantageous to continue a line of code in the code editing window to a second line so that the entire line can be read without scrolling. To continue a line of code onto a second or subsequent line, place a space in the statement and then place an underscore (_) character in the line of code. The underscore character indicates to the Visual Basic compiler that the line of code continues on the next line (see Figure 4-80).

As you can see, the price per download is declared as a constant that cannot be changed during program execution. If the price changes in the future, the developer can make one change to this declaration and all elements of the program that use the value will be correct.

To create the actual heading for the Digital Downloads program, the value in the variable declared in Figure 4-79 must be combined with the words Per Download and that result must be placed in the Text property of the lblCostHeading Label object. The process of joining two different values into a single string is called **concatenation**. Whenever you use concatenation, the values being concatenated must be String data types. You will note in Figure 4-79 that the cdecPricePerDownload variable is a Decimal data type. Therefore, it must be changed to a String data type before being joined with the words in the heading.

The statement in Figure 4-80 converts the Decimal data type to a String data type, concatenates (or joins) the two strings together, and then places that result in the Text property of the lblCostHeading Label object.

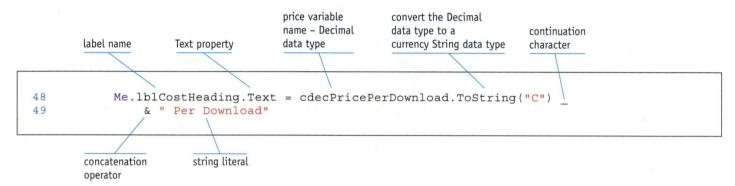

FIGURE 4-80

In Figure 4-80, the string generated on the right of the equal sign will be placed in the Text property of the lblCostHeading Label object. The first entry on the right of the equal sign is the price variable name (see Figure 4-79). Following the dot operator is the ToString procedure name, followed by the currency argument within parentheses. You will recall from earlier in this chapter that the ToString procedure converts a numeric value to a String data type. When the currency argument("C") is used, the String value returned is in a currency format (see 4-72 on page 241 for a detailed explanation).

Following the conversion statement is the **concatenation operator (&)**. Whenever the Visual Basic compiler encounters the concatenation operator, the string on the left of the operator is joined with the string data on the right of the operator to create a single concatenated string. The resulting concatenated string then is placed in the Text property of the lblCostHeading Label object.

The process that occurs on the right of the equal sign is illustrated in Figure 4-81.

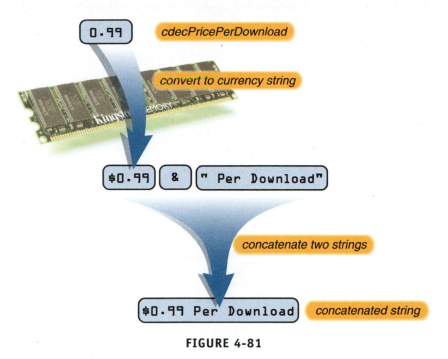

FIGURE 4-81

In Figure 4-81 you can see that to obtain the concatenated string, the Decimal value in the cdecPricePerDownload decimal variable is converted to a currency String data type. Then, that value is concatenated with the string literal to create the concatenated string. In the assignment statement in Figure 4-80, the concatenated string is assigned to the Text property of the lblCostHeading Label object.

CLASS SCOPE

You will recall from earlier in this chapter that when you declare a variable you also define the scope of the variable. The scope of a variable identifies where within the program the variable can be referenced. For example, if a variable is declared within an event handler procedure, the variable can be referenced only within that procedure.

Sometimes, a variable must be referenced in multiple event handlers. In the Digital Downloads program, the value in the cdecPricePerDownload variable is referenced in the Calculate button event handler when the total cost is calculated (see Figure 4-55 on page 232). The value also is referenced in the form load event when the heading is displayed (see Figure 4-80 on page 246). Because the variable is referenced in two different event handling procedures, it must be defined at the class level instead of the procedure (event handler) level. This means that the variable must be declared in the code prior to the first procedure, or event handler, in the program.

As you can see in Figure 4-82, the declaration of the cdecPricePerDownload variable follows the class definition statement but appears before the first event handler procedure.

beginning of program   class definition statement

```
1  ' Program:   Digital Downloads
2  ' Author:    Corinne Hoisington
3  ' Date:      April 14, 2012
4  ' Purpose:   This application calculates and displays
5  '            the total cost of music downloads
6
7  Option Strict On
8
9  Public Class frmDigitalDownloads
10
11     ' Cost per download - used in multiple procedures
12     Const _cdecPricePerDownload As Decimal = 0.99D
13
14     Private Sub btnCalculateCost_Click(ByVal sender As System.Object, ByVal e As System
       .EventArgs) Handles btnCalculateCost.Click
15         ' This event handler is executed when the user clicks the
16         ' Calculate Cost button. It calculates and displays the cost
17         ' of music downloads (number of downloads times the cost per download).
```

FIGURE 4-82

first event handler   declaration of Price Per Download variable

As a result of the code in Figure 4-82, the scope of the _cdecPricePerDownload variable will be all procedures within the class; that is, code within any event handler procedure within the class can reference the variable. Because the variable is declared as a constant, the value in the variable cannot be changed by code within the class; however, the value in the class can be referenced to calculate the total cost and to create the cost heading.

DEBUGGING YOUR PROGRAM

When your program processes numeric data entered by a user, you should be aware of several errors that can occur when users enter data that the program does not expect. The three errors that occur most often are: 1) Format Exception; 2) Overflow Exception; 3) Divide By Zero Exception.

A **Format Exception** occurs when the user enters data that a statement within the program cannot process properly. In the Digital Downloads program, you will recall that the user is supposed to enter a numeric value for the number of song downloads desired. When the user clicks the Calculate Cost button, the program converts the value entered to an integer and then uses the numeric value in the calculation (see Figure 4-52 on page 230). If the user enters a nonnumeric value, such as abc, the conversion process cannot take place because the argument passed to the Convert class is not a numeric value. When this occurs, a Format Exception error is recognized and the error box shown in Figure 4-83 is displayed.

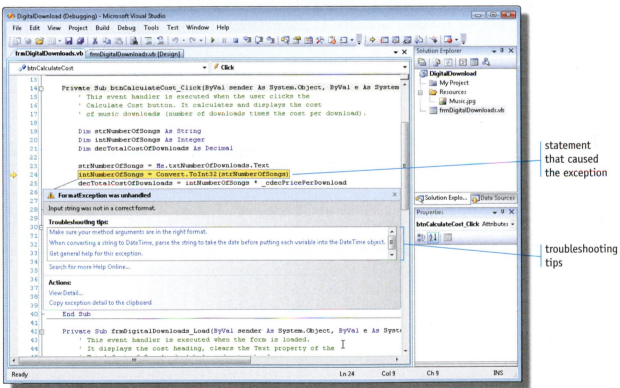

FIGURE 4-83

In Figure 4-83, the user entered the value abc and then clicked the Calculate Cost button. When control was passed to the ToInt32 procedure to convert the value from the String value entered in the text box to an Integer, the Format Exception was triggered because the value in the strNumberOfSongs was not numeric. When an exception occurs, the execution of the program is terminated. With Visual Studio running, click the Stop Debugging button on the Standard toolbar.

An **Overflow Exception** occurs when the user enters a value greater than the maximum value that can be processed by the statement. For example, in the Digital Downloads program, if the user enters a value in the text box that is greater than the value that can be converted by the ToInt32 procedure, an Overflow Exception occurs.

An Overflow Exception also can occur when a calculation creates a value larger than one that can be processed by a procedure. For example, if two large but valid numbers are multiplied, the product of the multiplication might be larger than can be processed.

The third type of common error is the **Divide By Zero Exception**. It is not possible to divide by zero, so if your program contains a division operation and the divisor is equal to zero, the Divide By Zero Exception will occur.

Whenever an exception occurs, a window similar to that shown in Figure 4-83 will be displayed.

To avoid exceptions, which should always be your goal, you can use certain techniques for editing the data and ensuring that the user has entered valid data that will not cause an exception. You will learn in Chapter 5 and Chapter 6 how to write code that checks user input to ensure exceptions do not occur because of the data users enter.

Program Design

As you have learned, the requirements document identifies the purpose of the program being developed, the application title, the procedures to be followed when using the program, any equations and calculations required in the program, any conditions within the program that must be tested, notes and restrictions that must be followed by the program, and any other comments that would be helpful to understanding the problem. The requirements document for the Digital Downloads application is shown in Figure 4-84.

REQUIREMENTS DOCUMENT

Date submitted: April 14, 2012

Application title: Digital Downloads

Purpose: The Digital Downloads program allows the user to enter the number of songs to be downloaded. The program calculates the total cost of the downloads based on a price of $0.99 per song.

Program Procedures: In a Windows application, the user enters the number of songs she wants to download. The program calculates the total cost of downloads. The user can clear the values on the screen and enter a new value for the number of downloads.

Algorithms, Processing, and Conditions:

1. The user must be able to enter the number of songs to be downloaded.
2. The user can initiate the calculation and display the total cost of the downloads.
3. The application computes the total cost of downloads by multiplying the number of downloads times the cost per download ($0.99).
4. The total cost of downloads is displayed as a currency value.
5. The user should be able to clear the value entered for the number of downloads and the total cost of downloads.
6. The user should be provided with a button to exit the program.

Notes and Restrictions:

Comments:

1. A graphic should depict a musical image named Music. The graphic is available at scsite.com/vb2008/ch4/images.

FIGURE 4-84

The use case definition identifies the steps the user will take when using the program. The use case definition for the Digital Downloads program is shown in Figure 4-85.

USE CASE DEFINITION

1. The Windows application opens with a text box where the user can enter the number of song downloads. The user interface includes the text box, an area to display the total cost of downloads, a Calculate Cost button, a Clear button, and an Exit button.
2. The user enters the number of songs downloads.
3. The user clicks the Calculate Cost button.
4. The program displays the total cost of the song downloads.
5. The user clicks the Clear button to clear the Number of Song Downloads text box and erase the total cost of downloads amount.
6. The user repeats steps 2-5 if desired.
7. The user clicks the Exit button to terminate the application.

FIGURE 4-85

EVENT PLANNING DOCUMENT

You will recall that the event planning document consists of a table that specifies an object in the user interface that will cause an event, the action taken by the user to trigger the event, and the event processing that must occur. The event planning document for the Digital Downloads program is shown in Figure 4-86.

EVENT PLANNING DOCUMENT

Program Name: Digital Downloads	Developer: Corinne Hoisington	Object: frmDigitalDownloads	Date: April 14, 2012
OBJECT	**EVENT TRIGGER**	**EVENT PROCESSING**	
btnCalculate	Click	Assign data entered in text box to a String variable Convert data entered to numeric integer Calculate total cost of downloads (number of downloads * price per download) Display total cost of downloads	
btnClear	Click	Clear number of song downloads text box Clear total cost of downloads label text Set focus on number of song downloads text box	
btnExit	Click	Close the window and terminate the program	
frmDigitalDownloads	Load	Display heading with price per download Clear the placement digits for total cost of downloads Label object Set focus on number of song downloads text box	

FIGURE 4-86

CODE THE PROGRAM

After identifying the events and tasks within the events, you are ready to code the program. As you have learned, coding the program means entering Visual Basic statements to accomplish the tasks specified on the event planning document. As you enter the code, you also will implement the logic to carry out the required processing.

Guided Program Development

To design the user interface for the Digital Downloads program and enter the code required to process each event in the program, complete the following steps:

NOTE TO THE LEARNER

As you will recall, in the following activity, you should complete the tasks within the specified steps. Each of the tasks is accompanied by a Hint Screen. The purpose of the Hint Screen is to indicate where in the Visual Studio window you should perform the activity; it also serves as a reminder of the method that you should use to create the user interface or enter code. If you need further help completing the step, refer to the figure number identified by the term ref: in the step.

Guided Program Development

Phase 1: Create User Interface Mockup

1

▶ **Create a Windows Application** Open Visual Studio using the Start button on the Windows taskbar and the All Programs submenu. Close the Start page by clicking the Start Page Close button. To create a Windows application, click the New Project button on the Standard toolbar; if necessary, click Visual Basic in the Project types pane; click Windows Forms Application in the Templates pane; double-click the term WindowsApplication1 in the Name text box and then type `DigitalDownload`. Click the OK button in the New Project dialog box.

▶ **Display Toolbox** Ensure the Toolbox is displayed in the Visual Studio window. If it is not, click the Toolbox button on the Standard toolbar. If necessary, click the plus sign next to the Common Controls category name in the Toolbox to display the tools *(ref: Figure 4-21)*.

▶ **Name the Windows Form Object** With the Windows Form object selected, scroll in the Properties window until the (Name) property is visible. Double-click in the right column of the (Name) property, type `frmDigitalDownloads`, and then press the ENTER key. In the Solution Explorer window, right-click the Form1.vb form file and select Rename. Type frmDigitalDownloads.vb and press the ENTER key.

▶ **Change the Title on the Title Bar** To change the title on the Windows Form object, click the form, scroll in the Properties window until the Text property is displayed, double-click in the right column of the Text property, type `Download Music`, and then press the ENTER key.

Guided Program Development *(continued)*

▶ **Resize the Windows Form Object** Drag the lower-right corner of the Windows Form object to resize it to approximately the size shown in Figure 4-87 on page 257. To match Figure 4-87 exactly, make the form size (397,338).

▶ **Add a PictureBox Object** Add a PictureBox object to the Windows Form object by dragging the PictureBox .NET component onto the Windows Form object. Place it in the upper-right corner of the Windows Form object.

▶ **Name the PictureBox Object** With the PictureBox object selected, scroll in the Properties window until the (Name) property is visible. Double-click in the right column of the (Name) property, type `picDownloadHeading`, and then press the ENTER key.

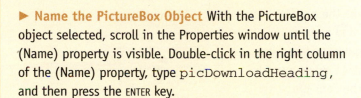

▶ **Resize the PictureBox Object** To resize the picDownloadHeading PictureBox object, if necessary select the PictureBox object. Point to the lower-left corner of the PictureBox object, and then drag the corner until the object's size is (81,110) as shown on the status bar.

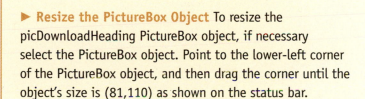

▶ **Add a Heading Label** To insert the Digital Downloads heading label, drag the Label .NET component from the Toolbox to the Windows Form object. Top-align the Label object and the PictureBox object through the use of blue snap lines. Position the PictureBox object and the Label object as shown in Figure 4-87.

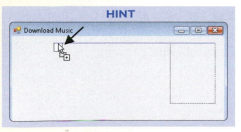
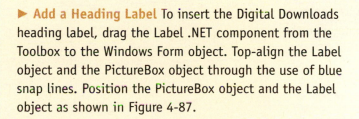

(continues)

Guided Program Development (continued)

▶ **Name the Label Object** Give the name lblDigitalDownloads to the Label object by scrolling to the (Name) property in the Properties window, double-clicking in the right column of the (Name) property, typing `lblDigitalDownloads` and then pressing the ENTER key.

▶ **Change the Text of the Label Object** To change the text displayed in the Label object, scroll until the Text property is visible, double-click in the right column of the Text property, type `Digital Downloads` and then press the ENTER key.

▶ **Change the Heading Font, Font Style, and Size** To make the heading stand out on the Windows form, its font should be larger and more prominent. To change the font to Cooper Black, its style to Regular, and its Size to 18, with the Label object selected, scroll in the Properties window until the Font property is visible. Click in the right column of the Font property, and then click the Ellipsis button that is displayed in the right column. In the Font dialog box that appears, scroll if necessary and then click Cooper Black (or a similar font) in the Font list, click Regular in the Font style list, and click 18 in the Size list. Then click the OK button in the Font dialog box.

▶ **Horizontally Center the PictureBox Object and the Label Object** The PictureBox object and the Label object should be centered horizontally as a group. To complete this task, click the Windows Form object to unselect any object, click the PictureBox object to select it, hold down the CTRL key and then click the Label object. Click Format on the menu bar, point to Center in Form on the Format menu, and then click Horizontally on the Center in Form submenu.

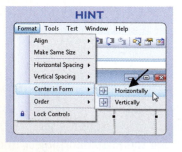

Guided Program Development *(continued)*

The PictureBox object and the Label object are placed on the re-sized Windows Form object (Figure 4-87). The font and font size for the Label object are appropriate for a heading in the window.

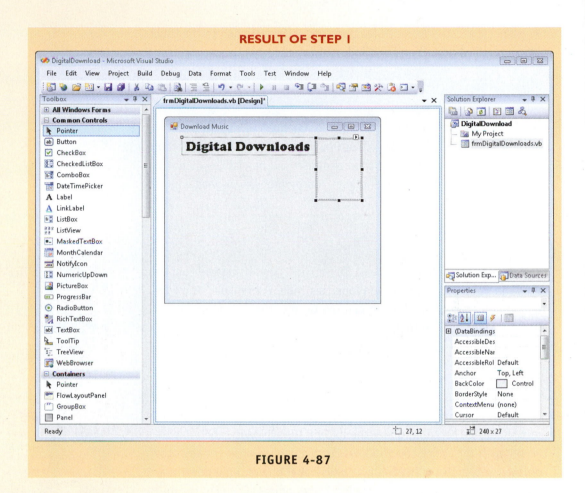

FIGURE 4-87

2

▶ **Add a Second Heading Label** To add the second heading label required for the Window, drag a Label .NET component from the Toolbox to the Windows Form object. Place the second Label object below the Digital Downloads Label object.

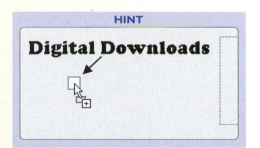

(continues)

Guided Program Development (continued)

▶ **Name the Label Object** Give the name lblCostHeading to the Label object you just placed on the Windows Form object.

▶ **Change the Text in the Label Object** Change the text in the lblCostHeading object to $X.XX Per Download. This text is a placeholder in the Label object so that the Label object will be visible when it is not selected, and so the Label object can be properly aligned.

▶ **Set the Font, Font style, and Size of the Font** Using the Font property and Ellipsis button in the Properties window to display the Font dialog box, change the font to Century Gothic, the Font style to Regular, and the Size to 12.

▶ **Center-Align the Two Label Objects** The lblCostHeading Label object should be centered under the lblDigitalDownloads Label object. To accomplish this, click the Windows Form object to unselect any other objects, select the lblDigitalDownloads Label object, hold down the CTRL key, and click the lblCostHeading Label object. Click Format on the menu bar, point to Align on the Format menu, and then click Centers on the Align submenu.

Guided Program Development *(continued)*

The PictureBox object and the Label objects are properly aligned in the Windows Form object (Figure 4-88).

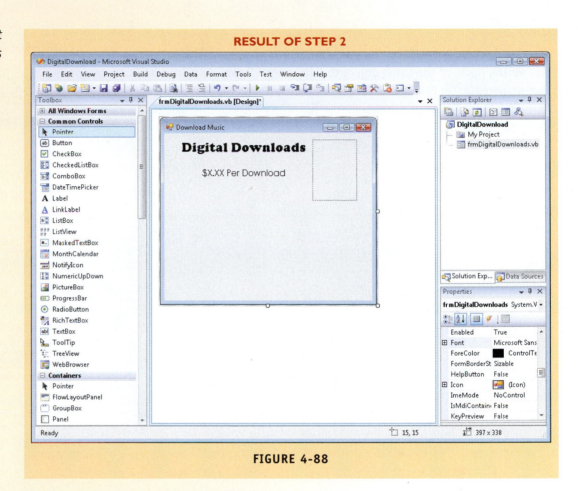

FIGURE 4-88

3

▶ **Add a Label for Number of Song Downloads** Add the Label object for the number of song downloads label by dragging it from the Toolbox. Place it below the lblDigitalDownloads object, and align the Label object using the blue snap lines.

(continues)

Guided Program Development (continued)

▶ **Change the Name, Enter Text, and Change the Font for Number of Song Downloads Label** Using techniques you have learned previously, change the name of the Label object to lblNumberOfDownloads. In the Text property, enter Number of Song Downloads:. Using the Font property in the Properties dialog box, change the font to Century Gothic, Regular style, 12 point Size.

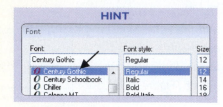

▶ **Add a TextBox Object for the Number of Song Downloads** Drag and drop a TextBox object onto the Windows Form object. Use the blue snap lines to align the top of the TextBox object with the top of the Number of Song Downloads Label object and align with the left edge of the picDownloadHeading Picture object. Name the TextBox object txtNumberOfDownloads *(ref: Figure 4-3)*.

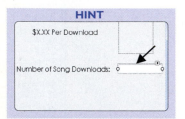

▶ **Enter Data into Text Property** As you learned in this chapter, even though the TextBox object will not contain text when the program begins execution, it still is necessary to enter text in the Text property of the TextBox object to size it properly. To enter text into the TextBox, select the TextBox object. Then, in the Properties window, change the Text property to 888 *(ref: Figure 4-6)*.

▶ **Change the Font and Size of the TextBox Object** Using the Properties dialog box, change the font for the TextBox object to Century Gothic, Regular style, 12 point Size. Drag the right border of the TextBox object so the numbers fit properly in the text box *(ref: Figure 4-8)*.

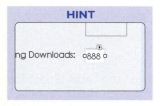

▶ **Align the Resized TextBox Object** To realign the resized TextBox object, drag it up until the red snap line indicates the text in the TextBox object is bottom-aligned with the label *(ref: Figure 4-9)*.

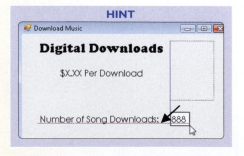

Guided Program Development (continued)

▶ **Center-Align Text in the TextBox Object** To center-align the text in the TextBox object, select the TextBox object, scroll in the Properties window until the TextAlign property is visible, click the list arrow in the right column of the TextAlign property, and then click Center on the TextAlign property list *(ref: Figure 4-10).*

▶ **Remove Text from TextBox Object** Because the TextBox object is sized properly, remove the digits from the TextBox object by selecting the digits in the Text property of the object and pressing the DELETE key *(ref: Figure 4-12).*

▶ **Add the Total Cost of Downloads Label Objects** The total cost of the downloads that is calculated by the program must be displayed as the Text property in a Label object. In addition, another label actually identifies the total cost. Drag two labels onto the Windows Form object and place them on the same horizontal line (use blue snap lines). Vertically align the left side of the left label with the label above it. Vertically align the left side of the right label with the text box above it. Name the Label object on the left lblTotalCostLabel. Name the label on the right lblTotalCostOfDownloads *(ref: Figure 4-18).*

▶ **Enter Text for the Labels and Change the Font** Select the lblTotalCostLabel Label object and then double-click in the right column of the Text property for the label. Type the text `Total Cost of Downloads:` and then press the ENTER key. Select the lblTotalCostOfDownloads Label object and then double-click in the right column of the Text property for the label. Enter the value **$888.88** because this represents the largest expected value for the label. With the right label selected, hold down the CTRL key and then click the left label. With both labels selected, change the font to Century Gothic, Regular style, 12 point Size.

(continues)

Guided Program Development *(continued)*

▶ **Add Buttons** Three buttons are required for the user interface—the Calculate Cost button, the Clear button, and the Exit button. Drag three buttons onto the Windows Form object below the labels. Use blue snap lines to horizontally align the tops of the buttons. Using the (Name) property for each button, name the first button btnCalculateCost, name the second button btnClear, and name the third button btnExit.

▶ **Change the Button Text and Change the Font Style** Using the Text property for each button, change the text for the btnCalculateCost Button object to Calculate Cost. Change the text for the btnClear button to Clear. Change the text for the btnExit button to Exit. Select all three buttons (click the Calculate Cost button, hold down the CTRL key, and then click the other two buttons), click the Font property, click the Ellipsis button in the right column of the Font property, and in the Font dialog box, change the Font style to Bold.

▶ **Change Button Size** The btnCalculateCost button does not display the entire Text property, so it must be enlarged. Drag the right border of the btnCalculateCost button until the entire Text property is visible.

▶ **Change the Size of the Other Buttons** Click the btnCalculateCost button first, and then hold down the CTRL key and click the other two buttons to select all three buttons. Make these buttons the same size by clicking Format on the menu bar, pointing to Make Same Size on the Format menu, and clicking Both on the Make Same Size submenu.

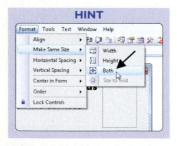

▶ **Space and Center the Buttons** With all three buttons selected, display the Format menu, point to Horizontal Spacing on the Format menu, and then click Make Equal on the Horizontal Spacing submenu. Display the Format menu, point to Center in Form on the Format menu, and then click Horizontally on the Center in Form submenu to center all three buttons horizontally in the Windows Form object.

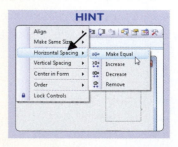

Guided Program Development (continued)

The mockup for the
user interface is com-
plete (Figure 4-89).

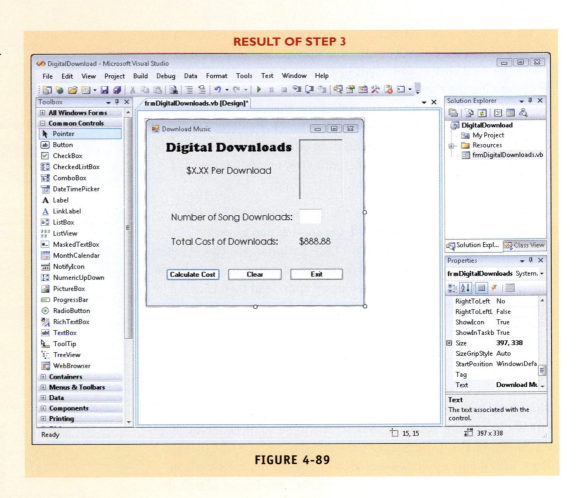

RESULT OF STEP 3

FIGURE 4-89

Phase 2: Fine-Tune the User Interface

4

▶ **Set the BackColor Property for the Windows Form Object** The user interface
must be finished by setting the colors, adding images, and preparing the user interface for program execution. To set the BackColor property for the user interface to
DarkSeaGreen, select the Windows Form object. In the Properties window, click the
BackColor property; click the BackColor arrow in the right column of the BackColor
property; if necessary, click the Web tab; scroll as required; and then click
DarkSeaGreen in the BackColor list.

▶ **Set the BackColor for the Button Objects** To set the BackColor for the button objects to White, select all three buttons. Click the BackColor property in the Properties
window; click the BackColor arrow in the right column of the BackColor property; if necessary, click the Web tab; scroll as required; and then click White in the BackColor list.

(continues)

Guided Program Development (continued)

▶ **Set the Calculate Cost Button Object as the Accept Button** When
the user enters the number of song downloads, she should able to calculate the total cost of downloads by clicking the Calculate Cost button
or by pressing the ENTER key on the keyboard. To assign the Calculate
Cost button as the Accept button, select the Windows Form object by
clicking anywhere in the window except on another object; scroll in the
Properties window until the AcceptButton property is visible; click the
AcceptButton property; click the AcceptButton property arrow; and
then click btnCalculateCost in the list *(ref: Figure 4-20)*.

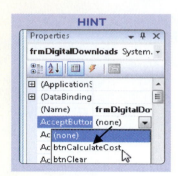

▶ **Set the Clear Button Object as the Cancel Button** When the user
presses the ESC key on the keyboard, the same action as clicking the
Clear button should occur. To set the Clear button as the Cancel button,
click the Windows Form object, click the CancelButton property in the
Properties window, click the CancelButton arrow, and then click
btnClear in the list *(ref: Page 211)*.

▶ **Insert the Music Image into the picDownloadHeading PictureBox
Object** The last step to ready the user interface for execution is to insert the image into the PictureBox object. To do so, if necessary download and save the Music image from scsite.com/vb2008/ch4/images.
Then, with the picture box selected, click the ellipsis button of the
Image property in the Properties window, click the Import button in
the Select Resource dialog box, locate the image, and then import the
image into the Resource folder. Click the OK button in the Select
Resource dialog box.

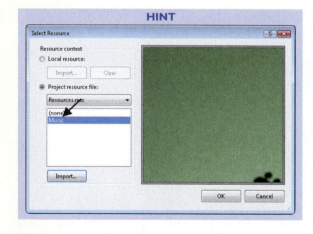

▶ **Resize the Image** To resize the Music image, with the
picDownloadHeading PictureBox object selected, in the Properties window
click the SizeMode property in the left column, click the SizeMode arrow in
the right column, and then click StretchImage in the list.

Guided Program Development (continued)

The user interface is complete (Figure 4-90).

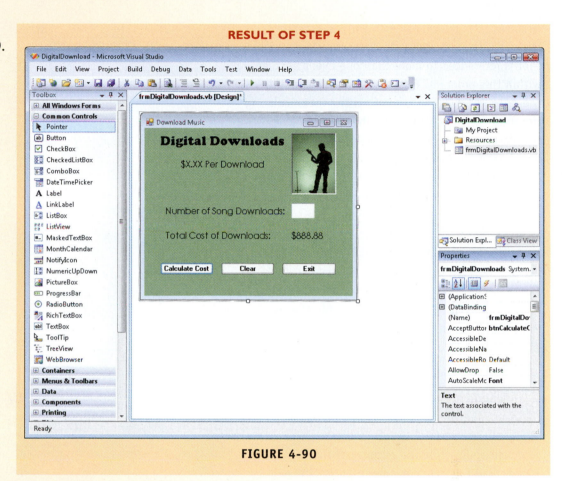

FIGURE 4-90

Phase 3: Code the Application

5

▶ **Code the Comments** Double-click the btnCalculateCost Button object on the frmDigitalDownloads Windows Form object to open the code editing window and create the btnCalculateCost_Click Event Handler. Click the Close button on the Toolbox title bar to close the Toolbox. Click in front of the first words, Public Class frmDigitalDownloads, and press the ENTER key to create a blank line. Press the UP ARROW key on your keyboard. Insert the first four standard comments. Insert the Option Strict On command at the beginning of the code to turn on strict type checking (ref: Figure 4-53).

(continues)

Guided Program Development (continued)

► **Enter the _cdecPricePerDownload Class Variable** The next step is to enter the class variable that is referenced in more than one event handler within this program. This variable, which contains the price per download, is referenced for calculating the total cost and also for the heading. To enter this variable, press the DOWN ARROW key on your keyboard until the insertion point is on the blank line following the Public Class command (line 9). Press the ENTER key to add a blank line, then type the comment that identifies the variable. Press the ENTER key and then write the declaration for the _cdecPricePerDownload variable. The constant decimal variable should contain the value 0.99. The underline character (_) in the variable name indicates the variable is a class variable that is referenced in multiple procedures within the class (ref: Figure 4-47).

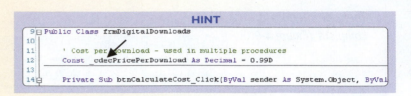

```
HINT
 9  Public Class frmDigitalDownloads
10
11         ' Cost per download - used in multiple procedures
12      Const _cdecPricePerDownload As Decimal = 0.99D
13
14      Private Sub btnCalculateCost_Click(ByVal sender As System.Object, ByVal
```

► **Comment the btnCalculateCost_Click Event Handler** Following the Private statement for the btnCalculateCost_Click event handler, enter a comment to describe the purpose of the btnCalculateCost_Click event.

```
HINT
14      Private Sub btnCalculateCost_Click(ByVal sender As System.Object, ByVal e A
15          ' This event handler is executed when the user clicks the
16          ' Calculate Cost button. It calculates and displays the cost
17          ' of music downloads (number of downloads times the cost per download).
```

► **Declare and Initialize the Variables** This event handler requires three variables: 1) strNumberOfSongs: Holds the number of song downloads entered by the user. 2) intNumberOfSongs: Holds the integer value for the number of song downloads entered by the user; 3) decTotalCostOfDownloads: Holds the calculated total cost of downloads. Declare these three variables (ref: Figure 4-22, Figure 4-35, Figure 4-37).

```
HINT
18
19          Dim strNumberOfSongs As String
20          Dim intNumberOfSongs As Integer
21          Dim decTotalCostOfDownloads As Decimal
```

Guided Program Development *(continued)*

▶ **Write the Statements to Place the Number of Downloads in a Variable and Convert the Value to an Integer** The first steps in the event handler are to move the number of songs value from the Text property of the txtNumberOfDownloads TextBox object to a string variable and then convert that value to an integer value. Using IntelliSense, write the code to complete these steps *(ref: Figure 4-29, Figure 4-52)*.

```
22
23        strNumberOfSongs = Me.txtNumberOfDownloads.Text
24        intNumberOfSongs = Convert.ToInt32(strNumberOfSongs)
```

▶ **Calculate Total Cost of Downloads** To calculate the total cost of downloads and place the result in the decTotalCostOfDownloads variable, the number of songs is multiplied by the price per download. Using IntelliSense, write the statement to perform this calculation *(ref: Figure 4-55)*.

```
25        decTotalCostOfDownloads = intNumberOfSongs * _cdecPricePerDownload
```

▶ **Convert the Decimal Total Cost of Downloads to a String Currency Value and Place It in the Text Property of the lblTotalCostOfDownloads Label Object** Once the total cost of downloads has been calculated, it must be converted from a Decimal value to a currency String value so it can be displayed as the value in the Text property of a Label object. Write the statement to perform this conversion and place the converted value in the Text property of the lblTotalCostOfDownloads Label object *(ref: Figure 4-72)*.

```
26        Me.lblTotalCostOfDownloads.Text = decTotalCostOfDownloads.ToString("C")
```

(continues)

Guided Program Development (continued)

The coding for the btnCalculateCost_Click event handler is complete (Figure 4-91).

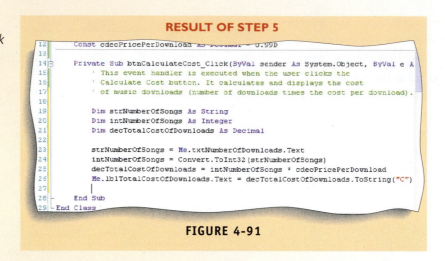

RESULT OF STEP 5

```
12      Const cdecPricePerDownload AS Decimal = 0.99D
13
14 ┌    Private Sub btnCalculateCost_Click(ByVal sender As System.Object, ByVal e A
15 │        ' This event handler is executed when the user clicks the
16 │        ' Calculate Cost button. It calculates and displays the cost
17 │        ' of music downloads (number of downloads times the cost per download).
18 │
19 │        Dim strNumberOfSongs As String
20 │        Dim intNumberOfSongs As Integer
21 │        Dim decTotalCostOfDownloads As Decimal
22 │
23 │        strNumberOfSongs = Me.txtNumberOfDownloads.Text
24 │        intNumberOfSongs = Convert.ToInt32(strNumberOfSongs)
25 │        decTotalCostOfDownloads = intNumberOfSongs * cdecPricePerDownload
26 │        Me.lblTotalCostOfDownloads.Text = decTotalCostOfDownloads.ToString("C")
27 │        |
28 └        End Sub
29  └ End Class
```

FIGURE 4-91

6

▶ **Run the Application** After you have entered code, you should run the application to ensure it is working properly. Run the Digital Downloads application by clicking the Start Debugging button on the Standard toolbar. Enter 10 for the number of song downloads and then click the Calculate Cost button. The Total Cost of Downloads should be $9.90. Enter 15 for the number of song downloads and then press the ENTER key on the keyboard.

When the number of downloads is 10 songs, the total cost of downloads is $9.90 (Figure 4-92).

RESULT OF STEP 6

FIGURE 4-92

Guided Program Development *(continued)*

7

▶ **Write the Code for the Clear Button Event Handler** Click the frmDigitalDownloads.vb[Design] tab in the coding window to return to the design window. Double-click the Clear button to create the event handler for the Clear button. The Clear button event handler must accomplish the following tasks: Clear the txtNumberOfDownloads text box; clear the value in the Text property of the lblTotalCostOfDownloads Label object; set the focus to the txtNumberOfDownloads text box. Write the comments for the event handler and then, using IntelliSense, write the code for the event handler *(ref: Figure 4-74, Figure 4-75, Figure 4-77)*.

```
HINT
30      Private Sub btnClear_Click(ByVal sender As System.Object, ByVal e As System
31          ' This event handler is executed when the user clicks the
32          ' Clear button. It clears the number of downloads text box
33          ' and the Text property of the Total Cost of Downloads label.
34          ' Then, it sets the focus on the txtNumberOfDownloads TextBox object.
35
36          Me.txtNumberOfDownloads.Clear()
37          Me.lblTotalCostOfDownloads.Text = ""
38          Me.txtNumberOfDownloads.Focus()
39
40      End Sub
```

▶ **Write the Code for the Form Load Event Handler** Click the frmDigitalDownloads.vb[Design] tab in the coding window to return to the design window. Double-click the Windows Form object to create the event handler for the Form Load event. The Form Load event handler must accomplish the following tasks: Using concatenation, create and display the Price per Download heading in the Text property of the lblCostHeading Label object; clear the Text property of the lblTotalCostOfDownloads Label object; set the focus in the txtNumberOfDownloads TextBox object. Write the comments for the event handler and then, using IntelliSense, write the code for the event handler *(ref: Figure 4-80, Figure 4-75, Figure 4-77)*.

```
HINT
42      Private Sub frmDigitalDownloads_Load(ByVal sender As System.Object, ByVal e
43          ' This event handler is executed when the form is loaded.
44          ' It displays the cost heading, clears the Text property of the
45          ' Total Cost of Downloads label, and sets the focus on
46          ' the txtNumberOfDownloads TextBox object.
47
48          Me.lblCostHeading.Text = _cdecPricePerDownload.ToString("C") _
49              & " Per Download"
50          Me.lblTotalCostOfDownloads.Text = ""
51          Me.txtNumberOfDownloads.Focus()
52
53      End Sub
```

▶ **Write the Code for the Exit Button Event Handler** Click the frmDigitalDownloads.vb[Design] tab in the coding window to return to the design window. Double-click the Exit button to create the event handler for the Exit button. The Exit button event handler must close the window and terminate the application. Write the comments and code for this event handler.

```
HINT
55      Private Sub btnExit_Click(ByVal sender As System.Object, ByVal
56          ' Close the window and terminate the application
57
58          Me.Close()
59
60      End Sub
61  End Class
```

(continues)

Guided Program Development (continued)

The coding is complete for the Clear button event handler, the Form load event handler, and the Exit button event handler (Figure 4-93).

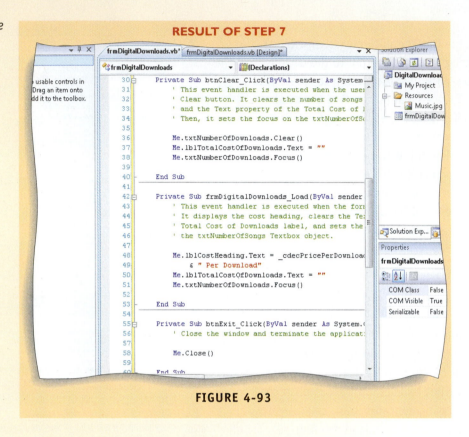

RESULT OF STEP 7

```
30     Private Sub btnClear_Click(ByVal sender As System
31         ' This event handler is executed when the user
32         ' Clear button. It clears the number of songs
33         ' and the Text property of the Total Cost of
34         ' Then, it sets the focus on the txtNumberOfS
35
36         Me.txtNumberOfDownloads.Clear()
37         Me.lblTotalCostOfDownloads.Text = ""
38         Me.txtNumberOfDownloads.Focus()
39
40     End Sub
41
42     Private Sub frmDigitalDownloads_Load(ByVal sender
43         ' This event handler is executed when the form
44         ' It displays the cost heading, clears the Te
45         ' Total Cost of Downloads label, and sets the
46         ' the txtNumberOfSongs Textbox object.
47
48         Me.lblCostHeading.Text = _cdecPricePerDownload
49             & " Per Download"
50         Me.lblTotalCostOfDownloads.Text = ""
51         Me.txtNumberOfDownloads.Focus()
52
53     End Sub
54
55     Private Sub btnExit_Click(ByVal sender As System.
56         ' Close the window and terminate the applicat:
57
58         Me.Close()
59
60     End Sub
```

FIGURE 4-93

8

▶ **Test the Program** After finishing the coding, you should test the program to ensure it works properly. Run the Digital Downloads application by clicking the Start Debugging button on the Standard toolbar. Enter the 20 for the number of song downloads and then click the Calculate Cost button. The Total Cost of Downloads should be $19.80. Click the Clear button to clear the text box and the label containing the total cost of downloads. Enter 5 for the number of song downloads and then press the ENTER key on the keyboard. The Total Cost of Downloads should be $4.95. Press the ESC key to clear the text box and the label containing the total cost of downloads. Enter other values to completely test the program.

The program runs properly (Figure 4-94).

RESULT OF STEP 8

FIGURE 4-94

Code Listing

The complete code for the sample program is shown in Figure 4-95.

```
1  ' Program:  Digital Downloads
2  ' Author:   Corinne Hoisington
3  ' Date:     April 14, 2012
4  ' Purpose:  This application calculates and displays
5  '           the total cost of music downloads
6
7  Option Strict On
8
9  Public Class frmDigitalDownloads
10
11     ' Cost per download - used in multiple procedures
12     Const _cdecPricePerDownload As Decimal = 0.99D
13
14     Private Sub btnCalculateCost_Click(ByVal sender As System.Object, ByVal e As System↙
       .EventArgs) Handles btnCalculateCost.Click
15        ' This event handler is executed when the user clicks the
16        ' Calculate Cost button. It calculates and displays the cost
17        ' of music downloads (number of downloads times the cost per download).
18
19        Dim strNumberOfSongs As String
20        Dim intNumberOfSongs As Integer
21        Dim decTotalCostOfDownloads As Decimal
22
23        strNumberOfSongs = Me.txtNumberOfDownloads.Text
24        intNumberOfSongs = Convert.ToInt32(strNumberOfSongs)
25        decTotalCostOfDownloads = intNumberOfSongs * _cdecPricePerDownload
26        Me.lblTotalCostOfDownloads.Text = decTotalCostOfDownloads.ToString("C")
27
28     End Sub
29
30     Private Sub btnClear_Click(ByVal sender As System.Object, ByVal e As System.      ↙
       EventArgs) Handles btnClear.Click
31        ' This event handler is executed when the user clicks the
32        ' Clear button. It clears the number of songs text box
33        ' and the Text property of the Total Cost of Downloads label.
34        ' Then, it sets the focus on the txtNumberOfDownloads Textbox object.
35
36        Me.txtNumberOfDownloads.Clear()
37        Me.lblTotalCostOfDownloads.Text = ""
38        Me.txtNumberOfDownloads.Focus()
39
40     End Sub
41
42     Private Sub frmDigitalDownloads_Load(ByVal sender As System.Object, ByVal e As      ↙
       System.EventArgs) Handles MyBase.Load
43        ' This event handler is executed when the form is loaded.
44        ' It displays the cost heading, clears the Text property of the
45        ' Total Cost of Downloads label, and sets the focus on
46        ' the txtNumberOfDownloads Textbox object.
47
48        Me.lblCostHeading.Text = _cdecPricePerDownload.ToString("C") _
49            & " Per Download"
50        Me.lblTotalCostOfDownloads.Text = ""
51        Me.txtNumberOfDownloads.Focus()
52
53     End Sub
```

FIGURE 4-95 (continues)

```
54
55      Private Sub btnExit_Click(ByVal sender As System.Object, ByVal e As System.    ↙
        EventArgs) Handles btnExit.Click
56          ' Close the window and terminate the application
57
58          Me.Close()
59
60      End Sub
61 End Class
62
```

FIGURE 4-95 (continued)

Summary

In this chapter you have learned to declare variables and write arithmetic operations. The items listed in the table in Figure 4-96 include all the new Visual Studio and Visual Basic skills you have learned in this chapter.

VISUAL BASIC SKILLS		
Skill	Figure Number	Web Address For Video
Place a TextBox object on the Windows Form object	Figure 4-3	scsite.com/vb2008/ch4/figure4-3
Size and position a TextBox object	Figure 4-6	scsite.com/vb2008/ch4/figure4-6
Align text in a TextBox object	Figure 4-10	scsite.com/vb2008/ch4/figure4-10
Create a MultiLine TextBox object	Figure 4-13	scsite.com/vb2008/ch4/figure4-13
Place a masked TextBox object on the Windows Form object	Figure 4-15	scsite.com/vb2008/ch4/figure4-15
Place and size a Label object on the Windows Form object	Figure 4-18	scsite.com/vb2008/ch4/figure4-18
Assign a Button object as the Accept button	Figure 4-20	scsite.com/vb2008/ch4/figure4-20
Assign a Button object as the Cancel button	Page 211	
Close the Toolbox	Figure 4-21	scsite.com/vb2008/ch4/figure4-21
Define a String variable	Figure 4-22	
Write an assignment statement	Figure 4-24	
Use IntelliSense to enter a variable and an assignment statement	Figure 4-25	scsite.com/vb2008/ch4/figure4-25
Declare an Integer data type	Figure 4-35	
Declare a Decimal data type	Figure 4-37	

VISUAL BASIC SKILLS (continued)		
Skill	**Figure Number**	**Web Address For Video**
Declare a Char data type	Figure 4-40	
Declare a Boolean data type	Figure 4-42	
Declare a constant variable	Figure 4-47	
Use an argument in a procedure call statement	Figure 4-49	
Write a procedure call statement for the ToInt32 procedure in the Convert class	Figure 4-52	
Enter the Option Strict On statement	Figure 4-53	
Perform arithmetic operations using arithmetic operators	Figure 4-56	
Display numeric output data	Figure 4-72	
Write a procedure call for the Clear procedure	Figure 4-74	
Write a procedure call for the Focus procedure	Figure 4-76	
Write a String concatenation statement	Figure 4-80	
Write a variable with class scope	Figure 4-82	
Understand a Format Exception	Figure 4-83	

FIGURE 4-96

Learn It Online

Start your browser and visit scsite.com/vb2008/ch4. Follow the instructions in the exercises below.

1. **Chapter Reinforcement TF, MC, SA** Click one of the Chapter Reinforcement links for Multiple Choice, True/False, or Short Answer below the Learn It Online heading. Answer each question and submit to your instructor.

2. **Practice Test** Click the Practice Test link below the Learn It Online heading. Answer each question, enter your first and last name at the bottom of the page, and then click the Grade Test button. When the graded practice test is displayed on your screen, submit the graded practice test to your instructor. Continue to take the practice test until you are satisfied with your score.

3. **Crossword Puzzle Challenge** Click the Crossword Puzzle Challenge link below the Learn It Online heading. Read the instructions, and then click the Continue button. Work the crossword puzzle. When you are finished, click the Submit button. When the crossword puzzle is redisplayed, submit it to your instructor.

Knowledge Check

1. Name three numeric data types that can contain a decimal point.

2. Write a Dim statement for each of the following variables using the variable type and variable name that would be best for each value.

   a. Population of the United States

   b. Your weekly pay

   c. The smallest data type you can use for your age

   d. A constant for the first initial of your first name

   e. The minimum wage

   f. The name of the city in which you live

   g. The answer to a true/false question

3. Determine if each of the following variable names is valid or invalid. Please state the error in the invalid variable names.

   a. _intRadian

   b. PercentOfSales#

   c. first_Input_Value

   d. R743-L56

   e. 3BZT477

   f. Close

   g. Name Of Client

Knowledge Check

(continued)

4. List the steps specifying how you would perfectly align a group of TextBox objects along their left edges.

5. Which data type would be best for currency amounts?

6. Explain the precedence for the order of operations.

7. What is the solution to each of the following arithmetic expressions?

   a. $5 + 8 * 3 + 1$

   b. $16 / 2 * 4 - 3$

   c. $40 - 6 \wedge 2 / 3$

   d. $74 \text{ Mod } 8$

   e. $9 \backslash 4 + 3$

   f. $2 \wedge 3 + (8 - 5)$

   g. $(15 \text{ Mod } 2) - 1 + 4 * (16 \backslash 5)$

8. What is the difference between a method and a procedure?

9. What is the difference between a variable and a literal?

10. Correct the following statements:

    a. `Dim itAge As Integr`

    b. `Dim dblDiscountRate As Dbl`

    c. `Constant cstrCollege As String = "CVCC"`

    d. `Dim strLastName As String`

       `strLastName = 'McNamara'`

    c. `1.5 * decHourlyPay = decOverTimePayRate`

11. Write a statement that sets the focus on the TextBox object txtLastName.

12. Write a statement that removes the contents of the txtAge TextBox object.

13. Write a statement that blanks the Text property of the lblEligibilityAge Label object.

14. Write a statement to convert the value in the String variable strWaistSize to an integer value and place the integer value in a variable named intWaistSize.

15. Write a statement to convert the value in the String variable named strHourlyPay to a Decimal value and place the Decimal value in a variable named decWage.

16. Write a statement that closes the form that currently is open.

17. Write a statement that declares a constant named decInsuranceDeductible as a Decimal data type and set its value to 250.00.

18. Which Windows Form property allows the user to press the ENTER key while the form is active and acti-vate a button's event handler?

(continues)

Knowledge Check

(continued)

19. What is a local variable? How does its scope differ from that of a global variable?

20. When the following statements are executed, what would be displayed in the lblHourlyWage Label object?

```
decHourlyWage = 12.637
Me.lblHourlyWage.Text = decHourlyWage.ToString("C")
```

Debugging Exercises

1. Fix the following code:

```
Option Strict On
Dim intDistance As Integer

intDistance = 17.5
```

2. Fix the following code:

```
Dim dblRegularPay As Double
Dim dblOvertimePay As Double

intRegularPay = 783.87
intOvertimePay = 105.92
lbl.TotalPay = (dblRegularPay + dblOvertimePay).ToString('C')
```

3. Analyze the following code and then correct it:

```
1 Public Class Form1
2
3     Private Sub btnCalculateArea_Click(ByVal sender As System.Object, ByVal e As System
      .EventArgs) Handles btnCalculateArea.Click
4         Dim strLengthOfSide As String
5         Dim intArea As Integer
6
7         strLengthOfSide = Me.txtLengthOfSide.Text
8         intArea = strLengthOfSide ^ 2
9         Me.lblArea.Text = intArea.ToString("C")
10
11     End Sub
12 End Class
```

FIGURE 4-97

Program Analysis

1. What will occur when the user clicks the btnSlope Button?

```
Private Sub btnSlope_Click(ByVal sender As System.Object, ByVal e As
System.EventArgs) Handles btnSlope.Click
    Dim decRise As Decimal
    Dim decRun As Decimal
    Dim decSlope As Decimal

    decRise = 12.3D
    decRun = 2.1D
    decSlope = decRise / decRun
    Me.lblSlope.Text = "The Line Slope is " & decSlope.ToString("F3")
End Sub
```

2. How would the number .0256 be displayed if the format specifier ("P") is used in a Convert.ToString statement?

3. How would the number 3746.35555 be displayed if the format specifier ("F3") is used in a Convert.ToString statement?

4. If you want the user to enter her telephone number with the area code, which .NET component would be best to use on the Windows Form object?

5. Using the Format Specification with the ToString procedure, write the statement that would display:

   a. The value in the decDvdCost variable with a dollar sign and two places to the right of the decimal place in a label named lblDvd.

   b. The value in the decWithholdingTaxRate variable with a percent sign and one place to the right of the decimal point in a label named lblWithholdingTaxRate.

   c. The value in the decOilRevenue variable with commas as needed, two places to the right of the decimal place, and no dollar sign in a label called lblOilRevenue.

6. Write a single line of code to declare a variable decWindSpeed as a Decimal data type and assign it the value 25.47. Use a forced literal to ensure the compiler views this number as a Decimal data type.

7. What would the values of the following variables be at the end of the code that follows:

   a. intParts

   b. intBoxes

   c. intLeftovers

   ```
   Dim intParts As Integer
   Dim intBoxes As Integer
   Dim intLeftovers As Integer

   intParts = 77
   intPartsPerBox = 9

   intBoxes = intParts \ intPartsPerBox
   intLeftovers = intParts Mod intBoxes
   ```

(continues)

Program Analysis

(continued)

8. Are the following statements written correctly? If not, how should they be written?

```
Dim dblPay as Double
Me.lblPay.Text = dblPay.ToString("C2")
```

9. For a Button object named btnCalories, write the click event handler to implement the following requirements to calculate the number of calories burned in a run:

   a. Declare variables named strMilesRan, decCaloriesConsumed, and decMilesRan.

   b. Declare a constant named cdecCaloriesBurnedPerHour and assign it the value 700 (you burn 700 calories for every mile you run).

   c. Allow the user to enter the number of miles she ran today.

   d. Convert the miles to a Decimal data type.

   e. Calculate the number of calories the user burned during their run.

   f. Display the result rounded to zero decimal places in a label named lblCaloriesBurned.

10. What would the output be when the user clicks the btnDrivingAge Button?

```
Private Sub btnDrivingAge_Click(ByVal sender As System.Object, ByVal e As
System.EventArgs) Handles btnDrivingAge.Click
    Dim intPresentAge As Integer
    Const cintDrivingAge As Integer = 16
    Dim intYearsToDrive As Integer

    intPresentAge = 13
    intYearsToDrive = cintDrivingAge - intPresentAge
    Me.lblYearsLeft.Text = intYearsToDrive.ToString() & " year(s) until you
can drive."
    End Sub
```

Case Programming Assignments

Complete one or more of the following case programming assignments. Submit
the program and materials you create to your instructor. The level of difficulty is
indicated for each case programming assignment.

● =	Easiest
● =	Intermediate
● ● ● =	Challenging

1 ●
CONCERT TICKETS

Design a Windows application and write the code that will execute according to the program requirements
in Figure 4-98 and the Use Case definition in Figure 4-99. Before writing the code, create an event planning document for each event in the program. The completed program is shown in Figure 4-100.

REQUIREMENTS DOCUMENT

Date submitted: January 31, 2010

Application title: Concert Tickets

Purpose: The concert tickets selection program allows a user to purchase tickets to a concert.

Program Procedures: From a window on the screen, the user chooses the number of tickets for her favorite artist/group and the total cost amount for the tickets will be displayed.

Algorithms, Processing, and Conditions:
1. The user must be able to enter the number of concert tickets for their favorite artist/group.
2. A picture of the artist/group performing at the concert will be displayed throughout the entire process.
3. After the user enters the number of tickets needed, the user clicks the Display Cost button.
4. The total cost of the tickets at $46.50 per ticket will be displayed in currency format (total cost = number of tickets * 46.50).

Notes and Restrictions:
1. The user can clear the number of tickets entered and the total cost of the tickets with a clear button and enter another number of tickets.
2. An exit button should close the application.
3. The cost per ticket can vary, so the program should allow a different price to be placed in any headings and be used in any calculations.

Comments:
1. The picture shown in the window should be selected from pictures available on the Web.

FIGURE 4-98

(continues)

Case Programming Assignments

Concert Tickets (continued)

USE CASE DEFINITION

1. The Windows Application opens.
2. The user enters the number of concert tickets.
3. The user clicks the Display Cost button.
4. The program displays the total cost of the concert tickets.
5. The user can click the Clear button and repeat steps 2–4.
6. The user terminates the program by clicking the Exit button.

FIGURE 4-99

FIGURE 4-100

Case Programming Assignments

2 ●
TAXI METER

Design a Windows application and write the code that will execute according to the program requirements in Figure 4-101 and the Use Case definition in Figure 4-102. Before writing the code, create an event planning document for each event in the program. The completed program is shown in Figure 4-103.

REQUIREMENTS DOCUMENT

Date submitted: October 19, 2012

Application title: Taxi Fare

Purpose: The Taxi Fare Windows application computes the cost of a taxi fare.

Program Procedures: From a window on the screen, the user enters the number of miles traveled in the taxi. The program calculates and displays the cost of the total fare.

Algorithms, Processing, and Conditions:
1. The user must be able to enter the number of miles traveled in a taxi cab.
2. The title and a taxi logo (logo is named Taxi and is found at scsite.com/vb2008/ch4/images) will be displayed throughout the entire process.
3. After entering the number of miles traveled, the user clicks the Display Fare button.
4. The formula for calculating the fare is: Flat fee ($1.25) + (number of miles * $2.25 per mile).
5. The program displays the fare in currency format.

Notes and Restrictions:
1. The user can clear the number of miles and make another entry.
2. An exit button should close the application.

Comments:

FIGURE 4-101

(continues)

Case Programming Assignments

Taxi Meter (continued)

USE CASE DEFINITION

1. The Windows Application opens.
2. The user enters the number of miles traveled.
3. The user clicks the Display Fare button.
4. The program displays the total fare.
5. The user can click the Clear button and repeat steps 2-4.
6. The user terminates the program by clicking the Exit button.

FIGURE 4-102

FIGURE 4-103

Case Programming Assignments

3 WEEKLY PAY CALCULATOR

Design a Windows application and write the code that will execute according to the program requirements in Figure 4-104 and the Use Case definition in Figure 4-105. Before writing the code, create an event planning document for each event in the program. The completed program is shown in Figure 4-106.

REQUIREMENTS DOCUMENT

Date submitted:	May 11, 2012
Application title:	Weekly Pay Calculator
Purpose:	The Weekly Pay Calculator Windows application computes the weekly pay for an hourly employee.
Program Procedures:	From a window on the screen, a payroll clerk enters the total minutes an employee worked in a week and the hourly pay rate. The program displays the weekly pay for the employee.
Algorithms, Processing, and Conditions:	1. The payroll clerk must be able to enter the total minutes worked during the week and the hourly pay rate. 2. The company name (Western Distribution) and the picture (company workers found at scsite.com/vb2008/ch4/images) will be displayed throughout the entire process. 3. After entering the total minutes worked and hourly pay rate, the payroll clerk clicks the weekly pay button. 4. The weekly pay is displayed in currency format together with the number of hours and minutes worked.
Notes and Restrictions:	1. The user can clear the total minutes worked, the hourly pay rate, the hours and minutes worked, and the weekly pay by clicking a clear button. He then can enter another employee's data. 2. An exit button should close the application. 3. In this application, if hours worked is greater than 40, the hourly pay rate still applies.
Comments:	

FIGURE 4-104

(continues)

Case Programming Assignments

Weekly Pay Calculator (continued)

USE CASE DEFINITION

1. The Windows Application opens.
2. The payroll clerk enters the total minutes worked by an employee and the employee's hourly pay rate.
3. The payroll clerk clicks the Weekly Pay button.
4. The program displays the hours worked, the minutes worked, and the employee's weekly pay.
5. The payroll clerk can click the Clear button and then repeat steps 2 through 4.
6. The user terminates the program by clicking the Exit button.

FIGURE 4-105

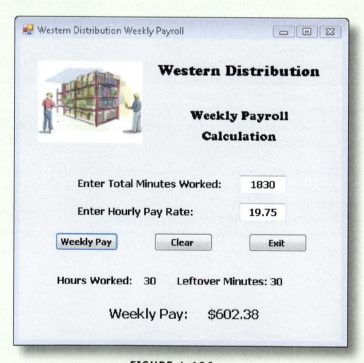

FIGURE 4-106

Case Programming Assignments

4 CASH REGISTER

Design a Windows application and write the code that will execute according to the program requirements in Figure 4-107. Before designing the user interface, create a Use Case definition. Before writing the code, create an event planning document for each event in the program.

REQUIREMENTS DOCUMENT

Date submitted: June 6, 2012

Application title: Cash Register

Purpose: The Cash Register Windows application will compute the tax and the final cost of a purchased item.

**Program
Procedures:**   From a window on the screen, the user enters the item name and amount of the item purchased. The program calculates the tax for the item and the final total, and then displays these values.

**Algorithms,
Processing, and
Conditions:**
1. The user must be able to enter the name of the item purchased and the cost of the item before tax.
2. The store name and store picture will be displayed throughout the entire process.
3. After the user enters the item name and the cost of the item, the user clicks the Display Cost button.
4. The program displays the item name with the cost, tax, and final total.
5. The cost, tax, and final total should appear in currency format.
6. The tax rate for all items is 7.75%.
7. The final total is calculated by adding the cost and the tax.

**Notes and
Restrictions:**
1. The user can clear the item name, cost, tax, and final total with a clear button.
2. The user can click an exit button to close the application.

Comments:
1. The store picture shown in the window should be selected from the pictures available on the Web.

FIGURE 4-107

Case Programming Assignments

5 ●●
GRADE CALCULATOR

Design a Windows application and write the code that will execute according to the program requirements in Figure 4-108. Before designing the user interface, create a Use Case definition. Before writing the code, create an event planning document for each event in the program.

REQUIREMENTS DOCUMENT

Date submitted: January 4, 2012

Application title: Grade Calculator

Purpose: The Grade Calculator Windows application will compute and display the average of four numeric test grades.

Program Procedures: From a window on the screen, the user enters the Social Security number of a student and the four numeric scores from four tests taken by the student. The program determines the average of the four test scores and displays the result.

Algorithms, Processing, and Conditions:
1. The user must be able to enter the Social Security number of the student and the four test scores.
2. The Social Security number must be formatted properly with hyphens.
3. To determine the average test score, add the four entered test scores and divide by four.
4. The average score should be shown with one position to the right of the decimal point.

Notes and Restrictions:
1. The user can clear the Social Security number, test scores, and average score; and then enter new data.
2. The user can use an exit button to close the application.

Comments:
1. The designer should design the user interface, including all graphics and words used.

FIGURE 4-108

Case Programming Assignments

6 ●●
CONVERT CURRENCY

Design a Windows application and write the code that will execute according to the program requirements in Figure 4-109. Before designing the user interface, create a Use Case definition. Before writing the code, create an event planning document for each event in the program.

REQUIREMENTS DOCUMENT

Date submitted: November 4, 2012

Application title: Convert Currency

Purpose: The Convert Currency Windows application will display the value of U.S. dollars in euros, English pounds, and Mexican pesos.

Program Procedures: From a window on the screen, the user should enter the number of U.S. dollars to be converted. The program will display the equivalent value in euros, British pounds, and Mexican pesos.

Algorithms, Processing, and Conditions:

1. The user must be able to enter the number of U.S. dollars to be converted.
2. After entering the number of U.S. dollars to be converted, the user clicks the Convert Currency button.
3. The program converts the number of U.S. dollars entered into the equivalent number of euros, English pounds, and Mexican pesos. The program displays all three currencies together with the U.S. dollars.
4. To find the conversion rates, the developer must consult the appropriate Web sites. A possible site is www.xe.com.
5. Because the currency rates change dynamically, the user should enter both the date and the time that the conversion rates were applied. The date and time should be displayed in U.S. format.
6. The user should be able to clear the date and time, the number of U.S. dollars entered, and the results of the calculations, and then enter new values.

Notes and Restrictions:

1. The user should be able to click an exit button to close the application.

Comments:

1. The designer must determine the design of the user interface, and the words and graphics used in the user interface.

FIGURE 4-109

Case Programming Assignments

7 ●●●
SWIMMING POOL FILL

Create a requirements document and a Use Case Definition document, and then design a Windows application based on the following case project. Before writing the code, create an event planning document for each event in the program.

Because filling a swimming pool with water requires much more water than normal usage, your local city charges a special rate of $0.77 per cubic foot of water to fill a swimming pool. In addition, it charges a one-time fee of $100.00 for pool filling. The city water works department has requested that you write a Windows application that allows the user to enter a swimming pool's length, width, and average depth to find the volume of the pool in cubic feet (volume = length * width * depth); and then display the pool's volume and the final cost of filling the pool, including the one-time fee. Allow the user to enter values with decimal places and compute the volume to one decimal place past the decimal point. The user should be able to clear all entries and then reenter data. To close the program, the user should be able to click a button.

FIGURE 4-110

Case Programming Assignments

8 ●●●
HOMEWORK HELPER

Create a requirements document and a Use Case Definition document, and then design a Windows application based on the following case project. Before writing the code, create an event planning document for each event in the program.

A teacher at the local elementary school would like you to write an application to help her students check their arithmetic skills. The application will allow the student to enter any two integer numbers and choose one of four buttons (add, subtract, multiply, divide) to add, subtract, multiply, or divide the two integers (show the quotient and the remainder in division). The result should display the entire problem such as: 12 + 17 = 29, 50 − 24 = 26; 12 * 8 = 96; 66 / 7 = 9, remainder 3. The student should be able to clear the entry, enter new values, and choose a different arithmetic operation. The teacher requested that you include an Exit button so her students can easily close the Windows application.

FIGURE 4-111

Case Programming Assignments

9 •••
HOURS AND YEARS SLEPT

Create a requirements document and a Use Case Definition document, and then design a Windows application based on the following case project. Before writing the code, create an event planning document for each event in the program.

The science museum has asked you to write a Windows application that children can use to find the total number of hours and years they have slept during their lifetime, assuming they sleep an average of 8 hours per night. The user should enter her first name, her birth date (ask for the month, day, and year separately in numeric form) and the current date (ask for the month, day, and year separately in numeric form). To calculate the number of hours slept, assume 360 days per year and 30 days per month. The program must display the user's name and the number of hours slept. Based on 360 days per year and 8 hours of sleep per day, the program also should show how many years, months, and days the user has slept in her lifetime. The user can click a Clear button to clear all entries and results. An Exit button must be available to close the application. Because children normally will use this program, the museum has asked you to develop a colorful and fun user interface.

FIGURE 4-112

CHAPTER FIVE

Mobile Applications Using Decision Structures

OBJECTIVES

You will have mastered the material in this chapter when you can:

- ► Write programs for devices other than a personal computer

- ► Understand the use of handheld technology

- ► Write handheld applications for a Personal Digital Assistant

- ► Use the Panel object

- ► Place RadioButton objects in applications

- ► Display a message box

- ► Make decisions using If…Then statements

- ► Make decisions using If…Then…Else statements

- ► Make decisions using nested If statements

- ► Make decisions using logical operators

- ► Make decisions using Case statements

- ► Insert code snippets

- ► Test input to ensure a value is numeric

HEADS UP

You can run the chapter project on the built-in Pocket PC simulator that is part of Visual Studio 2008 or without any changes in a Windows application. Running the application on a Pocket PC simulator allows programmers to experience multiplatform development.

Introduction

Developers can code Visual Basic applications to make decisions based on the input of users or other conditions that occur. Decision-making is one of the fundamental activities of a computer program. In this chapter, you will learn to write decision-making statements in Visual Basic 2008.

Today's computers are not limited to traditional personal computers. For mobile, on-the-go people, smaller handheld computers have evolved to become a major business tool. Handheld computers can manage personal information, such as contacts, appointments, and to-do lists. In addition, today's devices can connect to the Internet, run sophisticated applications, and provide multimedia services. The topics you will learn throughout this chapter are as applicable on a handheld device as they are in a Windows application.

Chapter Project

The sample program in this chapter is designed to run on a mobile device called a Pocket PC. The application, called the Wood Cabinet Estimate application, is written for a cabinetmaker who wants a program on the job site that can provide a cost estimate for building wood cabinets. The cabinetmaker requests that the program be developed for a handheld device because most job sites do not have an area to set up a laptop or desktop computer.

The application requests that the user enter the number of linear feet of cabinetry required and the wood type requested by the customer. The mobile application then computes the cost of the cabinets based on the rate of $100.00 per linear foot for pine, $150.00 per linear foot for oak, and $250.00 per linear foot for cherry. Figure 5-1 shows the user interface for the application.

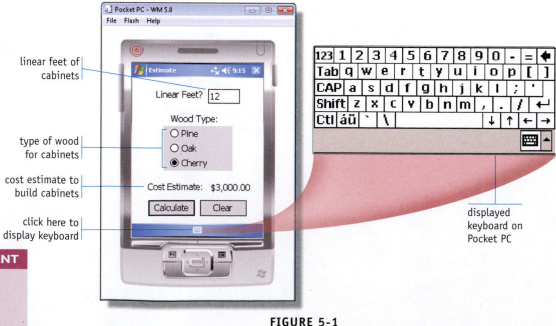

linear feet of cabinets

type of wood for cabinets

cost estimate to build cabinets

click here to display keyboard

displayed keyboard on Pocket PC

FIGURE 5-1

ONLINE REINFORCEMENT

To view a video of program execution, visit scsite.com/vb2008/ch5 and then select Figure 5-1.

In Figure 5-1, the Wood Cabinet Estimate Mobile application is running on a Pocket PC handheld device. The title in the title bar is Estimate. When designing the user interface for a handheld device, the developer must consider that space is limited on the title bar of a Pocket PC due to the built-in title bar components including connectivity symbols, a speaker control, and a clock.

The user enters the number of linear feet of cabinetry by pressing a pointing device called a **stylus** on a displayed keyboard (see inset). The linear footage the user enters in the TextBox object includes all cabinets for the job. Using the stylus, the user chooses the wood type by selecting a RadioButton from the following list: Pine (the most common choice), Oak, or Cherry. After the user has entered the number of linear feet of cabinetry and selected one of the three types of wood, the user clicks the Calculate button to obtain the cost estimate. The calculation is based on the linear feet multiplied by the cost of the selected wood. The cost estimate is displayed in currency format. In the example in Figure 5-1, the user entered 12 linear feet for the length of the cabinetry and selected cherry wood. After pressing the Calculate button, the application displayed a cost of $3,000.00 (12 x $250.00).

Clicking the Clear button will clear the linear footage, reset the RadioButton selection to Pine, which is the most common wood type, and clear the result of the calculation.

An important requirement of the chapter project program is to check the data the user enters to ensure it is valid. In Chapter 4, you learned that if you enter nonnumeric data and attempt to use it in a calculation, the program will be terminated. To check for invalid data, the Wood Cabinet Estimate program ensures that the user enters a numeric value greater than zero in the Linear Feet TextBox object. A warning dialog box appears if the user leaves the linear feet TextBox blank or does not enter a valid number. Figure 5-2 displays the warning dialog box called a Message Box that directs the user to enter the linear feet for the cabinets.

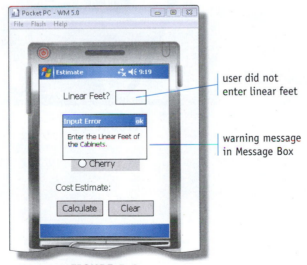

FIGURE 5-2

Checking input data for validity is an important task in Visual Basic programs. You will learn several data validation techniques in this chapter.

Pervasive Devices

Mobile applications are no more difficult to code than Windows applications because you use the same skills. It is not even necessary to use an actual Pocket PC handheld device because Visual Studio has a built-in **emulator** that displays a "working" Pocket PC.

A few years ago, mainstream software development was focused on coding desktop and server applications. In the past decade, smaller handheld computers called **pervasive devices** have become important in many business venues. Faster processing, increased storage, and improved interconnectivity make these mobile devices useful as business tools, entertainment machines, electronic guidance systems with GPS (Global Positioning System), and access devices for information retrieval from the Web or specific information systems. Developers of handheld applications are needed to program more than one billion cell phones and millions of PDAs (personal digital assistants) worldwide.

The health care industry is the largest user of PDAs (Figure 5-3). Medical staffs can use a medical dictionary, drug interaction information, patient records, medical research, and temperature probes loaded on a handheld device. These devices allow monitoring patients' clinical data and transmitting the captured data to a physician or hospital.

FIGURE 5-3

An increasing number of business and leisure travelers carry mobile devices when they travel to access the Internet, communicate with their office and customers, and even make travel arrangements on the fly (Figure 5-4).

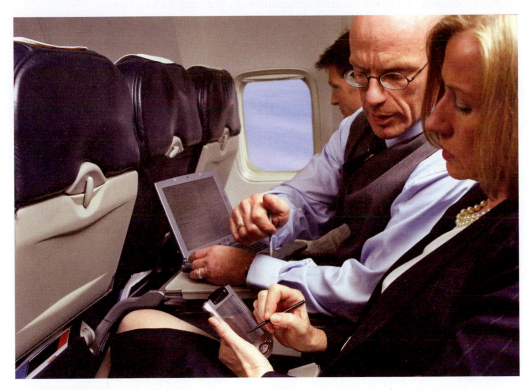

FIGURE 5-4

Emergency services providers such as police officers, firefighters, emergency medical technicians, and security officers use handheld devices for a variety of tasks ranging from crime prevention to saving lives (Figure 5-5).

FIGURE 5-5

PDAs and other mobile devices have become the electronic three-ring binders of choice for students at all levels of education. In response to this innovation, universities, colleges, and high schools are equipping classrooms, laboratories, dormitories, student lounges, and other campus locations with wireless technologies.

Pervasive devices are being integrated into the workplace. The applications to be written for these devices are yet to be imagined.

Create a Smart Device Application

The Wood Cabinet Estimate chapter project application calculates the cost of wood cabinets for a Pocket PC device at the job site. To place an application on a mobile device, you develop the project in Visual Basic 2008 using the same commands you would use for a Windows application. Instead of creating a Windows application, however, you develop the project as a **Smart Device** application for a Pocket PC. The newest version of the Pocket PC device software is the Pocket PC 5.0 Software Development Kit (SDK). To create a Smart Device application, you can complete the following steps:

STEP 1   With Visual Studio 2008 open, click the New Project button on the Standard toolbar and click Smart Device in the Project types pane on the left side of the New Project dialog box. Click Smart Device Project in the Templates pane.

The Smart Device application type and Smart Device Project are selected (Figure 5-6).

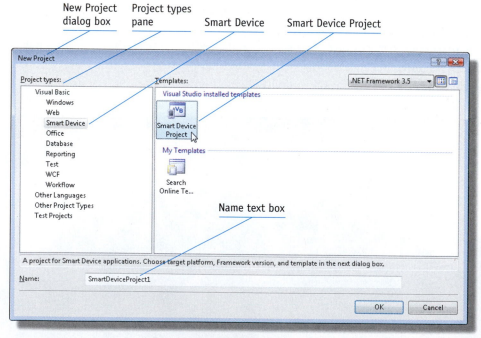

FIGURE 5-6

STEP 2 Change the Name of the Smart Device project from SmartDeviceProject1 to WoodCabinetEstimate. Click the OK button.

After the Smart Device project is named and the OK button is clicked, a new dialog box opens to request the type of smart device target platform such as a Pocket PC 2003, Windows CE, Windows Mobile 5.0 Pocket PC SDK, or Windows Mobile 5.0 SmartPhone SDK (Figure 5-7).

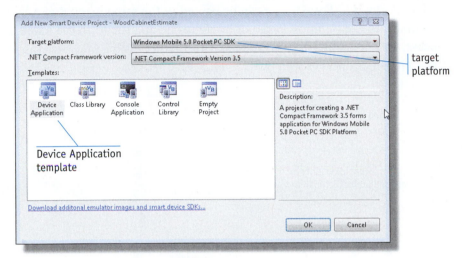

FIGURE 5-7

STEP 3 Click the Target platform list button and select Windows Mobile 5.0 Pocket PC SDK. Next, click Device Application and then click the OK button.

After the OK button is clicked, the Pocket PC 5.0 emulator form opens (Figure 5-8). The Pocket PC 5.0 emulator form object is similar to the Windows form. You can place objects from the Toolbox on this form as you design the mobile application.

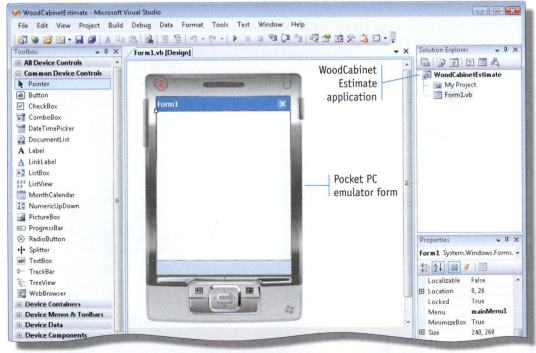

FIGURE 5-8

IN THE REAL WORLD

Visual Studio can be used to create mobile applications for over two hundred different devices from multiple vendors. The device must be a smart device that uses a form of the Windows operating system.

ONLINE REINFORCEMENT

To view a video of the process in the previous steps, visit scsite.com/vb2008/ch5 and then select Figure 5-6.

PLACING OBJECTS ON THE POCKET PC FORM OBJECT

As you create a user interface using a Pocket PC device, many of the same objects used in a Windows application can be placed on the Pocket PC Form object. Note, however, that you can resize a Windows Form object based on the need for the application, but a Pocket PC form must remain the same size because it is designed to fit the screen size of a standard Pocket PC device.

The Pocket PC Form object can be named in the same manner as a Windows Form object in the Solution Explorer by right-clicking the form file name, clicking Rename, and then entering a new name, which automatically updates the form (Name) in the Properties window (Figure 5-9).

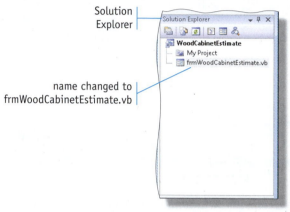

Solution Explorer

name changed to frmWoodCabinetEstimate.vb

FIGURE 5-9

The title bar text for the Pocket PC form in Figure 5-8 on page 297 is Form1. To change the title bar text, change the Text property of the Pocket PC Form object from Form1 to Estimate in the same manner used for the Windows Form object (Figure 5-10). Because the size of the Pocket PC Form object is set permanently, you have limited space on the Pocket PC title bar for the name. Therefore, it is best to limit the title bar text of a Pocket PC device to one word.

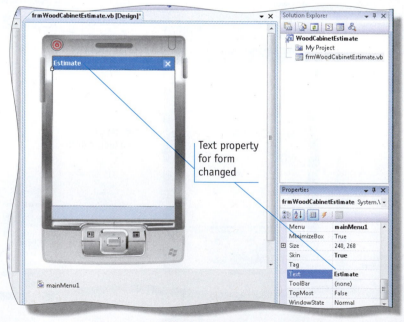

Text property for form changed

FIGURE 5-10

You can place objects such as a Label object, a TextBox object, and a Button object on the Pocket PC form by dragging them from the Toolbox to the Pocket PC form, as you did with a Windows application. Therefore, to place the labels, text box, and buttons on the form for the sample program, you can drag the objects from the Toolbox onto the form.

Similar to Windows forms, you can align the objects using snap lines and the align tools. The (Name) property, Text property, Visible property, and Enabled property work the same for a Pocket PC Form object as for a Windows Form object. Most objects in the Toolbox are identical in purpose for both Windows and mobile applications. The few exceptions are explained later in the chapter.

While creating the design is the same as a Windows application, one coding change in Smart Device applications involves the TextBox object. The Clear procedure you used in Chapter 4 to clear the TextBox object is not available for Smart Devices. When clearing a TextBox on a Pocket PC form, assign a null string ("") to the TextBox just as you do for the Label object.

USING THE PANEL OBJECT

The Wood Cabinet Estimate application requires two new types of objects: RadioButton objects and a Panel object (Figure 5-11).

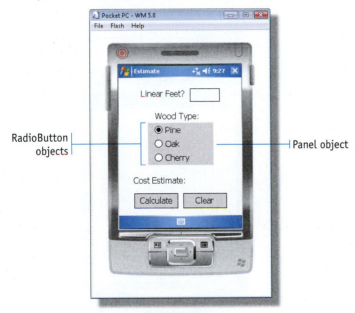

FIGURE 5-11

A Panel object associates items as a group, allowing the user to select one item from the group. RadioButton objects allow the user to make choices. In Figure 5-11, the Panel object groups the radio buttons with which the user can select the wood type. When RadioButton objects are contained in a panel, the user can select only one of the radio buttons. For example, in Figure 5-11 the Cherry radio button is selected. If the user clicks the Oak radio button, it will be selected and the Cherry radio button automatically will be deselected.

The Panel object is one of two **container objects** you can use in a Pocket PC application to group other objects. The other container object is the TabControl object, which generates tabbed pages where you can group objects on separate pages.

The Panel object shown in Figure 5-11 is displayed with a LightGray BackColor. The prefix for the Panel object (Name) property is pnl. To place a Panel object on the Pocket PC Form object, you can complete the following steps:

STEP 1 If necessary, open the Device Containers category of the Toolbox by clicking the plus sign next to the category name. Drag the Panel .NET component in the Device Containers category of the Toolbox over the Pocket PC Form object to the approximate location where you want to place the Panel object.

The mouse pointer changes when you place it over the Pocket PC Form object (Figure 5-12). The Panel object will be placed on the form at the location of the shaded square in the pointer.

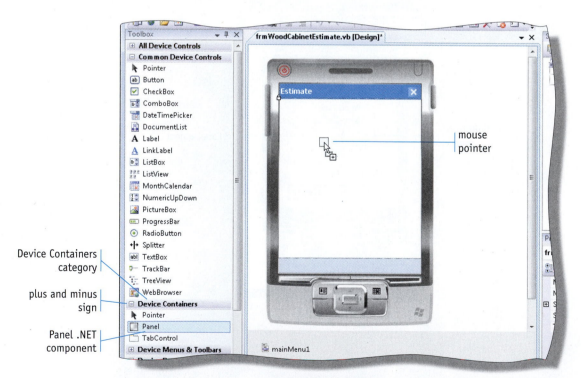

FIGURE 5-12

STEP 2 When the mouse pointer is in the correct location, release the left mouse button. Increase the size of the Panel object to the approximate size shown in Figure 5-13 by dragging the lower-right sizing handle.

The Panel object is placed and sized on the form (Figure 5-13). If you want to move the panel to another location on the form, place the mouse pointer over the drag box on the border of the panel and then drag the panel to the desired location.

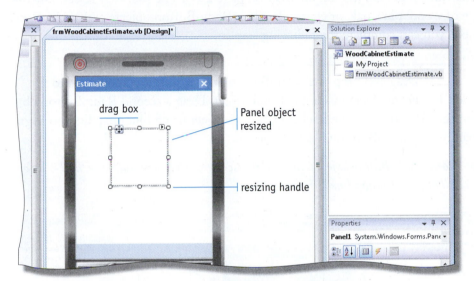

FIGURE 5-13

STEP 3 With the Panel object selected, scroll in the Properties window to the (Name) property. Double-click in the right column of the (Name) property and then enter the name `pnlWoodType`.

The name you entered is displayed in the (Name) property in the Properties window (Figure 5-14).

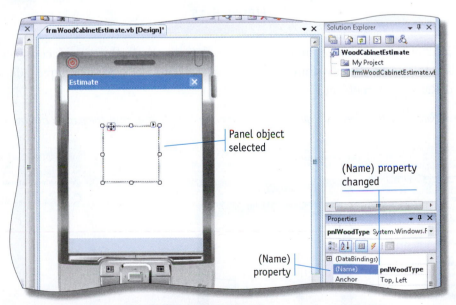

FIGURE 5-14

ONLINE REINFORCEMENT

To view a video of the process in the previous steps, visit scsite.com/vb2008/ch5 and then select Figure 5-12.

Grouping all options in a Panel object gives the user a logical visual cue. Also, when you move the Panel object, all its contained objects move as well.

ADDING THE RADIOBUTTON OBJECTS

Inside the Panel object in the Wood Cabinet Estimate application is a set of RadioButton objects (see Figure 5-11 on page 299). The user may select only one type of wood: pine, oak, or cherry. To place RadioButton objects within the Panel object, you can complete the following steps:

STEP 1 Drag and drop one RadioButton object from the Toolbox onto the Pocket PC Form object inside the Panel object. Drag a second RadioButton object from the Toolbox onto the Pocket PC Form object using blue snap lines to align and separate the RadioButton objects vertically.

The second RadioButton object is aligned vertically with a blue snap line, and is separated vertically by a blue snap line (Figure 5-15).

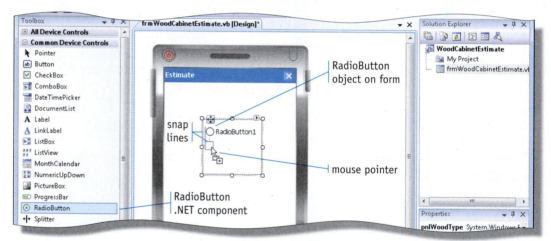

FIGURE 5-15

STEP 2 Release the left mouse button to place the RadioButton object on the Pocket PC Form object within the Panel object. Using the same technique, add a third RadioButton object.

Three RadioButton objects are placed on the form and aligned within the panel (Figure 5-16).

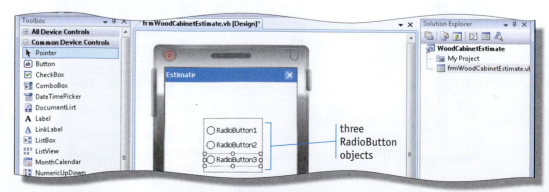

FIGURE 5-16

STEP 3 Name the RadioButton objects by selecting a RadioButton object, double-clicking in the right column of the (Name) property in the Properties window, and entering the name. The names for the radio buttons, from top to bottom, should be radPine, radOak, and radCherry.

The (Name) property is selected (Figure 5-17). The names radPine, radOak, and radCherry are entered.

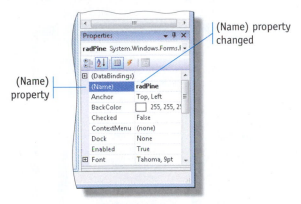

FIGURE 5-17

STEP 4 Change the Text property for each RadioButton by double-clicking in the right column of the Text property and typing `Pine` for the first RadioButton, `Oak` for the second RadioButton and `Cherry` for the third RadioButton.

The Text property has been changed to the types of wood available: Pine, Oak, and Cherry (Figure 5-18).

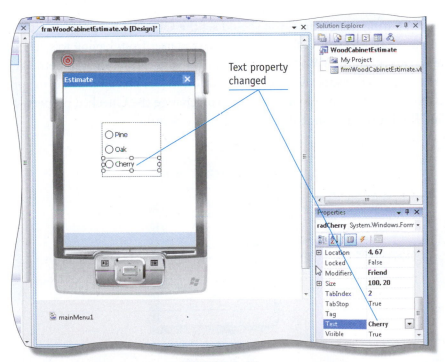

FIGURE 5-18

ONLINE REINFORCEMENT

To view a video of the process in the previous steps, visit scsite.com/vb2008/ch5 and then select Figure 5-15

USING THE CHECKED PROPERTY OF RADIOBUTTON OBJECTS

You will recall that the RadioButton objects in the Wood Cabinet Estimate application allow the user to select one wood type. When the user selects Cherry as the wood type as shown in Figure 5-19, the RadioButton is selected (the small circle in the radio button is shaded). When a RadioButton is selected, the Checked property of the Cherry RadioButton changes from False (unselected) to True (selected).

Cherry
selected

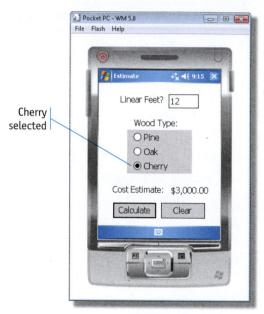

FIGURE 5-19

Often, during design time, you should set the Checked property to True for the most commonly selected RadioButton to save the user from having to select the most common choice. In the Wood Cabinet Estimate application, the cabinetmaker uses Pine most often. To cause the Pine RadioButton object named radPine to appear selected (shaded) when the program begins, you change the Checked property for the radPine RadioButton from False to True (Figure 5-20).

Checked
property is True

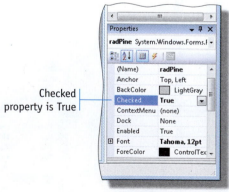

FIGURE 5-20

WINDOWS APPLICATION CONTAINER OBJECTS

The Panel object in a Windows application performs in the same manner as the Panel object in the Pocket PC application. For Windows applications, Visual Basic provides five additional container objects: FlowLayoutPanel, GroupBox, SplitContainer, TabControl, and TableLayoutPanel. The GroupBox object, which is not available in a Pocket PC application, is used most often. It provides several options not available with the Panel object. The table in Figure 5-21 shows the differences between the GroupBox and the Panel objects.

Option	GroupBox Object	Panel Object
Have a caption	Yes	No
Have scroll bars	Yes	No
Display a labeled border	Yes	No

FIGURE 5-21

Figure 5-22 shows the Windows application Toolbox, the Containers group of .NET components, and a GroupBox object and a Panel object in a Windows application. Notice in the Toolbox that the GroupBox and Panel objects are in a subcategory called Containers.

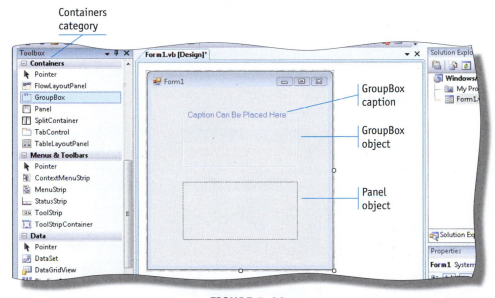

FIGURE 5-22

The GroupBox object in Figure 5-22 displays a border around the edges of the object with a text area in the upper-left for a caption. The Panel object has a black dashed border that does not appear when the application is executed. GroupBox and Panel objects have the same purpose of grouping RadioButtons and other objects, but they differ in their appearance.

Related RadioButtons should be placed in a separate container object so that the user can select one radio button from each group. Always place the container object on the form first, and then drag the RadioButton objects on top of the container object.

The Course Sign-Up example in Figure 5-23 displays a Windows application that allows the user to sign up for a Web Design course. Notice the two separate groups of RadioButton objects. In the Choose Course Level GroupBox object, the user should select a course level. In the Choose Semester GroupBox object, the user should identify the semester for the course. As you can see, the user selects one radio button from the left group and one radio button from the right group.

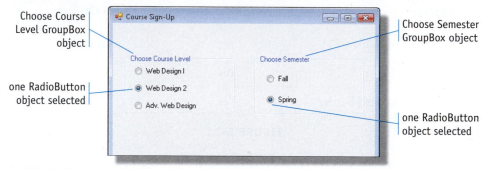

FIGURE 5-23

DISPLAYING A MESSAGE BOX

In the Wood Cabinet Estimate chapter project, a message box, also called a dialog box, opens if the user does not enter the length of the cabinets correctly. The dialog box displays an error message if the user omits the length of the cabinets or enters nonnumeric data (Figure 5-24).

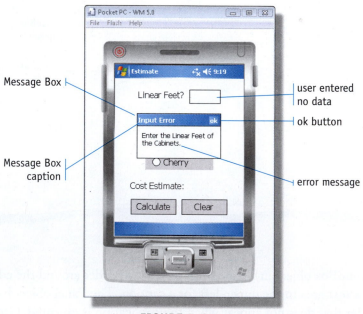

FIGURE 5-24

This message box reminds the user to enter the linear feet of the cabinets. A message box window must be closed before the application can continue. The user can continue the application by clicking ok in the upper-right corner of the message box.

In Visual Basic, the message to the user in a message box window is displayed using a procedure named Show that is found in the MessageBox class. The syntax for the statement to display a message in a message box is:

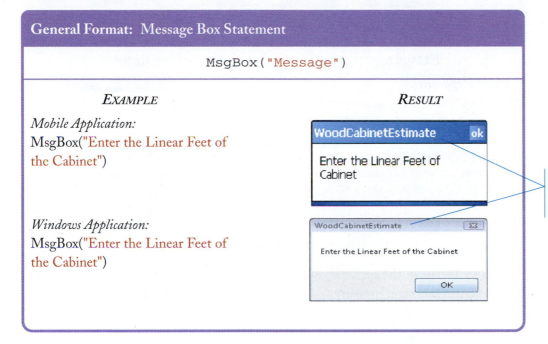

General Format: Message Box Statement

MsgBox("Message")

EXAMPLE	RESULT
Mobile Application: MsgBox("Enter the Linear Feet of the Cabinet")	**WoodCabinetEstimate** ok Enter the Linear Feet of Cabinet
Windows Application: MsgBox("Enter the Linear Feet of the Cabinet")	WoodCabinetEstimate ⊠ Enter the Linear Feet of the Cabinet OK

name of project is displayed in the title bar by default

FIGURE 5-25

The string message shown in the parentheses will appear in the message box when the code is executed. The string message is considered an argument of the procedure. You will recall that an argument is a value that is passed to a procedure. The first argument for the MsgBox command contains the message to be printed in the message box window on top of the form during execution.

The first example in Figure 5-25 illustrates the code that could be used in the Calculate button click event handler. This code could be executed if the user clicks the Calculate button without entering a numeric value in the Linear Feet text box (see Figure 5-24 on page 306).

Although a message box in a Smart Device application looks different from a message box in a Windows application, they are coded in the same way. In the second example in Figure 5-25, the message box is displayed in a Windows application.

Displaying Message Box Captions

A message box can be displayed during execution with a variety of arguments. For example, a message box can display a message and a caption in the title bar (two arguments with two commas between the two arguments) with the following syntax:

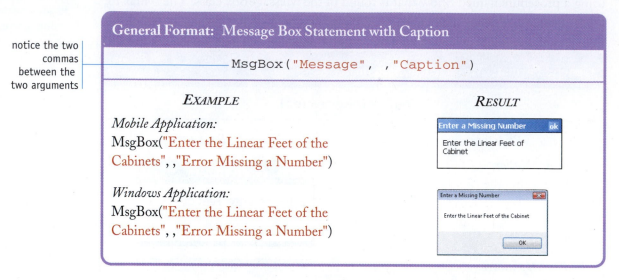

notice the two commas between the two arguments

General Format: Message Box Statement with Caption

MsgBox("Message", ,"Caption")

EXAMPLE

Mobile Application:
MsgBox("Enter the Linear Feet of the Cabinets", ,"Error Missing a Number")

Windows Application:
MsgBox("Enter the Linear Feet of the Cabinets", ,"Error Missing a Number")

RESULT

FIGURE 5-26

The title bars in the examples in Figure 5-26 display a caption and the message box displays a message. In many applications, the caption is used to give further information to the user.

Message Box Buttons

For message boxes displayed in a Windows application but not in a mobile application, buttons other than the OK button can be displayed. The general format for changing the button command from OK to another button type is shown in Figure 5-27. The button entry can be a command or a value representing a command.

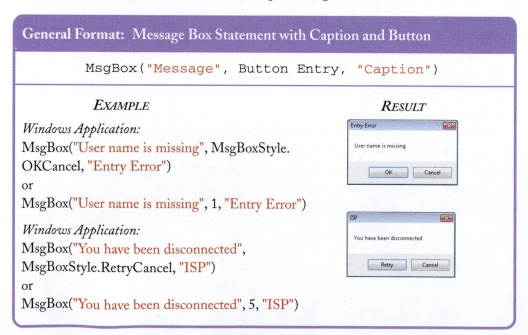

General Format: Message Box Statement with Caption and Button

MsgBox("Message", Button Entry, "Caption")

EXAMPLE

Windows Application:
MsgBox("User name is missing", MsgBoxStyle.
OKCancel, "Entry Error")
or
MsgBox("User name is missing", 1, "Entry Error")

Windows Application:
MsgBox("You have been disconnected",
MsgBoxStyle.RetryCancel, "ISP")
or
MsgBox("You have been disconnected", 5, "ISP")

RESULT

FIGURE 5-27

In the first example in Figure 5-27, the buttons specified are the OK button and the Cancel button. In the second example, the buttons shown are the Retry button and the Cancel button.

The table in Figure 5-28 shows all the possible entries that can be placed in the Button Entry portion of the argument passed to the Show procedure.

MsgBoxButtons Arguments	Value	Use
MsgBoxStyle.OKOnly	0	Displays an OK button — default setting
MsgBoxStyle.OKCancel	1	Displays an OK and Cancel button
MsgBoxStyle.AbortRetryIgnore	2	After a failing situation, the user can choose to Abort, Retry, or Ignore
MsgBoxStyle.YesNoCancel	3	Displays Yes, No, and Cancel buttons
MsgBoxStyle.YesNo	4	Displays Yes and No buttons
MsgBoxStyle.RetryCancel	5	After an error occurs, the user can choose to Retry or Cancel

FIGURE 5-28

Message Box Icons

In the button entry portion of the argument (the second argument), a message box icon can be added (Figure 5-29). The word "or" connects the button entry to the icon entry.

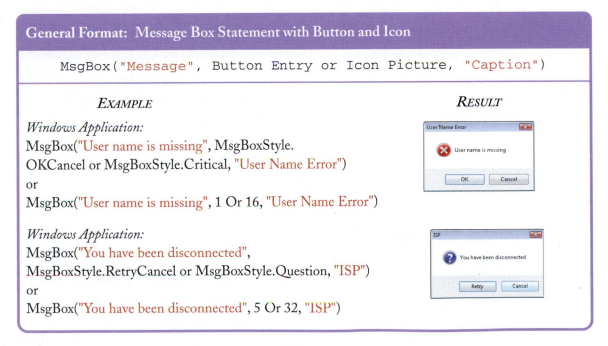

General Format: Message Box Statement with Button and Icon

MsgBox("Message", Button Entry or Icon Picture, "Caption")

EXAMPLE   RESULT

Windows Application:
MsgBox("User name is missing", MsgBoxStyle.
OKCancel or MsgBoxStyle.Critical, "User Name Error")
or
MsgBox("User name is missing", 1 Or 16, "User Name Error")

Windows Application:
MsgBox("You have been disconnected",
MsgBoxStyle.RetryCancel or MsgBoxStyle.Question, "ISP")
or
MsgBox("You have been disconnected", 5 Or 32, "ISP")

FIGURE 5-29

The picture icon represents the MsgBoxStyle that can be displayed as a graphic icon in the message box. Both examples in Figure 5-29 show a graphic icon added to the message box.

The picture icon in the second argument can contain any of the entries shown in Figure 5-30.

MsgBoxStyle Icons	Value	Icon	Use
MsgBoxStyle.Critical	16	❌	Alerts the user to an error
MsgBoxStyle.Question	32	❓	Displays a question mark
MsgBoxStyle.Exclamation	48	⚠️	Alerts the user to a possible problem
MsgBoxStyle.Information	64	ℹ️	Displays an information icon

FIGURE 5-30

In the general formats shown for a message box, you must follow the syntax of the statements exactly, which means the commas, quotation marks, and parentheses must be placed in the statement as shown in the general formats.

You can also add values to display both the buttons and a picture icon. In Figure 5-31, the value of the message button type AbortRetryIgnore is 2 and the value of the critical icon is 16. If you add 16 plus 2, the result is 18.

General Format: MsgBox("Message", Button Entry Value + Icon Picture Value, "Caption")

EXAMPLE

Windows Application:
MsgBox("Enter a Number Only", 18, "Illegal Operation")

RESULT

FIGURE 5-31

Message Box IntelliSense

When you enter the code for a message box, IntelliSense can assist you. To use IntelliSense to enter code for the message box shown in Figure 5-29 that contains a message, caption, and button, you can follow the steps on the next page:

STEP 1   In the code editing window, inside the event handler you are coding, type `msg` to display MsgBox in the IntelliSense list.

IntelliSense displays a list of the allowable entries (Figure 5-32). When you type msg, MsgBox is selected in the IntelliSense list.

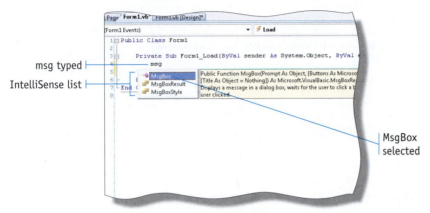

msg typed

IntelliSense list

MsgBox selected

FIGURE 5-32

STEP 2   Press the Tab key to select MsgBox from the IntelliSense list. Type the following text: (`"You have been disconnected from the Internet",`)

The first argument for the message box is entered (Figure 5-33). IntelliSense displays a list of the allowable entries for the second argument.

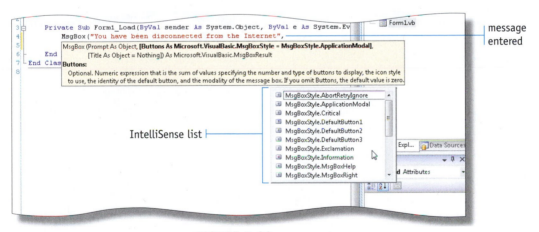

message entered

IntelliSense list

FIGURE 5-33

STEP 3 Type a space and then select the MsgBoxStyle.AbortRetryIgnore argument by pressing the DOWN ARROW key on the keyboard one time.

The MsgBoxStyle.AbortRetryIgnore argument is selected (Figure 5–34).

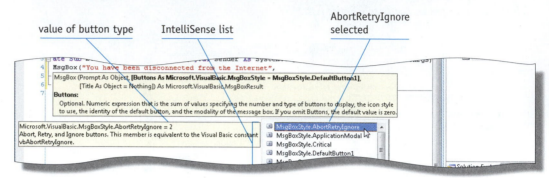

FIGURE 5-34

STEP 4 Type a comma. Then type "ISP" and a right parenthesis.

After the comma is typed following the second argument, the caption "ISP" is typed with a right parenthesis (Figure 5–35).

FIGURE 5-35

STEP 5 Click the Start Debugging button on the Standard toolbar.

The application runs, displaying the message box that shows the message, buttons, and caption (Figure 5-36).

FIGURE 5-36

STRING CONCATENATION

Recall that when the Wood Cabinet Estimate application runs, the user enters the linear footage of the wood cabinets. If the user enters a number that is not greater than zero, such as −10, a message box appears that states "You entered −10. Enter a Number Greater Than Zero." as shown in Figure 5-37.

message box with error message

message created using concatenation

FIGURE 5-37

To create the message in the message box, you can use concatenation, which you learned about in Chapter 4. In Figure 5-37, the string message is constructed by joining a string ("You entered"), a variable named decFootage containing the linear footage entered (which must be converted to a string), and a string for the final part of the message (". Enter a Number Greater Than Zero."). The code in Figure 5-38 creates the desired message box.

```
MsgBox("You entered " & decLinearFeet.ToString() & _
    ". Enter a Number Greater Than Zero.", "Input Error")
```

FIGURE 5-38

You will recall that the operator to concatenate strings is the ampersand (&). When the statement is executed, the three string elements are joined together (concatenated) to form the one string that is displayed in the message box.

Making Decisions with Conditional Statements

In the Wood Cabinet Estimate chapter project, which calculates the cost of wood cabinets, the application allows the user to select one of three different types of wood: pine, oak, or cherry. The price per square foot is based on the user's choice of wood. To select the wood type, the user must click one of three radio buttons titled Pine, Oak, and Cherry. Then, based on the choice, the application uses a different wood cost.

Visual Basic uses decision structures to deal with the different conditions that occur based on the values entered into an application. A **decision structure** is one of the three fundamental control structures used in computer programming. For example, if the user clicks the Pine radio button, the wood cost is set to $100.00 per linear foot. The statement that tests the radio button is called a **conditional statement**. The condition checked is whether the Pine radio button is selected. If so, the wood cost is set to $100.00.

When a condition is tested in a Visual Basic program, the condition either is true or false. For example, when checking to determine if the Pine radio button is selected, the condition can either be true (the Pine radio button is checked) or false (the Pine radio button is not checked). All conditional statements result in the tested condition either being true or false.

To implement a conditional statement and the statements that are executed when a condition is true and the statements that are executed when a condition is false, Visual Basic uses the If statement and its variety of formats. You will learn about the If statement in the following sections.

USING AN IF...THEN STATEMENT

In the sample program, an If...Then statement is used to determine the cost of the wood. The simplest form of the If...Then statement is shown in Figure 5-39.

```
5        If condition Then
6            Statement(s) executed when condition is true
7        End If
8
```

FIGURE 5-39

In Figure 5-39, when the condition tested in the If statement on line 5 is true, the statement(s) between the If and the End If keywords will be executed. If the condition is not true, no statements between the If and End If keywords will be executed, and program execution will continue with the statement(s) that follows the End If statement.

Visual Basic automatically indents statements to be executed when a condition is true or not true to indicate the lines of code are within the conditional If...Then structure. This is why the statement on line 6 in Figure 5-39 is indented. The End If keyword terminates the If...Then block of code. After executing the If...Then block of code, execution continues with any statements that follow the closing End If statement.

HEADS UP

If Visual Basic does not automatically indent the code in an If...Then statement, follow these steps:
1) Click Tools on the menu bar at the top of the screen and then click Options; 2) If necessary, click the triangle next to Text Editor in the left panel; 3) If necessary, click the triangle next to Basic in the left panel; 4) If necessary, click VB Specific in the left panel; 5) Ensure the Pretty listing (reformatting) of code check box contains a check mark; 6) Click the OK button in the Options dialog box.

RELATIONAL OPERATORS

In Figure 5-39 on page 314, the condition portion of the If...Then statement means a condition is tested to determine if it is true or false. The conditions that can be tested are:

1. Is one value equal to another value?
2. Is one value not equal to another value?
3. Is one value greater than another value?
4. Is one value less than another value?
5. Is one value greater than or equal to another value?
6. Is one value less than or equal to another value?

To test these conditions, Visual Basic provides relational operators that are used within the conditional statement to express the relationship being tested. The table in Figure 5-40 shows these relational operators.

	Relational Operator	Meaning	Example	Resulting Condition
1	=	Equal to	8 = 8	True
2	<>	Not equal to	6 <> 6	False
3	>	Greater than	7 > 9	False
4	<	Less than	4 < 6	True
5	>=	Greater than or equal to	3 >= 3	True
6	<=	Less than or equal to	7 <= 5	False

FIGURE 5-40

A condition tested using a relational operator is evaluated as true or false. Example 1 tests whether 8 is equal to 8. Because it is, the resulting condition is true. Example 2 tests if 6 is not equal to 6. Because they are equal, the resulting condition is false. Similarly, example 5 tests if 3 is greater than or equal to 3. Because they are equal, the resulting condition is true.

As an example of using a conditional operator, consider the following problem where an If statement is used to determine if someone is old enough to vote. If the value in the intAge variable is greater than or equal to 18, then the person is old enough to vote. If not, the person is not old enough to vote. The If...Then statement to test this condition is shown in Figure 5-41.

```
8        If intAge >= 18 Then
9            Me.lblVotingEligibility.Text = "You are old enough to vote"
10       End If
```

FIGURE 5-41

In Figure 5-41, if the value in the intAge variable is greater than or equal to 18, the string value "You are old enough to vote" is assigned to the Text property of the lblVotingEligibility Label object. If not, then no processing occurs based on the conditional statement and any statement(s) following the End If keyword will be executed.

You can see in Figure 5-41 that several keywords are required in an If...Then statement. The word If must be the first item. Then, the condition(s) to be tested are stated, followed by the word Then. This keyword is required in an If statement.

Following the statements to be executed when the condition is true is the End If keyword. This entry also is required. It signals to the Visual Basic compiler that statements following it are to be executed regardless of the result of the conditional statement; that is, the End If keyword is the last element within the If block and no subsequent statements depend on it for execution.

To enter the If...Then statement shown in Figure 5-41, you can complete the steps on the following pages:

STEP 1 With the insertion point in the correct location in the code, type `if` and then press the SPACEBAR.

The statement begins with the word if (Figure 5–42). The If command is displayed in blue because it is a Visual Basic keyword. You can type uppercase or lowercase letters. IntelliSense lists the possible entries.

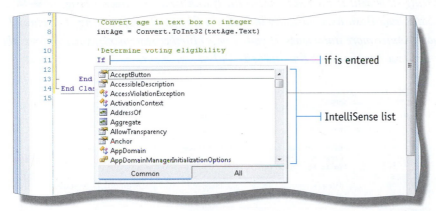

FIGURE 5-42

STEP 2 Type `inta` to select the variable named intAge in the IntelliSense list. Then, type `>=18` as the condition to be tested. Press the ENTER key.

The If…Then statement is entered in the code editing window (Figure 5–43). When the ENTER key is pressed, Visual Basic adds the keyword Then to the end of the If statement line of code and inserts spaces between the elements in the statement for ease of reading. In addition, Visual Basic inserts the End If keyword following a blank line. Notice the keywords Then and End If are capitalized and displayed in blue.

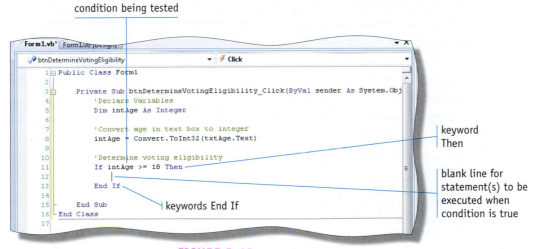

FIGURE 5-43

STEP 3 On the blank line (line 12 in Figure 5-43), enter the statement that should be executed when the condition is true. To place the message, "You are old enough to vote" in the Text property of the lblVotingEligibility Label object, insert the code shown in Figure 5-41 on page 316. Remember to use IntelliSense to reference the lblVotingEligibility Label object.

The resulting statement is entered between the If and End If keywords (Figure 5-44). Notice that Visual Basic automatically indents the line for ease of reading. The blank line allows you to enter more statements. If you have no further statements, you can press the DELETE key to delete the blank line in the If...Then statement.

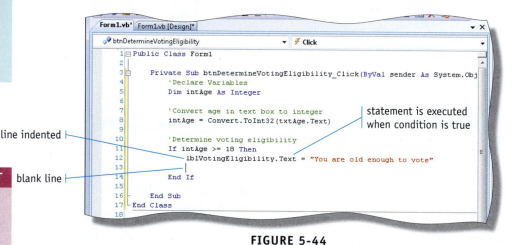

line indented

blank line

FIGURE 5-44

Comparing Strings

You also can write an If...Then statement using the relational operators shown in Figure 5-40 to compare string values. A string value comparison compares each character in two strings, starting with the first character in each string. For example, in the two strings in Figure 5-45, the comparison begins with the first character in each string, a. Because the characters are equal, the comparison continues with the second character in each string, b. Because these characters are equal, the comparison continues with the third characters in each string, c. Because all three character are equal, the strings are considered equal and the resulting condition from the If statement is true.

```
13        Dim String1 As String = "abc"
14        Dim String2 As String = "abc"
15
16        If String1 = String2 Then
17            Me.lblStringTest.Text = "Equal"
18        End If
```

FIGURE 5-45

All characters found in strings, including letters, numbers, and special characters are in a sequence from low to high based on the manner in which the characters are coded internally on the computer. When using Visual Studio 2008, characters are stored and sequenced in Unicode, which is a coding methodology that can accommodate more than 60,000 characters. Appendix A in this book shows the Unicode sequence for the standard keyboard characters. You will find that the numbers are considered less than uppercase letters, and uppercase letters are considered less than lowercase letters.

Using the If...Then statement, the following comparisons produce the following resulting conditions:

Example 1:

```
Dim String1 As String = "Powder"
Dim String2 As String = "Power"

If String1 < String2 Then
```

Resulting Condition: True because in the fourth character position, the letter d is less than the letter e.

Example 2:

```
Dim String1 As String = "6"
Dim String2 As String = "T"

If String1 < String2 Then
```

Resulting Condition: True because in a string comparison, a number is less than an uppercase letter.

Example 3:

```
Dim String1 As String = "12"
Dim String2 As String = "9"

If String1 < String2 Then
```

Resulting Condition: True because in a string comparison, the characters in the first position of the string are compared first. Because the value 1 in String1 is less than the value 9 in String2, the entire value in String1 is considered less than the value in String2.

Example 4:

```
Dim String1 As String = "anchor"
Dim String2 As String = "Anchorline"

If String1 > String2 Then
```

Resulting Condition: True because a lowercase letter (the a in the first position of String1) is considered greater than an uppercase letter (the A in the first position of String2).

COMPARING DIFFERENT DATA TYPES

Every type of data available in Visual Basic can be compared. Different numeric types can be compared to each other using an If statement. A single string character can be compared to a Char data type. The following examples illustrate some of the allowable comparisons.

Example 1: Decimal compared to Double

```
If decQuarterlySales > dblSalesQuota Then
```

If decQuarterlySales = 110,324.54 and dblSalesQuota = 112,435.54, the condition is false.

Example 2: Decimal compared to Integer

```
If decTirePressureReading > intTirePressureMaximum Then
```

If decTirePressureReading = 30.21 and intTirePressureMaximum = 30, the condition is true.

Example 3: Double compared to Integer

```
If dblCurrentTemperature >= intHeatDanger Then
```

If dblCurrentTemperature = 94.543 and intHeatDanger = 98, the condition is false.

Example 4: String compared to Char

```
If strChemistryGrade < chrPassingGrade Then
```

If strChemistryGrade = "B" and chrPassingGrade = "C", the condition is true.

Visual Basic allows comparisons between most data types. If you are unsure whether a comparison can be made, write an If statement to ensure the comparison is working properly.

USING THE IF...THEN...ELSE STATEMENT

An If...Then statement executes a set of instructions if a condition is true. If the condition is false, the instructions between the If statement and the End If statement are not executed and program execution continues with the statement(s) following the End If statement.

In many applications, the logic requires one set of instructions to be executed if a condition is true, and another set of instructions to be executed if a condition is false. For example, a requirement in a program could specify that if a student's test score is 70 or greater, a message stating "You passed the examination" should be displayed, while if the test score is less than 70, a message stating "You failed the examination" should be displayed.

To execute one set of instructions if a condition is true, and another set of instructions if the condition is false, you can use the If...Then...Else statement. Figure 5-46 illustrates the syntax of the If...Then...Else statement:

```
16          If condition Then
17              Statement(s) executed if condition is true
18          Else
19              Statement(s) executed if condition is false
20          End If
```

FIGURE 5-46

In the code in Figure 5-46, if the condition tested by the If statement is true, the statement(s) between the Then keyword and the Else keyword will be executed. If the condition tested is false, the statement(s) between the Else keyword and the End If keyword will be executed.

The example in Figure 5-47 shows the use of the If...Then...Else statement to calculate student fees by testing the student status.

statement is executed if
student is a graduate

```
27          If strStudentStatus = "Graduate" Then
28              decStudentFees = decGraduateFee * intNumberOfUnits
29          Else
30              decStudentFees = decUndergraduateFee * intNumberOfUnits
31          End If
```

statement is executed if
student is not a graduate

FIGURE 5-47

If the student is a graduate student, the student fees are calculated by multiplying the graduate fee times the number of units. If the student is not a graduate student, the student fees are calculated by multiplying the undergraduate fee times the number of units. Notice that a student cannot be both an undergraduate student and a graduate student, so either the statement following the Then keyword will be executed or the statement following the Else keyword will be executed.

HEADS UP

A condition cannot be true and false at the same time, so statements for a true condition and statements for a false condition cannot both be executed based on a single comparison.

Comparing to an Arithmetic Expression

An If statement can compare an arithmetic expression to a constant or other data type. For example, in Figure 5-48, the withdrawals from a bank account are compared to the value obtained by adding the current balance to deposits and then subtracting account charges.

```
41      If decWithdrawals > decCurrentBalance + decDeposits - decAccountCharges Then
42          Me.lblAccountStatus.Text = "Overdrawn"
43      Else
44          Me.lblAccountStatus.Text = "Balance is Positive"
45      End If
```

FIGURE 5-48

In Figure 5-48, if the value in the decWithdrawals variable is greater than the current balance plus the deposits minus the account charges, the Text property of the lblAccountStatus Label object is set to Overdrawn. If the value in decWithdrawals is less than or equal to the value from the arithmetic expression, the message Balance is Positive is placed in the Text property of the lblAccountStatus Label object. Notice that the arithmetic expression is evaluated prior to the comparison. If the condition is true, the statement between the Then and Else keywords is executed. If the condition is false, the statement between the Else and End If keywords is executed.

USING THE IF...THEN...ELSEIF STATEMENT

Complex logic problems might require a more complex structure than the If...Then...Else logic structure. For example, consider the following logical problem that must be solved in a computer program:

An online store charges a shipping amount based on the dollar amount of the order being shipped. The rules are: 1) If the order amount is above $500, the shipping cost is $30; 2) If the order amount is more than $400 and not greater than $500, the shipping cost is $25; 3) If the order amount is more than $200 and not greater than $400, the shipping cost is $20; 4) If the order amount is equal to or less than $200, the shipping cost is $15.

When one of the conditions is found to be true, the rest of the conditions are not tested because the correct condition has been found. To solve this problem, you should think this way:

1. If the order amount is greater than $500.00, then the shipping cost is $30.00 and no more processing must be done to determine the shipping cost.
2. If, however, the order amount is not greater than $500.00, I must check further to see if it is greater than $400.00 (400.01 through 500.00). If so, the shipping cost is $25.00.

3. If the order amount is not greater than $400.00, the next step is to check if it is greater than $200.00. Notice that if it is greater than $200.00 but not greater than $400.00, it must be in the range $201.00 to $400.00. If this is true, the shipping cost is $20.00
4. If none of the above is true, then the order amount must be less than or equal to $200. In this case, the shipping cost is $15.00.

As you can see, a simple If...Then...Else statement could not solve this logic problem because the If...Then...Else structure tests only a single condition and specifies the processing based on whether the condition is true or false. For a problem where multiple conditions must be tested, the If...Then...ElseIf statement might be appropriate. The general format of the If...Then...ElseIf statement is shown in Figure 5-49.

```
105         If decOrderAmount > 500D Then
106             Statement(s) executed if condition is true
107         ElseIf decOrderAmount > 400D Then
108             Statement(s) executed if condition is true
109         ElseIf decOrderAmount > 200D Then
110             Statement(s) executed if condition is true
111         ElseIf decOrderAmount > 0D Then
112             Statement(s) executed if condition is true
113         End If
```

FIGURE 5-49

Once a condition in the code in Figure 5-49 is true, Visual Basic bypasses the rest of the ElseIf statements. For example, assume the order amount is $455. The first condition tests if the order amount is greater than 500.00. The first condition would test false because 455.00 is not greater than 500.00.

Next, the ElseIf entry will test if 455.00 is greater than 400.00. Because the value 455.00 is greater than 400.00, the condition is true and the statement(s) on line 108 will be executed. The remaining ElseIf statements will not be evaluated because the true condition has been found.

Separate If...Then statements are not used in the example in Figure 5-49 because each condition would have to be tested even though a condition had already been found to be true. When using an If...Then...ElseIf statement, after the condition is found to be true, the rest of the conditions are not tested, making the process faster and more efficient.

HEADS UP

When testing conditions like those in the example in Figure 5-49, make sure you do not leave a number out of the range of numbers being tested. For example, if one ElseIf statement tests decAmountSpent > 400.00 and the next ElseIf statement tests < 400.00, the value 400.00 has not been tested and the program will not properly process the value 400.00.

Trailing Else Statements

You may want to include a trailing Else statement at the end of an If...Then...ElseIf conditional statement to handle a condition that does not meet any of the conditions tested. In the example in Figure 5-50, the code is determining if the user is eligible for Social Security benefits. If the user's age is greater than or equal to 65, the user receives full benefits. If the user's age is between 0 and 65, the user is not eligible for benefits.

```
115          If intAge >= 65 Then
116              Me.lblSocialSecurity.Text = "Full Benefits"
117          ElseIf intAge > 0 Then
118              Me.lblSocialSecurity.Text = "Not Eligible for Benefits"
119          Else
120              Me.lblSocialSecurity.Text = "Invalid Age"
121          End If
```

FIGURE 5-50

In Figure 5-50, the statement on line 120 that follows the trailing Else statement on line 119 is executed if the number in the intAge variable does not meet the conditions stated in the previous If statements. For example, if the intAge variable contains a negative value such as −12, the Text property of the lblSocialSecurity Label object will be set to "Invalid Age".

NESTED IF STATEMENTS

At times, more than one decision has to be made to determine what processing must occur. For example, if one condition is true, a second condition may need to be tested before the correct code is executed. To test a second condition only after determining a first condition is true (or false), you must place an If statement within another If statement. When you place one If statement within another If statement, the inner If statement is said to be nested within the outer If Statement. The syntax of a nested If statement is shown in Figure 5-51:

nested If statement – (first inner If statement)

```
123          If first condition Then
124              If second condition Then
125                  Statement(s) executed if condition 1 is true and condition 2 is true
126              Else
127                  Statement(s) executed if condition 1 is true and condition 2 is false
128              End If          ──── end of first inner If statement
129          Else
130              If third condition Then
131                  Statement(s) executed if condition 1 is false and condition 3 is true
132              Else
133                  Statement(s) executed if condition 1 is false and condition 3 is false
134              End If          ──── end of second inner If statement
135          End If
```

nested If statement – (second inner If statement)

end of first If statement

FIGURE 5-51

In Figure 5-51, if the first condition tested is true, the statements following the keyword Then are executed. The statement to be executed when the first condition is true is another If statement (line 124) that tests the second condition. This second If statement is said to be a nested If statement, and also is termed an inner If statement. If the second condition is true, the statement(s) on line 125 following the keyword Then for the first inner If statement are executed. If the second condition is not true, the statement(s) on line 127 following the keyword Else for the first inner If statement are executed. Following the first inner If statement is the End If entry (line 128), which indicates the end of the effect of the first inner If statement.

If the first condition is not true, then the statements following the keyword Else on line 129 for the first If statement are executed. The statement to be executed when the first condition is not true is an If statement that tests the third condition (line 130). If the third condition is true, the statement(s) on line 131 following the Then keyword of the second inner If statement are executed. Finally, if the second inner If statement that tests the third condition is false, the statement(s) on line 133 are executed for the case when condition 1 is false and condition 3 is false.

To illustrate a nested If statement, assume a college has the following admissions policy: If an applying student has a GPA greater than 3.5 and an SAT score greater than 1000, then that student is granted admission. If an applying student has a GPA greater than 3.5 but an SAT score of 1000 or lower, the student is advised to retake the SAT exam. If an applying student has a GPA of 3.5 or lower but an SAT score greater than 1200, the student is granted a probationary admission, which means a 2.5 GPA must be achieved in the first semester of college. If an applying student has a GPA lower than 3.5 and an SAT score of 1200 or lower, the student is denied admission. The nested If statement to process this admission policy is shown in Figure 5-52.

```
140          If decGPA > 3.5D Then
141              If intSatScore > 1000 Then
142                  lblAdmissionStatus.Text = "You have earned admission"
143              Else
144                  lblAdmissionStatus.Text = "Retake the SAT exam"
145              End If
146          Else
147              If intSatScore > 1200 Then
148                  lblAdmissionStatus.Text = "You have earned probationary admission"
149              Else
150                  lblAdmissionStatus.Text = "You have been denied admission"
151              End If
152          End If
```

FIGURE 5-52

Notice in Figure 5-52 that the test for greater than 1000 on the SAT (line 141) must take place only after the test for a GPA greater than 3.5 (line 140) because the test for greater than 1000 is required only after it has been determined that the GPS is greater than 3.5. Therefore, a nested If statement is required. In addition, the test for greater than 1200 (line 147) should occur only after it has been determined that the GPA is less than 3.5. As you can see, you should use a nested If statement when a condition must be tested only after another condition has been tested.

Other Nested If Configurations

You can use nested If statements in a variety of forms. Assume, for example, that the admissions policy for a different school is as follows: If an applying student has a GPA greater than 3.5 and an SAT score greater than 1100, then that student is granted admission. If an applying student has a GPA greater than 3.5 but an SAT score of 1100 or lower, the student is advised to retake the SAT exam. If an applying student has a GPA of 3.5 or lower, the student is denied admission. The nested If statement in Figure 5-53 solves this logic problem:

```
154        If decGPA > 3.5D Then
155            If intSatScore > 1100 Then
156                lblAdmissionStatus.Text = "You have earned admission"
157            Else
158                lblAdmissionStatus.Text = "Retake the SAT exam"
159            End If
160        Else
161            lblAdmissionStatus.Text = "You have been denied admission"
162        End If
```

FIGURE 5-53

In Figure 5-53, if the GPA is greater than 3.5, then the first inner If statement on line 155 is executed to determine if the SAT score is greater than 1100. If so, the person has earned admission. If not, the person is advised to retake the SAT exam. If the GPA is not greater than 3.5, the student is denied admission. Notice that an If statement does not follow the Else keyword on line 160. An inner If statement need not follow both the If and the Else keywords.

Sometimes, after a condition is found to be true, a statement must be executed before the inner If statement is executed. For example, assume that if the GPA for a student is greater than 3.5, then the student should be informed that their GPA is acceptable for admission. The code in Figure 5-54 implements this condition.

```
164        If decGPA > 3.5D Then
165            Me.lblGPAStatus.Text = "Your GPA is acceptable"
166            If intSatScore > 1100 Then
167                lblAdmissionStatus.Text = "You have earned admission"
168            Else
169                lblAdmissionStatus.Text = "Retake the SAT exam"
170            End If
171        Else
172            Me.lblGPAStatus.Text = "Your GPA is not acceptable"
173            lblAdmissionStatus.Text = "You have been denied admission"
174        End If
```

FIGURE 5-54

In Figure 5-54, on line 165 the message "Your GPA is acceptable" is assigned to the Text property of the lblGPAStatus Label object prior to checking the SAT score. As you can see, after the first condition has been tested, one or more statements can be executed prior to executing the inner If statement. This holds true for the Else portion of the If statement as well.

Matching If, Else, and End If Entries

When you write a nested If statement, the inner If statement must be fully contained within the outer If statement. To accomplish this, you must ensure that each Else entry has a corresponding If entry, and an inner If statement must be terminated with an End If entry before either the Else entry or the End If entry for the outer If statement is encountered. If you code the statement incorrectly, one or more entries in the nested If statement will be identified with a blue squiggly line, indicating an error in the structure of the statement.

You also must place the correct statements with the correct If and Else statements within the nested If statement. For example, in Figure 5-55, the code is *incorrect* because the statement following the Else statements has been switched.

```
164        If decGPA > 3.5D Then
165            Me.lblGPAStatus.Text = "Your GPA is acceptable"
166            If intSatScore > 1100 Then
167                lblAdmissionStatus.Text = "You have earned admission"
168            Else
169                lblAdmissionStatus.Text = "You have been denied admission"
170            End If
171        Else
172            Me.lblGPAStatus.Text = "Your GPA is not acceptable"
173            lblAdmissionStatus.Text = "Retake the SAT exam"          incorrect
174        End If                                                        statements
```

FIGURE 5-55

You must be precise when placing the executing statements in the nested If statement. It is easy to miscode a nested If statement.

Nesting Three or More Levels of If Statements

If statements are not limited to two levels of nesting. Three or more levels can be included in a nested If statement. When this is done, however, the nested If statement can become more difficult to understand and code. If more than two levels are required to solve a logic problem, great care must be taken to ensure errors such as the one shown in Figure 5-55 do not occur.

TESTING THE STATUS OF A RADIOBUTTON OBJECT IN CODE

In the Wood Cabinet Estimate chapter project, which finds the cost of wood cabinets, the user selects one RadioButton in the Panel object to select the wood type. The code must check each RadioButton to determine if that RadioButton has been selected by the user. When the user selects a radio button, the Checked property for that button is changed from False to True. In addition, the Checked property for other RadioButton objects in the same panel is set to False. This Checked property can be tested in an If statement to determine if the RadioButton object has been selected.

To test the status of the Checked Property for a RadioButton object, the general statement shown in Figure 5-56 can be written:

```
237        If Me.radPine.Checked Then
238            Statement(s) to be executed if radio button is checked
239        End If
```

FIGURE 5-56

Notice in Figure 5-56 that the RadioButton property is not compared using a relational operator. Instead, when a property that can contain only True or False is tested, only the property must be specified in the If statement. When the property contains True, then the If statement is considered true, and when the property contains False, the If statement is considered false.

Testing Radio Buttons with the If...Then...ElseIf Statement

When a program contains multiple RadioButton objects in a Panel object or a GroupBox object, only one of the radio buttons can be selected. The statement that can be used to check multiple radio buttons is the If...Then...ElseIf statement because once the checked radio button is detected, there is no reason to check the rest of the radio buttons.

In the Wood Cabinet Estimate application, the user will click one of three radio buttons (Pine, Oak, or Cherry) to select the type of wood to be used for cabinets. To use an If...Then...ElseIf statement to check the status of the radio buttons, the most likely choice should be checked first. By doing this, the fewest number of tests will have to be performed. Therefore, the first If statement should test the status of the Pine radio button (radPine). If the radPine button is checked, the Cost Per Foot should be set to the value in the decPineCost variable, which is 100.00. No further testing should be done (see Figure 5-57).

```
31          If Me.radPine.Checked Then
32              decCostPerFoot = decPineCost
33          ElseIf Me.radOak.Checked Then
34              decCostPerFoot = decOakCost
35          ElseIf Me.radCherry.Checked Then
36              decCostPerFoot = decCherryCost
37          End If
```

FIGURE 5-57

If the radPine button is not checked, then the radOak button should be tested. If it is checked, the Cost Per Foot should be set to the value in the decOakCost variable (150.00) and no further testing should be done. If the radOak button is not checked, then the radCherry button should be tested. If the other two buttons are not checked, then the radCherry button must be checked because one of the three must be checked. The Cost Per Foot will be set to the value in the decCherryCost variable (250.00).

As you learned earlier, during design time you can set the Checked property to True for the most often selected RadioButton to save the user from having to select the most common choice. In the Wood Cabinet Estimate program, after the Cost Per Linear Foot has been determined and the Cost Estimate has been calculated, the user can click the Clear button to clear the Linear Feet text box, clear the Cost Estimate, and reset the radio buttons so that the Pine button is selected. The code to reset the radio buttons is shown in Figure 5-58.

```
62      Me.radPine.Checked = True
63      Me.radOak.Checked = False
64      Me.radCherry.Checked = False
```

FIGURE 5-58

In Figure 5-58, the Checked property for the radPine RadioButton object is set to True using the same method you have seen in previous chapters for setting an object property. Similarly, the Checked property for the other two RadioButton objects is set to False. As a result of these statements, the Pine radio button will be selected in the user interface, and the Oak and Cherry radio buttons will not be selected.

BLOCK-LEVEL SCOPE

In Chapter 4 you learned that the scope of a variable means where a variable can be referenced within a program. Scope is defined by where the variable is declared within a program. For example, if a variable is declared within an event handler, then only code within that event handler can reference the variable. Code in one event handler within a program cannot reference a variable declared in another event handler.

Within an event handler, an If...Then...Else statement (the code beginning with the If keyword and ending with the corresponding Else keyword or the code beginning with the Else keyword and ending with the End If keyword) is considered a block of code. Variables can be declared within the block of code. When this occurs, the variable can be referenced only within the block of code where it is declared. For example, variables defined within an If...Then block of code fall out of scope (cannot be referenced) outside that block of code. To illustrate this concept, the code in Figure 5-59 shows a variable, intYears, declared within an If...Then block of code.

```
11        If intAge < 18 Then
12            Dim intYears As Integer
13            intYears = 18 - intAge
14            Me.lblMessage.Text = "You can vote in " & intYears & " years(s)."
15        Else
16            Me.lblMessage.Text = "You can vote!"
17        End If
```

FIGURE 5-59

In Figure 5-59, on line 12 the variable intYears is declared as an Integer variable. On line 13, the variable is used in an arithmetic statement to receive the result of the calculation, 18 - intAge, which determines the number of years less than 18 that is stored in intAge. The result in intYears is concatenated with literals in the statement on line 14. The intYears variable can be referenced in any statements between the If keyword and the Else keyword. It cannot be referenced anywhere else in the program. Note that it cannot be referenced even in the Else portion of the If statement. When a statement referencing the intYears variable is written outside the area between the If keyword and the Else keyword, a compilation error will occur and the program will not be able to be compiled and executed.

Although the scope of the intYears variable in Figure 5-59 is between the If keyword on line 11 and the Else keyword on line 15, you should realize that the variable itself perseveres during the execution of the event handler procedure. Therefore, if the If statement in Figure 5-59 is executed a second time, the value in the intYears variable will be the same as when the If statement was completed the first time. To avoid unexpected results when the If statement is executed the second time, you should initialize block variables at the beginning of the block. In Figure 5-59, the statement on line 13 sets the value in the intYears variable immediately after the variable is declared, which is good programming technique.

USING LOGICAL OPERATORS

The If statements you have seen thus far test a single condition. In many cases, more than one condition must be true or one of several conditions must be true in order for the statements in the Then portion of If...Then...Else statement to be executed. When more than one condition is included in an If...Then...Else statement, the conditions are called a **compound condition**. For example, consider the following business traveling rule: "If the flight costs less than $300.00 And the hotel is less than $120.00 per night, the business trip is approved." In this case, both conditions (flight less than $300.00 And hotel less than $120.00 per night) must be true in order for the trip to approved. If either condition is not true, then the business trip is not approved.

To create an If statement that processes the business traveling rule, you must use a **logical operator**. The most common set of logical operators are listed in Figure 5-60.

Logical Operator	Meaning
And	All conditions tested in the If statement must be true
Or	One condition tested in the If statement must be true
Not	Negates a condition

FIGURE 5-60

For the business traveling rule specified previously, you should use the And logical operator.

Using the And Logical Operator

The **And logical operator** allows you to combine two or more conditions into a compound condition that can be tested with an If statement. If any of the conditions stated in the compound condition is false, the compound condition is considered false and the statements following the Else portion of the If statement will be executed. The code in Figure 5-61 uses the And logical operator to implement the business traveling rule.

```
137        If decFlightCost < 300D And decHotelCost < 120D Then
138            Me.lblTripMessage.Text = "Your business trip is approved"
139        Else
140            Me.lblTripMessage.Text = "Your business trip is denied"
141        End If
```

FIGURE 5-61

In Figure 5-61, both conditions in the compound condition (flight cost < 300 and hotel cost < 120) must be true in order for the business trip to be approved. If one of the conditions is false, then the compound condition is considered false and the If statement would return a false indication. For example, if the flight cost is 300 or more, the trip will not be approved regardless of the hotel cost. Similarly, if the hotel cost is 120 or more, the trip will not be approved regardless of the flight cost. This process is illustrated in the diagram in Figure 5-62.

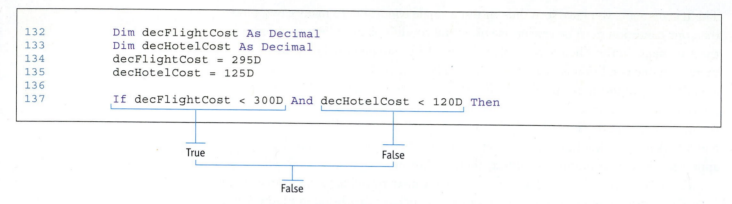

```
132        Dim decFlightCost As Decimal
133        Dim decHotelCost As Decimal
134        decFlightCost = 295D
135        decHotelCost = 125D
136
137        If decFlightCost < 300D And decHotelCost < 120D Then
```

True   False

False

FIGURE 5-62

In Figure 5-62, the flight cost is 295, so it is less than 300 and the first part of the compound condition is true. Following the And logical operator, the hotel cost (125) is not less than 120. Therefore, the second part of the compound condition is false. With the And logical operator, when either condition is false, the If statement considers the compound condition to be false. The result of the If statement in Figure 5-62 is that the compound condition is considered to be false.

Using the Or Logical Operator

When the **Or logical operator** is used to connect two or more conditions, the compound condition is true if any tested condition is true. Even if four conditional statements are included in the compound condition, if one conditional statement in the compound condition is true, the entire statement is considered true.

As an example, assume a college has an acceptance policy that states each student must either have a minimum of a 3.5 grade point average (GPA) or at least a 1080 score on the SAT college entrance exam to be accepted for enrollment. If the student meets one or both conditions, the student would be accepted. The If statement in Figure 5-63, which uses the Or logical operator, will solve this problem.

```
147        If decGPA >= 3.5D Or intSATScore >= 1080 Then
148            Me.lblAcceptance.Text = "You have been accepted"
149        Else
150            Me.lblAcceptance.Text = "You are not accepted"
151        End If
```

FIGURE 5-63

In Figure 5-63 if the GPA is 3.2, but the SAT score is 1130, the compound condition would be considered true because at least one of these conditions (SAT > 1080) is true (Figure 5-64).

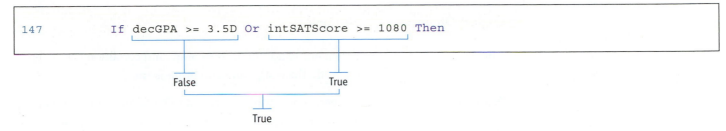

FIGURE 5-64

Using the Not Logical Operator

The **Not logical operator** allows you to state conditions that are best expressed in a negative way. In essence, the Not logical operator reverses the logical value of a condition on which it operates. For example, if a shoe store sells shoe sizes under size 14 from their showroom but requires special orders for larger sizes, the code could use the Not logical operator as shown in Figure 5-65 to negate the condition in the statement:

```
155        If Not decShoeSize >= 14 Then
156            Me.lblOrderPolicy.Text = "Showroom shoe style available"
157        Else
158            Me.lblOrderPolicy.Text = "Special order needed"
159        End If
```

FIGURE 5-65

The statement in Figure 5-65 works, but the use of the Not logical operator makes the If statement somewhat difficult to understand. Generally, a statement that avoids the Not logical operator is more easily understood. For example, the code in Figure 5-66 accomplishes the same task as the code in Figure 5-65, but is easier to understand:

```
162        If decShoeSize < 14 Then
163            Me.lblOrderPolicy.Text = "Showroom shoe style available"
164        Else
165            Me.lblOrderPolicy.Text = "Special order needed"
166        End If
```

FIGURE 5-66

IN THE REAL WORLD

Many developers avoid using the Not logical operator because it makes the code harder to understand. By removing the Not logical operator and reversing the relational operator, the statement becomes clearer.

Other Logical Operators

The Visual Basic programming language provides three other lesser used logical operators. These are shown in the table in Figure 5-67.

Logical Operator	Meaning
Xor	When one condition in the compound condition is true, but not both, the compound condition is true
AndAlso	As soon as a condition is found to be false, no further conditions are tested and the compound condition is false
OrElse	As soon as a condition is found to be true, no further conditions are tested and the compound condition is true

FIGURE 5-67

Order of Operations for Logical Operators

You can combine more than one logical operator in the same If...Then statement. In an If statement, arithmetic operators are evaluated first, relational operators are evaluated next, and logical operators are evaluated last. The order of operations for logical operators is shown in Figure 5-68:

Logical Operator	Order
Not	Highest Precedence
And, AndAlso	Next Precedence
Or, OrElse, Xor	Last Precedence

FIGURE 5-68

In most cases, if a developer uses multiple relational or logical operators in an If statement, the order of precedence should be established through the use of parentheses in order to clarify the sequence of evaluation. As in arithmetic expressions, conditional expressions within parentheses are evaluated before conditional expressions outside parentheses.

SELECT CASE STATEMENT

In some programming applications, different operations can occur based upon the value in a single field. For example, in Figure 5-69 the user enters the number of the day in the week and the program displays the name of the day. The program must evaluate the number of the day value and display the correct name of the day.

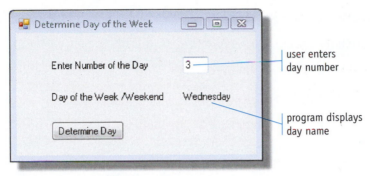

FIGURE 5-69

In Figure 5-69, if the number of the day is 1, then the value Monday should be displayed. If the number of the day is 2, then Tuesday should be displayed; and so on. If the number of the day is 6 or 7, then the value Weekend should be displayed. If the user does not enter a value of 1 through 7, the user should be told to enter a value between 1 and 7.

To solve this problem, a series of If...Then...ElseIf statements could be used. An easier and clearer way to solve the problem, however, is to use the Select Case statement.

When using a Select Case statement, the value in a single field, such as the day number, is evaluated and different action, such as displaying the name of the day, is taken based on the value in the field.

A general example of the Select Case statement is shown in Figure 5-70.

The coding for the Determine Day of Week application is shown in Figure 5-71.

```
168          Select Case Test Expression
169              Case First Expression
170                  Statement(s) for First Case
171              Case Second Expression
172                  Statement(s) for Second Case
173              Case Third Expression
174                  Statement(s) for Third Case
175              Case Else
176                  Statement(s) for when the Case Conditions do not match the
177                      test expressions above
178          End Select
```

FIGURE 5-70

```
13          Select Case intDayNumber
14              Case 1
15                  Me.lblDayOfWeek.Text = "Monday"
16              Case 2
17                  Me.lblDayOfWeek.Text = "Tuesday"
18              Case 3
19                  Me.lblDayOfWeek.Text = "Wednesday"
20              Case 4
21                  Me.lblDayOfWeek.Text = "Thursday"
22              Case 5
23                  Me.lblDayOfWeek.Text = "Friday"
24              Case 6
25                  Me.lblDayOfWeek.Text = "Weekend"
26              Case 7
27                  Me.lblDayOfWeek.Text = "Weekend"
28              Case Else
29                  Me.lblDayOfWeek.Text = "Enter 1 through 7"
30          End Select
```

FIGURE 5-71

The Select Case statement begins with the Select Case command. The test expression entry is used to specify the value or variable that contains the value to be tested in the Select Case statement. In Figure 5-71, the variable is intDayNumber. So, when the Select Case statement is executed, each of the cases will be compared to the value in the intDayNumber variable.

Each Case statement specifies the value for which the test expression is checked. For example, the first Case statement on line 14 in Figure 5-71 specifies the value 1. If the value in the variable intDayNumber is equal to 1, the statement(s) following the first Case statement up to the second Case statement (line 16) are executed. In Figure 5-71, the assignment statement on line 15 that sets the Text property of the lblDayOfWeek to Monday is executed if the value in intDayNumber is equal to 1. More than one statement can follow a Case statement.

If the expression following the first Case statement is not true, then the next Case statement is evaluated. In Figure 5-71, the Case statement on line 16 checks if the value in intDayNumber is equal to 2. If so, the Text property of the lblDayOfWeek is set to Tuesday. This process continues through the remainder of the Case statements.

The Case Else statement on line 28 is an optional entry that includes all conditions not specifically tested for in the other Case statements. In Figure 5-71, if the value in the intDayNumber variable is not equal to 1 through 7, then the statement following the Case Else statement is executed. While not required, good programming practice dictates that the Case Else statement should be used so that all cases are accounted for and the program performs a specific action regardless of the value found in the test expression.

The End Select statement is required to end the Select Case statement. When you enter the Select Case statement in Visual Studio 2008, IntelliSense automatically includes the End Select statement.

Select Case Test Expressions

The example in Figure 5-71 used an integer as the test expression value, but any data type can be used in the test expression. For example, the test expression in Figure 5-72 uses the Text property of the txtStudentMajor TextBox object as a string value.

```
217        Select Case Me.txtStudentMajor.Text
218            Case "Accounting"
219                Me.lblDepartment.Text = "Business"
220            Case "Marketing"
221                Me.lblDepartment.Text = "Business"
222            Case "Electrical Engineering"
223                Me.lblDepartment.Text = "Engineering"
224            Case "Biochemistry"
225                Me.lblDepartment.Text = "Chemistry"
226            Case "Shakespearean Literature"
227                Me.lblDepartment.Text = "English"
228            Case "Web Design and E-Commerce"
229                Me.lblDepartment.Text = "CIS"
230            Case Else
231                Me.lblDepartment.Text = "Other"
232        End Select
```

FIGURE 5-72

In Figure 5-72, the Select Case statement is used to test the value in the Text property of the txtStudentMajor TextBox object and move the corresponding department name to the Text property of the lblDepartment object. The Case statements specify the values to be tested in the text box. The use of a string for the Select Case statement works in the same manner as other data types.

Using Relational Operators in a Select Case Statement

You can use relational operators in a Select Case statement. You must, however, use the keyword Is with the relational operator. For example, in Figure 5-49 on page 323, an If...Then...ElseIf statement was used to determine the shipping cost. That same processing could be accomplished using a Select Case statement, as shown in Figure 5-73.

HEADS UP

If you forget to type Is in the Case Is statement, Visual Studio will insert the Is keyword for you.

```
191        Select Case decOrderAmount
192            Case Is > 500D
193                decShippingCost = 30D
194            Case Is > 400D
195                decShippingCost = 25D
196            Case Is > 200D
197                decShippingCost = 20D
198            Case Is > 0D
199                decShippingCost = 15D
200            Case Else
201                decShippingCost = 0D
202        End Select
203
```

FIGURE 5-73

Using Ranges in Select Case Statements

Another way to specify values in a Select Case statement is to use ranges. In Figure 5-74, the Case statements illustrate testing for six different conditions:

```
224        Select Case intGradeLevel
225            Case 1 To 3
226                Me.lblGradeLevelExam.Text = "Early elementary"
227            Case 4 To 6
228                Me.lblGradeLevelExam.Text = "Late elementary"
229            Case 7 To 8
230                Me.lblGradeLevelExam.Text = "Middle school"
231            Case 9 To 10
232                Me.lblGradeLevelExam.Text = "Early high school"
233            Case 11
234                Me.lblGradeLevelExam.Text = "Late high school"
235            Case 12
236                Me.lblGradeLevelExam.Text = "Final exam"
237            Case Else
238                Me.lblGradeLevelExam.Text = "Invalid grade level"
239        End Select
```

FIGURE 5-74

As you can see, a range of values in a Case statement is specified by stating the beginning value, the word To, and then the ending value in the range. The Case statements will test the value in the intGradeLevel variable and the appropriate statements will be executed.

You also can write Case statements with more than one distinct value being tested. In Figure 5-75, the Case statement tests the individual values of 1, 3, 8, 11, and 17 against the value specified in the intDepartmentNumber variable.

```
230        Select Case intDepartmentNumber
231            Case 1, 3, 8, 11, 17
232
```

FIGURE 5-75

Notice in Figure 5-75 that each value in the Case statement is separated by a comma.

The code in Figure 5-76 shows a mixture of the two techniques, using both commas and a To statement:

```
234        Select Case intDepartmentNumber
235            Case 2, 4, 7, 12 To 16, 22
```

FIGURE 5-76

Selecting Which Decision Structure to Use

In some instances, you might be faced with determining if you should use the Select Case statement or the If...Then...ElseIf statement to solve a problem. Generally, the Select Case statement is most useful when more than two or three values must be tested for a given variable. For example, in Figure 5-72 on page 337, six different values are checked in the Text property of the txtStudentMajor TextBox object. This is a perfect example of the use of the Select Case statement.

The If...Then...ElseIf statement is more flexible because more than one variable can be used in the comparison, and compound conditions with the And, Or, and Not logical operators can be used.

CODE SNIPPETS

Visual Basic includes a code library of almost five hundred pieces of code, called IntelliSense **code snippets**, that you can insert into an application. Each snippet consists of a complete programming task such as an If...Then...Else decision structure, sending an e-mail message, or drawing a circle. Inserting these commonly used pieces of code is an effective way to enhance productivity. You also can create your own snippets and add them to the library.

In addition to inserting snippets in your program, you also can display a code snippet to ensure you understand the syntax and requirements for a given type of statement. To display and insert a code snippet for the If...Then...Else statement, you can complete the following steps:

STEP 1   Right-click the line in the code editing window where you want to insert the snippet.

Visual Studio displays a shortcut menu (Figure 5-77). It is important to right-click in the code editing window in the exact location where you want the code snippet to appear. If you right-click outside this location, the shortcut menu might list choices that are customized to that area of code and not include the code snippet for which you were searching. In addition, if you click in the wrong place, the snippet will be positioned in the incorrect location in your program.

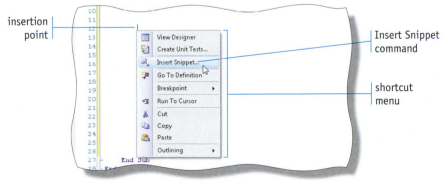

FIGURE 5-77

STEP 2 Click Insert Snippet on the shortcut menu.

Visual Studio displays a menu of folders containing snippets (Figure 5-78). The code snippets in each folder correspond to their folder titles.

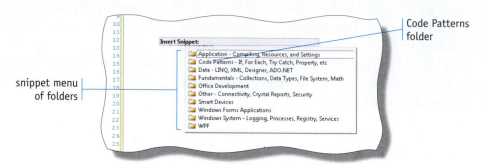

FIGURE 5-78

STEP 3 Double-click Code Patterns - If, For Each, Try Catch, Property, etc, which is a folder that contains commonly used code such as the If...Then...Else statement.

Visual Studio displays a menu of folders for code patterns (Figure 5-79).

FIGURE 5-79

STEP 4 Double-click the Conditionals and Loops folder because an If...Then...Else statement is a conditional statement.

Visual Studio displays the list of Conditionals and Loops code snippets (Figure 5-80). Some of these statements will be unfamiliar to you until you complete Chapter 6, but you can see that the list of code snippets includes a number of different types of If statements.

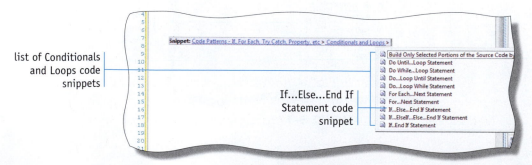

FIGURE 5-80

STEP 5   Double-click the If...Else...End If Statement code snippet.

The If...Else...End If Statement code snippet is inserted into the code on the line selected in step 1 (Figure 5-81). The highlighted text must be replaced by the condition(s) to be tested in the If statement. The code to be executed when the condition is true and the code to be executed when the condition is false must be added.

enter code to be executed when condition is true

enter code to be executed when condition is false

replace highlighted text with condition(s)

If...Else...End If Statement code snippet

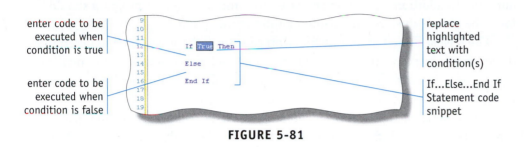

FIGURE 5-81

You must modify the code snippet shown in Figure 5-81 in order for the code to work properly. You may find that modifying the code in the snippet, particularly in a complicated code snippet, is more work than using IntelliSense to enter the statement.

But, you also can use code snippets to learn or review the format and syntax of a statement. For example, if you wanted to review the syntax of an If...ElseIf...Else...End If statement, you could insert the statement into the code editing window and examine it. You could then either click the Undo button to remove the statement or you could comment out the snippet code and keep it for your review. In many cases of checking syntax, reviewing a snippet is faster and clearer than consulting Visual Basic help.

VALIDATING DATA

Since the first days of computers, the phrase, "garbage in, garbage out" has described the fact that allowing incorrect input data into a program produces incorrect output. Developers should anticipate that users will enter invalid data. Therefore, developers must write code that will prevent the invalid data from being used in the program to produce invalid output.

For example, in the Wood Cabinet Estimate chapter project, the user is asked to enter the number of linear feet for the wood cabinets. If the user enters a negative number, a letter of the alphabet, or even leaves the text box blank, the program should inform the user of the input error and allow the user to reenter a proper value. If the program attempts to process invalid data, unexpected errors can occur, which is not the way a program should respond to invalid input data.

To properly check the linear feet value the user enters, two checks must be performed. First, the program must check the value entered by the user to ensure it is numeric. Second, the numeric value entered by the user must be checked to ensure it is greater than zero. These checks are explained in the following paragraphs.

Testing Input to Determine If the Value Is Numeric

In the Wood Cabinet Estimate program, if no check is performed on the input data and the user accidentally enters a nonnumeric character such as an "a" or fails to enter a value at all, the program will fail when Visual Basic attempts to convert that value to a number. An exception (error) screen will open and the program will be terminated. Therefore, the program must check the value entered by the user to ensure it is numeric. In addition, if the user enters a nonnumeric value, the program should inform the user of the error and request a valid numeric value.

The Visual Basic **IsNumeric function** can check the input value to determine if the value can be converted into a numeric value such as an Integer or Decimal data type. If so, it returns a True Boolean value. If the value is not recognized as a numeric value, the IsNumeric function returns a False Boolean value.

For example, the IsNumeric function can check the value in the Text property of the Linear Feet text box. If the user enters a letter such as "a" in the text box, the IsNumeric function would return a False Boolean value because the letter "a" is not numeric.

Because the IsNumeric function returns a Boolean value (True or False), it can be placed within an If statement as the condition to be tested. If the returned value is True, the condition in the If statement is considered true. If the returned value is False, the condition in the If statement is considered false. The code in Figure 5-82 uses an If statement to determine if the Text property of the txtLinearFeet TextBox object is numeric.

```
                IsNumeric          argument for
                function           IsNumeric function

27      If IsNumeric(Me.txtLinearFeet.Text) Then
  ⋮         Statement(s) executed when condition is true
50      Else
51          'Display MessageBox if user entered nonnumeric value
52          MsgBox("Enter the Linear Feet of the Cabinets.", , "Input Error")
53          Me.txtLinearFeet.Text = ""
54          Me.txtLinearFeet.Focus()
55      End If
```

FIGURE 5-82

In Figure 5-82, the If statement on line 27 calls the IsNumeric function. The Text property of the txtLinearFeet TextBox object is the argument for the IsNumeric function. As a result of this specification, the IsNumeric function will analyze the data in the Text property of the txtLinearFeet TextBox object. If the data can be converted to a numeric data type, then the function will return a Boolean value of True. If the data cannot be converted to a numeric data type, the function will return a Boolean value of False.

Once the function has returned a Boolean value, the If statement tests the Boolean value. If it is true, which means the value in the Text property of the txtLinearFeet TextBox object is numeric, the appropriate statements are executed. If the condition is false, meaning the value is not numeric, the statements on lines 51–55 are executed. The statement on line 52 displays a message box telling the user to enter the linear feet of the cabinet (see Figure 5-2 on page 293). The caption of the message box states, "Input Error". The statement on line 53 clears the Text property. The statement on line 54 sets the focus on the textbox so the user can reenter the value.

Checking for a Positive Number

If the condition in Figure 5-82 is true, the value in the Text property must be converted to a Decimal data type. Then, the program checks to ensure the value entered is greater than zero. These statements are shown in Figure 5-83.

```
27          If IsNumeric(Me.txtLinearFeet.Text) Then
28              decLinearFeet = Convert.ToDecimal(Me.txtLinearFeet.Text)
39
40              ' Is linear feet greater than zero
41              If decLinearFeet > 0 Then
  ⋮                 Statement(s) executed when condition is true
43              Else
44                  ' Display error message if user entered a negative value
45                  MsgBox("You entered " & decLinearFeet.ToString() &
46                      ". Enter a Number Greater Than Zero.", , "Input Error")
47                  Me.txtLinearFeet.Text = ""
48                  Me.txtLinearFeet.Focus()
49              End If
50          Else
51              ' Display error message if user entered a nonnumeric value
52              MsgBox("Enter the Linear Feet of the Cabinets.", , "Input Error")
53              Me.txtLinearFeet.Text = ""
54              Me.txtLinearFeet.Focus()
55          End If
```

FIGURE 5-83

When the value in the Text property is numeric, the value is converted to a decimal value (line 28). On line 31, the decimal value is compared to zero. If it is greater than zero, then the processing for a true statement is executed. If the value is not greater than zero, a message box is displayed informing the user an invalid entry was made (see Figure 5-37 on page 313). The user then can enter a valid value.

The process of validating input data is fundamental to programming when using a graphical user interface. A well-designed program must ensure the user enters valid data.

DEPLOYING THE APPLICATION

As you code the Wood Cabinet Estimate chapter project, you need to test and execute the application. Because the Wood Cabinet Estimate application is a Smart Device application that will be run on a Pocket PC device, executing the application is different from running a Windows application.

When you write an application for a handheld device such as the Pocket PC, you can deploy the application to an actual Pocket PC device and run the program on that device. In many cases, however, you may not have a Pocket PC device available, or you may not want to complete the device deployment steps when you merely are testing the program. Fortunately, Visual Studio provides a Pocket PC emulator that runs on your personal computer under the Windows operating system. The Pocket PC emulator looks and runs exactly like a genuine Pocket PC. You can easily deploy your program to the emulator to test the program without requiring an actual Pocket PC.

To deploy a program to the Pocket PC emulator, you can complete the following steps:

STEP 1 With Visual Studio open and the program you want to run loaded, click the Start Debugging button on the Standard toolbar.

The Deploy window opens (Figure 5-84). In the Device list, you must select the device on which you want to deploy the application. If you have an actual Pocket PC, you can select the Windows Mobile 5.0 Pocket PC Device R2. The Pocket PC would need to be plugged into the USB port with the Pocket PC drivers already installed. The second option in the list is the square emulator for devices with square displays.

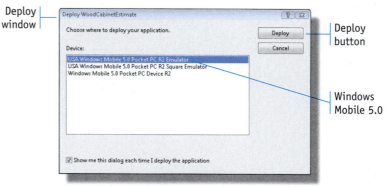

FIGURE 5-84

STEP 2 If necessary, select USA Windows Mobile 5.0 Pocket PC R2 Emulator in the Device list. Click the Deploy button.

After a wait, the Pocket PC emulator opens (Figure 5-85). As the program is downloaded to the emulator, the status bar in Visual Studio specifies that the program is deploying. The reason for the wait, which can take 1 to 2 minutes, is that the emulator works at the same speed as a real Pocket PC; and because some time is required to deploy the program to a remote device such as the Pocket PC, the emulator requires the time as well. While the program is deploying, the Pocket PC emulator functions as a real Pocket PC device. In the upper-left corner of the emulator window, you can click the Windows Start button to display the Start menu. The calendar, contacts, and browser in the emulator are working applications that you can open and use.

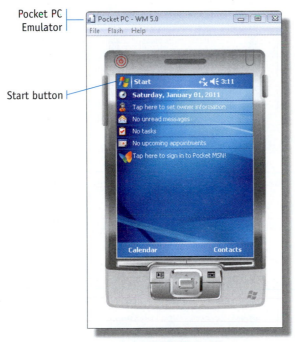

FIGURE 5-85

STEP 3   After the Wood Cabinet Estimate application loads and executes on the emulator device, type 15 in the Linear Feet text box.

The application is displayed within the Pocket PC emulator (Figure 5-86). The value 15 is displayed in the Linear Feet text box.

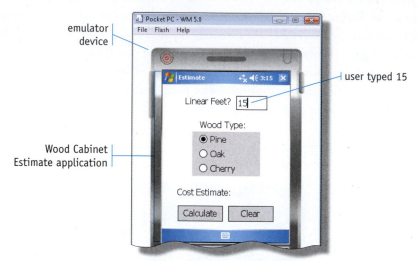

FIGURE 5-86

STEP 4   Using your mouse, click the Oak radio button, and then click the Calculate button.

When you click the Calculate button, the program multiplies the linear feet by the cost per foot for Oak and displays the cost estimate (Figure 5-87).

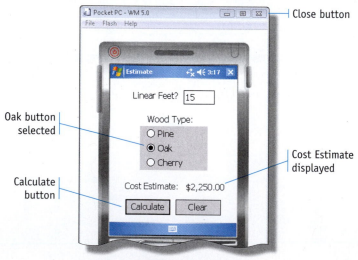

FIGURE 5-87

Using the Input Panel

When you use the emulator, you can enter data directly from the keyboard, but if you are deploying the application to an actual Pocket PC, you may not have a full keyboard available. The Pocket PC has the **input panel** shown in Figure 5-88 to enter data into applications. You can use a stylus to select the characters from the input panel. When you press the stylus on a character in the input panel, the character is entered into the focused object on the form.

Keyboard button opens and closes the keyboard display

FIGURE 5-88

Closing the Emulator

When you are finished with the application, close the emulator by clicking the Close button (X) in the upper-right corner of the Pocket PC emulator. The Device Emulator dialog box will open and ask if you want to save the emulator state before exiting (Figure 5-89). It is *critical* that you click the No button. If you click the Yes button and then subsequently make changes to the code, the new changes will not take effect the next time you run the application. Clicking the No button shown in Figure 5-89 resets the device and will cause any code to be sent to the emulator the next time you execute the application.

Device Emulator dialog box

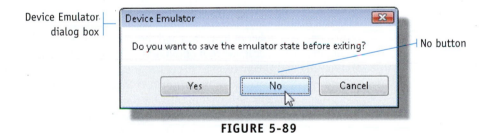

No button

FIGURE 5-89

Program Design

As you have learned, the requirements document identifies the purpose of the program being developed, the application title, the procedures to be followed when using the program, any equations and calculations required in the program, any conditions within the program that must be tested, notes and restrictions that must be followed by the program, and any other comments that would be helpful to understanding the problem. The requirements document for the Wood Cabinet Estimate application is shown in Figure 5-90.

REQUIREMENTS DOCUMENT

Date submitted: January 29, 2012

Application title: Wood Cabinet Estimate

Purpose: This application calculates the estimated cost of wood cabinetry for a job bid.

Program Procedures: From a Pocket PC handheld device, the user should enter the linear footage of cabinets needed and select the type of wood. The estimated cost for the cabinet job will be displayed.

Algorithms, Processing, and Conditions:
1. The user must be able to enter the number of linear feet of cabinetry.
2. The user must be able to select one of three wood types — pine, oak, or cherry.
3. The user can initiate the calculation and display the cost estimate for the wood cabinets.
4. The application computes the cost estimate of the cabinets based on the number of linear feet and the cost of the wood. Pine costs $100 per linear foot of cabinets, oak costs $150 per linear foot, and cherry costs $250 per linear foot.
5. The estimate calculation is: linear feet × cost per linear foot
6. The cost estimate is displayed in currency format.
7. The user should be able to clear the linear feet entered, reset the wood type to pine, and clear the cost estimate.

Notes and Restrictions:
1. If the user enters a non-numeric value for the linear feet or if the TextBox object is empty, the user should be advised and asked for a valid entry.
2. If the user enters a negative number for the linear feet, the user should be advised and asked for a valid entry.

Comments:
1. The application will be deployed on a Pocket PC.
2. The title of the Pocket PC form should be Estimate.

FIGURE 5-90

USE CASE DEFINITION

1. The Pocket PC window opens and displays the title, Estimate, a text box requesting the number of linear feet for the cabinets, radio buttons to select the wood type, and two buttons labeled Calculate and Clear.
2. The user enters the linear feet and selects one of the wood types.
3. The user clicks the Calculate button.
4. The user will be warned if a nonnumeric value is entered, the text box is left empty, or a negative number is entered.
5. The program displays the cost estimate for the cabinetry job.
6. The user clicks the Clear button to clear the Linear Feet text box, set the wood choice to Pine, and erase the cost estimate.
7. The user clicks the Close button to terminate the application.

FIGURE 5-91

EVENT PLANNING DOCUMENT

You will recall that the event planning document consists of a table that specifies an object in the user interface that will cause an event, the action taken by the user to trigger the event, and the event processing that must occur. The event planning document for the Wood Cabinet Estimate program is shown in Figure 5-92.

EVENT PLANNING DOCUMENT

Program Name: Wood Cabinet Estimate	Developer: Corinne Hoisington	Object: frmWoodCabinetEstimate	Date: January 29, 2012
OBJECT	EVENT TRIGGER	EVENT PROCESSING	
btnCalculate	Click	Ensure data entered is numeric Display error message if data is not numeric or text box is empty Convert data entered to numeric Ensure data entered is greater than zero Display error message if data is not greater than zero Assign wood cost per foot based on type of wood selection Calculate cost (linear feet × cost per foot) Display cost	
btnClear	Click	Clear input text box Clear cost estimate Set the Pine radio button to checked Clear the Oak radio button Clear the Cherry radio button Set focus on input text box	
frmWoodCabinetEstimate	Load	Set focus on input text box Clear the placement zeros for cost	

FIGURE 5-92

DESIGN AND CODE THE PROGRAM

After the events and tasks within the events have been identified, the developer is ready to create the program. As you have learned, creating the program means designing the user interface and then entering Visual Basic statements to accomplish the tasks specified on the event planning document. As the developer enters the code, she also will implement the logic to carry out the required processing.

Guided Program Development

To design the user interface for the Wood Cabinet Estimate program and enter the code required to process each event in the program, complete the steps on the following pages.

Guided Program Development

Phase 1: Design the Form

1

▶ **Create a Smart Device Application** Open Visual Studio using the Start button on the Windows taskbar and the All Programs submenu. Create a new Visual Basic Smart Device Pocket PC Application project by completing the following: Click the New Project button on the Standard toolbar; select and expand Visual Basic in the left pane under Project types; select Smart Device; select Smart Device Project in the right (Templates) pane; name the project WoodCabinetEstimate in the Name text box; then click the OK button in the New Project dialog box *(ref: Figure 5-6)*.

HINT

▶ **Choose Target Platform** Select Windows Mobile 5.0 Pocket PC SDK, select Device Application, and then click the OK button.

▶ **Name the Form** In the Solution Explorer pane, right-click Form1.vb and then click Rename. Type frmWoodCabinetEstimate.vb, and then press the ENTER key. Click the Yes button to automatically change the form (Name) in the Properties window.

HINT

▶ **Change the Title on the Title Bar** To change the title on the title bar, click the form, scroll down the Properties window until the Text property is displayed, double-click in the right column of the Text property, type Estimate, and then press the ENTER key.

HINT

HEADS UP

The title in the Text property for a Smart Device Form object must be short because the space provided on the title bar is limited.

▶ **Add a Label** Drag the first label onto the frmWoodCabinetEstimate Form object and name the label lblLinearFeet. Set the Text property for the Label object to Linear Feet? Set the font to Tahoma, Regular, Size 12. Position the label to resemble Figure 5-93 on the next page.

(continues)

Guided Program Development (continued)

▶ **Add TextBox Object** Drag a TextBox object onto the form. Using snap lines, align the top of the TextBox object with the top of the Label object. Name the TextBox object txtLinearFeet. Change the font to Tahoma, Regular, Size 12. Reduce the width of the TextBox object to closely resemble Figure 5-93. Center the Label object and the TextBox object horizontally in the frmWoodCabinetEstimate Form object.

The Label object and TextBox object occupy the first line of the frmWoodCabinetEstimate Form object (Figure 5-93). They are centered horizontally in the form.

RESULT OF STEP 1

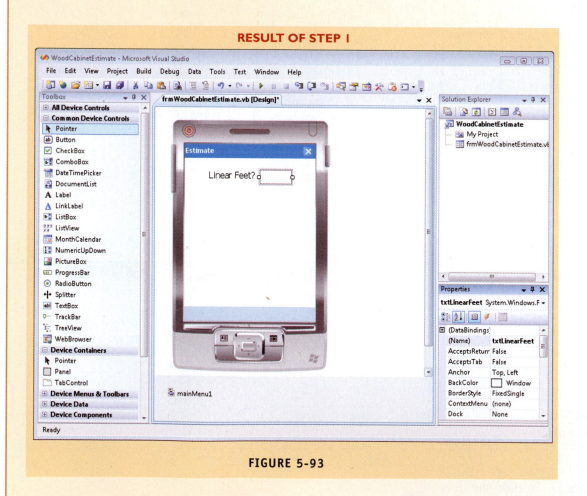

FIGURE 5-93

Guided Program Development *(continued)*

2

▶ **Add a Second Label** Drag a Label object onto the form below the lblLinearFeet Label object. Name the Label lblWoodType. Change the text in the Label to Wood Type:. Change the font to Tahoma, Regular, Size 12. Center the label horizontally in the frmWoodCabinetEstimate Form object.

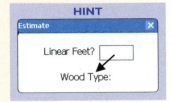

▶ **Add a Panel** Drag a Panel object onto the frmWoodCabinetEstimate Form object. Name the Panel pnlWoodType. Set the BackColor to LightGray so the panel will stand out on the form. Set the Size of the Panel object to 127,82. Center the Panel object horizontally in the frmWoodCabinetEstimate Form object *(ref: Figure 5-12)*.

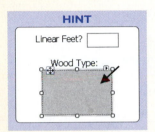

▶ **Add Radio Buttons** Place three RadioButton objects on the Panel object. Name the first RadioButton radPine and change its Text property to Pine. Name the second RadioButton radOak and change its Text property to Oak. Name the third RadioButton radCherry and change its Text property to Cherry. Select the three RadioButtons and change the font to Tahoma, Regular, Size 12 *(ref: Figure 5-15)*.

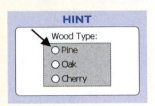

▶ **Set Radio Button Properties** Click the Pine RadioButton object and change its Checked property from False to True. Pine is the most commonly used wood by this cabinetmaker *(ref: Figure 5-20)*.

(continues)

Guided Program Development *(continued)*

The panel and radio buttons are included on the frmWoodCabinetEstimate Form object
(Figure 5-94). The light gray background of the Panel object helps it to stand out on the
form. The radPine radio button is selected because it is the most widely used wood type.

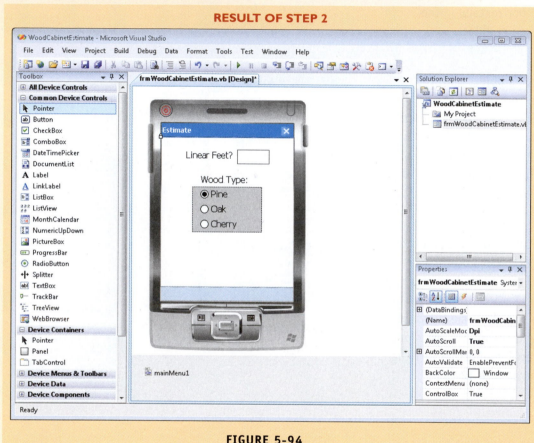

RESULT OF STEP 2

FIGURE 5-94

3

▶ **Add Estimate and Cost Labels** Drag two more Label objects below the
Panel object. Align these labels by their tops using snap lines. Name the
first label lblCostEstimateLabel and change its Text property to Cost
Estimate: and resize the Label object to view the text. Name the second
label lblCostEstimate and set its Text property to 0000.00. These placement
zeros allow you to view the Label object when it is not selected. The placement zeros will be cleared using code when the form is loaded. Change the
font for both Label objects to Tahoma, Regular, Size 12. Horizontally center
the labels as a unit on the frmWoodCabinetEstimate Form object.

HINT

Guided Program Development (continued)

▶ **Add Calculate and Clear Buttons** Drag two Button objects onto the form. Align the tops of the Button objects using snap lines. Name the first Button object btnCalculate and change its Text property to Calculate. Name the second Button object on the right btnClear and change its Text property to Clear. Change the font for these two buttons to Tahoma, Regular, Size 12. Change the size of each button to 85,29. Change the BackColor property for each button to LightGray.

The user interface is completed (Figure 5-95).

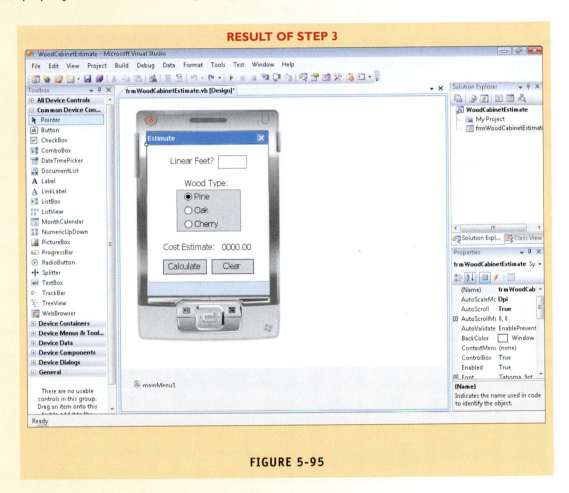

RESULT OF STEP 3

FIGURE 5-95

(continues)

Guided Program Development (continued)

Phase 2: Code the Application

4

▶ **Code the Comments** Double-click the btnCalculate Button object on the frmWoodCabinetEstimate Form object to open the code editing window and create the btnCalculate_Click Event Handler. Close the Toolbox. Click in front of the first words, Public Class frmWoodCabinetEstimate, and press the ENTER key to create a blank line. Insert the first four standard comments. Insert the Option Strict On command at the beginning of the code to turn on strict type checking.

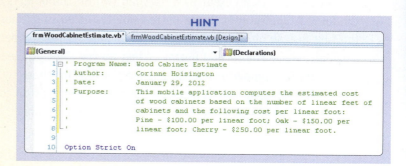

HINT

```
frmWoodCabinetEstimate.vb *   frmWoodCabinetEstimate.vb [Design]*

(General)                                    (Declarations)

 1 ⊟ ' Program Name: Wood Cabinet Estimate
 2   ' Author:       Corinne Hoisington
 3   ' Date:         January 29, 2012
 4   ' Purpose:      This mobile application computes the estimated cost
 5   '               of wood cabinets based on the number of linear feet of
 6   '               cabinets and the following cost per linear foot:
 7   '               Pine - $100.00 per linear foot; Oak - $150.00 per
 8 └ '               linear foot; Cherry - $250.00 per linear foot.
 9
10   Option Strict On
```

▶ **Comment btnCalculate_Click Event Handler** Enter a comment to describe the purpose of the btnCalculate_Click event.

HINT

```
14 ⊟      Private Sub btnCalculate_Click(ByVal sender As System.Object, ByVal e
15          ' The btnCalculate event handler calculates the estimated cost
16          ' of cabinets based on the linear feet and the wood type.
```

▶ **Declare and Initialize the Variables** This application requires six variables: 1) decLinearFeet: Holds the estimated linear footage of the cabinets. 2) decCostPerFoot: Holds the cost per linear foot based on the wood type; 3) decCostEstimate: Is assigned the calculated final estimated cost; 4) decPineCost: Is assigned the value 100.00; 5) decOakCost: Is assigned the value 150.00; 6) decCherryCost: Is assigned the value of 250.00. Declare and initialize these six variables.

HINT

```
18          ' Declaration section
19          Dim decLinearFeet As Decimal
20          Dim decCostPerFoot As Decimal
21          Dim decCostEstimate As Decimal
22          Dim decPineCost As Decimal = 100D
23          Dim decOakCost As Decimal = 150D
24          Dim decCherryCost As Decimal = 250D
```

▶ **Write the If Statement to Test for Numeric Data** When the user clicks the Calculate button, the program must first ensure that the user entered a valid numeric value in the txtLinearFeet TextBox object. If the user has entered a valid numeric value, the value must be converted from a string value into a decimal data type. Write the If statement and conversion statement required for this process *(ref: Figure 5-82)*.

HINT

```
26          ' Did user enter a numeric value?
27          If IsNumeric(Me.txtLinearFeet.Text) Then
28              decLinearFeet = Convert.ToDecimal(Me.txtLinearFeet.Text)
```

Guided Program Development *(continued)*

▶ **Write the If Statement to Test for Positive Number** If the value is numeric, then the converted numeric value must be checked to ensure it is a positive number. Write the If statement to check if the converted numeric value is greater than zero *(ref: Figure 5-83)*.

```
HINT
30          ' Is linear feet greater than zero
31          If decLinearFeet > 0 Then
```

▶ **Write the If Statements to Determine Cost Per Linear Foot** When the value is greater than zero, the cost per linear foot is determined by checking the status of the RadioButton objects and placing the appropriate cost per linear foot in the decCostPerFoot variable. Using the If...Then...ElseIf structure, write the statements to identify the checked radio button and place the appropriate cost in the decCostPerFoot variable *(ref: Figure 5-57)*.

```
HINT
32          ' Determine cost per foot of wood
33          If Me.radPine.Checked Then
34              decCostPerFoot = decPineCost
35          ElseIf Me.radOak.Checked Then
36              decCostPerFoot = decOakCost
37          ElseIf Me.radCherry.Checked Then
38              decCostPerFoot = decCherryCost
39          End If
```

▶ **Calculate and Display the Cost Estimate** The next step is to calculate the cost estimate by multiplying the value in the decCostPerFoot variable times the linear feet. Then you should display the cost estimate in the cost estimate label. Write the statements to calculate and display the cost estimate in the currency format.

```
HINT
40          ' Calculate and display the cost estimate
41          decCostEstimate = decLinearFeet * decCostPerFoot
42          Me.lblCostEstimate.Text = decCostEstimate.ToString("C")
```

▶ **Display Message Box If Value Entered Is Not Greater Than Zero** After the processing is finished for the true portion of the If statements, the Else portion of the If statements must be written. Write the code to display the message box containing the error message when the value entered by the user is not greater than zero *(ref: Figure 5-31)*.

```
HINT
43          Else
44              ' Display error message if user entered a negative value
45              MsgBox("You entered " & decLinearFeet.ToString() & _
46                  ". Enter a Number Greater Than Zero.", , "Input Error")
47              Me.txtLinearFeet.Text = ""
48              Me.txtLinearFeet.Focus()
49          End If
```

▶ **Display Error Message If Value Entered Is Not Numeric** Write the Else portion of the If statement if the value entered by the user is not numeric *(ref: Figure 5-31)*.

```
HINT
50          Else
51              ' Display error message if user entered a nonnumeric value
52              MsgBox("Enter the Linear Feet of the Cabinets.", , "Input Error")
53              Me.txtLinearFeet.Text = ""
54              Me.txtLinearFeet.Focus()
55          End If
56      End Sub
57
```

(continues)

Guided Program Development *(continued)*

The code for the click event of the Calculate Button is completed (Figure 5-96).

RESULT OF STEP 4

```
 1 ' Program Name:  Wood Cabinet Estimate
 2 ' Author:        Corinne Hoisington
 3 ' Date:          January 29, 2012
 4 ' Purpose:       This mobile application computes the estimated cost
 5 '                of wood cabinets based on the number of linear feet of
 6 '                cabinets and the following cost per linear foot:
 7 '                Pine - $100.00 per linear foot; Oak - $150.00 per
 8 '                linear foot; Cherry - $250.00 per linear foot.
 9
10 Option Strict On
11
12 Public Class frmWoodCabinetEstimate
13
14     Private Sub btnCalculate_Click(ByVal sender As System.Object, ByVal e As System.
        EventArgs) Handles btnCalculate.Click
15         ' The btnCalculate event handler calculates the estimated cost of
16         ' cabinets based on the linear feet and the wood type.
17
18         ' Declaration Section
19         Dim decLinearFeet As Decimal
20         Dim decCostPerFoot As Decimal
21         Dim decCostEstimate As Decimal
22         Dim decPineCost As Decimal = 100D
23         Dim decOakCost As Decimal = 150D
24         Dim decCherryCost As Decimal = 250D
25
26         ' Did user enter a numeric value?
27         If IsNumeric(Me.txtLinearFeet.Text) Then
28             decLinearFeet = Convert.ToDecimal(Me.txtLinearFeet.Text)
29
30             ' Is Linear Feet greater than zero
31             If decLinearFeet > 0 Then
32                 ' Determine cost per foot of wood
33                 If Me.radPine.Checked Then
34                     decCostPerFoot = decPineCost
35                 ElseIf Me.radOak.Checked Then
36                     decCostPerFoot = decOakCost
37                 ElseIf Me.radCherry.Checked Then
38                     decCostPerFoot = decCherryCost
39                 End If
40                 ' Calculate and display the cost estimate
41                 decCostEstimate = decLinearFeet * decCostPerFoot
42                 Me.lblCostEstimate.Text = decCostEstimate.ToString("C")
43             Else
44                 ' Display error message if user entered a negative value
45                 MsgBox("You entered " & decLinearFeet.ToString() & _
46                     ". Enter a Number Greater Than Zero.", , "Input Error")
47                 Me.txtLinearFeet.Text = ""
48                 Me.txtLinearFeet.Focus()
49             End If
```

FIGURE 5-96 (continues)

Guided Program Development *(continued)*

```
50              Else
51                  ' Display error message if user entered a nonnumeric value
52                  MsgBox("Enter the Linear Feet of the Cabinets.", , "Input Error")
53                  Me.txtLinearFeet.Text = ""
54                  Me.txtLinearFeet.Focus()
55              End If
56      End Sub
57 End Class
58
```

FIGURE 5-96 (continued)

5

▶ **Create the Clear Button Click Event Handler** The Clear Button click event includes the following processing: 1) Clear the txtLinearFeet Text property; 2) Clear the lblCostEstimate Text property; 3) Set the radPine Checked property to True; 4) Set the radOak and radCherry Checked properties to False; 5) Set the focus in the txtLinearFeet text box. To enter this code, click the frmWoodCabinetEstimate.vb [Design] tab and then double-click the Clear button. Using IntelliSense, enter the required code.

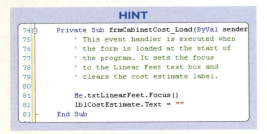

```
HINT
58   Private Sub btnClear_Click(ByVal sender As System.
59       ' This event handler is executed when
60       ' the user clicks the Clear button. It
61       ' clears the Linear Feet text box and the
62       ' cost estimate label, resets the radio
63       ' buttons with Pine selected, and sets  the
64       ' focus to the Linear Feet text box.
65
66       Me.txtLinearFeet.Text = ""
67       Me.lblCostEstimate.Text = ""
68       Me.radPine.Checked = True
69       Me.radOak.Checked = False
70       Me.radCherry.Checked = False
71       Me.txtLinearFeet.Focus()
72   End Sub
73
```

▶ **Create the Form Load Event Handler** When the frmWoodCabinetEstimate Form object loads, the following processing should occur: 1) The focus is in the txtLinearFeet text box; 2) The lblCostEstimate Text property is set to null. Click the frmWoodCabinetEstimate.vb [Design] tab to return to Design view and then double-click the form. Enter the code for the form load event handler.

```
HINT
74   Private Sub frmCabinetCost_Load(ByVal sender
75       ' This event handler is executed when
76       ' the form is loaded at the start of
77       ' the program. It sets the focus
78       ' to the Linear Feet text box and
79       ' clears the cost estimate label.
80
81       Me.txtLinearFeet.Focus()
82       lblCostEstimate.Text = ""
83   End Sub
```

6

▶ **Run the Application** After you have completed the code, you should run the application to ensure it works properly. Click the Start Debugging button on the Standard toolbar. A window opens requesting you to identify the device on which you will be running the application. Select the USA Windows Mobile 5.0 Pocket PC R2 Emulator and then click the Deploy button (*ref: Figure 5-84*). It will take up to 1 to 2 minutes for the emulator to display the execution of the project.

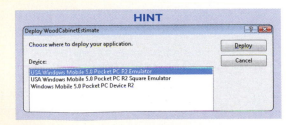

(continues)

Guided Program Development (continued)

▶ **Test the Application** When the emulator is displayed, test the application with the following data: 1) Linear feet: 25, wood type Oak; 2) Linear feet: 9, wood type Cherry; 3) Linear feet 100, wood type Pine; 4) Linear feet: Fifteen (use this word), wood type Cherry; 5) Linear feet: −21, wood type Oak; 6) Use other values to thoroughly test the program. After each test, click the Clear button before entering new data.

▶ **Close the Emulator** After testing the application, close the emulator by clicking the Close button (X) in the title bar of the Pocket PC Emulator window. When the Device Emulator dialog box opens, click the No button. When the Microsoft Visual Studio dialog box is displayed, click the OK button (ref: Figure 5-89).

IN THE REAL WORLD

This Pocket PC application would work completely without any change of code in a Windows Application.

Code Listing

The complete code for the sample program is shown in Figure 5-97.

```
1  ' Program Name:  Wood Cabinet Estimate
2  ' Author:        Corinne Hoisington
3  ' Date:          January 29, 2012
4  ' Purpose:       This mobile application computes the estimated cost
5  '                of wood cabinets based on the number of linear feet of
6  '                cabinets and the following cost per linear foot:
7  '                Pine - $100.00 per linear foot; Oak - $150.00 per
8  '                linear foot; Cherry - $250.00 per linear foot.
9
10 Option Strict On
11
12 Public Class frmWoodCabinetEstimate
13
14     Private Sub btnCalculate_Click(ByVal sender As System.Object, ByVal e As System.
       EventArgs) Handles btnCalculate.Click
```

FIGURE 5-97 (continues)

```
15        ' The btnCalculate event handler calculates the estimated cost of
16        ' cabinets based on the linear feet and the wood type.
17
18        ' Declaration Section
19        Dim decLinearFeet As Decimal
20        Dim decCostPerFoot As Decimal
21        Dim decCostEstimate As Decimal
22        Dim decPineCost As Decimal = 100D
23        Dim decOakCost As Decimal = 150D
24        Dim decCherryCost As Decimal = 250D
25
26        ' Did user enter a numeric value?
27        If IsNumeric(Me.txtLinearFeet.Text) Then
28            decLinearFeet = Convert.ToDecimal(Me.txtLinearFeet.Text)
29
30            ' Is Linear Feet greater than zero
31            If decLinearFeet > 0 Then
32                ' Determine cost per foot of wood
33                If Me.radPine.Checked Then
34                    decCostPerFoot = decPineCost
35                ElseIf Me.radOak.Checked Then
36                    decCostPerFoot = decOakCost
37                ElseIf Me.radCherry.Checked Then
38                    decCostPerFoot = decCherryCost
39                End If
40                ' Calculate and display the cost estimate
41                decCostEstimate = decLinearFeet * decCostPerFoot
42                Me.lblCostEstimate.Text = decCostEstimate.ToString("C")
43            Else
44                ' Display error message if user entered a negative value
45                MsgBox("You entered " & decLinearFeet.ToString() & _
46                    ". Enter a Number Greater Than Zero.", , "Input Error")
47                Me.txtLinearFeet.Text = ""
48                Me.txtLinearFeet.Focus()
49            End If
50        Else
51            ' Display error message if user entered a nonnumeric value
52            MsgBox("Enter the Linear Feet of the Cabinets.", , "Input Error")
53            Me.txtLinearFeet.Text = ""
54            Me.txtLinearFeet.Focus()
55        End If
56    End Sub
57
58    Private Sub btnClear_Click(ByVal sender As System.Object, ByVal e As System.
      EventArgs) Handles btnClear.Click
59        ' This event handler is executed when
60        ' the user clicks the Clear button. It
61        ' clears the Linear Feet text box and the
62        ' cost estimate label, resets the radio
63        ' buttons with Pine selected, and sets  the
64        ' focus to the Linear Feet text box.
65
```

FIGURE 5-97 (continues)

```
66              Me.txtLinearFeet.Text = ""
67              Me.lblCostEstimate.Text = ""
68              Me.radPine.Checked = True
69              Me.radOak.Checked = False
70              Me.radCherry.Checked = False
71              Me.txtLinearFeet.Focus()
72          End Sub
73
74          Private Sub frmCabinetCost_Load(ByVal sender As System.Object, ByVal e As System.  ↙
            EventArgs) Handles MyBase.Load
75              ' This event handler is executed when
76              ' the form is loaded at the start of
77              ' the program. It sets the focus
78              ' to the Linear Feet text box and
79              ' clears the cost estimate label.
80
81              Me.txtLinearFeet.Focus()
82              lblCostEstimate.Text = ""
83          End Sub
84
85      End Class
86
```

FIGURE 5-97 (continued)

Summary

In this chapter you have learned to make decisions based on the user's input. You now can write both Windows and Mobile applications.

The items listed in the table in Figure 5–98 on the next page include all the new Visual Studio and Visual Basic skills you have learned in this chapter.

VISUAL BASIC SKILLS

Skill	Figure Number	Web Address for Video
Explore the Wood Cabinet Estimate chapter project application	Figure 5-1	scsite.com/vb2008/ch5/figure5-1
Create a Smart Device application	Figure 5-6	scsite.com/vb2008/ch5/figure5-6
Use a Panel with RadioButton objects	Figure 5-12	scsite.com/vb2008/ch5/figure5-12
Add RadioButton objects to a Panel object	Figure 5-15	scsite.com/vb2008/ch5/figure5-15
Use Windows Application Container objects	Figure 5-22	
Code a Message Box command	Figure 5-32	scsite.com/vb2008/ch5/figure5-32
Concatenate strings	Figure 5-37	
Code an If...Then statement	Figure 5-39	
Turn on Pretty Listing for indentation	Page 315	
Use relational operators	Figure 5-40	
Enter an If...Then statement	Figure 5-42	scsite.com/vb2008/ch5/figure5-42
Compare strings	Figure 5-45	
Code If...Then...Else statements	Figure 5-46	
Compare values using an arithmetic expression	Figure 5-48	
Code an If...Then...ElseIf statement	Figure 5-49	
Code a nested If statement	Figure 5-51	
Test the status of a RadioButton object in code	Figure 5-56	
Understand block-level scoping	Figure 5-59	
Code logical operators	Figure 5-61	
Code Select Case statements	Figure 5-70	
Insert code snippets	Figure 5-77	scsite.com/vb2008/ch5/figure5-77
Validate input data	Figure 5-82	
Deploy a Smart Device Application on a Pocket PC	Figure 5-84	scsite.com/vb2008/ch5/figure5-84

FIGURE 5-98

Learn It Online

Start your browser and visit scsite.com/vb2008/ch5. Follow the instructions in the exercises below.

1. **Chapter Reinforcement TF, MC, SA** Click one of the Chapter Reinforcement links for Multiple Choice, True/False, or Short Answer below the Learn It Online heading. Answer each question and submit to your instructor.

2. **Practice Test** Click the Practice Test link below Chapter 5. Answer each question, enter your first and last name at the bottom of the page, and then click the Grade Test button. When the graded practice test is displayed on your screen, submit the graded practice test to your instructor. Continue to take the practice test until you are satisfied with your score.

3. **Crossword Puzzle Challenge** Click the Crossword Puzzle Challenge link below the Learn It Online heading. Read the instructions, and then click the Continue button. Work the crossword puzzle. When you are finished, click the Submit button. When the crossword puzzle is redisplayed, submit it to your instructor.

Knowledge Check

1. Name the six relational operators and state the purpose of each operator.

2. How is input entered on an actual Pocket PC device while an application is running?

3. Write an If...Then statement that tests if the value in the variable intTemp is between 32 and 95 degrees. If the number is in that range, set the Text property for the lblWarning Label object to "Normal Temperature".

4. Write an If...Then...Else statement that assigns 30 to a variable named intMinutes if strRoadway is equal to "Interstate". Otherwise, assign 60 to intMinutes.

5. List the three most common logical operators and explain their use.

6. Rewrite the following line of code without a Not logical operator but keeping the same logical processing:

```
If Not intHeight <= 72 Then
```

7. The intent of the following statement is to check if the radDeluxeRoom RadioButton object is checked. What is the error in the statement? Rewrite the statement so it is correct.

```
If Me.radDeluxeRoom = Checked Then
```

8. The intent of following statement is to check if the value in the intGrade variable is less than 0 or greater than 100. What is the error in the statement? Rewrite the statement so it is correct.

```
If intGrade < 0 And intGrade > 100 Then
```

9. Using the Internet for research, identify a Wi-Fi hotspot in a city near you that can be used for a Pocket PC. Is the hotspot free? Submit your findings to your instructor.

10. Using the Internet for research, find an advertisement for a new Pocket PC. Submit the advertisement to your instructor.

Knowledge Check

(continued)

11. Why do most developers indent the code within a decision structure?

12. Write a statement that creates the dialog box shown in Figure 5-99 in a Windows application. Use a single numerical value to create the button and picture icon.

FIGURE 5-99

13. What is the difference between a Panel object and a GroupBox object? Can you use both objects in a Windows application? In a Mobile application?

14. What is the difference between the Or logical operator and the Xor logical operator?

15. Write a data validation statement that would check to ensure the value in the intAge variable is between 1 and 120. If the age is not valid, display an error message box stating that the age is not valid.

16. How many radio buttons in a group can be selected at one time?

17. Using the concatenation operator (&), write a statement that would create the compound word teahouse from the following two strings: strFirst = "tea" and strSecond= "house". Assign the compound word to the strCompound string variable.

18. Write a statement that would clear the radio button named radSurfBoard.

19. Write a Select Case statement using the fewest Case statements possible to display the number of days in each month. The user enters the number of the month, such as 8, which is converted to an integer and assigned to the intMonth variable. The Select Case statement should display a message box that states the number of days in the month, such as "31 Days".

20. Which logical operator has the highest precedence in the order of operations?

Debugging Exercises

1. Explain how the two statements shown in Figure 5-100 are evaluated:

```
If strResponse = "Red" AndAlso strAnswer = "Green" Then

    If strResponse = "Red" And strAnswer = "Green" Then
```

FIGURE 5-100

(continues)

Debugging Exercises

(continued)

2. Explain the error in the code shown in Figure 5-101 and explain how to correct the code.

```
If dblCommission >= 2500 Then
    Dim intBonus As Integer
    intBonus = 500
Else
    intBonus = 0
End If
```

FIGURE 5-101

3. The Select Case statement shown in Figure 5-102 contains one or more errors. Identify the error(s) and rewrite the statements correctly.

```
Select Case intNumberOfSeats
    Case > 5000
        strVenueType = "Stadium"
    Case > 2000
        strVenueType = "Amphitheater"
    Case > 1000
        strVenueType = "Auditorium"
    Case > 200
        strVenueType = "Theater"
    Case > 0
        strVenueType = "Club"
    Else Case
        strVenueType = "Error"
Select End
```

FIGURE 5-102

4. The Select Case statement shown in Figure 5-103 contains one or more errors. Identify the error(s) and rewrite the statements correctly.

```
Select Case charFlightCode
    Case 'F', 'A'
        Me.lblFare.Text = 'First Class'
    Case 'B', 'Q'
        Me.lblFare.Text = 'Business Class'
    Case 'Y', 'S', 'M'
        Me.lblFare.Text = 'Full Fare Economy'
    Case 'K', 'C'
        Me.lblFare.Text = 'Preferred Economy'
    Case 'U', 'J', 'P', 'G'
        Me.lblFare.Text = 'Economy'
    Else
        Me.lblFare.Text = 'Unknown'
End Select
```

FIGURE 5-103

Debugging Exercises

(continued)

5. The If...Then...Else statement shown in Figure 5-104 contains one or more errors. Identify the error(s) and rewrite the statements correctly.

```
If strShippingMethod = "Overnite" Then
    If strDeliveryTime = "Morning"
        decDeliveryCost = 29.00D
    Else
        decDeliveryCost = 24.00D
Else
    If strShippingMethod = "Two Days" Then
        decDeliveryCost = 14.00D
    Else
        decDeliveryCost = 4.00D
End If
```

FIGURE 5-104

Program Analysis

1. Write an If...Then...Else decision structure to compare the two numbers in the intPay1 and intPay2 variables. Display a message box stating intPay1 is greater than intPay2, or intPay1 is less than or equal to intPay2.

2. Write an If statement that displays the message box "Snow is possible" if the value in the variable decTemp is within the range 0 to 32.

3. Write an If...Then...Else statement that checks the value in the variable chrGender for the value M (Male) or F (Female) and assigns the information shown in Figure 5-105 to lblCollegeExpectation.Text based on the gender. If the variable chrGender contains a value other than M or F, assign the message "Invalid Gender" to lblCollegeExpectation.Text.

Gender	College Expectation
Male	75% plan to graduate from college
Female	85% plan to graduate from college

FIGURE 5-105

(continues)

Program Analysis

(continued)

4. Write a Select Case statement that tests the user's age in a variable named intAge and assigns the name of the favorite snack of that age group to the variable strSnack, according to the preferences shown in Figure 5-106.

Age	Favorite Snack
Under age 7	Yogurt
Age 7 to 12	Potato Chips
Age 13 to 18	Chocolate
Over Age 18	Gum

FIGURE 5-106

5. Rewrite the Select Case statement shown in Figure 5-107 as an If...Then...Else statement.

```
Select Case chrDepartment
    Case "B", "b"
        strDept = "Baby / Infant Clothing"
    Case "T", "t"
        strDept = "Technology"
End Select
```

FIGURE 5-107

6. Rewrite the If...Then...Else statement shown in Figure 5-108 as a Select Case statement.

```
If intGrade >= 9 And intGrade <= 12 Then
    Me.lblSchool.Text = "High School"
ElseIf intGrade >= 7 Then
    Me.lblSchool.Text = "Middle School"
ElseIf intGrade >= 1 Then
    Me.lblSchool.Text = "Elementary School"
Else
    Me.lblSchool.Text = "Invalid Grade"
End If
```

FIGURE 5-108

7. What is the output of the code shown in Figure 5-109 if the word Black is entered in the txtSkiSlope text box?

Program Analysis

(continued)

```
Select Case Me.txtSkiSlope.Text
    Case "Green"
        MsgBox("Beginner Slope")
    Case "Blue"
        MsgBox("Intermediate Slope")
    Case "Black"
        MsgBox("Expert Slope")
    Case Else
        MsgBox("Invalid Entry")
End Select
```

FIGURE 5-109

8. After the execution of the Select Case structure in Figure 5-110, what value will be found in the Text property of lblFemaleHeight if the user enters the number 74 into the txtEnterHeight text box? If the number 81 is entered? If the number 59 is entered?

```
Dim intHeightInches As Integer
intHeightInches = Convert.ToInt32(Me.txtEnterHeight.Text)
Select Case intHeightInches
    Case Is < 61
        Me.lblFemaleHeight.Text = "Petite"
    Case 61 To 69
        Me.lblFemaleHeight.Text = "Average"
    Case 70 To 80
        Me.lblFemaleHeight.Text = "Tall"
    Case 80 To 120
        Me.lblFemaleHeight.Text = "Towering"
    Case Else
        Me.lblFemaleHeight.Text = "Not Possible"
End Select
```

FIGURE 5-110

9. In each of the following examples, is the condition True or False?

a. "C" >= "C"

b. "G" >= "g"

c. "Content" < "Contented"

d. "Apple" <> "apple"

e. "40" >= "Forty"

f. ("Paris" < "Barcelona") And ("Amsterdam" <= "Prague")

g. ("Ford" > "Chevrolet") Or ("Toyota" < "Honda")

h. 3 ^ 2 <= 3 * 2

i. Not ("CNN" >= "ABC")

j. Not ("Tim" > "Tom") And Not ("Great" <> "great")

Case Programming Assignments

Complete one or more of the following case programming assignments. Submit the program and materials you create to your instructor. The level of difficulty is indicated for each case programming assignment.

● = Easiest
●● = Intermediate
●●● = Challenging

1 ● PARKING TICKET FINES

Design a mobile application and write the code that will execute according to the program requirements in Figure 5-111. Before writing the code, create an event planning document for each event in the program. The completed Pocket PC Form object and other objects in the user interface are shown in Figure 5-114.

REQUIREMENTS DOCUMENT

Date submitted: May 6, 2011

Application title: Parking Ticket Fines

Purpose: This mobile application calculates a parking ticket fine.

Program Procedures: From a Pocket PC handheld device, the user selects the type of parking violation and indicates if the owner of the vehicle is a repeat offender. The user then requests that the program calculate and display the parking ticket fine.

Algorithms, Processing, and Conditions:
1. The user selects the type of parking violation.
2. If the owner of the vehicle has been ticketed previously for a parking offense in the city, the fine is doubled.
3. The user must be able to indicate the owner is a repeat offender.
4. The fine is calculated based on the chart in Figure 5-112.
5. The user must be able to initiate the display of the parking ticket fine.
6. The user should be able to clear the type of violation indicator, the repeat offender indicator, and the ticket fine.

Notes and Restrictions:

Comments: The application should be deployed on the Pocket PC emulator built into Visual Studio 2008.

FIGURE 5-111

Case Programming Assignments

Parking Violation	Fine
Expired Meter	$35
No Parking Zone	$75
Blocking Driveway	$150
Illegal Handicap Parking	$500

FIGURE 5-112

USE CASE DEFINITION

1. The Pocket PC window opens.
2. The user selects the type of parking offense.
3. The user selects whether the user is a repeat offender.
4. The user clicks the Display Fine button to display the parking ticket fine.
5. The user clears the input and the result by clicking the Clear button.
6. If desired, the user repeats the process.

FIGURE 5-113

FIGURE 5-114

Case Programming Assignments

2 CELL PHONE BILL

Design a mobile application and write the code that will execute according to the program requirements in Figure 5-115. Before writing the code, create an event planning document for each event in the program. The completed Pocket PC Form object and other objects in the user interface are shown in Figure 5-117.

REQUIREMENTS DOCUMENT

Date submitted: April 15, 2011

Application title: Cell Phone Bill

Purpose: This application calculates the cost of a cell phone bill.

Program Procedures: From a Pocket PC handheld device, the user should enter the number of minutes used during the past month in order to calculate the cost of the cell phone bill. The plan allows 300 minutes for $29.95 per month. For each minute that exceeds 300 minutes, the cost is 17 cents per minute. Taxes and other fees add up to $4.85 per month.

Algorithms, Processing, and Conditions:
1. The user enters the number of minutes used during the past month's billing cycle.
2. Based on the monthly plan rate of 300 minutes for $29.95 and 17 cents for each minute over 300, calculate the cost of the bill. Also add the fixed cost of $4.85 for taxes and other fees.
3. The user must be able to initiate the calculation and display of the individual charges and the total cost of the cell phone bill.
4. The user should be able to clear the number of cell phone minutes, the individual charges, and the bill total.

Notes and Restrictions:
1. If a negative number is entered for cell phone minutes, the user should be advised and asked for a valid entry.
2. If a nonnumeric value is entered for the cell phone minutes or if the input for the number of minutes is left blank, the user should be advised and asked for a valid entry.

Comments: The application should be deployed on the Pocket PC emulator built into Visual Studio 2008.

FIGURE 5-115

Case Programming Assignments

USE CASE DEFINITION

1. The Pocket PC window opens.
2. The user enters the number of minutes used.
3. The user clicks the Display Bill button.
4. The program displays the total cell phone bill and the individual costs.
5. Using a MsgBox, the user is warned if a negative number is entered for the minutes.
6. Using a MsgBox, the user is warned if a nonnumeric value is entered for the minutes or if the value is left blank.
7. The user can clear the input and the results by clicking the Clear button.

FIGURE 5-116

FIGURE 5-117

Case Programming Assignments

3 • PATIENT WEIGHT CONVERTER

Design a mobile application and write the code that will execute according to the program requirements in Figure 5-118. Before writing the code, create an event planning document for each event in the program. The completed Pocket PC Form object and other objects in the user interface are shown in Figure 5-120.

REQUIREMENTS DOCUMENT

Date submitted:	May 11, 2011
Application title:	Patient Weight Converter
Purpose:	This mobile application converts the weight of the patient from pounds to kilograms and kilograms to pounds.
Program Procedures:	From a Pocket PC handheld device, the user enters the weight of the patient, selects the conversion type (pounds to kilograms or kilograms to pounds) and displays the converted weight of the patient.
Algorithms, Processing, and Conditions:	1. A user must be able to enter the weight of the patient in pounds or kilograms.
	2. The user must be able to select the type of conversion: Pounds to Kilograms or Kilograms to Pounds.
	3. The user must be able to initiate the weight conversion and the display of the patient's converted weight.
	4. The conversion formulas are: kilograms = pounds / 2.2 pounds = kilograms × 2.2
	5. The user must be able to clear the entered weight, conversion choice, and results.
Notes and Restrictions:	1. If a nonnumeric value is entered or if the weight is left blank, the user should be advised and asked for a valid entry.
	2. If a negative number is entered for the weight, the user should be advised and asked for a valid entry.
	3. If the value entered is greater than 500 for the conversion from pounds to kilograms or greater than 225 for the conversion from kilograms to pounds, the user should be advised and asked for a valid entry.
	4. The default conversion choice should be pounds to kilograms.
	5. The converted weight should be displayed with one digit to the right of the decimal point.
Comments:	The application should be deployed on the Pocket PC emulator built into Visual Studio 2008.

FIGURE 5-118

Case Programming Assignments

USE CASE DEFINITION

1. The Pocket PC window opens.
2. The user enters the patient's weight.
3. The user selects the conversion type (pounds to kilograms or kilograms to pounds).
4. The user clicks the Display Weight button to display the converted weight value.
5. The user clears the input and the result by clicking the Clear button.
6. If desired, the user repeats the process.

FIGURE 5-119

FIGURE 5-120

Case Programming Assignments

4 ●● HEALTH CLUB MEMBERSHIP

Design a mobile application and write the code that will execute according to the program requirements in Figure 5-121. Before designing the user interface, create a Use Case definition. Before writing the code, create an event planning document for each event in the program.

REQUIREMENTS DOCUMENT

Date submitted: April 22, 2011

Application title: Health Club Membership

Purpose: This mobile application calculates the prepayment amount for a new member of a health club.

Program Procedures: From a Pocket PC handheld device, the user should enter the name of the new member, the number of months the new user would like to prepay, and the type of membership. The health club prepayment cost will be computed and displayed for the entered number of months. The per month costs for the three types of membership are:

Single Membership	$38 per month
Family Membership	$58 per month
Senior Membership	$27 per month

Algorithms, Processing, and Conditions:
1. The user must enter the name of the new member, the type of membership, and the number of months the new member would like to prepay.
2. Based on the type of membership, the prepayment cost is calculated using the following formula: number of prepay months x cost per month.
3. The user must be able to initiate the calculation and display of the prepay amount for the health club membership.
4. The user should be able to clear the name of the new member, the number of prepay months, the type of membership, and prepay amount for the new member.

Notes and Restrictions:
1. If the user enters a nonnumeric value for the number of months, the user should be advised and asked for a valid entry.
2. If the user enters a negative number for the number of months or if the user leaves the number of months input area blank, the user should be advised and asked for a valid entry.
3. If the user leaves the input area for the user name blank, the user should be advised and asked for a valid entry.
4. The default membership type is single membership.

Comments: The application must be deployed on the Pocket PC emulator built into Visual Studio 2008.

FIGURE 5-121

Case Programming Assignments

5 ●●
TWO-DAY PACKAGE SHIPPING

Design a mobile application and write the code that will execute according to the program requirements in Figure 5-122. Before designing the user interface, create a Use Case definition. Before writing the code, create an event planning document for each event in the program.

REQUIREMENTS DOCUMENT

Date submitted: May 6, 2011

Application title: Two-Day Package Shipping

Purpose: This application calculates the cost of shipping a package with two-day delivery.

Program Procedures: From a Pocket PC handheld device, the user enters the weight of the package (in pounds) and selects the destination of the package. The application will determine the cost of shipping. The destination of the package can be the continental U.S., Hawaii, or Alaska. If the package is going to Hawaii, a 20% surcharge is added to the shipping cost. If the package is going to Alaska, a 26% surcharge is added to the shipping cost.

Algorithms, Processing, and Conditions:
1. The user must be able to enter the number of pounds the package weighs and indicate that the package is being mailed to the continental U.S., Hawaii or Alaska.
2. The shipping costs are calculated based on the rates in the table in Figure 5-123 on the next page. A 20% surcharge is added if the shipping destination is Hawaii. A 26% surcharge is added if the shipping destination is Alaska.
3. The user must be able to initiate the calculation and the display of the shipping cost.
4. The user must be able to clear the weight of the package and the shipping cost.

Notes and Restrictions:
1. If the entry for the shipping weight is blank or nonnumeric, the user should be advised and asked for a valid entry.
2. The maximum weight for a package is 30 pounds. If the weight is greater than 30 pounds, or if the value entered is not greater than zero, the user should be advised and asked for a valid entry.

Comments: The application should be deployed on a Pocket PC emulator built into Visual Studio 2008.

FIGURE 5-122

(continues)

Case Programming Assignments

Two-Day Package Shipping (continued)

For Weight Not Over (Pounds)	2-Day Rate
2	$3.69
4	$4.86
6	$5.63
8	$5.98
10	$6.28
30	$15.72

FIGURE 5-123

Case Programming Assignments

6 ●● PAYROLL CALCULATOR

Design a Windows application and write the code that will execute according to the program requirements in Figure 5-124. Before designing the user interface, create a Use Case definition. Before writing the code, create an event planning document for each event in the program.

REQUIREMENTS DOCUMENT

Date submitted: May 11, 2011

Application title: Payroll Calculator

Purpose: This application calculates the payroll for employees of the Food For All local grocery store.

Program Procedures: In a Windows application, the user enters the employee's name, hours worked, and pay per hour. If the employee works more than 40 hours per week, the grocery store pays time-and-a-half for overtime. The tax rate can be the single rate (18%) or at the family rate (15%). The application should compute and display the gross pay, the tax based on the single or family rate, and the net pay.

Algorithms, Processing, and Conditions:
1. The user must be able to enter the employee's name, hours worked, and pay per hour.
2. The user must be able to indicate if the tax rate is at the single rate (18%) or the family rate (15%).
3. The user must be able to initiate the calculation and the display of the gross pay, the tax amount based on the single or family rate, and the net pay.
4. A Clear button will clear the user's input and final results.

Notes and Restrictions:
1. If the employee name, hours worked, or pay per hour are blank, the user should be advised and asked for a valid entry.
2. If the hours worked or pay per hour are nonnumeric, the user should be advised and asked for a valid entry.
3. The minimum value for hours worked is 5 hours. The maximum for hours worked is 60. If the user enters an hours worked value not within the range, the user should be advised and asked for a valid entry.
4. The minimum pay per hour is $8.00. The maximum pay per hour is $40.00 per hour. If the user enters a pay per hour value not within the range, the user should be advised and asked for a valid entry.
5. The user must be able to clear the employee's name, the hours worked, the pay per hour, and the pay information.

Comments:

FIGURE 5-124

Case Programming Assignments

7 ●●●
TECHNOLOGY CONFERENCE REGISTRATION

Create a requirements document and a Use Case Definition document, and then design a mobile application based on the following case project. Before writing the code, create an event planning document for each event in the program:

It is important that developers update their skills by attending developers' conferences. The Dynamic International Management Consortium (DIMC) runs and manages the ADSE (Active Developers Skill Enhancement) Conference two times per year. To encourage companies to send multiple employees to the conference, the cost per attendee is determined based on the number of attending developers from a given company. The table below specifies the cost per attendee.

Number of Conference Registrations per Company	Cost per Attendee
1	$695
2-4	$545
5-8	$480
8 or more	$395

DIMC has requested that you develop a mobile application that can determine and display the total cost per company for developers attending the conference. DIMC has a conference policy that states if any member of a company has attended a previous DIMC conference, the company receives a 15% discount from the total cost of its employees who attend. The policy also states that no more than 16 people from a single company can attend the conference. DIMC has asked that you design the program so that the user must enter valid data.

FIGURE 5-125

Case Programming Assignments

8 ●●●
CAR RENTAL

Create a requirements document and a Use Case Definition document, and then design a mobile application based on the following case project. Before writing the code, create an event planning document for each event in the program:

The Adventure Car Rental Company has asked that you create a Windows application for the rental of an adventure vehicle. The user selects the number of rental days, up to 7 days. The user also can select one of three types of vehicles. The types of vehicles and the cost per day for each vehicle is shown in the table below.

Vehicle Model	Cost per Day
Jeep Wrangler	$55.00
Jeep Grand Cherokee	$85.00
Land Rover	$125.00

The customer has a choice of filling the gas tank themselves at the end of their use, or prepaying for a full tank of gas ($52 total). If the vehicle will be driven by more than one driver, a multiple driver cost of $22 per day is added to the cost of the vehicle. Adventure has asked that the Windows application determine and display the total rental cost of the vehicle for the amount of time and the options chosen by the user. Adventure also has requested that you include all appropriate checking for invalid data entry by the user.

FIGURE 5-126

Case Programming Assignments

9 ● ● ●

MOVIE TICKETS

Create a requirements document and a Use Case Definition document, and then design a mobile application based on the following case project. Before writing the code, create an event planning document for each event in the program.

In the Dark Movies, Inc. is reducing ticket lines by installing ticket kiosks on Pocket PC devices outside the movie theatre where customers can purchase their tickets. In the Dark has asked you to create a mobile application that allows the customer to enter the number of tickets to be purchased (up to a maximum of 15), the name of one movie from a possible five movies, and indicate whether the ticket is for a matinee performance ($5.75 per ticket) or an evening performance ($8.50 per ticket). The application should compute and display the cost of the tickets along with the name of the movie selected. Lastly, the ticket kiosk can process cash to pay for the ticket(s). The application should ask the user for the amount of cash placed into the kiosk and then compute the change amount. The largest bill the kiosk can process is a $100 bill. In the Dark Movies, Inc. has asked that you include all appropriate data validation to ensure the user enters valid values.

FIGURE 5-127

CHAPTER SIX

Loop Structures

OBJECTIVES

You will have mastered the material in this chapter when you can:

- ► Add a MenuStrip object
- ► Use the InputBox function
- ► Display data using the ListBox object
- ► Understand the use of counters and accumulators
- ► Understand the use of compound operators
- ► Repeat a process using a For…Next loop
- ► Repeat a process using a Do loop

- ► Avoid infinite loops
- ► Prime a loop
- ► Validate data
- ► Create a nested loop
- ► Select the best type of loop
- ► Debug using DataTips at breakpoints
- ► Publish a finished application using ClickOnce technology

Introduction

In Chapter 5 you learned about the decision structure, one of the major control structures used in computer programming. In this chapter you will learn another major structure called the **looping structure**, or the **iteration structure**.

A fundamental process in a computer program is to repeat a series of instructions either while a condition is true (or not true) or until a condition is true (or not true). For example, if a company is printing paychecks for its 5,000 employees, it can use the same set of instructions to print the check for each employee, varying only the name of the employee and amount paid for each check. This process would continue until all checks are printed. Unique check-printing instructions for each employee in the company are not required.

The process of repeating a set of instructions while a condition is true or until a condition is true is called **looping**, and when the program is executing those instructions, it is said to be in a loop. Another term for looping is **iteration**.

CHAPTER PROJECT

The programming project in this chapter uses a loop to obtain input data and produce output information. A police department has requested a Windows application that determines the average speed for vehicles on a local highway. This application, called the Highway Radar Checkpoint application, computes the average speed for up to 10 vehicles that pass a checkpoint on a highway with a posted speed limit of 60 miles per hour (mph). The application uses a loop to request and display the speed for up to 10 vehicles. When the user has entered all vehicle speeds, the application displays the average speed of the vehicles (Figure 6-1).

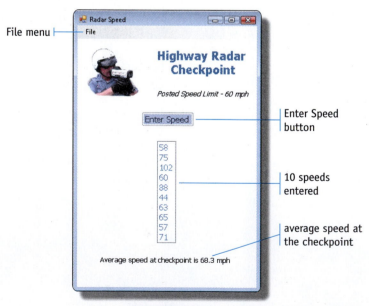

FIGURE 6-1

In Figure 6-1, the user entered the 10 vehicle speeds shown as a list. After the user entered the 10 speeds, the application calculated the average speed at the checkpoint.

When the Highway Radar Checkpoint application begins, the main window shows no speeds entered (Figure 6-2).

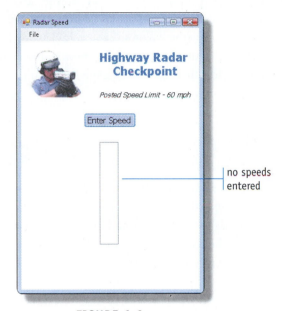

no speeds entered

FIGURE 6-2

When the user clicks the Enter Speed button, the Radar Speed dialog box shown in Figure 6-3 opens, allowing the user to enter the first vehicle's speed. This dialog box is called an **input box**.

user enters speed here

FIGURE 6-3

ONLINE REINFORCEMENT

To view a video of program execution, visit scsite.com/vb2008/ch6 and then select Figure 6-1.

After entering the first valid speed, the user clicks the OK button in the dialog box. The application lists the speed in the main window, and then displays the input box again, requesting the speed for the next vehicle. This process repeats for up to 10 vehicles. This repetitive process is implemented using a loop in the program and, when the user is entering vehicle speeds, the program is said to be in a loop. The loop is terminated when the user enters the speed for the tenth vehicle or clicks the Cancel button in the dialog box. After the loop is terminated, the Highway Radar Checkpoint application displays the average speed for the vehicles, as shown in Figure 6-1 on page 384.

The Highway Radar Checkpoint application has several other features. In Figure 6-1 you can see that a menu bar containing the File menu is displayed at the top of the window. The File menu contains the Clear command, which clears the list and the average speed; and the Exit command, which closes the window and terminates the application. In this chapter, you will learn to design and code a menu.

In addition, the application contains data editing features. For example, if a user enters a non-numeric or negative value for the vehicle speed, the user is asked for the speed of that vehicle again, until the entry is a reasonable value.

Finally, the application displays the average speed to one decimal place, such as 68.3 mph.

User Interface Design

The user interface for the Highway Radar Checkpoint application includes three new elements: a menu, the input box, and the list for the vehicle speeds. The menu and the list for vehicle speeds are objects placed on the Windows Form object. The input box is created through the use of a function call in the program code. Each of these items is explained in the following sections.

MENUSTRIP OBJECT

A **menu bar** is a strip across the top of a window that contains one or more menu names. A **menu** is a group of commands, or items, presented in a list. In the sample program, a File menu is created in the application window (Figure 6-4).

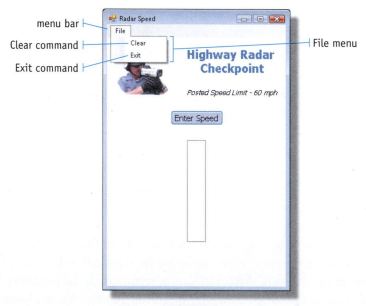

FIGURE 6-4

When the user clicks File on the menu bar during program execution, as shown in Figure 6-4, a menu appears with two commands: Clear and Exit. If the user clicks the Clear menu command, the entered speeds and the results are cleared. Clicking the Exit menu command closes the application. An advantage of a menu is that it conserves space instead of cluttering the form with objects such as buttons.

Using Visual Studio 2008, you can place menus at the top of a Windows Form using the MenuStrip object. To place a MenuStrip object on a Windows Form, you can complete the following steps:

STEP 1 With a Windows Form object open in the Visual Studio window, scroll in the Toolbox until the Menus & Toolbars category is visible. If the category is not open, click the + sign next to the Menus & Toolbars category name. Drag the MenuStrip .NET component from the Menus & Toolbars category in the Toolbox to the Windows Form object.

The pointer changes when you place it over the Windows Form object (Figure 6-5).

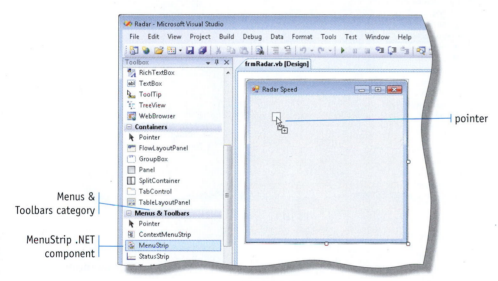

FIGURE 6-5

STEP 2 Release the mouse button.

Visual Studio places the MenuStrip object at the top of the form regardless of the location of the mouse pointer when you released the mouse button (Figure 6-6). The Component Tray, which is displayed below the form, organizes non-graphical Toolbox objects. It displays the MenuStrip1 object name.

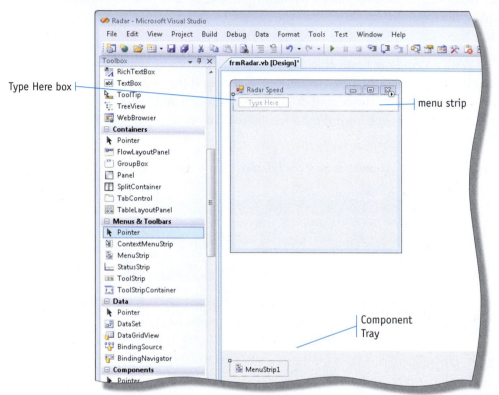

FIGURE 6-6

STEP 3 With the MenuStrip object selected, scroll in the Properties window until the (Name) property is visible. Change the MenuStrip object name to mnuHighwayRadarCheckpoint. (Note that the prefix for a MenuStrip object is mnu).

The name for the MenuStrip object is changed in the Properties window and in the Component Tray (Figure 6-7).

FIGURE 6-7

STEP 4 Click the Type Here box on the menu bar. Type **&File** to identify the File menu, and then press the ENTER key.

The menu name File is displayed in the upper-left corner of the MenuStrip object and new Type Here boxes are available to create other menu items (Figure 6-8). The ampersand (&) you entered preceding the F indicates that F is a hot key. A hot key provides a keyboard short-cut for opening the menu. Instead of clicking File to open the menu, the user can press and hold the ALT key and then press the designated hot key, such as ALT + F. After you enter the menu name, the character following the ampersand is underlined to indicate it is the hot key.

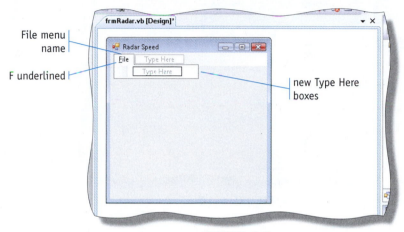

File menu name

F underlined

new Type Here boxes

FIGURE 6-8

STEP 5 Click File in the MenuStrip object to select it, scroll in the Properties window to the (Name) property, and then change the name to **mnuFileMenu.**

The name of the File menu is displayed in the (Name) property in the Properties window (Figure 6-9).

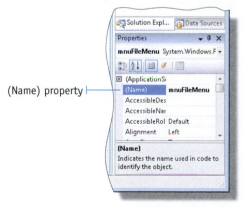

(Name) property

FIGURE 6-9

STEP 6 To add a menu item to the File menu, click the Type Here box below the File menu name. Type **&Clear** and then press ENTER to create a new menu item named Clear with C as the hot key.

The Clear menu item is displayed below the File menu (Figure 6-10). After you enter the item by pressing the ENTER key, the character following the ampersand is underlined to indicate it is the hot key.

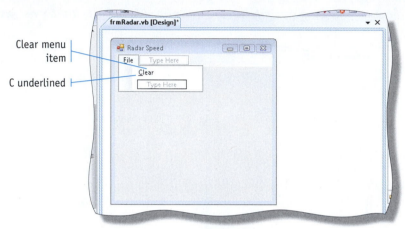

Clear menu item

C underlined

FIGURE 6-10

STEP 7 On the File menu, click Clear to select it, scroll in the Properties window until the (Name) property is visible, and then change the name to **mnuClearItem.**

The mnuClearItem name is displayed in the (Name) property in the Properties window (Figure 6-11).

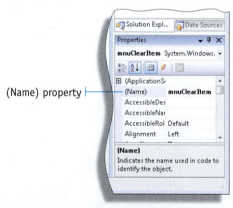

(Name) property

FIGURE 6-11

The letter representing a hot key appears underlined in the menu name, as shown in Figure 6-10. The first letter often is used for the hot key, but not always. For example, in the chapter project, the File menu includes the Exit item (see Figure 6-4 on page 386). The hot key typically used for the Exit item is the letter x. When entering the Exit menu item on the File menu, the developer can type E&xit, which assigns the letter following the & (x) as the hot key.

When assigning hot keys, you should be aware that menu item hot keys are not case-sensitive. Therefore, you should not assign "T" to one menu item and "t" to another.

Event Handlers for Menu Items

As you are aware, the design of the user interface occurs before you write the code for event handlers. When you are ready to write code, however, you must write an event handler for each menu item because clicking a menu item or using its hot key triggers an event. Writing a menu item event handler is the same as writing an event handler for a button click.

To code the event handler for the Exit menu item, you can complete the following steps:

STEP 1   In Design view, double-click the Exit menu item to open the code editing window.

The code editing window is displayed and the insertion point is located within the Exit item click event handler (Figure 6-12). When the user clicks the Exit item on the File menu, the code in the event handler will be executed. Note in Figure 6-12 that the Toolbox is closed.

mnuExitItem
event handler

FIGURE 6-12

STEP 2   Using IntelliSense, enter the Close procedure call to close the window and terminate the application.

When executed, the Close procedure will close the window and terminate the program (Figure 6-13).

Close()
procedure

FIGURE 6-13

ONLINE REINFORCEMENT

To view a video of the process in the previous steps, visit scsite.com/vb2008/ch6 and then select Figure 6-12.

Standard Items for a Menu

Developers often customize the MenuStrip object for the specific needs of an application. In addition, Visual Basic 2008 contains an **Action Tag** that allows you to create a full standard menu bar commonly provided in Windows programs, with File, Edit, Tools, and Help menus. In Visual Basic 2008, an Action Tag (▶) appears in the upper-right corner of many objects, including a MenuStrip. Action Tags provide a way for you to specify a set of actions, called **smart actions**, for an object as you design a form. For example, to insert a full standard menu, you can complete the following steps:

STEP 1 With a new Windows Form object open, drag the MenuStrip .NET component onto the Windows Form object. Click the Action Tag on the MenuStrip object.

The MenuStrip Tasks menu opens (Figure 6-14).

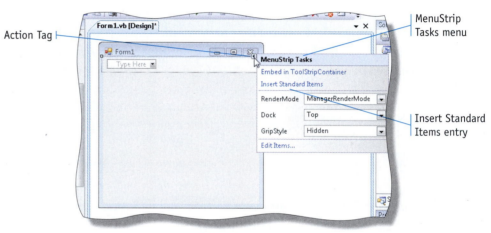

Action Tag

MenuStrip Tasks menu

Insert Standard Items entry

FIGURE 6-14

STEP 2 Click Insert Standard Items on the MenuStrip Tasks menu.

The MenuStrip object contains four menu names — File, Edit, Tools, and Help (Figure 6-15). These menus are the standard menus found on many Windows applications. Each menu contains the standard menu items normally found on the menus.

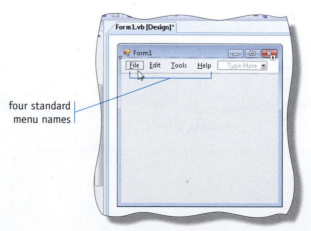

four standard menu names

FIGURE 6-15

STEP 3 Click File on the menu bar to view the individual menu items and their associated icons on the File menu.

The standard File menu items (New, Open, Save, Save As, Print, Print Preview, and Exit) are displayed with their associated icons and shortcut keys (Figure 6-16). The other menus also contain standard items. You can code an event handler for each menu item by double-clicking the item.

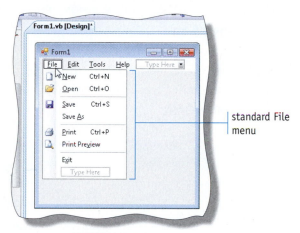

FIGURE 6-16

INPUTBOX FUNCTION

To calculate the average vehicle speed, the Highway Radar Checkpoint application uses an InputBox object where users enter the speed for each vehicle. The InputBox object is a dialog box that prompts the user to enter a value. Similar to a MessageBox object, you code the InputBox function to specify when the InputBox object appears. The InputBox function displays a dialog box that consists of a message asking for input, an input area, a title, an OK button, and a Cancel button (see Figure 6-3 on page 385). When the user enters the text and clicks the OK button, the InputBox function returns this text as a string. If the user clicks the Cancel button, the function returns a null string (""). The code shown in Figure 6-17 demonstrates the syntax of the InputBox function:

General Format: InputBox Function

```
strVariableName = InputBox("Question to Prompt User", "Title Bar")
```

FIGURE 6-17

For example, the code in Figure 6-18 creates a dialog box that requests the user's age for a driver's license application. The string returned by the InputBox function is assigned to the strAge variable.

```
5        Dim strAge As String
6
7        strAge = InputBox("Please enter your age", "Driver's License Agency")
```

FIGURE 6-18

When the application is executed, the InputBox object in Figure 6-19 opens, requesting that the user enter her age. The InputBox function can be used to obtain input instead of a TextBox object.

FIGURE 6-19

The InputBox object returns all entered data as a string, which then can be converted to the appropriate data type.

InputBox Object Default Value

The InputBox object can be assigned a default value. For example, if a college application for admission requests the student's home state and the college or university is located in Virginia, the most likely state, Virginia, can be the default value in the InputBox, as shown in Figure 6-20.

FIGURE 6-20

The code to produce this input box is shown in Figure 6-21.

```
9        Dim strState As String
10
11       strState = InputBox("Please enter the state in which you reside:", _
12           "College Application", "Virginia")
```

FIGURE 6-21

As you can see, the third argument for the InputBox function call is the default value that is placed in the input box. It must be a string value and follow the syntax shown in Figure 6-21.

InputBox Object for Highway Radar Checkpoint Application

The Highway Radar Checkpoint application uses an InputBox object that requests the speed of vehicles numbered 1-10, as shown in Figure 6-22.

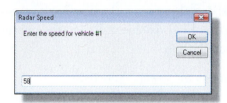

FIGURE 6-22

The code for the Radar Speed InputBox is shown in Figure 6-23. Notice that the prompt message for the user is assigned to the strInputBoxMessage variable, and the title bar text (Radar Speed) is assigned to the strInputBoxHeading variable.

```
15          Dim strVehicleSpeed As String
16          Dim strInputBoxMessage As String = "Enter the speed for vehicle #"
17          Dim strInputBoxHeading As String = "Radar Speed"
18          Dim intNumberOfEntries As Integer = 1
19
20          strVehicleSpeed = InputBox(strInputBoxMessage _
21              & intNumberOfEntries, strInputBoxHeading, " ")
```

FIGURE 6-23

The variable intNumberOfEntries identifies the vehicle number. It is included in the prompt message through the use of concatenation. The variable intNumberOfEntries is incremented later in the code so that it refers to the correct vehicle each time the InputBox function call is executed.

In Figure 6-23, the default value is specified as a space (" "). When the input box is displayed, a space will be selected in the input area. This space is required so that if a user clicks the OK button without entering any data, the InputBox will not return a null character (""), which indicates the user clicked the Cancel button. This normally is a good programming practice.

When the user clicks the Cancel button in an input box and the InputBox function returns a null character, the program can test for the null character to determine further processing.

DISPLAYING DATA USING THE LISTBOX OBJECT

In the Highway Radar Checkpoint application, the user enters the speed of each vehicle into the InputBox object, and the program displays these speeds in a list box (see Figure 6-1 on page 384). To create such a list, you use the ListBox object provided in the Visual Basic Toolbox. A ListBox displays a group of values, called items, with one item per line. To add a ListBox object to a Windows Form object, you can complete the following steps:

STEP 1　Drag the ListBox object from the Toolbox to the Windows Form object where you want to place the ListBox object. When the pointer is in the correct location, release the left mouse button.

The ListBox object is placed on the form (Figure 6-24).

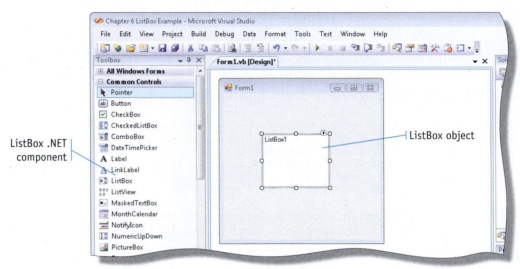

ListBox .NET component

ListBox object

FIGURE 6-24

STEP 2　With the ListBox object selected, scroll in the Properties window to the (Name) property. Name the ListBox object `lstRadarSpeed`.

The name you entered is displayed in the (Name) property in the Properties window (Figure 6-25). Notice a ListBox object name begins with lst.

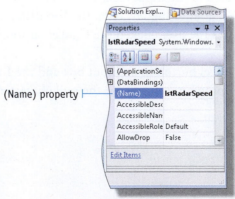

(Name) property

FIGURE 6-25

After placing a ListBox object on the Windows Form object, you can adjust the size as needed by dragging the size handles (see Figure 6-24). Be sure to resize the ListBox so that it is large enough to hold the application data. The ListBox object for the Highway Radar Checkpoint application is designed to be wide enough to hold three digits, and long enough to hold 10 numbers (Figure 6-26).

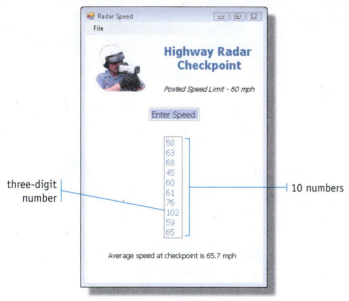

three-digit number　　　10 numbers

FIGURE 6-26

To display the speed of each vehicle in the list box, you must write code to add each item to the ListBox object. After an item is added, it is displayed in the list box. The general format of the statement to add an item to a ListBox object is shown in Figure 6-27.

General Format: Adding Items to a ListBox Object

```
lstListBoxName.Items.Add(Variable Name)
```

FIGURE 6-27

In Figure 6-27, the Add procedure will add the item contained in the variable identified by the Variable Name entry. The syntax for the statement must be followed precisely.

The code to add the vehicle speed to the lstRadarSpeed ListBox object and then display the speed of each vehicle (decVehicleSpeed) in the ListBox object is shown in Figure 6-28.

```
48          Me.lstRadarSpeed.Items.Add(decVehicleSpeed)
```

FIGURE 6-28

If the number of items exceeds the number that can be displayed in the designated space of the ListBox object, a scroll bar automatically is added to the right side of the ListBox object as shown in Figure 6-29.

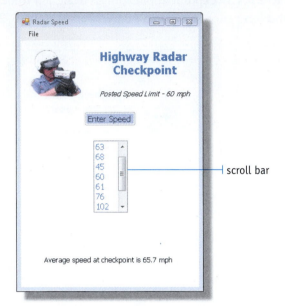

scroll bar

FIGURE 6-29

To clear the items in a ListBox object, the Clear method works as it does for the TextBox object. The syntax of the statement to clear the ListBox is shown in Figure 6-30.

General Format: Clear the ListBox Object

```
lstListBoxName.Items.Clear()
```

FIGURE 6-30

In the Highway Radar Checkpoint application, the user can select the Clear menu item to clear the form. The code in Figure 6-31 removes the items from the lstRadarSpeed ListBox.

```
87       Me.lstRadarSpeed.Items.Clear()
```

FIGURE 6-31

Add Items During Design

The Highway Radar Checkpoint application allows the user to add items to the
ListBox object during program execution, but you also can add items to a ListBox object
while designing the form. Adding items to the ListBox object during the design phase
allows the user to select an item from the ListBox object during execution. For example,
in an application to select a favorite clothing store, you can add items to a ListBox object
named lstStores during the form design by completing the following steps:

STEP 1   Assume the lstStores ListBox object already has been placed and named
on the Windows Form object. Select the ListBox object on the Windows Form object and then click the Items property in the Properties window.

*The Items property in the Properties window is selected. An ellipsis button appears to the
right of the (Collection) entry (Figure 6-32).*

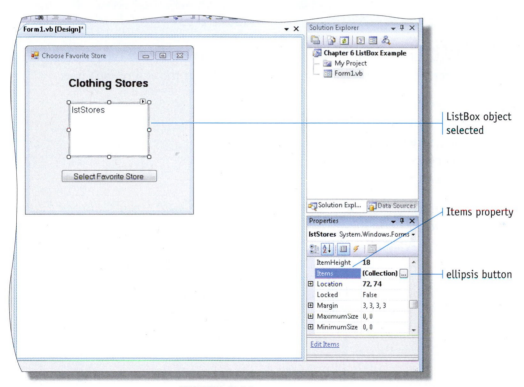

FIGURE 6-32

STEP 2 Click the ellipsis button in the right column of the Items property.

The String Collection Editor window opens, allowing you to enter items that will be displayed in the ListBox object named lstStores (Figure 6-33).

String Collection
Editor window

enter items to
be placed in the
ListBox object

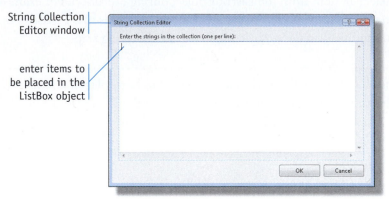

FIGURE 6-33

STEP 3 Click in the String Collection Editor window. Type the following items to represent popular retail stores, pressing ENTER at the end of each line:

```
Abercrombie & Fitch
Aeropostale
American Eagle
Express
Hollister
```

The items representing favorite retail stores appear in the String Collection Editor window on separate lines (Figure 6-34).

items entered for
ListBox object

OK button

FIGURE 6-34

STEP 4 Click the OK button.

The Windows Form object displays the stores in the lstStores ListBox object (Figure 6-35). The user can select one of the items in the ListBox object during execution.

items in ListBox object

FIGURE 6-35

Selected Item Property

The SelectedItem property identifies which item in the ListBox is selected. An assignment statement is used to assign that property to a variable, as shown in Figure 6-36.

General Format: Assign the Selected Item in a ListBox Object

```
strVariableName = lstListBoxName.SelectedItem
```

FIGURE 6-36

The actual code to show the user's selection of their favorite store from the ListBox object named lstStores in a message box is shown in Figure 6-37.

```
5        MsgBox("Your favorite store is " _
6        & Me.lstStores.SelectedItem & ".")
```

FIGURE 6-37

ACCUMULATORS, COUNTERS, AND COMPOUND OPERATORS

In the Highway Radar Checkpoint application, after the user enters the speeds of up to 10 vehicles, the application calculates the average speed (see Figure 6-1 on page 384). The formula to calculate the average speed is: (total of all speeds entered) / (number of vehicles). For example, if the total of all the speeds entered is 683 and 10 vehicle speeds were entered, the average speed is 68.3 mph.

To calculate the average, the program must add the speed of each vehicle to a variable. The variable that contains an accumulated value such as the total of all the speeds is called an **accumulator**.

To compute the average speed, the program also must keep track of how many vehicle speeds the user has entered. The variable that is used to keep track of this value is called a **counter**. A counter always is incremented with a constant value. This value can be positive or negative. In the Highway Radar Checkpoint program, the counter is incremented by 1 each time the user enters a speed for a vehicle.

You can use one of two techniques when you need to add a value to a variable and update the value in the variable, as with an accumulator or a counter. The first technique is shown in Figure 6-38.

```
26        decTotalVehicleSpeed = decTotalVehicleSpeed + decVehicleSpeedEntered
27        intNumberOfEntries = intNumberOfEntries + 1
```

FIGURE 6-38

In Figure 6-38, on line 26 the value in the decTotalVehicleSpeed variable is added to the value in the decVehicleSpeedEntered variable and the result is stored in the decTotalVehicleSpeed variable. This statement has the effect of accumulating the vehicle speed values in the decTotalVehicleSpeed accumulator. Similarly, the number of entries counter is incremented by 1 by the statement on line 27. The effect is that the value in the number of entries counter is increased by 1 each time the statement is executed.

A second method for accomplishing this task is to use a shortcut mathematical operator called a **compound operator** that allows you to add, subtract, multiply, divide, use modulus or exponents, or concatenate strings, storing the result in the same variable. An assignment statement that includes a compound operator begins with the variable that will contain the accumulated value, such as an accumulator or a counter, followed by the compound operator. A compound operator consists of an arithmetic operator and an equal sign. The last element in the assignment statement is the variable or literal containing the value to be used in the calculation.

This means that an assignment statement using a compound operator such as:

`intNumberOfEntries += 1`

which is an assignment statement using a compound operator, is the same as:

`intNumberOfEntries = intNumberOfEntries + 1`

The += compound operator adds the value of the right operand to the value of the left operand and stores the result in the left operand's variable. Similarly, the statement:

`decTotalVehicleSpeed += decVehicleSpeedEntered`

is the same as:

`decTotalVehicleSpeed = decTotalVehicleSpeed + decVehicleSpeedEntered`

The table in Figure 6-39 shows an example of compound operators used in code. Assume that intResult = 24, decResult = 24, and strSample = "tree".

Operation	Example with Single Operators	Example with Compound Operator	Result
Addition	intResult = intResult + 1	intResult += 1	intResult = 25
Subtraction	intResult = intResult − 3	intResult −= 3	intResult = 21
Multiplication	intResult = intResult * 2	intResult *= 2	intResult = 48
Decimal Division	intResult = decResult / 5	decResult /= 5	decResult = 4.8
Integer Division	intResult = intResult \ 5	intResult \ =5	intResult = 4
Exponents	intResult = intResult ^ 2	intResult ^= 2	intResult = 576
Concatenate	strSample = strSample & "house"	strSample &= "house"	strSample = "treehouse"

FIGURE 6-39

HEADS UP

The compound operators +=, −=, *=, /=, \=, ^=, and &= run faster than their regular longer equation counterparts because the statement is more compact.

Compound operators often are used by developers in Visual Basic coding. The coding example in Figure 6-40 uses several compound operators and a MsgBox object. When the following code is executed, the result shown in the MsgBox object is "Final Result = 2".

```
30          Dim intTotal As Integer
31          intTotal = 7
32          intTotal += 6
33          intTotal *= 2
34          intTotal /= 13
35          MsgBox("Final Result = " & intTotal.ToString(), , "Compound Operators")
```

FIGURE 6-40

Compound operators also can be used to connect two strings using the concatenation operator (&). The code in Figure 6-41 creates the phrase "To err is human!" in a MessageBox object by using compound operators to concatenate the strPhrase variable. Each compound operator joins another word to the end of the phrase assigned to the strPhrase variable.

```
30          Dim strPhrase As String
31          strPhrase = "To err"
32          strPhrase &= " is "
33          strPhrase &= "human!"
34          MsgBox(strPhrase, , "Compound Operators")
```

FIGURE 6-41

Using Loops to Perform Repetitive Tasks

In the Highway Radar Checkpoint application, the user enters up to 10 vehicle speeds using the InputBox function. The repetitive process of entering 10 vehicle speeds can be coded within a loop to simplify the task with fewer lines of code. Unlike If…Then statements that execute only once, loops repeat multiple times. Each repetition of the loop is called an **iteration**. An iteration is a single execution of a set of instructions that are to be repeated.

Loops are powerful structures used to repeat a section of code a certain number of times or until a particular condition is met. Visual Basic has two main types of loops: For…Next loops and Do loops.

REPEATING A PROCESS USING THE FOR…NEXT LOOP

You can use a For…Next loop when a section of code is to be executed an exact number of times. The syntax of a For…Next loop is shown in Figure 6-42.

General Format: For…Next loop

```
For Control Variable = Beginning Numeric Value To Ending Numeric Value

    ' Body of the Loop

Next
```

FIGURE 6-42

In Figure 6-42, the For…Next loop begins with the keyword For. Following this keyword is the control variable, which is the numeric variable that keeps track of the number of iterations the loop completes. To begin the loop, the For statement places the beginning numeric value in the control variable. The program then executes the code between the For and Next statements, which is called the body of the loop.

Upon reaching the Next statement, the program returns to the For statement and increments the value of the control variable. This process continues until the value in the control variable is greater than the ending numeric value. When this occurs, the statement(s) that follows the Next command are executed.

The first line of a For…Next loop that is supposed to execute four times is shown in Figure 6-43. The control value is a variable named intNumber.

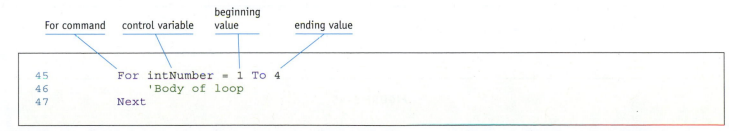

```
45        For intNumber = 1 To 4
46            'Body of loop
47        Next
```

FIGURE 6-43

The first line in the For...Next loop in Figure 6-43 specifies that the control variable (intNumber) is assigned the value 1 because the literal 1 is the beginning value. Then the section of code between the For and Next statement, which is called the body of the loop, is executed. When the Next statement is encountered, control returns to the For statement where, by default, the value 1 is added to the control variable. The code in the body of the loop is executed again. This process continues until the value in the control value becomes greater than 4, which is the ending value. When this occurs, the statement(s) in the program that follow the Next command are executed. The table in Figure 6-44 illustrates this looping process.

Loop Iteration	Value of intNumber	Process
1	intNumber = 1	Executes the code inside the loop
2	intNumber = 2	Executes the code inside the loop
3	intNumber = 3	Executes the code inside the loop
4	intNumber = 4	Executes the code inside the loop
5 (exits the loop)	intNumber = 5	The control variable value exceeds the ending value, so the application exits the For...Next loop. This means the statement(s) following the Next command are executed.

FIGURE 6-44

Step Value in a For...Next Loop

A Step value is the value in a For...Next loop that is added to or subtracted from the beginning value on each iteration of the loop. If you do not include a Step value in the For statement, such as in Figure 6-43, by default the value in the control variable is incremented by 1 after each iteration of the loop.

You can include a Step value in a For statement. For example, in the For header statement in Figure 6-45, the Step value is 2. The control variable intNumber is set to the initial value of 1, and the lines of code in the body of the loop are executed. After the first iteration of the loop, the Step value is added to the control variable, changing the value in the control variable to 3 (1 + 2 = 3). The For loop will continue until the value in intNumber is greater than 99.

step value

```
49        For intNumber = 1 To 99 Step 2
50            ' Body of loop
51        Next
```

FIGURE 6-45

The Step value can be negative. If so, the value in the control variable is decreased on each iteration of the loop. To exit the loop, you must specify an ending value that is less than the beginning value. This is illustrated in Figure 6-46.

```
                                              negative
                                              Step value

55          For intCount = 25 To -10 Step -5
56              ' Body of loop
57          Next
```

FIGURE 6-46

In the first iteration of the For...Next loop header in Figure 6-46, the control variable value is 25. The value in the control variable intCount is decreased by 5 each time the loop repeats. This repetition will continue until the value in the intCount control variable is less than −10. Then the loop exits.

The control variable in a For...Next loop can be assigned decimal values as well. The For loop header in Figure 6-47 has a starting value of 3.1. The loop ends when the value in the control variable is greater than 4.5. The Step value is 0.1, which means the value in decNumber increments by 0.1 each pass through the loop.

```
                                              decimal
                                              Step value

61          For decNumber = 3.1 To 4.5 Step 0.1
62              ' Body of loop
63          Next
```

FIGURE 6-47

A For...Next loop also can include variables and mathematical expressions as shown in Figure 6-48.

```
69          For intNumber = intBegin To (intEnd * 2) Step intIncrement
70              'Body of loop
71          Next
```

FIGURE 6-48

In Figure 6-48, the control variable (intNumber) is initialized with the value in the intBegin variable. Each time the Next statement is encountered and control is returned to the For statement, the value in intNumber will be incremented by the value in the intIncrement variable. The loop will continue until the value in intNumber is greater than the product of the value in intEnd times 2.

Entering the For...Next Loop Code Using IntelliSense

To show the process for entering the For...Next loop code using IntelliSense, assume that an application is designed to show in a list box the population growth over the next six years for Alaska. Assume further that the current population of Alaska is 675,000 people and is expected to grow at 5% per year for the next six years. The code in Figure 6-49 will accomplish this processing.

```
4        Dim intAlaskaPopulation As Integer = 675000
5        Dim intYears As Integer
6
7        For intYears = 1 To 6
8            intAlaskaPopulation += (intAlaskaPopulation * 0.05)
9            Me.lstGrowth.Items.Add("Year " & intYears & " Population " & _
10               intAlaskaPopulation)
11
12       Next
```

FIGURE 6-49

To use IntelliSense to enter the code shown in Figure 6-49, you can complete the following steps: (The following code assumes the lstGrowth ListBox object has been defined on the Windows Form object.)

STEP 1   In the code editing window, type `Dim intAlaskaPopulation As Integer = 675000` and then press the ENTER key. Type `Dim intYears As Integer` and then press the ENTER key two times. Type `for`, a space, and then an IntelliSense list opens.

The IntelliSense list shows all available entries (Figure 6-50).

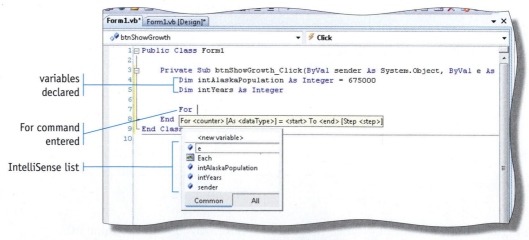

FIGURE 6-50

STEP 2 Type the first four letters of the intYears variable name (**intY**) to select intYears in the IntelliSense list. Type **= 1 to 6** and press the ENTER key to specify the beginning value and ending value for the loop.

Visual Basic automatically inserts the Next statement in the code (Figure 6-51). For, To, and Next are blue to indicate they are keywords.

```
Form1.vb*  Form1.vb [Design]*

btnShowGrowth                          Click

 1  Public Class Form1
 2
 3      Private Sub btnShowGrowth_Click(ByVal sender As System.Object, ByVal e As
 4          Dim intAlaskaPopulation As Integer = 675000
 5          Dim intYears As Integer
 6
 7          For intYears = 1 To 6 ──────┤ For statement entered
 8              |                       ┤ line indented
 9          Next ───────────────────────
10      End Sub
11  End Class
12                                      │ Next statement
                                        │ entered automatically
```

FIGURE 6-51

STEP 3 Use IntelliSense to select the appropriate variables. Enter the two new lines shown in Figure 6-52.

Each line of code automatically is indented between the For and Next statements (Figure 6-52).

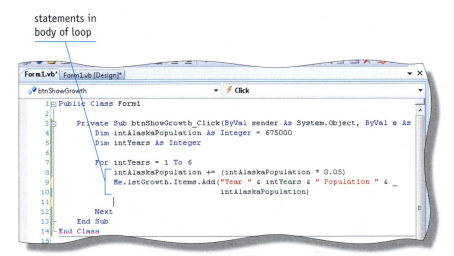

statements in body of loop

```
Form1.vb*  Form1.vb [Design]*

btnShowGrowth                          Click

 1  Public Class Form1
 2
 3      Private Sub btnShowGrowth_Click(ByVal sender As System.Object, ByVal e As
 4          Dim intAlaskaPopulation As Integer = 675000
 5          Dim intYears As Integer
 6
 7          For intYears = 1 To 6
 8              intAlaskaPopulation += (intAlaskaPopulation * 0.05)
 9              Me.lstGrowth.Items.Add("Year " & intYears & " Population " & _
10                              intAlaskaPopulation)
11              |
12          Next
13      End Sub
14  End Class
15
```

FIGURE 6-52

STEP 4   Run the program to see the results of the loop.

The loop calculates and displays the Alaskan population growth for six years based on 5% growth per year (Figure 6-53).

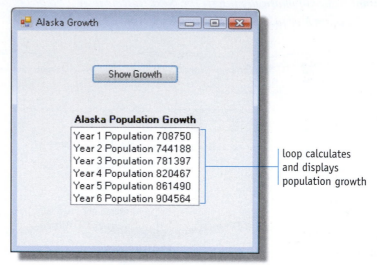

FIGURE 6-53

User Input and the For...Next Loop

The beginning, ending, and step values used in a For...Next loop can vary based on input from a user. For example, in Figure 6-54, the program displays the squared values of a range of numbers the user enters. The user enters the beginning (minimum) and ending (maximum) range of values, and then clicks the Calculate Values button to view the squares of the numbers in the range.

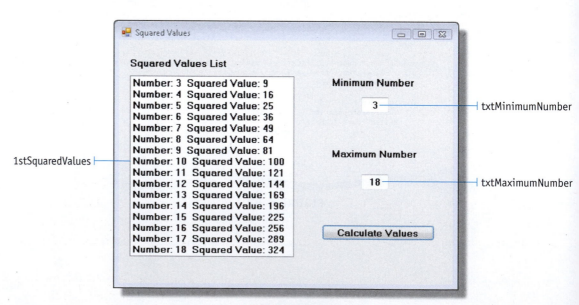

FIGURE 6-54

The code for the Squared Values application in Figure 6-54 is shown in Figure 6-55.

```
5          Dim intCount As Integer
6          Dim intBegin As Integer
7          Dim intEnd As Integer
8
9          intBegin = Convert.ToInt32(Me.txtMinimumNumber.Text)
10         intEnd = Convert.ToInt32(Me.txtMaximumNumber.Text)
11
12         For intCount = intBegin To intEnd
13             Me.lstSquaredValues.Items.Add("Number: " & intCount _
14                                     & "    Squared Value:" _
15                                     & (intCount ^ 2))
16         Next
```

FIGURE 6-55

In Figure 6-55, on line 9 the minimum value the user entered is converted to an integer and placed in the intBegin variable. Similarly, on line 10, the maximum value the user entered is converted to an integer and assigned to the intEnd variable. On line 12, the value in intBegin is used as the beginning value in the For...Next loop, and the value in intEnd is used as the ending value. As you can see, the number of iterations for the loop is determined by values the user entered.

Within the loop, the value in intCount, which begins with the value in intBegin and is incremented by the default value of one each time through the loop, is used as the number from which the squared value is calculated. As shown in Figure 6-54, this results in the squared values being calculated for all numbers beginning with the minimum number and ending with the maximum number.

REPEATING A PROCESS USING A DO LOOP

A For...Next loop is used when a process is repeated an exact number of times. In many applications, however, a loop should be repeated until a certain condition changes. For example, in the Highway Radar Checkpoint application, the process of entering the speed of each vehicle is repeated 10 times or until the user stops entering the speed of the next vehicle by clicking the Cancel button. The loop in the Highway Radar Checkpoint application continues until one of two conditions becomes true — either the count of the speeds entered reaches 10 or the user clicks the Cancel button on the InputBox object.

In a **Do loop**, the body of the loop is executed while or until a condition is true or false. The Do loop uses a condition similar to an If...Then decision structure to determine whether it should continue looping. In this way, you can use a Do loop to execute a body of statements an indefinite number of times. In the Highway Radar Checkpoint application, the Do loop runs an indefinite number of times because the user can end the loop at any time by clicking the Cancel button.

Visual Basic 2008 provides two types of Do loops: the Do While loop and the Do Until loop. Both Do loops execute statements repeatedly until a specified condition becomes true or false. Each loop examines a condition to determine whether the condition is true. The **Do While loop** executes as long as the condition is true. It is stated as, "Do the loop processing while the condition is true."

The **Do Until loop** executes until the condition becomes true. It is stated as, "Do the loop processing until a condition is true."

Do loops are either top-controlled or bottom-controlled, depending on whether the condition is tested before the loop begins or after the body of the loop has executed one time. A **top-controlled loop** is tested before the loop is entered. The body of a top-controlled loop might not be executed at all because the condition being tested might be true before any processing in the loop occurs.

Bottom-controlled loops test the condition at the bottom of the loop, so the body of a bottom-controlled loop is executed at least once. Visual Basic provides top-controlled and bottom-controlled Do While and Do Until loops, meaning it can execute four types of Do loops.

Top-Controlled Do While Loops

You use a top-controlled Do While loop if you want the body of the loop to repeat as long as a condition remains true. Figure 6-56 shows the syntax of a top-controlled Do While loop.

> **General Format: Do While Loop (Top-Controlled)**
>
> ```
> Do While condition
>
>     ' Body of loop
>
> Loop
> ```

FIGURE 6-56

A top-controlled Do While loop begins with the keywords Do While. Next, the condition is specified. The condition is expressed using the same relational operators that are available with the If statements that you learned in Chapter 5. Any condition that can be specified in an If statement can be specified in a Do While condition. The condition can compare numeric values or string values.

The body of the loop contains the instructions that are executed as long as the condition is true. The Loop keyword indicates the end of the loop. It is inserted automatically when you enter the Do While loop header statement.

You must ensure that a statement within the body of the Do While loop will, at some point, cause the condition to change so the loop ends. For example, in the statement Do While strColor = "Red" the loop will continue to process as long as the value in the strColor variable remains Red. Based on the processing in the body of the loop, at some point the value in the strColor variable must be changed from Red. If not, the loop will not terminate. A loop that does not end is called an **infinite loop**.

The code in Figure 6-57 is an example of a top-controlled Do While loop. It continues to add 1 to the variable intScore while intScore is less than 5. It is considered a top-controlled loop because the condition is checked at the top of the loop.

```
17          Dim intScore As Integer = 0
18          Do While intScore < 5
19              intScore += 1
20          Loop
```

FIGURE 6-57

The loop in Figure 6-57 begins by testing whether intScore is less than 5. Because intScore starts with the value 0, the condition tested is true because 0 is less than 5. Next, the variable intScore is incremented by 1, and the loop repeats. The table in Figure 6-58 displays the values that are assigned to intScore each time the condition is checked in the code in Figure 6-57.

Loop Iteration	Value of intScore	Result of Condition Tested
1	intScore = 0	True
2	intScore = 1	True
3	intScore = 2	True
4	intScore = 3	True
5	intScore = 4	True
6	intScore = 5	False

FIGURE 6-58

The loop in Figure 6-57 is executed five times because intScore is less than 5 during five iterations of the loop. As shown in Figure 6-57, if the value in the variable intScore is 5 or greater when the Do While statement is first executed, the body of the loop never will be executed because the condition is not true prior to the first iteration of the loop.

Entering a Do Loop Using IntelliSense

To use IntelliSense to enter the Do While loop in Figure 6-57 into the code editing window, you can complete the following steps:

STEP 1 In the code editing window, enter the intScore variable declaration and then press the ENTER key. Type **Do While** and a space, and then an IntelliSense list is displayed. Type **ints** to highlight intScore in the list.

The words Do While appear in blue because they are Visual Basic keywords (Figure 6-59). The IntelliSense list contains the valid entries and the intScore variable name is highlighted.

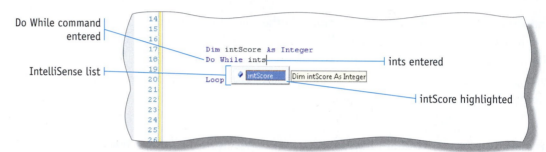

FIGURE 6-59

STEP 2 Type **< 5** and then press the ENTER key.

Visual Basic automatically inserts the intScore variable name and the characters you typed (Figure 6-60). The keyword Loop also is inserted and the insertion point is located inside the loop, ready to enter the body of the loop.

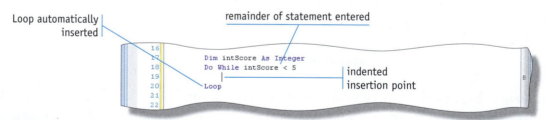

FIGURE 6-60

STEP 3 Type **ints** to highlight the intScore variable. Complete the statement by typing **+= 1** and then pressing the ENTER key. Press the DELETE key to delete the blank line.

The statement automatically is indented between the Do While and Loop statements (Figure 6-61). The intScore += 1 statement uses a compound operator to increment the intScore variable.

FIGURE 6-61

Bottom-Controlled Do While Loop

You can write a Do While loop where the condition is tested at the bottom of the loop. A bottom-controlled loop works the same way as the top-controlled Do While loop except that the body of the loop is executed before the condition is checked the first time, guaranteeing at least one iteration of a loop will be completed. The bottom-controlled Do While loop has the syntax shown in Figure 6-62.

General Format: Do While Loop (Bottom-Controlled)

```
Do

        ' Loop Body

Loop While condition
```

FIGURE 6-62

In the syntax shown in Figure 6-62, the word Do appears on its own line at the beginning of the loop. The loop body follows, and the Loop While statement is the last statement in the loop. The Loop While statement contains the condition that is tested to determine if the loop should be terminated. Because the While condition is in the last statement of the loop, the body of the loop is executed one time regardless of the status of the condition.

The code in Figure 6-63 is an example of a bottom-controlled Do While loop.

```
22          Dim intScore As Integer = 0
23          Do
24              intScore = intScore + 1
25          Loop While intScore < 5
```

FIGURE 6-63

The body of the Do loop in Figure 6-63 is executed one time before the condition in the Loop While statement is checked. The variable intScore begins with the initial value of 0 and is incremented in the body of the loop, changing the value to 1.

The condition is then tested and found to be true because 1 < 5. The loop repeats and the value of intScore increases, as shown in Figure 6-64.

Loop Iteration	Value of intScore at Start of the Loop	Value of intScore When Checked	Result of Condition Tested
1	intScore = 0	intScore = 1	True
2	intScore = 1	intScore = 2	True
3	intScore = 2	intScore = 3	True
4	intScore = 3	intScore = 4	True
5	intScore = 4	intScore = 5	False

FIGURE 6-64

The body of the loop in Figure 6-63 is executed five times because intScore is less than 5 during five iterations of the loop.

DO UNTIL LOOPS

A loop similar to a Do While loop is called a Do Until loop. The Do Until loop allows you to specify that an action repeats until a condition becomes true. When the condition in a Do Until loop becomes true, the loop ends.

Top-Controlled Do Until Loop

A Do Until loop can be both top-controlled and bottom-controlled. The syntax of the top-controlled Do Until loop is shown in Figure 6-65.

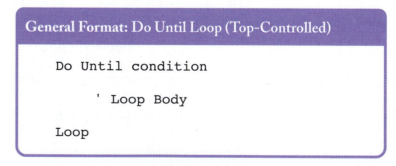

```
General Format: Do Until Loop (Top-Controlled)

    Do Until condition

            ' Loop Body

    Loop
```

FIGURE 6-65

A top-controlled Do Until loop begins with the keywords Do Until. Next, as with the Do While top-controlled loop, the condition is specified. The condition is expressed using the same relational operators that are available with If statements. Any condition that can be specified in an If statement can be specified in a Do Until condition. The condition can compare numeric values or string values.

The Do Until loop example shown in Figure 6-66 displays a parking meter application that computes the number of minutes a user can purchase based on the cost of 25 cents for each 15 minutes of parking. If the user only has 88 cents in pocket change, for example, the application computes how many minutes of parking time 88 cents will purchase.

```
4          Dim decAmount As Decimal = 0.88
5          Dim intQuarters As Integer = 0
6          Dim intTime As Integer = 15
7          Dim intParkingTime As Integer
8
9          Do Until decAmount < 0.25
10             intQuarters += 1
11             decAmount -= 0.25
12         Loop
13         intParkingTime = intQuarters * intTime
14         Me.lblParkingTime.Text = "Parking Time: " &
15                                  intParkingTime.ToString() & " minutes"
```

FIGURE 6-66

In the code example in Figure 6-66, the Do Until loop condition is checked before the body of the loop executes. The first time the condition is tested, the expression decAmount < 0.25 is false because the decAmount variable contains 0.88. The body of the loop is executed because the Do Until will be executed until the value in decAmount is less than 0.25. When the body of the loop is executed, it adds 1 to intQuarters to count the number of quarters the user has for the parking meter and 0.25 is subtracted from decAmount because a quarter is worth 25 cents. Because decAmount is first assigned the value 0.88, the loop executes three times (decAmount = 0.88, decAmount = 0.63, and decAmount = 0.38) and stops when decAmount becomes less than 0.25. The lblParkingTime Label object displays the text "Parking Time: 45 minutes".

Bottom-Controlled Do Until Loop

The last of the four Do loops is the bottom-controlled Do Until loop. This Do Until loop checks the condition after the body of the loop is executed. The loop continues until the condition becomes true. The syntax of the bottom-controlled Do Until loop is shown in Figure 6-67.

General Format: Do Until Loop (Bottom-Controlled)

```
Do

       ' Loop Body

Loop Until condition
```

FIGURE 6-67

As shown in Figure 6-67, the bottom-controlled Do Until loop begins with the word Do. The body of the loop is executed one time regardless of the condition being tested. The Loop Until statement checks the condition. The loop will be repeated until the condition is true.

User Input Loops

Do loops often are written to end the loop when a certain value is entered by the user, or the user performs a certain action such as clicking the Cancel button in an input box. The value or action is predefined by the developer. For example, the loop in Figure 6-68 continues until the user clicks the Cancel button in the input box. If the user clicks the Cancel button, the InputBox function returns a null string that is assigned to the strTestGrade variable. The Do Until statement tests the string. If it contains a null character, the loop is terminated. The Do Until loop accumulates the total of all the entered test scores until the user clicks the Cancel button.

```
40      Do Until strTestGrade = ""
41          strTestGrade = InputBox("Enter test grade", "Compute Average")
42          If IsNumeric(strTestGrade) Then
43              decGrade = Convert.ToDecimal(strTestGrade)
44              decTotal += decGrade
45          End If
46      Loop
```

FIGURE 6-68

AVOIDING INFINITE LOOPS

Recall that an **infinite loop** is a loop that never ends. It happens when the condition that will cause the end of a loop never occurs. If the loop does not end, it will continue to repeat until the program is interrupted. Figure 6-69 shows an example of an infinite loop.

```
22      Dim intProblem = 0
23      Do While intProblem <= 5
24          Box.Show("This loop will not end", "Infinite Loop")
25      Loop
```

FIGURE 6-69

The Do While loop in Figure 6-69 never ends because the value in the variable intProblem is never changed from its initial value of zero. Because the value in intProblem never exceeds 5, the condition in the Do While loop (intProblem <= 5) never becomes false. The processing in a loop eventually must change the condition being tested in the Do While loop so the loop will terminate. When working in Visual Basic 2008, you can interrupt an infinite loop by clicking the Stop Debugging button on the toolbar.

PRIMING THE LOOP

As you have learned, a top-controlled loop tests a condition prior to beginning the loop. In most cases, the value that is tested in that condition must be set before the condition is tested the first time in the Do While or Do Until statement. Starting a loop with a preset value in the variable(s) tested in the condition is called **priming the loop**. You have seen this in previous examples, such as in Figure 6-66 on page 417 where the value in decAmount is set before the condition is tested the first time.

In some applications, such as the Highway Radar Checkpoint application, the loop is primed with a value the user enters or an action the user takes. You will recall that the user enters the speed for a vehicle (up to 10 vehicles) or clicks the Cancel button in the input box to terminate the input operation. Prior to executing the Do Until statement the first time in the Do Until loop that processes the data the user enters, the InputBox function must be executed to obtain an initial value. Then, the Do Until statement can test the action taken by the user (enter a value or click the Cancel button). The coding to implement this processing is shown in Figure 6-70.

```
31          Dim strCancelButtonClicked As String = ""
32          Dim intMaximumNumberOfEntries As Integer = 10
33          Dim intNumberOfEntries As Integer = 1
⋮
39          strVehicleSpeed = InputBox(strInputBoxMessage & intNumberOfEntries, _
40                              strInputBoxHeading, " ")
41
42          Do Until intNumberOfEntries > intMaximumNumberOfEntries _
43              Or strVehicleSpeed = strCancelButtonClicked
⋮
50                      intNumberOfEntries += 1
⋮
59              If intNumberOfEntries <= intMaximumNumberOfEntries Then
60                  strVehicleSpeed = InputBox(strInputBoxMessage & intNumberOfEntries, _
61                                      strInputBoxHeading, " ")
62              End If
63
64          Loop
```

FIGURE 6-70

In the Do Until loop shown in Figure 6-70, you can see that the Do Until statement on line 42 tests two conditions: is the value in the intNumberOfEntries variable greater than the value in the intMaximumNumberOfEntries variable, or is the value in the strVehicleSpeed variable equal to the value in the strCancelButtonClicked variable, which is a null character (see line 31). If either of these conditions is true, the body of the loop will not be executed.

The Do Until loop must have two primed variables — the intNumberOfEntries variable and the strVehicleSpeed variable. The intNumberOfEntries variable is initialized to the value 1 on line 33. The strVehicleSpeed variable is initialized by the InputBox function call on lines 39 and 40. In this function call, either the user has entered a value or clicked the Cancel button. If the user clicked the Cancel button, the body of the loop should not be entered.

To continue the loop, the processing within the body of the loop eventually must change one of the conditions being tested in the Do Until statement or the loop never terminates. In the sample program, the conditions being tested are whether the user has entered 10 vehicle speeds or whether the user has clicked the Cancel button. Therefore, within the loop, the variable containing the number of vehicle speeds entered (intNumberOfEntries) must be incremented when the user enters a valid speed, and the user must be able to enter more speeds or click the Cancel button. On line 50 in Figure 6-70, the value in the intNumberOfEntries is incremented by 1 each time the user enters a valid value. In addition, the statement on lines 60 and 61 displays an input box that allows the user to enter a new value or click the Cancel button as long as the number of valid entries is not greater than the maximum number of entries.

VALIDATING DATA

As you learned in Chapter 5, you must test the data a user enters to ensure it is accurate and that its use in other programming statements, such as converting string data to numeric data, will not cause a program exception. When using an input box, the data should be checked using the IsNumeric function and If statements as discussed in Chapter 5. If the data is not valid, the user must be notified of the error and an input box displayed to allow the user to enter valid data.

For example, if the user enters non-numeric data, the input box in Figure 6-71 should be displayed.

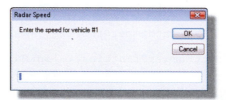

FIGURE 6-71

Similarly, if the user enters a negative number, the message in Figure 6-72 should be displayed in an input box.

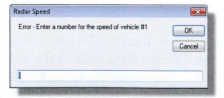

FIGURE 6-72

When error checking is performed within a loop and the user is asked to enter data through the use of an input box, the body of the loop must be executed each time the user enters data regardless of whether the data is valid or invalid. If the user enters valid data, then the data is processed according to the needs of the program.

If the user enters invalid data, an error message is displayed and the user is given the opportunity to enter valid data in the input box. The coding for the Highway Radar Checkpoint application that accomplishes these tasks is shown in Figure 6-73.

```
39      strVehicleSpeed = InputBox(strInputBoxMessage & intNumberOfEntries, _
40                            strInputBoxHeading, " ")
41
42      Do Until intNumberOfEntries > intMaximumNumberOfEntries _
43          Or strVehicleSpeed = strCancelButtonClicked
44
45          If IsNumeric(strVehicleSpeed) Then
46              decVehicleSpeed = Convert.ToDecimal(strVehicleSpeed)
47              If decVehicleSpeed > 0 Then
48                  Me.lstRadarSpeed.Items.Add(decVehicleSpeed)
49                  decTotalOfAllSpeeds += decVehicleSpeed
50                  intNumberOfEntries += 1
51                  strInputBoxMessage = strNormalBoxMessage
52              Else
53                  strInputBoxMessage = strNegativeNumberErrorMessage
54              End If
55          Else
56              strInputBoxMessage = strNonNumericErrorMessage
57          End If
58
59          If intNumberOfEntries <= intMaximumNumberOfEntries Then
60              strVehicleSpeed = InputBox(strInputBoxMessage & intNumberOfEntries,_
61                                strInputBoxHeading, " ")
62          End If
63
64      Loop
```

FIGURE 6-73

In Figure 6-73, the loop is primed by the InputBox function call on line 39. The Do Until statement on line 42 checks the two conditions — if the value in the intNumberOfEntries counter is greater than the maximum number of entries, or the user clicks the Cancel button, then the body of the loop is not entered.

When the body of the loop is entered, the data the user entered is checked to verify it is numeric. If it is numeric, the value is converted to a Decimal data type and then is checked to ensure it is greater than zero (line 47). If it is greater than zero, it is added to the lstRadarSpeed ListBox object, the decTotalOfAllSpeeds accumulator is incremented by the speed the user entered, the intNumberOfEntries counter is incremented by 1, and the normal message is moved to the strInputBoxMessage variable. This variable contains the message that is displayed in the input box (see line 39).

If the value the user entered is not greater than zero, the statement following the Else statement on line 52 moves the value in the strNegativeNumberErrorMessage variable to the strInputBoxMessage variable so that the next time the InputBox function is called, the message will indicate an error, as shown in Figure 6-72 on page 420.

If the value the user entered was not numeric (as tested by the statement on line 45), the statement on line 56 moves the value in the strNonNumericErrorMessage variable to the strInputBoxMessage variable so the next time the InputBox function is called, the message will indicate a non-numeric error, as shown in Figure 6-71 on page 420.

On lines 59 and 60, as long as the number of entries is not greater than the maximum number of entries, the InputBox function is called. The message that is displayed in the input box depends on whether an error occurred. The Do Until statement on line 42 then is executed again and the process begins again.

CREATING A NESTED LOOP

In the last chapter, you learned to nest If...Then...Else statements within each other. Loops also can be nested. You can place any type of loop within any other type of loop. Any loop can be placed within another loop under the following conditions: interior loops must be completely contained inside the outer loop and must have a different control variable. The example in Figure 6-74 uses a nested For loop to display a list of the weeks in the first quarter of the year (13 weeks) along with the day in each week. The outer For...Next loop counts from 1 to 13 for the 13 weeks, and the inner For...Next loop counts from 1 to 7 for the days in each of the 13 weeks.

```
6        Dim intOuterCount As Integer ' Counts the first 13 weeks in a quarter
7        Dim intInnerCount As Integer ' Counts the 7 days in a week
8        For intOuterCount = 1 To 13 ' For weeks in the 1st quarter of the year
9            For intInnerCount = 1 To 7 ' For the 7 days in a week
10               Me.lstDays.Items.Add("Week: " & intOuterCount.ToString() _
11                               & " Day: " & intInnerCount.ToString())
12           Next
13       Next
```

FIGURE 6-74

The code in Figure 6-74 displays the output shown in Figure 6-75.

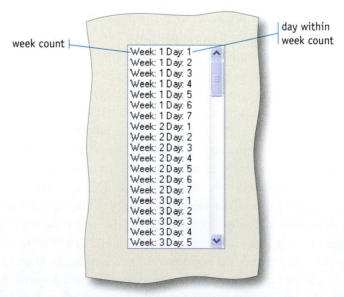

FIGURE 6-75

SELECTING THE BEST LOOP

When writing a program, you might have to make a decision regarding which loop structure to use. For...Next loops are best when the number of repetitions is fixed. Do loops are best when the condition to enter or exit the loop needs to be re-evaluated continually. When deciding which loop to use, keep the following considerations in mind:

1. Use a Do loop if the number of repetitions is unknown and is based on a condition changing; a For...Next loop is best if the exact number of repetitions is fixed.
2. If a loop condition must be tested before the body of the loop is executed, use a top-controlled Do While or Do Until loop. If the instructions within a loop must be executed one time regardless of the status of a condition, use a bottom-controlled Do While or Do Until loop.
3. Use the keyword While if you want to continue execution of the loop while the condition is true. Use the keyword Until if you want to continue execution until the condition is true.

Using a DataTip with Breakpoints

As programs become longer and more complex, the likelihood of errors increases, and you need to carefully find and remove these errors. Resolving defects in code is called **debugging**. When you debug a program, you collect information and find out what is wrong with the code in the program. You then fix that code.

A good way to collect information is to pause the execution of the code where a possible error could occur. One way to pause execution is to use breakpoints. **Breakpoints** are stop points placed in the code to tell the Visual Studio 2008 debugger where and when to pause the execution of the application. During this pause, the program is in break mode. While in break mode, you can examine the values in all variables that are within the scope of execution through the use of **DataTips**. In the Highway Radar Checkpoint program, you can insert a breakpoint in the assignment statement that increments the decTotalOfAllSpeeds accumulator to view its value after each iteration of the loop as the user enters vehicle speeds. To set a breakpoint in your code and then check the data at the breakpoint using DataTips, you can complete the following steps:

STEP 1 With the program open in the code editing window, right-click line 49, which contains the code where you want to set a breakpoint, and then point to Breakpoint on the shortcut menu.

A shortcut menu opens that contains the Breakpoint command (Figure 6-76). The Breakpoint submenu contains the Insert Breakpoint command. Setting a breakpoint in line 49 means that the program will pause at that line during execution so that the values in variables within the scope of execution can be examined.

set breakpoint
on line 49

shortcut menu

Breakpoint
submenu

Breakpoint
command

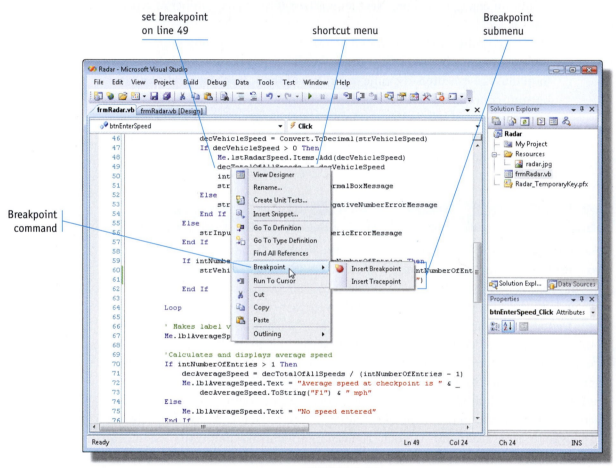

FIGURE 6-76

STEP 2   Click Insert Breakpoint on the submenu.

A breakpoint is set on line 49, which is the line inside the Do Until loop that adds the vehicle speed the user entered to the vehicle speed accumulator — decTotalOfAllSpeeds (Figure 6-77). The breakpoint is identified by the bullet to the left of the line numbers and the highlight on the code.

breakpoint set

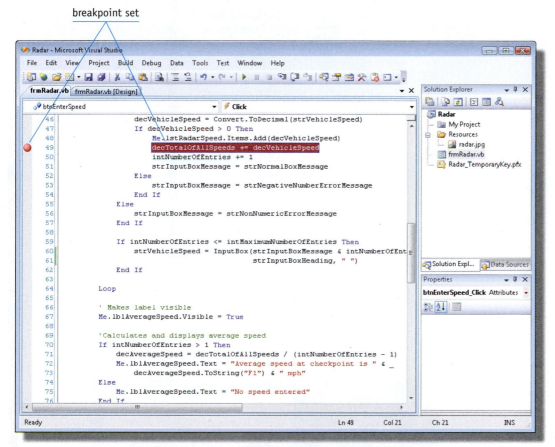

FIGURE 6-77

STEP 3   To run and test the program with the breakpoint, click the Start Debugging button on the Standard toolbar.

The program starts and the Radar Speed window opens (Figure 6-78).

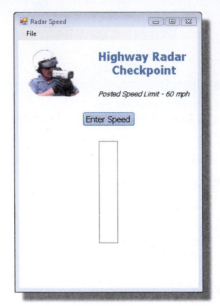

FIGURE 6-78

STEP 4   Click the Enter Speed button. Type 75 as the speed of the first vehicle.

The Radar Speed input box contains 75 as the speed of the first vehicle (Figure 6-79).

75 entered in
Radar Speed
input box

FIGURE 6-79

STEP 5   Click the OK button in the input box.

The program executes the lines of code in the event handler until reaching the breakpoint, where it pauses execution on the accumulator line (Figure 6-80). The application is now in break mode. Notice the breakpoint line is highlighted in yellow.

program execution
paused at breakpoint

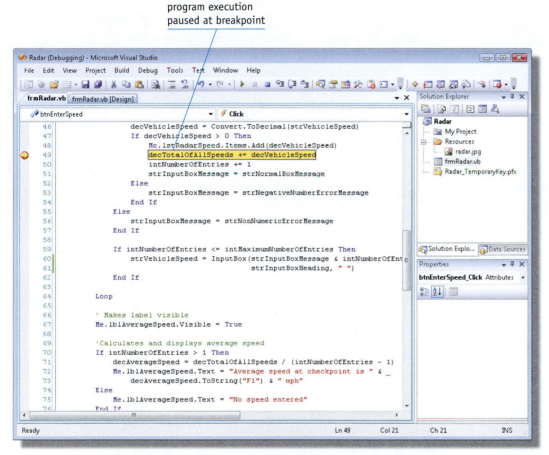

FIGURE 6-80

STEP 6   Point to the variable decVehicleSpeed on line 49.

A DataTip appears, displaying the value of the decVehicleSpeed variable at the time program execution was paused (Figure 6-81). The value is 75 because that is the value the user entered in Step 4. It is a decimal value (75D) because the value the user entered was converted to a decimal value by the statement on line 46.

pointer points to
decTotalOfAllSpeeds
variable

DataTip displays the value in the
decTotalOfAllSpeeds variable

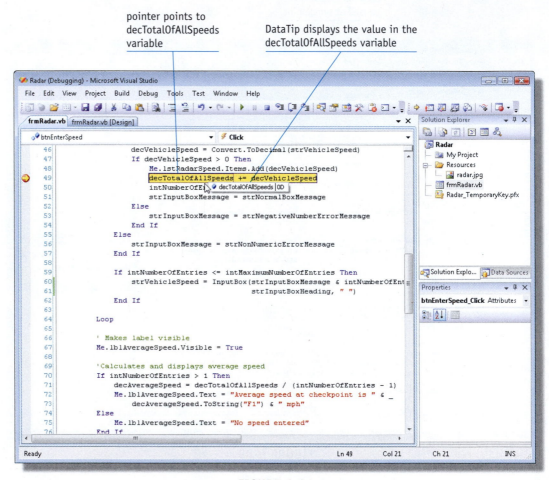

FIGURE 6-81

STEP 7   You can view the value in any other variable within execution scope by pointing to that variable. To illustrate, point to the variable decTotalOfAllSpeeds on line 49.

The value in the decTotalOfAllSpeeds variable is displayed (Figure 6-82). The value is zero, which means the assignment statement on line 49 has not yet been executed. When a breakpoint is set, the program pauses before executing the statement containing the breakpoint.

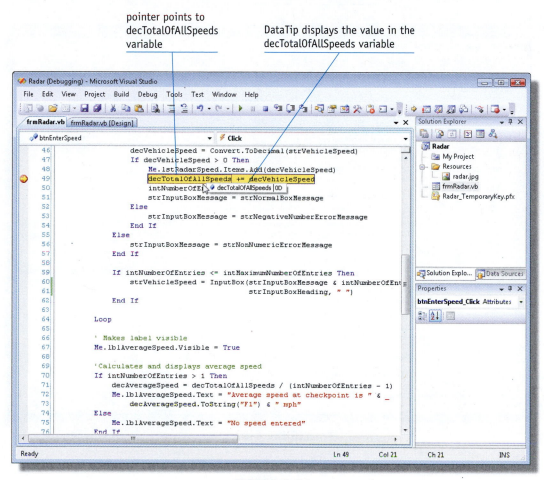

FIGURE 6-82

STEP 8   Continue the program by clicking the Continue button on the Standard toolbar. Notice that the Continue button is the same as the Start Debugging button.

The program continues by opening the next InputBox function where the user can enter the speed for the next vehicle. The program runs until it again reaches the breakpoint, where it pauses so you can point to any variable to view its present value in a DataTip (Figure 6-83).

program execution   Continue
paused again   button

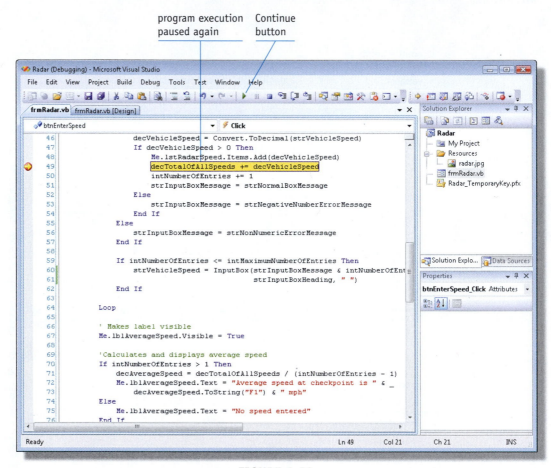

FIGURE 6-83

STEP 9   Point to the decTotalOfAllSpeeds variable.

The updated value in the decTotalOfAllSpeeds variable is shown (Figure 6-84). The value 75D is in the variable as a result of the processing in the first iteration of the loop. You also can examine the values in other variables by pointing to the variable name.

updated value
shown

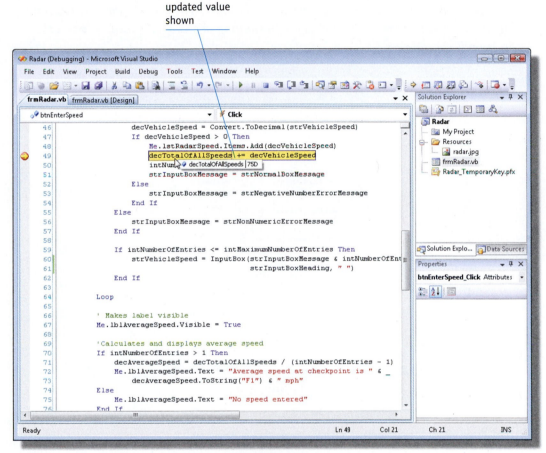

FIGURE 6-84

The preceding examples illustrated the use of one breakpoint, but you can include multiple breakpoints in a program if that will be useful. Sometimes, breakpoints before and after an instruction that you suspect is in error can pinpoint the problem.

ONLINE REINFORCEMENT

To view a video of the process in the previous steps, visit scsite.com/vb2008/ch6 and then select Figure 6-76.

To remove a breakpoint, you can complete the following steps:

STEP 1   Right-click the statement containing the breakpoint, and then point to Breakpoint on the shortcut menu.

The shortcut menu is displayed, the pointer is located on the Breakpoint entry, and the Breakpoint submenu is displayed (Figure 6-85). You can right-click the statement containing the breakpoint either when the program is running in Debugging mode or when the program is not running.

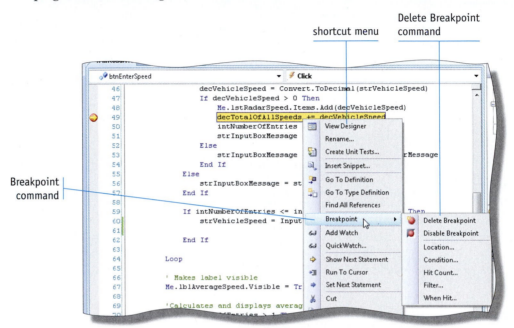

FIGURE 6-85

STEP 2   Click Delete Breakpoint on the Breakpoint submenu.

If the program is running in Debugging mode, the breakpoint is removed when you click the Continue button (Figure 6-86). If the program is not running, the breakpoint is removed immediately.

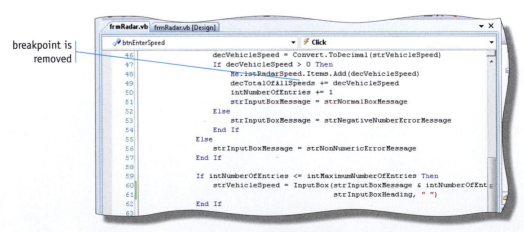

FIGURE 6-86

The use of breakpoints and DataTips allows you to examine any variables during the execution of the program. By moving step by step through the program, normally you will be able to identify any errors that might occur in the program.

Publishing an Application with ClickOnce Deployment

After an application is completely debugged and working properly, you can deploy the project. Deploying a project means placing an executable version of the program on your hard disk (which then can be placed on CD or DVD), on a Web server, or on a network server.

You probably have purchased software on a CD or DVD. To install the application on your computer, you insert the CD or DVD into your computer and then follow the setup instructions. The version of the program you receive on the CD or DVD is the deployed version of the program.

When programming using Visual Basic 2008, you can create a deployed program by using **ClickOnce Deployment**. The deployed version of the program you create can be installed and executed on any computer that has the .NET framework installed. The computer does not need Visual Studio 2008 installed to run the program.

To publish the Highway Radar Checkpoint program using ClickOnce Deployment, you can complete the following steps:

HEADS UP

Your application should be complete, debugged, and working properly before you deploy it. Users expect a deployed program to be error-free. While you are debugging your program in Visual Studio 2008, you should run it in Debugging mode.

STEP 1 With the program open, click Build on the menu bar.

The Build menu is displayed (Figure 6-87).

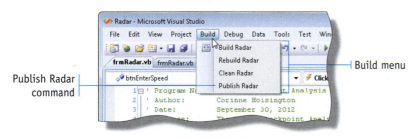

FIGURE 6-87

STEP 2   Click Publish Radar on the Build menu.

The Publish Wizard starts (Figure 6-88). The first Publish Wizard dialog box asks where you want to publish the application. The application can be published to a Web server, a network, or as a setup file on a hard disk or USB drive for burning on a CD or DVD. This dialog box includes publish\ as the default location, which you can change to a file location.

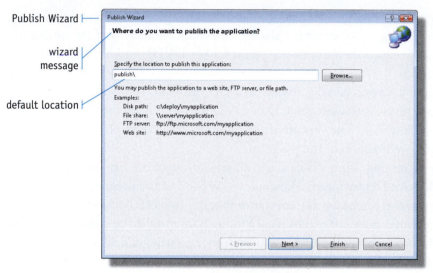

FIGURE 6-88

STEP 3   Change the default location from publish\ to a file location. To publish to a USB drive, type the drive letter. In this example, enter E: for a USB drive.

The Publish Wizard dialog box requests where the user intends to publish the application. The Radar application will be saved to the USB drive, which is drive E: in this example (Figure 6-89).

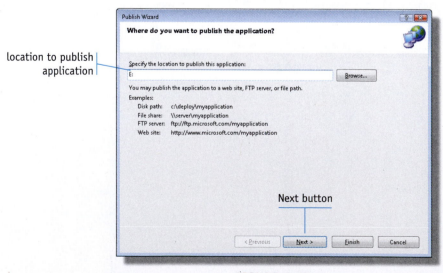

FIGURE 6-89

STEP 4   Click the Next button. If necessary, click the From a CD-ROM or DVD-ROM radio button.

Visual Basic displays a Publish Wizard dialog box that asks, How will users install the application? (Figure 6-90). When the user will install the application from a CD or DVD, such as when you purchase software, you should select the CD or DVD option.

From a CD-ROM
or DVD-ROM
selected

Next button

FIGURE 6-90

STEP 5   Click the Next button. If necessary, click the The application will not check for updates radio button.

The next Publish Wizard dialog box asks where will the application check for updates (Figure 6-91). You can select and enter a location, or indicate that the application will not check for updates. Generally, when an application will be deployed to a CD or DVD, the application will not check for updates. If the application is deployed to a Web server or network server, then it might check for updates before being executed on the user's computer.

application will
not check for
updates

Next button

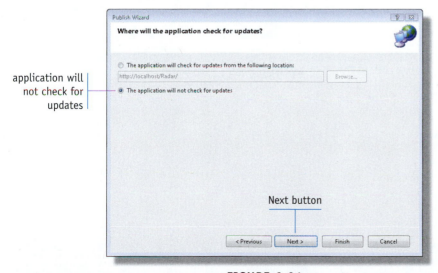

FIGURE 6-91

STEP 6 Click the Next button.

The Ready to Publish Wizard window is displayed (Figure 6-92). Notice the message in the Publish Wizard window — when the program is installed on the user's machine, a shortcut for the program will be added to the Start menu, and the program can be deleted using the Add/Remove Programs function in the Control Panel.

message describes what
will happen when the
application is installed

Finish button

FIGURE 6-92

STEP 7 Click the Finish button.

The Visual Basic window displays several messages indicating that the application is being published. The last message is "Publish succeeded" (Figure 6-93).

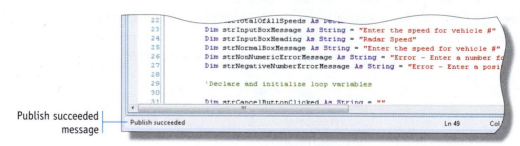

Publish succeeded
message

FIGURE 6-93

STEP 8 To view the finished result, minimize the Visual Studio window, and then click Computer on the Windows Vista Start menu. Double-click the USB drive icon to view the published installation folder.

Installation files are placed on the USB drive (Figure 6-94). If all of these files are copied to a computer with the .NET framework, the program can be installed by double-clicking the setup file to begin the installation.

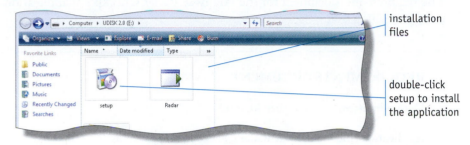

installation files

double-click setup to install the application

FIGURE 6-94

STEP 9 To install the application, double-click the setup file.

After double-clicking the setup file, the application installs on the local computer. During installation, Windows might display the security warning dialog box shown in Figure 6-95. This dialog box is intended to protect you from installing programs that might harm your computer. Because you know the source of this program, you can click the Install button to continue installing the program.

Install Warning dialog box

Install button

FIGURE 6-95

STEP 10 After installation, the program will run. To run the installed application again, click the Start button on the Windows taskbar. Point to All Programs, click Radar on the All Programs menu, and then click Radar on the Radar submenu.

Program Design

As you have learned, the requirements document identifies the purpose of the program being developed, the application title, the procedures to be followed when using the program, any equations and calculations required in the program, any conditions within the program that must be tested, notes and restrictions that must be followed by the program, and any other comments that would be helpful to understanding the problem. The requirements document for the Highway Radar Checkpoint application is shown in Figure 6-96.

REQUIREMENTS DOCUMENT

Date submitted: September 30, 2012

Application title: Highway Radar Checkpoint Application

Purpose: This application finds the average speed of vehicles on a highway with a posted speed limit of 60 mph.

Program Procedures: From a Windows application, the user enters the speed of up to 10 vehicles to compute the average speed on a highway with a posted speed limit of 60 mph.

Algorithms, Processing, and Conditions:
1. The user must be able to enter each of 10 vehicle's speeds after clicking the Enter Speed button.
2. Each speed is validated to confirm that the value is numeric and greater than zero.
3. Each vehicle speed is displayed in a ListBox object.
4. After the 10 speeds are entered or when the user clicks the Cancel button in an input box, the average speed is calculated and displayed.
5. A menu bar includes the File menu, which contains Clear and Exit items. The Clear menu item clears the result and the values representing vehicle speed. The Exit menu item closes the application.

Notes and Restrictions:
1. If a non-numeric or negative value is entered for the speed, the program should display an error message and ask the user to re-enter the value.
2. If the user clicks the Cancel button before entering any vehicle speeds, a message should indicate no speeds were entered. An average is not calculated when no speeds are entered.

Comments:
1. The picture shown in the window can be found on scsite.com/vb2008/ch6/images. The name of the picture is Radar.
2. The average speed should be formatted as a Decimal value with one decimal place.

FIGURE 6-96

The Use Case Definition shown in Figure 6-97 specifies the procedures the user will follow to use this application.

USE CASE DEFINITION

1. The Windows application opens, displaying the Highway Radar Checkpoint title, a ListBox object that will hold the numeric entries, and a Button object that allows the user to begin entering up to 10 vehicle speeds.
2. A menu bar displays the File menu, which has two menu items: Clear and Exit.
3. The user enters up to 10 values representing the vehicle speeds into an InputBox object.
4. The program asks the user for the vehicle speed again if a value is non-numeric or negative.
5. The user terminates data entry by entering 10 vehicle speeds or by clicking the Cancel button in the InputBox object.
6. The program calculates the average speed for the speeds that were entered.
7. The program displays the average vehicle speed in a Label object as a Decimal value with one decimal place.
8. The user can clear the input and the results by clicking the Clear menu item, and can then repeat steps 3 through 7.
9. The user clicks Exit on the File menu to close the application.

FIGURE 6-97

EVENT PLANNING DOCUMENT

You will recall that the event planning document consists of a table that specifies an object in the user interface that will cause an event, the action taken by the user to trigger the event, and the event processing that must occur. The event planning document for the Highway Radar Checkpoint program is shown in Figure 6-98.

EVENT PLANNING DOCUMENT

Program Name: Highway Radar Checkpoint Application	Developer: Corinne Hoisington	Object: frmRadar	Date: September 30, 2012
OBJECT	**EVENT TRIGGER**	**EVENT PROCESSING**	

btnEnterSpeed	Click	Display an InputBox object 10 times to obtain vehicle speeds or until the user clicks the Cancel button
		Check if strVehicleSpeed is numeric
		If vehicle speed is numeric, convert strVehicleSpeed to a decimal value
		If strVehicleSpeed is numeric, check if the value is positive
		If the vehicle speed is positive:
		  Display the vehicle speed in lstRadarSpeed
		  Accumulate the total of the speeds in decTotalOfAllSpeeds
		  Update the number of entries
		  Set the InputBox message to the normal message
		If the value entered is not numeric, display an error message in the input box
		If the value entered is not positive, display an error message in the input box
		After all speeds are entered, change the Visible property of lblAverageSpeed to true
		If one or more speeds were entered:
		  Calculate the average speed in decAverageSpeed
		  Display the average speed in lblAverageSpeed
		If no values were entered:
		  Display the text No Speed Entered
		Disable the btnEnterSpeed Button	

mnuClear	Click	Clear lstRadarSpeed ListBox Change Visible property of lblAverageSpeed to False Enable btnEnterSpeed Button	
mnuExit	Click	Exit the application	

FIGURE 6-98

DESIGN AND CODE THE PROGRAM

After the events and tasks within the events have been identified, the developer is ready to create the program. As you have learned, creating the program means designing the user interface and then entering Visual Basic statements to accomplish the tasks specified on the event planning document. As the developer enters the code, she also will implement the logic to carry out the required processing.

Guided Program Development

To design the user interface for the Highway Radar Checkpoint program and enter the code required to process each event in the program, complete the steps on the following pages:

NOTE TO THE LEARNER

As you will recall, in the following activity, you should complete the tasks within the specified steps. Each of the tasks is accompanied by a Hint Screen. The purpose of the Hint Screen is to indicate where in the Visual Studio window you should perform the activity; it also serves as a reminder of the method that you should use to create the user interface or enter code. If you need further help completing the step, refer to the figure number identified by the term ref: in the step.

Guided Program Development

Phase 1: Design the Form

1

▶ **Create a Windows Application** Open Visual Studio and then close the Start page. Create a new Visual Basic Windows Forms Application project by clicking the New Project button on the Standard toolbar, selecting Visual Basic as the project type, selecting Windows Forms Application as the template, naming the project Radar in the Name text box, and then clicking the OK button in the New Project dialog box.

▶ **Display the Toolbox** Ensure the Toolbox is displayed in the Visual Studio window and the Common Controls are accessible.

▶ **Name the Windows Form Object** In the Solution Explorer window, right-click Form1.vb, click Rename, and then rename the form frmRadar.

▶ **Change the Text on the Title Bar for the Windows Form Object** Change the title bar text of the Windows Form object to Radar Speed.

▶ **Change the Size of the Form Object** Resize the Form object by changing the Size property to 341, 509.

▶ **Add the MenuStrip Object** Drag a MenuStrip object from the Menus & Toolbars category of the Toolbox to the Windows Form object. The MenuStrip snaps into place below the title bar. Name the MenuStrip object mnuHighwayRadarCheckpoint in the Properties window. Click the Type Here box on the MenuStrip object, type &File, and then press the ENTER key. The ampersand creates a hot key for the letter F. Name the File menu item mnuFile (*ref: Figure 6-5*).

Guided Program Development (continued)

▶ **Add Menu Items** The next step is to add two menu items to the File menu. Click the Type Here box below the word File, and then enter &Clear. Name the Clear menu item mnuClearItem. Click the Type Here box below the Clear menu item, and then enter E&xit to make the "x" in Exit the hot key. Name the Exit menu item mnuExitItem (*ref: Figure 6-10*).

▶ **Add a PictureBox Object** Drag a PictureBox .NET component from the Toolbox to the left side of the Windows Form object. Name the PictureBox object picRadar. Change the Size property of the PictureBox object to 102, 89. Change the Location property of the PictureBox object to 13, 41.

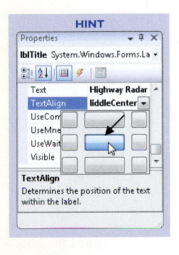

▶ **Add the Title Label Object** Drag a Label .NET component onto the Windows Form object. Name the label lblTitle. Enter the text for this label as Highway Radar Checkpoint on two lines (Hint: Click the Text property list arrow in the Properties window to enter a label with multiple lines. Press the ENTER key to move to a new line.) Choose the font Tahoma, Bold font style, and 18-point size. Change the TextAlign property to MiddleCenter by clicking the TextAlign list arrow and then clicking the Center block. Change the Location property of the lblTitle Label object to 133,41.

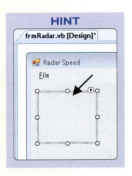

▶ **Add the Posted Speed Label** Place a Label object below the lblTitle Label object. Name the second Label lblPostedSpeed. In the Text property, enter Posted Speed Limit — 60 mph. Change the Font property to Tahoma, Italic font style, and 10-point size. Align the bottom of the lblPostedSpeed Label object with the bottom of the picRadar PictureBox object. Align the center of the lblPostedSpeed label with the center of the lblTitle Label object.

(continues)

Guided Program Development (continued)

▶ **Add the Enter Speed Button Object** Drag a Button object onto the Windows Form object below the picture box and labels. Name the Button btnEnterSpeed. Change the text of the button to Enter Speed. Change the font to 11-point Tahoma. Resize the Button object to view the complete text. Horizontally center the button in the Windows Form object.

▶ **Add the ListBox Object for the Vehicle Speeds** To add the ListBox object that displays the vehicle speeds, drag a ListBox object onto the Windows Form object below the Button object. Name the ListBox lstRadarSpeed. Change the font for the text in the ListBox object to 11-point Tahoma. Resize the ListBox to the width of three characters because the top speed of a vehicle could reach speeds such as 102 mph. Lengthen the ListBox object to display 10 numbers. The Size property for the ListBox object in the sample program is 34, 184. Horizontally center the ListBox object in the Windows Form object (*ref: Figure 6-24*).

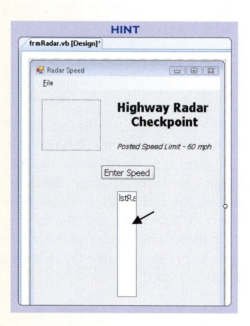

▶ **Add the Result Label** To add the label where the average speed message is displayed, drag a Label object onto the Windows Form object. Name the Label object lblAverageSpeed. Change the text to "Average speed at checkpoint is X.XX mph". Change the font to Tahoma 10-point. Horizontally center the message in the Windows Form object.

Guided Program Development (continued)

The user interface mockup is complete (Figure 6-99).

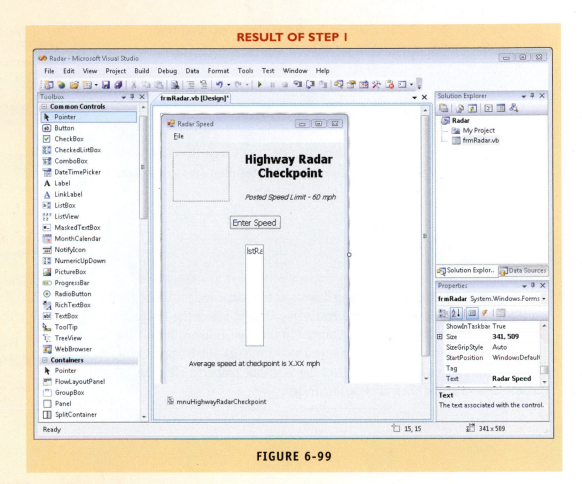

RESULT OF STEP 1

FIGURE 6-99

Phase 2: Fine-Tune the User Interface

2

▶ **Change the BackColor Property of the Windows Form Object** Select the Windows Form object and then change its BackColor property to White on the Web tab.

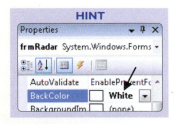

▶ **Change the Color for the Title Label** Change the ForeColor property for the lblTitle Label object to SteelBlue on the Web tab.

(continues)

Guided Program Development *(continued)*

▶ **Change the Button Color** Change the BackColor property of the btnEnterSpeed Button object to LightSteelBlue.

▶ **Change the Font Color for the List Box Object** Change the ForeColor property of the lstRadarSpeed ListBox object to SteelBlue on the Web tab.

▶ **Insert and Size the Radar Image into the PictureBox Object** Visit scsite.com/vb2008/ch6/images and download the Radar image. Select the picRadar PictureBox object. In the Properties window, select the Image property and then click the ellipsis button in the right column. Import the Radar image from the location where you saved it. Click the OK button in the Select Resource dialog box. Select the SizeMode property, click the SizeMode arrow, and then click StretchImage.

▶ **Change the Visible Property for the Average Speed Label** Select the lblAverageSpeed Label object and change its Visible property to False be-cause the Label object is not displayed until the average for the speeds entered is calculated.

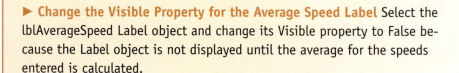

HEADS UP

As you work on your program, do not forget to save it from time to time. You can save the work you have done by clicking the Save All button on the Standard toolbar.

▶ **Make the Enter Speed Button the Accept Button** Click the background of the Windows Form object to select it. In the Properties window, click the AcceptButton list arrow to display the buttons in the user interface. Click btnEnterSpeed in the list. During program execution, when the user presses the ENTER key, the event handler for btnEnterSpeed executes.

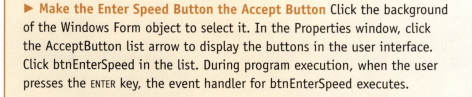

Guided Program Development (continued)

The user interface design is complete (Figure 6-100).

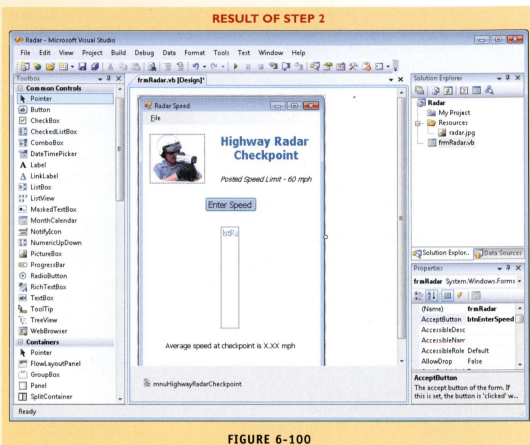

RESULT OF STEP 2

FIGURE 6-100

Phase 3: Code the Program

3

► **Enter the Comments for the Enter Speed Button Event Handler** Double-click the btnEnterSpeed Button object on the Windows Form object to open the button event handler. Insert the first four standard comments at the top of the code window. Insert the command Option Strict On at the beginning of the code to turn on strict type checking.

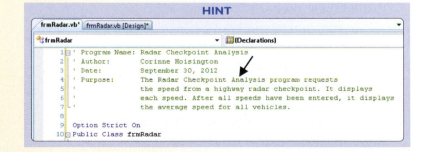

(continues)

Guided Program Development (continued)

▶ **Comment the btnEnterSpeed_Click Event Handler** Enter a comment to describe the purpose of the btnEnterSpeed_Click event handler.

```
13  Private Sub btnEnterSpeed_Click(ByVal sender As System.Object, ByVal e As S
14      ' The btnEnterSpeed click event accepts and displays up to ten speeds
15      ' from the user, and then calculates and displays the average speed
```

▶ **Declare and Initialize the Variables to Calculate the Average Speed** Four variables are used to calculate the average speed (besides the vehicle count). These variables are: 1) strVehicleSpeed: Is assigned the value from the InputBox function call; 2) decVehicleSpeed: Is assigned the converted vehicle speed; 3) decAverageSpeed: Contains the calculated average speed; 4) decTotalOfAllSpeeds: The accumulator used to accumulate the total speeds entered by a user. Declare and initialize these four variables.

HINT
```
17      ' Declare and initialize variables
18
19      Dim strVehicleSpeed As String
20      Dim decVehicleSpeed As Decimal
21      Dim decAverageSpeed As Decimal
22      Dim decTotalOfAllSpeeds As Decimal = 0D
```

▶ **Declare and Initialize the Variables Used with the InputBox Function Call** Five variables contain messages used in the input box to obtain the vehicle speeds. These variables are: 1) strInputBoxMessage: Is used in the function call to contain the message displayed in the input box; 2) strInputBoxHeading: Contains the message displayed in the title bar of the input box; 3) strNormalBoxMessage: The normal message that appears in the input box when no error has occurred; 4) strNonNumericErrorMessage: The message that appears in the input box when the user has entered a non-numeric value; 5) strNegativeNumberErrorMessage: The message that appears in the input box when the user has entered zero or a negative number. Declare and initialize these five variables.

HINT
```
23      Dim strInputBoxMessage As String = "Enter the speed for vehicle #"
24      Dim strInputBoxHeading As String = "Radar Speed"
25      Dim strNormalBoxMessage As String = "Enter the speed for vehicle #"
26      Dim strNonNumericErrorMessage As String = "Error - Enter a number for t
27      Dim strNegativeNumberErrorMessage As String = "Error - Enter a positive
```

Guided Program Development *(continued)*

▶ **Declare and Initialize Variables Used in the Loop Processing** Three variables are used for processing the loop in the program. These variables are: 1) strCancelButtonClicked: This variable contains a null string. It is used to determine if the user clicked the Cancel button in the input box; 2) intMaximumNumberOfEntries: Contains the maximum number of entries for vehicle speeds. Program requirements state the maximum number is 10; 3) intNumberOfEntries: The counter that counts the valid number of vehicle speeds entered by the user. This variable is used to determine when the maximum of entries has been made and to act as the divisor when calculating the average speed per vehicle.

HINT
```
29     'Declare and initialize loop variables
30
31     Dim strCancelButtonClicked As String = ""
32     Dim intMaximumNumberOfEntries As Integer = 10
33     Dim intNumberOfEntries As Integer = 1
```

▶ **Write Comments for the Do Until Loop and Write the Priming InputBox Function Call** You often can use comments to document a loop or other set of major processing statements. The comments here alert the reader to the role of the Do Until loop. The priming InputBox function call obtains the first vehicle speed, or allows the user to click the Cancel button. The normal message is displayed. The space at the end of the argument list places a space in the input box so if the user clicks the OK button without entering any data, it will not be treated the same as clicking the Cancel button *(ref: Figure 6-21)*.

HINT
```
35     ' This loop allows the user to enter the speed of up to 10 vehicles.
36     ' The loop terminates when the user has entered 10 speeds or the user
37     ' clicks the Cancel button or the Close button in the InputBox
38
39     strVehicleSpeed = InputBox(strInputBoxMessage & intNumberOfEntries, _
40                                strInputBoxHeading, " ")
```

▶ **Code the Do Until Loop** Because the application requests the speed of up to 10 vehicles, the Do Until loop should continue until 10 speeds are entered or until the user clicks the Cancel or Close Button in the input box. Enter the Do Until loop using IntelliSense *(ref: Figure 6-59, Figure 6-65, Figure 6-70)*.

HINT
```
42     Do Until intNumberOfEntries > intMaximumNumberOfEntries _
43         Or strVehicleSpeed = strCancelButtonClicked
44
```

(continues)

Guided Program Development *(continued)*

▶ **Validate the Entry is a Number** The first process in the Do Until loop is to validate that the vehicle speed entered by the user is a numeric value. Enter the If...Then statement to test if the value in the strVehicleSpeed variable is numeric.

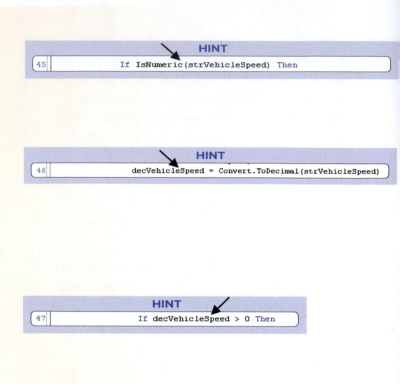

```
45        If IsNumeric(strVehicleSpeed) Then
```

▶ **Convert the Value Entered from String to Decimal Data Type** If the user entered a numeric value, the next step is to convert the string value the user entered to a Decimal data type. Using IntelliSense, enter the code to convert the value in the strVehicleSpeed variable from String to Decimal data type and place the result in the decVehicleSpeed variable.

```
46        decVehicleSpeed = Convert.ToDecimal(strVehicleSpeed)
```

▶ **Validate That the Entered Value is a Positive Number** After the value is converted, the program must validate that the number is positive. Write the If...Then statement to test whether the value in the decVehicleSpeed variable is greater than zero.

```
47        If decVehicleSpeed > 0 Then
```

▶ **Perform the Processing When the User Enters a Valid Speed** After ensuring the speed entered by the user is valid, the next steps are to perform the processing for valid speeds. Four steps are required: 1) Add the speed as an item to the lstRadarSpeed ListBox object *(ref: Figure 6-28)*; 2) Add the speed the user entered to the decTotalOfAllSpeeds accumulator *(Figure 6-39)*. The accumulated speed is used to calculate the average speed; 3) Increment the intNumberOfEntries counter by 1 because the user entered a valid speed *(Figure 6-39)*. This value is used as the divisor to determine the average speed, and also as one of the indicators that the loop should be terminated; 4) Because the user entered a valid speed, the normal message should be displayed in the input box the next time the input box is displayed. Therefore, the normal message should be moved to the strInputBoxMessage variable. Using IntelliSense, enter the code for these four activities.

```
48        Me.lstRadarSpeed.Items.Add(decVehicleSpeed)
49        decTotalOfAllSpeeds += decVehicleSpeed
50        intNumberOfEntries += 1
51        strInputBoxMessage = strNormalBoxMessage
```

Guided Program Development (continued)

▶ **Assign an Error Message if the User Entered a Negative Speed** If the user entered a negative speed, the next the input box that is displayed should show the negative number error message *(ref: Figure 6-72)*. Following the Else statement for the If statement that checks for a number greater than zero, enter the assignment statement that places the value in the strNegativeNumberErrorMessage variable in the strInputBoxMessage variable.

```
HINT
52         Else
53             strInputBoxMessage = strNegativeNumberErrorMessage
54         End If
```

▶ **Assign an Error Message If the User Entered a Non-Numeric Speed** If the user entered a non-numeric speed, the next the input box that is displayed should show the non-numeric error message *(ref: Figure 6-71)*. Following the Else Statement for the If statement that checks for numeric data, enter the assignment statement that places the value in the strNonNumericErrorMessage variable in the strInputBoxMessage variable.

```
HINT
55         Else
56             strInputBoxMessage = strNonNumericErrorMessage
57         End If
```

▶ **Code the InputBox Function Call** The first InputBox function call was placed before the Do Until loop to prime the loop. To continue the process after the first value is entered, another InputBox function is needed as the last statement inside the loop to request subsequent values. This statement should be executed only if the maximum number of entries has not been exceeded. So, an If structure is required to determine if the maximum number of entries has been reached. If not, the InputBox function call is executed *(ref: Figure 6-73)*.

```
HINT
59     If intNumberOfEntries <= intMaximumNumberOfEntries Then
60         strVehicleSpeed = InputBox(strInputBoxMessage & intNumberOfEntries, _
61                              strInputBoxHeading, " ")
62     End If
63
64 Loop
```

(continues)

Guided Program Development (continued)

The coding for the variables and Do Until loop that processes the data in the program is complete (Figure 6-101). It is important that you examine the code in Figure 6-101 and understand the loop processing. The priming of the loop by both setting the value in the intNumberOfEntries value (line 33) and calling the InputBox function (line 39) is critical for proper execution of the loop. Increasing the loop counter when a valid entry is made (line 50) also is fundamental in the loop processing because testing this counter is one way the Do Until loop can be terminated. Also, using variables for messages instead literals in the actual code demonstrates how professional programs are coded. You should follow these examples in your programming.

RESULT OF STEP 3

```
17          ' Declare and initialize variables
18
19          Dim strVehicleSpeed As String
20          Dim decVehicleSpeed As Decimal
21          Dim decAverageSpeed As Decimal
22          Dim decTotalOfAllSpeeds As Decimal = 0D
23          Dim strInputBoxMessage As String = "Enter the speed for vehicle #"
24          Dim strInputBoxHeading As String = "Radar Speed"
25          Dim strNormalBoxMessage As String = "Enter the speed for vehicle #"
26          Dim strNonNumericErrorMessage As String = "Error - Enter a number for the  ↙
        speed of vehicle #"
27          Dim strNegativeNumberErrorMessage As String = "Error - Enter a positive number ↙
        for vehicle #"
28
29          'Declare and initialize loop variables
30
31          Dim strCancelButtonClicked As String = ""
32          Dim intMaximumNumberOfEntries As Integer = 10
33          Dim intNumberOfEntries As Integer = 1
34
35          ' This loop allows the user to enter the speed of up to 10 vehicles.
36          ' The loop terminates when the user has entered 10 speeds or the user
37          ' clicks the Cancel button or the Close button in the InputBox
38
39          strVehicleSpeed = InputBox(strInputBoxMessage & intNumberOfEntries,
40                                  strInputBoxHeading, " ")
41
42          Do Until intNumberOfEntries > intMaximumNumberOfEntries _
43              Or strVehicleSpeed = strCancelButtonClicked
44
45              If IsNumeric(strVehicleSpeed) Then
46                  decVehicleSpeed = Convert.ToDecimal(strVehicleSpeed)
47                  If decVehicleSpeed > 0 Then
48                      Me.lstRadarSpeed.Items.Add(decVehicleSpeed)
49                      decTotalOfAllSpeeds += decVehicleSpeed
50                      intNumberOfEntries += 1
51                      strInputBoxMessage = strNormalBoxMessage
52                  Else
53                      strInputBoxMessage = strNegativeNumberErrorMessage
54                  End If
55              Else
```

FIGURE 6-101 (continues)

Guided Program Development *(continued)*

```
56                     strInputBoxMessage = strNonNumericErrorMessage
57            End If
58
59            If intNumberOfEntries <= intMaximumNumberOfEntries Then
60                strVehicleSpeed = InputBox(strInputBoxMessage & intNumberOfEntries,
61                                     strInputBoxHeading, " ")
62            End If
63
64        Loop
```

FIGURE 6-101 (continued)

4

▶ **Set the Result Label's Visible Property** When
you finish the Do Until loop, you must complete
three tasks to finish the Enter Speed button click
event handler: 1) The label that will contain the
average speed must be made visible; 2) The average
speed must be calculated and displayed; 3) The Enter
Speed button must be disabled. Using IntelliSense,
write the code to make the lblAverageSpeed label
visible.

HINT

```
66        ' Makes label visible
67        Me.lblAverageSpeed.Visible = True
```

▶ **Calculate the Average Speed** To calculate the
average of the speeds the user entered, the value in
the decTotalOfAllSpeeds variable must be divided by
the number of vehicles for which speeds were entered.
At the end of the loop shown in Figure 6-101, the
value in the intNumberOfEntries variable always will
be one greater than the actual number of vehicles entered, so the total of all speeds must be divided by the
value in the intNumberOfEntries less 1. This calculation
should occur only if one or more vehicle speeds were
entered, so an If statement must be used to check if
the value in the intNumberOfEntries variable is greater
than 1. If so, the average speed is calculated; if not,
the "No speed entered" message should be displayed.
Using IntelliSense, write the code to perform this
processing.

HINT

```
69        'Calculates and displays average speed
70        If intNumberOfEntries > 1 Then
71            decAverageSpeed = decTotalOfAllSpeeds / (intNumberOfEntries - 1)
72            Me.lblAverageSpeed.Text = "Average speed at checkpoint is " & _
73                decAverageSpeed.ToString("F1") & " mph"
74        Else
75            Me.lblAverageSpeed.Text = "No speed entered"
76        End If
```

(continues)

Guided Program Development (continued)

► **Change the Enter Speed Button Enabled Property to False** After the average speed is calculated and displayed, the Enabled property of the btnEnterSpeed button is set to False to dim the button. Using IntelliSense, write the code to accomplish this processing.

HINT

```
78       ' Disables the Enter Speed button
79       Me.btnEnterSpeed.Enabled = False
```

The code for the btnEnterSpeed button click event handler is completed (Figure 6-102).

RESULT OF STEP 4

```
13      Private Sub btnEnterSpeed_Click(ByVal sender As System.Object, ByVal e As System. ↵
        EventArgs) Handles btnEnterSpeed.Click
14          ' The btnEnterSpeed click event accepts and displays up to ten speeds
15          ' from the user, and then calculates and displays the average speed
16
17          ' Declare and initialize variables
18
19          Dim strVehicleSpeed As String
20          Dim decVehicleSpeed As Decimal
21          Dim decAverageSpeed As Decimal
22          Dim decTotalOfAllSpeeds As Decimal = 0D
23          Dim strInputBoxMessage As String = "Enter the speed for vehicle #"
24          Dim strInputBoxHeading As String = "Radar Speed"
25          Dim strNormalBoxMessage As String = "Enter the speed for vehicle #"
26          Dim strNonNumericErrorMessage As String = "Error - Enter a number for the       ↵
        speed of vehicle #"
27          Dim strNegativeNumberErrorMessage As String = "Error - Enter a positive number ↵
        for vehicle #"
28
29          'Declare and initialize loop variables
30
31          Dim strCancelButtonClicked As String = ""
32          Dim intMaximumNumberOfEntries As Integer = 10
33          Dim intNumberOfEntries As Integer = 1
34
35          ' This loop allows the user to enter the speed of up to 10 vehicles.
36          ' The loop terminates when the user has entered 10 speeds or the user
37          ' clicks the Cancel button or the Close button in the InputBox
38
39          strVehicleSpeed = InputBox(strInputBoxMessage & intNumberOfEntries, _
40                               strInputBoxHeading, " ")
41
42          Do Until intNumberOfEntries > intMaximumNumberOfEntries _
43              Or strVehicleSpeed = strCancelButtonClicked
44
45              If IsNumeric(strVehicleSpeed) Then
46                  decVehicleSpeed = Convert.ToDecimal(strVehicleSpeed)
47                  If decVehicleSpeed > 0 Then
48                      Me.lstRadarSpeed.Items.Add(decVehicleSpeed)
49                      decTotalOfAllSpeeds += decVehicleSpeed
```

FIGURE 6-102 (continues)

```
50                     intNumberOfEntries += 1
51                     strInputBoxMessage = strNormalBoxMessage
52                 Else
53                     strInputBoxMessage = strNegativeNumberErrorMessage
54                 End If
55             Else
56                 strInputBoxMessage = strNonNumericErrorMessage
57             End If
58
59             If intNumberOfEntries <= intMaximumNumberOfEntries Then
60                 strVehicleSpeed = InputBox(strInputBoxMessage & intNumberOfEntries, _
61                                         strInputBoxHeading, " ")
62             End If
63
64         Loop
65
66         ' Makes label visible
67         Me.lblAverageSpeed.Visible = True
68
69         'Calculates and displays average speed
70         If intNumberOfEntries > 1 Then
71             decAverageSpeed = decTotalOfAllSpeeds / (intNumberOfEntries - 1)
72             Me.lblAverageSpeed.Text = "Average speed at checkpoint is " & _
73                 decAverageSpeed.ToString("F1") & " mph"
74         Else
75             Me.lblAverageSpeed.Text = "No speed entered"
76         End If
77
78         ' Disables the Enter Speed button
79         Me.btnEnterSpeed.Enabled = False
80
81     End Sub
```

FIGURE 6-102 (continued)

Guided Program Development *(continued)*

5

▶ **Run the Program** After coding a major section of the program, you should run the program to ensure it is working properly. Click the Start Debugging button on the Standard toolbar to run the Highway Radar Checkpoint program. Click the Enter Speed button and then enter a vehicle speed 10 times. Verify the speeds are displayed properly and the average speed is correct. Close the program by clicking the Close button. Run the program again, click the Enter Speed button, enter four vehicle speeds, enter a non-numeric speed, enter a speed that is less than zero, and then click the Cancel button in the input box. Ensure the speeds are displayed properly, the average speed is correct, and the error messages are displayed properly in the input box. Close the program. Run the program again, click the Enter Speed button, and then click the Cancel button in the input box. Ensure the no speed entered message is displayed. Close the program and then run it as many times as necessary to ensure the program is working properly. If the program does not run properly, consider setting a breakpoint and checking the values in the variables *(ref: Figure 6-76)*.

HINT

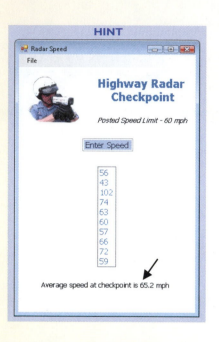

6

▶ **Enter the Code for the Clear Menu Item Click Event** Click the frmRadar.vb[Design]* tab in the code editing window to display the design window. Click File on the MenuStrip object, and then double-click the Clear menu item to open the Clear click event handler in the code editing window. The Clear click event handler must perform three tasks: 1) Clear the lstRadarSpeed list box; 2) Hide the average speed Label object; 3) Enable the Enter Speed Button object. Using IntelliSense, write the code for these three tasks.

HINT

```
84        ' The mnuClear click event clears the ListBox object and hides
85        ' the average speed label. It also enables the Enter Speed button
86
87        Me.lstRadarSpeed.Items.Clear()
88        Me.lblAverageSpeed.Visible = False
89        Me.btnEnterSpeed.Enabled = True
```

Guided Program Development *(continued)*

▶ **Enter the Code for the Exit Menu Item Click Event** Return to the design window. Double-click the Exit menu item. In the code window, enter a Close procedure call that will close the window and terminate the program.

The code for the Clear menu item click event and the Exit menu item click event is completed (Figure 6-103). The program code for the program is done.

RESULT OF STEP 4

```
83      Private Sub mnuClear_Click(ByVal sender As System.Object, ByVal e As System.      ↙
        EventArgs) Handles mnuClearItem.Click
84           ' The mnuClear click event clears the ListBox object and hides
85           ' the average speed label. It also enables the Enter Speed button
86
87           Me.lstRadarSpeed.Items.Clear()
88           Me.lblAverageSpeed.Visible = False
89           Me.btnEnterSpeed.Enabled = True
90
91      End Sub
92
93      Private Sub mnuExit_Click(ByVal sender As System.Object, ByVal e As System.      ↙
        EventArgs) Handles mnuExitItem.Click
94           ' The mnuExit click event closes the window and exits the application
95
96           Me.Close()
97
98      End Sub
```

FIGURE 6-103

(continues)

Guided Program Development *(continued)*

7

▶ **Publish the Highway Radar Checkpoint Program Option** After completing the program, you can publish it using ClickOnce deployment so it can be installed on multiple computers. To open the Publish Wizard and begin the deployment process, click Build on the menu bar and then click Publish Radar on the Build menu *(ref: Figure 6-87)*.

▶ **Select the Publish File Location** The Publish Wizard dialog box asks where you want to publish the application. Change the default location to the same file location that you used to save your Windows application by clicking the Browse button and then selecting the drive. For example, select the E: drive, a USB drive. After selecting the drive, click the Next button in the Publish Wizard dialog box *(ref: Figure 6-88)*.

▶ **Select How the Users Will Install the Application** In the next Publish Wizard dialog box, select the option that lets users install the application from a CD-ROM or DVD-ROM. Then, click the Next button *(ref: Figure 6-90)*.

Guided Program Development *(continued)*

▶ **Indicate the Application Will Not Check for Updates** Click the The application will not check for updates radio button to indicate no updates will be checked. This is the normal selection when programs are placed on CDs or DVDs. Then, click the Next button in the Publish Wizard dialog box *(ref: Figure 6-91)*.

▶ **View the Summary Window** The Publish Wizard summary is displayed. Click the Finish button to publish the application *(ref: Figure 6-92)*.

▶ **View the Installation Files** After the publishing succeeds, a folder is created with the installation files that could be placed on a CD, DVD, or other computer *(ref: Figure 6-94)*.

(continues)

Code Listing

The complete code for the sample program is shown in Figure 6-104.

```vb
1  ' Program Name:  Radar Checkpoint Analysis
2  ' Author:        Corinne Hoisington
3  ' Date:          September 30, 2012
4  ' Purpose:       The Radar Checkpoint Analysis program requests
5  '                the speed from a highway radar checkpoint. It displays
6  '                each speed. After all speeds have been entered, it displays
7  '                the average speed for all vehicles.
8
9  Option Strict On
10
11 Public Class frmRadar
12
13     Private Sub btnEnterSpeed_Click(ByVal sender As System.Object, ByVal e As System. ↵
       EventArgs) Handles btnEnterSpeed.Click
14         ' The btnEnterSpeed click event accepts and displays up to ten speeds
15         ' from the user, and then calculates and displays the average speed
16
17         ' Declare and initialize variables
18
19         Dim strVehicleSpeed As String
20         Dim decVehicleSpeed As Decimal
21         Dim decAverageSpeed As Decimal
22         Dim decTotalOfAllSpeeds As Decimal = 0D
23         Dim strInputBoxMessage As String = "Enter the speed for vehicle #"
24         Dim strInputBoxHeading As String = "Radar Speed"
25         Dim strNormalBoxMessage As String = "Enter the speed for vehicle #"
26         Dim strNonNumericErrorMessage As String = "Error - Enter a number for the      ↵
       speed of vehicle #"
27         Dim strNegativeNumberErrorMessage As String = "Error - Enter a positive number↵
       for vehicle #"
28
29         'Declare and initialize loop variables
30
31         Dim strCancelButtonClicked As String = ""
32         Dim intMaximumNumberOfEntries As Integer = 10
33         Dim intNumberOfEntries As Integer = 1
34
35         ' This loop allows the user to enter the speed of up to 10 vehicles.
36         ' The loop terminates when the user has entered 10 speeds or the user
37         ' clicks the Cancel button or the Close button in the InputBox
38
39         strVehicleSpeed = InputBox(strInputBoxMessage & intNumberOfEntries, _
40                                    strInputBoxHeading, " ")
41
42         Do Until intNumberOfEntries > intMaximumNumberOfEntries _
43             Or strVehicleSpeed = strCancelButtonClicked
44
45             If IsNumeric(strVehicleSpeed) Then
46                 decVehicleSpeed = Convert.ToDecimal(strVehicleSpeed)
47                 If decVehicleSpeed > 0 Then
48                     Me.lstRadarSpeed.Items.Add(decVehicleSpeed)
49                     decTotalOfAllSpeeds += decVehicleSpeed
50                     intNumberOfEntries += 1
51                     strInputBoxMessage = strNormalBoxMessage
52                 Else
53                     strInputBoxMessage = strNegativeNumberErrorMessage
```

FIGURE 6-104 (continues)

```
 54                     End If
 55                 Else
 56                     strInputBoxMessage = strNonNumericErrorMessage
 57                 End If
 58
 59             If intNumberOfEntries <= intMaximumNumberOfEntries Then
 60                 strVehicleSpeed = InputBox(strInputBoxMessage & intNumberOfEntries, _
 61                                     strInputBoxHeading, " ")
 62             End If
 63
 64         Loop
 65
 66         ' Makes label visible
 67         Me.lblAverageSpeed.Visible = True
 68
 69         'Calculates and displays average speed
 70         If intNumberOfEntries > 1 Then
 71             decAverageSpeed = decTotalOfAllSpeeds / (intNumberOfEntries - 1)
 72             Me.lblAverageSpeed.Text = "Average speed at checkpoint is " & _
 73                 decAverageSpeed.ToString("F1") & " mph"
 74         Else
 75             Me.lblAverageSpeed.Text = "No speed entered"
 76         End If
 77
 78         ' Disables the Enter Speed button
 79         Me.btnEnterSpeed.Enabled = False
 80
 81     End Sub
 82
 83     Private Sub mnuClear_Click(ByVal sender As System.Object, ByVal e As System.   ↙
        EventArgs) Handles mnuClearItem.Click
 84         ' The mnuClear click event clears the ListBox object and hides
 85         ' the average speed label. It also enables the Enter Speed button
 86
 87         Me.lstRadarSpeed.Items.Clear()
 88         Me.lblAverageSpeed.Visible = False
 89         Me.btnEnterSpeed.Enabled = True
 90
 91     End Sub
 92
 93     Private Sub mnuExit_Click(ByVal sender As System.Object, ByVal e As System.   ↙
        EventArgs) Handles mnuExitItem.Click
 94         ' The mnuExit click event closes the window and exits the application
 95
 96         Me.Close()
 97
 98     End Sub
 99 End Class
100
```

FIGURE 6-104 (continued)

Summary

In this chapter you have learned to design and write code to implement loops and to create menus, list boxes, and an input box. The items listed in the following table include all the new Visual Studio and Visual Basic skills you have learned in this chapter.

VISUAL BASIC SKILLS		
Skill	**Figure Number**	**Web Address for Video**
Place a MenuStrip object on the Windows Form object	Figure 6-5	scsite.com/vb2008/ch6/figure6-5
Code the Exit menu item event	Figure 6-12	scsite.com/vb2008/ch6/figure6-12
Insert a full standard menu	Figure 6-14	scsite.com/vb2008/ch6/figure6-14
Code the InputBox function	Figure 6-17	
Add a ListBox object	Figure 6-24	scsite.com/vb2008/ch6/figure6-24
Add an item to a ListBox object	Figure 6-27	
Add items to a ListBox object during design	Figure 6-32	scsite.com/vb2008/ch6/figure6-32
Assign a selected item from a ListBox object	Figure 6-36	
Write code using compound operators	Figure 6-39	
Write the code for a For...Next loop	Figure 6-42	
Use IntelliSense to enter the code for a For...Next loop	Figure 6-50	scsite.com/vb2008/ch6/figure6-50
Write code for a top-controlled Do While loop	Figure 6-56	
Use IntelliSense to code a Do While loop	Figure 6-59	scsite.com/vb2008/ch6/figure6-59
Write code for a bottom-controlled Do While loop	Figure 6-62	
Write code for a top-controlled Do Until loop	Figure 6-65	
Write code for a bottom-controlled Do Until loop	Figure 6-67	
Avoid infinite loops	Figure 6-69	
Prime a loop	Figure 6-70	
Validate data	Figure 6-73	
Create a nested loop	Figure 6-74	
Set a breakpoint and use a DataTip	Figure 6-76	scsite.com/vb2008/ch6/figure6-76
Publish an application with ClickOnce deployment	Figure 6-87	scsite.com/vb2008/ch6/figure6-87

FIGURE 6-105

Learn It Online

Start your browser and visit scsite.com/vb2008/ch6. Follow the instructions in the exercises below.

1. **Chapter Reinforcement TF, MC, SA** Click one of the Chapter Reinforcement links for Multiple Choice, True/False, or Short Answer below the Learn It Online heading. Answer each question and submit to your instructor.

2. **Practice Test** Click the Practice Test link below Chapter 6. Answer each question, enter your first and last name at the bottom of the page, and then click the Grade Test button. When the graded practice test is displayed on your screen, submit the graded practice test to your instructor. Continue to take the practice test until you are satisfied with your score.

3. **Crossword Puzzle Challenge** Click the Crossword Puzzle Challenge link below the Learn It Online heading. Read the instructions, and then click the Continue button. Work the crossword puzzle. When you are finished, click the Submit button. When the crossword puzzle is redisplayed, submit it to your instructor.

Knowledge Check

1. Write a statement that displays the default value of 12.50 in the input box shown in Figure 6-106 and assigns the return value from the InputBox function to a variable named strPayRate.

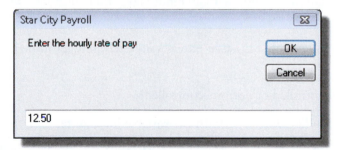

FIGURE 6-106

2. Write compound operators for the following equations:

   a. intTouchdown = intTouchdown + 6

   b. dblSquare = dblSquare ^ 2

   c. strFast = strFast & "Comet"

3. Write For...Next loops that calculate the sum of the following ranges and assign their sum to a variable named intSum:

   a. The first 100 numbers starting with number 1.

   b. The even numbers beginning at 10 and ending with 50.

   c. The numbers 20, 30, 40, 50, and 60.

(continues)

Knowledge Check

(continued)

4. Find the errors in the following For...Next header statements:

   a. For intCounter = "1" To "19"

   b. For intNumber = 98 To 71 Step 2

   c. For intValue = 12 To 52 Step −4

   d. For strCount = −15 To 5 Step 5

5. Explain the purpose of placing an ampersand before or within a MenuStrip item.

6. Write the command to clear a ListBox object named lstBaseballPlayers.

7. Write a command to add your favorite sports team to a ListBox object named lstFavoriteTeam.

8. Using a compound operator, write an assignment statement to increment the value in intAmount by 7.

9. Using a compound operator, write an assignment statement to decrease the value in intCounter by 4.5.

10. Using a compound operator, write an assignment statement to increment the value in intQuantity by 10.

11. Write a top-controlled Do Until loop with an empty body that would continue until intValue is greater than 19.

12. Write a bottom-controlled Do While loop with an empty body that continues while the user enters "Yes" into the strContinue variable.

13. Write a Do While loop to validate that the user enters a non-zero integer into an input box for a variable named intDenominator.

14. Is the For...Next loop top-controlled or bottom-controlled?

15. Write the code for an infinite Do Until loop with the variable intInfinite.

16. Which loop should be used if you know the required number of times the loop will be executed?

17. What is the fewest number of times a top-controlled Do Until loop is executed?

18. Write a data validation Do loop to check that the variable intAge entered from an input box is between 1 and 115.

19. A loop inside another loop is called a _____ _____.

20. When you insert standard items in a MenuStrip object, what File menu items are automatically created by default?

Debugging Exercises

1. The loop shown in Figure 6-107 should repeat 10 times. If it will not repeat 10 times, change the code so it will.

```
7           For intRepeat = 20 To 10
8               MsgBox("The value is " & intRepeat.ToString("C0"))
9           Next
```

FIGURE 6-107

2. What output does the code shown in Figure 6-108 produce? How would you change the code to produce a list box containing the values 12-20?

```
15          intRate = 12
16          Do While intRate <= 10
17              Me.lstDisplay.Items.Add(intRate)
18              intRate += 1
19          Loop
```

FIGURE 6-108

3. What is the output of the code shown in Figure 6-109?

```
5           Dim intAdd As Integer
6           Dim intOuterLoop As Integer
7           Dim intInnerLoop As Integer
8
9           intAdd = 0
10          For intOuterLoop = 1 To 8
11              For intInnerLoop = 3 To 7
12                  intAdd += 1
13              Next
14          Next
            MessageBox.Show("The final value is " & intAdd.ToString())
```

FIGURE 6-109

(continues)

Debugging Exercises

(continued)

4. What is the output of the code shown in Figure 6-110?

```
33          Dim intValue As Integer
34
35          intValue = 2
36          Do While intValue <= 9
37              Me.lstDisplay.Items.Add(intValue & " " & intValue ^ 3)
38              intValue += 2
39          Loop
```

FIGURE 6-110

5. Fix the errors in the loop shown in Figure 6-111.

```
41          Dim intStart As Integer = 8
42
43          Loop
44          intStart = +4
45          Do While intStart < 24
```

FIGURE 6-111

6. What is the output of the code shown in Figure 6-112?

```
53          intCount = 40
54          Do Until intCount < 26
55              intCount -= 2
56              Me.lstCount.Items.Add(intCount)
57          Loop
```

FIGURE 6-112

7. Fix the following errors in the code shown in Figure 6-113.

```
5           Dim decCost As Decimal = 3.5D
6
7           Do Until decCost > 10.5D
8               MsgBox("The cost is now " & decCost.ToString("F1"))
9               decCost -= 0.5
10          Loop
```

FIGURE 6-113

Debugging Exercises

(continued)

8. In the example shown in Figure 6-114, you want the code to count the odd numbers from 1 to 99. What is missing?

```
66        Dim intOddNumber As Integer = 1
67
68        Do While intOddNumber <= 99
69            Me.lstDisplay.Items.Add("Odd Numbers: " & intOddNumber.ToString())
70        Loop
```

FIGURE 6-114

Program Analysis

1. What is the value of lblResult after the code shown in Figure 6-115 is executed?

```
73        Dim intCounter As Integer = -20
74
75        Do While intCount < 25
76            intCount += 5
77            Me.lblResult.Text &= intCount.ToString() & " "
78        Loop
```

FIGURE 6-115

2. What is the value of lblResult after the code shown in Figure 6-116 is executed?

```
80        Dim intCountIt As Integer
81
82        intCountIt = 6
83        Do
84            intCountIt += 3
85            Me.lblResult.Text &= intCountIt.ToString() & " "
86        Loop Until intCountIt = 21
```

FIGURE 6-116

(continues)

Program Analysis

(continued)

3. Rewrite the top-controlled Do While loop shown in Figure 6-117 as a top-controlled Do Until loop.

```
88          Dim intQuantity As Integer
89
90          intQuantity = -5
91          Do While intQuantity < 30
92              intQuantity += 5
93          Loop
```

FIGURE 6-117

4. Convert the Do loop shown in Figure 6-118 to a For...Next loop:

```
95          Dim intIncrease As Integer
96
97          intIncrease = 10
98          Do While intIncrease < 40
99              Me.lstDisplay.Items.Add(intIncrease)
100             intIncrease += 2
101         Loop
```

FIGURE 6-118

5. How many times will the inner statement inside the nested loop in Figure 6-119 be executed?

```
103         For intOuterLoop = 3 To 5
104             For intInnerLoop = 6 To 10
105                 Me.lstDays.Items.Add("Value: " & intOuterLoop.ToString() & _
106                     " Count: " & intInnerLoop.ToString())
107             Next
108         Next
```

FIGURE 6-119

Program Analysis

(continued)

6. How many times will the loop in Figure 6-120 be executed?

```
110          Dim intQuantitySold As Integer
111          Dim decTax As Decimal
112
113          intQuantitySold = 1
114          Do Until intQuantitySold = 5
115              decTax = intQuantitySold * 0.07
116              Me.lstDisplay.Items.Add("Tax Amount: " & decTax.ToString())
117              intQuantitySold += 1
118          Loop
```

FIGURE 6-120

7. Write a For...Next loop that adds the odd numbers 1 through 49 and assigns their sum to the variable intSum. The program should start with the lines shown in Figure 6-121 (use the following variables in your code).

```
120          Dim intLoopValue As Integer
121          Dim intStartvalue As Integer
122          Dim intEndvalue As Integer
123          Dim intSum As Integer
124
125          intStartvalue = 1
126          intEndvalue = 49
127          intSum = 0
```

FIGURE 6-121

Case Programming Assignments

Complete one or more of the following case programming assignments.
Submit the program and materials you create to your instructor. The level of
difficulty is indicated for each case programming assignment.

1 ●

AVERAGE TEMPERATURE IN PARADISE

Design a Windows application and write the code that will execute according to the program requirements
shown in Figure 6-122. Before writing the code, create an event planning document for each event in the
program. The Use Case Definition document is shown in Figure 6-123. The completed user interface is
shown in Figure 6-124.

REQUIREMENTS DOCUMENT

Date submitted: March 17, 2012

Application title: Hawaiian Average Temperature

Purpose: This Windows application is written for the Hawaiian Tourism Board with the task of calculating the yearly average temperature in the Hawaiian Islands for one year.

**Program
Procedures:**   In a Windows application, the user enters up to 12 average monthly temperatures to compute
the annual average temperature in the Hawaiian islands.

**Algorithms,
Processing, and
Conditions:**
1. The user enters up to 12 monthly average temperatures for Hawaii in an InputBox object.
2. Each month's average temperature is displayed in a ListBox object.
3. After the 12 temperatures are entered, the average temperature is calculated and displayed.
4. A File menu contains a Clear and an Exit option. The Clear menu item clears the average
and the 12 values representing the monthly temperatures. The Exit menu item closes the
application.
5. If the user clicks the Cancel button before entering 12 values, compute the average for the
number of months entered.
6. If the user clicks the Cancel button before entering any temperatures, display a message
indicating the user did not enter a temperature.

**Notes and
Restrictions:**
1. Non-numeric values should not be accepted.
2. Negative values should not be accepted.
3. The average temperature should be rounded to the nearest tenth.

Comments:
1. The application allows decimal entries.
2. Obtain the image from scsite.com/vb2008/ch6/images. Its name is Beach.

FIGURE 6-122

Case Programming Assignments

USE CASE DEFINITION

1. The Windows application opens, displaying the Hawaiian Tourism Board Average Temperature title, a ListBox object that displays the temperatures, an image, and a Button object that allows the user to begin entering the temperatures.
2. A menu bar displays the File menu, which has two menu items: Clear and Exit.
3. The user enters up to 12 values in an InputBox object, with each value representing an Hawaiian monthly average temperature.
4. The program asks the user for the temperature again if the value is a negative number or the entry is a non-numeric value.
5. The program displays the average temperature rounded to one decimal place.
6. The user can clear the input and the result by clicking the Clear menu item, and then can repeat steps 3-5. If the user clicks the Cancel button, the average for the values entered is calculated. If the user did not enter any values, the program displays an appropriate message.
7. The user clicks the Exit menu item to close the application.

FIGURE 6-123

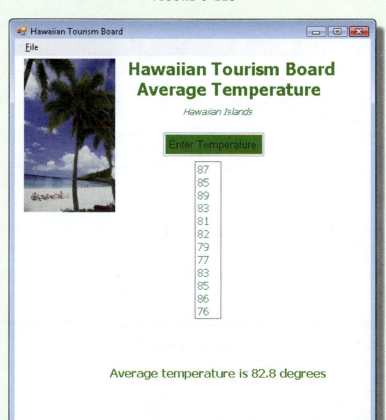

FIGURE 6-124

Case Programming Assignments

2 ● AVERAGE COMMISSION

Design a Windows application and write the code that will execute according to the program requirements shown in Figure 6-125. Before writing the code, create an event planning document for each event in the program. The Use Case Definition document is shown in Figure 6-126. The completed user interface is shown in Figure 6-127.

REQUIREMENTS DOCUMENT

Date submitted: July 31, 2012

Application title: Average Sales Commission Windows Application

Purpose: This Windows application finds the average commission of a team of up to eight software salespeople.

Program Procedures: In a Windows application, the user enters the monthly commission of up to eight software salespeople to compute the average commission of the team.

Algorithms, Processing, and Conditions:
1. The user clicks the Enter Commission button to enter the monthly commission for each of up to eight salespeople.
2. Each commission is displayed in a ListBox object.
3. After the eight commissions are entered, the average commission is displayed.
4. A File menu contains a Clear and an Exit option. The Clear menu item clears the average commission and the eight values representing the sales commissions. The Exit menu item closes the application.
5. If the user clicks the Cancel button after entering one but before entering eight commissions, use the commissions the user entered for the calculations.
6. If the user clicks the Cancel button before entering any commissions, display an appropriate message.

Notes and Restrictions:
1. The result should be rounded to the nearest dollar.
2. Non-numeric values should not be accepted.
3. Negative numbers should not be accepted.

Comments:
1. The application allows decimal entries.

FIGURE 6-125

Case Programming Assignments

USE CASE DEFINITION

1. The Windows application opens, displaying the software company name as the title, a ListBox object that will display the sales commissions, and a Button object that allows the user to enter the commissions.
2. A menu bar displays the File menu, which has two menu items: Clear and Exit.
3. In an InputBox object, the user enters up to eight values, one at a time, representing the salespeople's commissions.
4. The program asks the user for the commission again if the value is a negative or non-numeric number.
5. The program displays the average commission.
6. The user clicks the Clear menu item to clear the input and the result.
7. If the user clicks the Cancel button before entering eight commissions, the program uses the commissions entered for calculations. If the user entered no commissions, an appropriate message is displayed.
8. The user clicks the Exit menu item to close the application.

FIGURE 6-126

FIGURE 6-127

Case Programming Assignments

3 ●
FOOTBALL FEVER SCOREBOARD

Design a Windows application and write the code that will execute according to the program requirements shown in Figure 6-128. Before writing the code, create an event planning document for each event in the program. The Use Case Definition document is shown in Figure 6-129. The completed user interface is shown in Figure 6-130.

REQUIREMENTS DOCUMENT

Date submitted:	November 3, 2012
Application title:	Football Fever Scoreboard Windows Application
Purpose:	This application calculates the points scored during a football game by one team.
Program Procedures:	In a Windows application, the user enters each score one football team makes to display the team's score on the scoreboard.
Algorithms, Processing, and Conditions:	1. The user clicks the Enter Scores button in an InputBox object to enter a score after the football team scores points in a game. 2. Each score and the running total is displayed in a ListBox. 3. After the user clicks the Cancel button in the InputBox object to end the game scoring, the total final score is displayed. 4. A File menu contains a Clear and an Exit option. The Clear menu item clears the result and the football scores. The Exit menu item closes the application.
Notes and Restrictions:	1. Non-numeric values should not be accepted. 2. A negative value should not be accepted.
Comments:	

FIGURE 6-128

Case Programming Assignments

USE CASE DEFINITION

1. The Windows application opens, displaying your favorite football team's name, scoreboard subtitle, a ListBox object that will display the football team scores throughout the game, and a Button object that allows the user to enter the scores.
2. A menu bar displays the File menu, which has two menu items: Clear and Exit.
3. In an InputBox object, the user enters points a football team scores.
4. The program asks the user for the score again if the value is a negative or non-numeric number.
5. The program displays the total score.
6. The program displays the final score when the user clicks the Cancel button in the input box.
7. The user clicks the Clear menu item to clear the input and the result.
8. The user clicks the Exit menu item to close the application.

FIGURE 6-129

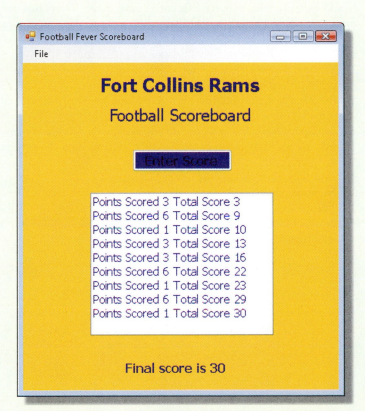

FIGURE 6-130

Case Programming Assignments

4 ●●
DOUBLE YOUR PAY

Design a Windows application and write the code that will execute according to the program requirements shown in Figure 6-131. Before writing the code, create an event planning document for each event in the program. Create a Use Case Definition document for the application.

REQUIREMENTS DOCUMENT

Date submitted: June 21, 2012

Application title: Double Your Pay Windows Application

Purpose: This Windows application finds the amount of your pay if your pay is doubled each day, starting with a penny a day or a nickel a day. Instead of one month's salary, a boss offers her new employees a penny the first day and experienced employees a nickel the first day under the new pay system. Each day the pay will double.

Program Procedures: In a Windows application, the user enters the number of days in a pay period and the pay for the first day. The program calculates and displays the amount of pay for the pay period.

Algorithms, Processing, and Conditions:
1. The user enters the number of days in the pay period.
2. The user selects a RadioButton object to indicate the pay amount of the first day: a penny or a nickel.
3. After the user enters the number of days and pay for the first day, the total amount earned is calculated and displayed.
4. A File menu contains a Clear and an Exit option. The Clear menu item clears the result and the RadioButton objects. The Exit menu item closes the application.

Notes and Restrictions:
1. Non-numeric values should not be accepted.
2. Negative values should not be accepted.
3. The minimum number of days for the pay period is 19 days for the new employees and 16 days for the experienced employees. The maximum number of days in a pay period is 22 days.

Comments:

FIGURE 6-131

Case Programming Assignments

5 ●●
DISTANCE TRAVELED CALCULATOR

Design a mobile application and write the code that will execute according to the program requirements shown in Figure 6-132. Before writing the code, create an event planning document for each event in the program. Create a Use Case Definition document for the application.

REQUIREMENTS DOCUMENT

Date submitted: December 5, 2012

Application title: Vacation Distance Calculator Mobile Application

Purpose: This application computes the number of miles traveled given the speed limit and the number of hours to be traveled in one day.

Program Procedures: In a mobile application, the user enters the speed limit and the number of hours of travel intended on the road for a day. The application displays the distance traveled for each hour within the time period.

Algorithms, Processing, and Conditions:
1. The application opens displaying a title. The user enters the vehicle speed and the amount of time to be traveled that day.
2. The user clicks the Compute Distance Traveled button to display the hour-by-hour distance in total miles traveled.
3. A File menu contains a Clear and an Exit option. The Clear menu item clears the result and the entered number of miles per hour and time traveled. The Exit menu item closes the application.

Notes and Restrictions:
1. Non-numeric values should not be accepted.
2. The number of hours for one day of travel should not exceed 20 hours.

Comments:
1. The application allows decimal entries.

FIGURE 6-132

Case Programming Assignments

6 ●● PAY CALCULATOR

Design a Windows application and write the code that will execute according to the program requirements shown in Figure 6-133. Before writing the code, create an event planning document for each event in the program. Create a Use Case Definition document for the application.

Requirements Document

Date submitted:	August 23, 2012
Application title:	The Next Decade Pay Calculator
Purpose:	This Windows application computes the amount of money an employee earns over the next decade based on a raise, which is a percentage amount.
Program Procedures:	In a Windows application, the user enters the present wage per hour and the raise percentage amount per year to compute the yearly pay over the next 10 years.
Algorithms, Processing, and Conditions:	1. The application opens displaying a title and requesting the amount of present pay per hour and the expected raise percentage per year. 2. When the Calculate Pay button is clicked, the program calculates the yearly pay based on 40 hours per week and 52 weeks per year. The raise increases each amount after the first year. 3. The yearly amount of pay earned is displayed for the next 10 years. 4. A File menu contains a Clear and an Exit option. The Clear menu item clears the result. The Exit menu item closes the application.
Notes and Restrictions:	1. Non-numeric values should not be accepted. 2. Negative numbers should not be allowed.
Comments:	1. The application allows decimal entries.

FIGURE 6-133

Case Programming Assignments

7 ●●●
ELEMENTARY SCHOOL MATH TUTOR

Create a requirements document and a Use Case Definition document, and design a Windows application based on the following case project:

Ms. Brea, a third grade teacher, asks you to write a Windows application to help her students learn their basic multiplication tables. The student can enter any number between 1 and 15. Ms. Brea would like the application to display the number the student entered and the result of multiplying that number by 1 through 12. Non-numeric values should not be accepted. For example, if the student enters the number 5, the ListBox object would display:

$5 \times 1 = 5$
$5 \times 2 = 10$
$5 \times 3 = 15$
$5 \times 4 = 20$
...
$5 \times 12 = 60$

FIGURE 6-134

Case Programming Assignments

8 ●●● GALAXY HOTEL

Create a requirements document and a Use Case Definition document, and design a Windows application based on the following case project:

The Galaxy Hotel asks you to write a Windows application that computes the occupancy rate of the hotel. Occupancy rate is a percentage that is equal to the number of rooms sold divided by the total number of rooms available. The hotel has seven floors. The user should use an InputBox function to respond to two questions about each floor: How many rooms are occupied on that floor? How many rooms on the floor are vacant? Display which floor you are asking about in each question. Display how many rooms are occupied and vacant on each floor in a ListBox object. After the user has entered all the information, display the following results: the total number of rooms at the hotel, the number of occupied rooms, and the number of vacant rooms. Also display the occupancy rate as a percentage, such as 61%. Non-numeric values should not be accepted. Do not accept negative numbers. Publish the application after testing the application.

FIGURE 6-135

9 ●●● BUYING A GAMING COMPUTER

Create a requirements document and a Use Case Definition document, and design a Windows application based on the following case project:

The newest gaming computer costs $5000 for 31-inch screen, two 120 GB hard drives, a metallic case, and a blazing fast processor. Ten years ago, your grandmother gave you $2500. The money has been in a savings CD that earns the compound interest of 7.5%. Write a Windows application that allows you to enter the amount in savings, the interest rate, and the number of years. Display a ListBox object with each year and the amount the entire account is worth at the end of that year. Determine whether you have saved enough money for the gaming computer. Non-numeric and negative values should not be accepted. Debug, and then publish the application. *Hint*: The formula for compound interest for one year is:

Amount = Principal * (1 + Rate). For 10 years of compound interest, this formula should be executed 10 times with the principal increasing to the new amount each year.

FIGURE 6-136

CHAPTER SEVEN

Creating Web Applications

OBJECTIVES

You will have mastered the material in this chapter when you can:

- ▶ Create a Web application
- ▶ Build a Web form using ASP.NET 3.5
- ▶ Set Web form properties
- ▶ Use the full screen view
- ▶ Add objects to a Web form
- ▶ Add a DropDownList object

- ▶ Add a Calendar object
- ▶ Add a custom table for layout
- ▶ Validate data on Web forms
- ▶ Use the <br> tag in Visual Basic code
- ▶ Use string manipulation methods in the String class

Introduction

Visual Studio allows you to create applications that can execute on the World Wide Web. Visual Basic 2008 includes ASP.NET 3.5 technology, with which you can create a user interface and a form for a Web application. A **Web form** is a page displayed in a Web browser, such as Internet Explorer and Firefox, that requests data from the user. The Visual Basic tools and techniques you use are familiar to you from what you have learned thus far in this course.

A practical example of a Web application developed using Visual Basic 2008 that can be delivered over the Internet is the project developed in this chapter — a bed-and-breakfast reservation form. This chapter project is based on a request from an inn called the Mystic Bed and Breakfast to create a Web application for guests who want to reserve rooms online. The application displays a Web form that requests the guest's first and last names, e-mail address, suite selection(s), the number of nights they want to stay, and the check-in date, as shown in Figure 7-1.

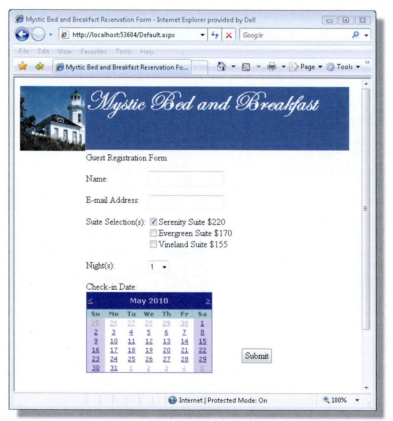

FIGURE 7-1

After the Web page is displayed in a browser, the user completes the form by entering the requested information, and then clicks the Submit button on the form. The application validates the information the user entered by confirming that the guest entered a name, provided an e-mail address in the correct format, and selected a valid check-in date. If the user makes an error, a message identifies the error, as shown in Figure 7-2.

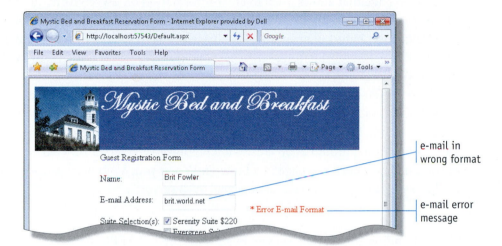

e-mail in wrong format

e-mail error message

FIGURE 7-2

When the validation is complete, the total cost of the stay is calculated and the reservation information is confirmed, as shown in Figure 7-3.

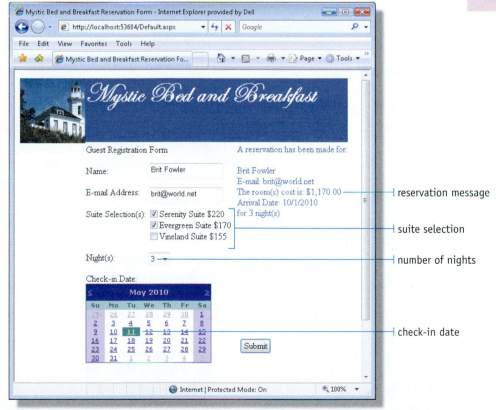

reservation message

suite selection

number of nights

check-in date

FIGURE 7-3

ONLINE REINFORCEMENT

To view a video of program execution, visit scsite.com/vb2008/ch7 and then select Figure 7-1.

Creating a Web Application

To develop a form such as the one shown in Figure 7-3 using Visual Basic, you create a Web application, which is similar to creating a Windows or Mobile application. When completed, a Visual Basic Web application is displayed as a Web page(s) in a browser.

A Web page that allows users to enter information on a Web form, like the Mystic Bed and Breakfast page in this chapter, is considered a **dynamic** Web page because the user enters data and the Web page reacts to the data. In contrast, a Web page that displays information such as text and pictures with no interactivity is called a **static** Web page.

After a Web page is created, the Web page is hosted (placed) on a Web server. A **Web server** is a computer that stores Web documents and makes them available to people on the Internet. When you test your Web application created using Visual Basic 2008, Visual Studio 2008 creates a temporary Web server on your computer so you can view your Web page in a browser. When your Web page is ready for the world to see, it must be placed on an actual Web server.

Understanding the Active Server Page (ASP.NET 3.5) Platform

The ASP.NET 3.5 technology used with Visual Basic 2008 creates an **active server page (ASP)**. When describing an active server page, developers speak of the server-side computer and the client-side computer. The server-side computer is the Web server that contains the actual active-server page and that will deliver the page to the client-side computer via the Internet. The client-side computer (often referred to as the client) runs the Web browser that requests a Web page from the Web server and displays the page.

An active server page has two primary components: the generated code component that executes on the Web server, and the HTML component that is interpreted and executed by a Web browser.

When Visual Basic compiles an active server page using ASP.NET 3.5 technology, the page contains both the server-side code that will operate on data entered by the user, such as computing the total cost of a reservation in the Mystic Bed and Breakfast Web application, and the HTML code that will display the page in a Web browser on the client-side computer. When the page is requested by a browser, ASP sends the HTML code to the client requesting the Web page, where the page is displayed. The user can interact with the page by entering data or making selections, such as selecting the check-in date. When, in the Mystic Bed and Breakfast application for example, the user clicks the Submit button, the data is sent to the Web server, where the coding within the application is executed. For example, the coding can calculate the total room cost and then display it on the Web form.

When you develop an ASP page in Visual Basic, the work you do on the design page to create the user interface will generate the HTML code for the active server page. This code includes the HTML to format and display the page, and might include JavaScript code to perform certain processing, such as ensuring that a text box contains data.

The event handler code that you write in Visual Basic for an event, such as clicking the Submit button, is executed on the Web server. So, in the Mystic Bed and Breakfast dynamic Web page, when the user clicks the Submit button, the control returns to the Web server and the event handler code written by the developer is executed. This code can perform calculations and other processing as you have seen in previous chapters. When the event handler code changes an object displayed in the Web page, such as changing the Label object that contains the reservation message, that change immediately is displayed on the Web page.

CREATING A WEB SITE WITH VISUAL STUDIO 2008

Visual Studio 2008 introduces a technology for creating Web pages that makes Web page design faster and simpler. A new Web component is now part of ASP.NET 3.5 that dramatically improves designing HTML layout. Microsoft Expression Web, the Web site software that replaces FrontPage, is built into the design portion of ASP.NET, making it easier for designers to open a Visual Basic 2008 Web page in Expression Web without any conversion issues. You can also open an Expression Web page directly in Visual Basic 2008. You do not need Expression Web to work with its Web pages in Visual Basic 2008, but Expression Web has many tools to add to enhance Web design.

CREATING A DYNAMIC WEB SITE USING VISUAL BASIC

Using Visual Basic 2008 to create a dynamic Web site is similar to creating an interactive Windows application — you drag objects from the Toolbox and place them in a design window to build a form. Some of the Web form objects are different from Windows objects because they are designed for use online. To create a Visual Basic Web project for the Mystic Bed and Breakfast application, you can complete the following steps:

STEP 1   Start Visual Studio. Click the New Web Site button on the Standard toolbar.

The New Web Site dialog box opens (Figure 7-4).

New Web Site
dialog box

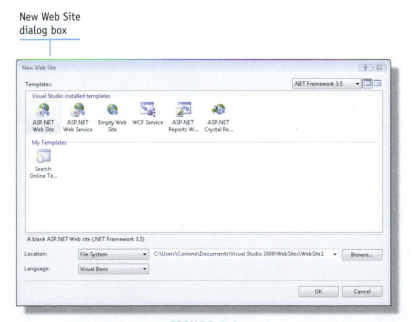

FIGURE 7-4

STEP 2 In the list of Visual Studio installed templates, click ASP.NET Web Site. Name the chapter project application MysticReservations in the Location text box. In Figure 7-5, the Web Site is placed on the e: drive.

The ASP.NET Web Site will be stored on the e: drive (Figure 7-5).

FIGURE 7-5

STEP 3   Click the OK button in the New Web Site dialog box.

The Web application Design window opens (Figure 7-6). The Default.aspx page is displayed. On the scroll bar at the bottom of the page, the Design button is selected, showing that the design window is displayed. The div tag is a division or container for objects placed in the Web page.

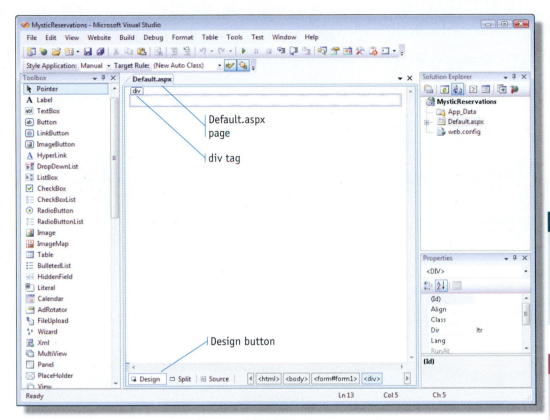

FIGURE 7-6

SETTING WEB FORM PROPERTIES

As with a Windows application, you can set the properties for a Web form to determine its appearance in a browser. Typically, you specify a title for the title bar and a background color for the Web page.

Specifying a Web Form Title

A Web form displays its title in the title bar of the browser used to display it. You specify the title bar text for a Web form using the Title property. To change the browser Title property from its default of Untitled to the title, Mystic Bed and Breakfast Reservation Form, you can complete the following steps:

STEP 1 In the design window of the Web form, click the background of the Web form below the div tag to select the form.

The Reservation Web form is selected (Figure 7-7).

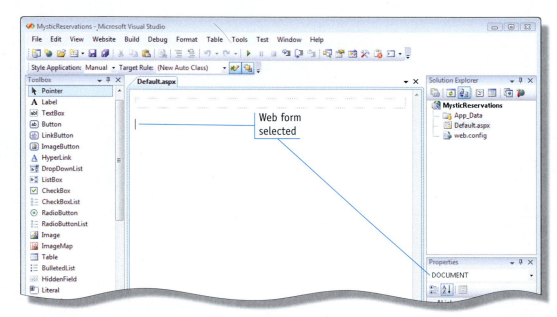

FIGURE 7-7

STEP 2 In the Properties window, scroll until the Title property is visible, and then click in the right column of the Title property. Enter the title `Mystic Bed and Breakfast Reservation Form`.

The title Mystic Bed and Breakfast Reservation Form is entered in the Title property of the Properties window (Figure 7-8). This title will be displayed in the title bar of the browser.

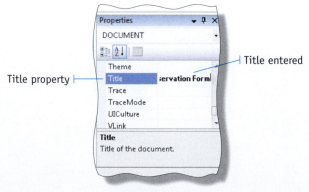

FIGURE 7-8

STEP 3 To view the title bar with the title Mystic Bed and Breakfast Reservation Form, click the Start Debugging button on the Standard toolbar. If the Debugging Not Enabled dialog box is displayed, select the Modify the Web.config file to enable debugging radio button and then click the OK button.

A browser opens and displays the title in the title bar (Figure 7-9).

Title displayed

FIGURE 7-9

STEP 4 To close the browser window, click the Close button on the title bar of the browser window.

ONLINE REINFORCEMENT

To view a video of the process in the previous steps, visit scsite.com/vb2008/ch7 and then select Figure 7-7.

Designing the Web Page

Before placing objects on the Web form, you must first design the Web page. A Web page often has a header, multiple columns, and possibly a footer.

NAMING THE PAGE DIVISIONS

A Web page can have the same types of objects that a Windows application contains, such as a TextBox object or a Button object. To hold these objects, containers called **div** elements are placed on the Web page. The term div is short for page division. By default, one div is already included on the background of the Web form. This div element will serve as the header of the Mystic Reservations Web page, so it should be re-named. Recall that in a Windows application, the property for naming an object is the (Name) property. When you are creating a Web form, however, you name objects using the (Id) property. To name the div element, you can complete the following steps:

STEP 1 Click in the div element, and then select the (Id) property in the Properties window.

The (Id) property in the Properties windows is selected (Figure 7-10).

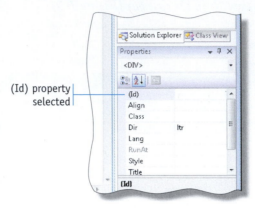

(Id) property selected

FIGURE 7-10

STEP 2 Type `leftcolumn` as the (Id) property.

You do not need to include a prefix on div element names, though Visual Basic 2008 adds div# to the beginning of div element names. The name div#leftcolumn is displayed above the div element (Figure 7-11).

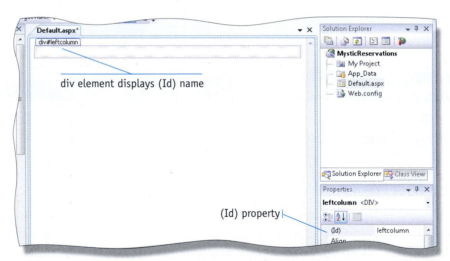

div element displays (Id) name

(Id) property

FIGURE 7-11

ONLINE REINFORCEMENT

To view a video of the process in the previous steps, visit scsite.com/vb2008/ch7 and then select Figure 7-10.

ARRANGING THE DIV CONTENTS OF THE WEB PAGE

A Web page typically has a header and multiple columns to hold the contents of the page. The div containers work behind the scenes, grouping objects together within a division. The chapter project has a header div to hold the opening graphic and the title and two column divs below the header. To lay out the page using divs, you can complete the following steps:

STEP 1   Click the div#leftcolumn heading above the div element. Position the mouse pointer over the sizing handle in the lower-right corner of the div element.

A two-headed arrow appears when the pointer is positioned over the sizing handle (Figure 7-12).

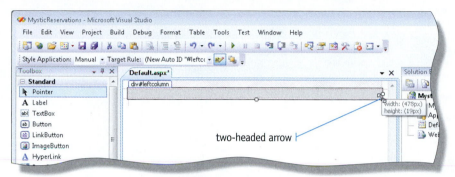

FIGURE 7-12

STEP 2   Resize the div#leftcolumn element until the width is 115px and the height is 600px.

The size of the div element changes to 115 × 600 pixels (Figure 7-13).

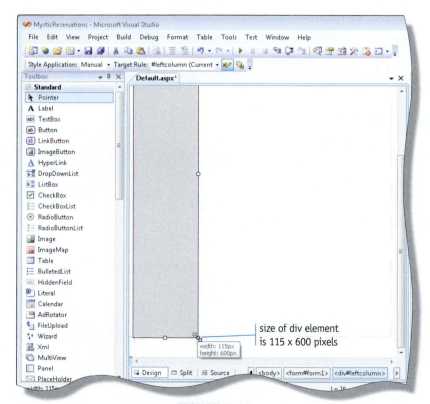

FIGURE 7-13

STEP 3 To add another div element, click the plus sign to open the HTML tools in the Toolbox, and then drag the Div element to the upper-left corner of the Web page. In the Properties window, select the (Id) property and type the name **header**.

A second div named div#header is added to the Web page (Figure 7–14).

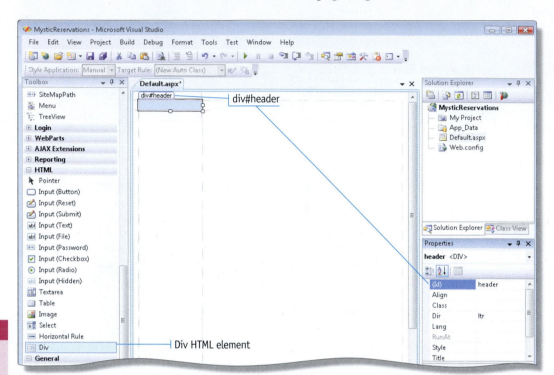

ONLINE REINFORCEMENT

To view of video of the process in the previous steps, visit scsite.com/vb2008/ch7 and then select Figure 7-12.

FIGURE 7-14

MOVING THE DIV ELEMENT

You can resize the div#header element and move it to another location on the page. By default, any object you add to the Web page from the Toolbox snaps to the left side of the page. To freely move the div element around the Web page, you must change the element's position setting to Absolute Positioning. To move the div element, you can complete the following steps:

STEP 1   Select the div#header element. Click Format on the menu bar, and then click Position on the Format menu. The Position dialog box opens. In the Positioning style section, click Absolute.

The Position dialog box opens after Position is selected on the Format menu. Absolute is selected in the Position dialog box (Figure 7-15).

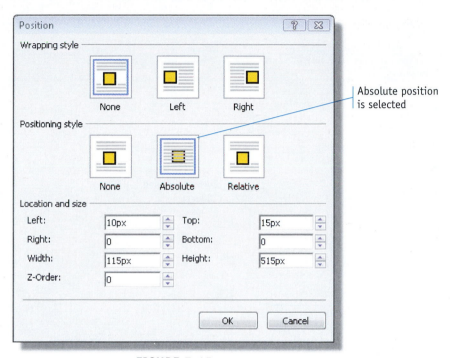

FIGURE 7-15

STEP 2   Click the OK button to close the Position dialog box. Click the middle-right sizing handle of div#header. Drag the two-headed arrow to the right until the width is 470 pixels, as noted in the ScreenTip. Click the middle-left sizing handle of div#header, and then drag so that the left side of div#header is slightly to the right of div#leftcolumn. Drag the lower-middle sizing handle down until the height is 115 pixels.

The div#header is resized on the Web form (Figure 7-16).

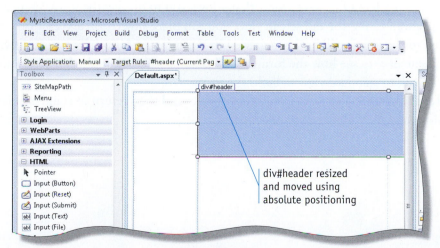

FIGURE 7-16

STEP 3   Add another div element and name it center. Click Format on the menu bar, click Position on the Format menu, and then click Absolute in the Position dialog box to change the position setting. Move the div#center element to the location shown in Figure 7-17. Resize div#center to 270 × 400 pixels. Add another div element and name it rightcolumn. Change the position of div#rightcolumn to absolute positioning. Resize div#rightcolumn to 200 × 400.

The four div elements are now set up to hold the objects for the Web form (Figure 7-17).

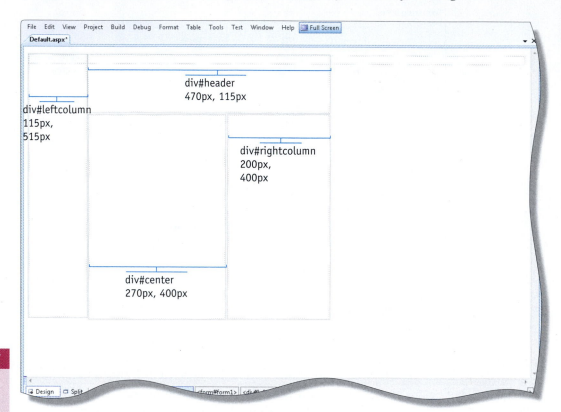

ONLINE REINFORCEMENT

To view of video of the process in the previous steps, visit scsite.com/vb2008/ch7 and then select Figure 7-15.

FIGURE 7-17

USING FULL SCREEN VIEW

ASP.NET 3.5 has a full screen view that allows you to display the full Web page as you design it. Using the full screen view, you can place objects on a Web form expanded to the size it will be when viewed in the browser. Generally, you can switch to full screen view to see how the form and its objects will look in the browser, and then switch back to standard view to build the form.

To display the Web form in full screen view and then return to standard view, you can complete the following steps:

STEP 1   Click View on the menu bar, and then click Full Screen.

The title bar and the Standard toolbar are hidden, and the Web page expands to full screen size (Figure 7–18).

FIGURE 7-18

STEP 2   To return to the standard view, click the Full Screen button on the menu bar.

The normal form reappears in the Visual Basic window (Figure 7–19).

FIGURE 7-19

ONLINE REINFORCEMENT

To view a video of the process in the previous steps, visit scsite.com/vb2008/ch7 and then select Figure 7-18.

ADDING A STYLE TO A DIV ELEMENT

Setting the style for each div section of a Web page makes designing a Web page much easier. A style can consist of formatting settings such as the background color, font color, font size, and font type. By setting a style, you can change the background color of every object within a div element, for example, by making one property change. Creating a style also reduces download time because the div contains the formatting information, not each object. To create a style in a div element, you can complete the following steps:

STEP 1   Select the div#header element by clicking the div#header name above the div element. In the Properties window, select the Style property, and then click its ellipsis button.

The Modify Style dialog box opens (Figure 7-20).

font-family
list arrow

Category list

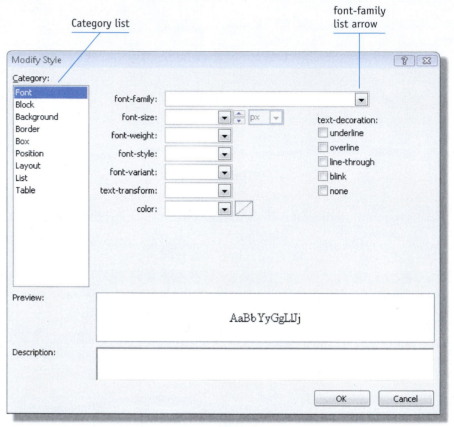

FIGURE 7-20

STEP 2 Click the font-family list arrow, and then click Edwardian Script ITC. Type 48 in the font-size box. Select bold for the font-weight and white for the color.

The Font styles are entered as shown in Figure 7-21. The color white was selected but appears as the hexadecimal value #FFFFFF.

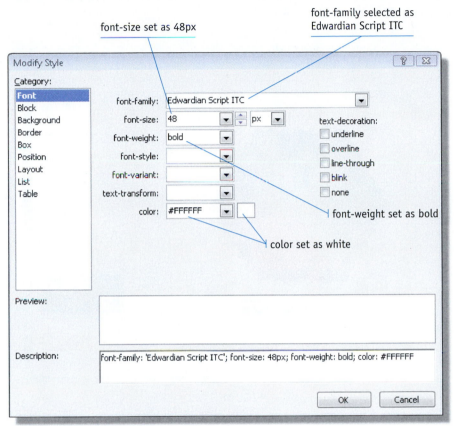

font-size set as 48px

font-family selected as Edwardian Script ITC

font-weight set as bold

color set as white

FIGURE 7-21

STEP 3 In the Category list, click Block. Set the vertical-align setting to top. In the Category list, click Background. Click the background-color list arrow, and then click More Colors. The More Colors dialog box appears. Select the second color from the left in the top row, a slate blue, as shown in Figure 7-22.

The text in div#header will be top-aligned. The shade of blue shown in Figure 7-22 is selected in the More Colors dialog box.

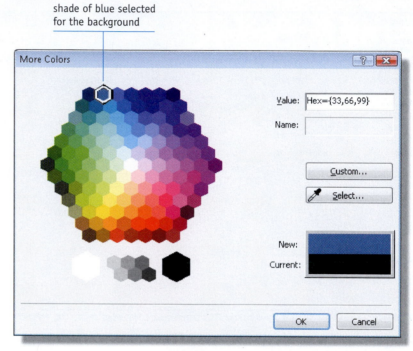

FIGURE 7-22

STEP 4   Click the OK button in the More Colors dialog box. A preview of the font background, font face, and font size is shown in the preview window. Click OK.

The div#header displays the blue background. When text is added later, it will appear in the specified font style, color, and size (Figure 7–23).

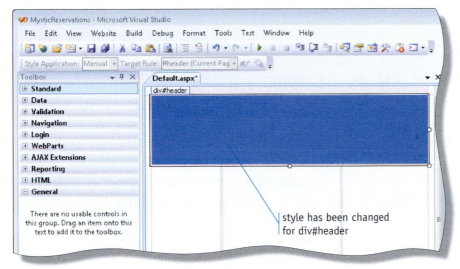

style has been changed for div#header

FIGURE 7-23

ONLINE REINFORCEMENT

To view of video of the process in the previous steps, visit scsite.com/vb2008/ch7 and then select Figure 7-20.

ADDING OBJECTS TO THE WEB FORM

Using Visual Studio's ASP.NET 3.5 objects and code, you can create interactive Web forms. You place objects on the Web form using a Toolbox similar to the one used for Windows applications, though its categories of tools are different. The Mystic Bed and Breakfast chapter project uses objects in the Standard and Validation categories of the Toolbox shown in Figure 7-24.

Toolbox

Standard category

Validation category

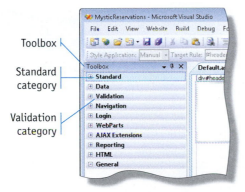

FIGURE 7-24

Toolbox objects unique to Web application objects include Login objects for allowing user access, Navigation objects for creating site maps, and Validation objects for checking Web form input. Some Windows application objects work the same, but have different object names in the Web environment. For example, in a Windows application you use a PictureBox object to display a picture, but in an ASP.NET 3.5 Web page, you use an Image object. Both the PictureBox object and the Image object place an image into the application, but the Image object needs a URL to specify where the picture resides.

ADDING AN IMAGE OBJECT

On the Mystic Bed and Breakfast reservation form, an image of the Mystic Bed and Breakfast Inn is displayed in an Image object in the upper-left corner of the page. The **Image** object is similar to the PictureBox object in a Windows application. The major difference is where the Image object is stored. Most Web pages reference a picture stored on a Web server connected to the Internet. On an ASP.NET Web form, you do this by specifying the entire URL (Web address) in the ImageUrl property of an Image object. To add an Image object that displays an image stored on a Web server, you can complete the following steps:

STEP 1   Drag the Image object from the Toolbox to the Web form. Resize the object so that it is about 115 × 115 pixels.

The Image object appears in the upper-left corner of the Web form and is resized (Figure 7-25). A placeholder appears in the Image object until you specify a URL or path to an image file.

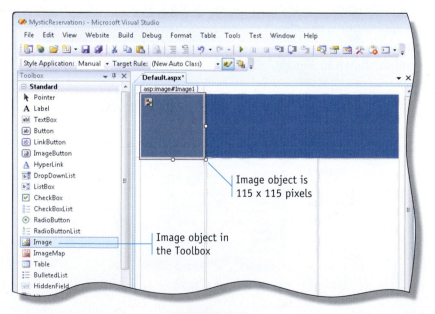

FIGURE 7-25

STEP 2 In the Properties window, name the Image object by entering `picMystic` in its (ID) property. Specify which image to display by entering the Web address `http://scsite.com/vb2008/ch7/images/bb.jpg` as the ImageUrl property.

The bb.jpg image appears in the Image object, replacing the placeholder (Figure 7-26).

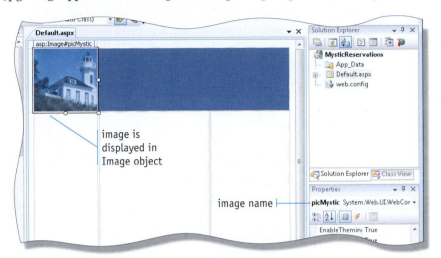

FIGURE 7-26

Entering Text Directly on the Web Form

ASP.NET 3.5 allows you to enter text directly on the Web form without creating labels. You should enter text directly on the form only if the text will not be changed by coded statements. Label objects are useful if you intend to change their contents after the user makes a selection on the Web form and the Web application needs to display a result. If the text is not going to change, type it directly on the form. As you type, use the **SPACEBAR** to add spaces and align text, and use the ENTER key to start a new line. To enter text directly on a Web form, follow these steps:

STEP 1 Click to the right of the Image object in the div#header at the top of the form. Type `Mystic Bed and Breakfast`. To display the full screen to view the full title of the page, click View on the menu bar, and then click Full Screen.

The words Mystic Bed and Breakfast appear in the div#header to the right of the picture, as shown in Figure 7-27. The font was set in the Style properties as shown in Figure 7-21 and 7-22.

FIGURE 7-27

STEP 2　Click in the div#center container. Type `Guest Registration Form`.

The words Guest Registration Form appear in the upper-left corner of the div#center container (Figure 7-28).

FIGURE 7-28

Adding TextBox and Button Objects

Like other Web form objects, TextBox and Button objects are similar to their Windows counterparts apart from a few exceptions. A TextBox object on a Web page usually is provided for data entry, allowing a user to enter a name, address, e-mail address, or zip code, for example. The Text property of a TextBox object, therefore, is blank. A Button object on a Web form serves the same purpose as it does in Windows applications. Because the user generally clicks the Button object after completing the Web form, the Text property for a Button object on a Web form often is "Submit." To name the TextBox and Button objects, you use the (ID) property. To move the objects freely around the form, make sure absolute positioning is set in the Position dialog box for each object. Figure 7-29 shows a TextBox and Button object created for a Web form.

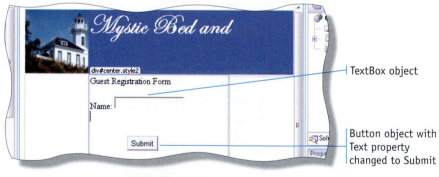

TextBox object

Button object with Text property changed to Submit

FIGURE 7-29

Adding CheckBox Objects

Three CheckBox objects are used in the Mystic Bed and Breakfast reservation form to determine which suite(s) the guest wants to reserve. The **CheckBox** object allows the user to choose from several options. It is similar to the RadioButton object, except the CheckBox object allows the user to pick more than one option. In contrast, you will recall that the RadioButton object allows a user to choose only one option from a group of related options. The CheckBox and RadioButton objects work the same in Web, Windows, and mobile applications.

When you name a CheckBox object, you should include the chk prefix in its (ID) property. In addition, you can specify that a check box is selected by default when a form opens. For example, because the Serenity suite is the most popular suite choice at the Mystic Bed and Breakfast Inn, the check box for the Serenity suite should be selected when the page first is displayed. To specify this setting, change the Checked property of the CheckBox object from False to True.

In the Mystic Bed and Breakfast application, the user can select one or more suites based on an individual or group reservation. For example, as shown in Figure 7-30, a family might select the Serenity suite for the parents and the Vineland suite for the children. RadioButton objects would not work in this example because only one RadioButton object can be selected at the same time within the same group.

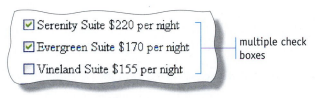

FIGURE 7-30

To place a CheckBox object on a Web form, you can complete the following steps:

STEP 1   Drag the CheckBox object from the Toolbox to the Web form, and then position it on the form. The CheckBox object is placed at the insertion point. You can move the insertion point by pressing ENTER or the SPACEBAR to place this object in the correct position. Absolute positioning is not an option with CheckBox objects.

The CheckBox object is placed on the Web form (Figure 7-31). The Placeholder text will remain until you change the Text property. It does not, however, appear on the Web page when the page is displayed in a Web browser.

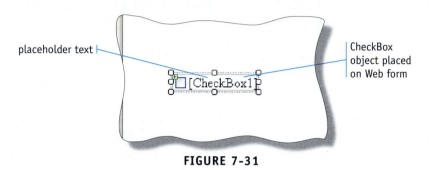

placeholder text

CheckBox object placed on Web form

FIGURE 7-31

STEP 2   Name the CheckBox object by clicking to the right of its (ID) property in the Properties window, and then entering `chkSerenity`.

The CheckBox object is named chkSerenity in the (ID) property (Figure 7-32).

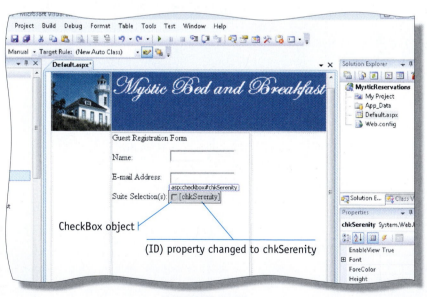

CheckBox object

(ID) property changed to chkSerenity

FIGURE 7-32

STEP 3   Change the Text property of the CheckBox object to `Serenity Suite $220`.

After changing the Text property of chkSerenity, the CheckBox object on the form displays the new text (Figure 7-33).

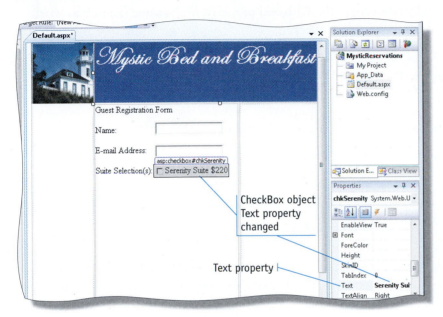

FIGURE 7-33

STEP 4   In the Mystic Bed and Breakfast application, the Serenity suite is the most popular suite. This suite, therefore, should be checked when the form opens to save time for the user. To select the Serenity suite check box, change the Checked property for the object from False to True.

The Serenity Suite CheckBox object appears with a check mark on the form, and the Checked property is set to True. (Figure 7-34).

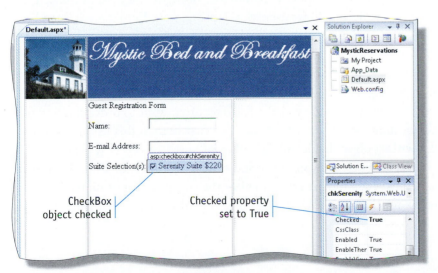

FIGURE 7-34

ONLINE REINFORCEMENT

To view a video of the process in the previous steps, visit scsite.com/vb2008/ch7 and then select Figure 7-31.

Coding for Check Box Objects

After the user selects one or more CheckBox objects representing the suite selections and clicks the Submit button on the Web form, control returns to the Web server where the event handler for the Submit button can evaluate which CheckBox objects are selected. The code shown in Figure 7-35 determines which CheckBox objects are selected by referring to the Checked property, in the same manner as when RadioButton objects are checked.

```
48              If Me.chkSerenity.Checked Then
49                  decRoomCost += _decSerenityRoomCost
50              End If
51              If Me.chkEvergreen.Checked Then
52                  decRoomCost += _decEvergreenRoomCost
53              End If
54              If Me.chkVineland.Checked Then
55                  decRoomCost += _decVinelandRoomCost
56              End If
```

FIGURE 7-35

HEADS UP

The code in Figure 7-35 uses separate If statements instead of a Nested If-Else structure because the user can select multiple CheckBox objects. Each If condition must be tested separately when using CheckBox objects.

In Figure 7-35, the statement on line 48 checks the Checked property for the chkSerenity check box. If it is checked, the Serenity room cost is added to the value in the decRoomCost variable. Similarly, if the chkEvergreen check box is checked, its room cost is added to the value in the decRoomCost variable. The same is true for the chkVineland check box. If all three check boxes are checked, the value in the decRoomCost variable will be the sum of the individual room costs for all three rooms.

Adding a DropDownList Object

On the Mystic Bed and Breakfast reservation Web form, guests can use a DropDownList object to specify the number of nights they plan to stay. The **DropDownList** object allows users to select one item from a predefined list. It is similar to the ListBox object used in Windows applications, except that for a DropDownList object, the list of items remains hidden until users click the list arrow button.

After adding a DropDownList object to a form and naming it, you can specify the items you want to display in the list. You often want to order these items alphabetically or numerically for ease of use. The first item in this list appears in the DropDownList object by default. The DropDownList object will not display the items in the list until you run the application and display the Web form in a browser. The user must click the list arrow to view the complete list of items during execution. The prefix for the name (ID) of the DropDownList object in Visual Basic is ddl.

In the Mystic Bed and Breakfast application, a DropDownList object is used to determine the number of nights the guests plan to stay at the inn. To add a DropDownList object to the Web form, you can complete the following steps:

STEP 1   Drag the DropDownList object to the Web form, and then click Format on the menu bar, click Position, and click Absolute in the Position dialog box so you can move the object on the form. Click OK in the Position dialog box.

A DropDownList object appears on the Web form (Figure 7-36).

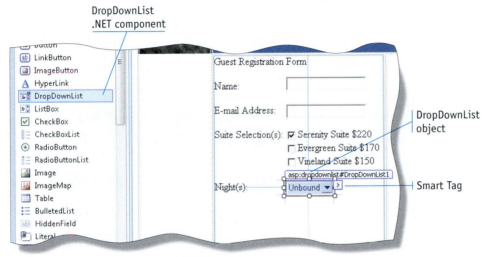

FIGURE 7-36

STEP 2   Name the DropDownList object by clicking to the right of the (ID) property in the object's Properties window, and then typing `ddlNights`.

The DropDownList object is named ddlNights (Figure 7-37).

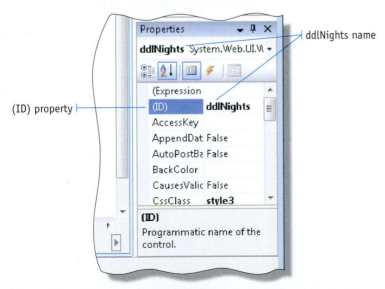

FIGURE 7-37

STEP 3 To fill the DropDownList object with list items, click the Smart Tag on the upper-right corner of the object.

The DropDownList Tasks menu opens (Figure 7-38).

FIGURE 7-38

STEP 4 Click Edit Items on the DropDownList Tasks menu.

The ListItem Collection Editor dialog box opens (Figure 7-39).

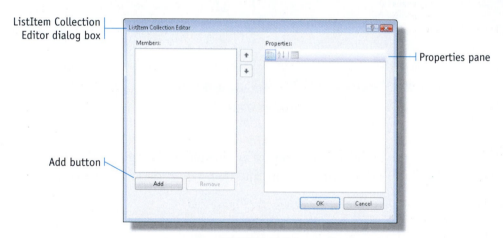

FIGURE 7-39

STEP 5 Click the Add button. In the ListItem properties pane on the right side of the dialog box, click to the right of the Text property and enter 1.

The number 1 is entered as the first item in the DropDownList object (Figure 7-40).

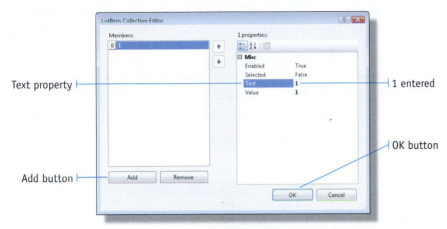

Text property — | — 1 entered

OK button

Add button — | — Add

FIGURE 7-40

STEP 6 Click the Add button and enter 2 as its Text property. Repeat this step, entering the numbers 3 through 7 to specify the number of nights users can select in the DropDownList object. Click the OK button in the ListItem Collection Editor dialog box. Resize the DropDownList object to the width of a single digit. To view the completed DropDownList object, run the application by clicking the Start Debugging button on the Standard toolbar. Click the list arrow on the DropDownList object in the Web page.

After clicking the Start Debugging button, the browser opens. After clicking the list arrow on the DropDownList object, the list item contents appear (Figure 7-41).

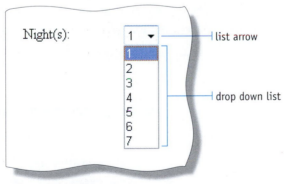

Night(s): — list arrow

— drop down list

FIGURE 7-41

ONLINE REINFORCEMENT

To view a video of the process in the previous steps, visit scsite.com/vb2008/ch7 and then select Figure 7-36.

Adding a Calendar Object

The Mystic Bed and Breakfast reservation form contains a calendar that allows guests to select their arrival date. Visual Basic provides an object to manipulate months, days, and years when specifying information such as reservations, anniversaries, or bill payments. The **Calendar** object is organized by month and displays the number of days in each month as appropriate for the year. For example, March has 31 days and

February includes an extra day when the year is a leap year. By default, the Calendar object displays the current month according to the system date and selects the current day when the application is executed.

You can use the Calendar object in any type of application, including Windows, mobile, and Web applications. When creating a Calendar object, use the prefix cld in the name. To place the Calendar object on a Web form, you can complete the following steps:

STEP 1 Drag the Calendar object from the Toolbox to the Web form, and then position it on the form. In the (ID) property, name the Calendar object cldArrival.

The Calendar object is placed on the Windows form (Figure 7–42).

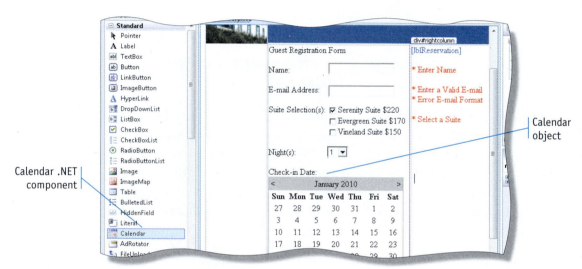

FIGURE 7-42

STEP 2 Select the Calendar object, if necessary, and then click the Smart Tag on the upper-right corner of the Calendar object.

The Calendar Tasks menu opens (Figure 7–43).

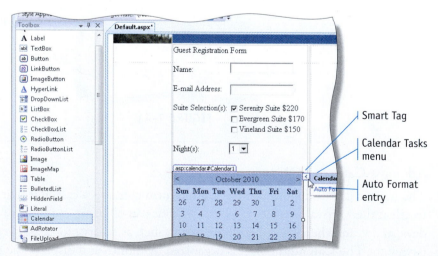

FIGURE 7-43

STEP 3 Click Auto Format on the Calendar Tasks menu. When the Auto Format dialog box opens, click the Colorful 2 scheme in the Select a scheme list.

The Auto Format dialog box previews the selected Colorful 2 scheme (Figure 7–44).

Auto Format
dialog box

Colorful 2
scheme

Colorful 2
scheme
preview

OK button

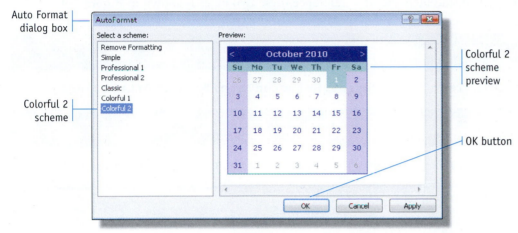

FIGURE 7-44

STEP 4 Click the OK button and resize the Calendar object as needed.

The Calendar object on the Web form appears with the Colorful 2 scheme (Figure 7–45).

Calendar object
with Colorful 2
scheme

FIGURE 7-45

ONLINE REINFORCEMENT

To view a video of the process in the previous steps, visit scsite.com/vb2008/ch7 and then select Figure 7-42.

Code for a Calendar Object

When using the Calendar object, two dates often are important — the selected date and the current date. In the Visual Basic code that you write in an event handler, you can include statements to reference both the selected date and the current date. The format of statements used to reference these two dates is shown in Figure 7-46.

General Format: SelectedDate Property

```
txtVariable.Text = cldObject.SelectedDate.ToShortDateString()
```

General Format: TodaysDate Property

```
txtVariable.Text = cldObject.TodaysDate.ToShortDateString()
```

FIGURE 7-46

In Figure 7-46, the SelectedDate property references the date the user clicked in the Calendar object. In the general format, the ToShortDateString() procedure changes the date to a String format so it can be displayed in a TextBox object. If you are referencing just the selected date without the need to change it to a string value, the procedure is not required.

Similarly, in Figure 7-46, the current date is referenced by the property TodaysDate.

In the Mystic Inn Bed and Breakfast application, it is important to ensure that the date the user selects is equal to or greater than the current date. A user cannot select a date for a reservation date that has already passed. One of the If statements used in the sample program to test this condition is shown in Figure 7-47.

```
38          If Me.cldArrival.SelectedDate < Me.cldArrival.TodaysDate Then
39              Me.lblCalendarError.Visible = True
40          Else
41              Me.lblCalendarError.Visible = False
42          End If
```

FIGURE 7-47

In Figure 7-47, the selected date for the cldArrival Calendar object is compared to the current date (TodaysDate) for the cldArrival Calendar object. If the selected date is less than the current date, an error message is displayed; otherwise the error message is not displayed.

If the user does not click a date on the calendar prior to clicking the Submit button and running the event handler code, the Calendar object automatically returns a date that is less than the current date. Therefore, the If statement on line 38 will detect both the case when the user selects a date less than the current date, and the case when the user does not select a date.

ADDING VALIDATION CONTROLS

An important part of creating Web forms is validating the data entered in the form to make sure the user has entered reasonable values. Instead of using a series of If statements or other complex code, ASP.NET 3.5 provides built-in validation control objects that compare a form's objects to a set rule using little or no code. The validation control objects check input forms for errors and display messages if users enter incorrect or incomplete responses. Built-in validation control objects include RequiredFieldValidator, which verifies that a required field contains data, and RangeValidator, which tests whether an entry falls within a given range.

Applying a Required Field Validator

The simplest validation control is the **RequiredFieldValidator** object, which finds a specified object to validate and determines whether the object is empty. For example, in the Mystic Bed and Breakfast application, the user must enter her first and last name. Otherwise, a reservation cannot be made. The RequiredFieldValidator object reminds the user to complete all required fields. You can customize this reminder by changing the ErrorMessage property, which often is helpful to let users know what they have done incorrectly. If the user enters a value in a field, the RequiredFieldValidator does not display an error message.

In the Mystic Bed and Breakfast reservation form, the first object to validate is the Name TextBox object, which is named txtName. You can add a RequiredFieldValidator object to the Web form that tests txtName to determine if it is empty. If it is, an error message appears reminding the user to enter a first name. After adding the RequiredFieldValidator object, you must specify that it validates the txtName TextBox object.

The prefix used for the RequiredFieldValidator is rfv. To validate a required TextBox object using a RequiredFieldValidator object, follow these steps:

STEP 1   In the Toolbox, hide the Standard tools by clicking the minus sign next to Standard. Expand the Validation tools by clicking the plus sign next to Validation.

The seven Validation tools are displayed (Figure 7–48).

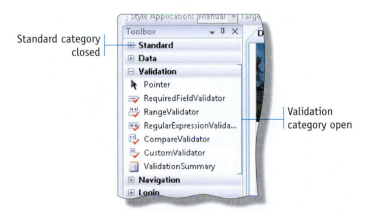

FIGURE 7-48

Click at the top of the div#rightcolumn. Press ENTER three times. Drag the RequiredFieldValidator to the right of the Name TextBox object.

The RequiredFieldValidator object is placed in the div#rightcolumn to the right of txtName (Figure 7–49).

RequiredFieldValidator added to div#rightcolumn

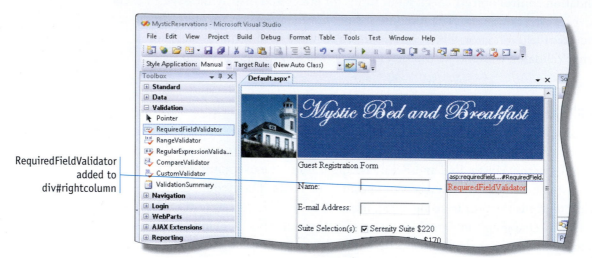

FIGURE 7-49

Name the RequiredFieldValidator by typing `rfvName` in its (ID) property.

The RequiredFieldValidator object is named rfvName (Figure 7-50).

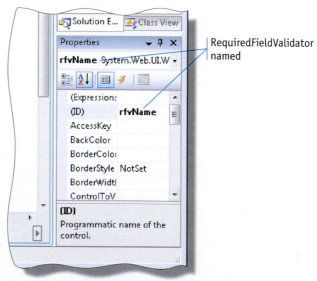

RequiredFieldValidator named

FIGURE 7-50

STEP 4   To specify that the rfvName RequiredFieldValidator object validates the txtName TextBox object, click to the right of the ControlToValidate property in the Properties window, click the list arrow, and then select txtName.

The ControlToValidate property is set to txtName (Figure 7-51).

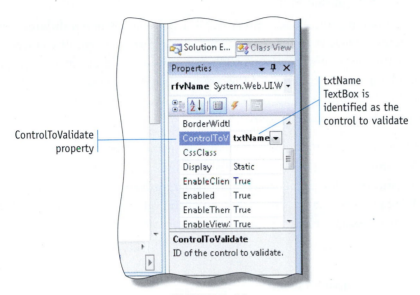

ControlToValidate property

txtName TextBox is identified as the control to validate

FIGURE 7-51

STEP 5   In the Properties window for the RequiredFieldValidator, change the ErrorMessage property to * Enter Name. If necessary, resize the RequiredFieldValidator to fit in the table cell.

*The ErrorMessage property is changed to * Enter Name (Figure 7-52).*

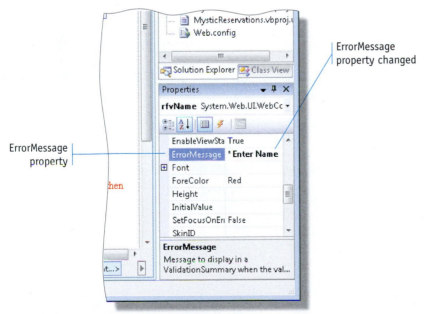

ErrorMessage property

ErrorMessage property changed

FIGURE 7-52

When the application is run on a Web browser with a Submit button, if the Submit button is clicked and no text has been entered in the txtName text box, the error message will be displayed.

Applying the Range Validator

Another validation control built into ASP.NET 3.5 is the **RangeValidator** control, which tests whether an input value falls within a given range. If you were testing whether a number entered on a Web page was a valid day in a month, the RangeValidator control could test if the day number is between 1 and 31. The RangeValidator control uses the prefix rgv in its name, and the following five properties to complete its validation:

- ▶ **ControlToValidate** property contains the name of the object you are validating.
- ▶ **MinimumValue** property contains the smallest value in the range.
- ▶ **MaximumValue** property contains the largest value in the range.
- ▶ **Type** property matches the data type of the value, such as Integer or String.
- ▶ **ErrorMessage** property explains to the user what value is requested.

Applying the Compare Validator

Another validation control is the **CompareValidator** object, which you use to compare an object's value with another object or a constant value. The CompareValidator control can also compare the value in one object to the value in another object. In the example shown in Figure 7-53, the user enters a password into a Web form, and re-enters the password to confirm that the two passwords are the same. You can use the CompareValidator control to verify that the passwords match.

> **HEADS UP**
>
> Remember to change the data type of the RangeValidator control to compare values properly. If you forget to change the Type property from String to Integer for data such as high school grade level (9, 10, 11, or 12), the validation range will not work properly. If you set the minimum value to 9 and the maximum value to 12, the application would create an error message that states that 9 is greater than 12. The reason for the error is that the string "9" is compared to only the "1" in the number 12, and 9 comes after 1.

FIGURE 7-53

The CompareValidator uses three properties to complete its validation:

▶ **ControlToValidate** property contains the name of the object that you are validating.

▶ **ControlToCompare** property contains the name of the object that you are comparing to the ControlToValidate property.

▶ **ErrorMessage** property contains a message stating that the value does not match.

In Figure 7-54, four properties are changed to apply the CompareValidator object to verify a password: The (ID), ControlToCompare, ControlToValidate, and ErrorMessage properties. This figure also shows that the prefix for the CompareValidator object is cmv.

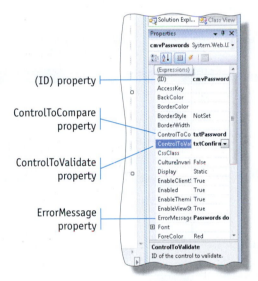

FIGURE 7-54

Applying the Regular Expression Validator

The **RegularExpressionValidator** control confirms whether the user entered data that matches standard formats such as a phone number, e-mail address, URL, zip code, or Social Security number. If the user does not enter the data in the proper format, an error message is displayed. The prefix rev is used for the RegularExpressionValidator control. The RegularExpressionValidator uses three properties to complete its validation:

▶ **ControlToValidate** property contains the name of the object that you are validating.

▶ **ErrorMessage** property contains a message stating that the value does not match the valid format.

▶ **ValidationExpression** property allows the user to select the format for the object.

In the Mystic Bed and Breakfast reservation form, the second TextBox object on the form requests the user's e-mail address. To confirm that the information entered is a possible e-mail address, a RegularExpressionValidator object can test the contents of the Text property of the txtEmail object and verify that it matches the format of a valid e-mail address, which follows the format of *name@isp.com*. To incorporate a RegularExpressionValidator object in a Web page, you can complete the following steps:

STEP 1   Drag the RegularExpressionValidator object from the Toolbox to the right of the E-mail Address TextBox object in the custom Table object. Resize the RegularExpressionValidator object to fit the table cell.

The RegularExpressionValidator object is placed in the div#rightcolumn to the right of txtEmail. (Figure 7-55).

txtEmail TextBox object   RegularExpressionValidator added

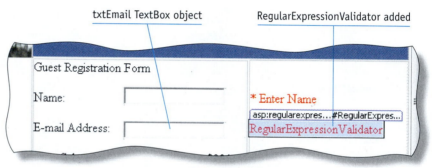

FIGURE 7-55

STEP 2   Name the RegularExpressionValidator by typing `revEmail` in its (ID) property.

The RegularExpressionValidator object is named revEmail (Figure 7-56).

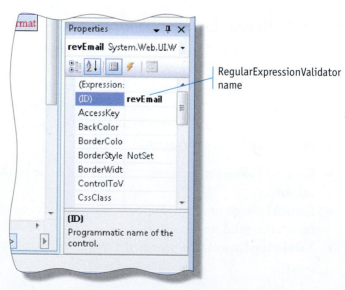

RegularExpressionValidator name

FIGURE 7-56

STEP 3   Click to the right of the ControlToValidate property, click the list arrow, and then click txtEmail.

The ControlToValidate property is set to txtEmail (Figure 7-57).

ControlToValidate property

txtEmail is control to validate

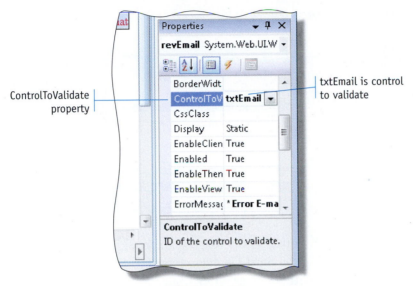

FIGURE 7-57

STEP 4   Change the ErrorMessage property to *`Error E-mail Format`.

*The ErrorMessage property is changed to * Error E-mail Format (Figure 7-58).*

ErrorMessage property

error message property changed

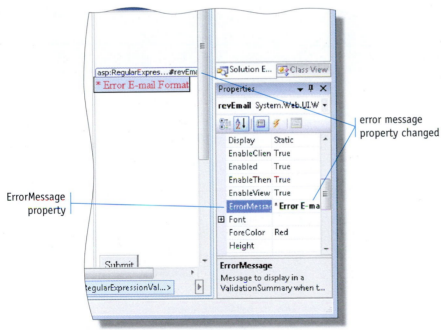

FIGURE 7-58

STEP 5 To set txtEmail to validate that it contains a standard e-mail address, click to the right of the ValidationExpression property, and then click its ellipsis button. In the Regular Expression Editor dialog box, select Internet e-mail address in the Standard expressions list.

The Internet e-mail address is selected as the standard expression to validate (Figure 7–59).

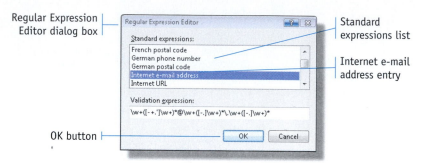

Regular Expression Editor dialog box · Standard expressions list · Internet e-mail address entry · OK button

FIGURE 7-59

STEP 6 Click the OK button in the Regular Expression Editor dialog box. Run the application by clicking the Start Debugging button on the Standard toolbar. Enter an e-mail address without an @ symbol, such as **brit.world.net**, and then press the ENTER key.

An error message appears to the right of the E-mail Address TextBox object (Figure 7-60). When a valid e-mail address is entered and the ENTER key is pressed again, the error message is removed.

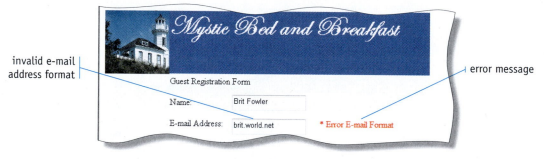

invalid e-mail address format · error message

FIGURE 7-60

Applying Multiple Validations

You can apply more than one type of validation control on an object to validate more than one aspect of the data. Often you may want to make a certain control required using the RequiredFieldValidator object, and to check the range using the RangeValidator object. In Figure 7-61, a RequiredFieldValidator confirms that the number of hours worked is not left blank, and the RangeValidator verifies that the number entered is between 1 and 60. Each validation control displays an error message if the object does not meet the specified criteria.

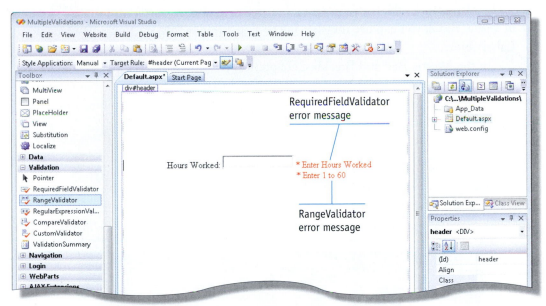

FIGURE 7-61

Displaying a Validation Summary Control

Instead of validating data, the **ValidationSummary** control lets you display validation error messages in a single location, creating a clean layout for the Web form. By default, each validation control displays an error message next to the object it validates. On a large or complex form, however, the error messages might interfere with data or other objects. You can use the ValidationSummary object to display all of the error messages in a different place, listing them in a blank area at the top or bottom of the form, for example, where they will appear together when the validation criteria for any control is not met.

To use a ValidationSummary object, drag the object to the location on the Web page where you want the summary to appear. The prefix used for naming the ValidationSummary object is vsm. You do not have to set any properties, such as ControlToValidate, because the summary displays the error messages for all the other validation objects.

USING THE
 TAG IN VISUAL BASIC CODE

One HTML tag often used when creating Web pages is the **
** tag, which stands for break; it breaks the text by starting a new line. When you are creating a Web form in Visual Basic, you can use the <br> tag to skip a line before starting a new one in a Label object.

In the Mystic Bed and Breakfast chapter project, after the user enters reservation information, a confirmation message is displayed that includes details about the reservation such as the name, e-mail address, cost of the rooms, date, and number of nights (Figure 7-62).

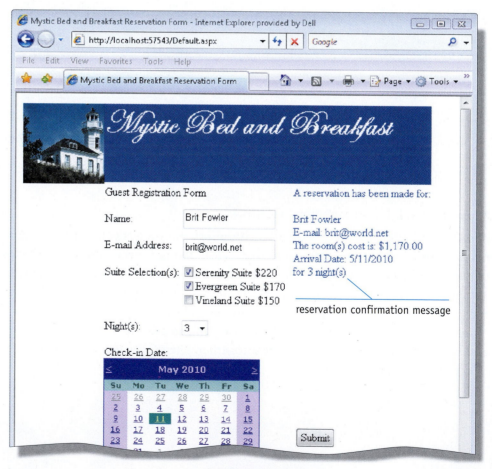

FIGURE 7-62

In Figure 7-62, the message consists of four lines. Each of the lines except the last line ends with the <br> tag so that the text that follows will be on the next line. The code to create the message is shown in Figure 7-63.

```
57          strReservationMessage = "A reservation has been made for: " & "<br>" _
58              & strName & "<br>" & "E-mail: " & strEmailAddress & "<br>"
59          strReservationMessage &= "The room(s) cost is: " _
60              & decRoomCost.ToString("C") & "<br>"
61          strReservationMessage &= "Arrival Date: " _
62              & cldArrival.SelectedDate.ToShortDateString() _
63              & "<br>" & " for " & intNumberOfNights & " night(s)"
64          Me.lblReservation.Text = strReservationMessage
```

FIGURE 7-63

In Figure 7-63, the message to be displayed is built in the strReservationMessage string variable. On line 57, the first line of the message is placed in the variable. The last item in the string is the <br> tag, which will cause the text that follows to be on the next line. Notice that the tag must be within double quotation marks because it is a string.

The statements on lines 58 and 60 also end with the <br> tag. As a result of the statements in Figure 7-63, a five-line message will be created.

Using String Manipulation Properties and Procedures in the String Class

The String class in Visual Basic has many properties and procedures that allow you to manipulate strings, which you often need to do when developing Web forms. For example, you might want to find the length of the string that the user entered or convert lowercase text to uppercase. The commands discussed in this section work with ASP.NET 3.5 as well as in any Windows or mobile application.

FINDING STRING LENGTH

You can use the **Length** property to determine the number of characters in a particular string. The syntax for determining string length is shown in Figure 7-64.

> **General Format: Determine String Length**
>
> ```
> intValue = strName.Length
> ```

FIGURE 7-64

In the statement intLength = "Visual Basic".Length, the value placed in the intLength Integer variable would be 12 because the Length property counts spaces as well as characters. The code shown in Figure 7-65 determines if the zip code entered in the txtZipCode TextBox object has a length of five characters.

```
8        Dim intCount As Integer
9
10       intCount = Me.txtZipCode.Text.Length
11       If intCount <> 5 Then
12           Me.lblError.Text = "You must enter 5 digits"
13       End If
14
```

FIGURE 7-65

If you enter only four digits in the zip code, as shown in Figure 7-66, a message appears reminding you to enter five digits.

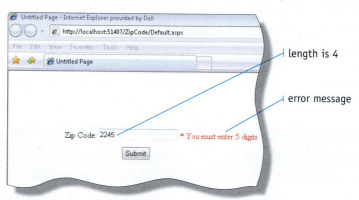

FIGURE 7-66

USING THE TRIM PROCEDURE

When entering information into a TextBox object, the user might accidentally add extra spaces before or after the input string. When that string is used later, the extra spaces might distort the format of the output. To prevent this, Visual Basic provides a procedure named **Trim** to remove spaces from the beginning and end of a string. The syntax for the Trim procedure is shown in Figure 7-67.

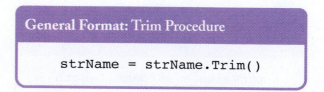

General Format: Trim Procedure

```
strName = strName.Trim()
```

FIGURE 7-67

In the Mystic Bed and Breakfast reservation form, the user enters a first name, a last name, and an e-mail address. If the user includes spaces before or after the entries, the spaces will appear in the final output. The Trim procedure shown in Figure 7-68 removes extra spaces.

```
30          ' Trim additional spaces entered by the user
31          strFirstName = Me.txtFirstName.Text.Trim
32          strLastName = Me.txtLastName.Text.Trim
33          strEmailAddress = Me.txtEmail.Text.Trim
```

FIGURE 7-68

CONVERTING UPPERCASE AND LOWERCASE TEXT

The **ToUpper** and **ToLower** procedures convert a string to all uppercase or all lowercase, respectively. The following syntax in Figure 7-69 shows how to use the ToUpper and ToLower procedures:

General Format: UpperCase and LowerCase Procedures

```
strName = strName.ToUpper()

strName = strName.ToLower()
```

FIGURE 7-69

When you compare a string, Visual Basic checks if you entered the word as specified. For example, if you enter YES in response to a question, but the code accepts only yes, the If statement as shown in Figure 7-70 would convert the response of YES to yes. The ToUpper() and ToLower() methods save coding time because all the possible ways to enter a response do not have to be compared.

```
87          If strAnswer.ToLower() = "yes" Then
```

FIGURE 7-70

Program Design

As you have learned, the requirements document identifies the purpose of the program being developed, the application title, the procedures to be followed when using the program, any equations and calculations required in the program, any conditions within the program that must be tested, notes and restrictions that must be followed by the program, and any other comments that would be helpful to understanding the problem. The requirements document for the Mystic Bed and Breakfast Web application is shown in Figure 7-71.

REQUIREMENTS DOCUMENT

Date submitted:	March 30, 2011
Application title:	Mystic Bed and Breakfast Web Application
Purpose:	This application allows the user to book a reservation at the Mystic Bed and Breakfast Inn using a Web form.
Program Procedures:	From a Web application, the user should complete an online reservation form to enter the guest's name, e-mail address, starting date, number of nights, and room preference. The total cost of the stay should be calculated and displayed.

Algorithms, Processing, and Conditions:

1. The user must be able to enter the requested reservation information on a Web form. The information should include the guest's name, e-mail address, starting date of the stay, number of nights, and which rooms they prefer. The user can select one or more rooms from the following choices: Serenity Suite $220 a night, Evergreen Suite $170 a night, and Vineland Suite $155 a night.
2. After entering the reservation information, the user clicks the Submit button.
3. The information entered is validated.
4. The application displays the final cost of the stay.

Notes and Restrictions:

1. Data in the Name TextBox object is required.
   The data in the E-mail TextBox object is required and is validated to confirm that it is in an e-mail address format. The Calendar object is checked to confirm that a date is selected and that the selected date is not before the current date. The maximum length of stay is 7 nights.

Comments:

1. Display a picture of the Mystic Bed and Breakfast Inn on the Web form.

FIGURE 7-71

USE CASE DEFINITION

1. The Web page opens, displaying the title Mystic Bed and Breakfast with a picture as well as TextBox objects to enter the guest's name and e-mail address. A Calendar object is used to select the beginning date of the reservation. A DropDownList object is used to enter the number of nights. The room preferences are entered with CheckBox objects.
2. User clicks the Submit button.
3. The data entered is checked and validated.
4. If necessary, the user makes corrections and resubmits the data.
5. The application confirms the reservation and displays the final cost of the stay.

FIGURE 7-72

EVENT PLANNING DOCUMENT

You will recall that the event planning document consists of a table that specifies an object in the user interface that will cause an event, the action taken by the user to trigger the event, and the event processing that must occur. The event planning document for the Mystic Bed and Breakfast Web program is shown in Figure 7-73.

EVENT PLANNING DOCUMENT

Program Name: Mystic Bed and Breakfast Web Application	Developer: Corinne Hoisington	Object: Default.aspx	Date: March 30, 2011
OBJECT	**EVENT TRIGGER**	**EVENT PROCESSING**	

btnSubmit	Click	Validate the name to confirm it is not empty
		Validate e-mail address to confirm it is not empty and is in the e-mail address format
		Trim extra spaces from name and e-mail data
		Blank the reservation message
		If a suite has not been selected
		   Display a suite error message
		   If arrival date is not valid
		      Display a calendar error message
		   Else
		      Hide the calendar error message
		Else
		   Hide suite error message
		   If arrival date is valid
		      Accumulate room costs
		      Convert number of nights to integer
		      Calculate cost of room (total room costs * number of nights)
		      Create the reservation message
		      Display the reservation message
		   Else
		      Display calendar error message	

Form	Form Load	Display suite selection check boxes and suite rates	

FIGURE 7-73

CODE THE PROGRAM

After identifying the events and tasks within the events, you are ready to create the program. As you have learned, creating the program means designing the user interface and then entering Visual Basic statements to accomplish the tasks specified on the event planning document. As you enter the code, you also will implement the logic to carry out the required processing.

Guided Program Development

To design the user interface for the Mystic Bed and Breakfast Web application and enter the code required to process each event in the program, complete the following steps:

NOTE TO THE LEARNER

As you will recall, in the following activity, you should complete the tasks within the specified steps. Each of the tasks is accompanied by a Hint Screen. The purpose of the Hint Screen is to indicate where in the Visual Studio window you should perform the activity; it also serves as a reminder of the method that you should use to create the user interface or enter code. If you need further help completing the step, refer to the figure number identified by the term ref: in the step.

Guided Program Development

Phase 1: Build the Form

1

▶ **Begin the Web Application** Start Visual Studio, and then create a Visual Basic Web Site Application project by clicking the New Web Site button on the Standard toolbar. In the New Web Site window, click ASP.NET Web Site. Enter the project name `MysticReservations` and store the program on the e: drive (or a network or USB drive of your choice). Click the OK button *(ref: Figure 7-4)*.

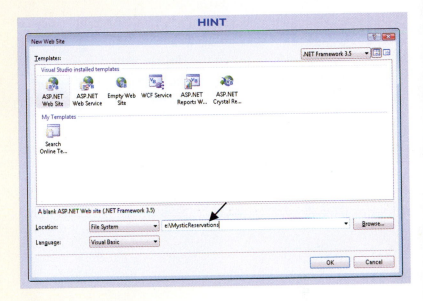

▶ **Specify the Web Page Document Title Property** Click the background of the Web page and change the Title property from Untitled Page to `Mystic Bed and Breakfast Reservation Form`. This title appears in the browser title bar at the top of the Web page when you execute the Web application *(ref: Figure 7-8)*.

▶ **Name and Resize the Div Element** Click inside the div element on the Web page. Name the div element leftcolumn in the (ID) property of the Properties window. Select the title div#leftcolumn at the top of the div element. Drag the sizing handles to resize the element to the size of 115 × 600 *(ref: Figure 7-13)*.

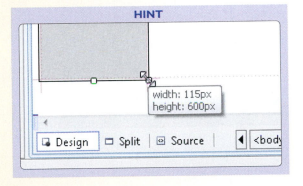

(continues)

Guided Program Development (continued)

▶ **Add a Div Element and Use Absolute Positioning** Drag a Div element from the HTML category on the Toolbox to the Web form. Name the div element `header` in the (Id) property. Select the div element heading div#center above the div element. Click Format on the menu bar, click Position, and then click Absolute in the Position dialog box. Click OK *(ref: Figure 7-15)*.

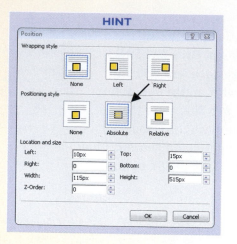

▶ **Add More Div Elements** Drag another div element to the form and name the (Id) Property `center`. Select the div#center element, click Format on the menu bar, click Position, and then click Absolute. Move the div element below the div#header and to the right of div#leftcolumn. Resize div#center to 270 × 400 pixels. Add another div element named `rightcolumn` to the Web form. Set Absolute positioning and move the div element to the right of div#center. Resize div#rightcolumn to 200 × 400 pixels *(ref: Figure 7-17)*.

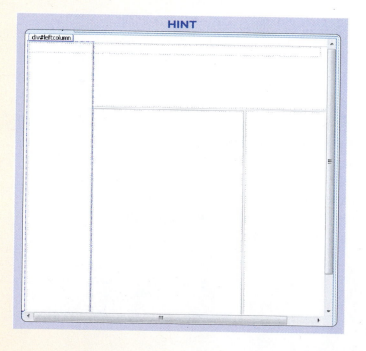

Guided Program Development *(continued)*

▶ **Add Style to a Div Element** Select the div#header element by clicking the heading name div#header above the upper-middle container. In the Properties window, select the Style property. Click the ellipsis button. In the Font category, change the font-family to Edwardian Script ITC. Change the font-size to 48 px. Change the font-weight to bold. Change the color to white. The color is shown as #FFFFFF, which represents white *(ref: Figure 7-21)*.

▶ **Change the Style Block** In the Modify Style dialog box, select the Block category. Change the vertical-align property to top.

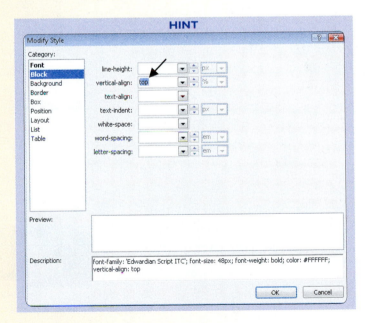

(continues)

Guided Program Development (continued)

▶ **Change the Style Background** Select the Background category. Click the background-color list arrow, and then select More Colors. Select the second color on the left *(ref: Figure 7-22)*.

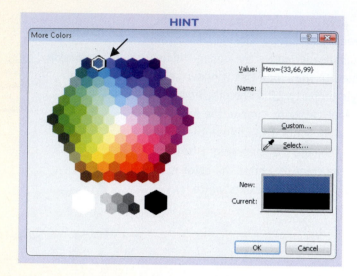

▶ **Add an Image Object** Drag an Image object to the upper-left corner of the Web form in the div#leftcolumn. Name the Image object `picMystic`. Resize the Image object to the size 115,115. Change its ImageUrl property to http://scsite.com/vb2008/ch7/images/bb.jpg. *(ref: Figure 7-26)*.

▶ **Type Text directly on the Web Form** Click in the div#header. Type `Mystic Bed and Breakfast`. At the top of the div#center section, type `Guest Registration Form`.

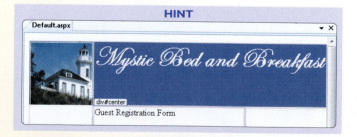

Guided Program Development *(continued)*

► **Add a TextBox Object** Press ENTER twice. Type
`Name:`. Drag a TextBox object to the Web form to the
right of Name:. In the (ID) property, name the TextBox
object `txtName`. To freely move the TextBox, click
Format on the menu bar, click Position, and then click
Absolute. Move the TextBox to the right as shown in
the Hint *(ref: Figure 7-29)*.

► **Add Another TextBox Object** Press ENTER twice
and type `E-mail Address:`. Drag another
TextBox object to the right of the text. In the (ID)
property, name the TextBox object `txtEmail`. Set
the TextBox to absolute positioning and move the
object.

► **Add CheckBox Objects** Press ENTER twice. Type
`Suite Selection(s):`. Press the SPACEBAR until
the insertion point is directly below the last TextBox
object. Drag a CheckBox object to the right of the
Suite Selection(s) text. Name the CheckBox object
`chkSerenity`, and change its Text property to
Serenity Suite $220. Change the Checked property for
the chkSerenity CheckBox object to True. (*ref:
Figure 7-34*). Press ENTER. Press the SPACEBAR to move
the insertion point directly below the first CheckBox.
Drag the second CheckBox object below the first
CheckBox object, and then name the second CheckBox
object `chkEvergreen`. Change its Text property to
Evergreen Suite $170. Press ENTER and then press the
SPACEBAR to move the insertion point below the last
CheckBox. Drag the third CheckBox object below the
second CheckBox object, and then name the third
CheckBox object `chkVineland`. Change its Text
property to Vineland Suite $155 *(ref: Figure 7-34)*.

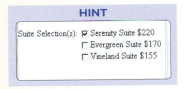

(continues)

Guided Program Development (continued)

▶ **Add DropDownList Object** Press ENTER twice. Type `Night(s)`. Drag a DropDownList object to the right of the Night(s) title. Change the name of the DropDownList object to `ddlNights`. Change the positioning to Absolute. Click the Smart Tag on the DropDownList object, and then click Edit Items. The ListItem Collection Editor dialog box opens. Click the Add button, and then enter the number 1 as the Text property. Click the Add button as necessary to add the numbers 2 through 7. After adding number 7, click the Remove button to remove the entry in the Members list. Click the OK button. Resize the object *(ref: Figure 7-37)*.

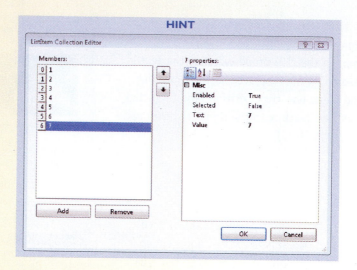

▶ **Add the Calendar Object** Press ENTER twice. Type `Check-in Date:`. Press ENTER. Drag a Calendar object onto the page. Change the Calendar object to Absolute positioning. Click the Smart Tag on the Calendar Object, and then click AutoFormat. Select Colorful 2, and then click OK. Resize the calendar object and move it as needed *(ref: Figure 7-42)*.

IN THE REAL WORLD

When you add objects to a Web form, often it is difficult to determine if the alignment of these objects is precise and up to your standards. A good way to ensure objects are placed properly on the form is to run the application. You will see immediately on the page in the browser window whether alignment is correct.

Guided Program Development (continued)

▶ **Add the Submit Button** Drag a Button object to the left side of the last row of the div#rightcolumn. Change the Button object (ID) property to btnSubmit. Change the Text property to Submit.

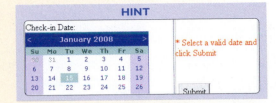

▶ **Add a Calendar Warning Label** Press ENTER in the div#rightcolumn until the insertion point is to the right of the top of the calendar. Drag a Label object to the div#rightcolumn, to the right of the Calendar object. Change the (ID) property of the Label object to lblCalendarError. Change the Text property to * Select a valid date and then click Submit. To change the warning message to red font, change the ForeColor property to red. The warning message is displayed only if a valid date is not selected. Change the Visible property to False.

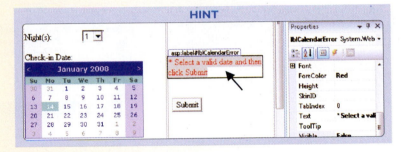

▶ **Add a Result Label** Select the div#rightcolumn header. Place the insertion point directly to the right of Guest Reservation Form. Drag a Label object to this position. Name the Label object lblReservation. Delete any value in the Text property. The lblReservation placeholder with the text[lblReservation] is displayed on the Web form, but will not appear in the actual Web page.

(continues)

Guided Program Development (continued)

The Guest Reservation Form includes labels, text boxes, a calendar, and a result label (Figure 7-74).

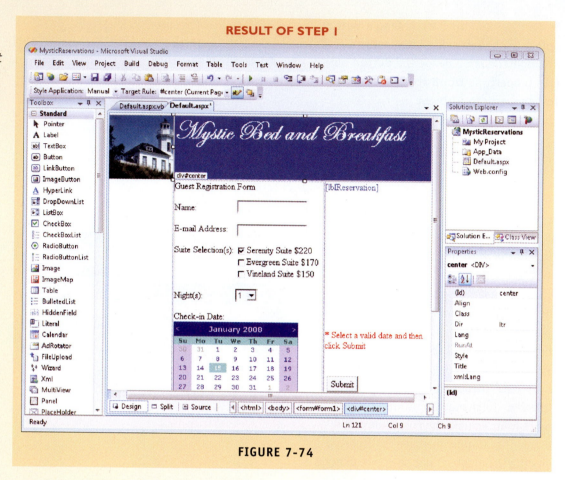

RESULT OF STEP 1

FIGURE 7-74

Phase 2: Add Validation Objects

2

▶ **Add the Required Validation Objects** In the Toolbox, expand the Validation controls by clicking the plus sign next to Validation (ref: Figure 7-49).

HINT

HEADS UP

When you run the Web application, a message may appear in a dialog box that states "Debugging Not Enabled". Select the "Modify the Web.config file to enable debugging" option button, and then click OK.

Guided Program Development *(continued)*

▶ **Validate the Name TextBox Object** Press ENTER until the insertion point is directly to the right of the Name TextBox object. Drag the RequiredFieldValidator object onto the Web form in the div#rightcolumn. Name the Validator Object `rfvName`. Change its ErrorMessage property to * `Enter Name` *(ref: Figure 7-50)*

▶ **Select the TextBox Object to Validate** In the Properties window for the rfvName object, click the list arrow in the ControlToValidate property and then click txtName *(ref: Figure 7-52)*.

(continues)

Guided Program Development (continued)

▶ **Validate the E-mail TextBox Object** Drag the RequiredFieldValidator object onto the Web form in the div#rightcolumn. Place the RequiredFieldValidator object to the right of the txtEmail TextBox object. Name the Validator object `rfvEmail`. Change its ErrorMessage property to `* Enter a Valid E-mail`. In the Properties window, click the list arrow in the ControlToValidate property and then click txtEmail.

▶ **Add Regular Expression Validator for E-Mail** Drag the RegularExpressionValidator object below the E-mail Address field. Name the Validator object `revEmail`. Change its ErrorMessage property to `* Error E-mail Format`. Click the list arrow in the ControlToValidate property, and then click txtEmail. Click the ellipsis button in the ValidationExpression property. When the Regular Expression Editor dialog box opens, select Internet e-mail address. Click the OK button (ref: Figure 7-55).

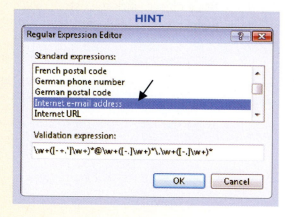

▶ **Add the Missing Suite Choice Message** Drag a Label object onto the Web form to the div#rightcolumn. Place the label in the same row as the Evergreen check box. Name the label `lblSuiteError`. Change the ForeColor for the Label object to red. Change the Text property to `* Select a Suite`. Set the Visible property for the label to False.

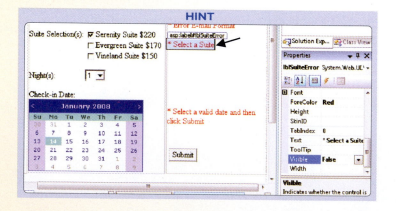

Guided Program Development *(continued)*

The validation objects and messages are part of the Web form (Figure 7-75).

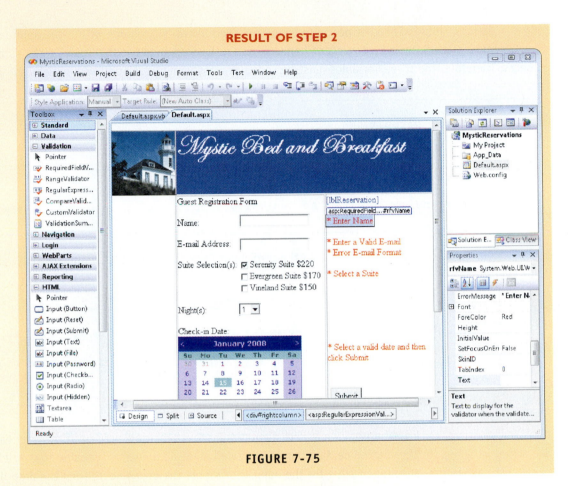

RESULT OF STEP 2

FIGURE 7-75

Phase 3: Code the Application

3

▶ **Code the Comments** Double-click the Submit button on the form to begin coding the btnSubmit_Click Event in the Web application. Insert the first four standard comments at the top of the Code window. Insert the command Option Strict On at the beginning of the code to turn on strict type checking.

HINT

```
1 ' Project:  Bed and Breakast Online Reservation Form
2 ' Author:   Corinne Hoisington
3 ' Date:     March 30, 2011
4 ' Purpose:  The following Web application will request reservation information
5 '           for the Mystic Bed and Breakfast. This web site will compute
6 '           the cost of the number of nights and room(s) selected.
7
8 Option Strict On
```

(continues)

Guided Program Development *(continued)*

▶ **Code the Class Variables** The cost per suite values are used in two procedures within the application — to calculate the room charges in the Submit button event handler, and in the form load event to display the suite costs in the check box objects. Therefore, the three variables must be coded as class variables. Code these variables.

HINT

```
 9  Partial Class _Default
10      Inherits System.Web.UI.Page
11
12      ' Define room costs per night - used in two event handlers
13      Dim _decSerenityRoomCost As Decimal = 220D
14      Dim _decEvergreenRoomCost As Decimal = 170D
15      Dim _decVinelandRoomCost As Decimal = 155D
```

▶ **Comment on the btnSubmit Click Event** In the btnSubmit Click Event, enter a comment that explains the purpose of the Click Event.

HINT

```
17      Protected Sub btnSubmit_Click(ByVal sender As Object, ByVal e As System.EventArgs) ↙
        Handles btnSubmit.Click
18          ' The btnSubmit Click Event will calculate the cost of the room based
19          ' on the type of suite selected and the number of nights reserved.
20
```

▶ **Initialize Variables** Click in the btnSubmit Click Event and enter the variables used in the application. These variables include string variables for the first name, last name, and email address; a decimal variable that will contain the result of the room cost calculation; an integer value for the number of nights the user selects from the drop down list; and a string variable in which to compose the reservation message.

HINT

```
21          ' Declare and initialize variables
22          Dim strName As String
23          Dim strEmailAddress As String
24          Dim decRoomCost As Decimal = 0D
25          Dim intNumberOfNights As Integer
26          Dim strReservationMessage As String
```

▶ **Trim the TextBox Object Data** Using the Trim procedure, write the code to remove excess spaces from the data the user entered. Place the trimmed Name from the TextBox object in the strName variable and the trimmed E-mail address in the strEmailAddress variable *(ref: Figure 7-67)*.

HINT

```
28          ' Trim additional spaces that are entered by the user
29          strName = Me.txtName.Text.Trim
30          strEmailAddress = Me.txtEmail.Text.Trim
```

Guided Program Development *(continued)*

▶ **Clear the Reservation Message** Write a statement to clear the strReservationMessage string variable.

HINT

```
32          Me.lblReservation.Text = ""
```

▶ **Ensure a Suite Type is Selected** Write an If statement that ensures a suite type has been selected. The Checked property of one or more of the CheckBox objects must be true. Use the Not operator to check for all three properties. If the suite type has not been selected, display the suite error message.

HINT

```
33          If Not (Me.chkVineland.Checked Or Me.chkSerenity.Checked Or Me.chkEvergreen.    ↙
         Checked) Then
34              Me.lblSuiteError.Visible = True
```

▶ **Ensure a Valid Date is Selected** Regardless of whether a valid suite was selected, the program must ensure a valid date was selected. Therefore, if a suite is not selected, write an If statement that ensures the date is valid (that is, the selected date is not less than the current date). If the date is invalid, display the calendar error message; otherwise, do not display the calendar error message.

HINT

```
33          If Not (Me.chkVineland.Checked Or Me.chkSerenity.Checked Or Me.chkEvergreen.    ↙
         Checked) Then
34              Me.lblSuiteError.Visible = True
35              If Me.cldArrival.SelectedDate < Me.cldArrival.TodaysDate Then
36                  Me.lblCalendarError.Visible = True
37              Else
38                  Me.lblCalendarError.Visible = False
39              End If
```

▶ **Hide Suite Error Message When Suite is Selected** If a suite is selected, the suite error message must be hidden; that is, the suite error message Visible property must be set to False. Write the statement to set the Visible property to False.

HINT

```
33          If Not (Me.chkVineland.Checked Or Me.chkSerenity.Checked Or Me.chkEvergreen.    ↙
         Checked) Then
34              Me.lblSuiteError.Visible = True
35              If Me.cldArrival.SelectedDate < Me.cldArrival.TodaysDate Then
36                  Me.lblCalendarError.Visible = True
37              Else
38                  Me.lblCalendarError.Visible = False
39              End If
40          Else
41              Me.lblSuiteError.Visible = False
```

(continues)

Guided Program Development (continued)

▶ **Ensure a Valid Date is Selected** When a suite has been selected, the program must ensure a valid date was selected. If a suite is selected and a valid date is selected, the data validity checking is complete and the room cost can be calculated. Write a statement to ensure that the selected date is greater than or equal to the current date, and if the date is valid, set the Visible property for the error message to False.

HINT

```
42              If Me.cldArrival.SelectedDate >= Me.cldArrival.TodaysDate Then
43                  Me.lblCalendarError.Visible = False
```

▶ **Determine Total of Room Costs** The user can select more than one suite type. For example, one room might be for parents and another room might be for their children. Therefore, the program must determine if each check box is checked, and if so, the room cost per night is accumulated. Write the statements to determine if a suite check box is checked and, if so, to accumulate the room costs in the decRoomCost variable.

HINT

```
44                  ' Calculate the cost of the room(s) selected by the user
45                  If Me.chkSerenity.Checked Then
46                      decRoomCost += _decSerenityRoomCost
47                  End If
48                  If Me.chkEvergreen.Checked Then
49                      decRoomCost += _decEvergreenRoomCost
50                  End If
51                  If Me.chkVineland.Checked Then
52                      decRoomCost += _decVinelandRoomCost
53                  End If
```

▶ **Calculate Total Room Cost** To calculate the total room cost, the number of nights selected by the user from the drop down list must be converted from a string to an integer. Then, the calculation to determine the total room costs (number of nights × room cost) must occur. Write the statements to perform these activities.

HINT

```
55              intNumberOfNights = Convert.ToInt32(Me.ddlNights.SelectedItem.Text)
56              decRoomCost = intNumberOfNights * decRoomCost
```

Guided Program Development (continued)

▶ **Create the Reservation Message** Write the code to create the reservation message, and place it in the strReservation string variable. Then, place the message stored in the strReservation variable in the Text property of the lblReservation Label object (ref: Figure 7-63).

HINT

```
57              strReservationMessage = "A reservation has been made for: " & "<br>" _
58                  & strName & "<br>" & "E-mail: " & strEmailAddress & "<br>"
59              strReservationMessage &= "The room(s) cost is: " _
60                  & decRoomCost.ToString("C") & "<br>"
61              strReservationMessage &= "Arrival Date: " _
62                  & cldArrival.SelectedDate.ToShortDateString() _
63                  & "<br>" & " for " & intNumberOfNights & " night(s)"
64              Me.lblReservation.Text = strReservationMessage
```

▶ **Show Calendar Error Message** If the user did not select a valid date for the check-in date, display the calendar error message by changing the Visible property for the error message label to True.

HINT

```
65          Else
66              Me.lblCalendarError.Visible = True
67          End If
68      End If
69  End Sub
```

Code Listing

The complete code for the sample program is shown in Figure 7-76.

```
 1 ' Project:   Bed and Breakast Online Reservation Form
 2 ' Author:    Corinne Hoisington
 3 ' Date:      March 30, 2011
 4 ' Purpose:   The following Web application will request reservation information
 5 '            for the Mystic Bed and Breakfast. This web site will compute
 6 '            the cost of the number of nights and room(s) selected.
 7
 8 Option Strict On
 9 Partial Public Class _Default
10     Inherits System.Web.UI.Page
11
12     ' Define room costs per night - used in two event handlers
13     Dim _decSerenityRoomCost As Decimal = 220D
14     Dim _decEvergreenRoomCost As Decimal = 170D
15     Dim _decVinelandRoomCost As Decimal = 155D
16
17     Protected Sub btnSubmit_Click(ByVal sender As Object, ByVal e As System.EventArgs) ↙
        Handles btnSubmit.Click
18         ' The btnSubmit Click Event will calculate the cost of the cost of the room
19         ' based on the type of suite selected and the number of nights reserved.
20
21         ' Declare and initialize variables
22         Dim strName As String
23         Dim strEmailAddress As String
24         Dim decRoomCost As Decimal = 0D
25         Dim intNumberOfNights As Integer
26         Dim strReservationMessage As String
27
28         ' Trim additional spaces that are entered by the user
29         strName = Me.txtName.Text.Trim
30         strEmailAddress = Me.txtEmail.Text.Trim
31
32         Me.lblReservation.Text = ""
33         If Not (Me.chkVineland.Checked Or Me.chkSerenity.Checked Or Me.chkEvergreen. ↙
        Checked) Then
34             Me.lblSuiteError.Visible = True
35             If Me.cldArrival.SelectedDate < Me.cldArrival.TodaysDate Then
36                 Me.lblCalendarError.Visible = True
37             Else
38                 Me.lblCalendarError.Visible = False
39             End If
40         Else
41             Me.lblSuiteError.Visible = False
42             If Me.cldArrival.SelectedDate >= Me.cldArrival.TodaysDate Then
43                 Me.lblCalendarError.Visible = False
44                 ' Calculate the cost of the room(s) selected by the user
45                 If Me.chkSerenity.Checked Then
46                     decRoomCost += _decSerenityRoomCost
47                 End If
48                 If Me.chkEvergreen.Checked Then
49                     decRoomCost += _decEvergreenRoomCost
50                 End If
51                 If Me.chkVineland.Checked Then
52                     decRoomCost += _decVinelandRoomCost
53                 End If
```

FIGURE 7-76 (continues)

```
54
55                    intNumberOfNights = Convert.ToInt32(Me.ddlNights.SelectedItem.Text)
56                    decRoomCost = intNumberOfNights * decRoomCost
57                    strReservationMessage = "A reservation has been made for: " & "<br>" _
58                        & strName & "<br>" & "E-mail: " & strEmailAddress & "<br>"
59                    strReservationMessage &= "The room(s) cost is: " _
60                        & decRoomCost.ToString("C") & "<br>"
61                    strReservationMessage &= "Arrival Date: " _
62                        & cldArrival.SelectedDate.ToShortDateString() _
63                        & "<br>" & " for " & intNumberOfNights & " night(s)"
64                    Me.lblReservation.Text = strReservationMessage
65                Else
66                    Me.lblCalendarError.Visible = True
67                End If
68            End If
69        End Sub
70
71  End Class
72
73
```

FIGURE 7-76 (continued)

Summary

In this chapter you have learned to create an online Web application using ASP.NET 3.5. The items listed in the table shown in Figure 7-77 include all the new Visual Studio and Visual Basic skills you have learned in this chapter.

VISUAL BASIC SKILLS

Skill	Figure Number	Web Address for Video
Examine the Mystic Bed and Breakfast chapter project application	Figure 7-1	scsite.com/vb2008/ch7/figure7-1
Create a Visual Basic Web project	Figure 7-4	scsite.com/vb2008/ch7/figure7-4
Change the Title property of the Web application	Figure 7-7	scsite.com/vb2008/ch7/figure7-7
Name the page divisions	Figure 7-10	scsite.com/vb2008/ch7/figure7-10
Arrange the div contents of a Web page	Figure 7-12	scsite.com/vb2008/ch7/figure7-12
Move a div element	Figure 7-15	scsite.com/vb2008/ch7/figure7-15
Display the Web form in full screen	Figure 7-18	scsite.com/vb2008/ch7/figure7-18
Set the style of a page division	Figure 7-20	scsite.com/vb2008/ch7/figure7-20
Add an Image object to the Web form	Figure 7-25	scsite.com/vb2008/ch7/figure7-25
Enter text directly on the Web form	Figure 7-27	scsite.com/vb2008/ch7/figure7-27
Add a TextBox object and a Button object	Figure 7-29	
Place a CheckBox object on a Web form	Figure 7-31	scsite.com/vb2008/ch7/figure7-31
Code a Check Box	Page 502	
Add a DropDownList object to a Web form	Figure 7-36	scsite.com/vb2008/ch7/figure7-36
Add a Calendar object to a Web form	Figure 7-42	scsite.com/vb2008/ch7/figure7-42
Write code for a Calendar object	Page 508	
Validate TextBox object using a RequiredFieldValidator object	Figure 7-48	scsite.com/vb2008/ch7/figure7-48
Validate the range using a RangeValidator object	Page 516	
Validate two objects with the CompareValidator object	Page 516	
Validate data using a RegularExpressionValidator object	Figure 7-55	scsite.com/vb2008/ch7/figure7-55
Validate data using multiple validations	Page 520	
Display a ValidationSummary	Page 520	
Use the tag in Visual Basic	Page 521	
Use the String Length property	Page 522	
Use the Trim procedure	Page 523	
Convert uppercase and lowercase text	Page 524	

FIGURE 7-77

Learn It Online

Start your browser and visit scsite.com/vb2008/ch7. Follow the instructions in the exercises below.

1. **Chapter Reinforcement TF, MC, SA** Click one of the Chapter Reinforcement links for Multiple Choice, True/False, or Short Answer below the Learn It Online heading. Answer each question and submit to your instructor.

2. **Practice Test** Click the Practice Test link below Chapter 7. Answer each question, enter your first and last names at the bottom of the page, and then click the Grade Test button. When the graded practice test is displayed on your screen, submit the graded practice test to your instructor. Continue to take the practice test until you are satisfied with your score.

3. **Crossword Puzzle Challenge** Click the Crossword Puzzle Challenge link below the Learn It Online heading. Read the instructions, and then click the Continue button. Work the crossword puzzle. When you are finished, click the Submit button. When the crossword puzzle is redisplayed, submit it to your instructor.

Knowledge Check

1. Name five Web sites that incorporate Web forms and state the purpose of each Web form (such as to enter customer information for purchasing an item). Do not list any sites that were mentioned in this chapter.

2. What type of Web page does ASP.NET 3.5 create? _aspx_

3. When you test a Web application, the page opens in a(n) _web browser_.

4. A Web page or Web site is hosted on a(n) _web server_.

5. A Web site that allows you to enter information is considered a(n) _dynamic_ Web page.

6. In an active server page, what computer executes the event handler code you write in Visual Basic 2008? _web server_

7. In a Windows application, each object has a (Name) property. In a Web application, each object has a _ID_ property, which is similar to the Name property.

8. Write a line of code that would display the date selected by the user in the TextBox shown in Figure 7-78.
txt Arrival.text = cldSelectDate.selectedDate.toShortDateString()

cldSelectDate

txtArrivalDate

Arrival Date:

FIGURE 7-78

Knowledge Check

(continued)

9. In the ListBox object shown in Figure 7-79, write the lines of code that would display in a Label named lblSizeDisplay "You have selected size: Large" if the user selects "L".

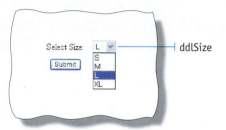

FIGURE 7-79

10. Explain the major difference between CheckBox and RadioButton objects.

11. What color are validation error messages by default?   *red*

12. Which control validator confirms that the user enters the constant value of 9.0?

13. Which control validator checks if a value is between 10 and 30?

14. Which control validator confirms that a TextBox object is not left blank?

15. Write a line of code that would convert strResponse to all uppercase letters.   *ToUpper()*

16. Write a line of code that would assign the length of a string named strCompany to the variable intSizeOfCompanyName.

17. Write a line of code that would display in a Label object named lblDisplayBirthday the date a user selected from a Calendar object named cldBirthdate.

18. How does the PictureBox object called an Image object in ASP.NET differ from an image in a Windows application?

19. In the browser window shown in Figure 7-80, name the type of validation and list any changes that were made in the Properties window.

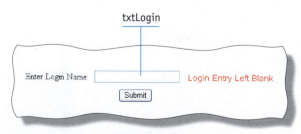

FIGURE 7-80

20. What three keys can you press simultaneously to open the full screen option?

Debugging Exercises

1. Fix the error in the following line of code.

   ```
   intFindLength = strHomeName.Text(Length)
   ```

2. Fix the error in the following lines of code.

   ```
   If (Me.chkDormStudent.Checked)= True Then
       decTuitionCost += 3400
   End If
   ```

3. What will be contained in the Text property of the lblResult Label object after executing the following code?

   ```
   Dim strPhrase As String
   strPhrase =  "              On the Wings"
   strPhrase += " of an Eagle!              "
   strPhrase = strPhrase.Trim()
   Me.lblResult.Text=strPhrase
   ```

4. What is the output of the following code?

   ```
   Dim strPhrase As String

   strPhrase = "Don't judge a book by its cover"
   Me.lblResult.Text= "Count =" & strPhrase.Length
   ```

5. Write the output that would be displayed in the Info label after the following statements are executed.

   ```
   lblInfo.Text = "Home Address: " & "<br>" & "3506 Wards Rd" & "<br>"
   & "Lynchburg, VA 24502"
   ```

Program Analysis

1. Name each of the property changes that are required in the Properties window for a Range Validator in order to validate that a TextBox named txtDeductibleRange contains a value in the range 250.00 up to and including 10,000.00. Display an error message that states "Please enter an acceptable deductible between 250 and 10,000".

2. Write a Visual Basic statement that displays the length of a variable named strSentence in a Label object named lblStringLength.

3. Write the section of code that would display a list of services in a Label object named lblService if the user selects any of the corresponding CheckBoxes shown in Figure 7-81.

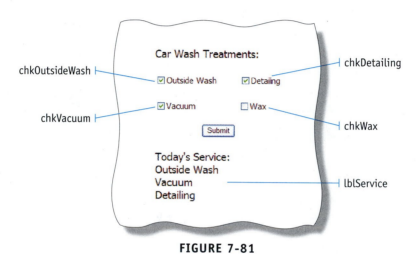

FIGURE 7-81

Case Programming Assignments

Complete one or more of the following case programming assignments.
Submit the program and materials you create to your instructor. The level of
difficulty is indicated for each case programming assignment.

● = Easiest
●● = Intermediate
●●● = Challenging

1 ●
CRUISE RESERVATION WEB APPLICATION

Design a Web application for a cruise reservation application using the options shown in Figure 7-82.
Write the code that will execute according to the program requirements shown in Figure 7-83 and the Use
Case Definition document shown in Figure 7-84. Before writing the code, create an event planning docu-
ment for each event in the program. The completed Web page is shown in Figure 7-85.

Cruise Option	Cost
First Three Nights Total for Inside Stateroom	$399
Each Additional Night for Inside Stateroom	$109
First Three Nights Total for Luxury Ocean View Cabin	$699
Each Additional Night for Luxury Ocean View Cabin	$159
Optional Shore Excursion to the Ancient Mayan Ruins in Mexico.	$179

FIGURE 7-82

REQUIREMENTS DOCUMENT

Date submitted: August 11, 2011

Application title: Cruise Reservation Form Web Application

Purpose: This application allows the user to book a reservation on a major cruise line.

**Program
Procedures:**   From a Web application, the user completes an online reservation form to select the type of
                         room, the number of nights, sailing date, and optional shore excursion.

**Algorithms,
Processing, and
Conditions:**
1. The user must be able to enter the requested reservation information on a Web form.
   The information should include their name, whether the user wants an
   inside stateroom or a luxury ocean view cabin, the number of nights spent on the cruise
   line (3–7 nights), the initial sail date, and whether they want to book an optional shore
   excursion. The prices are displayed in Figure 7-82.
2. After entering the reservation information, the user clicks the Submit button.
3. The information entered is validated.
4. The application displays the final cost of the cruise that has been selected.

FIGURE 7-83 (continues)

(continues)

Case Programming Assignments

Cruise Reservation Web Application (continued)

Notes and Restrictions:	1. Data Validation controls should be used. The name is validated to confirm that it is not left blank.
	2. The calendar object must have a date selected that is later than the current date.
	3. The number of nights must be 3 to 7 nights.
Comments:	1. Display a picture of a cruise ship on the Web form.

FIGURE 7-83 (continued)

USE CASE DEFINITION

1. The Web page opens, displaying this week's cruise options, a picture of the cruise ship, one TextBox object to request name, a DropDownList object displaying the length of the cruise (3-7 Nights), a Calendar object to select the sail date, a CheckBox object indicating whether they want the optional shore excursion, and a Submit button.
2. The user enters the information, makes the appropriate selections, and clicks the Submit button.
3. Validation controls check the data.
4. The application displays the final cost of the cruise package.

FIGURE 7-84

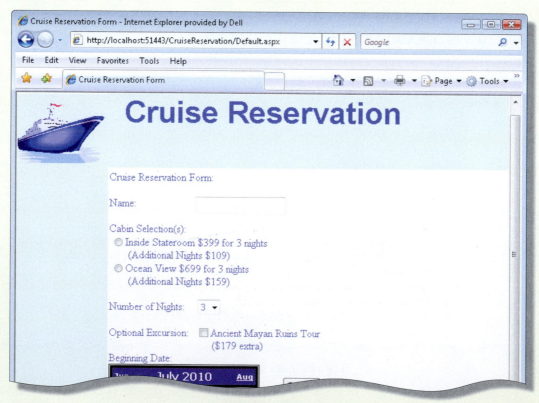

FIGURE 7-85

Case Programming Assignments

2 ● NEW EMPLOYEE E-MAIL WEB APPLICATION

Design a Web application and write the code that will execute according to the program requirements shown in Figure 7-86 and the Use Case Definition document shown in Figure 7-87. Before writing the code, create an event planning document for each event in the program. The completed Web page is shown in Figure 7-88.

REQUIREMENTS DOCUMENT

Date submitted:	July 31, 2011
Application title:	New Employee E-mail Web Application
Purpose:	This application allows a new employee to set up an e-mail address at the Webside Company.
Program Procedures:	From a Web application, the user should enter their first name and last name to create an e-mail address in the format: jim.bellweather@Webside.com, with the first and last name in lowercase letters.
Algorithms, Processing, and Conditions:	1. The user must be able to enter their first name and their last name. 2. The user must select a department from a DropDownList object with the following choices: Accounting, Executive, Marketing, Sales, and Warehouse. 3. The user clicks the Submit button. 4. The information entered is validated. 5. The application displays the department and the new e-mail address in the format first name, dot, last name (all lowercase) @ sign, Webside.com.
Notes and Restrictions:	1. Data validation tools should be used. The first and last names are validated to confirm that they are not left blank.
Comments:	1. The e-mail address will be displayed in lowercase letters.

FIGURE 7-86

(continues)

Case Programming Assignments

New Employee E-Mail Web Application (continued)

USE CASE DEFINITION

1. The Web page opens, displaying the title Webside New Employee E-mail Web page, two TextBox objects to enter the user's name, a DropDownList object for selecting the department, and a Submit button.
2. User enters their first name and last name.
3. User selects the department.
4. User clicks the Submit button.
5. Validation controls check that the data was entered.
6. The application displays the department and the e-mail address.

FIGURE 7-87

FIGURE 7-88

Case Programming Assignments

3 ONLINE SERVICE

Design a Web application and write the code that will execute according to the program requirements shown in Figure 7-89 and the Use Case Definition document in Figure 7-90. Before writing the code, create an event planning document for each event in the program. The completed Web page is shown in Figure 7-91.

REQUIREMENTS DOCUMENT

Date submitted: January 4, 2013

Application title: Online Service Web Application

Purpose: This Web application allows the user to sign up for an Internet service provider for home connectivity.

Program Procedures: From a Web application, the user should select one of two types of home online service.

Algorithms, Processing, and Conditions:

1. The user must be able to select information about the Internet service provider on a Web form. The information should include the first and last name of the user, whether the user wants dial-up service or a DSL connection, the connection date, and whether they want options of hosting a personal Web site and renting a wireless router.

2. The cost for the service is as follows:

Dial-up Connection (56K):		Optional Services:	
Initial Connection:	$29.99	Host Personal Site:	$2.99 per month
Basic Monthly Service:	$9.99	Wireless Router:	$3.99 per month
Digital Subscriber Line (DSL):			
Initial Connection:	$49.99		
Basic Monthly Service:	$19.99		

3. After the selection is entered, the user clicks the Submit button.
4. The information entered is validated.
5. The application displays the first month's cost (includes the initial connection fee), and the subsequent month's cost (does not include the initial connection fee).

Notes and Restrictions:

1. Data Validation controls should be used. The first and last names are validated to confirm they are not left empty.
2. One type of connection service must be selected. No optional service is required.
3. The selected connection date must be later than the current date.
4. Fees change consistently, so a change in fees must be easily accommodated within the application.

Comments:

1. Display a picture representing the World Wide Web on the Web form.

FIGURE 7-89

(continues)

Case Programming Assignments

Online Service (continued)

USE CASE DEFINITION

1. The Web page opens, displaying an Internet service provider order form for a home connection, a picture representing the World Wide Web, two TextBox objects requesting the user's first and last names, two radio buttons offering a choice of dial-up connection or DSL connection and their prices, a Calendar object to select the connection date, a CheckBox object for selecting whether the user wants a personal site, a CheckBox object for indicating the user wants to rent a wireless router, and a Submit button.
2. User clicks the Submit button.
3. Validation controls check the data.
4. The application displays the first month cost of connectivity to an Internet service provider with the services selected, and the subsequent month's cost for the service.

FIGURE 7-90

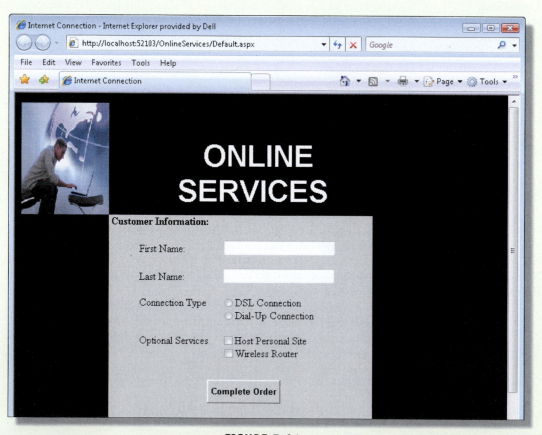

FIGURE 7-91

Case Programming Assignments

4 ●● HELP DESK

Design a Web application and write the code that will execute according to the program requirements shown in Figure 7-92. Before writing the code, create an event planning document for each event in the program. Create a Use Case Definition document for the application.

REQUIREMENTS DOCUMENT

Date submitted: February 22, 2012

Application title: Help Desk Work Ticket Web Application

Purpose: This Web application allows college staff to fill in a Web form requesting help from a computer help desk.

Program Procedures: From a Web application, the user should enter their name, e-mail address, lab number (1 – 15), computer station number (1 – 30), the operating system (DropDownList object with 3 options), and a large TextBox object to describe the problem in order to create a work ticket for the help desk.

Algorithms, Processing, and Conditions:
1. The user must be able to enter information about the requested computer repair on a Web form. The user will enter their first and last name, e-mail address, telephone number, lab number (1 – 15), computer station number (1 – 30), the operating system (DropDownList object with the choices of Vista, Windows XP, Windows 2000), and a large TextBox object to describe the problem in order to create a work ticket for the help desk.
2. After the information is entered, the user can click the Submit button.
3. The information entered is validated.
4. The application displays a help desk work ticket below the Submit button.

Notes and Restrictions:
1. Data Validation tools should be used. The first and last names are validated to confirm that they are not left blank.
2. The e-mail address is checked to verify it is not blank and that it conforms to the proper e-mail format.
3. The phone number is checked to verify it is not blank and that it conforms to a U.S. phone number.
4. The lab number and computer number are to be validated to confirm they are within the proper ranges.

Comments:
1. Display a picture of representing your college logo on the Web form.

FIGURE 7-92

Case Programming Assignments

5 ●●
LIL CUCCI'S PIZZERIA ONLINE

Design a Web application that calculates the cost of pizza according to the prices listed in Figure 7-93. Write the code that will execute according to the program requirements shown in Figure 7-94. Before writing the code, create an event planning document for each event in the program. Create a Use Case Definition document for the application.

Pizza Size	Cost
Small	$7.99
Medium	$9.99
Large	$12.99
Extra Large	$15.99
Each Extra Topping (Cheese Included)	$0.99

FIGURE 7-93

Case Programming Assignments

REQUIREMENTS DOCUMENT

Date submitted: July 24, 2011

Application title: Lil Cucci's Pizzeria Web Application

Purpose: This Web application allows a customer to fill out a pizza order form.

Program Procedures: From a Web application, the user should enter their name, address, and phone number. They also should select the size pizza they would like to order and the toppings. The final cost of the order will be displayed.

Algorithms, Processing, and Conditions:
1. The user must be able to enter information to order a pizza using a Web form. The user will enter their first and last name, address, phone number, the size of the pizza from a DropDownList object and CheckBoxes displaying pizza topping choices (at least six kinds of toppings).
2. After the information is entered, the user clicks the Submit button.
3. The information entered will be validated.
4. The application displays the final cost of the pizza order and a message that the pizza will be delivered in 45 minutes.

Notes and Restrictions:
1. Data Validation tools should be used. The first and last names are validated to confirm that they are not left blank.
2. The phone number is checked to ensure it is not blank and that it conforms to a U.S. phone number.

Comments:
1. A picture of a pizza will be displayed on the Web form.

FIGURE 7-94

Case Programming Assignments

6 ●●
THE LION GOLF PRO SHOP

Design a Web application and write the code that will execute according to the program requirements shown in Figure 7-95. Before writing the code, create an event planning document for each event in the program. Create a Use Case Definition document for the application.

REQUIREMENTS DOCUMENT

Date submitted: January 4, 2012

Application title: The Lion Golf Pro Shop Order Form Web Application

Purpose: This Web application allows the user to select a golf shirt for purchase online.

Program Procedures: From a Web application, the user should enter their name, address, and phone number. They also should select the size, color, and quantity of the golf shirts. The final cost of the order is displayed.

Algorithms, Processing, and Conditions:
1. The user must be able to view a graphic of a golf shirt, a description of the product, a DropDownList object with the sizes (S, M, L, XL), a DropDownList object of four colors, and a TextBox object allowing the quantity (check to make sure the number is between 1 and 12).
2. After the information is entered, the user clicks the Submit button.
3. The information entered will be validated.
4. The application will display a summary of their order. The subtotal for this item will be shown based on the cost of $39.99 per shirt. The shipping cost of 12% of the order will also be displayed and used in the total cost.

Notes and Restrictions:
1. Data Validation tools should be used. The range of the quantity ordered is to be 1-12.
2. The name, address, and phone number must be present.
3. The phone number must conform to a U.S. phone number.

Comments:
1. A picture of a golf shirt will be shown on the Web form.

FIGURE 7-95

Case Programming Assignments

7 ••• RECREATE AN ONLINE FORM

Create a requirements document and a Use Case Definition document, and design a Web application, based on the following case project.

Find an online form on the Internet you would like to re-create that has varied objects such as a Label, RadioButton, CheckBox, TextBox, and DropDownList objects. Use a similar layout of the existing Web site and at least eight objects on the form to display your own version of the Web site for practice. Validate the form using validation objects as needed.

FIGURE 7-96

8 ••• MOORE'S LAW

Create a requirements document and a Use Case Definition document, and create a Web application, based on the following case project.

Create a Web application that displays Moore's Law, which states that the computing power or the number of transistors within the same silicon processor doubles every 18 months. In other words, computing speed doubles every 18 months. As shown in the following table, allow the user to enter the current average speed in GHz and display the next 15 years of projected speed. Use the validation controls to make sure the entry is filled in and that the decimal entered is between 1.0 and 10.0.

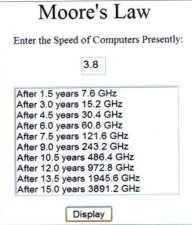

FIGURE 7-97

Case Programming Assignments

9 ●●●
JAVA SHOP

Create a requirements document and a Use Case Definition document, and create a Web application, based on the following case project.

To speed up the ordering process, a local coffee shop will allow customers to order their coffee on a touch screen while standing in line. The Web application will display the cost of the coffee. Allow the customer to enter their first name, display a DropDownList object with five coffee flavors, and allow the user to select the size of the coffee: Tall, Huge, and Bucket. Prices for these sizes are shown in the table below. Use validation controls. The coffee shop also provides options such as a double shot, flavored syrups, whipped cream, and soy milk for 49 cents each. Display the person's name and order with the purchase price with a 6.5% sales tax.

Size	Price
Tall	$2.59
Huge	$3.09
Bucket	$3.59

FIGURE 7-98

CHAPTER EIGHT

Using Procedures and Exception Handling

OBJECTIVES

You will have mastered the material in this chapter when you can:

- ► Create a splash screen

- ► Pause the splash screen

- ► Add a ComboBox object to a Windows Form

- ► Write Code for a SelectedIndexChanged event

- ► Code a Sub procedure

- ► Pass an argument to a procedure by value

- ► Pass an argument to a procedure by reference

- ► Code a Function procedure to return a value

- ► Create a class-level variable

- ► Catch an exception using a Try-Catch block

Introduction

The programs you have written thus far in this course were relatively small applications. Most real-world software, however, solves more expansive problems. As an application grows, it is important to divide each facet of a problem into separate sections of code called **procedures**. By using the principle of divide and conquer to create procedures, the code becomes more manageable.

In previous programs you have learned about data verification to ensure the user enters valid data before the data is processed. To expand your knowledge of data verification, you need to understand exception handling using Try-Catch blocks, which can check for any error a user might commit. By managing exceptions using Try-Catch blocks, you build high-quality, robust applications.

Finally, one way to make your programs more professional is to display a splash screen while the full program loads. In this chapter, you will learn to design and write procedures, include Try-Catch blocks in your program, and create a splash screen.

Chapter Project

The sample program in this chapter displays two Windows forms and is more complex than previous applications. A travel agent has requested a Windows application that provides pricing information for an island water-sports company named Ocean Tours. The purpose of the Windows application is to display the pricing information for water sports at different island locations. Ocean Tours is located in Aruba, Jamaica, and Key West in the Caribbean. Each island specializes in different water sports activities. The table in Figure 8-1 shows the available tours for each island, the length of the tour, and the tour cost.

Location	Tour Type	Tour Length	Tour Cost
Aruba	Deep Sea Fishing	8 hours	$199
	Kayaking	2 hours	$89
	Scuba	3 hours	$119
	Snorkeling	4 hours	$89
Jamaica	Glass Bottom Boat	2 hours	$39
	Parasailing	2 hours	$119
	Snorkeling	3 hours	$59
Key West	Deep Sea Fishing	4 hours	$89
	Glass Bottom Boat	2 hours	$29
	Scuba	3 hours	$119
	Snorkeling	3 hours	$59

FIGURE 8-1

The program begins with an opening screen called a splash screen. Shown in Figure 8-2, this splash screen displays the company title and image logo for approximately five seconds.

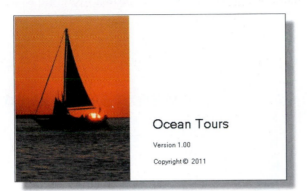

FIGURE 8-2

After the splash screen closes, the main form of the application opens requesting that the user select the island location. When the user clicks the ComboBox arrow, the three island locations of Aruba, Jamaica, and Key West appear in the drop-down list, as shown in Figure 8-3.

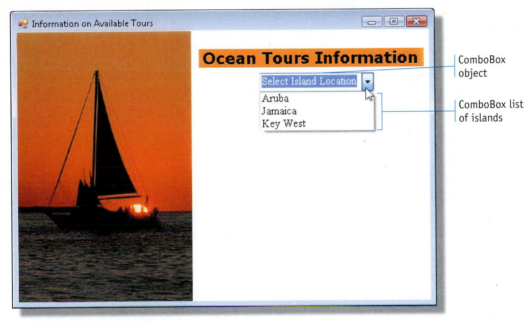

FIGURE 8-3

ONLINE REINFORCEMENT

To view a video of program execution, visit scsite.com/vb2008/ch8 and then select Figure 8-2.

After the user selects the island location, the Windows form displays form controls that request the number of guests in the party and the type of tour. The user enters the number of guests, selects the type of tour in which she will be traveling, and then clicks the Find Cost of Tour button. As shown in Figure 8-4, the program displays the cost and length of the tour.

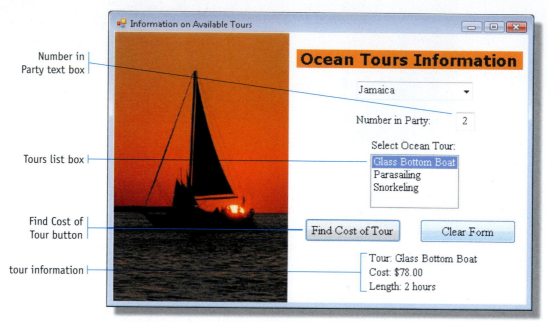

FIGURE 8-4

CREATING A SPLASH SCREEN

A **splash screen** is an opening screen that appears as an application is loading, signaling that the program is about to start and displaying an image and information to engage the user. In the Ocean Tours chapter project, the splash screen displays a sailboat image and the title, the version, and the copyright information (see Figure 8-2 on page 565).

Visual Basic provides a generic splash screen template you can add to your project with or without modification. You can change the generic graphic on the splash screen by changing the BackgroundImage property on the Properties window. To use the generic splash screen, you can complete the following steps:

STEP 1   Create a Windows application named Ocean Tours. Name the form frmTours. Click Project on the menu bar and then click Add New Item on the Project menu.

The Add New Item dialog box is displayed (Figure 8–5).

Add New Item dialog box   Splash Screen template

FIGURE 8-5

STEP 2   In the Add New Item dialog box, select Splash Screen in the Templates section.

The Splash Screen template is selected (Figure 8–6).

Splash Screen selected

Add button

FIGURE 8-6

STEP 3 Click the Add button in the Add New Item dialog box.

A form preconfigured by Visual Studio as a splash screen opens as a new tab named SplashScreen1.vb[Design] in the Design window (Figure 8-7). The splash screen can be customized with different graphics and text to suit an application.

FIGURE 8-7

STEP 4 Click the splash screen form in the left side of the form to select the form. To set the application to display the splash screen first, right-click OceanTours in the Solution Explorer.

The splash screen form is selected (Figure 8-8). A shortcut menu opens.

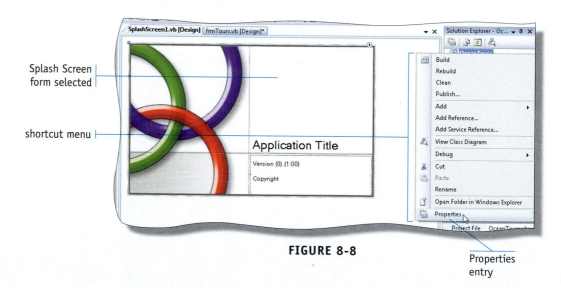

FIGURE 8-8

STEP 5 Click Properties on the shortcut menu.

*The Project Designer opens displaying the Application tab (Figure 8-9). The Project
Designer provides a central location for managing project properties, settings, and resources.
The Project Designer appears as a single window in the Visual Studio IDE. It contains a
number of pages that are accessed through tabs on the left.*

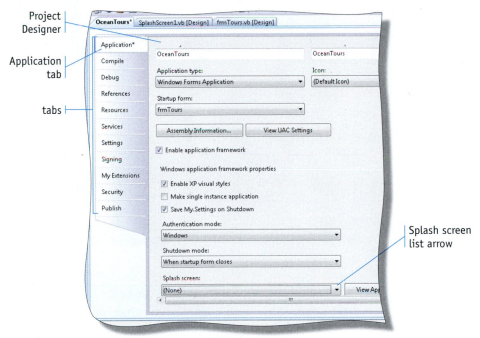

FIGURE 8-9

STEP 6 In the Windows application framework properties section, click the
Splash screen list arrow, and then click SplashScreen1 to select the form as the splash
screen used for project.

SplashScreen1 is selected in the Splash screen list (Figure 8-10).

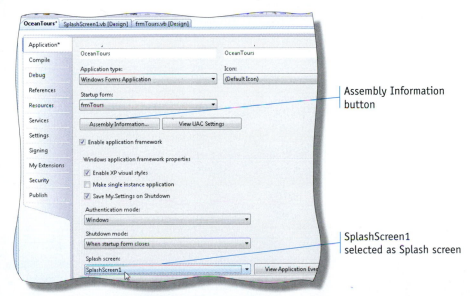

FIGURE 8-10

STEP 7 Click the Assembly Information button on the Properties Designer to open the Assembly Information dialog box.

The Assembly Information dialog box opens (Figure 8–11).

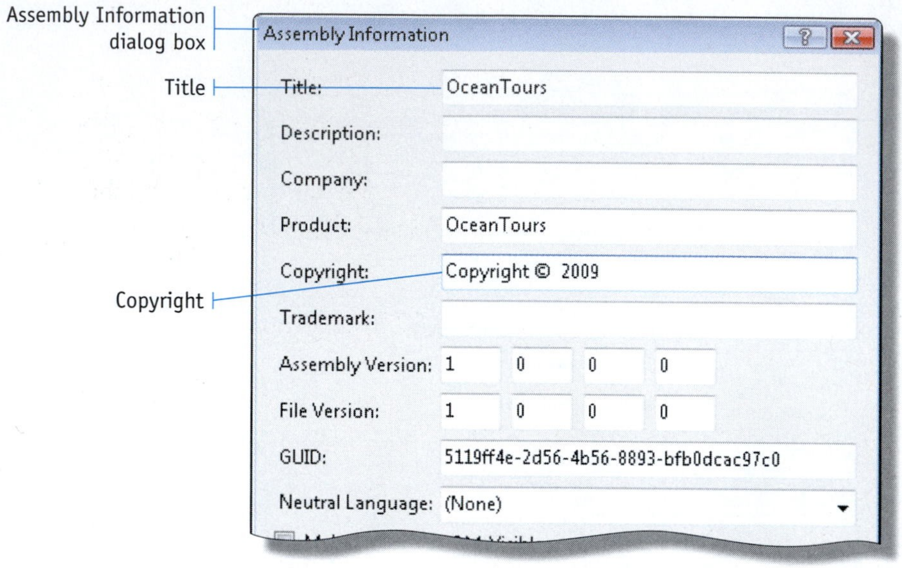

Assembly Information dialog box

Title

Copyright

Assembly Information	? ✕
Title:	OceanTours
Description:	
Company:	
Product:	OceanTours
Copyright:	Copyright © 2009
Trademark:	
Assembly Version:	1 0 0 0
File Version:	1 0 0 0
GUID:	5119ff4e-2d56-4b56-8893-bfb0dcac97c0
Neutral Language:	(None) ▼

FIGURE 8-11

STEP 8 To customize the splash screen, change the Title to Ocean Tours and the Copyright to the present year. The File Version can be changed as you update the application.

The Title and Copyright year are changed. The text on the splash screen form will not change until the application runs (Figure 8–12).

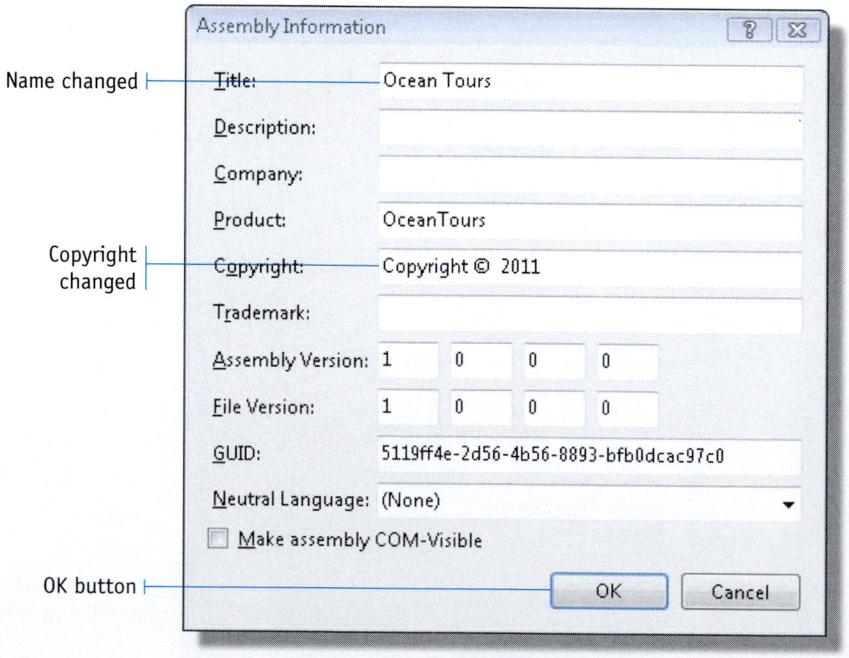

Name changed

Copyright changed

OK button

Assembly Information	? ✕
Title:	Ocean Tours
Description:	
Company:	
Product:	OceanTours
Copyright:	Copyright © 2011
Trademark:	
Assembly Version:	1 0 0 0
File Version:	1 0 0 0
GUID:	5119ff4e-2d56-4b56-8893-bfb0dcac97c0
Neutral Language:	(None) ▼
☐ Make assembly COM-Visible	
	OK Cancel

FIGURE 8-12

STEP 9   Click the OK button on the Assembly Information dialog box. Close the OceanTours* Project Designer window. To change the predefined image, first download the ocean.jpg picture from the scsite/vb2008/ch8/images Web site and store the image in a location you remember. Then, click the SplashScreen1.vb [Design] tab. Click the left side of the splash screen, making sure to select the entire splash screen form. The Properties window should identify MainLayoutPanel if you have selected the entire splash screen form. Click to the right of the Background Image property in the Properties window, and then click the ellipsis button. In the Select Resource dialog box, click the Project resource file radio button if necessary. Import the ocean.jpg picture by clicking the Import button in the Select Resource dialog box and selecting the ocean.jpg image from the location where you stored it. Click the OK button in the Select Resource dialog box.

The splash screen background image changes from the predefined image to the ocean.jpg image (Figure 8-13).

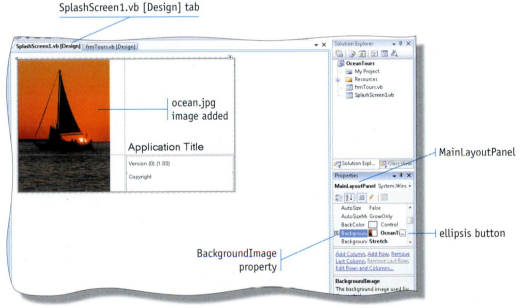

FIGURE 8-13

STEP 10   Run the application by clicking the Start Debugging button on the Standard toolbar.

The application begins to run. The splash screen appears for a moment and immediately closes (Figure 8-14). The amount of time the splash screen is displayed is based on the time needed to open the main form.

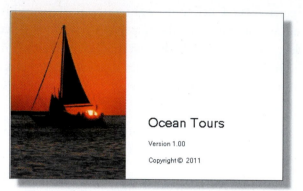

Ocean Tours

Version 1.00

Copyright© 2011

FIGURE 8-14

PAUSING THE SPLASH SCREEN

The user needs enough time to read the splash screen before it closes and the main form opens. To pause the splash screen for a specific time period, you can call the Sleep procedure. In fact, you can pause the execution of any application by calling the Thread.Sleep procedure. The Sleep procedure uses an integer value that determines how long the application should pause. To pause the splash screen, you can complete the following steps:

STEP 1   After the splash screen loads, the application executes any code in the form load event handler. To display the splash screen for five seconds, the code that calls the Sleep procedure should be in the form load event handler. To open the code editor window and the form load event handler, double-click the background of the frmTours Windows Form object in the Design window.

The frmTours_Load event handler opens in the code editor window (Figure 8-15).

frmTours load event handler

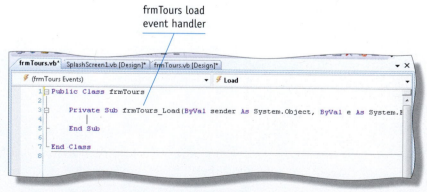

FIGURE 8-15

STEP 2   Click inside the frmToursLoad event handler. Type `Threading.` to cause IntelliSense to display a list of possible entries. If necessary, type T to select Thread from the IntelliSense list. Type .S to select Sleep from the IntelliSense list. Type `(5000)`.

The call for the Sleep procedure is entered (Figure 8-16). When the program executes and the frmTours load event is executed, the Sleep procedure suspends the execution of the application for 5000 milliseconds (5 seconds). This means that while the splash screen is displayed, the form will not be loaded for five seconds. You can increase the number of milliseconds if you want a longer pause.

Sleep procedure call   5000 milliseconds

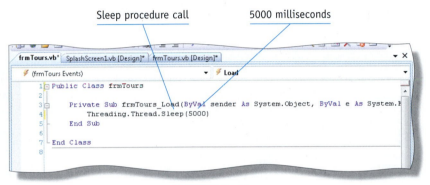

FIGURE 8-16

ADDING A COMBOBOX OBJECT

The Ocean Tours sample program requires a new type of object, a ComboBox object, in the Windows form to determine which island the user will be touring (Figure 8-17).

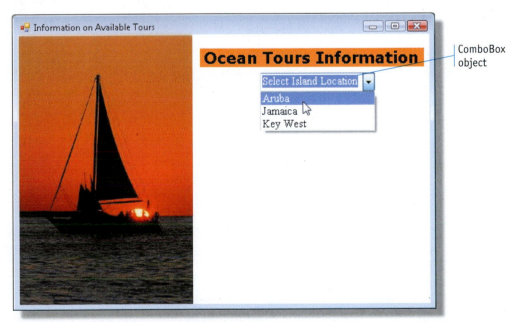

ComboBox object

FIGURE 8-17

A ComboBox object consists of two parts. The top part is a text box that allows the user to enter text. The second part is a list box that, when the user clicks the box arrow, displays a list of items from which the user can select one item. To save space on a form, use a ComboBox object because the full list is not displayed until the user clicks the list arrow. The prefix for the ComboBox object (Name) property is cbo. To place a ComboBox object on a Windows Form object, you can complete the following steps:

STEP 1 Drag the ComboBox .NET component from the Common Controls category of the Toolbox to the approximate location where you want to place the ComboBox object.

The ComboBox object is placed on the Windows Form object (Figure 8-18).

FIGURE 8-18

STEP 2 With the ComboBox object selected, scroll in the Properties window to the (Name) property. Double-click in the right column of the (Name) property and then enter the name `cboIsland`.

The name you entered is displayed in the (Name) property in the Properties window (Figure 8-19).

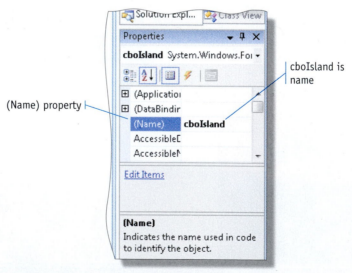

FIGURE 8-19

STEP 3 In the Properties window, scroll to the Text property. Click to the right of the Text property and enter `Select Island Location:` to specify the text that appears in the combo box. Resize the ComboBox object as needed to display the data in the box.

The Text property is changed to the instructions to select an island location (Figure 8-20).

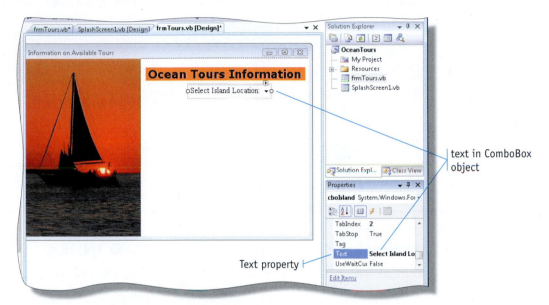

FIGURE 8-20

STEP 4 In the Properties window, scroll to the Items property, and click to the right of the Items property on the word (Collection). Click the ellipsis button. The String Collection Editor dialog box opens. Enter the island locations `Aruba` (press ENTER), `Jamaica` (press ENTER), and `Key West`.

The three items for the ComboBox list are shown in the String Collection Editor dialog box (Figure 8-21).

FIGURE 8-21

STEP 5 In the String Collection Editor dialog box, click the OK button. Click the Start Debugging button on the Standard toolbar to run the application. Click the list arrow on the right of the ComboBox object to view the contents. You can select a choice from the list.

The list in the ComboBox object contains the names previously entered in the String Collection Editor dialog box (Figure 8-22). The user can select one of the items in the list.

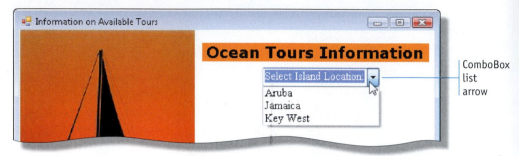

FIGURE 8-22

DETERMINING THE COMBOBOX SELECTED INDEX

To determine the cost of the tour selected in the Ocean Tours sample program, the user first selects the island location from the ComboBox object list. Code for the program must determine both that a value was selected and which one was selected. When the user selects an item in the ComboBox object list, the **SelectedIndex** property for the ComboBox object is assigned to the number that represents a zero-based index of the selected item. For example, if the user selects Aruba as shown in Figure 8-23, the index of 0 is the SelectedIndex for the ComboBox object which can be assigned to an Integer data type variable.

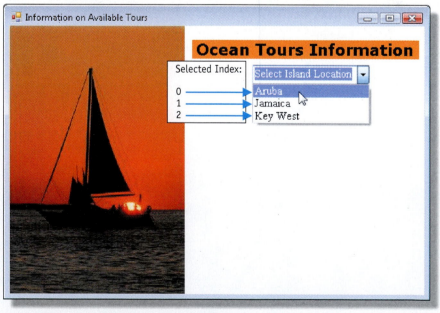

FIGURE 8-23

If the user has not made a selection, the SelectedIndex property is set to −1. To assign the item that the user selects using the SelectedIndex property, you can use a statement as shown in Figure 8-24.

```
32          intIslandChoice = Me.cboIsland.SelectedIndex()
```

FIGURE 8-24

HANDLING SELECTEDINDEXCHANGED EVENTS

In the Ocean Tours chapter project, the user's first action is to select the vacation island location. When the Ocean Tours application opens, the user views the main title and a ComboBox object named cboIsland, as shown in Figure 8-25.

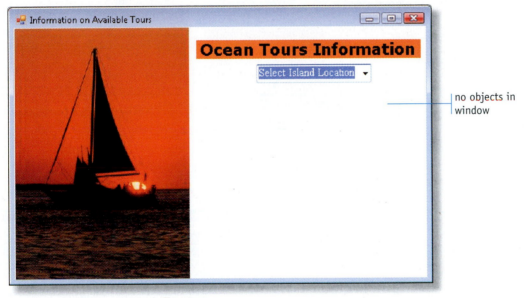

FIGURE 8-25

Notice that a Button object is not displayed in the window shown in Figure 8-25. When the user selects the island location, the application displays other objects on the form that request the number of people in the party, display the list of possible tour choices for that selected island, and request the month that the user is taking the tour. Instead of using a button click event to begin this process, another type of event handler called the **SelectedIndexChanged** event handler is executed when the user selects the island location of the tour. The SelectedIndexChanged event is triggered by the user selecting an item in the ComboBox object because the selected index in the ComboBox object is changed when the user makes a selection. To create a SelectedIndexChanged event, you can complete the following steps:

STEP 1   Select the ComboBox object named cboIsland on the Windows Form object.

The cboIsland ComboBox object is selected on the form (Figure 8-26).

ComboBox object selected

FIGURE 8-26

STEP 2   Double-click the ComboBox object. Close the Toolbox.

The code editing window is opened and the code generated by Visual Studio for the SelectedIndexChanged event handler is displayed (Figure 8-27). Within the event handler, you can write any code that should be executed when the user make a selection in the cboIsland ComboBox object.

cboIsland SelectedIndexChanged event handler

FIGURE 8-27

By executing an event handler when the user selects a particular item in the cboIsland ComboBox object, the program works efficiently without multiple user clicks. Many objects, such as the ListBox and DropDownList objects, can be used in the same manner as the ComboBox object with a SelectedIndexChanged event handler.

Procedures

The Ocean Tours application is a larger and more complex program than in previous chapters. Because the code for each event handler will be long, you should divide the code into smaller parts, each of which completes a specific task for the event handler. It is easier to deal with a larger program if you can focus on code that accomplishes a single task.

When a program is broken into manageable parts, each part is called a **procedure**. A procedure is a named set of code that performs a given task. In previous programs, you have called procedures, such as the Clear procedure and the ToString procedure, that have been written by the developers of Visual Studio. In the Ocean Tours program in this chapter, you will both write and call procedures.

Visual Basic provides two types of procedures: Sub procedures and Function procedures. The following sections explain these two type of procedures and how to code them.

CODING A SUB PROCEDURE

A **Sub procedure** is a procedure that completes its task but does not return any data to the calling procedure. A Sub procedure in Visual Basic 2008 is defined by using the Sub keyword. A **Sub** procedure is the series of Visual Basic statements enclosed by the Sub and End Sub statements. Each time the Sub procedure is called, its statements are executed, starting with the first executable statement after the Sub statement and ending with the first End Sub statement. A Sub procedure is called with a statement consisting of the procedure name and a set of parentheses in the form of a **procedure call**, as shown in Figure 8-28.

General Format: Procedure Call

The procedure call is made:

```
ProcedureName()
```

The **procedure declaration** that begins the Sub procedure has the form:

```
Private Sub ProcedureName()

        ' Line(s) of code

End Sub
```

FIGURE 8-28

In the Ocean Tours application, each island provides ocean tour selections. Based on the user's selection of an island location, the ListBox object in Figure 8-29 is filled with the various water tours available. For example, if the user selects Aruba, the tours Deep Sea Fishing, Kayaking, Scuba, and Snorkeling are displayed in the ListBox object.

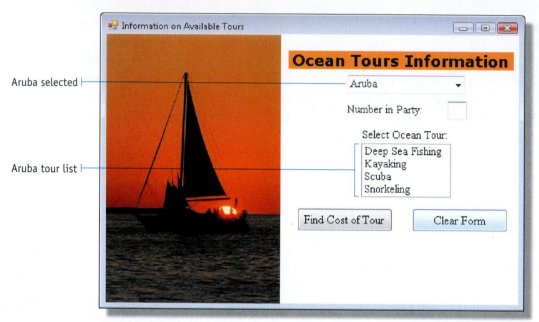

FIGURE 8-29

The items in the ListBox object are different based on the island selected. Figure 8-30 shows the code in the SelectedIndexChanged event handler that calls a Sub procedure to fill in the items in the ListBox object based on the island location selected by the user.

```
23    Private Sub cboIsland_SelectedIndexChanged(ByVal sender As System.Object, ByVal e  ↵
      As System.EventArgs) Handles cboIsland.SelectedIndexChanged
24        ' This event handler allows the user to enter the island choice
25        ' and then calls subprocedures to place the island activities in the list.
26
27        Dim intIslandChoice As Integer
28
29        intIslandChoice = Me.cboIsland.SelectedIndex ───── Selected Index
                                                              assigned to
30        Me.lstTours.Items.Clear()                         intIslandChoice
31        Select Case intIslandChoice
32            Case 0                        ArubaTours Sub
33                ArubaTours()              procedure call
34            Case 1                        JamaicaTours Sub
35                JamaicaTours()            procedure call
36            Case 2                        KeyWestTours Sub
37                KeyWestTours()            procedure call
38        End Select
```

FIGURE 8-30

In Figure 8-30, the selected index for the cboIsland ComboBox is assigned to the integer variable named intIslandChoice. Then, in the Case Select statement, the appropriate Sub procedure is called based on the island the user selected. When the selected index is equal to zero, the first item in the ComboBox list was selected, which is Aruba, so the ArubaTours Sub procedure is called. Notice that the name of the Sub procedure is specified followed by open and closed parentheses. As you learned previously, the Visual Basic compiler recognizes a procedure call by the parentheses.

The ArubaTours Sub procedure code is shown in Figure 8-31.

```
58      Private Sub ArubaTours()
59          ' This procedure fills in the possible ocean tours for Aruba
60          Me.lstTours.Items.Add(_strDeepSeaFishing)
61          Me.lstTours.Items.Add(_strKayaking)
62          Me.lstTours.Items.Add(_strScuba)
63          Me.lstTours.Items.Add(_strSnorkeling)
64
65      End Sub
```

FIGURE 8-31

In the code in Figure 8-31, the string values for the types of tours available on Aruba are added as items in the lstTours ListBox object. Notice that the string variables contain an underscore as the first character. You will recall that this designation identifies the variables as class variables that can be referenced in any procedure within the class.

In Figure 8-30, if the SelectedIndex value is 1, the Jamaica Sub procedure is called, and if the SelectedIndex value is 2, the Key West Sub procedure is called. Each of those Sub procedures adds items to the lstTours ListBox object, depending on what tours are available on each island.

A Sub procedure call may be used within a loop, If statements, or even Select Case statements as shown in Figure 8-30. When a Sub procedure is called, the program gives control to the called Sub procedure and executes the lines of code within that Sub procedure. After the Sub procedure has completed its execution, program control returns to the calling procedure and program execution resumes in the calling procedure.

HEADS UP

A Sub procedure call is like a detour on the highway. After the Sub procedure is completed, control returns to the calling procedure.

PASSING ARGUMENTS

Earlier chapters defined and used the term scope, and explained that variables declared within a procedure are limited in scope to their procedure. Code outside a procedure cannot interact with the variables declared within another procedure.

When a procedure is called, however, the call statement can pass an argument to the called procedure. You have experienced this in previous chapters when you passed a string value to the ToInt32 procedure to convert the string value to an integer value (Figure 8-32).

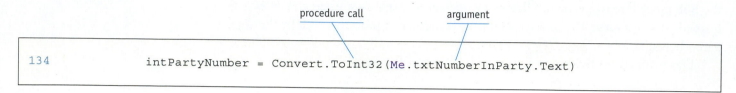

```
134          intPartyNumber = Convert.ToInt32(Me.txtNumberInParty.Text)
```

FIGURE 8-32

In Figure 8-32, the argument is contained within parentheses. In this example, the argument is the Text property of the txtNumberInParty TextBox object.

In many applications, passing variables to another procedure is essential because the called procedure requires the value(s) in order to complete its processing. For example, in Figure 8-33, the btnDaysOfWeek click event determines whether a certain day of the week is a weekday or a weekend day. When the Weekday Sub procedure is called, a variable named intNumericDayOfWeek is passed to the Weekday Sub procedure because the Sub procedure must know the numeric day in order to perform its processing.

```
20    Private Sub btnDaysOfWeek_Click(ByVal sender As System.Object, ByVal e As System. ↙
      EventArgs) Handles btnDaysOfWeek.Click
21        Dim intNumericDayOfWeek As Integer
22
23        intNumericDayOfWeek = Convert.ToInt32(Me.txtDay.Text)
24        Weekday(intNumericDayOfWeek)
25        MsgBox("Have a Great Week!", "Goodbye")
26    End Sub
27
28    Private Sub Weekday(ByVal intDay As Integer)
29        If intDay = 1 Or intDay = 7 Then
30            Me.lblDisplayDay.Text = "Weekend"
31        End If
32        If intDay >= 2 And intDay <= 6 Then
33            Me.lblDisplayDay.Text = "Weekday"
34        End If
35    End Sub
```

FIGURE 8-33

In Figure 8-33, the variable named intNumericDayOfWeek is passed to the Weekday Sub procedure by the calling statement on line 24. The value in the intNumericDayOfWeek variable should be 1 for Sunday, 2 for Monday, 3 for Tuesday, 4 for Wednesday, 5 for Thursday, 6 for Friday, and 7 for Saturday.

When a value is passed to a Sub procedure, the Sub procedure declaration, which identifies the name of the Sub procedure, also must contain an entry that defines the argument for use within the Sub procedure. In the Weekday Sub procedure in Figure 8-33, the parentheses following the Sub procedure name -Weekday- on line 28 contain the command ByVal intDay as Integer within parentheses. This entry defines an integer variable name (intDay) for use within the Sub procedure.

Visual Basic treats variables passed from a calling procedure to a called procedure in one of two ways: ByVal or ByRef. The following sections explain these two methods.

Passing Arguments by Value (ByVal)

When an argument is passed ByVal, it means the Sub procedure has access to the value of the passed argument, but does not actually reference the variable declared in the calling procedure. Instead, the value is copied into a variable whose name is specified in the Sub procedure declaration statement. Thus, in Figure 8-33, since the argument is passed ByVal, the value in the intNumericDayOfWeek is copied to the variable defined in the procedure declaration of the called Sub procedure (intDay).

The intDay variable contains the value passed from the calling procedure only so long as the called Sub procedure has processing control. When the Sub procedure has completed processing and passes control back to the calling procedure, the variable is lost. If the Sub procedure is called again, the variable is created again as a new variable with no preexisting value. So, you can consider the variable defined in the Sub procedure declaration as a temporary variable that exists only during processing within the Sub procedure when the argument is passed ByVal.

The temporary variable can be given any name, including the name of the variable in the calling procedure, but most developers use different names to avoid confusion. Notice that the name used in the calling procedure is intNumericDayOfWeek and the name used in the Sub procedure for the temporary variable is intDay.

When the argument is passed ByVal, the Sub procedure code can change the value in the temporary variable and use it in any manner required. The original value of the variable in the calling procedure is not affected because the value is copied into the temporary Sub procedure variable and the variable in the calling procedure is never referenced in the Sub procedure.

ByVal is the default for all passed arguments. The keyword ByVal is added automatically if you do not enter it when you code the Sub procedure declaration.

The code in Figure 8-34 illustrates the fact that the Sub procedure can change the passed value, but that value is not changed in the calling procedure when the value is passed ByVal.

```
22    Private Sub btnShowMessages Click(ByVal sender As System.Object, ByVal e As System.↙
      EventArgs) Handles btnShowMessages.Click
23        Dim strMessage As String
24
25        strMessage = "The Original Welcome Message"
26        MsgBox(strMessage, ,"First Message")
27        DisplayMessage(strMessage)
28        MsgBox(strMessage, ,"Fourth Message")
29    End Sub
30
31    Private Sub DisplayMessage(ByVal strShowMessage As String)
32        MsgBox(strShowMessage, ,"Second Message")
33        strShowMessage = "The Changed Welcome Message"
34        MsgBox(strShowMessage, ,"Third Message")
35    End Sub
36  End Class
```

FIGURE 8-34

The output for the code in Figure 8-34 is shown in Figure 8-35.

FIGURE 8-35

In Figure 8-35 you can see that the DisplayMessage Sub procedure in Figure 8-34 changed the message and the third message box displays this changed message, "The Changed Welcome Message". When the Sub procedure is finished and control is passed back to the calling procedure, however, the value in the strMessage variable, which was passed to the Sub procedure, was not changed, as shown in the Fourth Message window.

You can call the same Sub procedure repeatedly, as shown in Figure 8-36. The Sub procedure DisplayMessage is called once and the Square Sub procedure is called three times. Notice that either literals or variables can be passed to a Sub procedure.

```
23      Private Sub btnSquare_Click(ByVal sender As System.Object, ByVal e As System.
        EventArgs) Handles btnSquare.Click
24
25          Dim decNum As Decimal
26
27          decNum = 3.3
28          DisplayMessage()
29          Square(7.9)
30          Square(4.0)
31          Square(decNum)
32
33      End Sub
34
35      Private Sub Square(ByVal decValue As Decimal)
36          Me.lstResult.Items.Add("The square of " & decValue & " is " & _
37            (decValue * decValue))
38
39      End Sub
40
41      Private Sub DisplayMessage()
42          Me.lstResult.Items.Add("Squares:")
43      End Sub
```

FIGURE 8-36

After executing the code in Figure 8-36, the ListBox object in Figure 8-36 would contain the values shown in Figure 8-37.

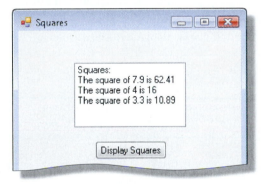

FIGURE 8-37

Passing Arguments by Reference (ByRef)

The second way in which to pass an argument from a calling procedure to a called Sub procedure is **by reference.** You specify you want to pass a value by reference by entering the keyword ByRef in the Sub procedure declaration.

Passing a value by reference allows code in the Sub procedure to modify the contents of the variable that is being passed because when you use ByRef, you are passing a reference to the variable that holds the value instead of the value as when you use ByVal. Thus, if a Sub procedure changes the value of a variable passed ByRef, the original variable in the calling procedure is changed. You should select the option to pass a variable by reference if you intend to change the original value when it is passed to the Sub procedure.

In the code example in Figure 8-38, the calling procedure assigns the value Vincent Van Gogh to the strFavoriteArtist variable (line 49) and then passes the variable ByRef (line 51).

```
46      Private Sub btnDisplayMessage_Click(ByVal sender As System.Object, ByVal e As
        System.EventArgs) Handles btnDisplayMessage.Click
47          Dim strFavoriteArtist As String
48
49          strFavoriteArtist = "Vincent Van Gogh"
50          MsgBox("Favorite Artist is " & strFavoriteArtist, , "First Message")
51          DisplayMessage(strFavoriteArtist)
52          MsgBox("Favorite Artist is now " & strFavoriteArtist, , "Fourth Message")
53      End Sub
54
55      Private Sub DisplayMessage(ByRef strshowArtist As String)
56          MsgBox("Favorite Artist is " & strshowArtist, , "Second Message")
57          ' The artist name is changed
58          strshowArtist = "Paul Cezanne "
59          MsgBox("Favorite Artist is " & strshowArtist, , "Third Message")
60      End Sub
61 End Class
```

FIGURE 8-38

The Sub procedure changes the value of the passed variable to Paul Cezanne (line 58). Because the variable is passed By Reference (ByRef), the value in the variable that is passed from the calling procedure is changed to Paul Cezanne. In the output shown in Figure 8-39, the changed value is displayed in the fourth message box when the btnDisplayMessage click event displays the last message box (line 52).

WATCH OUT FOR

Passing ByVal means the Sub procedure cannot change the original value. Passing ByRef means the Sub procedure can change the original value.

FIGURE 8-39

Passing Multiple Arguments

You can pass as many arguments as needed to a Sub procedure. If you have more than one argument, the variables are passed in the same order in which they appear in the procedure call statement.

FUNCTION PROCEDURES

A **Function procedure** is similar to a Sub procedure except that a Function procedure returns a single value to the calling procedure. Just like a Sub procedure, you can pass variables to the Function procedure using ByVal and ByRef. A Function procedure uses the keyword Function (instead of the keyword Sub) in the procedure declaration. You also must specify a return data type in the procedure declaration to define the type of variable that is being returned to the calling procedure by the Function procedure. The Function procedure call has the syntax shown in Figure 8-40:

General Format: Function Procedure Call

The Function procedure call is made:

```
VariableName = FunctionProcedureName()
```

The **procedure declaration** that begins the Function procedure has the form:

```
Private Function FunctionProcedureName() as DataType
        ' Line(s) of code
        Return VariableName
End Function
```

FIGURE 8-40

The Private keyword is optional in the Function procedure declaration. If it is omitted, the default is Public, which means any code in any class can reference the Function procedure. In many instances, this is not desirable so the Private access modifier is used.

In the Function procedure call statement in Figure 8-40, the FunctionProcedureName on the right of the assignment statement is replaced by the value that is returned from the Function procedure. That value then is assigned to the variable on the left side of the equal sign.

HEADS UP

You can exclude the receiving variable in the procedure call if you use the value immediately, as in Me.lblResult.Text = "Price: " & FindPrice(intValue).ToString().

The Function procedure is different in appearance from a Sub procedure in the following ways:

1. The Function procedure call has a receiving variable that is assigned the returned value from the Function procedure.
2. The data type of the return value is listed in the procedure declaration.
3. The keyword Return is used in the Function procedure to return a single value.

A Function procedure can pass only one value back to the calling procedure. The coding example in Figure 8-41 determines the gas mileage of a vehicle by dividing the number of miles driven by the number of gallons of gas used. The ComputeGasMileage Function procedure returns one value representing the gas mileage (Return statement on line 87). When the gas mileage value is returned, it is assigned to the receiving variable decMilesPerGallon (line 76 in the btnCompute click event).

```
69    Private Sub btnCompute_Click(ByVal sender As System.Object, ByVal e As System.      ↙
      EventArgs) Handles btnCompute.Click
70        Dim decMiles As Decimal
71        Dim decGallons As Decimal
72        Dim decMilesPerGallon As Decimal
73
74        decMiles = Convert.ToDecimal(Me.txtMiles.Text)
75        decGallons = Convert.ToDecimal(Me.txtGallons.Text)
76        decMilesPerGallon = ComputeGasMileage(decMiles, decGallons)
77        MsgBox("You are getting " & decMilesPerGallon.ToString("F1") & " miles per   ↙
      gallon",,"MPG")
78
79    End Sub
80
81    Function ComputeGasMileage(ByVal decMiles As Decimal, ByVal decGallons As Decimal)
      As Decimal
82        Dim decMileage As Decimal
83
84        decMileage = decMiles / decGallons
85        ' The following statement returns control to the calling
86        ' procedure and returns the value in the decMileage variable.
87        Return decMileage
88
89    End Function
```

FIGURE 8-41

When writing a Function procedure, do not place any lines of code after the Return statement because control returns to the calling procedure when the Return statement is executed.

It is best to use a Function procedure when you plan to return a value from a called procedure. In the Ocean Tours chapter project, a Function procedure returns the final cost of the selected tour as shown in Figure 8-42.

Calling Procedure

```
105                    Select Case intIslandChoice
106                        Case 0
107                            decTotalCost = ArubaFindCost(intTourChoice, _
108                                              intGroupSize, intLengthOfTour)
```

Called Procedure

```
182     Private Function ArubaFindCost(ByVal intTourSelection As Integer, _
183       ByVal intGroupSize As Integer, ByRef intTourLength As Integer) As Decimal
184         ' This function calculates the cost of the tours to Aruba
185
186         Dim decTourCost As Decimal
187         Dim decFinalCost As Decimal
188         Dim decArubaDeepSeaCost As Decimal = 199D
189         Dim decArubaKayakCost As Decimal = 89D
190         Dim decArubaScubaCost As Decimal = 119D
191         Dim decArubaSnorkelCost As Decimal = 89D
192
193         Select Case intTourSelection
194             Case 0
195                 decTourCost = decArubaDeepSeaCost
196                 intTourLength = _intEightHours
197             Case 1
198                 decTourCost = decArubaKayakCost
199                 intTourLength = _intTwoHours
200             Case 2
201                 decTourCost = decArubaScubaCost
202                 intTourLength = _intThreeHours
203             Case 3
204                 decTourCost = decArubaSnorkelCost
205                 intTourLength = _intFourHours
206         End Select
207         decFinalCost = decTourCost * intGroupSize
208         Return decFinalCost
209
210     End Function
```

FIGURE 8-42

In Figure 8-42, the function call on line 107 calls the ArubaFindCost Function procedure. The arguments include the integer value of the user choice in the list box (intTourChoice), the integer value of the number in the party (intGroupSize), and a variable to contain the length of the chosen tour (intLengthOfTour).

In the called Function procedure, the tour choice and group size are passed ByVal. The length of the tour is passed ByRef. Therefore, when the Function procedure changes a value in the length of tour a change is made in the passed variable.

You can use Sub procedures and Function procedures in any Visual Basic application including Windows applications, Mobile applications, Web applications, and VSTO applications.

CREATING A PRIVATE CLASS-LEVEL VARIABLE

In previous programs within this book you have defined class level variables for use in multiple procedures or event handlers within the class. In those programs, the variable was declared using the Dim statement (for an example, see the Chapter 7 program). You will recall that a class-level variable is defined within the class but outside any procedure. When a class-level variable is declared using the Dim statement, it can be referenced by any code within any procedure within the class.

It cannot, however, be referenced by any code outside the class (in larger projects, multiple classes can be created). When a class-level variable cannot be referenced outside the class in which it is declared, the variable is said to have Private access. Generally, it is a good programming practice to limit the scope of a class-level variable to the class in which it is declared.

By default, then, a class-level variable declared using the Dim statement has Private access. You also can declare class-level variables by using the Private keyword instead of the Dim keyword. The class-level variables used in the Ocean Tours program in this chapter are shown in Figure 8-43.

```
11      ' Class variables
12      Private _intTwoHours As Integer = 2
13      Private _intThreeHours As Integer = 3
14      Private _intFourHours As Integer = 4
15      Private _intEightHours As Integer = 8
16      Private _strDeepSeaFishing As String = "Deep Sea Fishing"
17      Private _strKayaking As String = "Kayaking"
18      Private _strScuba As String = "Scuba"
19      Private _strSnorkeling As String = "Snorkeling"
20      Private _strGlassBottomBoat As String = "Glass Bottom Boat"
21      Private _strParasailing As String = "Parasailing"
```

FIGURE 8-43

As you can see in Figure 8-43, each of the variables is declared using the Private keyword. All of the variables will have Private access, which means code in any procedure within the class can reference the variables but code in another class cannot.

Exception Handling

In previous programs in this book, you have learned that ensuring users enter valid data is an essential task within the program. You have used loops and If statements to check the values entered by users to ensure that data they enter does not cause an exception within the program.

Visual Basic provides another tool you can use to detect exceptions and take corrective action. This tool is called the **Try-Catch** set of statements. The Try keyword means "Try to execute this code." The Catch keyword means "Catch errors here." A Try-Catch block includes a statement or statements that are executed in the Try block and the statements that are executed in the Catch block(s) when an exception occurs. The format of the Try-Catch block is shown in Figure 8-44.

General Format: Try-Catch block

Try

      'Try Block of Code – Executable statement(s) that may generate an exception.

Catch (filter for possible exceptions)

      'Catch Block of Code for handling the exception

[Optional: Additional Catch blocks]

[Optional Finally]

      'Optional statements that will always execute before finishing the Try block

End Try

FIGURE 8-44

To illustrate the use of a Try-Catch block, assume the value in one variable is being divided by the value in another variable. As you will recall, it is invalid to divide by zero. If an attempt is made to divide by zero, a DivideByZero exception will occur. Therefore, the divide operation should be placed in a Try block and the Catch block should be set for a divide by zero exception.

If the exception occurs, the code in Figure 8-45 will open a message box opens stating that an attempt was made to divide by zero.

```
91          Dim decNumerator As Decimal
92          Dim decDenominator As Decimal
93          Dim decDivision As Decimal
94
95          decNumerator = Convert.ToDecimal(Me.txtNum.Text)
96          decDenominator = Convert.ToDecimal(Me.txtDen.Text)
97          Try
98              decDivision = decNumerator / decDenominator
99          Catch Exception As DivideByZeroException
100             MsgBox("Attempt to divide by zero")
101         End Try
102
103     End Sub
104 End Class
```

FIGURE 8-45

In Figure 8-45, the divide operation occurs by the statement on line 98. Note that the divide operation is within the Try-Catch block, as defined by the Try keyword on line 97, the Catch keyword on line 99, and the End Try statement on line 101. You can define the particular class of exception in a Catch block by mentioning the name of the exception with the Catch keyword. In Figure 8-48, DivideByZeroException was stated to catch that specific exception. If the value in decDenominator is zero when the divide operation occurs, the code in the Catch block will display a message box with an error message. More importantly, the program will not be terminated. A Try-Catch block allows the program to handle exceptions elegantly so that the program does not abruptly terminate.

Different types of exceptions can occur. The table shown in Figure 8-46 identifies some of the possible exceptions.

Exception Type	Condition when Exception Occurs	Code Example
ArgumentNullException	A variable that has no value is passed to a procedure	`Dim strTerm As String` `Me.lstDisplay.Items.Add(strTerm)`
DivideByZeroException	A value is divided by zero	`intResult = intNum / 0`
FormatException	A variable is converted to another type that is not possible	`strTerm = "Code"` `intValue = Convert.ToInt32(strTerm)`
NullReferenceException	A procedure is called when the result is not possible	`Dim strTerm as String` `intValue = strTerm.Length`
OverflowException	A value exceeds its assigned data type	`Dim intCost as Integer` `intCost = 58 ^ 4000000000`
SystemException	Generic	`Catches all other exceptions`

FIGURE 8-46

In another example of a Try-Catch Block, in Figure 8-47 a very large number assigned to the variable intBaseValue is squared within a Try-Catch block. Notice that when the value intBaseValue is squared, the result will exceed the range for an Integer data type, causing an OverflowException. When the exception occurs within the Try block, the Catch block is called to deal with the OverflowException.

```
105        Dim intBaseValue As Integer
106        Dim intSquaredValue As Integer
107
108        intBaseValue = 50000000
109        Try
110            intSquaredValue = intBaseValue ^ 2
111        Catch Exception As OverflowException
112            'This catch block detects an overflow of the range of the data type
113            MsgBox("The value exceeds the range of the data type", , "Error")
114        End Try
```

FIGURE 8-47

Multiple Catch blocks can be defined for a single Try block where each Catch block will catch a particular class of exception. This is useful when you want to state which type of error occurred, identifying to users the particular mistake that was made. It is best to order exceptions in Catch blocks from the most specific to the least specific. In other words, place the Catch block that is most likely to be needed for the most common exception first in a series of Catch statements. If an exception occurs during the execution of the Try block, Visual Basic examines each Catch statement within the Try-Catch block until it finds one whose condition matches that error. If a match is found, control transfers to the first line of code in the Catch block. If no matching Catch statement is found, the search proceeds to the next Catch statement in the Try-Catch block. This process continues through the entire code block until a matching Catch block is found in the current procedure. If no match is found, an exception that stops the program is produced.

In the Ocean Tours chapter project, the variable that is assigned the value of the number in the party needs to be validated. You want to make sure the user enters a number, not a letter or other symbol, and the number should be 1–99.

The code in Figure 8-48 displays a Try-Catch block used within a Function procedure named ValidateNumberInParty. It uses three Catch blocks.

```
124   Private Function ValidateNumberInParty() As Boolean
125      ' This procedure validates the value entered for the number in party
126
127      Dim intPartyNumber As Integer
128      Dim blnValidityCheck As Boolean = False
129      Dim strNumberInPartyErrorMessage As String = _
130         "Please enter the number of people in your party (1-99)"
131      Dim strMessageBoxTitle As String = "Error"
132
133      Try
134         intPartyNumber = Convert.ToInt32(Me.txtNumberInParty.Text)
135         If intPartyNumber > 0 And intPartyNumber < 100 Then
136            blnValidityCheck = True
137         Else
138            MessageBox.Show(strNumberInPartyErrorMessage, _
139               strMessageBoxTitle)
140            Me.txtNumberInParty.Focus()
141            Me.txtNumberInParty.Clear()
142         End If
143      Catch Exception As FormatException
144         MessageBox.Show(strNumberInPartyErrorMessage, _
145            strMessageBoxTitle)
146         Me.txtNumberInParty.Focus()
147         Me.txtNumberInParty.Clear()
148      Catch Exception As OverflowException
149         MessageBox.Show(strNumberInPartyErrorMessage, _
150            strMessageBoxTitle)
151         Me.txtNumberInParty.Focus()
152         Me.txtNumberInParty.Clear()
153      Catch Exception As SystemException
154         MessageBox.Show(strNumberInPartyErrorMessage, _
155            strMessageBoxTitle)
156         Me.txtNumberInParty.Focus()
157         Me.txtNumberInParty.Clear()
158      End Try
159
160      Return blnValidityCheck
161
162   End Function
```

FIGURE 8-48

The Boolean variable, blnValidityCheck (line 128 in the code in Figure 8-48) is initially set to false, but it is set to true if an exception is not thrown (line 136); in other words, the Catch block was not executed because an exception was not thrown. This Boolean variable set to True then is returned to the calling procedure (line 160) and the calling procedure can continue its processing.

If an exception is thrown when the value in the Text property of the txtNumberInParty TextBox is converted to an integer (line 134), the statements below the Convert.ToInt32 statement will not be executed because control is passed to the appropriate Catch statement. The processing in each of the Catch blocks displays a message box with an error message, places the focus on the text box where the user enters the number in the party, and clears the text box.

When the processing in the Try-Catch block is complete, the Return statement on line 160 returns the value of the Boolean variable. If the data was valid, the

Boolean variable contains the True value. If the data was not valid, it contains False because the variable initially was set to False (line 128) and its value was not changed by the Catch block processing.

An optional portion of the Try-Catch block is the Finally statement. The code in the Finally section always executes last regardless of whether the code in the Catch blocks has been executed. Place cleanup code, such as closing files, in the Finally section. Code in the Finally section always is executed, no matter what happens in the Try-Catch blocks.

Program Design

As you have learned, the requirements document identifies the purpose of the program being developed, the application title, the procedures to be followed when using the program, any equations and calculations required in the program, any conditions within the program that must be tested, notes and restrictions that must be followed by the program, and any other comments that would be helpful to understanding the problem. The requirements document for the Ocean Tours application is shown in Figure 8-49.

REQUIREMENTS DOCUMENT

Date submitted: June 22, 2012

Application title: Ocean Tours Trip Selection

Purpose: This Windows application allows a customer to view ocean tours available in the Caribbean islands.

Program Procedures: From a Windows application, the user can select ocean tours and find out pricing information.

Algorithms, Processing, and Conditions:
1. The user first selects the island location. No other objects are displayed at this time.
2. When the user selects an island, the following items are displayed in the window: Number in party text box and a custom list of the available tours on the chosen island. In addition, a button to find the cost of the tour and a button to clear the form are included.
3. The user enters the number of guests in their party.
4. From the custom list of tours that are available for the chosen island, the user selects the tour desired.
5. The total price for the ocean tour for the group is displayed.

Notes and Restrictions:
1. Validate numeric input with Try-Catch blocks.
2. Use multiple procedures to break the application into manageable sections.

Comments:
1. The ocean.jpg picture used in the Window is available at scsite/vb2008/ch8/images.
2. A splash screen is shown for approximately 5 seconds before the main window is displayed.

FIGURE 8-49

The use case definition for the application is shown in Figure 8-50.

USE CASE DEFINITION

1. A splash screen welcomes the user for approximately 5 seconds.
2. The user selects an island location.
3. The program displays a text box for the number of people in the party and a list of available ocean tours for the selected island.
4. The user enters the number of people in the party, selects a tour, and clicks the Find Cost of Tour button.
5. The program identifies the tour, calculates and displays the tour cost for the entire party, and specifies the length in hours of the tour.
6. The user can change any of the entries (island choice, number in party, and tour) and click the Find Cost of Tour button to recalculate the tour cost.
7. The user can clear the form by clicking the Clear Form button.

FIGURE 8-50

The table in Figure 8-51 contains the data for the tour type for each island, the tour length, and the tour cost.

Location	Tour Type	Tour Length	Tour Cost
Aruba	Deep Sea Fishing	8 hours	$199
	Kayaking	2 hours	$89
	Scuba	3 hours	$119
	Snorkeling	4 hours	$89
Jamaica	Glass Bottom Boat	2 hours	$39
	Parasailing	2 hours	$119
	Snorkeling	3 hours	$59
Key West	Deep Sea Fishing	4 hours	$89
	Glass Bottom Boat	2 hours	$29
	Scuba	3 hours	$119
	Snorkeling	3 hours	$59

FIGURE 8-51

PROGRAM DESIGN WHEN USING SUB AND FUNCTION PROCEDURES

As noted previously, when a program becomes larger, often it is advantageous to break the program into procedures, which perform specific tasks within the program. The goal of using procedures is to make the program easier to read and understand, and therefore make the program easier to debug. The final result is a program that is more reliable and easier to maintain.

The developer must determine what code should be placed in a procedure. Several rules are important to follow when creating procedures in a program; otherwise, the use of procedures might make the program more difficult and more confusing. These rules include:

1. The Sub procedure or the Function procedure should perform a single, defined task, such as checking the validity of a specific user input, or calculating the cost of a tour on an island. Procedures which perform multiple tasks tend to become large and difficult to design and code.

2. A Sub procedure or a Function procedure must perform reasonably substantial processing. It makes little sense to place a procedure call statement in a calling procedure and have the called procedure contain one or two program statements. It would be easier and clearer just to place the statements in the calling procedure.

3. When deciding whether a set of programming steps should be placed in a Sub procedure or a Function procedure, ask yourself the following questions: 1) Will the program be easier to read and understand if the code is placed in a separate procedure? 2) Does the proposed code perform a single task and does this task require more than three or four programming statements? 3) Can the Sub procedure or Function procedure perform its processing by receiving data as arguments, and by returning data either using the Return statement or by using ByRef arguments?

If the answers to these questions are yes, then the code is a good candidate for a procedure within your program.

In the Ocean Tours program developed in this chapter, four event handlers are required: 1) Selected Index Change: This event handler is executed when the user selects an island location from a combo box; 2) Find Cost Button: This event handler is executed when the user clicks the btnFindCost Button object; 3) Clear Button: This event handler is executed when the user clicks the btnClear Button object; 4) frmTours Load Event: This event handler is executed when the Windows Form object is loaded.

Within each event handler, the Event Planning Document is used to identify the tasks that must be accomplished. As each of the tasks is identified, you should ask the questions from above. If it appears the task should be accomplished in a procedure, the procedure must be included on the event planning document.

EVENT PLANNING DOCUMENT

You will recall that the event planning document consists of a table that specifies an object in the user interface that will cause an event, the action taken by the user to trigger the event, and the event processing that must occur. The event planning document for the program in this chapter must specify two forms and the events that occur for objects on each form. In addition, the tasks that must be accomplished for each event must be identified and a decision made on whether that task will be accomplished in a Sub or Function procedure. The Event Planning Document for the Ocean Tours Trip Selection program is shown in Figure 8-52 and Figure 8-53.

EVENT PLANNING DOCUMENT

Program Name: Ocean Tours Trip Selection	Developer: Corinne Hoisington	Object: SplashScreen1	Date: June 22, 2012
OBJECT	**EVENT TRIGGER**	**EVENT PROCESSING**	
SplashScreen1_Load	Load	An opening splash screen opens with the company name, version number, and year	

FIGURE 8-52

EVENT PLANNING DOCUMENT

Program Name: Ocean Tours Trip Selection	Developer: Corinne Hoisington	Object: frmTours	Date: June 22, 2012
OBJECT	**EVENT TRIGGER**	**EVENT PROCESSING**	
cboIsland_SelectedIndexChanged	Select Index	Assign island choice selection to an Integer SUB (Aruba(), Jamaica(), KeyWest()): Based on the island selection, display a list of the available tours on the island. Change Visible property for all objects on the form to True Clear the labels that provide trip information Set the focus on the number in party text box	
ArubaTours()	Sub procedure call	Display list of available tours (deep sea fishing, kayaking, scuba, and snorkeling) in list box	
JamaicaTours()	Sub procedure call	Display list of available tours (glass bottom boat, parasailing, snorkeling) in list box	
KeyWestTours()	Sub procedure call	Display list of available tours (deep sea fishing, glass bottom boat, scuba, snorkeling) in list box	

FIGURE 8-53 (continues)

Program Name: Ocean Tours Trip Selection	Developer: Corinne Hoisington	Object: frmTours	Date: June 22, 2012
OBJECT	**EVENT TRIGGER**	**EVENT PROCESSING**	

btnFindCost	Click	SUB (ValidateNumberInParty): Validate the value in the number in party text box is valid
		FUNCTION (ValidateTourSelection): Ensure the user has selected a tour in the list box
		If the number in party is valid and a tour is selected:
		    Convert number in party to an integer
		    Set month to selected month +1
		    If the month is greater than zero
		        Change selected island index to integer
		            FUNCTION(ArubaFindCosts,
		                JamaicaFindCost, KeyWestFindCost):
		                Calculate cost based on island choice
		        Display tour, cost, and length
		    Else display error message	

ValidateNumberInParty()	Function procedure call	Set Boolean indicator to False
		Convert number in party to integer
		If conversion valid
		    If number >0 and <100
		        Set Boolean indicator to True for valid number
		If conversion not valid
		    Catch format, overflow, and system exceptions
		    Display error message boxes
		    Place focus in number in party text box
		    Clear number in party text box
		Return Boolean indicator	

ValidateTourSelection()	Function procedure call	Convert tour selection index to integer
		If conversion successful
		    Place selected item string in ByRef variable
		    Set Boolean validity indicator to True
		Else Display error message box
		    Set Boolean validity indicator to False
		Return ocean tour selected index integer	

ArubaFindCost()	Function procedure call	If tour selected is deep sea fishing
		    Set cost to Aruba deep sea cost for one person
		    Set length to Aruba deep sea length
		If tour selected is kayaking
		    Set cost to Aruba kayak for one person
		    Set length to Aruba kayak
		If tour selected is scuba
		    Set cost to Aruba scuba for one person
		    Set length to Aruba scuba
		If tour selected is snorkel
		    Set cost to Aruba snorkel for one person
		    Set length to Aruba snorkel
		Calculate cost of trip: cost * number in party
		Return cost of trip	

FIGURE 8-53 (continues)

Program Name: Ocean Tours Trip Selection	Developer: Corinne Hoisington	Object: frmTours	Date: June 22, 2012
OBJECT	**EVENT TRIGGER**	**EVENT PROCESSING**	

JamaicaFindCost()	Function procedure call	If tour selected is glass bottom boat
		    Set cost to Jamaica glass bottom boat cost for one person
		    Set length to Jamaica glass bottom length
		If tour selected is parasail
		    Set cost to Jamaica parasail for one person
		    Set length to Jamaica parasail
		If tour selected is snorkel
		    Set cost to Jamaica snorkel for one person
		    Set length to Jamaica snorkel
		Calculate cost of trip: cost * number in party
		Return cost of trip	

KeyWestFindCost()	Function procedure call	If tour selected is deep sea fishing
		    Set cost to Key West deep sea cost for one person
		    Set length to Key West deep sea length
		If tour selected is glass bottom boat
		    Set cost to Key West glass bottom boat for one person
		    Set length to Key West glass bottom
		If tour selected is scuba
		    Set cost to Key West scuba for one person
		    Set length to Key West scuba
		If tour selected is snorkel
		    Set cost to Key West snorkel for one person
		    Set length to Key West snorkel
		Calculate cost of trip: cost * number in party
		Return cost of trip	

btnClear	Click	Set Select Item cbo text to "Select Island Location" Clear text boxes, list, and labels Hide all objects except Select Island cbo	
frmTours_Load	Load	Set sleeping period to 5000 milliseconds	

FIGURE 8-53 (continued)

DESIGN AND CODE THE PROGRAM

After identifying the events and tasks within the events, you are ready to create the program. As you have learned, creating the program means designing the user interface and then entering Visual Basic statements to accomplish the tasks specified on the event planning document. As you enter the code, you also will implement the logic to carry out the required processing.

Guided Program Development

To design the user interface for the Ocean Tours program and enter the code required to process each event in the program, complete the following steps:

NOTE TO THE LEARNER

As you will recall, in the following activity, you should complete the tasks within the specified steps. Each of the tasks is accompanied by a Hint Screen. The purpose of the Hint Screen is to indicate where in the Visual Studio window you should perform the activity; it also serves as a reminder of the method you should use to create the user interface or enter code. If you need further help completing the step, refer to the figure number identified by the term ref: in the step.

Guided Program Development

1

▶ **Create a New Windows Project** Open Visual Studio
using the Start button on the Windows taskbar and the
All Programs submenu. Close the Start page. Click the New
Project button on the Standard toolbar. Begin a Windows
Application project and title the project OceanTours.
Name the Form object frmTours.vb.

▶ **Add a New Item to the Project** Click Project on the
menu bar and then click Add New Item on the Project
menu *(ref: Figure 8-5)*.

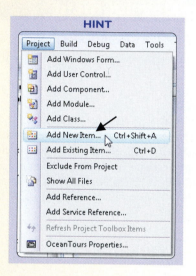

▶ **Select Splash Screen as the New Item** Select the
Splash Screen Template. Click the Add button
(ref: Figure 8-6).

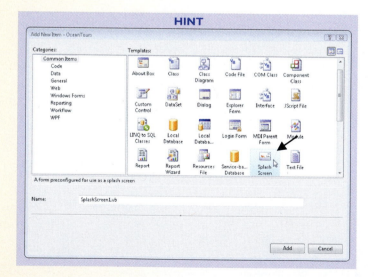

Guided Program Development (continued)

▶ **Select the Generic Splash Screen**
When the generic splash screen opens,
click the left side of the screen to select
it *(ref: Figure 8-8)*.

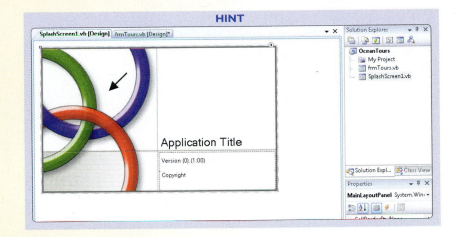

▶ **Prepare to Set the Contents of the
Splash Screen** Right-click the application
name OceanTours in Solution Explorer, and
then click Properties on the shortcut menu
to open the Project Designer window *(ref:
Figure 8-9)*.

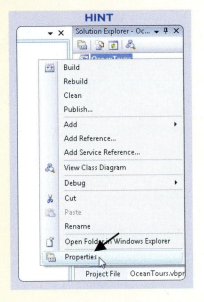

(continues)

Guided Program Development (continued)

▶ **Set the Splash Screen** On the Application tab, click the Splash screen list arrow to change the setting of (None) to SplashScreen1 *(ref: Figure 8-10)*.

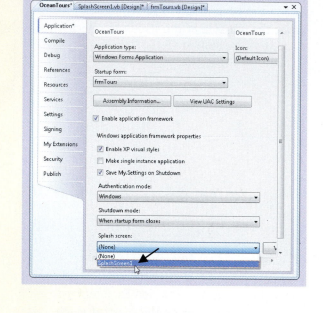

▶ **Add Text to the Splash Screen** To change the text of the splash screen, click the Assembly Information button in the Project Designer window *(ref: Figure 8-11)*.

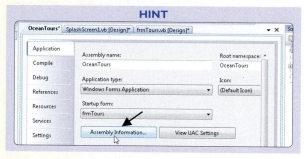

▶ **Set the Assembly Information** In the Assembly Information dialog box, change the title to `Ocean Tours` and change the copyright to the current year *(ref: Figure 8-12)*. Click the OK button to close the dialog box. Close the properties window. The information on the Splash Screen form does not change. The changes appear when the application is executed.

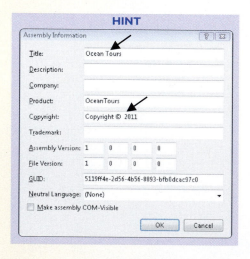

Guided Program Development *(continued)*

▶ **Change the Background Image** To customize the picture, click the background on the left side of the splash screen and select the BackgroundImage property in the Properties window. Click the ellipsis button *(ref: Figure 8-13)*.

▶ **Select the Project Resource File** The Select Resource dialog box opens. Click the Project resource file option button, if necessary, and ensure the Resources.resx file is selected.

▶ **Select an Image File** Click Import and select the graphic image ocean.jpg. You can download and save the ocean image used in the Ocean Tours application from scsite/vb2008/ch8/images. Click the OK button in the Select Resource dialog box.

(continues)

Guided Program Development (continued)

The splash screen is
designed (Figure 8-54).

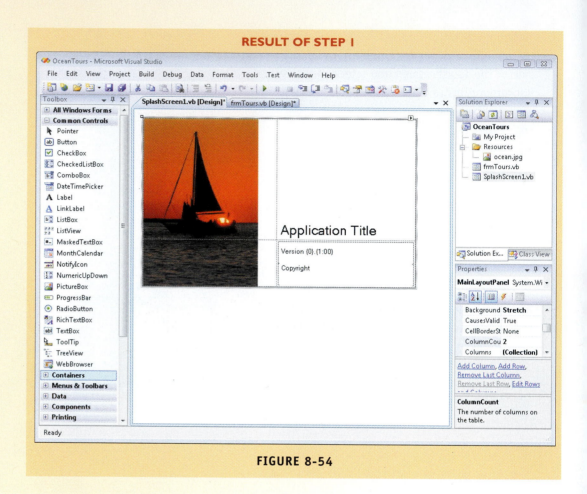

FIGURE 8-54

2

▶ **Title the Form Object** With the Windows Form object selected, change its Text property to
`Information on Available Tours`.

▶ **Add a Background Image** With the Windows Form object selected, click the ellipsis button for
the BackgroundImage property. Select the ocean image in the Select Resource dialog box. Click
the OK button in the Select Resource dialog box.

▶ **Resize the Windows Form Object** Resize the Windows Form object to (574,374) to view the
entire image.

Guided Program Development (continued)

▶ **Add a Panel Object** Drag a Panel object in the
Containers category from the Toolbox to the portion of
the Window object not covered by the image. Resize the
Panel object so it covers the white space where no image
displays.

▶ **Change Panel Object's BackColor to Transparent**
In the BackColor property for the Panel object, click the
BackColor property arrow, click the Web tab if necessary,
and then click Transparent on the Web palette. Making
the panel transparent allows all the objects placed on
the Windows Form object to be visible but allows you to
center and align objects within the Panel object instead
of the entire Windows Form object.

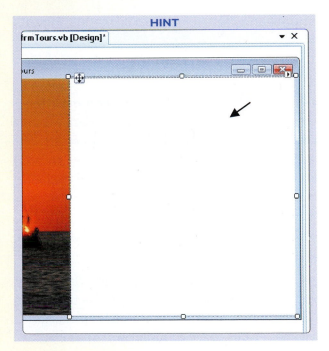

(continues)

Guided Program Development (continued)

▶ **Add a Label and a ComboBox Object** Add a Label object on the right side of the Form object. Change the Text property to `Ocean Tours Information`. Name the Label `lblTitle`. Change the font property to Verdana, Bold, 16pt. Change the BackColor property of the Label object to Dark Orange in the Web palette. The location of the Label object can be (10,18). Add a ComboBox object under the Label object. The location is (91,51). Name the ComboBox object `cboIsland`. Change the Text property to `Select Island Location:`. Resize the ComboBox object to see all the text *(ref: Figure 8-18)*. Change the font size to 11pt.

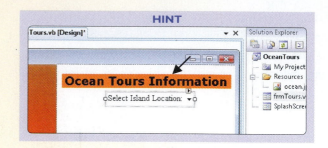

▶ **Add the Terms in the Items Property** Enter the following terms in the Items property of the ComboBox object: `Aruba`, `Jamaica`, and `Key West` on separate lines *(ref: Figure 8-21)*.

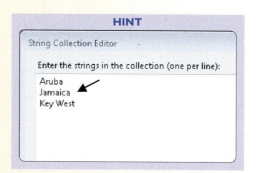

▶ **Add a Label Object** Drag a Label object from the Visual Basic Toolbox to the Form object. Place the Label object at location (87,89) within the Panel object. Change the Text property to `Number in Party:`. Name the Label object `lblParty`. Change the font size to 11pt.

▶ **Add a TextBox Object for the Number in Party** Drag a TextBox object from the Visual Basic Toolbox to the Panel object on the Windows Form object. Place the TextBox object at location (225,86). Resize the TextBox object to fit the length of approximately two numbers. Name the TextBox object `txtNumberInParty`. Change the font size to 11pt.

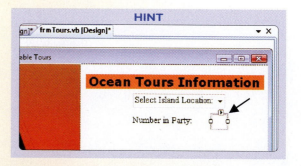

Guided Program Development *(continued)*

▶ **Add the Select Ocean Tour Label Object** Drag a Label object
from the Visual Basic Toolbox to the Windows Form object. The location is (108,23). Change the Text property to `Select Ocean`
`Tour:`. Name the Label Object `lblSelect`. Change the font size
to 11pt.

▶ **Add the Tours ListBox Object** Drag a ListBox object from the
Visual Basic Toolbox to the Windows Form object. The location is
(110,143). Name the ListBox `lstTours`. Change the font size
to 11pt.

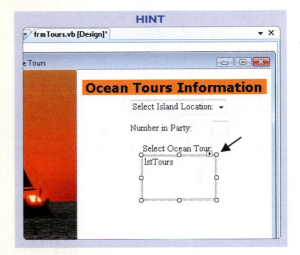

▶ **Add the Find Cost Button Object** Drag a Button object from the
Visual Basic Toolbox to the Windows Form object. The location is
(23,230). Name the Button Object `btnFindCost` and change the
Text property to `Find Cost of Tour`. Resize the button until the
Text is visible.

(continues)

Guided Program Development (continued)

▶ **Add the Clear Button Object** Drag a Button object from the Visual Basic Toolbox to the Windows Form object. The location is (178,230). Name the Button Object `btnClear` and change the Text property to `Clear Form`.

▶ **Add a Label Object for the Tour Type** Drag a Label object from the Visual Basic Toolbox to the Windows Form object. The location is (106,274). Name the Label object `lblTourType`. Enter 10 X's for the Text property.

▶ **Add a Label Object for the Cost** Drag a Label object from the Visual Basic Toolbox to the Windows Form object. The location is (106,293). Name this Label object `lblCost`. Enter 10 X's for the Text property.

▶ **Add a Label Object for the Tour Length** Drag a Label object from the Visual Basic Toolbox to the Windows Form object. The location is (106,312). Name this Label object `lblLength`. Enter 10 X's for the Text property.

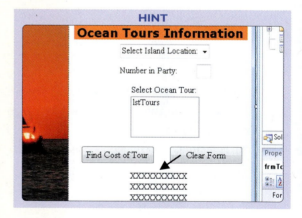

Guided Program Development (continued)

▶ **Change the Font** Select all the objects on the form except lblTitle and change the font to Times New Roman, size 11pt. Resize any objects required so that the text is visible. Resize both buttons to (129,31).

▶ **Set the Visible Properties** Change the Visible property to False for the following objects: lblParty, txtNumberInParty, lblSelect, lstTours, lblMonth, ~~cboMonth~~, btnFindCost, btnClear, lblTourType, and lblCost. These objects are not displayed until the tour is selected.

▶ **Set the Accept Button** Click the background of the Windows Form object on its title bar and change the AcceptButton property to the Button object btnFindCost.

▶ **Set the Cancel Button** Click the background of the Windows Form object on its title bar and change the CancelButton property to the Button object btnClear.

The Form object frmTours is designed (Figure 8-55).

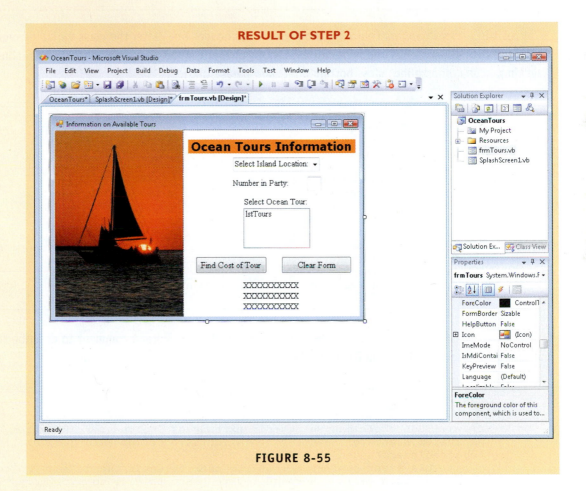

RESULT OF STEP 2

FIGURE 8-55

(continues)

Guided Program Development *(continued)*

3

▶ **Code the Comments** Double-click the cboIsland ComboBox object on the frmTours.vb [Design] tab to open the code editing window and create the cboIsland_SelectedIndexChanged Event Handler. Close the Toolbox. Click before the first word in Public Class frmTours, and then press the ENTER key to create a blank line. Insert the first four standard comments. Insert the Option Strict On command following the comments to turn on strict type checking.

HINT

```
1 ' Program Name: Ocean Tours Trip Selection
2 ' Author:       Corinne Hoisington
3 ' Date:         June 22, 2012
4 ' Purpose:      The Ocean Tours Trip Selection application determines the
5 '               ocean tours available and calculates the cost of the tour.
6
7 Option Strict On
```

▶ **Enter the Class Variables** Following the Public Class header line, enter the class variables required for the program. These class variables are: a) The hours for the length of the tours; b) The types of tours available (deep sea fishing, kayaking, scuba, snorkeling, glass bottom boat, and parasailing).

HINT

```
 9 Public Class frmTours
10
11     ' Class variables
12     Private _intTwoHours As Integer = 2
13     Private _intThreeHours As Integer = 3
14     Private _intFourHours As Integer = 4
15     Private _intEightHours As Integer = 8
16     Private _strDeepSeaFishing As String = "Deep Sea Fishing"
17     Private _strKayaking As String = "Kayaking"
18     Private _strScuba As String = "Scuba"
19     Private _strSnorkeling As String = "Snorkeling"
20     Private _strGlassBottomBoat As String = "Glass Bottom Boat"
21     Private _strParasailing As String = "Parasailing"
```

▶ **Comment the cboIsland_SelectedIndexChanged Event Handler** Enter a comment to describe the purpose of the cboIsland_SelectedIndexChanged Event Handler.

HINT

```
22
23     Private Sub cboIsland_SelectedIndexChanged(ByVal sender As System.Object, ByVal e ↙
        As System.EventArgs) Handles cboIsland.SelectedIndexChanged, cboIsland. ↙
        SelectedIndexChanged
24         ' This event handler allows the user to enter the island choice
25         ' and then calls subprocedures to place the island activities in the list.
26
```

Guided Program Development *(continued)*

▶ **Code the Sub Procedure Calls to Place the Appropriate Tours in the List Box** When the user selects an island in the cboIsland ComboBox object, the SelectedIndexChanged event is triggered. In that event handler, the island choice as indicated by the selected index must be changed to an integer. Then, based on that integer, the appropriate Sub procedure is called to place the correct tours in the lstTours list box. Write the code to obtain the selected index integer, clear the lstTours ListBox object of any previous entries, and then call the appropriate Sub procedure *(ref: Figure 8-30)*.

HINT

```
27          Dim intIslandChoice As Integer
28
29          intIslandChoice = Me.cboIsland.SelectedIndex
30          Me.lstTours.Items.Clear()
31          Select Case intIslandChoice
32              Case 0
33                  ArubaTours()
34              Case 1
35                  JamaicaTours()
36              Case 2
37                  KeyWestTours()
38          End Select
```

▶ **Set the Visibility and Focus** After the user selects the island location from the ComboBox object and the event handler calls the Sub procedures to load the ListBox object with the correct tours, the objects on the Windows Form object must become visible. In addition, the Label objects for the type of tour, the cost of the tour, and the length of the tour must be cleared of the X's placed in them during design. Finally, the focus should be set on the txtNumberInParty TextBox object. Enter the code to complete this processing.

HINT

```
39          ' Make items visible in the window
40          Me.lblParty.Visible = True
41          Me.txtNumberInParty.Visible = True
42          Me.lblSelect.Visible = True
43          Me.lstTours.Visible = True
44          Me.btnFindCost.Visible = True
45          Me.btnClear.Visible = True
46          Me.lblTourType.Visible = True
47          Me.lblCost.Visible = True
48          Me.lblLength.Visible = True
49          ' Clear the labels
50          Me.lblTourType.Text = ""
51          Me.lblCost.Text = ""
52          Me.lblLength.Text = ""
53          ' Set focus on number in party text box
54          Me.txtNumberInParty.Focus()
55
56      End Sub
```

(continues)

Guided Program Development (continued)

▶ **Code the Sub Procedures for Aruba Tour Options** After the first event handler is completed, the Sub procedures called by the event handler should be written. The event handler that handles the cboIsland_SelectedIndexChanged event calls three Sub procedures. Code the first referenced Sub procedure, which is called ArubaTours. To do so, click below the End Sub statement for the event handler, press the ENTER key to insert a blank line, and then write the Sub procedure declaration. It begins with the word Private, followed by the word Sub, and then the name of the Sub procedure. Press the ENTER key, write a comment that explains the purpose of the Sub procedure, and then write the statements that put the Aruba tours in the lstTours ListBox object *(ref: Figure 8-31)*.

HINT

```
58      Private Sub ArubaTours()
59          ' This procedure fills in the possible ocean tours for Aruba
60          Me.lstTours.Items.Add(_strDeepSeaFishing)
61          Me.lstTours.Items.Add(_strKayaking)
62          Me.lstTours.Items.Add(_strScuba)
63          Me.lstTours.Items.Add(_strSnorkeling)
64
65      End Sub
66
```

▶ **Code the Sub Procedures for the Jamaica and Key West Tour Options** In a similar manner, write the code for the Jamaica and Key West Sub procedures that place the appropriate tour names in the lstTours ListBox object.

HINT

```
67      Private Sub JamaicaTours()
68          'This procedure fills in the possible ocean tours for Jamaica
69          Me.lstTours.Items.Add(_strGlassBottomBoat)
70          Me.lstTours.Items.Add(_strParasailing)
71          Me.lstTours.Items.Add(_strSnorkeling)
72
73      End Sub
74
75      Private Sub KeyWestTours()
76          'This procedure fills in the possible ocean tours for Key West
77          Me.lstTours.Items.Add(_strDeepSeaFishing)
78          Me.lstTours.Items.Add(_strGlassBottomBoat)
79          Me.lstTours.Items.Add(_strScuba)
80          Me.lstTours.Items.Add(_strSnorkeling)
81
82      End Sub
```

Guided Program Development *(continued)*

▶ **Initialize the btnFindCost_Click Event and Write the Event Handler Variables** Click the Form1.vb [Design] tab and then double-click the Find Cost of Tour button to create the event handler for the button click event. The first step is to write a comment describing the purpose of the event handler. Then, code the variable declarations for the variables required in the event handler. These variables include: a) Integer variables for the group size, tour choice, month, and island choice; b) Boolean variables to indicate the validity of number in the party and the tour selection; c) A string variable to contain the name of the selected tour; d) A decimal variable to contain the total cost of the selected tour. Write the code to create and initialize these variables.

HINT

```
83
84       Private Sub btnFindCost_Click(ByVal sender As System.Object, ByVal e As System.        ↙
         EventArgs) Handles btnFindCost.Click
85            ' This button event handler determines the cost of the ocean
86            ' tour and displays the tour, the cost, and the length
87
88         Dim intGroupSize As Integer
89         Dim blnNumberInPartyIsValid As Boolean = False
90         Dim blnTourIsSelected As Boolean = False
91         Dim intTourChoice As Integer
92         Dim strSelectedTour As String = ""
93         Dim intIslandChoice As Integer
94         Dim intLengthOfTour As Integer = 0
95         Dim decTotalCost As Decimal
96
```

▶ **Validate the User Input** The next steps are to call two Function procedures, the first of which verifies the value entered in the txtNumberInParty TextBox object is valid, and the second of which verifies a tour was selected. Write the two Function calls for these Function procedures. The ValidateNumberInParty Function procedure returns a Boolean value indicating whether the number entered is valid (True) or not valid (False). The ValidateTourSelection Function procedure returns the number of the tour selected by the user when a tour has been selected. It also sets a Boolean value in the blnTourIsSelected Boolean variable to indicate if a tour has been selected (true) or not selected (False). This value is set because the blnTourIsSelected variable is passed to the Function procedure ByRef.

HINT

```
97          ' Call a function to ensure the number of people in the party is valid
98          blnNumberInPartyIsValid = ValidateNumberInParty()
99          ' Call a function to ensure a tour was selected
100         intTourChoice = ValidateTourSelection(blnTourIsSelected, strSelectedTour)
```

(continues)

Guided Program Development *(continued)*

▶ **Code the Rest of the btnFindCost Click Event** Upon return from the procedure calls, the Find Cost click event handler must determine if both the number of people in a party is valid and that a tour was selected. If both are true, the Text property of the txtNumberInParty TextBox is converted to an Integer value named intGroupSize. The Function procedures are passed three variables that are needed in the Function procedure. The variables intTourChoice and intGroupSize are passed by value because the values are not changed in the Function procedures. The variable intLengthOfTour is passed by reference because the value is changed in the Function procedures. The value returned from the Function procedures as the total cost of the tour is assigned to the variable decTotalCost. After the Function procedures are called, the event handler displays the information for tour chosen, cost, and length of tour. Write the code to implement this processing.

HINT

```
101              ' If number of people and the tour selection are valid, calculate the cost
102          If (blnNumberInPartyIsValid And blnTourIsSelected) Then
103              intGroupSize = Convert.ToInt32(Me.txtNumberInParty.Text)
104              intIslandChoice = Me.cboIsland.SelectedIndex
105              Select Case intIslandChoice
106                  Case 0
107                      decTotalCost = ArubaFindCost(intTourChoice, _
108                                                   intGroupSize, intLengthOfTour)
109                  Case 1
110                      decTotalCost = JamaicaFindCost(intTourChoice, _
111                                                   intGroupSize, intLengthOfTour)
112                  Case 2
113                      decTotalCost = KeyWestFindCost(intTourChoice, _
114                                                   intGroupSize, intLengthOfTour)
115              End Select
116              ' Display the cost of the ocean tour
117              Me.lblTourType.Text = "Tour: " & strSelectedTour
118              Me.lblCost.Text = "Cost: " & decTotalCost.ToString("C")
119              Me.lblLength.Text = "Length: " & intLengthOfTour.ToString() & " hours"
120          End If
121
122      End Sub
```

Guided Program Development *(continued)*

▶ **Code the ValidateNumberInParty Function Procedure** The next step is to code the ValidateNumberInParty Function procedure. Click below the btnFindCost_Click event handler and enter the Function procedure declaration. The Function procedure returns a Boolean value that indicates whether the number the user entered is valid. The value must be an integer value that is greater than 0 and less than 100. A Try-Catch block is used for the conversion to an integer operation to catch any invalid data the user entered. Multiple Catch blocks are used to catch specific exceptions. If an exception occurs, the error message is displayed in a message box, the focus is placed on the txtNumberInParty TextBox object, and the value in the TextBox object is cleared. Write the code for this Function procedure *(ref: Figure 8-52)*.

HINT

```vb
124     Private Function ValidateNumberInParty() As Boolean
125         ' This procedure validates the value entered for the number in party
126
127         Dim intPartyNumber As Integer
128         Dim blnValidityCheck As Boolean = False
129         Dim strNumberInPartyErrorMessage As String = _
130             "Please enter the number of people in your party (1-99)"
131         Dim strMessageBoxTitle As String = "Error"
132
133         Try
134             intPartyNumber = Convert.ToInt32(Me.txtNumberInParty.Text)
135             If intPartyNumber > 0 And intPartyNumber < 100 Then
136                 blnValidityCheck = True
137             Else
138                 MessageBox.Show(strNumberInPartyErrorMessage, _
139                     strMessageBoxTitle)
140                 Me.txtNumberInParty.Focus()
141                 Me.txtNumberInParty.Clear()
142             End If
143         Catch Exception As FormatException
144             MessageBox.Show(strNumberInPartyErrorMessage, _
145                 strMessageBoxTitle)
146             Me.txtNumberInParty.Focus()
147             Me.txtNumberInParty.Clear()
148         Catch Exception As OverflowException
149             MessageBox.Show(strNumberInPartyErrorMessage, _
150                 strMessageBoxTitle)
151             Me.txtNumberInParty.Focus()
152             Me.txtNumberInParty.Clear()
153         Catch Exception As SystemException
154             MessageBox.Show(strNumberInPartyErrorMessage, _
155                 strMessageBoxTitle)
156             Me.txtNumberInParty.Focus()
157             Me.txtNumberInParty.Clear()
158         End Try
159
160         Return blnValidityCheck
161
162     End Function
```

(continues)

Guided Program Development (continued)

▶ **Code the ValidateTourSelection Function Procedure** Click below the ValidateNumberInParty function and enter the ValidateTourSelection procedure declaration. The ValidateTourSelection Function procedure ensures the user selected a tour from the lstTours ListBox object and then returns an integer value for the list selection to the calling procedure. To determine if a tour was selected, the procedure uses a Try-Catch block to convert the selected index value to an integer. If the conversion is successful, a choice was made and the choice is returned. In addition, a Boolean variable in the calling procedure is set to True because the variable was passed ByRef. If the selected index is not converted, the user did not make a choice. A error message box is displayed and the Boolean variable is set to False. One Catch block is used because the only error using the ListBox object is if the user does not select a tour.

HINT

```
164     Private Function ValidateTourSelection(ByRef blnTour As Boolean, _
165         ByRef strTour As String) As Integer
166         ' This function ensures the user selected a tour
167
168         Dim intOceanTour As Integer
169         Try
170             intOceanTour = Convert.ToInt32(Me.lstTours.SelectedIndex)
171             strTour = Me.lstTours.SelectedItem.ToString()
172             blnTour = True
173         Catch Exception As SystemException
174             ' Detects if tour not selected
175             MessageBox.Show("Select an Ocean Tour", "Error")
176             blnTour = False
177         End Try
178         Return intOceanTour
179
180     End Function
181
```

Guided Program Development *(continued)*

▶ **Code the ArubaFindCost Function Procedures to Find the Cost of an Aruba Island Tour** Click below the
ValidateTourSelection Function procedure and enter the ArubaFindCost Function procedure declaration. The purpose of the
ArubaFindCost Function procedure is to determine the cost for an Aruba tour. Three variables are passed to the function.
Two are passed ByVal: the tour selection, and the group size. Tour length is passed ByRef. The ArubaFindCost Function pro-
cedure uses the tour selection and group size to determine the cost for the tour based on published rates (see Figure 8-51
on page 596). It also changes the values in the tour length field for use in the calling procedure. Write the code for the
ArubaFindCost Function procedure.

HINT

```
182      Private Function ArubaFindCost(ByVal intTourSelection As Integer, _
183       ByVal intGroupSize As Integer, ByRef intTourLength As Integer) As Decimal
184          ' This function calculates the cost of the tours to Aruba
185
186          Dim decTourCost As Decimal
187          Dim decFinalCost As Decimal
188          Dim decArubaDeepSeaCost As Decimal = 199D
189          Dim decArubaKayakCost As Decimal = 89D
190          Dim decArubaScubaCost As Decimal = 119D
191          Dim decArubaSnorkelCost As Decimal = 89D
192
193          Select Case intTourSelection
194              Case 0
195                  decTourCost = decArubaDeepSeaCost
196                  intTourLength = _intEightHours
197              Case 1
198                  decTourCost = decArubaKayakCost
199                  intTourLength = _intTwoHours
200              Case 2
201                  decTourCost = decArubaScubaCost
202                  intTourLength = _intThreeHours
203              Case 3
204                  decTourCost = decArubaSnorkelCost
205                  intTourLength = _intFourHours
206          End Select
207          decFinalCost = decTourCost * intGroupSize
208          Return decFinalCost
209
210      End Function
```

(continues)

Guided Program Development (continued)

▶ **Code the JamaicaFindCost Function Procedure to Find the Cost of a Jamaica Island Tour** Click below the ArubaFindCost Function procedure and enter the JamaicaFindCost Function procedure declaration. The purpose of the JamaicaFindCost Function procedure is to determine the cost for a Jamaica tour. It uses the same three passed variables as the ArubaFindCost Function procedure. It also uses similar logic and returns the same values. Write the code for the JamaicaFindCost Function procedure.

HINT

```
212        Private Function JamaicaFindCost(ByVal intTourSelection As Integer, _
213        ByVal intGroupSize As Integer, ByRef intTourLength As Integer) As Decimal
214            ' This function calculates the cost of the tours to Jamaica
215
216            Dim decTourCost As Decimal
217            Dim decFinalCost As Decimal
218            Dim decJamaicaGlassBottomCost As Decimal = 39D
219            Dim decJamaicaParasailCost As Decimal = 119D
220            Dim decJamaicaSnorkelCost As Decimal = 59D
221
222            Select Case intTourSelection
223                Case 0
224                    decTourCost = decJamaicaGlassBottomCost
225                    intTourLength = _intTwoHours
226                Case 1
227                    decTourCost = decJamaicaParasailCost
228                    intTourLength = _intTwoHours
229                Case 2
230                    decTourCost = decJamaicaSnorkelCost
231                    intTourLength = _intThreeHours
232            End Select
233            decFinalCost = decTourCost * intGroupSize
234            Return decFinalCost
235
236        End Function
```

Guided Program Development *(continued)*

▶ **Code the KeyWestFindCost Function Procedure to Find the Cost of a Key West Island Tour** Click below the JamaicaFindCost Function procedure and enter the KeyWestFindCost Function procedure declaration. The purpose of the KeyWestFindCost Function procedure is to determine the cost for a Key West tour. It uses the same three passed variables as the JamaicaFindCost Function procedure. It also uses similar logic and returns the same values. Write the code for the KeyWestFindCost Function procedure.

HINT

```
238        Private Function KeyWestFindCost(ByVal intTourSelection As Integer, _
239         ByVal intGroupSize As Integer, ByRef intTourLength As Integer) As Decimal
240            ' This function calculates the cost of the tours to Key West
241
242            Dim decTourCost As Decimal
243            Dim decFinalCost As Decimal
244            Dim decKeyWestDeepSeaCost As Decimal = 89D
245            Dim decKeyWestGlassBottomCost As Decimal = 29D
246            Dim decKeyWestScubaCost As Decimal = 119D
247            Dim decKeyWestSnorkelCost As Decimal = 59D
248
249            Select Case intTourSelection
250                Case 0
251                    decTourCost = decKeyWestDeepSeaCost
252                    intTourLength = _intFourHours
253                Case 1
254                    decTourCost = decKeyWestGlassBottomCost
255                    intTourLength = _intTwoHours
256                Case 2
257                    decTourCost = decKeyWestScubaCost
258                    intTourLength = _intThreeHours
259                Case 3
260                    decTourCost = decKeyWestSnorkelCost
261                    intTourLength = _intThreeHours
262            End Select
263            decFinalCost = decTourCost * intGroupSize
264            Return decFinalCost
265
266        End Function
```

(continues)

Guided Program Development (continued)

▶ **Code the Clear Button Click Event** After the Function procedures that are called from the btnFindCost click event handler have been coded, the next step is to write the code for the Clear Button click event handler. This event handler must reset the Windows Form object and objects on the form so it is displayed the same as when the program starts. This includes resetting the message in the cboIsland ComboBox object, clearing the number in party text box and the tours list box, blanking the labels that display the results, and removing all the objects except the cboIsland ComboBox object from view. Display the design window and then double-click the btnClear object to open the btnClear click event handler. Write the code for the event handler.

HINT

```
268    Private Sub btnClear_Click(ByVal sender As System.Object, ByVal e As System.
       EventArgs) Handles btnClear.Click
269        ' This event handler clears the form and resets the form for
270        ' reuse when the user clicks the Clear button.
271
272        Me.cboIsland.Text = "Select Island Location"
273        Me.txtNumberInParty.Clear()
274        Me.lstTours.Items.Clear()
275        Me.lblTourType.Text = ""
276        Me.lblCost.Text = ""
277        Me.lblLength.Text = ""
278        Me.lblParty.Visible = False
279        Me.txtNumberInParty.Visible = False
280        Me.lblSelect.Visible = False
281        Me.lstTours.Visible = False
282        Me.btnFindCost.Visible = False
283        Me.btnClear.Visible = False
284        Me.lblTourType.Visible = False
285        Me.lblCost.Visible = False
286        Me.lblLength.Visible = False
287
288    End Sub
```

Guided Program Development *(continued)*

▶ **Code the frmTours_Load Event** The last bit of code to write for the Ocean Tours program is the event handler for the frmTours load event. You will recall that when the application begins execution, a splash screen opens first. To display the splash screen longer than by default, you must add a sleep timer. Return to the frmTour.vb [Design] window and double-click the Windows Form object. Assuming you want the splash screen to be displayed for 5 seconds, code the statement to delay program execution for 5000 milliseconds *(ref: Figure 8-16)*.

HINT

```
290    Private Sub frmTours_Load(ByVal sender As System.Object, ByVal e As System.    ↙
       EventArgs) Handles MyBase.Load
291        ' Hold the splash screen for 5 seconds
292
293        Threading.Thread.Sleep(5000)
294
295    End Sub
```

Code Listing

The complete code for the sample program is shown in Figure 8-56.

```
1  ' Program Name:  Ocean Tours Trip Selection
2  ' Author:        Corinne Hoisington
3  ' Date:          June 22, 2012
4  ' Purpose:       The Ocean Tours Trip Selection application determines the
5  '                ocean tours available and calculates the cost of the tour.
6
7  Option Strict On
8
9  Public Class frmTours
10
11     ' Class variables
12     Private _intTwoHours As Integer = 2
13     Private _intThreeHours As Integer = 3
14     Private _intFourHours As Integer = 4
15     Private _intEightHours As Integer = 8
16     Private _strDeepSeaFishing As String = "Deep Sea Fishing"
17     Private _strKayaking As String = "Kayaking"
18     Private _strScuba As String = "Scuba"
19     Private _strSnorkeling As String = "Snorkeling"
20     Private _strGlassBottomBoat As String = "Glass Bottom Boat"
21     Private _strParasailing As String = "Parasailing"
22
23     Private Sub cboIsland_SelectedIndexChanged(ByVal sender As System.Object, ByVal e ↵
       As System.EventArgs) Handles cboIsland.SelectedIndexChanged
24         ' This event handler allows the user to enter the island choice
25         ' and then calls subprocedures to place the island activities in the list.
26
27         Dim intIslandChoice As Integer
28
29         intIslandChoice = Me.cboIsland.SelectedIndex
30         Me.lstTours.Items.Clear()
31         Select Case intIslandChoice
32             Case 0
33                 ArubaTours()
34             Case 1
35                 JamaicaTours()
36             Case 2
37                 KeyWestTours()
38         End Select
39         ' Make items visible in the window
40         Me.lblParty.Visible = True
41         Me.txtNumberInParty.Visible = True
42         Me.lblSelect.Visible = True
43         Me.lstTours.Visible = True
44         Me.btnFindCost.Visible = True
45         Me.btnClear.Visible = True
46         Me.lblTourType.Visible = True
47         Me.lblCost.Visible = True
```

FIGURE 8-56 (continues)

```vbnet
48          Me.lblLength.Visible = True
49          ' Clear the labels
50          Me.lblTourType.Text = ""
51          Me.lblCost.Text = ""
52          Me.lblLength.Text = ""
53          ' Set focus on number in party text box
54          Me.txtNumberInParty.Focus()
55
56      End Sub
57
58      Private Sub ArubaTours()
59          ' This procedure fills in the possible ocean tours for Aruba
60          Me.lstTours.Items.Add(_strDeepSeaFishing)
61          Me.lstTours.Items.Add(_strKayaking)
62          Me.lstTours.Items.Add(_strScuba)
63          Me.lstTours.Items.Add(_strSnorkeling)
64
65      End Sub
66
67      Private Sub JamaicaTours()
68          'This procedure fills in the possible ocean tours for Jamaica
69          Me.lstTours.Items.Add(_strGlassBottomBoat)
70          Me.lstTours.Items.Add(_strParasailing)
71          Me.lstTours.Items.Add(_strSnorkeling)
72
73      End Sub
74
75      Private Sub KeyWestTours()
76          'This procedure fills in the possible ocean tours for Key West
77          Me.lstTours.Items.Add(_strDeepSeaFishing)
78          Me.lstTours.Items.Add(_strGlassBottomBoat)
79          Me.lstTours.Items.Add(_strScuba)
80          Me.lstTours.Items.Add(_strSnorkeling)
81
82      End Sub
83
84      Private Sub btnFindCost_Click(ByVal sender As System.Object, ByVal e As System.↙
        EventArgs) Handles btnFindCost.Click
85          ' This button event handler determines the cost of the ocean
86          ' tour and displays the tour, the cost, and the length
87
88          Dim intGroupSize As Integer
89          Dim blnNumberInPartyIsValid As Boolean = False
90          Dim blnTourIsSelected As Boolean = False
91          Dim intTourChoice As Integer
92          Dim strSelectedTour As String = ""
93          Dim intIslandChoice As Integer
94          Dim intLengthOfTour As Integer = 0
95          Dim decTotalCost As Decimal
96
97          ' Call a function to ensure the number of people in the party is valid
98          blnNumberInPartyIsValid = ValidateNumberInParty()
99          ' Call a function to ensure a tour was selected
100         intTourChoice = ValidateTourSelection(blnTourIsSelected, strSelectedTour)
101         ' If number of people and the tour selection are valid, calculate the cost
```

FIGURE 8-56 (continues)

```
102          If (blnNumberInPartyIsValid And blnTourIsSelected) Then
103              intGroupSize = Convert.ToInt32(Me.txtNumberInParty.Text)
104              intIslandChoice = Me.cboIsland.SelectedIndex
105              Select Case intIslandChoice
106                  Case 0
107                      decTotalCost = ArubaFindCost(intTourChoice, _
108                                          intGroupSize, intLengthOfTour)
109                  Case 1
110                      decTotalCost = JamaicaFindCost(intTourChoice, _
111                                          intGroupSize, intLengthOfTour)
112                  Case 2
113                      decTotalCost = KeyWestFindCost(intTourChoice, _
114                                          intGroupSize, intLengthOfTour)
115              End Select
116              ' Display the cost of the ocean tour
117              Me.lblTourType.Text = "Tour: " & strSelectedTour
118              Me.lblCost.Text = "Cost: " & decTotalCost.ToString("C")
119              Me.lblLength.Text = "Length: " & intLengthOfTour.ToString() & " hours"
120          End If
121
122      End Sub
123
124      Private Function ValidateNumberInParty() As Boolean
125          ' This procedure validates the value entered for the number in party
126
127          Dim intPartyNumber As Integer
128          Dim blnValidityCheck As Boolean = False
129          Dim strNumberInPartyErrorMessage As String = _
130              "Please enter the number of people in your party (1-99)"
131          Dim strMessageBoxTitle As String = "Error"
132
133          Try
134              intPartyNumber = Convert.ToInt32(Me.txtNumberInParty.Text)
135              If intPartyNumber > 0 And intPartyNumber < 100 Then
136                  blnValidityCheck = True
137              Else
138                  MessageBox.Show(strNumberInPartyErrorMessage, _
139                      strMessageBoxTitle)
140                  Me.txtNumberInParty.Focus()
141                  Me.txtNumberInParty.Clear()
142              End If
143          Catch Exception As FormatException
144              MessageBox.Show(strNumberInPartyErrorMessage, _
145                      strMessageBoxTitle)
146              Me.txtNumberInParty.Focus()
147              Me.txtNumberInParty.Clear()
148          Catch Exception As OverflowException
149              MessageBox.Show(strNumberInPartyErrorMessage, _
150                      strMessageBoxTitle)
151              Me.txtNumberInParty.Focus()
152              Me.txtNumberInParty.Clear()
153          Catch Exception As SystemException
154              MessageBox.Show(strNumberInPartyErrorMessage, _
155                      strMessageBoxTitle)
156              Me.txtNumberInParty.Focus()
157              Me.txtNumberInParty.Clear()
158          End Try
159
160          Return blnValidityCheck
161
162      End Function
```

FIGURE 8-56 (continues)

```
163
164        Private Function ValidateTourSelection(ByRef blnTour As Boolean, _
165            ByRef strTour As String) As Integer
166            ' This function ensures the user selected a tour
167
168            Dim intOceanTour As Integer
169            Try
170                intOceanTour = Convert.ToInt32(Me.lstTours.SelectedIndex)
171                strTour = Me.lstTours.SelectedItem.ToString()
172                blnTour = True
173            Catch Exception As SystemException
174                ' Detects if tour not selected
175                MessageBox.Show("Select an Ocean Tour", "Error")
176                blnTour = False
177            End Try
178            Return intOceanTour
179
180        End Function
181
182        Private Function ArubaFindCost(ByVal intTourSelection As Integer, _
183         ByVal intGroupSize As Integer, ByRef intTourLength As Integer) As Decimal
184            ' This function calculates the cost of the tours to Aruba
185
186            Dim decTourCost As Decimal
187            Dim decFinalCost As Decimal
188            Dim decArubaDeepSeaCost As Decimal = 199D
189            Dim decArubaKayakCost As Decimal = 89D
190            Dim decArubaScubaCost As Decimal = 119D
191            Dim decArubaSnorkelCost As Decimal = 89D
192
193            Select Case intTourSelection
194                Case 0
195                    decTourCost = decArubaDeepSeaCost
196                    intTourLength = _intEightHours
197                Case 1
198                    decTourCost = decArubaKayakCost
199                    intTourLength = _intTwoHours
200                Case 2
201                    decTourCost = decArubaScubaCost
202                    intTourLength = _intThreeHours
203                Case 3
204                    decTourCost = decArubaSnorkelCost
205                    intTourLength = _intFourHours
206            End Select
207            decFinalCost = decTourCost * intGroupSize
208            Return decFinalCost
209
210        End Function
211
212        Private Function JamaicaFindCost(ByVal intTourSelection As Integer, _
213         ByVal intGroupSize As Integer, ByRef intTourLength As Integer) As Decimal
214            ' This function calculates the cost of the tours to Jamaica
215
216            Dim decTourCost As Decimal
217            Dim decFinalCost As Decimal
218            Dim decJamaicaGlassBottomCost As Decimal = 39D
219            Dim decJamaicaParasailCost As Decimal = 119D
220            Dim decJamaicaSnorkelCost As Decimal = 59D
```

FIGURE 8-56 (continues)

```
221
222          Select Case intTourSelection
223              Case 0
224                  decTourCost = decJamaicaGlassBottomCost
225                  intTourLength = _intTwoHours
226              Case 1
227                  decTourCost = decJamaicaParasailCost
228                  intTourLength = _intTwoHours
229              Case 2
230                  decTourCost = decJamaicaSnorkelCost
231                  intTourLength = _intThreeHours
232          End Select
233          decFinalCost = decTourCost * intGroupSize
234          Return decFinalCost
235
236      End Function
237
238      Private Function KeyWestFindCost(ByVal intTourSelection As Integer, _
239       ByVal intGroupSize As Integer, ByRef intTourLength As Integer) As Decimal
240          ' This function calculates the cost of the tours to Key West
241
242          Dim decTourCost As Decimal
243          Dim decFinalCost As Decimal
244          Dim decKeyWestDeepSeaCost As Decimal = 89D
245          Dim decKeyWestGlassBottomCost As Decimal = 29D
246          Dim decKeyWestScubaCost As Decimal = 119D
247          Dim decKeyWestSnorkelCost As Decimal = 59D
248
249          Select Case intTourSelection
250              Case 0
251                  decTourCost = decKeyWestDeepSeaCost
252                  intTourLength = _intFourHours
253              Case 1
254                  decTourCost = decKeyWestGlassBottomCost
255                  intTourLength = _intTwoHours
256              Case 2
257                  decTourCost = decKeyWestScubaCost
258                  intTourLength = _intThreeHours
259              Case 3
260                  decTourCost = decKeyWestSnorkelCost
261                  intTourLength = _intThreeHours
262          End Select
263          decFinalCost = decTourCost * intGroupSize
264          Return decFinalCost
265
266      End Function
267
268      Private Sub btnClear_Click(ByVal sender As System.Object, ByVal e As System.
         EventArgs) Handles btnClear.Click
269          ' This event handler clears the form and resets the form for
270          ' reuse when the user clicks the Clear button.
271
272          Me.cboIsland.Text = "Select Island Location"
273          Me.txtNumberInParty.Clear()
274          Me.lstTours.Items.Clear()
275          Me.lblTourType.Text = ""
276          Me.lblCost.Text = ""
277          Me.lblLength.Text = ""
278          Me.lblParty.Visible = False
279          Me.txtNumberInParty.Visible = False
```

FIGURE 8-56 (continues)

```
280            Me.lblSelect.Visible = False
281            Me.lstTours.Visible = False
282            Me.btnFindCost.Visible = False
283            Me.btnClear.Visible = False
284            Me.lblTourType.Visible = False
285            Me.lblCost.Visible = False
286            Me.lblLength.Visible = False
287
288        End Sub
289
290        Private Sub frmTours_Load(ByVal sender As System.Object, ByVal e As System.      ↙
           EventArgs) Handles MyBase.Load
291            ' Hold the splash screen for 5 seconds
292
293            Threading.Thread.Sleep(5000)
294
295        End Sub
296
297  End Class
298
```

FIGURE 8-56 (continued)

Summary

In this chapter you have learned to create applications using procedures. The items listed in the table in Figure 8-57 include all the new Visual Studio and Visual Basic skills you have learned in this chapter.

VISUAL BASIC SKILLS		
Skill	**Figure Number**	**Web Address for Video**
Examine the Ocean Tours chapter project application	Figure 8-2	scsite.com/vb2008/ch8/figure8-2
Add the generic splash screen	Figure 8-5	scsite.com/vb2008/ch8/figure8-5
Pause the splash screen	Figure 8-15	scsite.com/vb2008/ch8/figure8-15
Place a ComboBox object on a form	Figure 8-18	scsite.com/vb2008/ch8/figure8-18
Use Assignment statement to obtain SelectedIndex	Page 576	
Create a SelectedIndexChanged Event	Figure 8-26	scsite.com/vb2008/ch8/figure8-26
Code a Procedure Call and a Sub Procedure	Figure 8-28	
Pass an argument to a called procedure	Figure 8-33	
Pass an argument by value	Figure 8-34	
Passing an argument by reference	Figure 8-38	
Code a Function procedure	Figure 8-40	
Code a Try-Catch Block	Figure 8-44	

FIGURE 8-57

Learn It Online

Start your browser and visit scsite.com/vb2008/ch8. Follow the instructions in the exercises below.

1. **Chapter Reinforcement TF, MC, SA** Click one of the Chapter Reinforcement links for Multiple Choice, True/False, or Short Answer below the Learn It Online heading. Answer each question and submit to your instructor.

2. **Practice Test** Click the Practice Test link below Chapter 8. Answer each question, enter your first and last name at the bottom of the page, and then click the Grade Test button. When the graded practice test is displayed on your screen, submit the graded practice test to your instructor. Continue to take the practice test until you are satisfied with your score.

3. **Crossword Puzzle Challenge** Click the Crossword Puzzle Challenge link below the Learn It Online heading. Read the instructions, and then click the Continue button. Work the crossword puzzle. When you are finished, click the Submit button. When the crossword puzzle is redisplayed, submit it to your instructor.

Knowledge Check

1. Write the line of code that would hold frmSplashScreen for approximately three seconds.

2. What is the name of the property that allows you to place a graphic on the background of the Windows Form object?

3. What is the difference between passing by value and passing by reference?

4. What is the least number of arguments you can pass to a Sub procedure?

5. What is the section of code called that performs a specific task and does not return a value?

6. What is the section of code called that performs a specific task and does return a value?

7. What happens to the variables that were passed by value when you leave a Sub procedure?

8. Name the two types of procedures.

9. How many value(s) can a Function procedure return?

10. Write the Visual Basic statements that will declare a Sub procedure called VotingBooth that receives one variable called intCount. The variable intCount will be changed in the procedure. Write only the first and last lines of the Sub procedure.

11. What is the name of a variable that is passed to a procedure?

12. If you want a copy of a variable passed to a procedure, which way should you pass it?

13. You must have a return statement in a Function procedure. True or false?

14. When multiple arguments are passed to a procedure, the order is not important. True or false?

(continues)

Knowledge Check

(continued)

15. Which type of exception would be detected if you use the conversion command Convert.ToInt32 to convert a non-integer value?

16. Which type of exception would be detected in the code in Figure 8-58?

```
Dim intMultiple As Integer
Dim intProduct As Integer

intMultiple = 2000000000
intProduct = intMultiple ^ 10
```

FIGURE 8-58

17. Which type of exception would be detected if you used the conversion command Convert.ToDecimal to try to convert a letter of the alphabet?

18. If you use multiple Catch blocks in a Try-Catch block of code, how do you determine the order of the Catch blocks?

19. If you include an optional Finally block, it should follow directly after the Try block. True or false?

20. When deciding whether a set of programming steps should be placed in a Sub procedure or a Function procedure, what are three questions you should ask?

Debugging Exercises

1. Fix the code in Figure 8-59:

```
Private Sub btnItemPrice_Click(ByVal sender As System.Object, ByVal e As
System.EventArgs) Handles btnItemPrice.Click
        Dim decPrice As Decimal
        Dim decTax As Decimal

        decPrice = Convert.ToDecimal(Me.txtCost.Text)
        TaxCost(decPrice, decTax)
        Me.lblDisplay.Text("The tax amount is " & decTax.ToString())
End Sub

Private Sub TaxCost(price, tax)
        tax = price * .06
End Sub
```

FIGURE 8-59

Debugging Exercises

2. Fix the code in Figure 8-60:

```
Private Sub btnBaseball_Click(ByVal sender As System.Object, ByVal e As
System.EventArgs) Handles btnBaseball.Click
        Dim decHits As Decimal = 200
        Dim decTimesAtBat As Decimal = 498
        Dim decBattingAverage As Decimal

        decBattingAverage=FindRunsBattedIn(decHits, decTimesAtBat)
        Me.lblHits.Text("The batting average is " & _
            decBattingAverage.ToString())
End Sub


Private Function BattingAverage(byVal decHitsCount as Decimal, byVal
decNumberAtBat as Decimal)
        Dim decAverageAtBat as Decimal
        decAverage = decHitsCount / decNumberAtBat
        Return decAverage
End Sub
```

FIGURE 8-60

3. Fix the code in Figure 8-61:

```
Private Sub btnInventory_Click(ByVal sender As System.Object, ByVal e As
System.EventArgs) Handles btnInventory.Click
        Dim intItemNumber As Integer
        Dim decCost As Decimal
        decCost = Convert.ToDecimal(Me.txtPrice.Text)
        DisplayProducts(intItemNumber, decCost)
End Sub


Private Sub DisplayProducts(ByRef decCostValue As Decimal, ByRef intItem As
Integer)
        Me.lblItemDisplay.Text("Item: " & intItem & " Costs: " & _
            decCostValue.ToString())
End Sub
```

FIGURE 8-61

Analysis Exercises

1. What is the output of the code in Figure 8-62?

```
Private Sub btnSevens_Click(ByVal sender As System.Object, ByVal e As
System.EventArgs) Handles btnSevens.Click
    Dim intCount As Integer
    For intCount = 1 To 7
        CalculateSevens(intCount)
    Next
End Sub


Private Sub CalculateSevens(ByVal intCountValue As Integer)
    Dim intResult As Integer
    intResult = intCountValue ^ 3
    Me.lstAnswer.Items.Add(intResult.ToString())
End Sub
```

FIGURE 8-62

2. What is the output of the code in Figure 8-63?

```
Private Sub btnJoke_Click(ByVal sender As System.Object, ByVal e As
System.EventArgs) Handles btnJoke.Click
    DisplayRiddle()
    DisplayAnswer()
End Sub


Private Sub DisplayAnswer()
    Me.lblAnswer.Text = "Because it has a spring in it"
End Sub


Sub DisplayRiddle()
    Me.lblRiddle.Text = "Why should you carry a watch when crossing a
desert?"
End Sub
```

FIGURE 8-63

Analysis Exercises

3. What is the output of the code in Figure 8-64?

```
Private Sub btnBedrock_Click(ByVal sender As System.Object, ByVal e As
System.EventArgs) Handles btnBedrock.Click
        Dim strFullName As String = "Fred Flintstone"
        Dim strSecondName As String = "Barney Rubble"

        CountLength(strFullName, strSecondName)
        Me.lblEnd.Text = "My favorite was " & strSecondName
End Sub


Private Sub CountLength(ByVal strFullName As String, ByRef strSecondName As
String)
        Me.lblFirst.Text = "The first name has " & strFullName.Length & "
letters."
        Me.lblSecond.Text = "The second name has " & strSecondName.Length &
" letters."
        strSecondName = "Dino"
End Sub
```

FIGURE 8-64

(continues)

Analysis Exercises

4. What is the output of the code ini Figure 8-65?

```
Private Sub btnStrangeFacts_Click(ByVal sender As System.Object, ByVal e As
System.EventArgs) Handles btnStrangeFacts.Click
        Dim intHangerLength As Integer = 44
        Dim intMen As Integer = 2000
        Dim intWomen As Integer = 7000
        Dim intValue As Integer

        intValue = Talk(intMen, intWomen)
        Me.lblResponse.Text = "The couple would say " & intValue & " words a
day"
        AverageHanger(intHangerLength)
    End Sub


Private Sub AverageHanger(ByVal intHanger As Integer)
        Me.lblPhrase.Text = "The average length of a coat hanger when
straightened is " & intHanger & " inches."
    End Sub


    Function Talk(ByVal intM As Integer, ByVal intW As Integer) As Integer
        Me.lblPhrase1.Text = "The average man says " & intM & " words a day"
        Me.lblPhrase2.Text = "The average woman says " & intW & " words a
day"
        Return intM + intW
    End Function
```

FIGURE 8-65

5. A program contains the procedure declaration shown in Figure 8-66. Write the Function call statement that assigns the returned value to intCubed and passes a variable named intValue.

```
Private Function Cube(ByVal intNum As Integer) As Integer
      Return intNum * intNum * intNum
End Function
```

FIGURE 8-66

6. Write a statement that passes the variable intBase to a procedure and assigns the return value to a variable named intSolution. Write the code that would declare a variable named intPopulation as an Integer. Allow the user to enter the population of their city in a TextBox object named txtCityPopulation. Convert the value to an integer within a Try block. Write a Try-Catch block with an overflow Catch block first, a format exception Catch block second, and a generic exception last. Each Catch block should display a message box explaining the problem with the user's input.

7. Write the code for a Sub procedure named FindHeight that will calculate the total number of inches based on the height of a person when given the feet and inches. For example, if a person is 5'10", they are 70 inches tall. Display the result in a message box.

Case Programming Assignments

Complete one or more of the following case programming assignments. Submit the program and materials you create to your instructor. The level of difficulty is indicated for each case programming assignment.

● = Easiest
●● = Intermediate
●●● = Challenging

1 ● COMPARE FUEL COST

Design a Windows application and write the code that will execute according to the program requirements in Figure 8-67 and the Use Case definition in Figure 8-68. Before writing the code, create an event planning document for each event in the program. The completed Windows Form object and other objects in the user interface are shown in Figure 8-69 and Figure 8-70.

REQUIREMENTS DOCUMENT

Date submitted: September 24, 2012

Application title: Compare the cost of fuel for a sports utility vehicle and a compact car.

Purpose: This Windows application compares the cost of fuel for a sports utility vehicle with the cost of fuel for a compact car over the life of the vehicles.

Program Procedures: From a Windows application, a consumer can enter the miles per gallon of two vehicles, the cost of gas, the mileage driven each year, and the years that they intend to own the car to calculate total fuel cost for the life of each vehicle. The difference in the cost is also displayed.

Algorithms, Processing, and Conditions:
1. The consumer enters the present fuel price, miles traveled per year, the years of vehicle ownership (years 1–10), and the miles per gallon of a sports utility vehicle and compact car.
2. The same Function procedure will be called twice to calculate the total fuel cost over the life for each car.
3. Display the total cost over the life of the vehicle for each of the two cars and the difference between the two values.

Notes and Restrictions:
1. Validate input by using Try-Catch blocks in separate procedures as needed.

Comments:
1. The picture shown in the application should be selected from a picture available on the Web.
2. The program opens with a splash screen that is displayed for approximately five seconds.

FIGURE 8-67

(continues)

Case Programming Assignments

Compare Fuel Cost (continued)

USE CASE DEFINITION

1. The user views the opening splash screen for approximately five seconds.
2. The user enters the present fuel cost, miles traveled per year, the number of years the vehicle will be owned, and the miles per gallon for their favorite sports utility vehicle and compact car.
3. The user clicks the Compare Life of Vehicle Cost button and the fuel cost per car is displayed.
4. User views the difference in costs between the two vehicles.

FIGURE 8-68

Compute Gas
Mileage

Version 1.00

Copyright © 2012

FIGURE 8-69

FIGURE 8-70

Case Programming Assignments

2
ALUMINUM RECYCLING CAMPAIGN

Design a Windows application and write the code that will execute according to the program requirements in Figure 8-71 and the Use Case definition in Figure 8-72. Before writing the code, create an event planning document for each event in the program. The completed Windows Form object and other objects in the user interface are shown in Figure 8-73, Figure 8-74, and Figure 8-75.

REQUIREMENTS DOCUMENT

Date submitted: August 11, 2012

Application title: Aluminum Recycling Campaign Windows Application

Purpose: This Windows application calculates the number of cans that must be collected to make the recycling campaign's goal amount and finds the amount earned based on the number of cans collected.

Program Procedures: From a Windows application, the user can select whether to calculate the number of cans needed to earn a target amount or find the amount earned based on the number of cans collected.

Algorithms, Processing, and Conditions:
1. The user first selects whether they want to compute their collection goal or the amount earned by aluminum collection.
2. After the user selects the recycling option, display the necessary objects based on the selected need. If the user selects the collection goal, request the target amount they hope to earn. If the user chooses to find the amount earned based on their aluminum collection, request the number of cans collected.
3. Based on approximately 24 aluminum cans in a pound and the cost paid for one pound of aluminum cans is currently $0.75, calculate the number of cans to collect to make the goal or calculate the amount of money the collected cans are worth in separate procedures.
4. Display the result for the calculation on the form.

Notes and Restrictions:
1. A Clear Form button should clear the Form.
2. The data the user enters should be validated in Try–Catch blocks in separate procedures as needed.

Comments:
1. The pictures shown in the table should be selected from pictures available on the Web.
2. The application should begin with a splash screen that holds for approximately 4 seconds.

FIGURE 8-71

(continues)

Case Programming Assignments

Aluminum Recycling Campaign (continued)

USE CASE DEFINITION

1. User views opening splash screen for four seconds.
2. User selects whether to calculate the number of cans that need to be collected to make the recycling campaign's goal amount or find the amount earned based on the number of cans collected.
3. User provides the following information: the target amount they hope to earn or the amount earned based on the number of cans collected.
4. User clicks the Find Target Amount of Cans button or Find Amount Earned button and result is displayed.
5. User clicks the Clear Form button to clear the responses.

FIGURE 8-72

FIGURE 8-73

FIGURE 8-74

FIGURE 8-75

Case Programming Assignments

3

BASEBALL TICKET SALES

Design a Windows application and write the code that will execute according to the program requirements and the chart in Figure 8-76, the Program Requirements in Figure 8-77, and the Use Case definition in Figure 8-78. Before writing the code, create an event planning document for each event in the program. The completed Windows Form object and other objects in the user interface are shown in Figure 8-79 and Figure 8-80.

Type of Ticket	Seat Type	Cost
Season Tickets	Box Seats	$2500
	Lower Deck	$1500
Single Game Tickets	Box Seats	$55
	Lower Deck	$35
	Upper Deck	$25
	Standing Room Only	$15

FIGURE 8-76

(continues)

Case Programming Assignments

Baseball Ticket Sales (continued)

REQUIREMENTS DOCUMENT

Date submitted:　　June 21, 2012

Application title:　　Baseball Ticket Sales Application

Purpose:　　This Windows application computes the cost of baseball tickets.

Program Procedures:　　From a Windows application, allow the user to select season or single-game baseball tickets and compute the cost of the tickets.

Algorithms, Processing, and Conditions:

1. The user is requested to select whether to purchase season or single-game tickets from a ComboBox object. The other objects are not visible until the user selects this option.
2. The user is requested to enter the number of tickets needed in a TextBox object.
3. The user is requested to select the type of seats from a ListBox object.
4. One of two Function procedures will be called for season or single-game tickets to compute and pass back the final cost of the tickets.

Notes and Restrictions:

1. A Clear Form button should clear the Form.
2. A Try-Catch block in separate procedures will validate the input.

Comments:

1. The picture should be selected from a picture available on the Web.
2. A splash screen begins this application.

FIGURE 8-77

Case Programming Assignments

USE CASE DEFINITION

1. User views opening splash screen for five seconds.
2. User selects whether to purchase season tickets or single-game tickets.
3. User enters the number of tickets needed and the type of seats based on whether they selected season or single-game tickets.
4. User clicks the Compute Ticket Cost button to display the final cost.
5. User clicks the Clear Form button to clear the responses.

FIGURE 8-78

FIGURE 8-79

FIGURE 8-80

Case Programming Assignments

4 ●●
FRACTIONS CALCULATOR

Design a Windows application and write the code that will execute according to the program requirements in Figure 8-81. Before designing the user interface, create a Use Case definition. Before writing the code, create an event planning document for each event in the program.

Bug: Divide By Zero Exception Only works with t not /

REQUIREMENTS DOCUMENT

Date submitted: October 19, 2012

Application title: Fractions Calculator — Addition, Subtraction, Multiplication, and Division

Purpose: This Windows application allows the user to enter two fractions with the choice of four operations: addition, subtraction, multiplication, or division.

Program Procedures: From a Windows form, the user will enter two fractions (a numerator and denominator for the first fraction and a numerator and denominator for the second fraction).

Algorithms, Processing, and Conditions:

1. The user first views a Windows Application that displays a title, a math graphic, and labels to enter information such as two numerators and two denominators for two fractions.
2. Four radio buttons will display the symbols for a basic calculator. $(+, -, *, /)$.
3. When the user enters the required data and selects the mathematical operation, a button displaying an equal sign can be selected to calculate the correct computation.
4. A Sub procedure should be called to handle the input and conversion of the four numbers entered.
5. Using Select Case statements, four Function procedures should be called based on the operation selected. Each Function procedure will calculate the correct operation and return the Decimal value to the calling procedure. The original procedure will print the result.

Notes and Restrictions:

1. The result should be calculated to the hundredths place.
2. The input values should be validated by a Try-Catch block.

Comments:

1. The picture shown should be selected from a picture available on the Web.
2. Do not allow division by zero. Catch this exception with a Try-Catch block.

FIGURE 8-81

Case Programming Assignments

5 •• HOTEL BILLING APPLICATION

Design a Windows application and write the code that will execute according to the program requirements in Figure 8-82. Before designing the user interface, create a Use Case definition. Before writing the code, create an event planning document for each event in the program.

REQUIREMENTS DOCUMENT

Date submitted: March 17, 2012

Application title: Hotel Billing Application for a Cancun Resort in Mexico

Purpose: This application allows the hotel clerk to calculate the hotel bill for a Cancun resort. The application will calculate the hotel cost and convert the bill into Mexican pesos or American dollars based on the customer's nationality.

Program Procedures: The hotel clerk can select the type of room, number of days, and whether the final bill should be figured in Mexican pesos or American dollars.

Algorithms, Processing, and Conditions:
1. The hotel clerk first views a Windows form that displays a hotel name, a picture of the hotel, a ComboBox object requesting the type of room: King Suite ($280), 2 Queen Beds Suite ($310), King Standard Room ($235), and 2 Queen Beds Standard Room ($255), the number of nights (TextBox object), and the currency type (Mexican pesos or American dollars).
2. After the clerk has entered the information needed, a Sub procedure displays the labels: Subtotal Billing Amount for Your Stay, Taxes for Your Stay, and Final Total.
3. Pass the cost of the type of room selected and the number of nights to a Sub procedure to calculate the subtotal of the room. Do not display the amount in this procedure.
4. Pass the subtotal and the currency type to a Function procedure. Determine the subtotal based on the type of currency (pesos or dollars). Pass that amount back to the calling method.
5. Another Function procedure should compute an 18.5% Mexican tax. Pass that value back to the calling method.
6. Pass the subtotal, tax, and final cost to a Sub procedure to print the results.

Notes and Restrictions:
1. The hotel is an American chain, so the billing will be in English.
2. The input values should be validated in a separate procedure by a Try-Catch block.

Comments:
1. The picture should be selected from pictures available on the Web.
2. The conversion calculation from dollars to pesos should be researched on the Internet.

FIGURE 8-82

Case Programming Assignments

6 ●●
CALCULATE YOUR COMMUTE

Design a Windows application and write the code that will execute according to the program requirements in Figure 8-83. Before designing the user interface, create a Use Case definition. Before writing the code, create an event planning document for each event in the program.

REQUIREMENTS DOCUMENT

Date submitted:	March 2, 2012
Application title:	Calculate your Commute Application
Purpose:	This Windows application computes the cost of a yearly commute based on car, train, or bus travel.
Program Procedures:	From a Windows application, the user selects how they commute to work, and also answers questions based on that commute to compute the cost of traveling to and from work for one year.

Algorithms, Processing, and Conditions:

1. The user first views a Windows application with a title and a ComboBox object requesting the way they commute — car, train, or bus. The other objects on the form are not visible at this time.
2. After the users select the mode of travel, the questions related to that type of travel are displayed immediately.
3. The following customized questions based on the user's choice are requested:
   Car: Daily round trip distance, days worked per month, miles per gallon of auto, cost per gallon of gas, monthly maintenance cost/insurance and monthly parking cost.
   Train: Round trip transit fare, days worked per month.
   Bus: Round trip transit fare, days worked per month.
4. After the values have been validated, calculate the cost of commuting for one year for the selected commuting choice.

Notes and Restrictions:

1. All values the user enters should be validated.

Comments:

1. The picture shown should be selected from a picture available on the Web.
2. A splash screen should open the application.

FIGURE 8-83

Case Programming Assignments

7 ●●●
BALANCE A CHECKBOOK

Create a requirements document and a Use Case Definition document, and then design a Windows application based on the following case project. Before writing the code, create an event planning document for each event in the program.

Your college wants you to write a Windows Application that students can use to balance their checkbooks. This program will be installed on all computers in the student union. The application should allow the user to enter a starting balance and indicate whether the account has a monthly interest rate. Validate the beginning balance to verify that the number is possible. Allow the user to enter checks, ATM cash withdrawals, and deposits. Also calculate the interest for one month and add the interest amount to the final balance. The user can make multiple debits and deposits and continue until indicating that they are finished making transactions. The interest for the final balance will be added to the last balance after the transactions are completed. Data validation is needed for all input. An opening splash screen will be displayed as well.

FIGURE 8-84

8 ●●●
BALANCE A CHECKBOOK ON A POCKET PC

Create a requirements document and a Use Case Definition document, and then design a mobile application based on the following case project. Before writing the code, create an event planning document for each event in the program.

Your college wants you to write a Smart Device Application that students can use to balance their checkbooks. This program will be installed on all college handheld devices. The application should allow the user to enter a starting balance and indicate whether the account has a monthly interest rate. Validate the beginning balance to verify that the number is possible. Allow the user to enter checks, ATM cash withdrawals, and deposits. Also calculate the interest for one month and add the interest amount to the final balance. The user can make multiple debits and deposits and continue until indicating that they are finished making transactions. The interest for the final balance will be added to the last balance after the transactions are completed. Data validation is needed for all input. An opening splash screen will be displayed as well.

FIGURE 8-85

Case Programming Assignments

9 ●●●
POPULATION ANALYSIS

Create a requirements document and a Use Case Definition document, and then design a Windows application based on the following case project. Before writing the code, create an event planning document for each event in the program.

The United States Census Bureau would like to you to create a Windows Application that will display the population demographic data for many countries across the world. The Census Bureau has provided the information in the following table.

Country	Last Census (2008) Population	Annual Rate of Population Change Expected	Life Expectancy	Annual Rate of Life Expectancy Change Expected
China	1,323,420,000	0.6%	72.3	0.00023%
France	64,473,140	0.4%	79.6	0.00021%
Mexico	106,535,000	1.6%	75.2	0.00015%
South Africa	47,850,700	−0.3%	43.3	0.00019%
United States	303,232,774	0.9%	77.7	0.00020%

Allow the user to enter a year in the next hundred years and select a country from the list of countries shown in the table. Gather the correct population and other statistics. Calculate the future population and life expectancy for the year entered. Validate all entries. An opening splash screen will be displayed as well.

FIGURE 8-86

CHAPTER NINE

Using Arrays and File Handling

OBJECTIVES

You will have mastered the material in this chapter when you can:

- ▶ Initialize an array
- ▶ Initialize an array with default values
- ▶ Access array elements using a loop
- ▶ Use ReDim to resize an array
- ▶ Determine the number of elements in an array using the Length command
- ▶ Use the For Each loop
- ▶ Initialize two-dimensional arrays
- ▶ Read a text file
- ▶ Write to a text file
- ▶ Calculate depreciation
- ▶ Use multiple Form objects
- ▶ Access variable objects on other forms

Introduction

You can use Visual Basic to create applications ranging from those for small home businesses to those for large international businesses. As programming applications grow in size, the role of organizing, storing, and retrieving large amounts of data becomes vital. This chapter introduces topics that allow you to develop applications that can keep data for later processing, including sorting, calculating, and displaying.

Chapter Project

In the sample chapter project, a small business named Light Span Computers requires a Windows application to compute the depreciation of their computers, computer components, office machinery, and company vehicles. **Depreciation** is an accounting term that describes the decline in value of a physical asset over a certain period of time. Most assets lose value due to use, aging, obsolescence, and impairment. Depreciation is an estimate of this declining value and is used for tax and other financial purposes.

Light Span repairs computers, and its inventory consists of computers, computer components, office equipment, and company vehicles. Each item is assigned a four-character identifying code. A table listing these items and associated codes is stored in a text file, which is a grouping of the data stored on a storage medium such as a USB drive.

When the Windows application for Light Span Computers starts, it opens the text file and fills the Select Inventory Item ComboBox object with the item numbers. Before calculating depreciation, the user selects an item and a depreciation method, as shown in Figure 9-1.

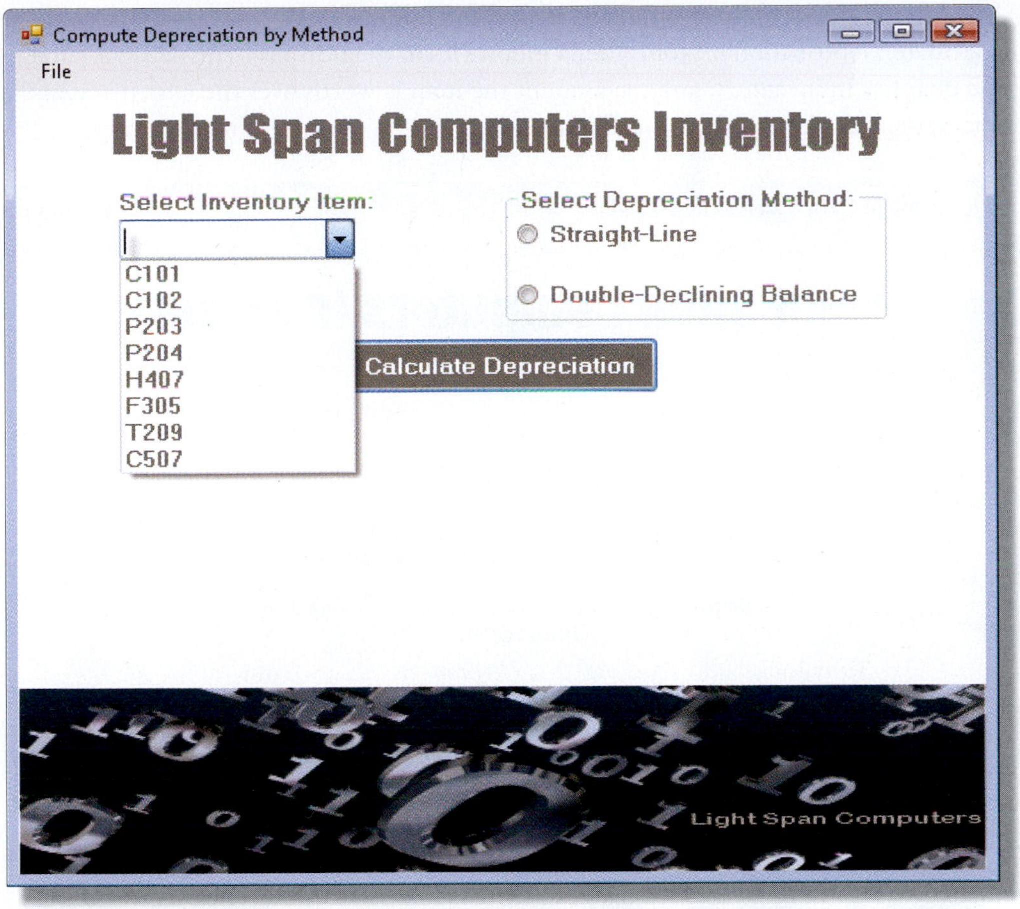

FIGURE 9-1

In Figure 9-1, the user clicks the combo box arrow to display the items in inventory. After selecting an item, the user can click a radio button to select either the Straight-Line or the Double-Declining Balance depreciation method.

In straight-line depreciation, the asset is depreciated the same amount each year for the life of the asset. In double-declining depreciation, the depreciation is accelerated.

After selecting an item number and method of depreciation, the user clicks the Calculate Depreciation button. The Windows form then displays the product name, the quantity in inventory, and the amount the item is worth over the next five years due to depreciation, as shown in Figure 9-2.

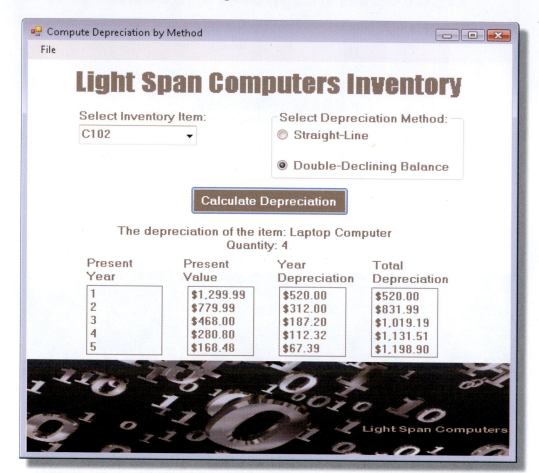

FIGURE 9-2

Light Span Computers purchased the items shown in Figure 9-3 in their first year of business.

Inventory Item	Item Number	Initial Cost	Quantity
Desktop Computer	C101	$ 699.99	12
Laptop Computer	C102	$ 1299.99	4
Laser Printer	P203	$ 299.99	6
Photocopier	P204	$ 3800.00	1
Pocket PC	H407	$ 229.99	9
Fax Machine	F305	$ 688.18	2
Delivery Van	T209	$22999.00	1
Company Car	C507	$18606.77	2

FIGURE 9-3

Each item in Figure 9-3 is depreciated each year for tax reasons. The Internal Revenue Service allows for depreciation deductions for five years because the average useful life of these types of items is five years. The items in table Figure 9-3 are stored in a text file named inventory.txt. Figure 9-4 shows this file in Notepad. The Windows application opens the inventory.txt text file and reads the information for use in the program.

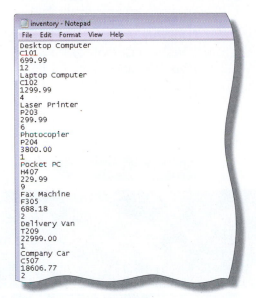

FIGURE 9-4

The Light Span Computers Depreciation Windows application also contains a File menu that displays the following menu items: Display Inventory, Clear, and Exit (Figure 9-5).

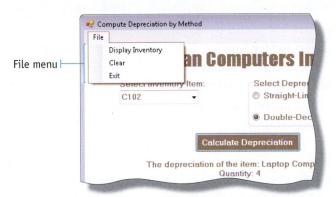

FIGURE 9-5

When the user clicks the Display Inventory menu item, the application opens a second Windows Form object that shows the items in inventory in sorted alphabetical order (Figure 9-6).

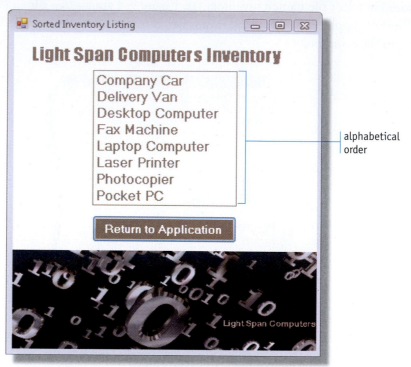

FIGURE 9-6

Introduction to Arrays

After completing Chapters 1-8 in this book, you know how to create the user interface for the chapter project, which involves ComboBox, Button, ListBox, Label, and RadioButton objects. The challenge in this chapter is in writing code to add data to the form efficiently and accurately. To do so, you must understand arrays and file handling. The next section provides background on arrays.

ARRAYS

Every application you have developed thus far involved a limited number of variables and data, but in professional programming projects, applications deal with much larger sets of data needing numerous variables. You have learned that data type variables can store only one value at a time. Therefore, you have not used data types that contain more than one memory location to store more than one value at a time. If you changed a variable's value, the previous value was erased because a typical variable can only store one value at a time. For example, if you wanted to create an application that recorded dinner reservations at a restaurant for named groups with different numbers of people in the group, you would need a unique variable name for each reservation, as shown in Figure 9-7 on the next page.

```
5              Dim intBakerReservation As Integer = 4
6              Dim intLopezReservation As Integer = 5
7              Dim intBuckReservation As Integer = 12
8              Dim intChanReservation As Integer = 2
9              Dim intTirrellReservation As Integer = 8
```

FIGURE 9-7

In a large restaurant, you would need to create hundreds of variables to hold hundreds of reservations each night. Having hundreds of variables just to record each night's reservations is impractical and difficult to manage. As you can see, a different kind of variable that can hold more than one value is required.

The solution to developing applications with larger amounts of data is to use an array. An **array** variable is simply a variable that can store more than one value. In fact, in Visual Basic an array can hold more than a million values. Each individual item in array that contains a value is called an **element**.

Arrays provide access to data by using a numeric **index**, or **subscript**, to identify each element in the array. Using an array, you can store a sequence of values of similar data type. For example, you can store six values of type Decimal without having to declare six different variables. Instead, each of the six values is stored in an individual element of the array, and you refer to each element according to its index within the array. The index used to reference a value in the first element within an array is zero. Each subsequent element is referenced by an increasing index value, as shown in Figure 9-8.

decShoeSize(0)	decShoeSize(1)	decShoeSize(2)	decShoeSize(3)	decShoeSize(4)	decShoeSize(5)
9.0	11.5	6.0	7.5	13.0	8.0

FIGURE 9-8

In Figure 9-8, an array named decShoeSize holds six shoe sizes. Each shoe size is stored in an array element, and each element is assigned a unique index. The first value (9.0) is stored in the element with the index of 0. The element is identified by the term, decShoeSize(0), pronounced "decShoeSize sub zero." The second shoe size (11.5) is stored in the second element of the array, which is referenced as decShoeSize(1). The same scheme is used for all elements in the array.

INITIALIZING AN ARRAY

To declare an array in a program, you must include an array declaration statement, which states the name of the array, how many items it can store, and what sort of data it can store. To initialize or declare an array, just as in declaring any other variable, you must reserve the amount of memory that will be needed to store the array. The syntax for declaring an array begins with the word Dim (Figure 9-9).

General Format: Declare an Array

```
Dim intReservations(300) as Integer
```

intReservations assigns the array name

300 is the index or subscript reserving the amount of memory needed – it is the highest numbered index

Integer determines the data type of the entire array

FIGURE 9-9

The statement in Figure 9-9 declares intReservations as an array of Integers that holds 301 elements. The first array element is intReservations(0), then intReservations(1), and so on to the last element in the array, intReservations(300). All arrays in Visual Basic 2008 are zero based, meaning that the index of the first element is zero; and the indexes increase sequentially by 1. You must specify the number of array elements by indicating the upper-bound index of the array. The upper-bound number specifies the index of the last element of the array. Setting the size of an array is called dimensioning the array.

If you know the values to be placed in each element in the array, you can declare an array by assigning values to each element, as shown in Figure 9-10.

```
13        Dim strNames() As String = {"Baker", "Lopez", "Buck", "Chan", "Tirrell"}
14        Dim intReservations() As Integer = {4, 5, 12, 2, 8}
```

FIGURE 9-10

The data to be placed in each element is contained within curly brackets. An array can be any data type. In Figure 9-10, the first array is a String data type and the second array is an Integer data type. strNames() is an array of String variables and contains five names, with Baker stored in strNames(0), Lopez in strNames(1), and so on. intReservations() is an array of Integer variables and contains five values, with 4 stored in intReservations(0), 5 in intReservations(1), and so on.

These two arrays are **parallel arrays**. Parallel arrays store related data in two or more arrays. The information for one reservation includes strNames(0) for the Baker reservation and the number of people associated with that reservation (4) is found in intReservations(0). The same subscript is used for the corresponding array elements. This is shown in Figure 9-11 and Figure 9-12, which illustrate the arrays created by the code in Figure 9-10.

strNames(0)	strNames(1)	strNames(2)	strNames(3)	
strNames(4)				
Baker	Lopez	Buck	Chan	Tirrell

FIGURE 9-11

intReservations(0)	intReservations(1)	intReservations(2)	intReservations(3)	intReservations(4)
4	5	12	2	8

FIGURE 9-12

Visual Basic determines the size of the array by counting the number of items within the curly brackets. In this case, each array has five elements, and each element has an index number ranging from 0 to 4. The upper-bound index is 4, which specifies the last element of the array. When a number is not used in the declaration statement to state the size of the array, the array is **implicitly sized**, meaning that the number of values is determined at execution. Instead of stating the size, you list the values stored in the array.

Another way to declare an array is to specify its upper-bound index and assign each item of an array one by one, as shown in Figure 9-13. Each sport is assigned to a different array element of the strAthlete() array.

HEADS UP

When declaring an implicitly sized array, do not place an upper-bound index in the parentheses following the array name in the array declaration. An error will occur if you place an upper-bound index in the declaration when the array is assigned elements in the array.

```
17          Dim strAthlete(5) As String
18
19          strAthlete(0) = "Football"
20          strAthlete(1) = "Soccer"
21          strAthlete(2) = "Lacrosse"
22          strAthlete(3) = "Baseball"
23          strAthlete(4) = "Tennis"
24          strAthlete(5) = "Hockey"
```

FIGURE 9-13

Initializing an Array with Default Values

When you initialize an array, if you do not assign values immediately, each element is assigned a default value. The table in Figure 9-14 shows the default value assigned to each data type.

Data Type	Default Value
All numeric data types	0
String data type	Null
Boolean data type	False

FIGURE 9-14

After the array has been initialized, specific values can be assigned to each element, replacing the default value for each item. You can assign explicit values to the first few elements of the array and allow the remaining elements of the array to be assigned to the default values automatically.

ACCESSING ARRAY ELEMENTS USING A LOOP

Because an array can contain multiple elements, in code you can use a loop to reference each element of an array. Loops can save valuable time when processing a large array because you don't have to write code for each array element. For example, if you were recording the lowest temperature for each day of the month of January to use in later calculations, the code in Figure 9-15 allows the user to enter all 31 temperatures.

```
26        Dim intDailyTempJanuary(31) As Integer
27        Dim strTemp As String
28        Dim intDays As Integer
29
30        For intDays = 0 To 30
31            strTemp = InputBox("Enter the lowest temperature on January " _
32                & intDays + 1, "Obtain Temperatures")
33            intDailyTempJanuary(intDays) = Convert.ToInt32(strTemp)
34        Next
```

FIGURE 9-15

The array intDailyTempJanuary can hold the low temperature for each of the 31 days in January by using the elements referenced by the subscripts of 0 to 30. The loop counts from 0 to 30 using the variable intDays. The first time through the loop, the temperature obtained in an InputBox is assigned to a string named strTemp. Then, the value in strTemp is converted to an integer and assigned to the element intDailyTempJanuary(0). On each subsequent pass through the loop, the temperature obtained is placed in the next element, moving from intDailyTempJanuary(1) to intDailyTempJanuary(2), and so on until the final value for January 31 is assigned to the array element intDailyTempJanuary(30).

By using a loop in this manner, the program can process items in a large array with a few simple lines.

Array Boundaries

The Visual Basic compiler determines if each subscript is within the boundaries set when you initialized the array. For example, if you initialize an array to contain 31 elements, but attempt to reference an element outside that boundary, as shown in Figure 9-16, an exception is produced when the code is executed.

```
37          Dim intDailyTempJanuary(30) As Integer
38          Dim strTemp As String
39          Dim intDays As Integer
40
41          For intDays = 0 To 31
42              strTemp = InputBox("Enter the lowest temperature on January " _
43                  & intDays + 1, "Obtain Temperatures")
44              intDailyTempJanuary(intDays) = Convert.ToInt32(strTemp)
45          Next
```

FIGURE 9-16

The exception occurs when the loop tries to reference an element with the subscript 31. This element does not exist because the array contains 31 elements with an upper-bound index of 30 (remember: an array's elements always are numbered beginning with zero). The exception created by the code in Figure 9-16 is an IndexOutOfRangeException (Figure 9-17). A Try-Catch statement can catch this exception, but it is best to stay within the array boundaries of zero and the upper-bound array subscript.

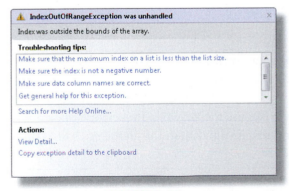

FIGURE 9-17

Upper-Bound Index Constant

HEADS UP

A subscript for an array cannot be less than the value 0.

An array can use a constant value representing the upper-bound index of the array. By using a constant, the size of several arrays can be specified quickly and, as you will learn in the next section, can be changed quickly. In Figure 9-18, the arrays strFirstNames() and strLastNames() are sized to hold 41 elements (indexes are from 0 to 40).

```
Const intUpperBound As Integer = 40
Dim strFirstNames(intUpperBound) As String
Dim strLastNames(intUpperBound) As String
```

FIGURE 9-18

Reinitializing an Array

Although you usually set the number of elements in an array when you declare it, you can alter the size of the array later in the code. Every array in Visual Basic is considered **dynamic**, which means that you can resize the array at run time. When you change the number of elements in an existing array, you redimension it. The **ReDim** statement assigns a new array size to the specified array variable. You use a ReDim statement to change the number of elements in an array. The code in Figure 9-19 reinitializes the strEmployees array.

```
Dim strEmployees(50) As String
' Later in the code
ReDim strEmployees(65)
```

FIGURE 9-19

HEADS UP

If you redimension an array to a smaller size and use the Preserve command, you still will lose the items between the original upper-bound array size and the new smaller upper-bound array size.

The strEmployees array originally is sized to hold 51 values, but is reinitialized later in the code to hold 66 values. When you use the ReDim statement, all the data contained in the array is lost when the array is redimensioned. If you want to preserve the existing data you can use the keyword **Preserve** as shown in Figure 9-20. Preserve resizes the array and retains the data in the elements from 0 through 50.

```
Dim strEmployees(50) As String
' Later in the code
ReDim Preserve strEmployees(65)
```

FIGURE 9-20

Using the Length Property

The Length property of an array contains the number of elements in an array. The code shown in Figure 9-21 displays 51 as the array size.

```
59          Dim strBranchOffices(50) As String
60
61          Me.lblArraySize.Text = "The array size is " & (strBranchOffices.Length)
```

FIGURE 9-21

You can use the Length property in a loop to determine the exact number of iterations needed to cycle through each element in the array. Using the Length property can prevent the program from throwing the IndexOutOfRange exception. In the code in Figure 9-22, the For loop uses the Length property to determine the number of iterations of the loop.

```
63          Dim intYear(99) As Integer
64          Dim intCount As Integer
65
66          ' Assigns the years from 2001 to 2100 to the elements in the table
67          For intCount = 0 To (intYear.Length - 1)
68              intYear(intCount) = 2001 + intCount
69          Next
```

FIGURE 9-22

In the code in Figure 9-22, intYear.Length is equal to 100 (elements 0 through 99), one more than the array's upper-bound index number. In the For loop, the loop count will run from zero through 99 (intYear.Length − 1), which means the loop will be executed 100 times, once for each element in the array.

Because an array can be resized at any time, the Length property is useful when you are unsure of an array's size.

Using Arrays

Arrays can be useful in many situations, such as when dealing with large amounts of data and finding totals and averages. For example, the code in Figure 9-23 computes the total yearly income and average yearly income for 10 employees in the warehouse department:

```
71      Dim intYearlySalary(9) As Integer
72      Dim intNumberOfEmployees As Integer
73      Dim intAdd As Integer
74      Dim intTotal As Integer
75
76      ' Allows the user to enter the 10 yearly salaries
77      For intNumberOfEmployees = 0 To (intYearlySalary.Length - 1)
78          intYearlySalary(intNumberOfEmployees) = _
79              InputBox("Enter Salary #" & intNumberOfEmployees + 1, _
80              "Warehouse Dept.")
81      Next
82
83      ' Finds the total amount of salaries entered
84      For intAdd = 0 To (intYearlySalary.Length - 1)
85          intTotal += intYearlySalary(intAdd)
86      Next
87
88      Me.lblDisplayTotalSalary.Text = intTotal.ToString("C2")
89      Me.lblDisplayAverageSalary.Text = _
90          (intTotal / intYearlySalary.Length).ToString("C2")
```

FIGURE 9-23

The reason the value accumulated in the intTotal variable is divided by the Length property is that the intTotalSalary array contains ten elements. To find the average, you add all the numbers and divide by the number of elements. The line of code that finds the average (line 89) is outside of the loop because the average should be determined once, not repeatedly within the loop.

In the chapter project, the Items property of the cboInventoryId ComboBox object must be filled with the inventory item numbers. The inventory item numbers are contained in the _strItemId array. The code in Figure 9-24 places the inventory item numbers in the Items property of the ComboBox object. The Length property of the _strItemId array is used to determine the number of iterations in the For loop.

```
43      ' The ComboBox object is filled with the Inventory IDs
44      For intFill = 0 To (_strItemId.Length - 1)
45          Me.cboInventoryId.Items.Add(_strItemId(intFill))
46      Next
```

FIGURE 9-24

On line 44, the For loop begins with the intFill variable containing the value 0, which references the first element in the _strItemId array. On each pass through the loop, the value in intFill is incremented by 1 so it references the next element in the array. The loop terminates when the value in intFill is greater than the length of the array minus 1. Recall that the length of the array counts from 1 but the subscript counts from 0. Therefore, the length of the array minus 1 references the last element in the array.

The results of the code in Figure 9-24 is shown in Figure 9-25.

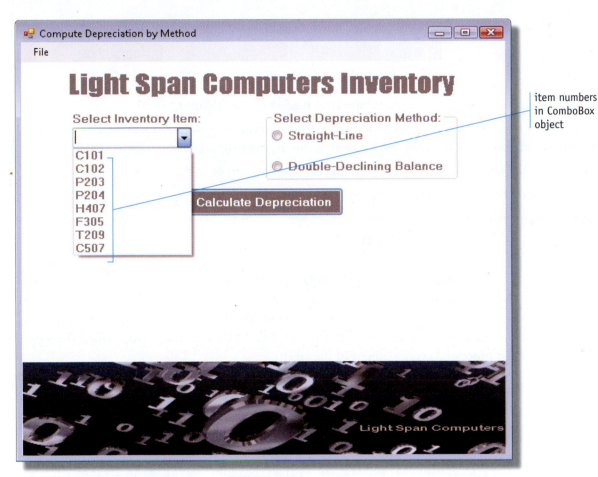

item numbers in ComboBox object

FIGURE 9-25

THE FOR EACH LOOP

Recall from earlier chapters that a loop repeats a process. A special loop designed specifically for arrays is called a **For Each** loop. The loop syntax is shown in Figure 9-26.

General Format: For Each

For Each *Control Variable Name* in *Array Name*

    ' Lines of Code

Next

For Each — This type of loop iterates through an array until the array reaches the last element.

Control Variable Name — This variable will contain each individual element of the array without a subscript as the loop is processed. During the first iteration of the loop, the first element in the array is assigned to the control variable.

Array Name( ) — The name of the array that the loop cycles through. The array must be initialized first.

Next — This statement continues the loop to its next iteration.

FIGURE 9-26

A For Each loop cycles through each element in the array until the end of the array is reached. In Figure 9-27, each element in the array is assigned to the variable strPioneer as the For Each loop is executed. The For Each loop does not require the program to keep track of the subscript for each element, and it stops when the loop has processed every element in the array.

Because each element in the array is assigned to the control variable, the elements and the variable must be the same data type. For example, in Figure 9-27, the array elements and the control variable are both Strings.

```
93      Private Sub btnHistory_Click(ByVal sender As System.Object, ByVal e As System.
        EventArgs) Handles btnHistory.Click
94
95          Dim strFamousComputerPioneers() As String = {"Pascal", _
96              "Babbage", "Ada", "Aiken", "Jobs"}
97          Dim strHeading As String = "Computer Pioneers:"
98          Dim strPioneer As String
99
100         Me.lstPioneers.Items.Add(strHeading)
101         Me.lstPioneers.Items.Add("")
102
103         For Each strPioneer In strFamousComputerPioneers
104             Me.lstPioneers.Items.Add(strPioneer)
105         Next
106
107     End Sub
```

FIGURE 9-27

When the loop is executed, the first element of the FamousComputerPioneers array is placed in the strPioneer variable and the body of the loop is executed. In the body of the loop, the value in strPioneer is added to the Items property of the lstPioneers ListBox object. On the second iteration of the loop, the second element of the array is placed in the strPioneer variable and the body of the loop is executed. This looping continues until all elements within the array have been processed.

After the loop processing is complete, the lstPioneers ListBox object displays the output shown in Figure 9-28.

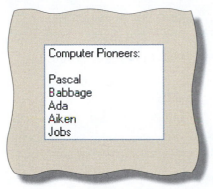

FIGURE 9-28

SCOPE OF ARRAYS

The scope of an array declared within a procedure is local to that procedure, but an array can be declared as a class level variable. As with other variables, an array declared as a class level variable is visible to all procedures within the class. For example, in the chapter project, multiple procedures will use the contents of the arrays that hold the inventory information for Light Span Computers. Therefore, these arrays should be declared as class level arrays, as shown in Figure 9-29.

```
 9 Public Class frmDepreciation
10
11     ' Class Level Private variables
12     Private _intLifeOfItems As Integer = 5
13     Private _intSizeOfArray As Integer = 7
14     Private _strInventoryItem(_intSizeOfArray) As String
15     Private _strItemId(_intSizeOfArray) As String
16     Private _decInitialPrice(_intSizeOfArray) As Decimal
17     Private _intQuantity(_intSizeOfArray) As Integer
```

FIGURE 9-29

The arrays in Figure 9-29 can be referenced in any procedure following the declaration within the class. Notice that the size of the arrays is determined by the value in the _intSizeOfArray variable, which is declared on line 13.

PASSING AN ARRAY

An array can be passed as an argument to a Sub procedure or a Function procedure. For example, if you need the sum of a salesperson's commission, you can pass to a Sub procedure the array holding the amounts of the commission earned. The Sub procedure named ComputeDisplayTotal in Figure 9-30 accepts a decimal array. The For Each loop in the Sub procedure ComputeDisplayTotal accumulates the sum of the commission amounts.

```
109    Private Sub btnCommission_Click(ByVal sender As System.Object, ByVal e As System. ↙
       EventArgs) Handles btnCommission.Click
110
111        Dim decCommissionAmounts() As Decimal = {1345.99, 7800.16, _
112            5699.99, 3928.09, 1829.45}
113
114        ComputeDisplayTotal(decCommissionAmounts)
115
116    End Sub
117
118    Private Sub ComputeDisplayTotal(ByVal decValueOfCommission() As Decimal)
119
120        Dim decAmount As Decimal
121        Dim decTotal As Decimal = 0
122
123        For Each decAmount In decValueOfCommission
124            decTotal += decAmount
125        Next
126
127        Me.lblTotalCommission.Text = "The Total Commission is " _
128            & decTotal.ToString("C")
129    End Sub
```

FIGURE 9-30

Notice the array was passed using the ByVal keyword, but with arrays ByVal has a different meaning. Arrays can be passed by value or by reference; however, the ByVal keyword does not restrict a Sub procedure or Function procedure from changing the array's elements. Whether you pass an array by value or by reference, the original array can be accessed and modified within the Sub or Function procedure. When passing arrays using ByVal, the array is not duplicated. If you change the value of any element of an array in a procedure, the original array is changed.

In Figure 9-31 on the next page, the decCommissionAmounts array is defined on line 133. The third element is given the value 5699.99. On line 147 in the ChangeValue Sub procedure, the third element in the array, referenced as decValueOfCommission(2), is changed. When the array is displayed in the btnCommission click event (line 140), the third element has been changed (see Figure 9-32).

```
131     Private Sub btnCommission_Click(ByVal sender As System.Object, ByVal e As System. ↙
        EventArgs) Handles btnCommission.Click
132
133         Dim decCommissionAmounts() As Decimal = {1345.99, 7800.16, _
134             5699.99, 3928.09, 1829.45}
135         Dim decDisplay As Decimal
136
137         ChangeValue(decCommissionAmounts)
138
139         For Each decDisplay In decCommissionAmounts
140             Me.lstDisplay.Items.Add(decDisplay.ToString("C"))
141         Next
142
143     End Sub
144
145     Private Sub ChangeValue(ByVal decValueOfCommission() As Decimal)
146
147         decValueOfCommission(2) = 4599.99
148
149     End Sub
```

FIGURE 9-31

FIGURE 9-32

SORTING AN ARRAY

The data in an array often is sorted for an organized display. For example, the telephone white pages are sorted by last name, making it easier to search and locate friends and family members. To sort array contents in Visual Basic, you use a procedure named **Sort**. When the Sort procedure is applied to an array, the lowest value is placed in the first element in the array with an index of zero, the next lowest is placed in the second element, and so on until the largest value is stored in the highest element of the array. The syntax for the Sort procedure is shown in Figure 9-33.

General Format: Sort Procedure
Array.Sort(ArrayName)
Coding Example: Dim intAges() as Integer = {16, 64, 41, 8, 19, 81, 23} Array.Sort(intAges)
After the sort executes, the values in the array are in the order 8, 16, 19, 23, 41, 64, and 81.

FIGURE 9-33

In the Light Span Computers Inventory Depreciation application, the array _strInventoryItem is declared as a class level private variable containing String data, as shown in Figure 9-34. The size of the array is specified by the value in the _intSizeOfArray variable.

```
13      Private _intSizeOfArray As Integer = 7
14      Private _strInventoryItem(_intSizeOfArray) As String
```

FIGURE 9-34

The array is filled with data from a text file in another procedure. The inventory items in the text file are not sorted but the items should be sorted before being displayed in a ComboBox object. Therefore, the array is sorted using the Array.Sort procedure, as shown in Figure 9-35 on the next page. After sorting, a For Each loop displays the elements in the array in ascending alphabetic (A to Z) order, as shown in Figure 9-36.

```
11          Dim strItem As String
12
13          ' Sorts the _strInventoryItem array
14          Array.Sort(frmDepreciation._strInventoryItem)
15
16          ' Displays the _strInventoryItem array
17          For Each strItem In frmDepreciation._strInventoryItem
18              Me.lstDisplay.Items.Add(strItem)
19          Next
```

FIGURE 9-35

FIGURE 9-36

SEARCHING AN ARRAY

Arrays provide an excellent way to store and process information. Suppose an array holds 5,000 student names in alphabetical order. If you searched for one name in that array, the search could take some time because the array contains 5,000 elements. One search approach is to begin with the first name in index zero, and evaluate each name until you find a match. Searching each element in an array is called a **sequential** search. Theoretically, you might have to search 5,000 names before you find a match or discover that the name is not even in the array. For these reasons, a sequential search is not the most efficient way of searching for an element.

If an array is large and requires many repeated searches, you need a more efficient search approach. The **BinarySearch** method searches a sorted array for a value using a binary search algorithm. The binary search algorithm searches an array by repeatedly dividing the search interval in half. In an array with the contents shown in Figure 9-37, if you were searching for the value 405, the BinarySearch method would quickly find the value.

searching for this value

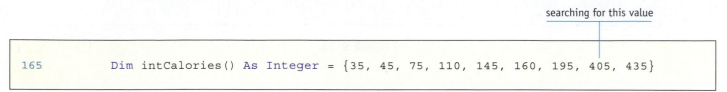

```
165         Dim intCalories() As Integer = {35, 45, 75, 110, 145, 160, 195, 405, 435}
```

FIGURE 9-37

The steps for the BinarySearch method are:

1. Determine the halfway point of the array, which is the number 145 in Figure 9-37. Compare that value first: 145 is less than 405.
2. If the first comparison is not equal to the number being searched, determine whether the value of the search number is less than the middle value. If the search value is less, narrow the search interval to the lower half. Otherwise narrow the search to the upper half of the array. The search value 405 is greater than the middle value 145, so the process narrows the search to the upper half of the array, which contains 160, 195, 405, and 435.
3. Repeatedly check each interval until the value is found or until the halving process evaluates the entire element list of the array.

The BinarySearch procedure returns the matching index value if the element is found. If the array does not contain the specified value, the method returns a negative integer. The BinarySearch procedure syntax is shown in Figure 9-38:

General Format: BinarySearch Procedure

```
intValue = Array.BinarySearch(arrayname, value)
```

If intValue returns a positive number or zero, a match was found at the subscript number equal to intValue.

If intValue returns a negative number, a match was not found

FIGURE 9-38

In another example, a user enters the number of calories to consume, and the code in Figure 9-39 determines if the number of calories is found in the intCalories() array. The code also displays the food item index location if it finds a match to the number of calories entered. If the number of calories is not found, a message stating that the food item is not found is displayed.

```
165        Dim intCalories() As Integer = {35, 45, 75, 110, 145, 160, _
166            195, 405, 435}
167        Dim strFoods() As String = {"Carrots", "Kiwi", "Egg", "Orange", _
168            "Cola", "Taco", "Yogurt", "Apple Pie Slice", "Raisins"}
169        Dim intSelection As Integer
170        Dim intIndexLocation As Integer
171
172        intSelection = Convert.ToInt32(Me.txtCalories.Text)
173        intIndexLocation = Array.BinarySearch(intCalories, intSelection)
174        If intIndexLocation >= 0 Then
175            Me.lblLocation.Text = "The search item is found in subscript number " _
176                & intIndexLocation
177            Me.lblFood.Text = strFoods(intIndexLocation)
178        Else
179            Me.lblLocation.Text = "The food item not found"
180        End If
```

FIGURE 9-39

If the calorie value of 405 is entered into the txtCalories TextBox object, the message "The search item is found in subscript number 7" is displayed in lblLocation. The second Label object displays Apple Pie Slice.

CREATING A TWO-DIMENSIONAL ARRAY

Recall that an array that has a single index, or subscript, is called a one-dimensional array, but arrays can be multidimensional and hold complex information. An array that has two-dimensions has two subscripts. A **two-dimensional** array holds data that is arranged in rows and columns as shown in Figure 9-40. In other words, two-dimensional arrays store the elements of tables. The array intVal is initialized with three rows and four columns in Figure 9-41 (recall that the values in parentheses specify the highest numbered element).

```
182        Dim intVal(2, 3) As Integer
```

FIGURE 9-40

	column 0	column I	column 2	column 3
row 0	intVal(0,0)	intVal(0,1)	intVal(0,2)	intVal(0,3)
row I	intVal(1,0)	intVal(1,1)	intVal(1,2)	intVal(1,3)
row 2	intVal(2,0)	intVal(2,1)	intVal(2,2)	intVal(2,3)

FIGURE 9-41

The table in Figure 9-42 shows the four busiest airports in the United States. The numbers are represented in millions, identifying the number of passengers traveling through each airport each year, according to the Bureau of Transportation Services. The table shows that Atlanta is the busiest airport in the United States with over 35 million passengers flying a year. The table has 4 rows and 2 columns.

	column 0 2008	column 1 2007	
Atlanta	35	34	**row(0)**
Chicago	28	27	**row(1)**
Dallas	24	23	**row(2)**
Los Angeles	20	19	**row(3)**

FIGURE 9-42

The array declared to hold the contents of the busiest airport table is the same as a one-dimensional array except for the two subscripts that hold the row and column index values. The declaration statement in Figure 9-43 initializes an array with four rows (0, 1, 2, 3) and two columns (0, 1) named intPassengers.

```
184        Dim intPassengers(3, 1) As Integer
```

FIGURE 9-43

After the array has been initialized, users can enter the values into a TextBox object from the table information or the program can assign the values by using an implicitly sized array such as the one shown in Figure 9-44.

```
192        Dim intPassengers(,) As Integer = {{35, 34}, {28, 27}, {24, 23}, _
193            {20, 19}}
```

FIGURE 9-44

In the code shown in Figure 9-45, the array representing the busiest airports in the country is totaled by column to find the number of passengers who flew through the five airports in each of the two years. A nested loop is used to total the two columns of the two-dimensional array. The outer loop controls the column index and the inner loop controls the row index of the array.

```
192        Dim intPassengers(,) As Integer = {{35, 34}, {28, 27}, {24, 23}, _
193            {20, 19}}
194        Dim intTotalColumn As Integer = 0
195        Dim intCol As Integer
196        Dim intRow As Integer
197
198        For intCol = 0 To 1
199            'Resets the total to 0
200            intTotalColumn = 0
201            For intRow = 0 To 3
202                intTotalColumn += intPassengers(intRow, intCol)
203            Next
204            MsgBox("The Sum of Column #" & intCol + 1 & " is " _
205                & intTotalColumn.ToString & " million.")
206        Next
```

FIGURE 9-45

The output for the airport program is shown in Figure 9-46 and Figure 9-47.

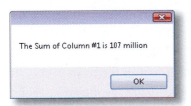

FIGURE 9-46

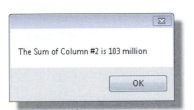

FIGURE 9-47

HEADS UP

In Visual Basic, an array can have up to 32 dimensions.

File Handling

In the applications you created in this book so far, the information entered has originated from assigning data to variables or requesting the user to enter data in objects on the form. In many business applications, entering information can be time-consuming if you must enter data for thousands of items. To process data more efficiently, many developers use text files to store and access information to use within an application. Text files have an extension that ends in **.txt**. The Windows operating system provides a basic text editor called Notepad that allows you to save files with the .txt extension. A simple text file is called a **sequential file**.

For example, in the chapter project, Light Span Computer's inventory is stored in a text file. By gaining access to that information, the depreciation program can manipulate the data and compute the depreciation for items in the inventory. The text file is available at scsite.com/vb2008/ch9. Visual Basic can access many types of files, including text files, as discussed in this chapter, or various types of databases, which are covered in Chapter 10.

With Visual Basic 2008, the System.IO (input/output) namespace in the .NET Framework provides several classes for working with text files, binary files, directories, and byte streams. The System.IO namespace allows you to create, copy, move, and delete files. The file handler supports all types of data, both string and numeric data types. The most commonly used classes are FileStream, BinaryReader, BinaryWriter, StreamReader, and StreamWriter.

READING A TEXT FILE

To open a text file, you need an object available in the System.IO called a **StreamReader**. As its name suggests, this object reads streams of text. You create a StreamReader to provide access to standard input and output files.

A variable object is first created for a data type called StreamReader. The prefix used for an object is obj in the format used in Figure 9-48.

```
24          Dim objReader As IO.StreamReader
```

FIGURE 9-48

After the object variable is declared, an If statement in the form IO.File.Exists("*filename*") determines if the file is available, as shown in Figure 9-49. The command IO.File.OpenText("*filename*") opens the text file and assigns it to the object variable objReader.

```
31          If IO.File.Exists("e:\inventory.txt") = True Then
32              objReader = IO.File.OpenText("e:\inventory.txt")
33          Else
34              MsgBox("The file is not available. Restart the program when the  ↙
      file is available",, "Error")
35              Me.Close()
36          End If
```

FIGURE 9-49

To read each line of the text file, you use a ReadLine procedure. The first line of data in the text file is assigned to the first element in the array _strInventoryItem (see Figure 9-50).

```
35          _strInventoryItem(intCount) = objReader.ReadLine()
```

FIGURE 9-50

To determine whether the end of the file has been reached, use the Peek procedure of the StreamReader object. The Peek procedure reads the next character in the file without changing position. If the end of the file is reached, the Peek procedure returns the value of −1. You can use a Do While loop to determine if all the lines in the file have been read. When the Peek procedure reaches the end of the file and returns a −1, the Do While loop ends as shown in Figure 9-51.

```
34          Do While objReader.Peek <> -1
35              _strInventoryItem(intCount) = objReader.ReadLine()
36              _strItemId(intCount) = objReader.ReadLine()
37              _decInitialPrice(intCount) = Convert.ToDecimal(objReader.ReadLine())
38              _intQuantity(intCount) = Convert.ToInt32(objReader.ReadLine())
39              intCount += 1
40          Loop
```

FIGURE 9-51

Before closing the application, be sure to close the file to terminate communications with it, as shown in Figure 9-52.

```
40          objReader.Close()
```

FIGURE 9-52

The Light Span Computers application opens and reads a file named inventory.txt. To read data from a text file, you can complete the following steps:

STEP 1 Open the code editing window by clicking the View Code button on the Solution Explorer toolbar. Click inside the frmDepreciation_Load event.

The code editing window opens and the insertion point appears in the frmDepreciation load event handler (Figure 9-53).

insertion point

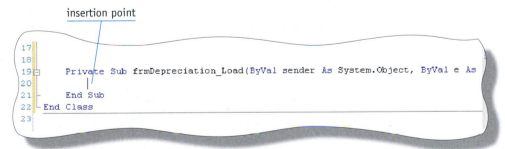

```
17
18
19      Private Sub frmDepreciation_Load(ByVal sender As System.Object, ByVal e As
20          |
21      End Sub
22  End Class
23
```

FIGURE 9-53

STEP 2 Initialize the variables. Assign an object variable to the IO.StreamReader object. Initialize the StreamReader object by typing `Dim objReader As IO.` and an IntelliSense window opens. Select StreamReader. Press ENTER. Finish declaring the rest of the variable names.

By initializing the objReader variable object in the IO namespace, IntelliSense opens a listing of IO procedures. The variables are initialized (Figure 9-54).

```
17
18
19    Private Sub frmDepreciation_Load(ByVal sender As System.Object, ByVal e As
20
21        ' Initialize an instance of the StreamReader object
22        Dim objReader As IO.StreamReader
23        Dim intCount As Integer = 0
24        Dim intFill As Integer
25
26    End Sub
27  End Class
28
```

FIGURE 9-54

STEP 3 Verify that the inventory.txt data file is available by typing `If IO.` and an IntelliSense window opens. Complete the rest of the line using IntelliSense as shown in Figure 9-55. Assign the objReader variable by typing `objR` and then pressing CTRL + SPACEBAR to complete the variable name. Type `= IO.` and IntelliSense opens. Type `F`.

The If statement confirms that the data file exists. The objReader is assigned to open the inventory.txt file (Figure 9-55).

IntelliSense list

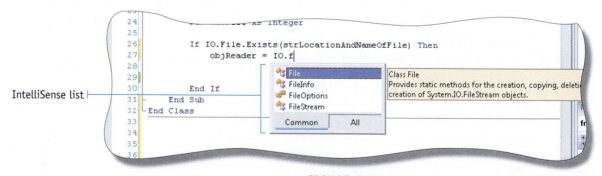

FIGURE 9-55

STEP 4   Select File by typing a period and select OpenText from the IntelliSense list. Type `("e:\inventory.txt")` to access the inventory text file from the USB drive (drive E).

The inventory.txt file is opened on the USB drive (Figure 9-56).

```
25
26          If IO.File.Exists("e:\inventory.txt") = True Then
27              objReader = IO.File.OpenText("e:\inventory.txt")
28              |
29          End If
30      End Sub
31  End Class
32
```
open the text file

FIGURE 9-56

STEP 5   To read each line of the text file, insert a Do While loop that continues until the Peek procedure returns the value of −1. Specify that the ReadLine() procedure reads each line of the text file. Use the variable intCount to determine the index of each array element.

The code is entered to read inventory item names, item IDs, initial price, and quantity from the text file and assign them to class module-level array variables until the last item of the file is read (Figure 9-57).

```
33
34          ' The file is read line by line until the file is completed
35          Do While objReader.Peek <> -1
36              _strInventoryItem(intCount) = objReader.ReadLine()
37              _strItemId(intCount) = objReader.ReadLine()
38              _decInitialPrice(intCount) = Convert.ToDecimal(objReader.ReadLi
39              _intQuantity(intCount) = Convert.ToInt32(objReader.ReadLine())
40              intCount += 1
41          Loop
42
```
read each line of the text file into the appropriate array element

FIGURE 9-57

STEP 6   After the data file has been read, close the file. Insert an Else statement that informs the user if the file cannot be opened and closes the application.

The object variable objReader file is closed and the Else statement informs the user that the file is not available (Figure 9-58).

if no file available, inform the user and close the application window

if file was opened, close the file

```
42
43              objReader.Close()
44          Else
45              MsgBox("The file is not available. Restart when the file is available.")
46              Me.Close()
47          End If
48
```

FIGURE 9-58

WRITING TO A TEXT FILE

Writing to a text file is similar to reading a text file. The System.IO namespace also includes the **StreamWriter**, which is used to write a stream of text to a file. The following example writes a file of users with their name and logon password to a new text file named NewAccounts.txt. Each name and password is written to a line in the file. The btnCreateAccount click event creates a text file with the new customer information, as shown in Figure 9-59. The Notepad text file named NewAccounts.txt is displayed in Figure 9-60.

```
53    Private Sub btnCreateAccount_Click(ByVal sender As System.Object, ByVal e As System↙
      .EventArgs) Handles btnCreateAccount.Click
54        ' Initialize Variables
55        Dim strCustomerName(5) As String
56        Dim strPassword(5) As String
57        Dim objWriter As New IO.StreamWriter("e:\NewAccounts.txt")
58        Dim intCount As Integer
59
60        For intCount = 0 To (strCustomerName.Length - 1)
61            strCustomerName(intCount) = InputBox("Please enter your name:", "Login   ↙
      Information")
62            strPassword(intCount) = InputBox("Please enter a password:", "Password   ↙
      Information")
63            If IO.File.Exists("e:\NewAccounts.txt") Then
64                ' Write the file line by line until the file is completed
65                objWriter.WriteLine(strCustomerName(intCount))
66                objWriter.WriteLine(strPassword(intCount))
67            Else
68                MsgBox("The file is not available. Restart the program when   ↙
      the file is available",,"Error")
69                Me.Close()
70            End If
71        Next
72
73        ' The file is closed
74        objWriter.Close()
75
76    End Sub
```

FIGURE 9-59

FIGURE 9-60

COMPUTING DEPRECIATION

Depreciation is the decrease in property value and the reduction in the balance sheet value of a company asset to reflect its loss of value through age and wear and tear. The United States Internal Revenue Service states that the life of office equipment for depreciation purposes is five years. The two common ways of computing depreciation are the straight-line method and the double-declining balance method.

The simplest and most common, **straight-line depreciation**, is calculated by dividing the purchase or acquisition price of an asset by the total productive years the asset can reasonably be expected to benefit the company, which is called the life of the asset. In the chapter project, each asset in the inventory file has a life of five years. Figure 9-61 shows the formula for computing straight-line depreciation.

```
94              decStraightDepreciationAmount = _decInitialPrice(intItemId) / _intLifeOfItems
```

FIGURE 9-61

The depreciation for a laser printer valued at $299.99 calculated using the straight-line depreciation method is shown in Figure 9-62.

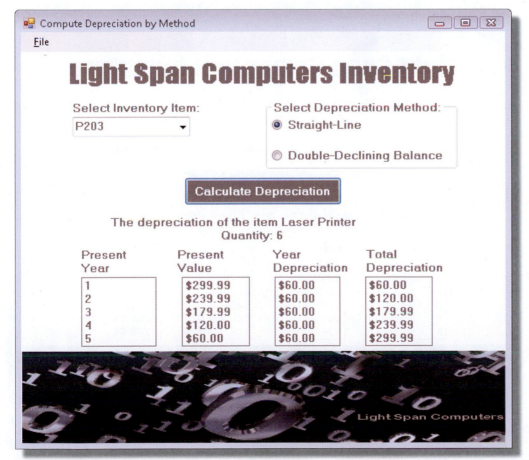

FIGURE 9-62

The double-declining balance depreciation method is like the straight-line method doubled. To use the double-declining balance method, first calculate depreciation using the formula in Figure 9-63. Notice that the price is doubled and divided by the life in years of the item. After that asset is depreciated the first year, subtract the depreciation amount from the initial price for each subsequent year. The present value after subtracting the depreciation is used in the formula for each year.

```
127          ' The loop repeats for the life of the items
128         For intDoublePresentYear = 1 To  intLifeOfItems
129            ' The formula for double-declining depreciation inside the loop to repeat ↙
        the process
130              decDoubleDepreciationAmount = (decDoublePresentYearValue * 2D) / _intLifeOfItems
131              ' Accumulates the total of depreciation
132              decDoubleTotal += decDoubleDepreciation
133              ' Displays the depreciation amounts
134         Next
```

FIGURE 9-63

The depreciation for a laser printer valued at $299.99 calculated using the double-declining balance depreciation method is shown in Figure 9-64.

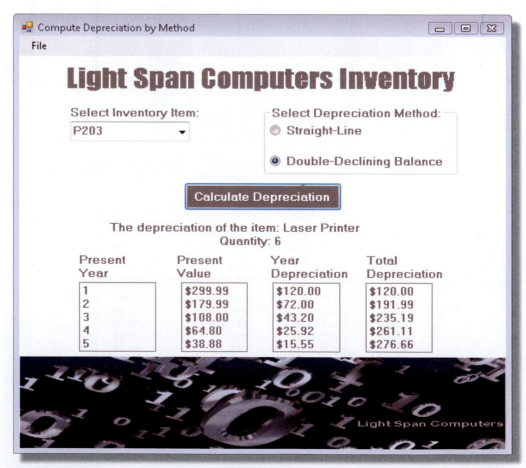

FIGURE 9-64

USING MULTIPLE FORM OBJECTS

As program applications become larger, more than one Windows Form object often is needed to display information. A Windows Form object such as frmDepreciation.vb shown in Figure 9-65 is associated with code with a .vb extension displayed in the Solution Explorer. The code stored in the frmDepreciation.vb file is displayed in the code window when you click the frmDepreciation.vb tab in the design window.

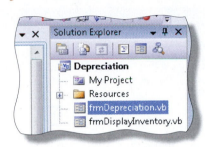

FIGURE 9-65

Visual Basic 2008 allows you to add multiple Windows Form objects to an application. To add a second Windows Form object to an application, you can complete the following steps:

STEP 1 In the Solution Explorer, right-click the project file name Depreciation. Point to Add on the shortcut menu, and then point to New Item on the submenu.

New Item is selected on the Add submenu of the Depreciation shortcut menu (Figure 9-66).

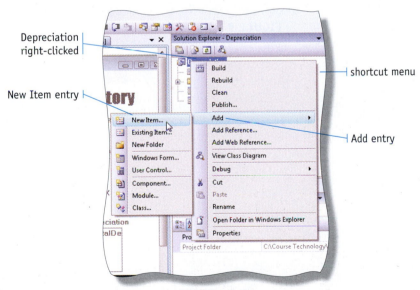

FIGURE 9-66

STEP 2 Click New Item. In the Add New Item dialog box, scroll down to Windows Form, click Windows Form in the Templates area, and then type `frmDisplayInventory.vb` in the Name text box.

A Windows Form is selected to add as a new item to the Depreciation project. The form is named frmDisplayInventory.vb (Figure 9-67).

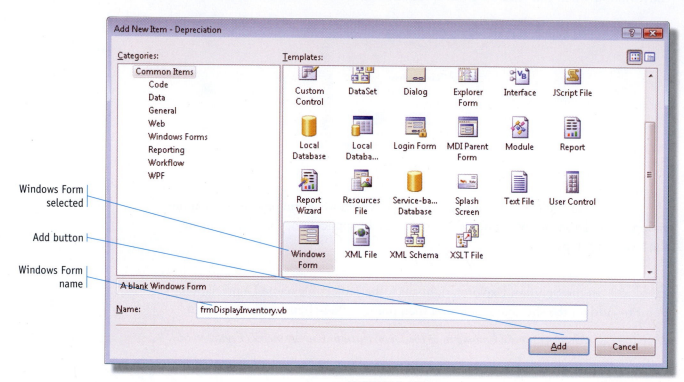

FIGURE 9-67

STEP 3 Click the Add button in the Add New Item dialog box. A second Form object opens in the Visual Basic 2008 window named frmDisplayInventory.vb. In the Properties window, change the Text property of the frmDisplayInventory object to Sorted Inventory Listing.

The second Form object opens and its Text property is changed (Figure 9-68).

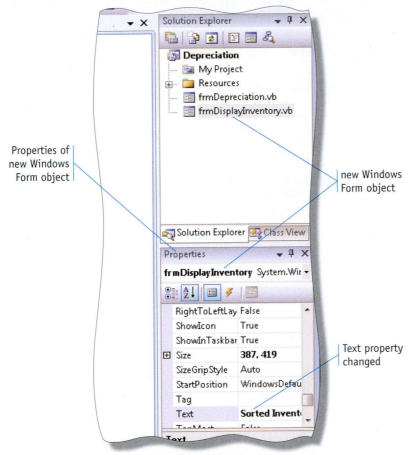

Properties of new Windows Form object

new Windows Form object

Text property changed

FIGURE 9-68

Startup Objects

Every application begins executing a project by displaying the object designated as the **Startup** object. For the Depreciation application, the default Startup object is frmDepreciation.vb. You can, however, change the Startup object if you want a different Form object to open first. To do so, right-click the project name in Solution Explorer and then click Properties on the shortcut menu. Click the Application tab as shown in Figure 9-69, click the Startup form list arrow, and then click the object you want to open when the application starts.

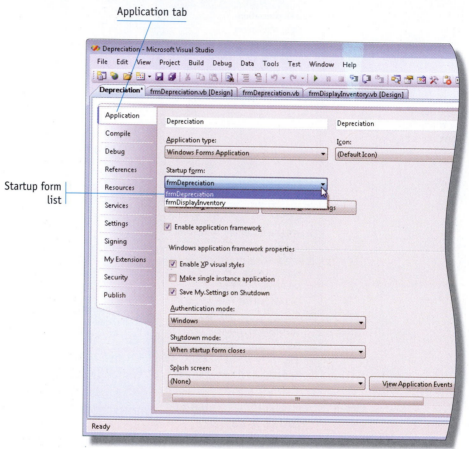

FIGURE 9-69

CREATING AN INSTANCE OF A WINDOWS FORM OBJECT

Now that you have multiple Windows Form objects in the application, you must write code that opens the Form objects as needed in the project. As you create each Form object, code associated with the Form object creates a class declaration. Figure 9-70 displays the code.

```
96  Public Class frmDepreciation
97
98  End Class
```

FIGURE 9-70

The class frmDepreciation holds the object's properties and the procedures for that class. To display a second or subsequent form, the initial step in displaying the form is to create an **instance** of the Windows Form object. An instance is an object variable that references the second form's class name to access the object's procedures and properties. For example, in the code for the chapter project shown in Figure 9-71, when the user clicks the Display Inventory menu item, the mnuDisplay click event opens. The click event declares an instance of the second form, which is named frmDisplayInventory. The object variable frmSecond references the instance of the Form object frmDisplayInventory. An object named frmSecond is created and can be used to perform operations with the second Windows Form object named frmDisplayInventory.

```
163     Private Sub mnuDisplay_Click(ByVal sender As System.Object, ByVal e As System.
        EventArgs) Handles mnuDisplay.Click
164
165         ' The mnuDisplay click event creates an instance of the frmDisplayInventory
166         Dim frmSecond As New frmDisplayInventory
```

FIGURE 9-71

After the instance of the Form object is created, another statement must be written to display the instance of the second form. When creating multiple Windows Form objects, Visual Basic allows you to generate two types of forms: **modal** and **modeless**. A modal form retains the input focus while open. The user cannot switch between Form objects until the first form is closed. You create a modal form with the ShowDialog procedure. In the code example in Figure 9-72, the second Form object named frmSecond is displayed using the ShowDialog procedure. The line preceding the ShowDialog() procedure hides the first form with **Hide** procedure. The Hide procedure removes the first form from the user's screen. The Me keyword refers to the current form being displayed. The Hide procedure conceals the first form so it is not visible on the screen without deleting the information it references.

> **HEADS UP**
>
> Command lines placed after the ShowDialog method call are not executed until the second Form object is closed.

```
167         'Hide this form and show the Display Inventory form
168         Me.Hide()
169         frmSecond.ShowDialog()
```

FIGURE 9-72

IN THE REAL WORLD

Modeless forms are used more often than modal forms in Windows applications.

The second method used for displaying a multiple form is referred to as a modeless Form object. A modeless form allows you to switch the input focus to another window. The first form stays open when you switch to another form, and lets you use the two forms at the same time. A modeless form is useful for a help window that displays instructions. You create a modeless Form object with the Show procedure as shown in Figure 9-73. A Hide method is not necessary because both Form objects are displayed at the same time.

```
        frmSecond.Show()
```

FIGURE 9-73

ACCESSING VARIABLES ON OTHER FORMS

When you create multiple Form objects, you might need to access the variable objects used in one form when you are working in another form. In the chapter project about depreciation, the user can click the Display Inventory menu item and a second Form object opens displaying the sorted inventory items. The second form needs to reference the array initialized in the first form's code. You control the availability of a variable by specifying its access level, or **access specifier**. The access level determines what code has permission to read or write to the variable. To access a variable object on a different form, you can declare a class module-level variable with a different access specifier other than Private. The access specifier Private determines that the variable can only be used with the class in which it is declared. For example, the variable _intLifeOfItems declared in Figure 9-74 can only be accessed within the class frmDepreciation because it has the access specifier Private.

```
Public Class frmDepreciation

    ' Class Module-Level variable
    Private _intLifeOfItems As Integer = 5
```

FIGURE 9-74

If you want to declare a variable object that can be used in the class that it is declared within and also in different classes within other Form objects, a variable can be declared using the access specifier Public Shared. A Public Shared variable is shared by all instances of a Form's class. If you initialize the array that holds the inventory items in the Depreciation chapter project with the access specifier Public Shared in the frmDepreciation class as shown in Figure 9-75, the Integer _intSizeOfArray and the array _strInventoryItem are now accessible in the second form. By using the Public Shared access specifier, the variable's values are shared across all objects within the Inventory Depreciation application.

```
13        Public Shared _intSizeOfArray As Integer = 7
14        Public Shared _strInventoryItem(_intSizeOfArray) As String
```

FIGURE 9-75

After the variables are initialized with the access specifier Public Shared, they can be used within a different class on more than one form. To access the shared variable on another form, specify the name of the originating Form object followed by the name of the variable object. In the chapter project, a second Form object named frmDisplayInventory accesses the _strInventoryItem array. To access the array in the second form, the array name must begin with the originating form, frmDepreciation. The originating Form object and the variable name are separated by the dot operator as shown in Figure 9-76. The array is sorted and displayed on the second Form object.

```
 7 Private Sub frmDisplayInventory_Load(ByVal sender As System.Object, ByVal e As System. ↙
       EventArgs) Handles MyBase.Load
 8        ' The frmDisplayInventory load event is a second forms that
 9        ' displays the sorted inventory items
10
11        Dim strItem As String                        originating
12                                                      form name
13        ' Sorts the _strInventoryItem array
14        Array.Sort(frmDepreciation._strInventoryItem)
15
16        ' Displays the _strInventoryItem array
17        For Each strItem In frmDepreciation._strInventoryItem
18            Me.lstDisplay.Items.Add(strItem)
19        Next
20
21    End Sub                                  dot operator        variable name
```

FIGURE 9-76

When you type frmDepreciation and the dot operator, IntelliSense displays the name of the shared variables from that Form object (see Figure 9-77).

originating form name   shared variable name

```
15
16        ' Displays the _strInventoryItem array
17        For Each strItem In frmDepreciation._s
18            Me.lstDisplay.Items.Add(strIt    ● _strInventoryItem    Public Shared _strInventoryItem
19        Next
20
21    End Sub                                                        IntelliSense list
22
23    Private Sub btnReturn_Click(ByVal sender As System.Object, ByVal e As Syst
24        ' This Sub procedure opens the first form
25        Dim frmFirst As New frmDepreciation
26
27        Me.Hide()
28        frmFirst.ShowDialog()
29
```

FIGURE 9-77

After the second form opens, the user can click the Return to Application button (Figure 9-78) to close the second Form object and return to the first Form object frmDepreciation. The code used in Figure 9-79 is executed when the Return to Application button is clicked. An instance of the first form, frmFirst, is created for frmDepreciation. The second form is hidden and the first form is opened again.

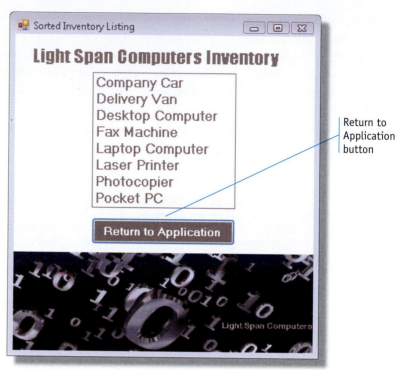

Return to Application button

FIGURE 9-78

```
23    Private Sub btnReturn_Click(ByVal sender As System.Object, ByVal e As System.
      EventArgs) Handles btnReturn.Click
24        ' This Sub procedure opens the first form
25        Dim frmFirst As New frmDepreciation
26
27        Me.Hide()
28        frmFirst.ShowDialog()
29
30    End Sub
```

FIGURE 9-79

Program Design

The requirements document for the Light Span Computers Inventory Depreciation Windows application is shown in Figure 9-80, and the Use Case Definition document is shown in Figure 9-81.

REQUIREMENTS DOCUMENT

Date submitted: April 14, 2012

Application title: Light Span Computer Inventory Depreciation Application

Purpose: This Windows application opens an inventory data file and computes item depreciation based on the straight-line and double-declining balance methods.

Program Procedures: In a Windows application, the inventory text file is opened and the user can select an item and the type of depreciation method. The depreciation is calculated for the five-year life of the inventory item.

Algorithms, Processing, and Conditions:

1. The user first views a Windows application that includes a title; File menu that includes Display Inventory, Clear, and Exit commands; a ComboBox object that displays the inventory item IDs filled from the inventory text file; and a GroupBox object with two RadioButton options of straight-line and double-declining balance depreciation methods. A Calculate Depreciation Button object is available. The Light Span Computers logo is displayed at the bottom of the Form object.
2. After selecting an item ID and the depreciation method and clicking the Button object, the selected inventory item and quantity are displayed. ListBox objects display the present year, present value, year depreciation, and total depreciation.
3. If the user selects the Display Inventory menu item, a second Form object opens displaying the sorted inventory items list. The first Form object closes. The second Form object provides a Return to Application Button object to reopen the first Form object.
4. The user can select the Clear menu item to clear and reset the first Form object. The user can also select the Exit menu item to close the application.

Notes and Restrictions:

1. The inventory.txt file is located on the USB drive on E: drive.

Comments:

1. The image shown in the window should be selected from a picture available on the Web.

FIGURE 9-80

USE CASE DEFINITION

1. The user selects the inventory item ID and the type of depreciation.
2. The user clicks the Calculate Depreciation button to display the inventory item selected and quantity below the Calculate Depreciation button.
3. The depreciation values of the present year, present value, year depreciation, and total depreciation values are displayed.
4. The user clicks the menu item Display Inventory to view the sorted inventory items.
5. The user clicks the menu item Clear to clear and reset the form or Exit to close the application.

FIGURE 9-81

Design the Program Processing Objects

The event planning documents for the Light Span Computers Inventory Depreciation Windows application are shown in Figure 9-82 and Figure 9-83.

EVENT PLANNING DOCUMENT

Program Name: Light Span Computers Inventory Depreciation Windows Application	Developer: Corinne Hoisington	Object: frmDepreciation	Date: April 14, 2012
OBJECT	**EVENT TRIGGER**	**EVENT PROCESSING**	
frmDepreciation_Load	Load	Open the inventory.txt file from the USB drive using If...Else statements to handle possible errors when opening the file Assign each line of the text file to array variables Continue to read the text file until all items are assigned If the text file is not available, display a message Fill the ComboBox object with the array of inventory item IDs	

FIGURE 9-82 (continues)

Program Name: Light Span Computers Inventory Depreciation Windows Application	Developer: Corinne Hoisington	Object: frmDepreciation	Date: April 14, 2012
OBJECT	EVENT TRIGGER	EVENT PROCESSING	
btnCalculateDepreciation	Click	If the ComboBox object and one RadioButton object are selected, call the appropriate Sub procedure based on the depreciation method selected If either one of the objects is not selected, display a message reminding the user to make a selection	
StraightLineDepreciation	Called Sub procedure	Make objects needed for results visible by calling the MakeObjectsVisible Sub procedure Display the inventory item selected and the quantity of that item Calculate the straight-line depreciation based on the formula initial price / life of the items in years Assign the initial price to the present year value In a loop that repeats five times due to the assigned life of the items, accumulate the total of depreciation Display the present years in a ListBox object Display the present values in a ListBox object Display the year depreciation in a ListBox object Display the total depreciation in a ListBox object	

FIGURE 9-82 (continues)

Program Name: Light Span Computers Inventory Depreciation Windows Application	Developer: Corinne Hoisington	Object: frmDepreciation	Date: April 14, 2012
OBJECT	**EVENT TRIGGER**	**EVENT PROCESSING**	
DoubleDecliningDepreciation	Called Sub procedure	Show objects needed for results by calling the MakeObjectsVisible Sub procedure Display the inventory item selected and the quantity of that item Assign the initial price to the pre sent year value In a loop that repeats five times due to the assigned life of the items, calculate the double-declining balance depreciation based on the formula initial price * 2 / life of the items in years Accumulate the total of depreciation Display the present years in a ListBox object Display the present values in a ListBox object Display the year depreciation in a ListBox object Display the total depreciation in a ListBox object	
MakeObjectsVisible	Called Sub procedure	Change the Visible property of the result objects to true Clear the ListBox objects	
mnuDisplay	Click	Create an instance of the second Form object Hide the first Form object Show the second Form object	
mnuClear	Click	Reset the ComboBox SelectedIndex property to −1, clearing the user's selection Set the Checked property of the RadioButton objects to false, clearing the user's selection Change the Visible property of all the result objects to false Clear all the ListBox objects	
mnuExit	Click	Close the application	

FIGURE 9-82 (continued)

EVENT PLANNING DOCUMENT

Program Name: Light Span Computers Inventory Depreciation Windows Application	Developer: Corinne Hoisington	Object: frmDisplayInventory	Date: April 14, 2012
OBJECT	**EVENT TRIGGER**	**EVENT PROCESSING**	
frmDisplayInventory_Load	Load	Sort the inventory item array Display the inventory item array in sorted order in a ListBox object	
btnReturn	Click	Hide the second Form object Open the first Form object	

FIGURE 9-83

Guided Program Development

To design the user interface for the Light Span Computers Inventory Depreciation Windows application and enter the code required to process each event in the program, complete the steps in this section.

NOTE TO THE LEARNER

As you will recall, in the following activity, you should complete the tasks within the specified steps. Each of the tasks is accompanied by a Hint Screen. The purpose of the Hint Screen is to indicate where in the Visual Studio window you should perform the activity; it also serves as a reminder of the method that you should use to create the user interface or enter code. If you need further help completing the step, refer to the figure number identified by the term ref: in the step.

Guided Program Development

Phase 1: Design the Form

1

▶ **Create a New Office Project** Open Visual Studio using the Start button on the Windows taskbar and the All Programs submenu. Click the New Project button on the Standard toolbar. Select and expand Visual Basic in the Project types list; select Windows in the left pane; select Windows Form Application in the right (Templates) pane; name the project Depreciation in the Name text box; click the OK button in the New Project dialog box.

▶ **Name the Form Object** Select the Form object. Change the (Name) property of the Form object to frmDepreciation.

▶ **Title the Form Object** Open the main Form object. Select the Form object and change the Text property to frmDepreciation by Method.

▶ **Create the User Interface** Using the skills you have acquired in this course, create the user interface for the frmDepreciation Windows Form object as shown in Figure 9-84a and Figure 9-84b.

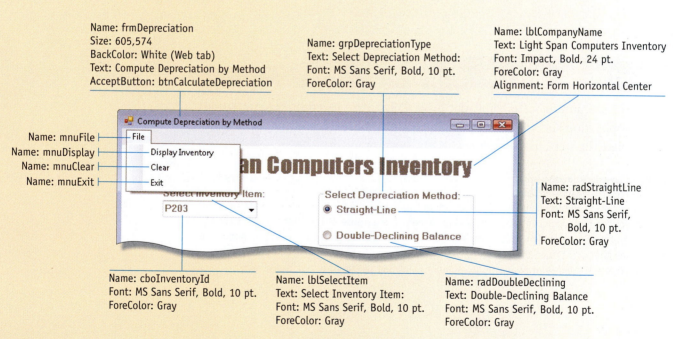

Name: frmDepreciation
Size: 605,574
BackColor: White (Web tab)
Text: Compute Depreciation by Method
AcceptButton: btnCalculateDepreciation

Name: grpDepreciationType
Text: Select Depreciation Method:
Font: MS Sans Serif, Bold, 10 pt.
ForeColor: Gray

Name: lblCompanyName
Text: Light Span Computers Inventory
Font: Impact, Bold, 24 pt.
ForeColor: Gray
Alignment: Form Horizontal Center

Name: mnuFile
Name: mnuDisplay
Name: mnuClear
Name: mnuExit

Name: radStraightLine
Text: Straight-Line
Font: MS Sans Serif,
        Bold, 10 pt.
ForeColor: Gray

Name: cboInventoryId
Font: MS Sans Serif, Bold, 10 pt.
ForeColor: Gray

Name: lblSelectItem
Text: Select Inventory Item:
Font: MS Sans Serif, Bold, 10 pt.
ForeColor: Gray

Name: radDoubleDeclining
Text: Double-Declining Balance
Font: MS Sans Serif, Bold, 10 pt.
ForeColor: Gray

FIGURE 9-84a

Guided Program Development

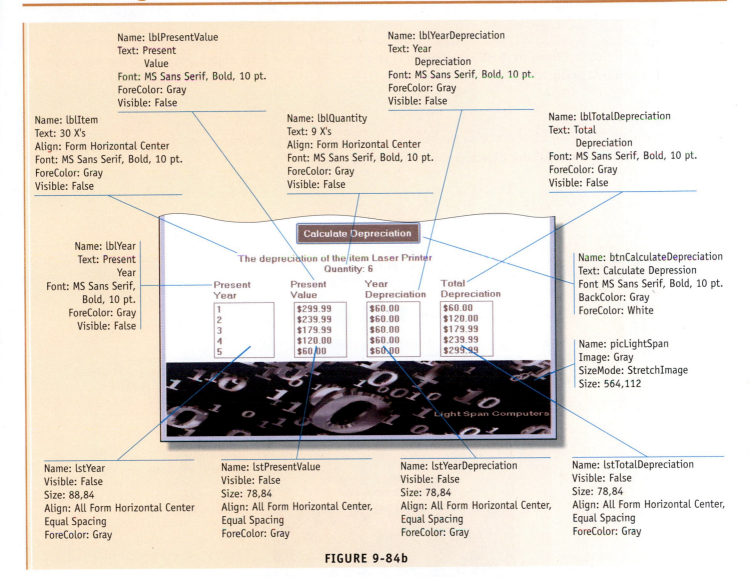

Name: lblPresentValue
Text: Present
      Value
Font: MS Sans Serif, Bold, 10 pt.
ForeColor: Gray
Visible: False

Name: lblYearDepreciation
Text: Year
      Depreciation
Font: MS Sans Serif, Bold, 10 pt.
ForeColor: Gray
Visible: False

Name: lblItem
Text: 30 X's
Align: Form Horizontal Center
Font: MS Sans Serif, Bold, 10 pt.
ForeColor: Gray
Visible: False

Name: lblQuantity
Text: 9 X's
Align: Form Horizontal Center
Font: MS Sans Serif, Bold, 10 pt.
ForeColor: Gray
Visible: False

Name: lblTotalDepreciation
Text: Total
      Depreciation
Font: MS Sans Serif, Bold, 10 pt.
ForeColor: Gray
Visible: False

Name: lblYear
Text: Present
      Year
Font: MS Sans Serif,
      Bold, 10 pt.
ForeColor: Gray
Visible: False

Name: btnCalculateDepreciation
Text: Calculate Depression
Font MS Sans Serif, Bold, 10 pt.
BackColor: Gray
ForeColor: White

Name: picLightSpan
Image: Gray
SizeMode: StretchImage
Size: 564,112

Name: lstYear
Visible: False
Size: 88,84
Align: All Form Horizontal Center
Equal Spacing
ForeColor: Gray

Name: lstPresentValue
Visible: False
Size: 78,84
Align: All Form Horizontal Center,
Equal Spacing
ForeColor: Gray

Name: lstYearDepreciation
Visible: False
Size: 78,84
Align: All Form Horizontal Center,
Equal Spacing
ForeColor: Gray

Name: lstTotalDepreciation
Visible: False
Size: 78,84
Align: All Form Horizontal Center,
Equal Spacing
ForeColor: Gray

FIGURE 9-84b

2

▶ **Add a Second Form Object** Right-click
Depreciation in the Solution Explorer, point to
Add, and then click New Item. In the Templates
section of the Add New Item dialog box, click
Windows Form. Name the Windows Form object
frmDisplayInventory.vb. Click the Add button
(*ref: Figure 9-66*).

(continues)

Guided Program Development (continued)

▶ **Title the Form Object** Open the frmDisplayInventory.vb object. Select the Form object and change the Text property to Sorted Inventory Listing.

▶ **Create the Windows Form Object** Using the skills you have learned in this course, create the user interface for the frmDisplayInventory Windows Form object as shown in Figure 9-85.

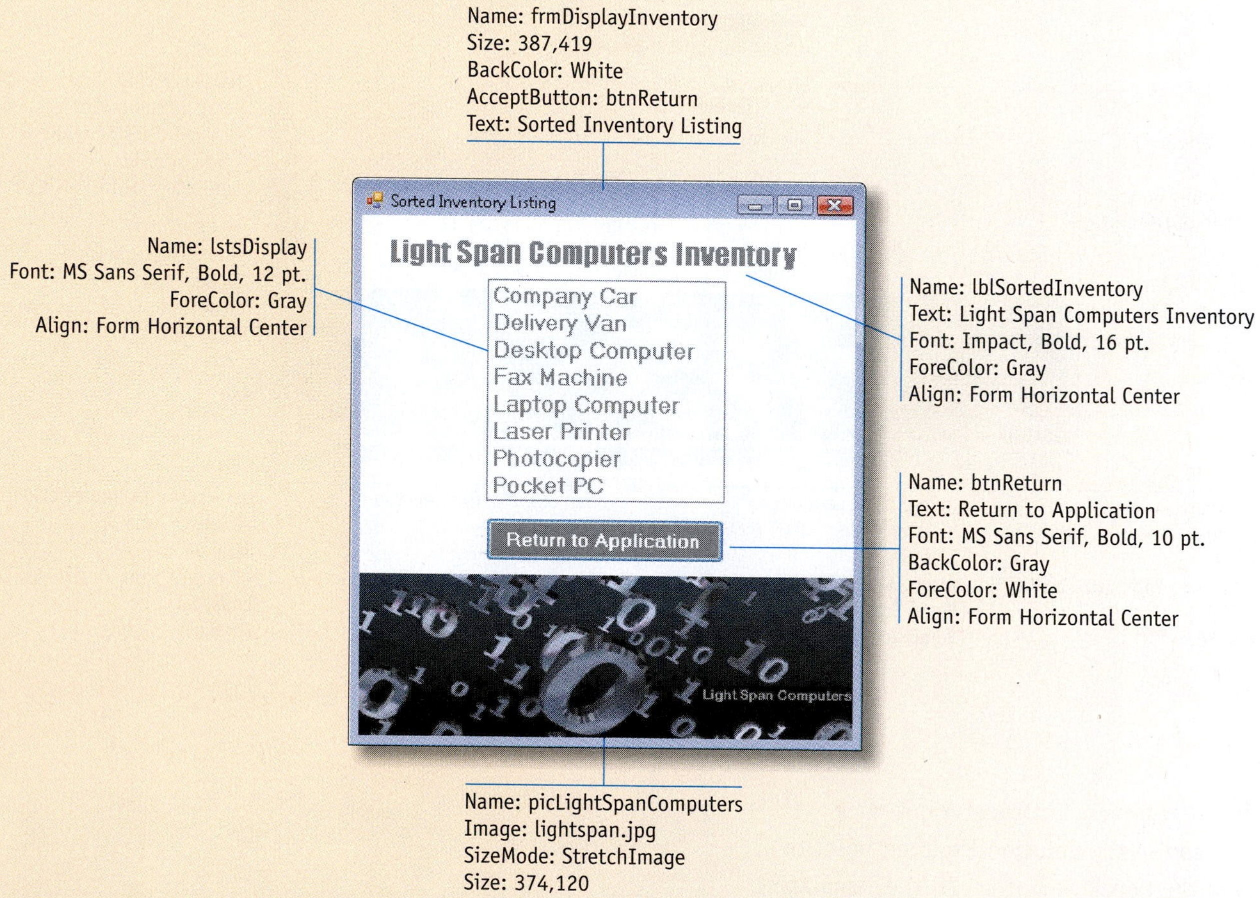
Name: frmDisplayInventory
Size: 387,419
BackColor: White
AcceptButton: btnReturn
Text: Sorted Inventory Listing
Sorted Inventory Listing
Light Span Computers Inventory
Company Car
Delivery Van
Desktop Computer
Fax Machine
Laptop Computer
Laser Printer
Photocopier
Pocket PC
Return to Application
Light Span Computers
Name: lstsDisplay
Font: MS Sans Serif, Bold, 12 pt.
ForeColor: Gray
Align: Form Horizontal Center
Name: lblSortedInventory
Text: Light Span Computers Inventory
Font: Impact, Bold, 16 pt.
ForeColor: Gray
Align: Form Horizontal Center
Name: btnReturn
Text: Return to Application
Font: MS Sans Serif, Bold, 10 pt.
BackColor: Gray
ForeColor: White
Align: Form Horizontal Center
Name: picLightSpanComputers
Image: lightspan.jpg
SizeMode: StretchImage
Size: 374,120

FIGURE 9-85

Guided Program Development *(continued)*

Phase 2: Code the Application

3

▶ **Coding the Comments** Click the View Code button to begin coding the application on frmDepreciation.vb. Type the first four standard comments at the top of the code editing window. Insert the command Option Strict On at the beginning of the code to turn on strict type checking.

HINT

```
1  ' Program Name: Light Span Computers Depreciation Windows Application
2  ' Author:       Corinne Hoisington
3  ' Date:         April 14, 2012
4  ' Purpose:      The Light Span Inventory Windows Application determines
5  '               the depreciation based on a 5 year life of items in inventory
6  '               using the straight-line and double-declining balance methods.
7
8  Option Strict On
```

▶ **Initialize the Variables** Enter the comments shown in the corresponding Hint Screen and initialize the class module-level private variables in the code editing window within the frmDepreciation class *(ref: Figure 9-29)*.

HINT

```
 9  Public Class frmDepreciation
10
11      ' Class Level Private variables
12      Private _intLifeOfItems As Integer = 5
13      Public Shared _intSizeOfArray As Integer = 7
14      Public Shared _strInventoryItem(_intSizeOfArray) As String
15      Private _strItemId(_intSizeOfArray) As String
16      Private _decInitialPrice(_intSizeOfArray) As Decimal
17      Private _intQuantity(_intSizeOfArray) As Integer
```

▶ **Code the frmDepreciation Load Event** To initialize the variables of this event, type the comments and code shown in the corresponding Hint Screen.

HINT

```
19      Private Sub frmDepreciation Load(ByVal sender As System.Object, ByVal e As System. ↵
        EventArgs) Handles MyBase.Load
20          ' The frmDepreciation load event reads the inventory text file and
21          ' fills the ComboBox object with the inventory items
22
23          ' Initialize an instance of the StreamReader object and declare variables
24          Dim objReader As IO.StreamReader
25          Dim strLocationAndNameOfFile As String = "e:\inventory.txt"
26          Dim intCount As Integer = 0
27          Dim intFill As Integer
28          Dim strFileError As String = "The file is not available. Restart when the file ↵
        is available."
```

(continues)

Guided Program Development (continued)

▶ **Code the If...Else Statements** Inside the frmDepreciation load event after the variables are initialized, insert an If statement that validates whether the inventory.txt file exists. The inventory file is opened from the USB drive and assigned to the instance of the StreamReader named objReader. The Do While loop continues to read each item in the file until the file is completed (Peek <>−1). Each line of the file is read and assigned to a unique array subscript by the ReadLine command. The counter intCount increments after each iteration of the loop to increased the subscript number *(ref: Figure 9-55)*.

HINT

```
30          ' Verify the file exists
31          If IO.File.Exists(strLocationAndNameOfFile) Then
32              objReader = IO.File.OpenText(strLocationAndNameOfFile)
33              ' Read the file line by line until the file is completed
34              Do While objReader.Peek <> -1
35                  _strInventoryItem(intCount) = objReader.ReadLine()
36                  _strItemId(intCount) = objReader.ReadLine()
37                  _decInitialPrice(intCount) = Convert.ToDecimal(objReader.ReadLine())
38                  _intQuantity(intCount) = Convert.ToInt32(objReader.ReadLine())
39                  intCount += 1
40              Loop
41              objReader.Close()
```

▶ **Fill the ComboBox Object** Inside the frmDepreciation load event, after the If...Else statements, a For loop counts from the beginning of the array starting at the index of 0 until the end of the array is reached. The statement within the loop fills the inventory IDs in cboInventory ComboBox object. Because the file might not be found, include an Else statement to inform the user that the file is not available and closes the application.

HINT

```
43              ' The ComboBox object is filled with the Inventory IDs
44              For intFill = 0 To (_strItemId.Length - 1)
45                  Me.cboInventoryId.Items.Add(_strItemId(intFill))
46              Next
47          Else
48              MsgBox(strFileError, , "Error")
49              Me.Close()
50          End If
51
52      End Sub
```

Guided Program Development (continued)

▶ **Code the btnCalculateDepreciation Click Event** Click the frmDepreciation.vb [Design] tab. Double-click the Calculate Depreciation Button object. The btnCalculateDepreciation_Click event opens. If the cboInventoryId ComboBox and one of the RadioButton objects have been selected by the user, one of the depreciation methods is called. A message box is displayed reminding the user to select one of the objects if they are left blank.

HINT

```vb
54    Private Sub btnCalculateDepreciation Click(ByVal sender As System.Object, ByVal e  ↙
      As System.EventArgs) Handles btnCalculateDepreciation.Click
55        ' The btnCalculateDepreciation click event calls the depreciation Sub  ↙
      procedures
56        ' Declare variables
57        Dim intSelectedItemId As Integer
58        Dim strMissingSelection As String ="Missing Selection"
59        Dim strSelectDepreciation Error As String = "Select a Depreciation Method"
60        Dim strSelectInventoryItemIDError As String = "Select an Inventory Item ID"
61
62        ' If the ComboBox and a Depreciation RadioButton object are selected,
63        ' call the depreciation procedures
64        If Me.cboInventoryId.SelectedIndex >= 0 Then
65            intSelectedItemId = Me.cboInventoryId.SelectedIndex
66            If Me.radStraightLine.Checked Then
67                StraightLineDepreciation(intSelectedItemId)
68            ElseIf Me.radDoubleDeclining.Checked Then
69                DoubleDecliningDepreciation(intSelectedItemId)
70            Else
71                MsgBox(strSelectDepreciationError, , strMissingSelection)
72            End If
73        Else
74            MsgBox(strSelectInventoryItemIDError, , strMissingSelection)
75        End If
76
77    End Sub
```

Guided Program Development *(continued)*

► **Code the StraightLineDepreciation Sub Procedure** Begin a new Sub procedure that calculates the depreciation when the straight-line method is selected. The result objects are displayed in the MakeObjectsVisible Sub procedure. The cost of straight-line depreciation is calculated and displayed in the ListBox objects on the Form object *(ref: Figure 9-61)*.

HINT

```
79    Private Sub StraightLineDepreciation(ByVal intItemId As Integer)
80        'This Sub procedure computes and displays the straight line depreciation for
      the item selected
81        ' Declare variables
82        Dim intStraightPresentYear As Integer
83        Dim decStraightPresentYearValue As Decimal = 0
84        Dim decStraightDepreciation As Decimal
85        Dim decStraightTotal As Decimal
86        Dim strDepreciationItem As String = "The depreciation of the item "
87        Dim strQuantityMessage As String = "Quantity: "
88
89        ' The procedure MakeObjectsVisible is called to display the Form objects
90        MakeObjectsVisible()
91        ' Display the item and quantity of the selected item
92        Me.lblItem.Text = strDepreciationItem & _strInventoryItem(intItemId)
93        Me.lblQuantity.Text = strQuantityMessage & intQuantity(intItemId).ToString()
94        ' The formula for straight-line depreciation
95        decStraightDepreciation = decInitialPrice(intItemId) / intLifeOfItems
96        decStraightPresentYearValue = _decInitialPrice(intItemId)
97
98        ' The loop repeats for the life of the items
99        For intStraightPresentYear = 1 To _intLifeOfItems
100           ' Accumulates the total of depreciation
101           decStraightTotal += decStraightDepreciation
102           ' Displays the depreciation amounts
103           Me.lstYear.Items.Add(intStraightPresentYear.ToString())
104           Me.lstPresentValue.Items.Add(decStraightPresentYearValue.ToString("C"))
105           Me.lstYearDepreciation.Items.Add(decStraightDepreciation.ToString("C"))
106           Me.lstTotalDepreciation.Items.Add(decStraightTotal.ToString("C"))
107           decStraightPresentYearValue -= decStraightDepreciation
108        Next
109
110    End Sub
111
```

Guided Program Development *(continued)*

▶ **Code the DoubleDecliningDepreciation Sub Procedure** Begin a new Sub procedure that calculates the depreciation when the straight-line method is selected. The result objects are displayed in the MakeObjectsVisible Sub procedure. The cost of double-declining balance depreciation is calculated and displayed in the ListBox objects on the Form object *(ref: Figure 9-63).*

HINT

```
112     Private Sub DoubleDecliningDepreciation(ByVal intItemId As Integer)
113         ' This Sub procedure computes and displays the double declining
114         ' balance depreciation for the item selected
115         Dim intDoublePresentYear As Integer
116         Dim decDoublePresentYearValue As Decimal = 0
117         Dim decDoubleDepreciation As Decimal
118         Dim decDoubleTotal As Decimal
119
120         ' The procedure MakeObjects Visible is called to display the Form objects
121         MakeObjectsVisible()
122         ' Display the item and quantity of the selected item
123         Me.lblItem.Text = "The depreciation of the item: " &_strInventoryItem
        (intItemId)
124         Me.lblQuantity.Text = "Quantity: " & intQuantity(intItemId).ToString()
125         decDoublePresentYearValue = _decInitialPrice(intItemId)
126
127         ' The loop repeats for the life of the items
128         For intDoublePresentYear = 1 To  intLifeOfItems
129             ' The formula for double-declining depreciation inside the loop to repeat
        the process
130             decDoubleDepreciation = (decDoublePresentYearValue * 2D)/ _intLifeOfItems
131             ' Accumulates the total of depreciation
132             decDoubleTotal += decDoubleDepreciation
133             ' Displays the depreciation amounts
134             Me.lstYear.Items.Add(intDoublePresentYear.ToString())
135             Me.lstPresentValue.Items.Add(decDoublePresentYearValue.ToString("C"))
136             Me.lstYearDepreciation.Items.Add(decDoubleDepreciation.ToString("C"))
137             Me.lstTotalDepreciation.Items.Add(decDoubleTotal.ToString("C"))
138             decDoublePresentYearValue -= decDoubleDepreciation
139         Next
140
141     End Sub
142
```

(continues)

Guided Program Development *(continued)*

▶ **Code the MakeObjectsVisible Sub Procedure** The Form objects displaying the results are made visible. The ListBox objects are also cleared.

HINT

```
143    Private Sub MakeObjectsVisible()
144        ' This procedure displays the objects showing the results
145        Me.lblItem.Visible = True
146        Me.lblQuantity.Visible = True
147        Me.lblYear.Visible = True
148        Me.lstYear.Visible = True
149        Me.lblPresentValue.Visible = True
150        Me.lstPresentValue.Visible = True
151        Me.lblYearDepreciation.Visible = True
152        Me.lstYearDepreciation.Visible = True
153        Me.lblTotalDepreciation.Visible = True
154        Me.lstTotalDepreciation.Visible = True
155        ' The previous data is removed
156        Me.lstYear.Items.Clear()
157        Me.lstPresentValue.Items.Clear()
158        Me.lstYearDepreciation.Items.Clear()
159        Me.lstTotalDepreciation.Items.Clear()
160
161    End Sub
162
```

▶ **Code the mnuDisplay Click Event** An instance of the second Form object frmDisplayInventory is named frmSecond. The first form is hidden and the second form is opened. *(ref: Figure 9-79)*.

HINT

```
163    Private Sub mnuDisplay Click(ByVal sender As System.Object, ByVal e As System.    ↙
       EventArgs) Handles mnuDisplay.Click
164        ' The mnuDisplay click event creates an instance of the frmDisplayInventory
165        Dim frmSecond As New frmDisplayInventory
166
167        'Hide this form and show the Display Inventory form
168        Me.Hide()
169        frmSecond.ShowDialog()
170
171    End Sub
```

Guided Program Development (continued)

▶ **Code the mnuClear Click Event** The mnuClear click event clears the Form object for the next set of input.

```
173    Private Sub mnuClear_Click(ByVal sender As System.Object, ByVal e As System.         ↙
       EventArgs) Handles mnuClear.Click
174        ' The mnuClear click event clears and resets the form
175        Me.cboInventoryId.SelectedIndex = -1
176        Me.radStraightLine.Checked = False
177        Me.radDoubleDeclining.Checked = False
178        Me.lblItem.Visible = False
179        Me.lblQuantity.Visible = False
180        Me.lblYear.Visible = False
181        Me.lstYear.Visible = False
182        Me.lstYear.Items.Clear()
183        Me.lblPresentValue.Visible = False
184        Me.lstPresentValue.Visible = False
185        Me.lstPresentValue.Items.Clear()
186        Me.lblYearDepreciation.Visible = False
187        Me.lstYearDepreciation.Visible = False
188        Me.lstYearDepreciation.Items.Clear()
189        Me.lblTotalDepreciation.Visible = False
190        Me.lstTotalDepreciation.Visible = False
191        Me.lstTotalDepreciation.Items.Clear()
192
193    End Sub
```

▶ **Code the mnuExit Click Event** The mnuExit click event closes the application.

```
195    Private Sub mnuExit_Click(ByVal sender As System.Object, ByVal e As System.          ↙
       EventArgs) Handles mnuExit.Click
196        ' The mnuExit click event closes the application
197        Application.Exit()
198
199    End Sub
200
201 End Class
```

(continues)

Guided Program Development (continued)

The frmDepreciation code is completed (Figure 9-86).

RESULT OF STEP 3

```
 1 ' Program Name: Light Span Computers Depreciation Windows Application
 2 ' Author:       Corinne Hoisington
 3 ' Date:         April 14, 2012
 4 ' Purpose:      The Light Span Inventory Windows Application determines
 5 '               the depreciation based on a 5 year life of items in inventory
 6 '               using the straight-line and double-declining balance methods.
 7
 8 Option Strict On
 9 Public Class frmDepreciation
10
11     ' Class Level Private variables
12     Private _intLifeOfItems As Integer = 5
13     Public Shared _intSizeOfArray As Integer = 7
14     Public Shared _strInventoryItem(_intSizeOfArray) As String
15     Private _strItemId(_intSizeOfArray) As String
16     Private _decInitialPrice(_intSizeOfArray) As Decimal
17     Private _intQuantity(_intSizeOfArray) As Integer
18
19     Private Sub frmDepreciation_Load(ByVal sender As System.Object, ByVal e As System.↙
    EventArgs) Handles MyBase.Load
20         ' The frmDepreciation load event reads the inventory text file and
21         ' fills the ComboBox object with the inventory items
22
23         ' Initialize an instance of the StreamReader object and declare variables
24         Dim objReader As IO.StreamReader
25         Dim strLocationAndNameOfFile As String = "e:\inventory.txt"
26         Dim intCount As Integer = 0
27         Dim intFill As Integer
28         Dim strFileError As String = "The file is not available. Restart when the file↙
    is available."
29
30         ' Verify the file exists
31         If IO.File.Exists(strLocationAndNameOfFile) Then
32             objReader = IO.File.OpenText(strLocationAndNameOfFile)
33             ' Read the file line by line until the file is completed
34             Do While objReader.Peek <> -1
35                 _strInventoryItem(intCount) = objReader.ReadLine()
36                 _strItemId(intCount) = objReader.ReadLine()
37                 _decInitialPrice(intCount) = Convert.ToDecimal(objReader.ReadLine())
38                 _intQuantity(intCount) = Convert.ToInt32(objReader.ReadLine())
39                 intCount += 1
40             Loop
41             objReader.Close()
42
43             ' The ComboBox object is filled with the Inventory IDs
44             For intFill = 0 To (_strItemId.Length - 1)
45                 Me.cboInventoryId.Items.Add(_strItemId(intFill))
46             Next
47         Else
48             MsgBox(strFileError, , "Error")
49             Me.Close()
```

FIGURE 9-86 (continues)

Guided Program Development *(continued)*

```
50          End If
51
52      End Sub
53
54      Private Sub btnCalculateDepreciation_Click(ByVal sender As System.Object, ByVal e ↙
        As System.EventArgs) Handles btnCalculateDepreciation.Click
55          ' The btnCalculateDepreciation click event calls the depreciation Sub          ↙
        procedures
56          ' Declare variables
57          Dim intSelectedItemId As Integer
58          Dim strMissingSelection As String = "Missing Selection"
59          Dim strSelectDepreciationError As String = "Select a Depreciation Method"
60          Dim strSelectInventoryItemIDError As String = "Select an Inventory Item ID"
61
62          ' If the ComboBox and a Depreciation RadioButton object are selected,
63          ' call the depreciation procedures
64          If Me.cboInventoryId.SelectedIndex >= 0 Then
65              intSelectedItemId = Me.cboInventoryId.SelectedIndex
66              If Me.radStraightLine.Checked Then
67                  StraightLineDepreciation(intSelectedItemId)
68              ElseIf Me.radDoubleDeclining.Checked Then
69                  DoubleDecliningDepreciation(intSelectedItemId)
70              Else
71                  MsgBox(strSelectDepreciationError, , strMissingSelection)
72              End If
73          Else
74              MsgBox(strSelectInventoryItemIDError, , strMissingSelection)
75          End If
76
77      End Sub
78
79      Private Sub StraightLineDepreciation(ByVal intItemId As Integer)
80          'This Sub procedure computes and displays the straight line depreciation for   ↙
        the item selected
81          ' Declare variables
82          Dim intStraightPresentYear As Integer
83          Dim decStraightPresentYearValue As Decimal = 0
84          Dim decStraightDepreciation As Decimal
85          Dim decStraightTotal As Decimal
86          Dim strDepreciationItem As String = "The depreciation of the item "
87          Dim strQuantityMessage As String = "Quantity: "
88
89          ' The procedure MakeObjectsVisible is called to display the Form objects
90          MakeObjectsVisible()
91          ' Display the item and quantity of the selected item
92          Me.lblItem.Text = strDepreciationItem & _strInventoryItem(intItemId)
93          Me.lblQuantity.Text = strQuantityMessage & _intQuantity(intItemId).ToString()
94          ' The formula for straight-line depreciation
95          decStraightDepreciation = _decInitialPrice(intItemId) / _intLifeOfItems
96          decStraightPresentYearValue = _decInitialPrice(intItemId)
97
```

FIGURE 9-86 (continues)

(continues)

Guided Program Development (continued)

```vbnet
 98          ' The loop repeats for the life of the items
 99          For intStraightPresentYear = 1 To _intLifeOfItems
100              ' Accumulates the total of depreciation
101              decStraightTotal += decStraightDepreciation
102              ' Displays the depreciation amounts
103              Me.lstYear.Items.Add(intStraightPresentYear.ToString())
104              Me.lstPresentValue.Items.Add(decStraightPresentYearValue.ToString("C"))
105              Me.lstYearDepreciation.Items.Add(decStraightDepreciation.ToString("C"))
106              Me.lstTotalDepreciation.Items.Add(decStraightTotal.ToString("C"))
107              decStraightPresentYearValue -= decStraightDepreciation
108          Next
109
110      End Sub
111
112      Private Sub DoubleDecliningDepreciation(ByVal intItemId As Integer)
113          ' This Sub procedure computes and displays the double declining
114          ' balance depreciation for the item selected
115          Dim intDoublePresentYear As Integer
116          Dim decDoublePresentYearValue As Decimal = 0
117          Dim decDoubleDepreciation As Decimal
118          Dim decDoubleTotal As Decimal
119
120          ' The procedure MakeObjectsVisible is called to display the Form objects
121          MakeObjectsVisible()
122          ' Display the item and quantity of the selected item
123          Me.lblItem.Text = "The depreciation of the item: " & _strInventoryItem ↙
     (intItemId)
124          Me.lblQuantity.Text = "Quantity: " & _intQuantity(intItemId).ToString()
125          decDoublePresentYearValue = _decInitialPrice(intItemId)
126
127          ' The loop repeats for the life of the items
128          For intDoublePresentYear = 1 To _intLifeOfItems
129              ' The formula for double-declining depreciation inside the loop to repeat ↙
     the process
130              decDoubleDepreciation = (decDoublePresentYearValue * 2D) / _intLifeOfItems
131              ' Accumulates the total of depreciation
132              decDoubleTotal += decDoubleDepreciation
133              ' Displays the depreciation amounts
134              Me.lstYear.Items.Add(intDoublePresentYear.ToString())
135              Me.lstPresentValue.Items.Add(decDoublePresentYearValue.ToString("C"))
136              Me.lstYearDepreciation.Items.Add(decDoubleDepreciation.ToString("C"))
137              Me.lstTotalDepreciation.Items.Add(decDoubleTotal.ToString("C"))
138              decDoublePresentYearValue -= decDoubleDepreciation
139          Next
140
141      End Sub
142
143      Private Sub MakeObjectsVisible()
144          ' This procedure displays the objects showing the results
145          Me.lblItem.Visible = True
146          Me.lblQuantity.Visible = True
```

FIGURE 9-86 (continues)

Guided Program Development (continued)

```
147        Me.lblYear.Visible = True
148        Me.lstYear.Visible = True
149        Me.lblPresentValue.Visible = True
150        Me.lstPresentValue.Visible = True
151        Me.lblYearDepreciation.Visible = True
152        Me.lstYearDepreciation.Visible = True
153        Me.lblTotalDepreciation.Visible = True
154        Me.lstTotalDepreciation.Visible = True
155        ' The previous data is removed
156        Me.lstYear.Items.Clear()
157        Me.lstPresentValue.Items.Clear()
158        Me.lstYearDepreciation.Items.Clear()
159        Me.lstTotalDepreciation.Items.Clear()
160
161    End Sub
162
163    Private Sub mnuDisplay_Click(ByVal sender As System.Object, ByVal e As System.    ↙
       EventArgs) Handles mnuDisplay.Click
164        ' The mnuDisplay click event creates an instance of the frmDisplayInventory
165        Dim frmSecond As New frmDisplayInventory
166
167        'Hide this form and show the Display Inventory form
168        Me.Hide()
169        frmSecond.ShowDialog()
170
171    End Sub
172
173    Private Sub mnuClear_Click(ByVal sender As System.Object, ByVal e As System.    ↙
       EventArgs) Handles mnuClear.Click
174        ' The mnuClear click event clears and resets the form
175        Me.cboInventoryId.SelectedIndex = -1
176        Me.radStraightLine.Checked = False
177        Me.radDoubleDeclining.Checked = False
178        Me.lblItem.Visible = False
179        Me.lblQuantity.Visible = False
180        Me.lblYear.Visible = False
181        Me.lstYear.Visible = False
182        Me.lstYear.Items.Clear()
183        Me.lblPresentValue.Visible = False
184        Me.lstPresentValue.Visible = False
185        Me.lstPresentValue.Items.Clear()
186        Me.lblYearDepreciation.Visible = False
187        Me.lstYearDepreciation.Visible = False
188        Me.lstYearDepreciation.Items.Clear()
189        Me.lblTotalDepreciation.Visible = False
190        Me.lstTotalDepreciation.Visible = False
191        Me.lstTotalDepreciation.Items.Clear()
192
```

FIGURE 9-86 (continues)

(continues)

Guided Program Development (continued)

```
193      End Sub
194
195      Private Sub mnuExit_Click(ByVal sender As System.Object, ByVal e As System.    ↙
         EventArgs) Handles mnuExit.Click
196          ' The mnuExit click event closes the application
197          Application.Exit()
198
199      End Sub
200
201 End Class
202
```

FIGURE 9-86 (continued)

Guided Program Development *(continued)*

4

▶ **Code the Comments for the Second Form frmDisplayInventory** Click the frmDisplayInventory tab to return to Design view. Double-click the Form object to open the code editing window. Code the comments for the form processing. Code the Option Strict On statement.

HINT

```
1 ' The frmDisplayInventory class is opened by frmDepreciation
2 ' and displays the inventory file in sorted order
3
4 Option Strict On
5 Public Class frmDisplayInventory
```

▶ **Code the frmDisplayInventory Load Event** The _strInventoryItem array is sorted. The For Each loop starts at the beginning element and continues until the last item is displayed in the ListBox object *(ref: Figure 9-35).*

HINT

```
7     Private Sub frmDisplayInventory_Load(ByVal sender As System.Object, ByVal e As
      System.EventArgs) Handles MyBase.Load
8         ' The frmDisplayInventory load event is a second forms that
9         ' displays the sorted inventory items
10
11        Dim strItem As String
12
13        ' Sorts the _strInventoryItem array
14        Array.Sort(frmDepreciation._strInventoryItem)
15
16        ' Displays the _strInventoryItem array
17        For Each strItem In frmDepreciation._strInventoryItem
18            Me.lstDisplay.Items.Add(strItem)
19        Next
20
21    End Sub
```

▶ **Code the btnReturn Click Event** Click the frmDisplayInventory [Design]* tab. Double-click the Return to Application button. Inside the btnReturn click event, create a instance of the frmDepreciation Form object named frmFirst. Hide the second form and open the first form.

HINT

```
23    Private Sub btnReturn_Click(ByVal sender As System.Object, ByVal e As System.
      EventArgs) Handles btnReturn.Click
24        ' This Sub procedure opens the first form
25        Dim frmFirst As New frmDepreciation
26
27        Me.Hide()
28        frmFirst.ShowDialog()
29
30    End Sub
```

(continues)

Guided Program Development (continued)

The frmDisplayInventory code is completed (Figure 9-87).

RESULT OF STEP 4

```
 1 ' The frmDisplayInventory class is opened by frmDepreciation
 2 ' and displays the inventory file in sorted order
 3
 4 Option Strict On
 5 Public Class frmDisplayInventory
 6
 7     Private Sub frmDisplayInventory_Load(ByVal sender As System.Object, ByVal e As    ↙
     System.EventArgs) Handles MyBase.Load
 8         ' The frmDisplayInventory load event is a second forms that
 9         ' displays the sorted inventory items
10
11         Dim strItem As String
12
13         ' Sorts the _strInventoryItem array
14         Array.Sort(frmDepreciation._strInventoryItem)
15
16         ' Displays the _strInventoryItem array
17         For Each strItem In frmDepreciation._strInventoryItem
18             Me.lstDisplay.Items.Add(strItem)
19         Next
20
21     End Sub
22
23     Private Sub btnReturn_Click(ByVal sender As System.Object, ByVal e As System.    ↙
     EventArgs) Handles btnReturn.Click
24         ' This Sub procedure opens the first form
25         Dim frmFirst As New frmDepreciation
26
27         Me.Hide()
28         frmFirst.ShowDialog()
29
30     End Sub
31 End Class
```

FIGURE 9-87

Summary

In this chapter you have learned to create a Windows application using arrays and data files. The items listed in the table in Figure 9-88 include all the new Visual Studio and Visual Basic skills you have learned in this chapter.

VISUAL BASIC SKILLS		
Skill	**Figure Number**	**Web Address for Video**
Examine the Light Span Computers Depreciation chapter project application	Figure 9-1	scsite.com/vb2008/ch9/figure9-1
Read data from a text file	Figure 9-52	scsite.com/vb2008/ch9/figure9-52
Use multiple Form objects	Figure 9-65	scsite.com/vb2008/ch9/figure9-65

FIGURE 9-88

Learn It Online

Start your browser and visit scsite.com/vb2008/ch9. Follow the instructions in the exercises below.

1. **Chapter Reinforcement TF, MC, SA** Click the Chapter Reinforcement link below Chapter 9. Then, at the top of the page, select the type of reinforcement you want to use (True and False, Multiple Choice, Short Answer). Answer the questions and then grade your answers. Take as many quizzes as you want.

2. **Practice Test** Click the Practice Test link below Chapter 9. Answer each question, enter your first and last name at the bottom of the page, and then click the Grade Test button. When the graded practice test is displayed on your screen, submit the graded practice test to your instructor. Continue to take the practice test until you are satisfied with your score.

3. **Crossword Puzzle Challenge** Click the Crossword Puzzle Challenge link below Chapter 9. Read the instructions, and then enter your first and last name. Click the Play button. Work the crossword puzzle. When you are finished, click the Submit button. When the crossword puzzle is redisplayed, submit it to your instructor.

Knowledge Check

1. Using implicit sizing, assign the integers 4, 18, 31, 26, 17 to an array named intLotteryWinners.

2. Write a statement that assigns the length of the array named strAddressBook to a variable named intAddressCount.

3. What is the upper-bound of an array whose size is 75?

4. Write a line of code that initializes an array named intEvenNumbers with the first five even numbers starting with the number 2.

5. Answer the following questions about the following initialized array:

   Dim strCityNames(6) as String

   a. Assign Detroit to the first array location. What is the index number?

   b. Assign Miami to the fourth location in the array. What would the assignment statement look like?

   c. What value does strCityNames.Length have?

   d. How many cities can this array hold?

   e. What would happen if you assigned strCityNames(7) = "Houston"?

6. Can you have a Boolean data type array?

7. Write a line of code that assigns the values Fred, Wilma, and Pebbles to the elements in the array strFlintstones().

8. Which of the three Flintstones in #7 would be assigned to strFlintstones(1)?

9. What is the lower index of an array?

10. Write a statement that assigns the length of the array named intMovieTimes to intSpan.

Knowledge Check

(continued)

11. Write a statement that assigns the elements shown in Figure 9-89 to a two-dimensional array with implicit sizing named intPinNumbers.

1659	2916	9876	3928
1117	9665	5397	4488
1211	0767	2956	2041

FIGURE 9-89

12. How many elements can be stored in the array in Figure 9-90?

```
Dim decRoomSize(4, 6) As Decimal
```
FIGURE 9-90

13. Write a statement that assigns the value 12.3 to the very last item in the array in question 12.

14. Write a statement thats assigns the first line of an opened text file to the first element in an array named strCartoon.

15. Write a statement that opens a text file named E:\accesscodes.txt and assigns the instance of the StreamReader to objReader.

16. Write a Sort statement to sort an array named strStreetNames.

17. If a binary search returns a negative value, what does that mean?

18. What is the default value of the elements in an array called intTopSpeed()?

19. Write the statement that hides the Windows Form object that is presently open in an application.

20. Write the statement that would initialize the variable intFinalExam as a Public Shared class level variable that can be accessed in other Windows Form objects.

Debugging Exercise

1. Correct the lines of code in Figure 9-91:

```
Dim intJellyBeans() As Integer = (23, 77, 89, 124, 25)
ReDim intJellyBeans(10) As Integer
```
FIGURE 9-91

2. Correct the line of code in Figure 9-92:

```
Dim strHighwayNumbers() As String = {95, 81, 605, 5}
```
FIGURE 9-92

(continues)

Debugging Exercise

(continued)

3. Rewrite the code shown in Figure 9-93 correctly:

```
Dim strFriends(4) = {"Brea", "Eric", "Daniel", "Ryan", "Brittany"}
```

FIGURE 9-93

4. Rewrite the code shown in Figure 9-94 correctly:

```
objReader = IO.File.OpenText{E:\testresults.txt}
```

FIGURE 9-94

5. Rewrite the code shown in Figure 9-95 correctly:

```
For Each intPulseRate In intHeartRate()
        Me.lstPulse.Items.Add(intHeartRate)
Next
```

FIGURE 9-95

6. What exception would the code shown in Figure 9-96 produce?

```
Dim intPlaneType(300) As Integer
Dim intCount As Integer

For intCount = 0 To 301
    intPlaneType(intCount)=767
Next
```

FIGURE 9-96

7. Rewrite the code in Figure 9-97 to read each line of a text file into an array named strFordModel.

```
Do While objReader.Peek = -1
    strFordModel(intCount) = objReader.ReadLine()
    intCount += 1
Loop
```

FIGURE 9-97

8. Rewrite the statement in Figure 9-98 to fix the error.

```
Dim intEvenNumbers(4),(8) As Integer
```

FIGURE 9-98

Program Analysis

1. What is the output of the code shown in Figure 9-99?

```
Private Sub btnSuperHero_Click(ByVal sender As System.Object, ByVal e
As System.EventArgs) Handles btnSuperHero.Click

        Dim strName() As String = {"Wonder Woman", "Superman", "Spiderman",
"Green Lantern", "Batman"}

        Array.Sort(strName)
        Me.lblFavorite.Text = "My favorite super hero is " & strName(3)
End Sub
```

FIGURE 9-99

2. What are the values for every element by subscript in the array when the code in Figure 9-100 has been executed?

```
Dim intJellyBeans() As Integer = {23, 77, 89, 124, 25}
intJellyBeans(3) = 59
ReDim intJellyBeans(6)
intJellyBeans(2) = 24
```

FIGURE 9-100

3. What are the values for every element by subscript in the array when the code in Figure 9-101 has been executed?

```
Dim intJellyBeans() As Integer = {23, 77, 89, 124, 25}
intJellyBeans(3) = 59
ReDim Preserve intJellyBeans(6)
intJellyBeans(2) = 24
```

FIGURE 9-101

4. In the array shown in Figure 9-102, what value would be displayed for these lines of code?

```
Dim intInsuranceQuotes() As Integer = {456, 398, 412, 508, 612}
Me.lblResult.Text = "The Insurance Rate is " & _
        (intInsuranceQuotes(intInsuranceQuotes.Length - 1))
```

FIGURE 9-102

(continues)

Program Analysis

(continued)

5. What is the output of the code shown in Figure 9-103?

```
Private Sub frmCompute_Load(ByVal sender As System.Object, ByVal e As
System.EventArgs) Handles MyBase.Load
    Dim intQuantity() As Integer = {17, 22, 3, 7, 51, 27}
    Me.lstResults.Items.Add(intQuantity(3))
    Me.lstResults.Items.Add(intQuantity(1) + intQuantity(3))
    Me.lstResults.Items.Add(intQuantity(2 + 3))
End Sub
```

FIGURE 9-103

6. Write a For Each loop that displays every element of an array named strSongNames in a ListBox named lstDisplay. The loop variable is named strPlay.

7. Write a section of code that declares an array named strStocksOwned initialized with the values in the table in Figure 9-104. Sort the array. Write the contents of the sorted array to a new file named e:\stockportfolio.txt. Close the file when the file has been created with the stock names.

Stocks Owned
Microsoft
Cisco
Coca-Cola
Disney
Exxon
Merck

FIGURE 9-104

8. Write a For Next loop using the Length command that computes the sum of an array named decMaySales. After the loop, display the average (use Length in the formula) in a Label object named lblAverage with the currency format.

Program Analysis

(continued)

9. What is the output of the code shown in Figure 9-105?

```
Dim intDoubleArray(3, 2) As Integer
Dim strDisplay As String = " "
Dim intOuter As Integer
Dim intInner As Integer

For intOuter = 0 To 3
    For intInner = 0 To 2
        intDoubleArray(intOuter, intInner) = intOuter + intInner
        strDisplay &= intDoubleArray(intOuter, intInner) & " "
    Next
Next
Me.txtValues.Text = strDisplay
```

FIGURE 9-105

10. Write the code to implicitly size an array named strDay and to determine the day of the week such as Monday if the user enters the number 1 into a TextBox object named txtDayOfWeek and is converted to an Integer variable named intDay. The day of the week is displayed in a Label object named lblFullDay.

11. An array is declared with the following Dim statement: Dim intSeniorGrades(12,8). After values have been assigned to this array, write a loop named intCount that computes the sum of the seventh row of the array. Assign the sum to intSeniorSum.

12. In the statement Me.lblDisplay.Text = "The result is " & frmInitial.intBloodPressure, what was the name of the original Windows Form object that initialized intBloodPressure?

Case Programming Assignments

Complete one or more of the following case programming assignments. Submit the program and materials you create to your instructor. The level of difficulty is indicated for each case programming assignment.

● = Easiest
●● = Intermediate
●●● = Challenging

1 ●

FLICK'S FICTIONAL BOOK PUBLISHING COMPANY

Design a Windows application and write the code that will execute according to the program requirements in Figure 9-106 and the Use Case definition in Figure 9-107. Before writing the code, create an event planning document for each event in the program. The completed Windows application and other objects in the user interface are shown in Figure 9-108. A file named warehouse.txt is needed for this application and can be downloaded from scsite.com/vb2008/ch9.

REQUIREMENTS DOCUMENT

Date submitted:	January 24, 2012
Application title:	Flick's Fictional Book Publishing Windows Application
Purpose:	This Windows application determines the total books on hand, the total books on order, the total present retail value of books on hand, and the total present retail value of books on order.
Program Procedures:	In a Windows application, the manager of Flick's Fictional Book Publishing company has a text file of the current book inventory in the warehouse. The application determines and displays the inventory totals.
Algorithms, Processing, and Conditions:	1. The manager views a Windows application that contains a title and a company logo for Flick's Fictional Book Publishing company. The application opens a text file named warehouse.txt from the USB drive (drive E:).
	2. The program assigns the text file contents to four arrays that hold the title of the book, the retail price of the book, the number of books on hand in the warehouse, and the number of books on order. The arrays will each have 17 elements.
	3. When the Compute Inventory Totals button is clicked, the program computes the total books on hand in the warehouse, the total books on order, the total present retail value of the books on hand, and the total present retail value of books on order.
	4. The program displays the titles of the books in sorted order and the inventory totals that were computed.
	5. A File menu with the menu items Clear and Exit is displayed which clears the results from the Form object and exits the application.
Notes and Restrictions:	1. Close the opened text file before the program exits.
Comments:	1. The warehouse.txt file is available from scsite.com/vb2008/ch9.

FIGURE 9-106

Case Programming Assignments

USE CASE DEFINITION

1. The manager clicks the Compute Inventory button.
2. The manager views the sorted book titles and inventory totals.
3. The manager clicks the Clear menu item to clear the results on the Windows Form object.
4. The manager clicks the Exit menu item to close the application.

FIGURE 9-107

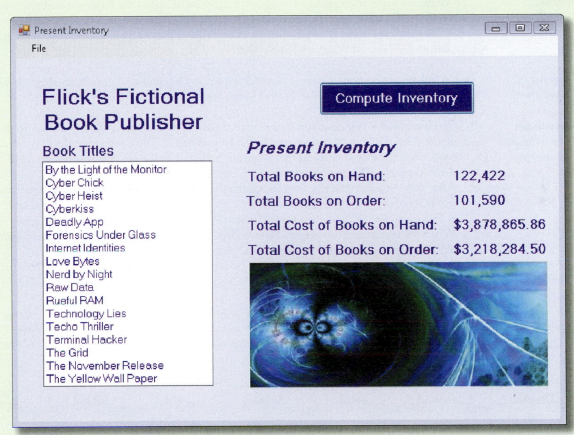

FIGURE 9-108

Case Programming Assignments

2 LARGEST CITIES IN THE UNITED STATES

Design a Windows application and write the code that will execute according to the program requirements in Figure 9-109 and the Use Case definition in Figure 9-110. Before writing the code, create an event planning document for each event in the program. The completed Windows application and other objects in the user interface are shown in Figure 9-111. The file named cities.txt is needed for this application and can be downloaded from scsite.com/vb2008/ch9.

REQUIREMENTS DOCUMENT

Date submitted:	April 2, 2012
Application title:	U.S. Largest Cities Windows Application
Purpose:	The Windows application opens a text file with the populations of the 10 largest cities in the United States. The user selects a city and displays the population for next five years with a projected 3% growth per year. A menu selection also can show the top 10 cities and their present populations on a second Windows Form object.
Program Procedures:	In a Windows application, a user can view the expected 3% population growth for the next five years for any of the 10 largest cities in the United States.
Algorithms, Processing, and Conditions:	1. The user views a Windows application that contains a title, graphic, and a ComboBox object filled with the 10 largest cities in the United States. The ComboBox object is filled from a text file named cities.txt that is opened and read by the application from the USB drive (drive E:). The text file contains each city name with the present population.
	2. After the user selects the city from the ComboBox object, a ListBox object displays the next five years of projected population based on a 3% growth for each year for the selected city.
	3. A File menu also displays the Display Present Population, Clear, and Exit menu items. When the user selects the Display Present Population menu item, a second Windows Form object opens and displays the current 10 largest cities and their populations.
Notes and Restrictions:	1. The user must select one city from the ComboBox object before the population of that city is displayed.
Comments:	1. The pictures shown in the table should be selected from graphics available on the Web.
	2. The second Form object displays a Return to Application button to reopen the initial Form object.

FIGURE 9-109

Case Programming Assignments

USE CASE DEFINITION

1. User selects the city to display the expected 3% population growth.
2. User selects the Display Present Population menu item to open a second form to display the 10 largest cities and their populations.
3. User selects the Clear menu item to clear the form.
4. User selects the Exit menu item to exit the application.

FIGURE 9-110

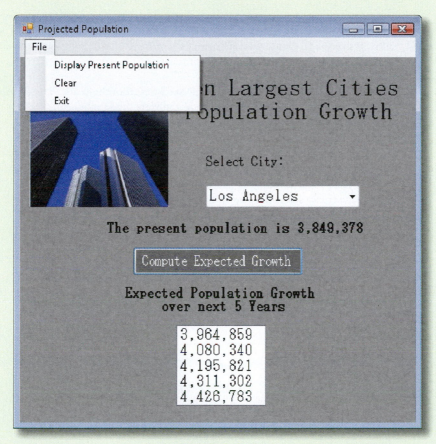

FIGURE 9-111

Case Programming Assignments

3 · HURRICANE STATISTICS

Design a Windows application and write the code that will execute according to the program requirements in Figure 9-112 and the Use Case definition in Figure 9-113. Before writing the code, create an event planning document for each event in the program. The completed Windows application and other objects in the user interface are shown in Figure 9-114. The file named hurricanes.txt is needed for this application and can be downloaded from scsite.com/vb2008/ch9.

REQUIREMENTS DOCUMENT

Date submitted:	August 17, 2012
Application title:	Hurricane Season Statistics by Year Windows Application
Purpose:	This application uses a text file that contains the 1990-2008 hurricane season statistics of named storms to find the average number of storms during the time period and to find the most active year. The user can also select the year within the range and the application will display the number of named storms for that year.
Program Procedures:	In a Windows application, the hurricane statistics from the years 1990-2008 are analyzed. The user can select a year from the range and view the number of named storms. The average and the most active year are displayed.
Algorithms, Processing, and Conditions:	1. The application first opens the information from the National Weather Service saved **in** a text file named hurricane.txt representing the number of named storms during the years 1990–2008.
	2. The user can select the year in the range of data to view the number of named storms for that year.
	3. The average of storms within the range and the year and number of the most active storm season are displayed when the appropriate button is pressed.
Notes and Restrictions:	1. The text file hurricanes.txt is available at scsite.com/vb2008/ch9.
	2. Two Sub methods are used to compute the average and the most active year.
Comments:	

FIGURE 9-112

Case Programming Assignments

USE CASE DEFINITION

1. The user selects a year from the range 1990-2008 from a list box.
2. The program displays the number of named storms for that year.
3. The user clicks the Display Statistics button to view the average number of storms between the years 1990–2008 and the year with the most active storm season is displayed from the text file.

FIGURE 9-113

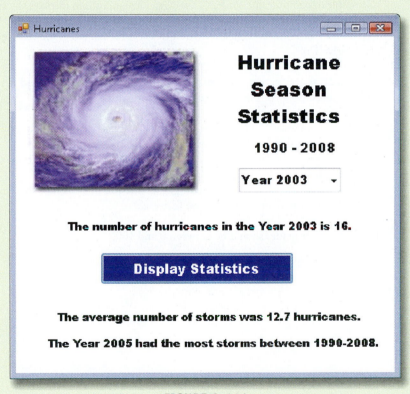

FIGURE 9-114

Case Programming Assignments

4 ●●
SEMESTER FINAL AVERAGES

Design a Windows application and write the code that will execute according to the program requirements in Figure 9-115. Before designing the user interface, create a Use Case definition. Before writing the code, create an event planning document for each event in the program.

REQUIREMENTS DOCUMENT

Date submitted: May 17, 2013

Application title: Final Averages for Semester

Purpose: This Windows application allows an instructor to enter 10 project scores from a course for a semester to compute one student's average. The application displays the final average for the semester with the two lowest scores removed from the average. The eight grades in sorted order and final average are written to a text file named grades.txt stored on a USB drive (drive E:).

Program Procedures: In a Windows application, the average of a student's grade is computed with the lowest two project scores dropped. The results are written to a text file.

Algorithms, Processing, and Conditions:
1. The user views a Windows application that displays a title, a picture of a grade book, and an InputBox function, which requests the 10 project grades.
2. The program displays the final average for the semester with the two lowest scores dropped.
3. The program saves the sorted eight grades and the final average to a text file named grades.txt stored on the USB drive (drive E:).

Notes and Restrictions:
1. The project grades should be between 0 and 100.

Comments:

FIGURE 9-115

Case Programming Assignments

5 ●●
PATIENT CHOLESTEROL LEVELS

Design a Windows application and write the code that will execute according to the program requirements in Figure 9-116. Before designing the user interface, create a Use Case definition. Before writing the code, create an event planning document for each event in the program. This program requires the use of a text file located at scsite.com/vb2008/ch9.

REQUIREMENTS DOCUMENT

Date submitted: February 14, 2012

Application title: Patient Cholesterol Levels

Purpose: This Windows application determines which patients' cholesterol is considered high.

Program Procedures: In a Windows application, a text file containing patient information named patient.txt is opened. The patients that have a cholesterol level above 200 are written to a second text file for consultation named consult.txt.

Algorithms, Processing, and Conditions:

1. Each day a text file named patient.txt is opened from the USB drive. The patient.txt file contains the names, patient ID numbers, and cholesterol level results from the lab. An opening graphic and title is displayed on the Windows Form object.
2. A File menu includes the options to Display Patient Information, Clear, and Exit. The Display Patient Information option displays the contents of the patient.txt file on a second Windows Form object.
3. The patient name, patient ID number, and the cholesterol level is assigned to an array that holds 15 elements each.
4. The cholesterol level is tested to see if the blood cholesterol level is above the value 200.
5. The patient name, patient ID number, and the cholesterol level for the patients who have a cholesterol level above 200 is written to a text file named consult.txt on the USB drive. A nurse will contact these patients with the elevated cholesterol levels for further evaluation.
6. The program displays the number of patients who had an elevated cholesterol level above 200 and the average cholesterol rate of today's patients.

Notes and Restrictions:

1. A picture should be selected from a graphic available on the Web.
2. The text file patient.txt is available on scsite.com/vb2008/ch9.

Comments:

FIGURE 9-116

Case Programming Assignments

6 ●● DJ PLAY LIST

Design a Windows application and write the code that will execute according to the program requirements in Figure 9-117. Before designing the user interface, create a Use Case definition. Before writing the code, create an event planning document for each event in the program. This program requires the use of a text file located at scsite.com/vb2008/ch9.

REQUIREMENTS DOCUMENT

Date submitted: March 4, 2013

Application title: DJ Play List Windows Application

Purpose: The DJ Play List Windows application opens a text file that contains song names ordered by popularity, music genre, and song length in minutes. The application determines how many songs from the play list can be played during the event and displays the songs to be played during the event. A list of songs displayed by a particular genre can also be displayed.

Program Procedures: In a Windows application, the user can enter the length of the event to view the songs that will be played from the play list. The user can also select the type of music and the songs on the play list can be displayed in sorted order.

Algorithms, Processing, and Conditions:
1. The application opens and reads the values from the song list named songs.txt which include the song titles, genres, and length of each song. The time length of each song is represented as 3.12 which represents 3 minutes and 12 seconds.
2. The user can enter the length of the event and select the Display Play List button to display the songs that will be played from the play list during the event.
3. A drop-down list of the music genres is available to select a music genre and display the songs in the play list of that music type.
4. The user can select the Display Song List menu item to open a second Form object displaying the choice of displaying the play list in the present play order or a sorted song list. The first Form object closes. The second Form object provides a button to return to the first Form object.
5. The user can select the Clear menu item which clears and resets the first Form object. The user can also select the Exit menu item which closes the application.

Notes and Restrictions:
1. The songs.txt file is located on scsite.com/vb2008/ch9.

Comments:

FIGURE 9-117

Case Programming Assignments

7 ●●●
SNOWBALL STAND

Create a requirements document and a Use Case Definition document, and then design a Windows application based on the following case project. Before writing the code, create an event planning document for each event in the program:

A local summer snow cones stand sells almost 5,000 snow cones in 10 flavors each week. Develop a Windows application that allows the manager of the stand to record (input) how many snow cones were sold in each of the 10 flavors. The application will compute the total amount of snow cones sold for the week, the most popular flavor, the least popular flavor, and the average number of each flavor sold. Display name for the snow cone stand with a picture logo. (Use two parallel arrays to hold the flavor and the amount sold. A different procedure for each of the results should be used.)

FIGURE 9-118

8 ●●●
BOX OFFICE MOST TICKETS SOLD

Create a requirements document and a Use Case Definition document, and then design a Windows application based on the following case project. Before writing the code, create an event planning document for each event in the program:

Download the text file named movies.txt from scsite.com/vb2008/ch9. The text file contains the names of the top 10 grossing movies and the domestic sales in millions for each film. Open the text file and assign the contents to arrays identifying the name of the movie. Allow the user to enter a movie name and determine if it is one of the top 10 grossing movies. Display the amount made for the movie if a match is made. Sort the array alphabetically by movie name and display the sorted array on a second form. Compute the total amount of money made by the top 10 movies and display that value on the second form.

FIGURE 9-119

Case Programming Assignments

9 ●●●
JOB GROWTH IN THE INFORMATION TECHNOLOGY FIELD

Create a requirements document and a Use Case Definition document, and then design a Windows application based on the following case project. Before writing the code, create an event planning document for each event in the program:

The U.S. Department of Labor has projected that the Information Technology job sector is growing. Enter the information from the table below into Notepad and save the text file.

Job Title	Jobs in 2000	Jobs Projected for 2010
Computer Developers	697,000	1,361,000
Computer Support	506,000	996,000
Systems Analyst	459,000	729,000
Database Administrators	106,000	176,000
Network Administrators	229,000	416,000
High Tech Managers	313,000	463,000

Calculate the total changes in position numbers and display the values. Compute the average number of positions available in these fields for each year. Fill a ComboBox object with the job titles and allow the user to select the job title to see the number of jobs for both the year 2000 and 2010 on a second form.

FIGURE 9-120

CHAPTER TEN

Incorporating Databases with ADO.NET

OBJECTIVES

You will have mastered the material in this chapter when you can:

- ► Understand database files
- ► Connect to a database using ADO.NET 3.5
- ► Use multiple database types
- ► Connect Form objects to the data source
- ► Bind database fields to the Windows Form object
- ► Access database information on a Windows Form object

- ► Add a record
- ► Delete a record
- ► Select records from a list
- ► Program beyond the Database Wizard
- ► Create the OleDbDataAdapter object

Introduction

As you have learned, information used in Visual Basic 2008 can originate from any source, including data entered into objects such as a TextBox, data assigned within the code, or data read from a text file. Large applications often need to connect to the large amounts of data required in business today. Businesses store huge volumes of data in databases, and information technology must manage this data and perform database operations such as change, add, and delete. It also must retrieve the database information for viewing and decision making. Increasingly, developers use Visual Basic 2008 to connect to databases and allow users to perform these operations and more. Within the Visual Studio environment, applications can connect to a variety of database sources through the data access technology of ADO.NET.

Chapter Project

In the sample chapter project, a company named Intuition Financial Services requires a Windows application to access their employee travel database, which documents the approved travel planned for business meetings, conferences, training, recruitment, and technology updates for hardware and software.

The information in the employee travel database is stored as a Microsoft Access database. By placing the information in a simple to use Windows application, the staff of Intuition Financial Services can easily view, update, and delete travel plans. By accessing the Approved Travel Windows application, the entire staff can determine whether their travel plans have been approved, the accounting department can pay for the travel expenses, and managers can approve and add travel plans.

The Approved Travel Windows application loads the existing travel plans from a Microsoft Access 2007 database named Travel.accdb, which is stored on a USB drive. When the Windows form opens, it displays the first record, which indicates the first approved travel request, as shown in Figure 10-1.

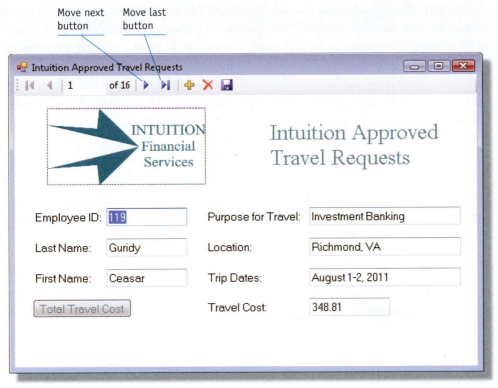

Move next button

Move last button

FIGURE 10-1

The user can use the navigation toolbar at the top of the Windows form to continue through the rest of the approved travel requests. The Windows form displays each of the 16 records that currently are saved in the ApprovedTravelRequests table, which was created using Microsoft Access 2007, as shown in Figure 10-2.

ApprovedTravelRequests Table

Employee	Last Name	First Name	Purpose for Travel	Location	Trip Dates	Travel Cost
119	Guridy	Caesar	Investment Banking	Richmond, VA	August 1-2, 2011	$348.81
123	Dunford	Janet	Stock & Annuties Meeting	Charleston, West Virginia	November 19-23, 2011	$1,945.91
128	Swanson	Kaylee	H.R. Convention	Chicago, Illinois	March 10-12, 2011	$1,208.42
221	Hall	Jan	International Mgmt. Meeting	Atlanta, Georgia	February 2-6, 2011	$2,900.29
242	Tirrell	Madison	Annuities Investments	Albany, New York	April 26-29, 2011	$2,275.18
324	James	Austin	Utilities Investments	Salem, Oregon	March 20-23, 2011	$1,740.10
365	Douglas	Braelyn	Technology Recruiting Event	Houston, Texas	September 29-30, 2012	$628.91
378	Coveny	Ramona	Financial Seminar	Trenton, New Jersey	July 25, 2011	$850.13
426	Henry	Daniel	Communications Symposium	Sacramento, California	June 6, 2011	$943.26
429	Dhiren	Keshav	Microsoft Event	Redmond, Washington	July 9-15, 2011	$2,143.02
628	Ellis	Sean	Interactive Marketing	Los Angeles, California	November 6–10, 2012	$1,670.89
656	Roberts	Faith	Online Marketing Event	Richmond, Virgina	August 21, 2011	$599.95
736	Ramsey	Jordan	Risk Assement and Management	Raleigh, North Carolina	August 22-25, 2012	$1,855.66
924	Tucker	Cordell	Method Validation	Baton Rouge, Louisiana	May 3-6, 2011	$1,555.11
941	Marcos	Desean	Stock Systems Conference	Columbus, Ohio	September 15-19, 2011	$2,330.59
949	Marques	Davon	Information Management	Providence, Rhode Island	September 30, 2011	$759.42
*						$0.00

FIGURE 10-2

The Travel.accdb database also can be updated to include new approved travel requests. The user can click the Add new button on the navigation toolbar at the top of the Windows form to open a blank record. Figure 10-3 shows a new record entered into the Windows form to represent a newly approved travel request by Eric Matthews. After entering the record, the user can add the record to the database by clicking the Save Data button on the navigation toolbar. The original Access database is permanently updated.

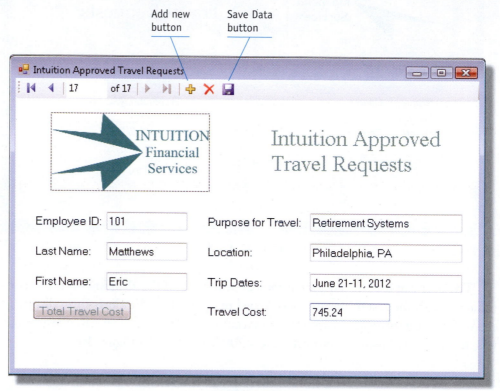

FIGURE 10-3

A user also can change the Travel.accdb Access database by deleting records using the Windows form interface. The user can delete a record by clicking the Delete button on the navigation toolbar. Clicking the Delete button removes the record currently displayed in the Windows form. For example, if Kaylee Swanson cannot travel to Chicago due to illness, the record of Kaylee's travel needs to be removed from the Access database. The user clicks the buttons on the navigation toolbar to access Kaylee's travel request record, and then clicks the Delete button shown in Figure 10-4 to permanently remove any record of Kaylee's travel request.

FIGURE 10-4

TextBox objects are not the only objects that can be used to display database data. In Figure 10-5, a ComboBox object is used to display the Last Name. When a field such as the Last Name is displayed in a ComboBox object, the user can click the ComboBox arrow to display a list of the values in the field. The user then can click a name in the list for the Last Name field to navigate directly to the individual record for the selected last name. For example, the user can view the travel request of Ramona Coveny by selecting Coveny from the ComboBox object in the Last Name field as shown in Figure 10-5.

FIGURE 10-5

Intuition Financial Services intends to keep close tabs on the amount of requested travel throughout the year. A Total Travel Cost button allows the user to compute the total cost of travel for the presently approved travel records within the database. Figure 10-6 shows the Approved Travel Requests form after the Total Travel Cost button has been clicked. A total of $23,755.65 currently is approved in the travel data base.

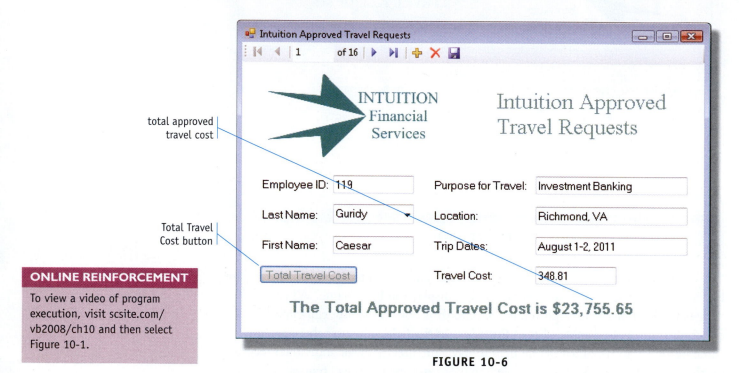

total approved travel cost

Total Travel Cost button

FIGURE 10-6

DATABASE FILES

A **database** is a collection of related information stored in a structured format. Common examples of business databases include a customer list, product information, mailing list, or reservation system. A database organizes data in **tables**. A table is a collection of data about a specific topic, such as a listing of approved travel requests or business contacts for the Intuition Financial Services company. Using a separate table for each topic means that you store that data only once, which makes a database efficient and reduces data-entry errors.

The chapter project creates a user interface that accesses the data from the Intuition Financial Services employee travel database. The travel database contains a table shown in Figure 10-2 on page 731 that contains the approved travel requests for the employees. A table structures data into rows and columns. Each row is referred to as a **record**. A record in a table contains information about a given employee, product, or event.

Each record in the ApprovedTravelRequests table in the Travel database contains information about one approved business trip to be taken by a particular employee. In Figure 10-7, the selected record shows all the information about Janet Dunford's business trip.

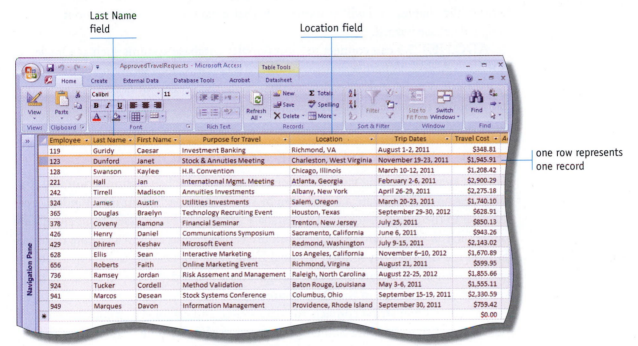

FIGURE 10-7

Each record begins with the Employee ID, which is a unique number that identifies each employee. The Employee ID is contained in the Employee ID field. Each column in a table is referred to as a **field**. A field contains a specific piece of data within a record. For example, in the ApprovedTravelRequests table, the column listing the location of each employee's trip is the Location field. Each column in the table such as the names of the employees, the dates of travel, and total cost of the travel, are all fields.

Each table in a relational database must contain a unique value. Therefore, no two employees in the travel database are assigned the same Employee ID. A unique field is an identifier that represents the **primary key** for the table. The Employee ID is the primary key for the ApprovedTravelRequests table in the Travel database. A primary key is used in relational databases to avoid problems such as duplicate records and conflicting values in fields.

CONNECTING TO A DATABASE USING ADO.NET

To support databases using Visual Basic 2008, a library called ActiveX Data Objects works within all Windows, Mobile, Office, and Web applications. The current version, ADO.NET 3.5, allows the developer to create, administer, and manipulate almost any type of database. ADO.NET 3.5 can open a connection to a database and also can disconnect from that database.

Visual Studio provides tools to connect an application to data from many sources, such as databases, Web services, and objects. If you are using ADO.NET 3.5 in Visual Basic 2008, you often do not need to create a coded connection for the Windows form. Instead, you can use a database wizard to create the connection object for you, and then drag data objects onto the Windows form. Later in the chapter, you will examine code that makes a connection without using a database wizard.

ADO.NET 3.5 can connect to most popular database systems such as Oracle, SQL, and Access. Whether you are creating data connections with one of the Visual Basic data wizards or coding a connection, the process of defining a connection is the same for all types of databases.

ESTABLISHING A DATABASE CONNECTION

The first step in accessing database information is to establish a **connection** with the database source. You create a connection by specifying a path from the Windows application to the database source. The database source can be accessed from any digital source such as a local hard drive, network drive, or a connection to a remote database through the Internet. To connect a Visual Basic 2008 application to data in a database, you can use the **Data Source Configuration Wizard**. After you complete the wizard, data is available in the **Data Sources** window for dragging onto a Windows form. A connection string contacts the data source and establishes a connection with the database using the Data Source Configuration Wizard. The wizard uses the Fill method to fill a DataSet object with table rows and columns from a selected table within a database. A **DataSet** object is a temporary cache storage for data retrieved from a data source. The DataSet object is a major component of the ADO.NET 3.5 architecture.

In the Intuition Travel chapter project, a Windows application must connect to the Access database table named ApprovedTravelRequests in the Travel.accdb database. To connect to the database using the Data Source Configuration Wizard, you can complete the following steps:

STEP 1   With Visual Studio 2008 open, click the New Project button on the Standard toolbar and then click Windows in the Project types area on the left side of the New Project dialog box. Name the project ApprovedTravelRequests. Click the OK button. When the Windows Form object opens, name it frmApprovedTravel. Change the Text property to Intuition Approved Travel Requests. Resize the form to a size of 586, 392. Change the BackColor property to White on the Web tab. An image representing the Intuition Financial Services company logo named intuitionlogo.gif is available at scseries.com/vb2008/ch10/images. Place a PictureBox object on the left side of the window. Name the PictureBox object picIntuitionLogo. Change the Size property to 223,109. Make the location 25,33. Using the Image property, import the intuitionlogo.gif image for the PictureBox object. Change the SizeMode to StretchImage. On the right side of the form, place a Label object named lblTitle. Change the Text property to Intuition Approved Travel Requests on two lines. Make the Font property Times New Roman, size 20, and the ForeColor property CadetBlue on the Web tab. Change the Location property of the lblTitle Label object to 308,56. Close the Toolbox. Click Data on the menu bar.

The Windows form is created and the Data menu is opened (Figure 10–8).

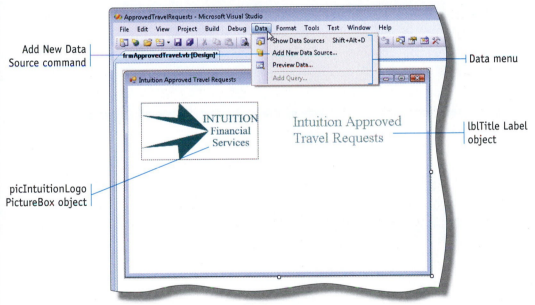

FIGURE 10-8

STEP 2 Click Add New Data Source on the Data menu.

The Data Source Configuration Wizard window opens requesting the Data Source Type. (Figure 10-9).

Data Source
Configuration
Wizard

Database is
source of data

Next button

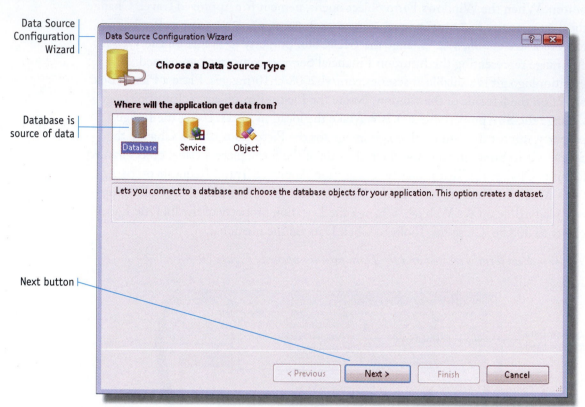

FIGURE 10-9

STEP 3   In the Choose a Data Source Type dialog box, click Database, and then click Next.

After selecting the Database option and clicking the Next button, the Choose Your Data Connection dialog box opens. (Figure 10-10).

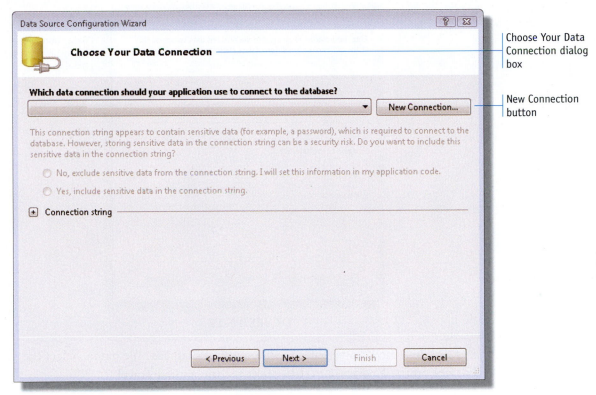

FIGURE 10-10

STEP 4   Click the New Connection button. In the Add Connection dialog box, click the Change... button to select the data source.

After the New Connection button is clicked, the Add Connection dialog box opens. After clicking the Change... button, the Change Data Source dialog box opens. (Figure 10-11).

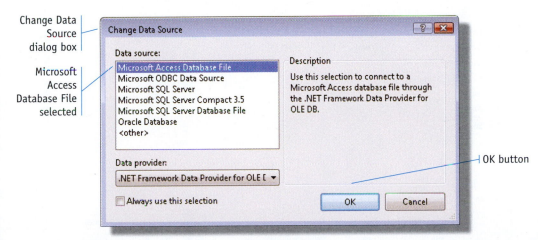

FIGURE 10-11

STEP 5 In the Change Data Source dialog box, select Microsoft Access Database
File because the Intuition Travel database is an Access database. Click the OK button.

*The Add Connection dialog box reopens (Figure 10-12). The Data source appears as
Microsoft Access Database File.*

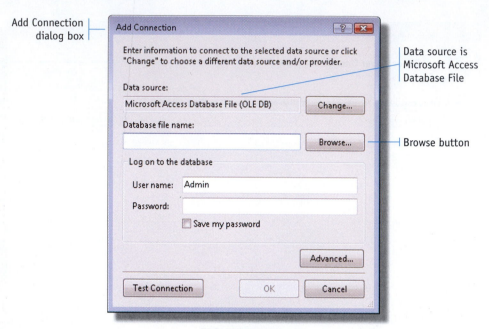

FIGURE 10-12

STEP 6 Click the Browse button to the right of Database file name. Select the
USB device on the E: drive, and then select the file named Travel.

*The Access database file Travel on the USB E: drive is selected. (Figure 10-13). The files
and folders on your USB drive might be different than those shown here.*

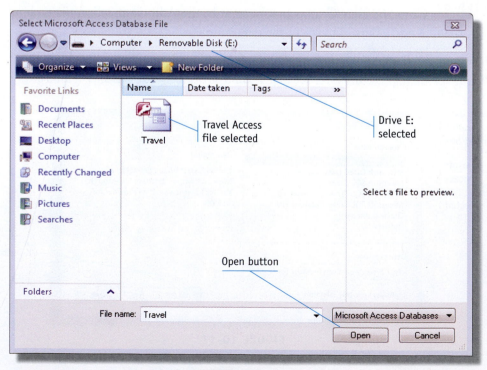

FIGURE 10-13

STEP 7   Click the Open button. The Add Connection dialog box reopens. Click the OK button in the Add Connection dialog box.

The Choose Your Data Connection dialog box reopens (Figure 10-14). The data connection path name begins with the database type ACCESS.

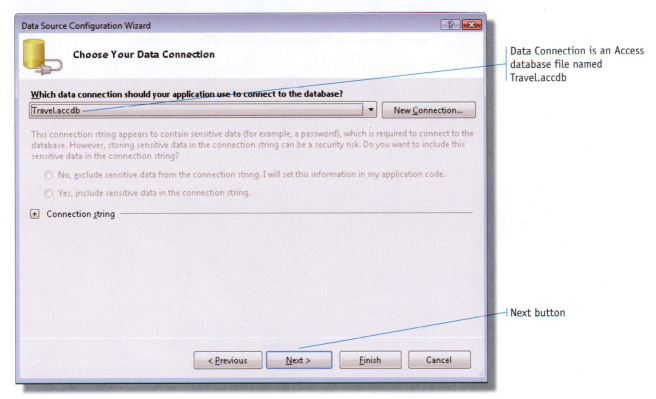

Data Connection is an Access database file named Travel.accdb

Next button

FIGURE 10-14

STEP 8   Click the Next button.

A reminder dialog box opens stating that the connection uses a local data file that is not in the current project (Figure 10-15). The dialog box also asks if you want to copy the file to your project. You do not want to add data and update the copied database. It is best to up-date the original database file.

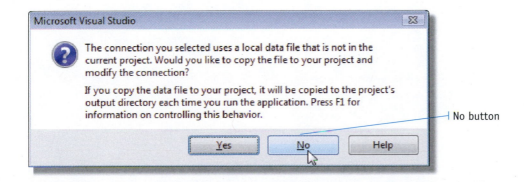

No button

FIGURE 10-15

STEP 9   Click the No button.

A dialog box opens and asks if you want to save the connection string (Figure 10-16). The connection string is named TravelConnectionString automatically.

Yes check box
is selected

Connection
String for
Travel database

Next button

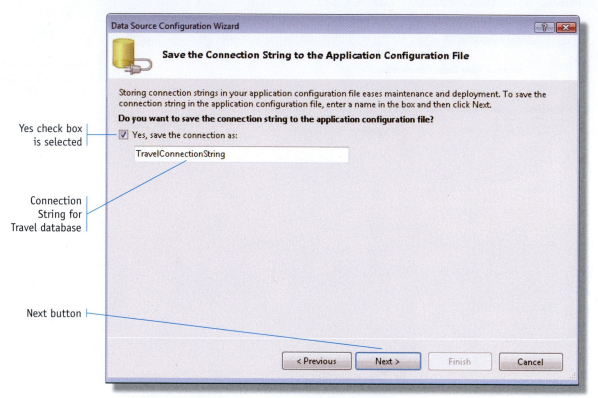

FIGURE 10-16

STEP 10   Click the Next button. The Choose Your Database Objects dialog box opens. You need to select which database objects you want in the DataSet. Click the plus sign next to the Tables option. Click the ApprovedTravelRequests check box to select that table. A connection is made from the Visual Basic application to the ApprovedTravelRequests table within the Travel.accdb database.

After the plus sign is clicked to expand the Tables available, the ApprovedTravelRequests check box is checked (Figure 10–17).

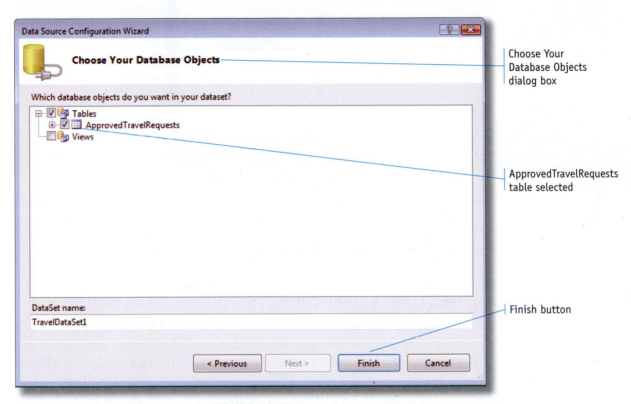

FIGURE 10-17

STEP 11 Click the Finish button.

The dialog box closes, and a connection to the ApprovedTravelRequests table is made. The Solution Explorer displays the DataSet named TravelDataSet.xsd (Figure 10-18).

TravelDataSet added to the program

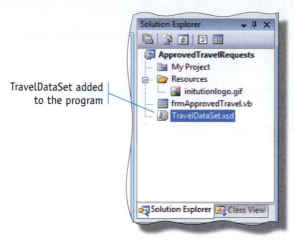

FIGURE 10-18

After a connection is established, you can design programs using the open connection and retrieve and manipulate the data accessed with the database file.

CONNECTING FORM OBJECTS TO THE DATA SOURCE

After a connection is created to an existing data source, the DataSet can provide the application with the ability to interface with the database. The DataSet temporarily stores the data in the application while you work with it. After you have configured a DataSet with the Data Source Configuration Wizard, the next step is to load the DataSet with the data stored in the database. After the DataSet is filled with the table information, the data can be displayed on the Windows form. Loading the DataSet string is called **data binding**. Data binding allows you to display each field as an object on the form. You can complete data binding by dragging the fields on the form or by coding. To view the data available in the source database, you can complete the following steps:

STEP 1 In the ApprovedTravelRequest project window, click Data on the menu bar.

The Data menu opens (Figure 10-19).

Show Data Sources command

Data menu

FIGURE 10-19

STEP 2 Click Show Data Sources on the Data menu.

The left side of the screen displays the Data Sources (Figure 10–20). A DataSet named TravelDataSet is displayed showing a connection to the ApprovedTravelRequests table.

Data Sources window

TravelDataSet

ApprovedTravelRequests table

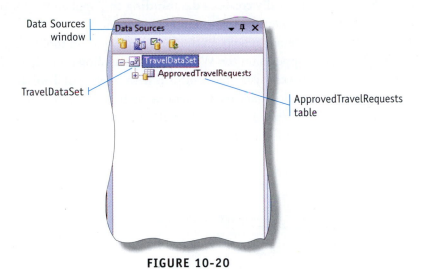

FIGURE 10-20

STEP 3 Click the plus sign in front of the ApprovedTravelRequests table to expand the listing of the field names within the table. Each bindable field item in the Data Sources window can be placed on the Windows Form object.

The fields of the ApprovedTravelRequests table are displayed (Figure 10–21). Each field is displayed by default with an icon that designates each database item as a TextBox object.

fields in the ApprovedTravelRequests table

abl identifies each field as a default TextBox object

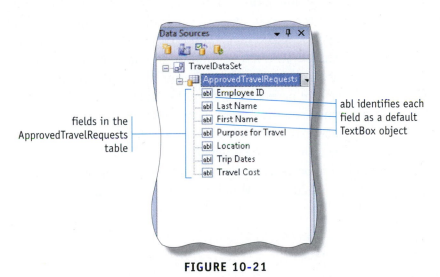

FIGURE 10-21

BINDING DATABASE FIELDS TO THE WINDOWS FORM

After a connection is created to link the database to the Windows application and the data source displays the existing field objects, you can drag the field objects to the Windows Form object. When you drag field objects from the Data Sources window, the Visual Studio automatically creates a **databinding** to populate the form by binding the form object to the DataSet information.

After the first field item is placed on the form, a navigation toolbar control called the **BindingNavigator** appears on the Windows form as shown in Figure 10-22. The BindingNavigator control consists of a ToolStrip with a series of ToolStripItem objects for most of the common data-related actions such as navigating through data, adding data, and deleting data. By default, the BindingNavigator control contains the standard buttons shown in Figure 10-22.

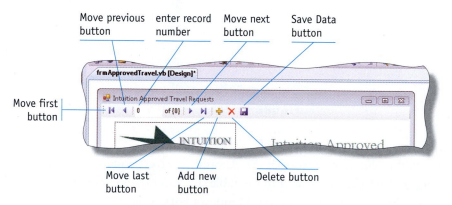

FIGURE 10-22

The first four arrow navigation buttons on the BindingNavigator control allow the user to move throughout the data in the associated table and to interact with the records. A user also can type the record number directly in the textbox to navigate quickly to the associated record. The Add new button inserts a new row to add a new record to the original database table. The Delete button deletes the current record displayed in the Windows form permanently from the database table. The Save Data button saves any changes made on the current form such as changing the spelling of a field item or updating the cost. If a record is added or deleted, the Save Data button must be clicked to save the change to the original database table.

The BindingNavigator appears when the first table field is bound to the Windows form. To bind each database field to the Windows form object, follow these steps:

STEP 1   Select the Employee ID field in the Data Sources window. Drag the Employee ID field to the Windows Form object at the location 22,166.

The Employee ID is placed on the Windows form (Figure 10-23). The Employee ID TextBox object is now bound to the data in the table. A navigation toolbar called a BindingNavigator control automatically is added to the top of the Windows Form object. A TravelDataSet, ApprovedTravelRequestsBindingSource, ApprovedTravelRequestsTableAdapter, and ApprovedTravelRequestsBindingNavigator appear in the component tray and bind the database data to the Windows Form object.

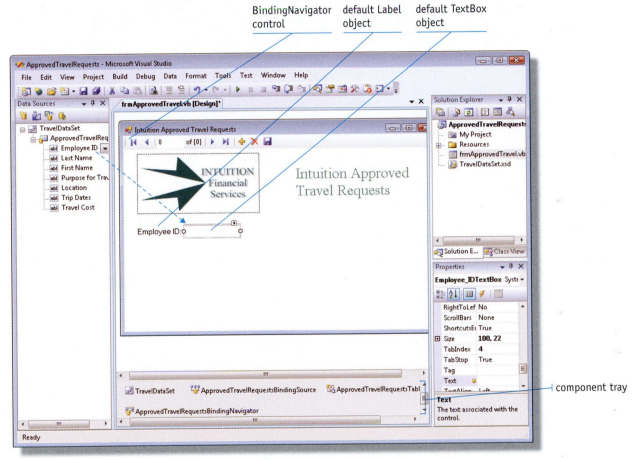

FIGURE 10-23

STEP 2   Drag the rest of the field objects from the Data Sources window to the Windows form. Select all the field labels and field TextBox objects and change the font to size 10. Use the formatting tools in the Format menu to equally distribute the bound objects. You can select the Label and the TextBox objects separately to move them independently of each other. Use the layout shown in Figure 10-24.

All of the field objects are placed on the Windows form and formatted to align with one another (Figure 10–24).

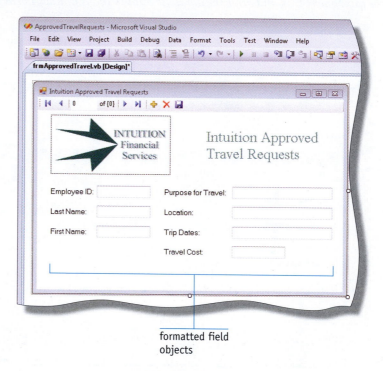

formatted field objects

FIGURE 10-24

STEP 3 Run the application by clicking the Start Debugging button on the Standard toolbar to fill the Windows Form object with the data from the ApprovedTravelRequests table. Use the Move next button on the navigation toolbar to move through the records. Click the Move last button to display the last record.

The Windows form opens with the first record filling the TextBox objects. The Move next button on the navigation toolbar is clicked to view records. The last record is displayed (Figure 10–25).

last record displayed

FIGURE 10-25

ADDING A RECORD

By running the application, the user can view every record within the database. For the Intuition Approved Travel Request application, the Windows form can allow the user to update the database by adding new approved travel requests. To add a new record to the database table, you can follow these steps:

STEP 1   Click the Start Debugging button on the Standard toolbar to run the Intuition Approved Travel Requests application.

The Windows form opens, displaying the first record (Figure 10-26).

FIGURE 10-26

STEP 2   Click the Add new button to add a new record to the database table.

A blank record opens displaying 17 as the record number in the navigation toolbar (Figure 10-27).

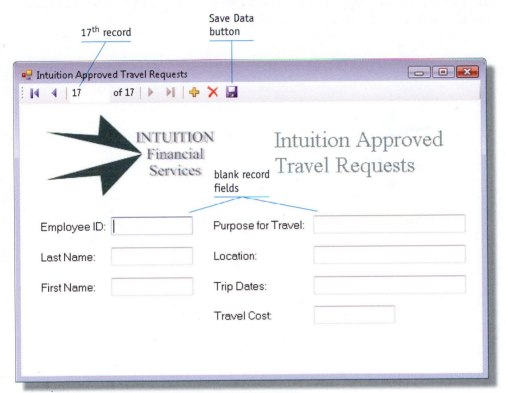

FIGURE 10-27

STEP 3 Add a new record by typing the Employee ID, 101. Type the rest of the information as displayed in Figure 10-28. After the record is complete, click the Save Data button on the BindingNavigator control to save the new record to the original database.

After the new record is typed into the Windows form, the Save Data button is clicked to append the original database table (Figure 10-28).

data entered for
new record

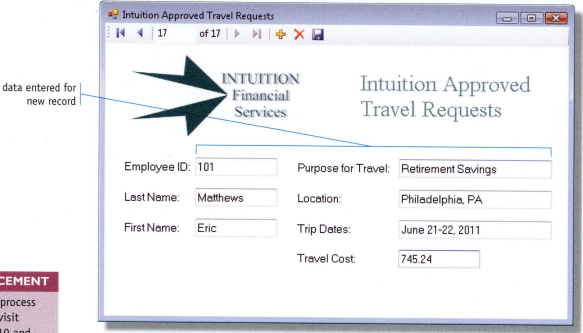

FIGURE 10-28

DELETING RECORDS

In the chapter project, users might need to delete a travel request if the employee cannot travel on the prearranged date. To delete an existing record in the database table, follow these steps:

STEP 1 Click the Start Debugging button on the Standard toolbar to execute the Intuition Approved Travel Requests application.

The Windows form opens displaying the first record (Figure 10-29).

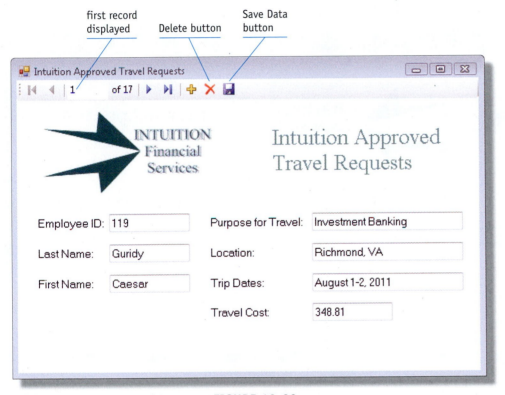

FIGURE 10-29

STEP 2 Use the navigation buttons to move to Kaylee Swanson's record. Her travel request should be deleted because she is ill and unable to travel. Click the Delete button on the BindingNavigator control to delete her record from the database table. Then click the Save Data button to remove the record from the original database.

After the Delete button is clicked, the record of Kaylee Swanson is deleted from the Windows form and the record of Jan Hall is displayed (Figure 10-30). Notice that there are now 16 records instead of 17 records in the database.

16 records in database

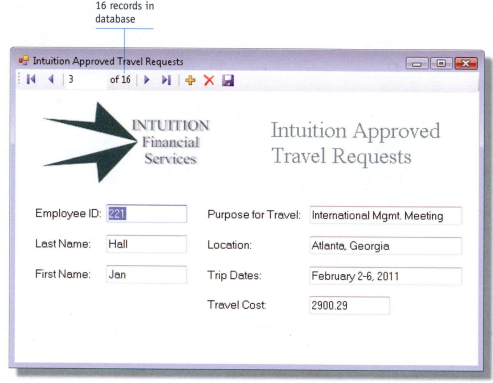

FIGURE 10-30

HEADS UP

In the Visual Studio design window, you can right-click any control on the BindingNavigator control to delete the button. For example, if you want the user only to read the information in the Windows form and not add or delete a record, the Add Record and Delete Record buttons can be removed from the navigation toolbar.

ONLINE REINFORCEMENT

To view a video of the process in the previous steps, visit scsite.com/vb2008/ch10 and then select Figure 10-29.

SELECTING RECORDS FROM A LIST

By default, the Data Sources window displays each table item as a TextBox object, but Visual Basic 2008 allows you to change the default TextBox object to another Toolbox object of your choice. In Figure 10-31 on the next page, when Employee ID is selected in the Data Sources window, a list arrow appears to the right of the field. When the list arrow is clicked, a listing of common Toolbox objects is available. The Customize option lets you select other Toolbox objects not already listed. For example, you can select Customize to add a MaskedTextBox instead of the default TextBox option if you are including a phone number or zip code.

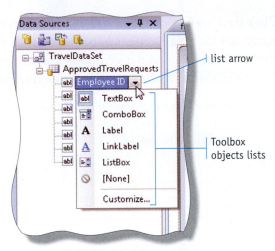

FIGURE 10-31

In Figure 10-30 on page 754, the only way to navigate through the records is to use the BindingNavigator control or enter a record number, but a quicker way to move directly to a particular record is to select that record from a ComboBox object. For example, in Figure 10-5 on page 733, the last name is displayed in a ComboBox object. The user clicks the list arrow to view the items in the Last Name list, and then clicks a last name. The record matching the selected last name is displayed immediately. To change the Toolbox object type, you can complete the following steps:

STEP 1   Select the Last Name Label object and TextBox object on the Windows form. Press the DELETE key to delete the Last Name objects from the Windows form. Select the Last Name table field in the Data Sources window and then click its list arrow.

The Last Name objects are deleted from the Windows Form object (Figure 10-32). The Last Name field in the Data Sources window displays a list of possible Toolbox object selections.

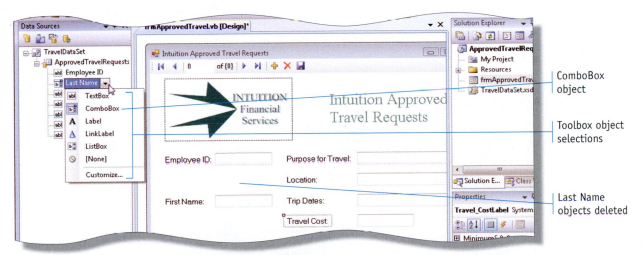

FIGURE 10-32

STEP 2   Click the ComboBox object from the Toolbox object listing for the Last Name field. Drag the Last Name field ComboBox object to the original location of the Last Name TextBox object on the Windows Form object. Change the font size to 10 and then align the ComboBox on the Windows Form object.

The Last Name ComboBox object is placed on the Windows Form object (Figure 10–33).

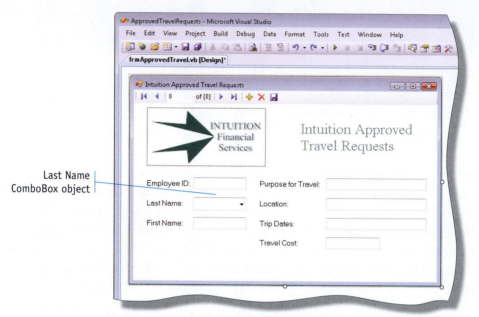

FIGURE 10-33

STEP 3   To fill the ComboBox object with the last names of the employees, the ComboBox object must be bound to the Last Name field. To bind the items to the ComboBox object, select the Last Name object on the Windows form and click the Action tag on the Last Name ComboBox object.

The ComboBox Tasks menu appears (Figure 10–34).

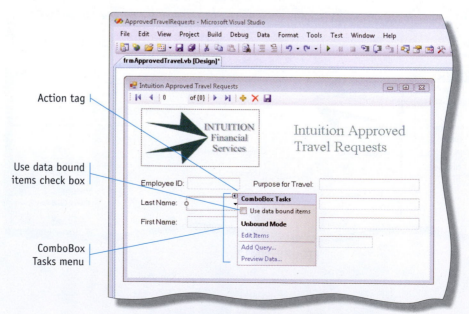

FIGURE 10-34

STEP 4 Click the Use data bound items check box on the ComboBox Tasks menu. The Data Binding Mode list is displayed. Click the Data Source list arrow under the Data Binding Mode and then select the ApprovedTravelRequestsBindingSource to connect the table to the ComboBox object. Next, click the Display Member list arrow and then select Last Name. Click the Value Member list arrow and then click Last Name in the list. Do not change the Selected value entry.

The ComboBox object is now bound to the Last Name fields in the ApprovedTravelRequests table (Figure 10-35).

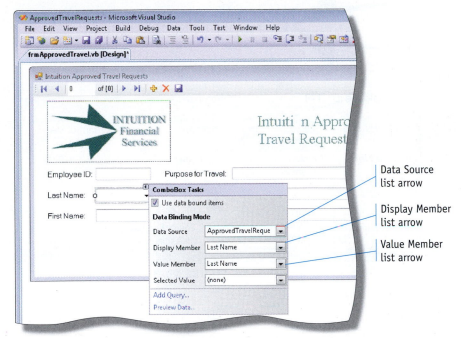

FIGURE 10-35

STEP 5 Click the Start Debugging button on the Standard toolbar to run the application. After the Windows form opens, click the list arrow on the Last Name ComboBox object.

The Last Name ComboBox object displays the employee last names (Figure 10–36).

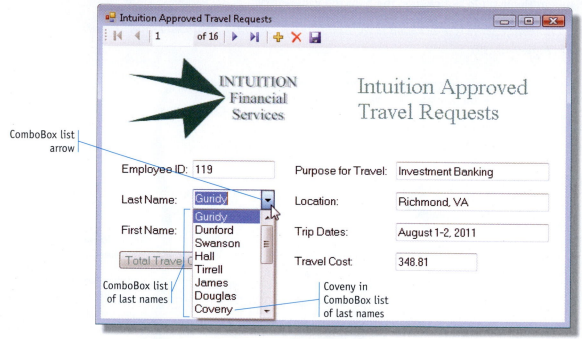

FIGURE 10-36

STEP 6 Click Coveny to move directly to the record containing the information for Ramona Coveny's approved travel request.

The application navigates directly to the selected record (Figure 10-37).

FIGURE 10-37

PROGRAMMING BEYOND THE DATABASE WIZARD

Although the Database Wizard allows you to view, update, and delete records from a database, often other operations such as calculating an average or determining how many records meet a certain criteria will need to be programmed. For example, in the chapter project, the travel office at Intuition Financial Services would like to use a Button object on the Approved Travel Request Windows form to compute the total cost of approved travel. The travel office then can calculate and track their present allocation of travel funds. Code must be written to handle that specific request.

HEADS UP

If you are using Access 2003, the path in Figure 10-38 would be: Dim strPath As String = "Provider=Microsoft.Jet.OLEDB. 4.0:" & "Data Source=E:Travel.mdb"

Creating the OleDbDataAdapter Object

The Database Wizard creates a bridge between the DataSet and the database that contains the data. The bridge that carries the database table information is called an **OleDbDataAdapter**.

The OleDbDataAdapter has two parts. The first part represents a set of data commands programmed using a SQL Select command. **SQL** stands for Structured Query Language, and is the language that communicates with databases. The second part of an OleDbDataAdapter is a path statement to connect to the database that fills the DataSet. The general format for the code that defines the two parts of the OleDbDataAdapter is shown in Figure 10-38.

General Format: OleDbDataAdapter

```
Dim odaName As New OleDb.OleDbDataAdapter(SQL Select command, Path statement)
```

Code:

```
'strSql is a SQL statement that selects all the fields from the
ApprovedTravelRequests table
Dim strSql As String = "SELECT * FROM ApprovedTravelRequests"

' strPath provides the database type and path of the Travel database
Dim strPath As String = "Provider=Microsoft.ACE.OLEDB.12.0 ;" & "Data
Source=E:\Travel.accdb"

Dim odaTravel As New OleDb.OleDbDataAdapter(strSql, strPath)
```

The SQL statement assigned to strSql ("SELECT * FROM ApprovedTravelRequests") is a query statement that requests that the entire table named ApprovedTravelRequests is opened for use by the application. The * symbol represents the wildcard symbol, which means all fields within the table are available.

The Path statement assigned to strPath ("Provider=Microsoft.ACE.OLEDB.12.0 ;" & "Data Source=E:\Travel.accdb") has two portions. The first portion represents the database source. Microsoft.ACE.OLEDB.12.0 assigns the drivers needed to create a connection to an Access database. The second portion represents the path of where the database resides.

An instance of the OleDbDataAdapter is assigned to the variable odaTravel. The prefix oda is used for an OleDbDataAdapter.

FIGURE 10-38

Filling a DataTable Object

After the OleDbDataAdapter makes a connection to the database, a **DataTable** is needed to hold the data that is retrieved from that connection. The DataTable is a crucial object in the ADO.NET 3.5 library. The DataSet used in the database wizard is a collection of DataTable objects. The DataTable is initialized using the dat prefix.

After the DataTable is initialized, it must be filled using the **Fill** command with the data from the selected table. When the DataTable is filled, the appropriate tables and columns are created for the table data. As soon as you connect to the database and fill the DataTable object, the next statement should disconnect the application from the database. To keep the maximum number of connections available, you should keep connections open only as long as necessary. By using the database in disconnected form, the system resources of the computer and network are not overloaded. To disconnect from the database, use the **Dispose** command.

The code in Figure 10-39 can be executed in a program without using the database wizard or you can run the wizard to access the data. The code opens a connection to the ApprovedTravelRequests table in the Travel.accdb Access database on the USB drive. A DataTable named datCost is initialized. The DataTable datCost is then filled with the data from the ApprovedTravelRequests table. The Dispose procedure closes the connection for the datCost DataTable.

```
37    Private Sub btnTotalTravelCost_Click_1(ByVal sender As System.Object, ByVal e As ↙
      System.EventArgs) Handles btnTotalTravelCost.Click
38        ' strSql is a SQL statement that selects all the fields from the
39        ' ApprovedTravelRequests table
40
41        Dim strSql As String = "SELECT * FROM ApprovedTravelRequests"
42
43        'strPath provides the database type and path of the Travel database
44        Dim strPath As String = "Provider=Microsoft.ACE.OLEDB.12.0 ;" _
45            & "Data Source=E:\Travel.accdb"
46        Dim odaTravel As New OleDb.OleDbDataAdapter(strSql, strPath)
47        Dim datCost As New DataTable
48        Dim intCount As Integer
49        Dim decTotalCost As Decimal = 0D
50
51        ' The DataTable name datCost is filled with the table data
52        odaTravel.Fill(datCost)
53        'The connection to the database is disconnected
54        odaTravel.Dispose()
```

FIGURE 10-39

After the DataTable is created, commands can access the data stored in its rows and columns. The number of rows or columns in the DataTable can be computed with the **Count** property. In a DataTable named datCost, the code entered with IntelliSense in Figure 10-40 determines the number of rows in the DataTable object. The ApprovedTravelRequests table contains 16 rows numbered 0 to 15.

```
46        Dim intNumberOfRows As Integer
47        intNumberOfRows = datCost.Rows.Count
```

FIGURE 10-40

The number of rows in the code in Figure 10-40 is equal to the number of records in the DataTable object. You can also compute the number of columns in a DataTable by entering the code in Figure 10-41.

```
49        Dim intNumberOfColumns As Integer
50        intNumberOfColumns = datCost.Columns.Count
```

FIGURE 10-41

The DataTable object can also be used to access individual fields within a database by using the Rows procedure. For example, if you wanted to determine the first value in the Travel Cost field for the first record, the field name "Travel Cost" can be used with the DataTable Rows procedure. In Figure 10-42, the variable decFirstValue is assigned to the first record's travel cost.

```
52        Dim decFirstValue As Decimal
53        decFirstValue = Convert.ToDecimal(datCost.Rows(0)("Travel Cost"))
```

FIGURE 10-42

In Figure 10-42, the first argument for the Rows procedure, (0), references the first row (row zero) in the data table, which is the first record in the table. The entry in the second parentheses ("Travel Cost") identifies the field within the first row.

In the original database shown in Figure 10-2 on page 731, if datCost represents the DataTable for the ApprovedTravelRequests table, the first field value for the field Travel Cost is assigned to decFirstValue. The value 348.81 is assigned to the variable decFirstValue in Figure 10-42.

Using the Rows method and the field name, you also can compute the sum or average of the entire Travel Cost values for all the records in the table. In the chapter project, when the user clicks a button on the Windows Form object, the event handler for the button click computes the total cost of the travel requests. To code a connection with a database and compute the sum, you can complete the following steps:

STEP 1   Download the original Access database file Travel.accdb again to overwrite any data you added or deleted from the database. Open the Approved Travel Windows application. Add a Button object named btnTotalTravelCost to the Windows Form object and change the Text property to `Total Travel Cost`. Change the font size to 10 and the ForeColor property to CadetBlue. Set the Location property to 22,273, and set the Size property for the button to 121,23. Add a Label object named lblTotalTravelCost with the Text property of 30 "X's". Change the font size to 14 and Bold. Change the ForeColor property to CadetBlue. Change the Location property to 55,312. Set the Visible property for the lblTotalTravelCost Label object to False because the X's should not be displayed when the program begins.

A Button object and Label object are added to the Windows Form object (Figure 10–43).

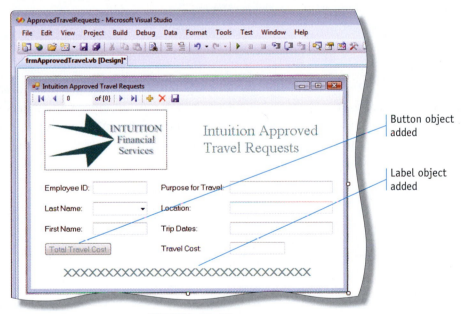

FIGURE 10-43

STEP 2 Double-click the Total Travel Cost button to create the btnTotalTravelCost_Click event handler. To initialize the OleDbDataAdapter, enter the code in Figure 10-44 inside the click event. The first variable strSql is assigned the SQL statement that queries all the fields in the ApprovedTravelRequests table. The second variable strPath is assigned the database driver for Access and the path to the Travel.accdb file. The third variable odaTravel is an instance of the OleDbDataAdapter.

Inside the btnTotalTravelCost_Click event, the variables are initialized for the OleDbDataAdapter (Figure 10-44).

```
36
37     Private Sub btnTotalTravelCost_Click_1(ByVal sender As System.Object, ByVal
38         ' strSql is a SQL statement that selects all the fields from the
39         ' ApprovedTravelRequests table
40
41         Dim strSql As String = "SELECT * FROM ApprovedTravelRequests"
42
43         'strPath provides the database type and path of the Travel database
44         Dim strPath As String = "Provider=Microsoft.ACE.OLEDB.12.0 ;" _
45             & "Data Source=F:\Travel.accdb"
46         Dim odaTravel As New OleDb.OleDbDataAdapter(strSql, strPath)
47         Dim datCost As New DataTable
48                         Integer
```

FIGURE 10-44

STEP 3 After the first three variables are initialized, initialize the rest of the variables needed for the Button object event handler. An instance named datCost is initialized to represent the DataTable object. The variable intCount is used to count through a For loop. The last variable, decTotalCost, will contain the total amount of the approved travel costs.

The rest of the variables are initialized (Figure 10-45).

```
47         Dim datCost As New DataTable
48         Dim intCount As Integer
49         Dim decTotalCost As Decimal = 0D
50
```

FIGURE 10-45

STEP 4 Continuing inside the btnTotalTravelCost_Click event handler, enter the code in Figure 10-46 to fill the DataTable with the contents of the ApprovedTravelRequests table. In the next line of code, the Dispose method is used to closed the connection.

The DataTable is filled and the connection is disconnected (Figure 10–46).

```
50
51          ' The DataTable name datCost is filled with the table data
52          odaTravel.Fill(datCost)
53          'The connection to the database is disconnected
54          odaTravel.Dispose()
55          For intCount = 0 To datCost.Rows.Count - 1
56              lCost += Convert.ToDecim        Rows(intCount)("Travel C
```

FIGURE 10-46

STEP 5 Enter the code in Figure 10-47 to create a For loop to increment through each record in the ApprovedTravelRequests table. Because the rows are numbered 0 to 15, the upper range is one less than the numbers of rows in the table, making 16 records. The value in each Travel Cost field is added to the value in the decTotalCost variable.

The total travel request cost is computed in the For loop (Figure 10–47).

```
54          odaTravel.Dispose()
55          For intCount = 0 To datCost.Rows.Count - 1
56              decTotalCost += Convert.ToDecimal(datCost.Rows(intCount)("Travel Cost"))
57          Next
58          lCost.Visible = True
```

FIGURE 10-47

STEP 6 Enter the code in Figure 10-48 to display the total approved travel request cost.

The total approved travel request cost is displayed (Figure 10–48).

```
58          Me.lblTotalTravelCost.Visible = True
59          Me.lblTotalTravelCost.Text = "The Total Approved Travel Cost is " _
60              & decTotalCost.ToString("C")
61
```

FIGURE 10-48

HEADS UP

You can use the process described beginning in Figure 10-43 with or without using a database wizard.

ONLINE REINFORCEMENT

To view a video of the process in the previous steps, visit scsite.com/vb2008/ch10 and then select Figure 10-43.

Program Design

The requirements document for the Intuition Financial Services Approved Travel Requests Windows application is shown in Figure 10-49, and the Use Case Definition document is shown in Figure 10-50.

REQUIREMENTS DOCUMENT

Date submitted: February 22, 2011

Application title: Intuition Financial Services Approved Travel Requests Windows Application

Purpose: This Windows application opens an Access database with the approved company travel requests in a Windows form. The data in the database can be viewed, updated, and deleted. The application also computes the total of approved travel costs.

Program Procedures: In a Windows application, the Travel Access database file is opened and the user can view, add, and delete records as needed. The total cost of approved travel is calculated.

Algorithms, Processing, and Conditions:
1. The user first views a Windows application that loads an existing Access database table that includes the information about each employee's approved travel request. A navigation toolbar appears at the top of the Windows form, allowing the user to move from record to record. The Windows form also includes a title and company logo.
2. The user can click the Add new button on the navigation toolbar to add an employee's travel request. The record is saved when the user clicks the Save Data button on the navigation toolbar.
3. The user can click the Delete button on the navigation toolbar to delete an employee's approved travel request. The record is permanently deleted when the user clicks the Save Data button on the navigation toolbar.
4. The user can click the Total Travel Cost button to compute the total cost of the approved travel requests.

Notes and Restrictions:
1. The Access database named Travel.accdb file is located on the USB drive on the E: drive.

Comments:
1. The image shown in the Windows application (intuitionlogo.gif) is available at scseries.com/vb2008/ch10/images.
2. The Access database file named Travel.accdb is available at scseries.com/vb2008/ch10.

FIGURE 10-49

USE CASE DEFINITION

1. The user views the Access database information displaying the approved travel requests.
2. The user clicks the Add new button to add employee approved travel requests and clicks the Save Data button to permanently save the request to the original database.
3. The user clicks the Delete button to delete employee approved travel requests and clicks the Save Data button to permanently delete the request from the original database.
4. The user clicks the Total Travel Cost button to display the total cost of the approved travel requests in the database.

FIGURE 10-50

EVENT PLANNING DOCUMENT

The event planning document for the Intuition Financial Services Approved Travel Requests Windows application is shown in Figure 10-51.

EVENT PLANNING DOCUMENT

Program Name: Intuition Financial Services Approved Travel Requests Windows Application	Developer: Corinne Hoisington	Object: frmApprovedTravel	Date: February 22, 2011

OBJECT	EVENT TRIGGER	EVENT PROCESSING
frmApprovedTravel_Load	Load	Fill the DataSet object using the Data Source Configuration Wizard
btnTotalTravelCost	Click	Initialize the OleDbDataAdapter with the type of database and the path statement Fill the data table Disconnect the database For each record in the database Add each record's cost to the total cost Display the total approved travel cost

FIGURE 10-51

Guided Program Development

To design the user interface for the Intuition Approved Travel Requests Windows application and enter the code required to process each event in the program, complete the steps in this section.

NOTE TO THE LEARNER

As you will recall, in the following activity, you should complete the tasks within the specified steps. Each of the tasks is accompanied by a Hint Screen. The purpose of the Hint Screen is to indicate where in the Visual Studio window you should perform the activity; it also serves as a reminder of the method that you should use to create the user interface or enter code. If you need further help completing the step, refer to the figure number identified by the term ref: in the step.

Guided Program Development

Phase 1: Design the Form

1

▶ **Create a New Windows Project** Open Visual Studio using the Start button on the Windows taskbar and the All Programs submenu. Close the Start page. Click the New Project button on the Standard toolbar. Select and expand Visual Basic in the Project types list; select Windows in the left pane; select Windows Form Application in the right (Templates) pane; name the project ApprovedTravelRequests in the Name text box; and then click the OK button in the New Project dialog box.

▶ **Name the Form Object** Select the Windows Form object. In the Solution Explorer, rename Form1.vb to frmApprovedTravel.vb.

▶ **Title the Form Object** Select the Windows Form object and change the Text property to Intuition Approved Travel Requests.

▶ **Build the Top Portion of the Windows Form Object** Using the skills you have learned in this course, complete the top portion of the Windows Form object. For detailed specifications, see Figure 10-8 on page 737.

The top of the form is completed (Figure 10-52).

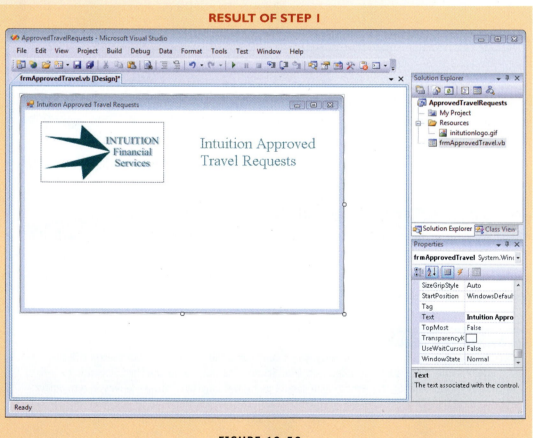

FIGURE 10-52

Guided Program Development (continued)

2

▶ **Create a Connection Using the Data Source Configuration Wizard** In the ApprovedTravelRequests project window, click Data on the menu bar, and then click Add New Data Source on the Data menu (ref: Figure 10-8).

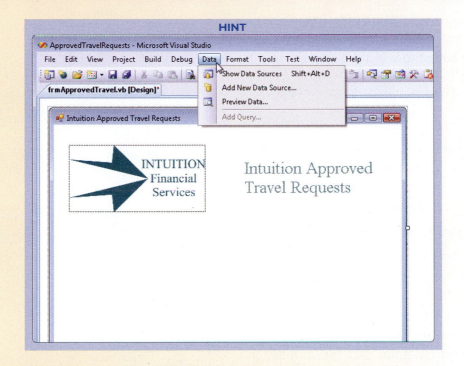

▶ **Choose the Data Source** Select Database in the Where will the application get data from group. Click the Next button.

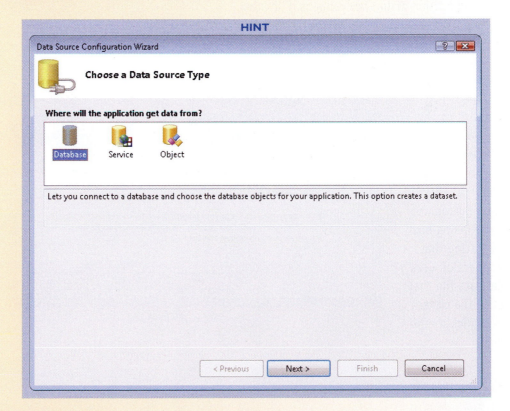

(continues)

Guided Program Development (continued)

▶ **Add a Connection** Click the New Connection button. In the Add Connection dialog box, click the Change button to select the Data source.

▶ **Change the Data Source** In the Change Data Source dialog box, select Microsoft Access Database File because the Travel database was created in Microsoft Access.

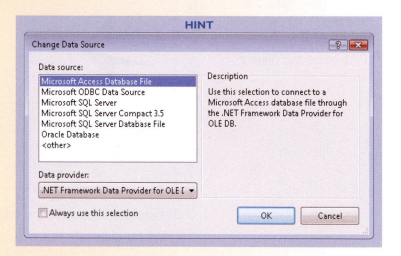

▶ **Select the Database File** Click the OK button. Click the Browse button to the right of Database filename. Select the USB device in drive E, and then select the Travel file. Click the Open button. The Add Connection dialog box reopens. Click the OK button.

▶ **Respond to the Dialog Box Question** The Choose Your Data Connection dialog box reopens. Click the Next button. A reminder dialog box opens stating that the connection uses a local data file that is not in the current project. Click the No button.

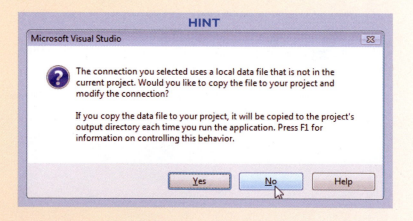

Guided Program Development (continued)

▶ **Save the Connection String**
The next dialog box opens requesting if you want to save the connect string to the application configuration file. Click the Next button.

HINT

▶ **Connect to the ApprovedTravelRequests Table** The Choose Your Database Object dialog box opens. Click the plus sign next to the Tables option. Click the ApprovedTravelRequests check box to select the ApprovedTravelRequests table. Click the Finish button.

The TravelDataSet is displayed in the Solution Explorer. (Figure 10-53).

HINT

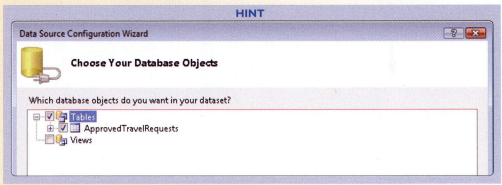

FIGURE 10-53

(continues)

Guided Program Development (continued)

3

▶ **Open the Data Menu** In the ApprovedTravelRequests project window, click Data on the menu bar *(ref: Figure 10-19)*.

▶ **Display the Data Sources Window** Click Show Data Sources on the Data menu.

▶ **Display the Field Names** Click the plus sign next to the table named ApprovedTravelRequests to expand the listing of the field names within the table.

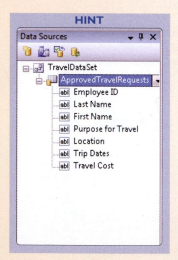

Guided Program Development *(continued)*

▶ **Bind a Field to the Windows Form** Select the Employee ID field in the Data Sources window. Drag the Employee ID field to the Windows Form object *(ref: Figure 10-23)*.

▶ **Bind All the Fields to the Windows Form** Drag the remaining field objects in the Data Sources window to the Windows Form object. Select the field Labels and TextBox objects and change the font to size 10. Resize the Label and TextBox objects. Use the formatting tools on the Format menu to equally distribute the bound objects. Use the layout shown in Figure 10-54.

▶ **Add a Button Object** Add a Button object to the Windows form named btnTotalTravelCost with the Text property changed to `Total Travel Cost`. Change the font size to 10 and the ForeColor property to CadetBlue. Add a Label object named lblTotalTravelCost with the Text property of 30 X's. Change the font size to 14 and Bold. Change the ForeColor property to CadetBlue. Center the Label object on the form (see Figure 10-54 for layout).

The Windows Form object is designed (Figure 10-54).

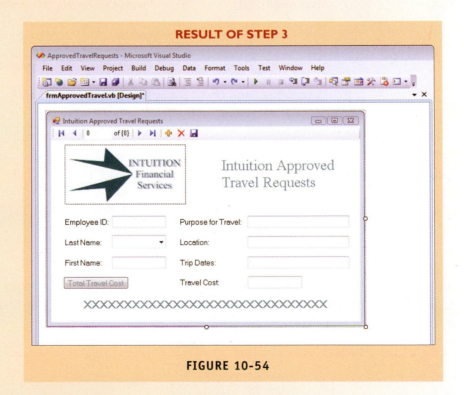

FIGURE 10-54

(continues)

Guided Program Development (continued)

4

▶ **Execute the Application to Load the Database Data** Click the Start Debugging button on the Standard toolbar to run the application. The data fills the Windows form (see Figure 10-55).

▶ **Use the Navigation Toolbar** With the application running, navigate through the database records. Add a record. Delete a record.

The Windows form is designed and the database is connected to the application (Figure 10-55).

RESULT OF STEP 4

FIGURE 10-55

Phase 2: Code the Application

5

▶ **Code the Comments** Click the View Code button on the Solution Explorer toolbar to begin coding the application. Type the first four standard comments at the top of the code editing window. Insert the Option Strict On command at the beginning of the code to turn on strict type checking.

HINT

```
 1 ' Program Name:  Intuition Approved Travel Windows Application
 2 ' Author:        Corinne Hoisington
 3 ' Date:          February 22, 2011
 4 ' Purpose:       The Approved Travel Requests Windows Application opens an
 5 '                Access database with the approved company travel requests in
 6 '                a Windows form. The database can be viewed, updated, and
 7 '                deleted. The application also computes the total of the
 8 '                travel costs that have been entered into the database.
 9
10 Option Strict On
```

Guided Program Development *(continued)*

▶ **Comment the Code Created by the Database Wizard** The Data Source Configuration Wizard creates two Sub methods. Enter the comments in the first line of the two Sub methods as shown in the adjacent Hint Screen.

HINT

```
12  Public Class frmApprovedTravel
13
14      Private Sub ApprovedTravelRequestsBindingNavigatorSaveItemClick(ByVal sender As    ↙
        System.Object, ByVal e As System.EventArgs) Handles                               ↙
        ApprovedTravelRequestsBindingNavigatorSaveItemClick
15          ' This click event is created by the database wizard
16
17          Me.Validate()
18          Me.ApprovedTravelRequestsBindingSource.EndEdit()
19          Me.ApprovedTravelRequestsTableAdapter.Update(Me.TravelDataSet.                 ↙
        ApprovedTravelRequests)
20
21      End Sub
22
23      Private Sub frmApprovedTravel_Load(ByVal sender As System.Object, ByVal e As System↙
        .EventArgs) Handles MyBase.Load
24          ' The frmApprovedTravel_Load event uses the Data Source Configuration
25          ' Wizard to fill the Windows form
26
27          Me.ApprovedTravelRequestsTableAdapter.Fill(Me.TravelDataSet.                    ↙
        ApprovedTravelRequests)
28
29      End Sub
```

▶ **Code a Try-Catch Block** Inside the frmApprovedTravel_Load event, place a Try statement before the Fill statement that was created by the database wizard. The Try-Catch block will catch an exception created by the file not being available. Code the Catch statement to catch an exception. If an exception is caught, a MessageBox states that the database file is unavailable and the application closes.

HINT

```
23      Private Sub frmApprovedTravel_Load(ByVal sender As System.Object, ByVal e As System↙
        .EventArgs) Handles MyBase.Load
24          ' The frmApprovedTravel_Load event uses the Data Source Configuration
25          ' Wizard to fill the Windows form
26
27          ' The Try Catch block catches an exception caused by a missing database file
28          Try
29              Me.ApprovedTravelRequestsTableAdapter.Fill(Me.TravelDataSet.                ↙
        ApprovedTravelRequests)
30          Catch ex As Exception
31              MsgBox("The Database File is Unavailable", , "Error")
32              Me.Close()
33          End Try
34
35      End Sub
```

(continues)

Guided Program Development *(continued)*

▶ **Code the OleDbDataAdapter for the btnTotalTravelCost_Click Event** Double-click the Total Travel Cost button in the
Design window to create the btnTotalTravelCost_Click event handler. To initialize the OleDbDataAdapter, enter the code in
the adjacent Hint Screen inside the click event. The first variable, strSql, is assigned the SQL statement that queries all
the fields in the ApprovedTravelRequests table. The second variable, strPath, is assigned the database driver for Access and
the path to the Travel.accdb file. The third variable, odaTravel, is an instance of the OleDbDataAdapter *(ref: Figure 10-45)*.

HINT

```
37      Private Sub btnTotalTravelCost_Click_1(ByVal sender As System.Object, ByVal e As    ↙
            System.EventArgs) Handles btnTotalTravelCost.Click
38          ' strSql is a SQL statement that selects all the fields from the
39          ' ApprovedTravelRequests table
40
41          Dim strSql As String = "SELECT * FROM ApprovedTravelRequests "
42
43          'strPath provides the database type and path of the Travel database
44          Dim strPath As String = "Provider=Microsoft .ACE.OLEDB.12.0 ;" _
45              & "Data Source =E:\Travel .accdb"
46          Dim odaTravel As New OleDb.OleDbDataAdapter(strSql, strPath)
```

▶ **Fill the DataTable Object** Inside the btnTotalTravelCost_Click event, after initializing the OleDbDataAdapter,
initialize an instance named datCost to represent the DataTable object. Declare the variable intCount for use in counting
through a For loop. Initialize the last variable, decTotalCost, which will contain the total of the approved travel costs.
Write the statement to fill the DataTable with the contents of the ApprovedTravelRequests table. Code the Dispose
method to close the open connection.

HINT

```
47          Dim datCost As New DataTable
48          Dim intCount As Integer
49          Dim decTotalCost As Decimal = 0D
50
51          ' The DataTable name datCost is filled with the table data
52          odaTravel.Fill(datCost)
53          'The connection to the database is disconnected
54          odaTravel.Dispose()
```

Guided Program Development *(continued)*

▶ **Calculate and Display the Sum of the Approved Travel Requests** Write a For loop statement to increment the count for each record in the ApprovedTravelRequests table. Because the rows number 0 to 15, the upper range is one less than the numbers of rows in the table, making 16 records. Write the code within the loop to add the value in each Travel Cost field to the value in the decTotalCost variable. Write the code to display the total approved travel costs in the lblTotalTravelCost Label object, including making the Label object visible.

HINT

```
55            For intCount = 0 To datCost.Rows.Count - 1
56                decTotalCost += Convert.ToDecimal(datCost.Rows(intCount)("Travel Cost"))
57            Next
58            Me.lblTotalTravelCost.Visible = True
59            Me.lblTotalTravelCost.Text = "The Total Approved Travel Cost is " _
60                & decTotalCost.ToString("C")
61        End Sub
62  End Class
```

The code is completed (Figure 10-56).

RESULT OF STEP 5

```
1  ' Program Name: Intuition Approved Travel Windows Application
2  ' Author:       Corinne Hoisington
3  ' Date:         February 22, 2011
4  ' Purpose:      The Approved Travel Requests Windows Application opens an
5  '               Access database with the approved company travel requests in
6  '               a Windows form. The database can be viewed, updated, and
7  '               deleted. The application also computes the total of the
8  '               travel costs that have been entered into the database.
9
10 Option Strict On
11
12 Public Class frmApprovedTravel
13
14     Private Sub ApprovedTravelRequestsBindingNavigatorSaveItem_Click(ByVal sender As  ↙
       System.Object, ByVal e As System.EventArgs) Handles                               ↙
       ApprovedTravelRequestsBindingNavigatorSaveItem.Click
15         ' This click event is created by the database wizard
16
17         Me.Validate()
18         Me.ApprovedTravelRequestsBindingSource.EndEdit()
19         Me.ApprovedTravelRequestsTableAdapter.Update(Me.TravelDataSet.              ↙
       ApprovedTravelRequests)
20
21     End Sub
22
```

FIGURE 10-56 (continues)

(continues)

Guided Program Development (continued)

RESULT OF STEP 5

```
23      Private Sub frmApprovedTravel_Load(ByVal sender As System.Object, ByVal e As System ↙
        .EventArgs) Handles MyBase.Load
24          ' The frmApprovedTravel_Load event uses the Data Source Configuration
25          ' Wizard to fill the Windows form
26
27          ' The Try Catch block catches an exception caused by a missing database file
28          Try
29              Me.ApprovedTravelRequestsTableAdapter.Fill(Me.TravelDataSet.            ↙
        ApprovedTravelRequests)
30          Catch ex As Exception
31              MsgBox("The Database File is Unavailable", , "Error")
32              Me.Close()
33          End Try
34
35      End Sub
36
37      Private Sub btnTotalTravelCost_Click(ByVal sender As System.Object, ByVal e As    ↙
        System.EventArgs) Handles btnTotalTravelCost.Click
38          ' strSql is a SQL statement that selects all the fields from the
39          ' ApprovedTravelRequests table
40
41          Dim strSql As String = "SELECT * FROM ApprovedTravelRequests"
42
43          'strPath provides the database type and path of the Travel database
44          Dim strPath As String = "Provider=Microsoft.ACE.OLEDB.12.0 ;" _
45              & "Data Source=F:\Travel.accdb"
46          Dim odaTravel As New OleDb.OleDbDataAdapter(strSql, strPath)
47          Dim datCost As New DataTable
48          Dim intCount As Integer
49          Dim decTotalCost As Decimal = 0D
50
51          ' The DataTable name datCost is filled with the table data
52          odaTravel.Fill(datCost)
53          'The connection to the database is disconnected
54          odaTravel.Dispose()
55          For intCount = 0 To datCost.Rows.Count - 1
56              decTotalCost += Convert.ToDecimal(datCost.Rows(intCount)("Travel Cost"))
57.         Next
58          Me.lblTotalTravelCost.Visible = True
59          Me.lblTotalTravelCost.Text = "The Total Approved Travel Cost is " _
60              & decTotalCost.ToString("C")
61
62      End Sub
63
64  End Class
65
```

FIGURE 10-56 (continued)

Summary

In this chapter you have learned to create a Windows application using database files and ADO.NET 3.5. The items listed in the table in Figure 10-57 include all the new Visual Studio and Visual Basic skills you have learned in this chapter.

	VISUAL BASIC SKILLS	
Skill	**Figure Number**	**Web Address for Video**
Examine Intuition Approved Travel Request chapter project application	Figure 10-1	scsite.com/vb2008/ch10/figure10-1
Connect to the database using the Data Source Configuration Wizard	Figure 10-8	scsite.com/vb2008/ch10/figure10-8
View the data available in the source database	Figure 10-19	scsite.com/vb2008/ch10/figure10-19
Bind each database field to the Windows Form object	Figure 10-23	scsite.com/vb2008/ch10/figure10-23
Add a new record to the database table	Figure 10-26	scsite.com/vb2008/ch10/figure10-26
Delete an existing record in the database table	Figure 10-29	scsite.com/vb2008/ch10/figure10-29
Change Toolbox object type	Figure 10-32	scsite.com/vb2008/ch10/figure10-32
Code a connection with a database and compute the sum	Figure 10-43	scsite.com/vb2008/ch10/figure10-43

FIGURE 10-57

Learn It Online

Start your browser and visit scsite.com/vb2008/ch10. Follow the instructions in the exercises below.

1. **Chapter Reinforcement TF, MC, SA** Below the Learn It Online heading, click one of the Chapter Reinforcement links for Multiple Choice, True/False, or Short Answer. Answer each question and submit your answers to your instructor.

2. **Practice Test** Click the Practice Test link below the Learn It Online heading. Answer each question, enter your first and last name at the bottom of the page, and then click the Grade Test button. When the graded practice test is displayed on your screen, submit the graded practice test to your instructor. Continue to take the practice test until you are satisfied with your score.

3. **Crossword Puzzle Challenge** Click the Crossword Puzzle Challenge link below the Learn It Online heading. Read the instructions, and then click the Continue button. Work the crossword puzzle. When you are finished, click the Submit button. When the crossword puzzle is redisplayed, submit it to your instructor.

Knowledge Check

1. ADO.NET 3.5 can only connect to local databases stored on a computer's hard drive. True or false?

2. Define ADO.

3. Define SQL.

4. What is the name of a unique field that must be present in each relational database?

5. Name three types of databases that can connect with ADO.NET 3.5.

6. What is a DataSet object?

7. Does a row in a database table represent a record or a field?

8. Name five types of objects that can be dragged from a data field in the Data Sources window to the Windows Form object, without using the Customize option.

9. What is the object name of the navigation toolbar?

10. When you add a record to a database using the Add new button on the navigation toolbar, the record is not added to the original database. What action must take place to add the record to the original data source?

11. How many records does the database table named SouthernStates displayed in Figure 10-58 contain?

Knowledge Check

APPROXIMATE POPULATION OF THE SOUTHERN STATES

AutoNumber	State Name	State Capital	Population
1	Florida	Tallahassee	20,066,000
2	Georgia	Atlanta	10,962,000
3	South Carolina	Columbia	4,574,000
4	North Carolina	Raleigh	9,916,000
5	Virginia	Richmond	8,165,000
6	Alabama	Montgomery	5,224,000
7	Louisiana	Baton Rouge	5,111,000
8	Tennessee	Nashville	7,249,000
9	West Virginia	Charleston	1,864,000
10	Mississippi	Jackson	3,413,000
11	Kentucky	Lexington	4,314,000

Source: http://www.census.gov/population/projections/state/stpjpop.txt

FIGURE 10-58

12. In the table in Figure 10-58, name the field labels.

13. For the table in Figure 10-58, write a statement that references the North Carolina state capital city and assign the value to the strCapitalCity variable.

14. What properties under the Data Binding Mode must you set when you bind a ComboBox object to a Windows form?

15. What procedure places data in the Data Table?

16. What command disconnects a database connection?

17. Write a line of code to initialize a String variable named strOrder to a Select SQL statement that would select all the fields from a table named Coffee.

18. What is the wildcard symbol used in a Select statement?

19. What does the wildcard symbol mean in the Select statement?

20. Write the statement that would fill a DataTable object named datCoins if an instance of the OleDbDataAdapter is named odaCollection.

Debugging Exercise

1. The code shown in Figure 10-59 is designed to increment through each row in a database table. Correct the error in the code.

```
For intRecordCount = 0 To datInventory.Rows.Count
    ' Processing statements

Next
```

FIGURE 10-59

2. Correct the line of code shown in Figure 10-60:

```
strNumberOfRows = datCityName.Rows.Count
```

FIGURE 10-60

3. Rewrite the code shown in Figure 10-61 correctly:

```
strNumberOfRows = Convert.ToString(datCityName.Rows(5)(City))
```

FIGURE 10-61

Program Analysis

1. Write a command that assigns an Access database named usedcarparts.accdb and a path located on E: drive to a string named strConnect for use later in an instance of an OleDbDataAdapter.

2. Consider the database table named BaseballStadiums shown in Figure 10-62. If the instance of the DataTable is named datStadium, what value would the statement in Figure 10-63 assign to the variable intCount?

Stadium Number	Stadium Name	Location	Team
203	Dodgers Stadium	Los Angeles, CA	Dodgers
304	Petco Field	San Diego, CA	Padres
425	Wrigley Field	Chicago, IL	Cubs
509	Camden Yards	Baltimore, MD	Orioles
698	Fenway Park	Boston, MA	Red Sox
756	Shea Stadium	New York City, NY	Mets

FIGURE 10-62

```
intCount = datStadium.Rows.Count
```

FIGURE 10-63

Program Analysis

3. Using the database table in Figure 10-62, what value would be assigned to strTeamName in the code in Figure 10-64?

```
strTeamName = Convert.ToString(datStadium.Rows(3)("Team"))
```
FIGURE 10-64

4. Using the database table in Figure 10-62, what value would be assigned to strLocation in the code in Figure 10-65?

```
strLocation = Convert.ToString(datStadium.Rows(1)("Location"))
```
FIGURE 10-65

5. Using the database table in Figure 10-62, what value would be assigned to intNumber in the code in Figure 10-66?

```
intNumber = datStadium.Columns.Count
```
FIGURE 10-66

Case Programming Assignments

Complete one or more of the following case programming assignments. Submit the program and materials you create to your instructor. The level of difficulty is indicated for each case programming assignment.

● = Easiest
●● = Intermediate
●●● = Challenging

1 ● FLORIST DATABASE

Design a Windows application and write the code that will execute according to the program requirements in Figure 10-67 and the Use Case definition in Figure 10-68. Before writing the code, create an event planning document for each event in the program. The completed Windows application and other objects in the user interface are shown in Figure 10-69. An Access database file named flower.accdb is needed for this application and can be downloaded from scsite.com/vb2008/ch10.

REQUIREMENTS DOCUMENT

Date submitted: October 30, 2012

Application title: Bonita Florist Shop Flower Meanings Windows Application

Purpose: This Windows application opens an Access database with 17 flower types and what each flower meaning represents, for example an iris means faith. The database can be viewed, updated, and deleted. The application can be used by a customer looking for a symbolic flower for a special occasion.

Program Procedures: In a Windows application, the Access database file is opened and the user can view, add, and delete records as needed.

Algorithms, Processing, and Conditions:
1. The user first views a Windows application that loads an existing Access database table that includes the flower number, flower name, and flower meaning. A navigation toolbar appears at the top of the Windows form, allowing the user to move from record to record. The Windows form also includes a title and a graphic background image.
2. The user can click the Add new button on the navigation toolbar to add a new flower. The record is saved when the user clicks the Save Data button on the navigation toolbar.
3. The user can click the Delete button on the navigation toolbar to delete a flower and its meaning. The record is permanently deleted when the user clicks the Save Data button on the navigation toolbar.

Notes and Restrictions:
1. The flower.accdb file is located on the USB drive on E: drive.
2. Use a Try-Catch statement to catch an exception if the database is not available.

Comments:
1. The flower.accdb Access database file can be downloaded from scsite.com/vb2008/ch10.
2. The background picture (sunflower.jpg) is available for download at scsite.com/vb2008/ch10/images.

FIGURE 10-67

Case Programming Assignments

USE CASE DEFINITION

1. The user views the Access database information displaying the flowers and their meanings.
2. The user clicks the Add new button to add a new flower and clicks the Save Data button to save the item to the original database.
3. The user clicks the Delete button to delete a flower and permanently deletes the record from the original database by clicking the Save Data button.

FIGURE 10-68

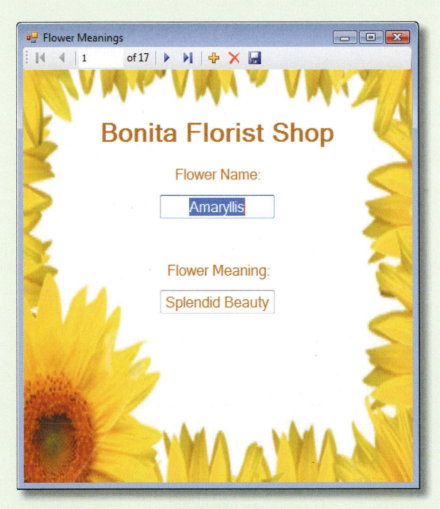

FIGURE 10-69

Case Programming Assignments

2 ● PHYSICIANS REFERRAL NETWORK

Design a Windows application and write the code that will execute according to the program requirements in Figure 10-70 and the Use Case definition in Figure 10-71. Before writing the code, create an event planning document for each event in the program. The completed Windows application and other objects in the user interface are shown in Figure 10-72. The Access file named physicians.accdb is needed for this application and can be downloaded from scsite.com/vb2008/ch10.

REQUIREMENTS DOCUMENT

Date submitted:	April 22, 2011
Application title:	HMO Physicians Referral Network Windows Application
Purpose:	This Windows application opens an Access database with 18 Texas physicians and their practice information. The database can be viewed, updated, and deleted. The application can be used for the referral network to search for a physician in an HMO network.
Program Procedures:	In a Windows application, the Access database file is opened and the user can view, add, and delete records as needed.
Algorithms, Processing, and Conditions:	1. The user first views a Windows application that loads an existing Access database table that includes the medical ID, the physician name, city, physician specialty, and phone number. A navigation toolbar appears at the top of the Windows form, allowing the user to move from record to record. The Windows form also includes a title and a graphic image.
	2. The user can click the Add new button on the navigation toolbar to add a new physician to the network. The record is saved when the user clicks the Save Data button on the navigation toolbar.
	3. The user can click the Delete button on the navigation toolbar to delete a physician. The record is permanently deleted when the user clicks the Save Data button on the navigation toolbar.
	4. The user can click a list arrow to move directly to a physician's record.
Notes and Restrictions:	1. The physicians.accdb file is located on the USB drive on E: drive.
	2. Use a Try-Catch statement to catch an exception if the database file is not available.
Comments:	1. The physicians.accdb Access database file can be downloaded from scsite.com/vb2008/ch10.
	2. The background picture (doctor.jpg) is available for download at scsite.com/vb2008/ch10/images.

FIGURE 10-70

Case Programming Assignments

USE CASE DEFINITION

1. The user views the Access database information displaying the physicians in the Texas HMO referral system.
2. The user clicks the Add new button to add a physician to the HMO network and clicks the Save Data button to save the item to the original database.
3. The user clicks the Delete button to delete a physician from the HMO network and permanently deletes it from the original database by clicking the Save Data button.
4. The user can click a list arrow to display physician names to move directly to a particular physician's record.

FIGURE 10-71

FIGURE 10-72

Case Programming Assignments

3 SPANISH FOOD STORE

Design a Windows application and write the code that will execute according to the program requirements in Figure 10-73 and the Use Case definition in Figure 10-74. Before writing the code, create an event planning document for each event in the program. The completed Windows application and other objects in the user interface are shown in Figure 10-75. An Access database file named spanishfood.accdb is needed for this application and can be downloaded from scsite.com/vb2008/ch10.

REQUIREMENTS DOCUMENT

Date submitted: August 1, 2011

Application title: Spanish Food Store Inventory Windows Application

Purpose: This Windows application opens an Access database with 22 food items in the store inventory in a Windows form. The database can be viewed, updated, and deleted. The application also computes the total value of the inventory in stock.

Program Procedures: In a Windows application, the Access database file is opened and the user can view, add, and delete records as needed. The total present store value of the Spanish foods in the inventory also can be displayed.

Algorithms, Processing and Conditions: 1. The user first views a Windows application that loads an existing Access database table that includes the product number, English food name, Spanish food name, quantity, cost per item, and department. A navigation toolbar appears at the top of the Windows form, allowing the user to move from record to record. The Windows form also includes a title and a graphic image.
2. The user can click the Add new button on the navigation toolbar to add a new food item to the inventory. The record is saved when the user clicks the Save Data button on the navigation toolbar.
3. The user can click the Delete button on the navigation toolbar to delete a food item. The record is permanently deleted when the user clicks the Save Data button on the navigation toolbar.
4. The user can click the Compute Total Value of Inventory Button object to compute the total value of the store's inventory.
5. The total value of inventory is computed by multiplying the cost per item times the quantity of the item and then adding the result to the value in an accumulator variable.

Notes and Restrictions: 1. The spanishfood.accdb file is located on the USB drive on E: drive.
2. Use a Try-Catch statement to catch an exception if the file is not available.

Comments: 1. The spanishfood.accdb Access database file can be downloaded from scsite.com/vb2008/ch10.
2. The picture (peppers.jpg) is available for download at scsite.com/vb2008/ch10/images.

FIGURE 10-73

Case Programming Assignments

USE CASE DEFINITION

1. The user views the Access database information displaying the Spanish food inventory items.
2. The user clicks the Add new button to add a new food item and clicks the Save Data button to save the item to the original database.
3. The user clicks the Delete button to delete a Spanish food item and permanently deletes the record from the original database by clicking the Save Data button.
4. The user clicks the Compute Total Value of Inventory button to display the total value of inventory in the database.

FIGURE 10-74

FIGURE 10-75

Case Programming Assignments

4 ●●
SPORTS LEAGUE BASEBALL TEAM

Design a Windows application and write the code that will execute according to the program requirements in Figure 10-76. Before designing the user interface, create a Use Case definition. Before writing the code, create an event planning document for each event in the program. This program requires the use of an Access database file named sportsleague.accdb located at scsite.com/vb2008/ch10.

REQUIREMENTS DOCUMENT

Date submitted:	May 13, 2013
Application title:	Sports League Baseball National All-Stars Co-ed Team Windows Application
Purpose:	This Windows application opens an Access database with 23 boys and girls ages 12-14 who are playing in the national Sports league co-ed championship. The database can be viewed, updated, and deleted in the Windows form. The application also computes the number of 12, 13, and 14 year olds on the team in three separate counts and the average age of the team.
Program Procedures:	In a Windows application, the Access database file is opened and the user can view, add, and delete records as needed. The total of each age in the database also can be displayed.
Algorithms, Processing, and Conditions:	1. The user first views a Windows application that loads an existing Access database table that includes the player number, first name, last name, parent's name, address, city, state, zip, telephone, and age. A navigation toolbar appears at the top of the Windows form, allowing the user to move from record to record. The Windows form also includes a title and a graphic image.
	2. The user can click the Add new button on the navigation toolbar to add a new player to the team. The record is saved when the user clicks the Save Data button on the navigation toolbar.
	3. The user can click the Delete button on the navigation toolbar to delete a team player. The record is permanently deleted when the user clicks the Save Data button on the navigation toolbar.
	4. The user can click the Find Total of Each Age Group Button object to compute the total number of 12, 13, and 14 year olds. The user also can compute the average age of the team.
Notes and Restrictions:	1. The sportsleague.accdb file is located on the USB drive on E: drive.
	2. Use a Try-Catch statement to catch an exception if the file is not available.
Comments:	1. The sportsleague.accdb Access database file can be downloaded from scsite.com/vb2008/ch10.

FIGURE 10-76

Case Programming Assignments

5 ●●
COLLEGE MAJORS

Design a Windows application and write the code that will execute according to the program requirements in Figure 10-77. Before designing the user interface, create a Use Case definition. Before writing the code, create an event planning document for each event in the program. This program requires the use of an Access database file named college.accdb located at scsite/vb2008/ch10.

REQUIREMENTS DOCUMENT

Date submitted: March 9, 2011

Application title: College Majors Windows Application

Purpose: This Windows application opens an Access database with 36 college majors in a Windows form. The database can be viewed, updated, and deleted. The application also computes the total number of students attending the college. The user can select a major from a combo box list and the application displays the percentage of students participating in that major.

**Program
Procedures:**   In a Windows application, the Access database file is opened and the user can view, add, and delete records as needed. The total student population and percent of students in a particular major also can be displayed.

**Algorithms,
Processing, and
Conditions:**   1. The user first views a Windows application that loads an existing Access database table that includes the department, college major, and the number of students in that major. A navigation toolbar appears at the top of the Windows form, allowing the user to move from record to record. The Windows form also includes a title and a graphic image.
                        2. The user can click the Add new button on the navigation toolbar to add a new major to the college. The record is saved when the user clicks the Save Data button on the navigation toolbar.
                        3. The user can click the Delete button on the navigation toolbar to delete a major. The record is permanently deleted when the user clicks the Save Data button on the navigation toolbar.
                        4. The user can click the Student Population of College Button object to compute the total number of students presently in majors.
                        5. The user can select the college major from a combo box list and the application will display the percentage of students at the college participating in that major.

**Notes and
Restrictions:**   1. The college.accdb file is located on the USB drive on E: drive.
                        2. Use a Try-Catch statement to catch an exception if the file is not available.

Comments: 1. The college.accdb Access database can be downloaded from scsite.com/vb2008/ch10.
                        2. Use a graphic image you obtain from the Web.

FIGURE 10-77

Case Programming Assignments

6 ●● KID FRIENDLY STOCKS

Design a Windows application and write the code that will execute according to the program requirements in Figure 10-78. Before designing the user interface, create a Use Case definition. Before writing the code, create an event planning document for each event in the program. This program requires the use of an Access database file named kidfriendlystocks.accdb located at scsite.com/vb2008/ch10.

REQUIREMENTS DOCUMENT

Date submitted: August 17, 2012

Application title: Kid Friendly Stocks Windows Application

Purpose: This Windows application opens an Access database in a Windows form with 16 child-centered stock picks from an investment portfolio. The database can be viewed, updated, and deleted. The application also computes the total investment made in the portfolio and lists the name of the stocks with the selected rating which have been entered into the database.

Program Procedures: In a Windows application, the Access database file is opened and the user can view, add, and delete records as needed. The total portfolio investment is calculated.

Algorithms, Processing, and Conditions:

1. The user first views a Windows application that loads an existing Access database table that includes the stock symbol, the name of the stock, the price per share, number of shares, and the earning potential rating. A navigation toolbar appears at the top of the Windows form, allowing the user to move from record to record. The Windows form also includes a title and graphic image.
2. The user can click the Add new button on the navigation toolbar to add a new stock purchase. The record is saved when the user clicks the Save Data button on the navigation toolbar.
3. The user can click the Delete button on the navigation toolbar to delete a stock purchase. The record is permanently deleted when the user clicks the Save Data button on the navigation toolbar.
4. The user can select the stock symbol using the list arrow on a ComboBox object to move directly to the record needed.
5. The user can click the Compute Total Investment Button object to compute the total worth of stock owned.
6. The stock ratings list includes Exceptional, High, Average, and Low, and can be selected by the user. The application will display all the stock names in the selected rating in a ListBox object.

Notes and Restrictions:

1. The kidfriendlystocks.accdb file is located on the USB drive on E: drive.
2. Use a Try-Catch statement to catch an exception if the file is not available.

Comments:

1. The kidfriendlystocks.accdb Access database can be downloaded at scsite.com/vb2008/ch10.
2. Use a graphic image you obtain from the Web.

FIGURE 10-78

Case Programming Assignments

7 ●●● CALORIES CONSUMED

Create a requirements document and a Use Case Definition document, and then design a Windows application, based on the following case project. Before writing the code, create an event planning document for each event in the program.

A nutritionist often has patients create a food diary to see the amount of calories consumed each day. Create an Access database with the following fields: an item number as an autonumber, food consumed, and number of calories. On the Web, research the amount of calories each food contains. Enter calorie data into the database of all food and beverages consumed in one day (at least 12 items). Develop a Windows application that displays the Access database table of calories consumed in one day. The application will compute the total number of calories consumed. The Department of Health estimates the average requirement of a daily calorie intake is 1,940 calories per day for women and 2,550 for men. The application should request whether the user is a male or female. When the total number of calories is displayed, the percentage of calories consumed above or below the recommended daily calorie intake also should be shown.

FIGURE 10-79

8 ●●● GRADUATION PARTY EVENT

Create a requirements document and a Use Case Definition document, and then design a Windows application, based on the following case project. Before writing the code, create an event planning document for each event in the program.

Create an Access database that holds the invitation information for 15 people you would like to invite to a graduation party. The main table should have a primary key and include an autonumber, first name, last name, address, city, state, zip, and phone number field for each family invited. Create a Windows form that will display the families who are invited to the graduation party. Include a field in the database that also requests the number who RSVP for the party. This number will be added to the Windows form as you receive RSVP responses. Compute the total amount of people attending the party.

FIGURE 10-80

Case Programming Assignments

9 ●●●
CURRENCY CALCULATOR

Create a requirements document and a Use Case Definition document, and then design a Windows application, based on the following case project. Before writing the code, create an event planning document for each event in the program.

Create an Access database with the following information. Enter the information from the following table into a database table. Visit *www.xe.com/ucc* to research the amount equivalent to $1 U.S. in the currency from other countries and enter that value in the same database table. Allow the user to enter a U.S. dollar amount and the type of currency from a list from the database. Using the conversion amount from the table, convert the amount of U.S. dollars entered into the selected country's currency. Display the amount.

Country	Name of Currency
Canada	Canadian dollar
Australia	Australian dollar
Japan	Yen
India	Rupee
Switzerland	Franc
South Africa	Rand
Mexico	Peso
Iraq	Dinar
Indonesia	Rupiah
Malaysia	Ringgit
Thailand	Baht
Vietnam	Dong

FIGURE 10-81

CHAPTER ELEVEN

Multiple Classes and Inheritance

OBJECTIVES

You will have mastered the material in this chapter when you can:

- ▶ Use the TabIndex Property
- ▶ Edit input, including MaskedTextBox, TextBox, and ComboBox objects
- ▶ Describe the three-tier program structure
- ▶ Understand a class
- ▶ Create a class
- ▶ Instantiate an object
- ▶ Pass arguments when instantiating an object

- ▶ Write a class constructor
- ▶ Call a procedure in a separate class
- ▶ Code a base class and a subclass incorporating inheritance
- ▶ Call procedures found in a base class and a subclass
- ▶ Write overridable and overrides procedures
- ▶ Create and write a comma-delimited text file

Introduction

In previous chapters you have learned that a class is a named group of program code. Within a class such as Form1 that you have seen often, you can define attributes and you also can define sub procedures and function procedures. The classes you have used thus far have either been generated by the design feature of Visual Basic, such as the two form classes developed in Chapter 10, or were used from a library of classes supplied by Visual Studio 2008. In this chapter, you will define a class in code and will develop the code in the class to help complete the chapter project.

When you define classes, you have the option of using a feature of object-oriented programming languages such as Visual Basic called inheritance. Inheritance allows one class, called a subclass, to use attributes and procedures defined in another class called a base class.

Finally, when you define your own classes, you have the opportunity to design a three-tier structure for your program so it is more reliable, more robust, and more easily understood. The sample program in this chapter uses the three-tier program structure.

Chapter Project

In the sample chapter project, a Registration Costs window is displayed (Figure 11-1).

FIGURE 11-1

In the window in Figure 11-1, a student or a worker assisting the student enters the Student ID (which is the social security number), the Student Name, the Number of Units the student is registering for, identifies if the student is living off-campus or on-campus, identifies the housing and board an on-campus student is using, and identifies the student's major.

Then, when the user clicks the Calculate Costs button, the application calculates the total semester costs by multiplying the number of units times the cost per unit ($450.00). If the student is an on-campus resident, the cost for room and board also is calculated and placed in the final cost. The cost for Cooper Dorm is $2,900.00 per semester, the cost for Percey Hall is $3,400.00 per semester, and the cost for Julian Suites is $4,000.00 per semester. The total semester costs are shown below the buttons (see Figure 11-2).

FIGURE 11-2

The user is required to enter valid values for each of the items on the Registration form. If the user either does not enter a value, or enters an invalid value such as not entering a numeric value for Number of Units, a message box is displayed to inform the user to enter a valid value (see Figure 11-3).

Number Of
Units is blank

FIGURE 11-3

In Figure 11-3, the user failed to enter the Number Of Units, so the message box directs the user to enter the Number Of Units.

In addition to calculating the total semester costs, this program also creates a log on disk for the students whose costs have been calculated. This log is kept as a text file. The program must write records in the text file as students use this program.

USER INTERFACE AND THE TABINDEX PROPERTY

The user interface in the Registration Costs program does not contain any objects that you have not seen in previous programs. But a new property is implemented that users often find useful.

When users enter data into a Windows Form object, they usually enter the data in sequence on the form. For example, in Figure 11-2 on page 798, the user can enter the Student ID first, followed by the Student Name and then the Number Of Units, and so on. Often, users will prefer to press the Tab key to move the insertion point from one object on the Windows Form object to the next. To specify the sequence of objects that will be selected when the Tab key is pressed, the TabIndex property used. To implement the TabIndex property for the Windows Form object in Figure 11-2, you can complete the following steps:

ONLINE REINFORCEMENT

To view a video of the program execution, visit scsite.com/ vb2008/ch11, and then select Figure 11-1.

STEP 1   Select the object that will be selected when program execution begins. In the example, this is the txtStudentID MaskedTextBox object. Scroll in the Properties window until the TabIndex property is visible and then double-click in the right column of the TabIndex property.

The TabIndex property for the MaskedTextBox object is selected (Figure 11–4).

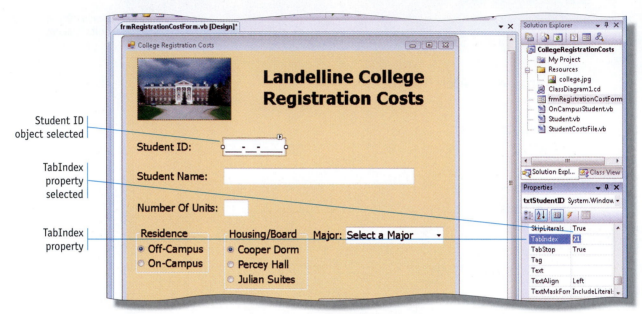

Student ID object selected

TabIndex property selected

TabIndex property

FIGURE 11-4

STEP 2   Type 1 and then press the ENTER key.

The value 1 in the TabIndex property of an object indicates the object will be selected when the program begins execution (Figure 11-5). When program execution begins, the insertion point will be located in the txtStudentID MaskedTextBox object.

TabIndex property changed to 1

FIGURE 11-5

STEP 3 Select the object which should be selected when the user presses the Tab key. In the sample program, the txtStudentName TextBox object should be selected. Double-click the right column of the TabIndex property for the txtStudentName TextBox object, type 2 and then press the ENTER key.

The TabIndex value for the txtStudentName object is set to 2 in the Properties window (Figure 11-6). When the user enters the Student ID value and presses the TAB key, the insertion point will be in the Student Name text box. Using these same techniques, you can continue to identify objects on the Windows Form object that will be selected when the user presses the TAB key.

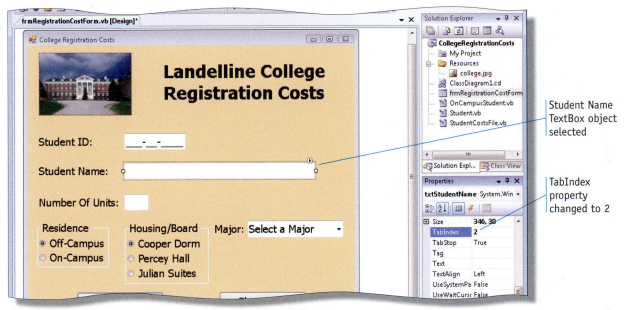

FIGURE 11-6

EDITING INPUT DATA

Like other applications in this book, in the Registration Costs program the data users enter through the use of the user interface must be checked to ensure valid data is entered. When the user clicks the Calculate Costs button, the following items must be checked:

1. Student ID: The student ID object is a masked text box and the mask is for the social security number, so the mask ensures that the user can enter only numbers. But, the social security mask does not ensure the user enters all nine numbers. Therefore, a check must be included in the program to require the user to enter all 9 numeric digits.

2. Student Name: The program must ensure the user enters characters in this TextBox object. In addition, spaces cannot be entered instead of actual alphabetic characters.

3. Number of Units: The user must enter a numeric value from 1 through 24 for the number of units the student is taking.

4. Major: The user must select a major from the list in the Major ComboBox object.

ONLINE REINFORCEMENT

To view a video of the process in the previous steps, visit scsite.com/vb2008/ch11 and then select Figure 11-4.

The code to implement these editing requirements is shown in Figure 11-7.

```
19          Dim InputError As Boolean = False
20
21          ' Is student ID entered properly
22          If Me.txtStudentID.MaskFull = False Then
23              MsgBox("Enter your Student ID in the Student ID box", , _
24                  "Error")
25              Me.txtStudentID.Clear()
26              Me.txtStudentID.Focus()
27              InputError = True
28              ' Is student name entered properly
29          ElseIf Me.txtStudentName.TextLength < 1 Or _
30                  Me.txtStudentName.Text < "A" Then
31              MsgBox("Enter your name in the Student Name box", , "Error")
32              Me.txtStudentName.Clear()
33              Me.txtStudentName.Focus()
34              InputError = True
35              ' Is number of units entered properly
36          ElseIf Not IsNumeric(Me.txtNumberOfUnits.Text) Then
37              MsgBox("Enter the units in the Number of Units box", , _
38                  "Error")
39              Me.txtNumberOfUnits.Clear()
40              Me.txtNumberOfUnits.Focus()
41              InputError = True
42              ' Has 1-24 units been entered
43          ElseIf Convert.ToInt32(Me.txtNumberOfUnits.Text) < 1 _
44                  Or Convert.ToInt32(Me.txtNumberOfUnits.Text) > 24 Then
45              MsgBox("Units must be 1 - 24", , "Error")
46              Me.txtNumberOfUnits.Clear()
47              Me.txtNumberOfUnits.Focus()
48              InputError = True
49              ' Has a major been selected
50          ElseIf Me.cboMajor.SelectedIndex < 0 Then
51              MsgBox("Please select a major", , "Error")
52              Me.cboMajor.Focus()
53              InputError = True
54          End If
```

FIGURE 11-7

In Figure 11-7, on line 19, a Boolean variable named InputError is defined and given the value False. This variable will be set to a value of True if an error is found in the editing statements. If any input area contains an error, the registration costs will not be calculated.

The editing checks are completed within an If...Else If statement. By placing the checks in this statement, each of the fields must contain valid data before the next field is checked; that is, until the Student ID field contains valid data, the Student Name field is not checked. This approach ensures that each field will contain valid data before the registration costs are calculated.

To ensure the Student ID masked text box contains all 9 numeric digits, the MaskFull property is tested, as shown in Figure 11-8.

```
21              ' Is student ID entered properly
22              If Me.txtStudentID.MaskFull = False Then
23                  MsgBox("Enter your Student ID in the Student ID box", , _
24                      "Error")
25                  Me.txtStudentID.Clear()
26                  Me.txtStudentID.Focus()
27                  InputError = True
```

FIGURE 11-8

The MaskFull property identifies if all digits have been entered into the mask. For the Student ID, if all nine numeric digits have been entered into the masked text box, the property will be true; otherwise, the property will be false. If the MaskFull property is false, a message box will be displayed that directs the user to enter the student ID in the Student ID box. In addition, the masked text box is cleared, the focus is placed in the masked text box, and the InputError Boolean variable is set to True, indicating an error occurred.

If the Student ID field is correct, the next check is to ensure the Student Name text box contains data. The Else...If statement to check the Student Name text box is shown in Figure 11-9.

```
28                  ' Is student name entered properly
29              ElseIf Me.txtStudentName.TextLength < 1 Or _
30                  Me.txtStudentName.Text < "A" Then
31                  MsgBox("Enter your name in the Student Name box", , "Error")
32                  Me.txtStudentName.Clear()
33                  Me.txtStudentName.Focus()
34                  InputError = True
```

FIGURE 11-9

The If statement tests if the length of the data in the text box is less than zero and if the first character entered is less than the letter, A. If the length is less than zero, no data was entered in the text box. If the first character is less than A, then either a space or a special character was entered as the first character, all of which are invalid. If either of these conditions is true, a message box instructing the user to enter a student name is displayed, the text box is cleared, focus is placed back on the Student Name text box, and the InputError Boolean variable is set to true.

If the Student Name text box contains valid data, the Number of Units TextBox object is checked to ensure it contains a numeric value from 1 through 24. To make this check, two If statements are required, one to check for numeric data (line 36 in Figure 11-10) and one to ensure the value is 1 through 24 (lines 43-44 in Figure 11-10). If either of these tests finds an error, once again a message box is displayed, the TextBox object is cleared, the focus is placed in the text box and the InputError variable is set to true.

```
35                       ' Is number of units entered properly
36             ElseIf Not IsNumeric(Me.txtNumberOfUnits.Text) Then
37                 MsgBox("Enter the units in the Number of Units box", , _
38                     "Error")
39                 Me.txtNumberOfUnits.Clear()
40                 Me.txtNumberOfUnits.Focus()
41                 InputError = True
42                 ' Has 1-24 units been entered
43             ElseIf Convert.ToInt32(Me.txtNumberOfUnits.Text) < 1 _
44                     Or Convert.ToInt32(Me.txtNumberOfUnits.Text) > 24 Then
45                 MsgBox("Units must be 1 - 24", , "Error")
46                 Me.txtNumberOfUnits.Clear()
47                 Me.txtNumberOfUnits.Focus()
48                 InputError = True
```

FIGURE 11-10

The last data editing step is to ensure the user selected a major in the Major ComboBox object (Figure 11-11).

```
50             ElseIf Me.cboMajor.SelectedIndex < 0 Then
51                 MsgBox("Please select a major", , "Error")
52                 Me.cboMajor.Focus()
53                 InputError = True
54             End If
55
```

FIGURE 11-11

As you have learned, when testing for a selection in a ComboBox object, the SelectedIndex property will contain the value −1 if a selection has not been made, and will contain the index value of the selected entry if a selection has been made. If the SelectedIndex property is less than zero, then a selection has not been made, so a message box displays an error message, the focus is placed on the ComboBox object, and the InputError Boolean variable is set to true.

If all tests are passed, the processing to compute the registration costs and other processing can occur.

Program Structure Using Classes

In previous programs, the Form class has been the basis of the program. It presented the user interface and has contained the Visual Basic statements that have processed data the user entered. In some programs, multiple procedures have been included in the class to complete the required processing.

When programs become larger and more complex, often you will divide the processing necessary to accomplish the program's requirements into classes. This can have several benefits: 1) The program is easier to read, understand, and maintain; 2) A class can be used in more than one program for the same purpose. For example, the Button class that is used to create buttons in the user interface is used each time a Button object is placed on the Windows Form object; 3) The processing accomplished in a class is separated from other classes, making the program easier to maintain and less prone to error; 4) Variables defined in one class can be hidden from processing in other classes so there is less likelihood of programming errors. Controlling the use of these variables, often called attributes or properties, by other classes reduces the inadvertent or purposeful inappropriate use of the attributes.

The concept of separating processing and hiding data within specific classes is called **encapsulation**, and is a major contributor to reliable and robust programs.

When developing programs with multiple classes, a starting point for determining what classes should appear in a program is the three-tier program structure. The three-tier structure specifies that a program is divided into three separate tiers: Presentation, Business, and Persistence (Figure 11-12).

Presentation Tier	Business Tier	Persistence Tier
User Interface, Forms	Logic, Calculations	Data Storage (Files and Databases)

FIGURE 11-12

The **presentation tier** contains the classes that display information for the user and accept user input. In many programs, the presentation tier consists of one or more forms and the objects placed on the forms. In a Web application, the presentation tier is the Web form and Web page that appear to the user. In addition, the processing in the presentation tier ensures that valid data is entered into the program for processing in the business tier.

The business tier contains the logic and calculations that must occur in order to fulfill the requirements of the program. The class(es) in the business tier generally use data entered by users and data obtained from storage to perform the logic and calculations. The business tier is so-called because the business tier implements the "business rules" required for the application.

The **persistence tier**, sometimes called the **data access tier**, contains the code required to read and write data from permanent storage. Data that is stored in a file or database on disk often is called persistent data because the data remains after the program is terminated.

When designing a program using the three-tier approach, a primary rule is that classes in the presentation tier can communicate only with classes in the business tier. They never can communicate with classes in the persistence tier. In the same manner, classes in the persistence tier cannot communicate with classes in the presentation tier.

By following this rule, a program is much easier to maintain if changes must be made. For example, if a program currently writes data to a text file, such as the Registration Costs program in this chapter, and a decision is made to instead write the data in a database, only the class(es) in the persistence tier must be examined and changed. The user interface classes should have nothing to do with how data is stored. Therefore, the developer can be confident that if the correct changes are made to the persistence classes, the program will run properly regardless of the processing in the presentation classes.

Similarly, the business classes need not be concerned with how the data is obtained or stored. While the business classes will decide what data is needed and what data should be written to storage, it is only the persistence classes that will actually read or write data.

This same thinking holds true for the separation of the business and presentation tiers. The classes in the business tier, where the logic and calculations occur, should not have to be concerned with the functionality of the user interface; nor should the user interface classes be concerned with how the data is manipulated by the business classes.

By placing classes in one of the three tiers, depending on the class's function, the program becomes much easier to design, develop, and maintain.

SAMPLE PROGRAM CLASSES

In the Registration Costs program in this chapter, the three-tier approach is used. The classes in each of the tiers are as follows:

1. Presentation tier: The presentation tier contains the frmRegistrationCostForm class. This class displays the user interface in a Windows Form object and also edits the user input data to ensure its validity.

2. Business tier: The business tier contains two classes: the Student class and the OnCampusStudent class. The Student class contains data for each registered student and calculates the registration costs for some students. The OnCampusStudent class is used for registered students who live in on-campus residence halls.

3. Persistence tier: The persistence tier consists of one class, StudentCostsFile, which creates and writes the Student Costs File.

CREATING A CLASS

The class in the presentation tier, the frmRegistrationCostForm class, is created when the new Windows Application is started. The other classes are created using the technique shown in the following steps:

STEP 1   With Visual Studio open and a Window Application project begun, right-click the project name in the Solution Explorer window and then point to Add on the shortcut menu.

The shortcut menu is displayed (Figure 11-13). When you point to the Add menu item, the Add submenu also is displayed.

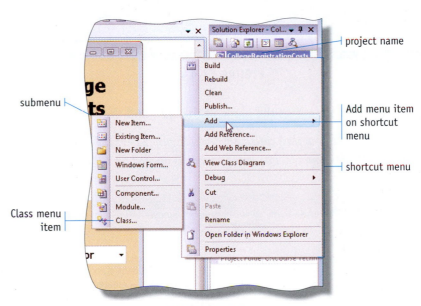

FIGURE 11-13

STEP 2 Click Class on the Add submenu.

The Add New Item dialog box is displayed (Figure 11-14). Class is selected in the Visual Studio installed template pane and the Name text box is highlighted.

Add New Item dialog box

Class selected

Add button

Name text box highlighted

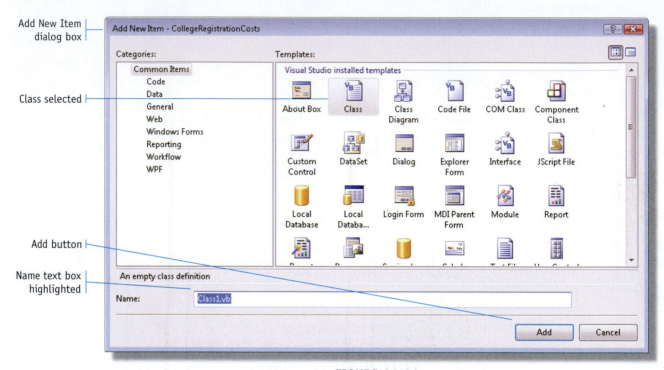

FIGURE 11-14

STEP 3 Type Student as the name of the class and then click the Add button.

Visual Studio creates a new class called Student (Figure 11-15). The class is identified in the Solution Explorer window. The code window is opened for the class.

Student class tab

Student class code window

Student class created

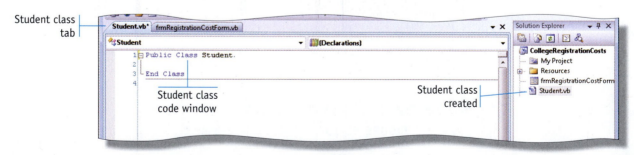

FIGURE 11-15

STEP 4   Using the same techniques, create the OnCampusStudent class and the
StudentCostsFile classes.

The Solution Explorer window now shows the four classes for the program —
OnCampusStudent, frmRegistrationCostForm, Student, and StudentCostsFile (Figure
11–16). To select a class and display its coding window, double–click the class name in
the Solution Explorer.

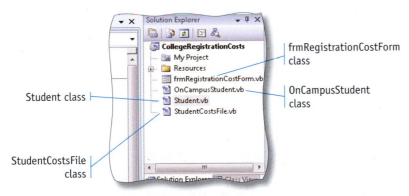

FIGURE 11-16

Coding Classes

After the classes have been defined, you must write the code for each class. You can
write code for each class using the same techniques you have used for previous programs. Before beginning the code for each class, however, you must consider how
classes communicate so you can write the correct code.

INSTANTIATING A CLASS AND CLASS COMMUNICATION

As you have learned, the code in a class acts as a template for an object. For example,
when you drag the Button .NET component from the Toolbox to the Windows
Form object, the Button object is created, or instantiated, based on the code in the
Button class. Properties of the Button object, such as the text shown in the button,
are processed using the code in the Button class.

Similarly, whenever you define a class in your Visual Basic program, you must instantiate, or create, an object based on that class in order for the processing within the object to take place. To instantiate an object, you can use the New statement, as shown in Figure 11-17.

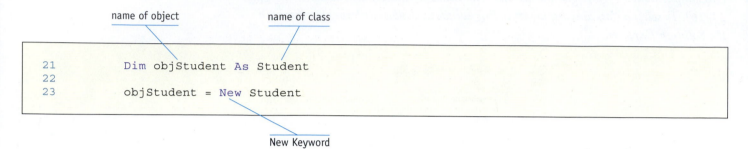

```
21          Dim objStudent As Student
22
23          objStudent = New Student
```

FIGURE 11-17

In Figure 11-17, the Dim statement on line 21 specifies a variable named objStudent that will contain the address of the Student object when it actually is created. The name of the class from which the object will be instantiated (Student) must follow the As keyword. As you have learned previously, an object name begins with the prefix, obj.

The assignment statement on line 23 creates the new object from the Student class and places the address of the object in the variable called objStudent. The keyword New must follow the equal sign, followed by the name of the class. Once the object is created, public procedures, public variables or attributes, and properties of the object can be referenced by other objects within the project.

A single statement also can be used to create an object, as shown in Figure 11-18.

```
25          Dim objStudent As New Student
```

FIGURE 11-18

The Dim statement on line 25 in Figure 11-18 both creates a variable to hold the address of the object (objStudent) and instantiates the object by using the keyword New followed by the name of the class.

The technique shown in Figure 11-17 is more widely used because the variable can be defined in the variables section of the code and the object is not instantiated until it is needed.

CONSTRUCTORS IN NEW INSTANTIATED CLASSES

When a class is instantiated into an object using the New keyword, a special procedure in the instantiated class called a constructor is executed. The **constructor** prepares the object for use in the program. The code in the constructor executes before any other code in the object. In addition to processes automatically completed by the constructor, the user can choose to write code for the constructor as well.

If the developer writes no code for a class constructor, Visual Basic automatically generates whatever processing must be accomplished to prepare the object for use. The developer can include a constructor with no executing code, as shown in Figure 11-19.

```
 1 Public Class Student
 2
 3     Sub New()
 4          'Constructor for Student class
 5
 6          'If required, initializing statements go here
 7
 8     End Sub
 9
10 End Class
```

FIGURE 11-19

Note in Figure 11-19 that the constructor begins with the statement Sub New(). No name is required for the constructor - the New keyword identifies the sub procedure as the constructor.

Because the code in the constructor executes before any other code in the object, it is a good place to place initializing code statements that prepare the object for execution.

PASSING ARGUMENTS WHEN INSTANTIATING AN OBJECT

Often when instantiating an object, data must be passed to the object. For example, in the Registration Costs program, the user enters the Student ID, Student Name, and other data into the user interface form. The Student object requires this data in order to calculate the registration costs and also cause the StudentCostsFile object to write the required text file. When an object requires data when it is instantiated, the data can be passed as part of the instantiation code. For example to pass the Student ID, the Student Name, the Major, and the Number of Units from the Form object to the Student object when the Student object is instantiated in the Form object, the statement in Figure 11-20 can be used.

new keyword   arguments

```
55            objStudent = New Student(txtStudentID.Text, txtStudentName.Text,
       cboMajor.SelectedItem, txtNumberOfUnits.Text)
```

FIGURE 11-20

In Figure 11-20, the assignment statement that is specified in the Form class uses the New keyword in a manner similar to that shown in Figure 11-17 on page 810 except that arguments are included within the parentheses following the New keyword. You will notice that the format for the arguments for the New statement are identical to the format used when passing arguments to a procedure as you saw in Chapter 8. In Figure 11-20, the value in the txtStudentID Text property, the value in the txtStudentName Text property, the value in the cboMajor.SelectedItem property, and the value in the txtNumberOfUnits Text property are passed to the instantiated object.

In the Student class, the New statement must be written with corresponding arguments; that is, the "signature" of the instantiating statement (Figure 11-20) must be the same as the constructor heading in the class. The New statement for the Student class is shown in Figure 11-21.

```
12        Sub New(ByVal strStudentID As String, ByVal strStudentName As String, ByVal     ↙
          strMajor As String, ByVal intUnits As String)
```

FIGURE 11-21

Note in Figure 11-21 that the arguments for the New statement in the Student class match up to the arguments in the instantiation statement in Figure 11-20. The arguments are passed ByVal, which you recall means a copy of the value is passed to the instantiated object but the original value is not used.

Once the object is instantiated and the arguments are passed, the constructor can use the values in the arguments to set the values in variables within the class. The coding in Figure 11-22 illustrates the assignment statements in the constructor to set the value of the variables defined in the Student class to the values passed from the calling object by the statement in Figure 11-21.

```
12        'Class variables                                                                 ↙
13        Private _strStudentID As String
14        Private _strStudentName As String
15        Private _strMajor As String
16        Private _intUnits As Integer
17
18        Sub New(ByVal strStudentID As String, ByVal strStudentName As String, _
19              ByVal strMajor As String, ByVal intUnits As String)
20           ' This subprocedure is a constructor for the Student class. It is
21           ' called when the object is instantiated with arguments
22
23           'The following code assigns the arguments to class variables
24           _strStudentID = strStudentID
25           _strStudentName = strStudentName
26           _strMajor = strMajor
27           _intUnits = Convert.ToInt32(intUnits)
28
29        End Sub
```

FIGURE 11-22

In the constructor shown in Figure 11-22, the assignment statements on lines 24 through 27 place the values passed from the instantiation statement into the variables defined in the Student class (line 13 through line 16). When the object based on the Student class is instantiated, the constructor code ensures the variables in the object contain data entered by the user.

Notice that the variables in the Student class are defined with Private access. Generally, when using multiple classes within a program, variables (also called attributes) should not be available to code within other classes within the program. The only way other classes can reference attributes within another class is if the class containing the attributes allows it. Techniques that you will learn later in this chapter can allow this, but generally attributes should be defined with Private access.

CALLING A PROCEDURE IN A SEPARATE CLASS

Most of the time, separate classes in a program contain procedures that must be executed. For example, in the Registration Costs program, the Student class must contain a procedure that calculates the registration costs. This procedure is shown in Figure 11-23.

```
16      Private _intUnits As Integer
17      Private _decCost As Decimal
18      Private _decCostPerUnit As Decimal = 450D
.
.
.
35      Function ComputeCosts() As Decimal
36          ' This function computes the registration costs, and
37          ' returns the registration costs
38
39          _decCost = _intUnits * _decCostPerUnit
40
41          Return _decCost
42
43      End Function
```

FIGURE 11-23

In Figure 11-23, the ComputeCosts function in the Student class multiplies the number of units (_intUnits) times the cost per unit (_decCostPerUnit) to determine the cost (_decCost). The cost then is returned as a decimal value to the calling class by the Return statement on line 41.

You might ask why the statement on line 39 cannot be included in the Form class that calls the Student class instead of calling the Compute Costs function in the Student class. The short answer is that it could be. But when designing larger and more robust programs, it is important that the tasks of each class be kept separate.

In this case, the Presentation tier of the three-tier structure, represented by the Form object, should have no knowledge of how the registration costs for a student are calculated. In the sample program of this chapter, the calculation is a simple multiplication statement. In the future the calculation of the registration costs might involve multiple lookups in a database, complex calculations based on major, in-state or out-of-state residence, and so on. The presentation class(es) should have nothing to do with these processes; the Student class should be the class in the program that knows how to perform all activities regarding a student. Therefore, even when the calculation is simple, as in the sample program, these tasks should be contained within the correct class.

To call the ComputeCosts procedure in the Student object, a statement in the Form object must identify both the object and the procedure within the object. The statement on lines 75-76 calls the ComputeCosts procedure.

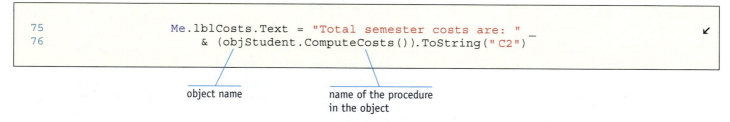

```
75        Me.lblCosts.Text = "Total semester costs are: " _
76            & (objStudent.ComputeCosts()).ToString("C2")
```

object name   name of the procedure
                     in the object

FIGURE 11-24

On line 76 in Figure 11-24, the statement objStudent.ComputeCosts() identifies the object (objStudent — see Figure 11-17 on page 810) and the procedure (ComputeCosts — see Figure 11-23 on page 813) separated by the dot operator (.). The statement says, "Pass control to the ComputeCosts procedure found in the objStudent object." The ComputeCosts procedure is a Function procedure, and the value returned from the procedure call is converted to a string and then assigned to the Text property of the lblCosts Label object so it is displayed in the Windows Form object (see Figure 11-2 on page 798).

In the previous section, you have seen the entire process for creating a class, instantiating a class, and calling a procedure in a class. This process is fundamental when designing larger and more robust programs.

Inheritance

In the Registration Costs program, the Student object contains student information from the Form object and performs calculations for the student. A student living on campus is a specialized student whose costs include housing and board. Therefore, the calculation for the on-campus student is different than that for an off-campus student. In addition, the On-Campus Student object must include Boolean indicators to indicate the type of housing selected.

Because the Student and On-Campus Student objects contain some different attributes and the cost calculation processing for them is different, logically they could be separate objects — if the student lives off-campus, a Student object will be instantiated, and if the student lives on-campus, an On-Campus Student object will be instantiated. Visual Basic, as well as other object-oriented programming languages, offers an alternative, however. This alternative is inheritance.

Inheritance allows one class to inherit attributes and procedures from another class. For example, the Student object contains the Student ID, the Student Name, the Major, and the Number of Units. These same values are required for the on-campus student. In addition, the On-Campus Student object contains indicators for the housing selected. By using inheritance, the attributes of the Student object can be used by the On-Campus Student object as well. This is illustrated in Figure 11-25.

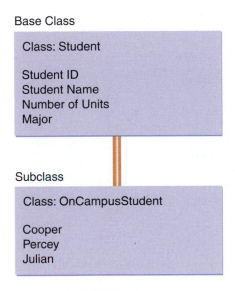

FIGURE 11-25

HEADS UP

Whenever inheritance is used, the subclass must fit into an "is-a" relationship with the base class. For example, an on-campus student (subclass) is a student (base class). A subclass is always in an "is-a" relationship with the base class. Further examples: An hourly worker (subclass) is an employee (base class); a scholarship athlete (subclass) is a student (base class); a computer teacher (subclass) is a faculty member (base class).

In Figure 11-25, the Student class contains the Student ID, Student Name, Number of Units, and Major attributes. Since the On-Campus Student class inherits from the Student class, the On-Campus Student class can reference the Student ID variable in the Student class as if that variable were defined in the On-Campus Student class. This is true of the other variables as well. As you can see, the On-Campus Student class inherits the attributes it can use from the Student class, and then defines the unique attributes it requires as well.

In the example in Figure 11-25, the Student class is called the **base** class. The On-Campus Student class is called the **subclass**. The subclass can use attributes from the base class as if those attributes were defined in the subclass.

The coding for the attributes in the Student base class and the OnCampusStudent subclass is shown in Figure 11-26.

```
 1 ' Class:        Student
 2 ' Developer:    Corinne Hoisington
 3 ' Date:         August 29, 2012
 4 ' Purpose:      This business class for a registering college student
 5 '               calculates the semester costs for tuition. It also causes the
 6 '               student costs file to be written.
 7
 8 Option Strict On
 9
10 Public Class Student
11
12     'Class variables
13     Protected _strStudentID As String
14     Protected _strStudentName As String
15     Protected _strMajor As String
16     Protected _intUnits As Integer
17     Protected _decCost As Decimal
18     Protected _decCostPerUnit As Decimal = 450D
19
20     Dim objStudentCostsFile As StudentCostsFile
```

FIGURE 11-26a

```
 1 ' Class:        OnCampusStudent
 2 ' Developer:    Corinne Hoisington
 3 ' Date:         August 29, 2012
 4 ' Purpose:      This business class for a registering an on-campus college
 5 '               student calculates the semester costs, including tuition
 6 '               and housing. It also causes the student costs file to be written.
 7
 8 Option Strict On
 9
10 Public Class OnCampusStudent
11     Inherits Student
12
13     ' Class variables
14     Private _Cooper As Boolean
15     Private _Percey As Boolean
16     Private _Julian As Boolean
17
18     Dim objStudentCostsFile As StudentCostsFile
```

FIGURE 11-26b

After the usual comment statements for the Student class, the variables required for the Student class are declared. You can see the string variables for Student ID, Student Name, and Major are declared, together with an integer variable for the Number of Units. In addition, the _decCost Decimal variable will contain the result of the calculation, and the _decCostPerUnit is a Decimal variable that contains the fixed cost per unit (450D) used in the calculation for semester costs.

Note that the variables in the Student class are declared with Protected access. Protected means statements in the subclasses of the base class can reference the variable as if the referencing statement were declared in the base class instead of the subclass. Statements outside the base class and the subclasses, however, cannot reference the variables.

In the OnCampusStudent subclass, the Class statement on line 10 includes the Inherits entry on line 11. This required entry indicates that the OnCampusStudent class inherits from the Student class. Any subclass must include the Inherits entry to indicate the class from which it inherits.

The three Boolean variables required in the subclass are declared but no declarations are made for Student ID, Student Name, etc. The reason is that these variables are declared in the Student base class and can be used as if they are part of the OnCampusStudent subclass.

CONSTRUCTORS

Both the base class and the subclass must have constructors. The coding for the base class constructor and the subclass constructor are shown in Figure 11-27 and Figure 11-28.

BASE CLASS CONSTRUCTOR

```
22      Sub New(ByVal strStudentID As String, ByVal strStudentName As String, _
23          ByVal strMajor As String, ByVal intUnits As String)
24          ' This subprocedure is a constructor for the Student class. It is
25          ' called when the object is instantiated with arguments
26
27          'The following code assigns the arguments to class variables
28          _strStudentID = strStudentID
29          _strStudentName = strStudentName
30          _strMajor = strMajor
31          _intUnits = Convert.ToInt32(intUnits)
32
33      End Sub
```

FIGURE 11-27

SUBCLASS CONSTRUCTOR

```
20      Sub New(ByVal StudentID As String, ByVal StudentName As String, _
21          ByVal Major As String, ByVal Units As String, _
22          ByVal Cooper As Boolean, ByVal Percey As Boolean, _
23          ByVal Julian As Boolean)
24          ' This subprocedure is a constructor for the Student class. It is called when
25          ' instantiated with arguments
26
27          MyBase.New(StudentID, StudentName, Major, Units)
28
29          'The following code assigns the arguments to class variables
30          _Cooper = Cooper
31          _Percey = Percey
32          _Julian = Julian
33
34      End Sub
```

FIGURE 11-28

In the constructor for the Student base class, the student ID, Student Name, Major, and Number of Units are passed when the object is instantiated. The constructor places the Student ID, Student Name, and Major in string variables, and converts the Number of Units to an integer.

In the constructor for the OnCampusStudent subclass, the Student ID, Student Name, Major, Number of Units, and the Boolean indicators for Cooper, Percey, and Julian are passed by the instantiating statement. The required first statement in the subclass constructor is the MyBase.New statement (line 27 in Figure 11-28). This statement calls the coding in the base class (Student) constructor and executes it. Therefore, when the subclass is instantiated, both the base class and the subclass constructors are executed.

In Figure 11-28, after the base class constructor is executed, the OnCampusStudent constructor places the Boolean indicators in variables so they can be tested in the class processing.

Again, it should be emphasized that the Student ID, Student Name, Major, and Number of Units variables are available to the OnCampusStudent subclass even though these variables are not declared within the class. They are available because of inheritance.

INHERITANCE AND PROCEDURES

When using inheritance, the subclass can use the procedures within the base class as well as the variables within the base class. Between the base class and the subclass, five different techniques for referencing and calling a procedure from an outside class such as a Form class can be used. After the base class and the subclass have been instantiated, the following techniques are available:

Base Class:

    1. Call a named procedure in the base class.
        Example: `objBaseClass.RegularBaseClassFunction()`

    2. Call an Overridable procedure in the base class.
        Example: `objBaseClass.OverridableBaseClassFunction()`

Subclass:

    3. Call an Overridable Procedure in the subclass:
        Example: `objSubClass.OverridableBaseClassFunction()`

    4. Call a named procedure in the subclass.
        Example: `objSubClass.RegularSubClassFunction()`

5. Call a base class procedure in the subclass:
   Example: `objSubClass.RegularBaseClassFunction()`

Each of these methods is explained in the following sections.

Call a Named Procedure in the Base Class

A procedure (either a Sub procedure or a Function procedure) in the base class can be called from another class in the manner you have seen previously. Thus, if a base class contains a Function procedure called RegularBaseClassFunction, another class can call the function using the statement, objBaseClass.RegularBaseClassFunction(), where objBaseClass is the instantiated base class object, and RegularBaseClassFunction is the name of the Function procedure.

An example of the coding for this process is shown in Figure 11-29.

FORM CLASS

```
4         Dim objSubClass As SubClass
5         Dim objBaseClass As BaseClass
6
7         objSubClass = New SubClass
8         objBaseClass = New BaseClass
9
10        MsgBox(objBaseClass.RegularBaseClassFunction())
```

FIGURE 11-29a

BASE CLASS

```
3      Function RegularBaseClassFunction() As String
4          Return "Regular base class function"
5      End Function
```

FIGURE 11-29b

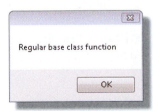

FIGURE 11-29c

In Figure 11-29a, the objBaseClass object is instantiated on line 8 of the Form class. The statement on line 10 in Figure 11-29a calls the RegularBaseClassFunction in the objBaseClass object. When the function returns the text value, the value is displayed in the message box in Figure 11-29c. The process shown in Figure 11-29 is the normal process for calling a procedure in another class.

Call an Overridable Procedure in a Base Class

When a procedure is written in the base class, the procedure will perform its assigned processing. Sometimes, the subclass might require basically the same task to be completed but with some differences in how that task is accomplished. For example, in the Registration Costs sample program, to determine the costs, the Student base class procedure multiplies the number of units times the cost per unit. In the OnCampusStudent subclass, the costs are calculated by multiplying the number of units times the cost per unit, and then adding the housing/board costs.

Even though the process (compute costs) accomplishes the same task, the calculations are different. When a task is accomplished in a different manner in a base class than in a subclass, the procedure in both the base class and the subclass can be named the same, but if the procedure in the subclass is called, it overrides the procedure in the base class. If the procedure in the base class is called, it is executed as a normal procedure call. This is shown in Figure 11-30.

FORM CLASS

```
4        Dim objSubClass As SubClass
5        Dim objBaseClass As BaseClass
6
7        objSubClass  = New SubClass
8        objBaseClass = New BaseClass
9
10       MsgBox(objBaseClass .OverridableBaseClassFunction ())
```

FIGURE 11-30a

BASE CLASS

```
7     Overridable Function OverridableBaseClassFunction() As String
8         Return "Overridable base class function"
9     End Function
```

FIGURE 11-30b

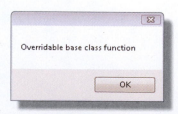

FIGURE 11-30c

Notice in Figure 11-30b the keyword Overridable precedes the Function keyword. Overridable means a subclass can contain a procedure with the same procedure name. If the procedure in the subclass is called (i.e.: SubClassName.ProcedureName) then the procedure in the subclass is executed even though it has the same name as the procedure in the base class. In Figure 11-30, however, the procedure named OverridableBaseClassFunction in the base class is called from the Form class, so that procedure is executed.

Call an Overridable Procedure in a Subclass

In Figure 11-31, a call is made to the OverridableBaseClassFunction that is defined in the subclass. Notice in Figure 11-31c that the Function name in the subclass is preceded by the Overrides keyword, which indicates the function in the subclass will override the function in the base class when the function in the subclass is called.

FORM CLASS

```
4        Dim objSubClass As SubClass
5        Dim objBaseClass As BaseClass
6
7        objSubClass = New SubClass
8        objBaseClass = New BaseClass
9
10       MsgBox(objSubClass.OverridableBaseClassFunction())
```

FIGURE 11-31a

BASE CLASS

```
7        Overridable Function OverridableBaseClassFunction() As String
8            Return "Overridable base class function"
9        End Function
```

FIGURE 11-31b

SUBCLASS

```
8        Overrides Function OverridableBaseClassFunction() As String
9            Return "Overrode the base class overridable function"
10       End Function
```

FIGURE 11-31c

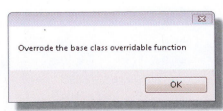

FIGURE 11-31d

In Figure 11-31b you can see that the function defined on line 7 of the base class is called OverridableBaseClassFunction, and the name is preceded by the Overridable keyword. In Figure 11-31c, the function with the same name on line 8 of the subclass overrides the function in the base class. As a result, when the subclass function is called (line 10 in the Form class — Figure 11-31a), the subclass message appears in the message box.

Call a Named Procedure in the Subclass

As with any other public procedure in a class, a named procedure in a subclass can be called (Figure 11-32).

FORM CLASS

```
4        Dim objSubClass As SubClass
5        Dim objBaseClass As BaseClass
6
7        objSubClass = New SubClass
8        objBaseClass = New BaseClass
9
10       MsgBox(objSubClass.RegularSubClassFunction())
```

FIGURE 11-32a

SUBCLASS

```
4     Function RegularSubClassFunction() As String
5        Return "Regular subclass function"
6     End Function
```

FIGURE 11-32b

FIGURE 11-32c

The example in Figure 11–32 is a straightforward procedure call to a procedure in another class.

Call a Base Class Procedure in the Subclass

The last common procedure call involving inheritance is when a procedure in the base class is called by referencing the subclass, as shown in Figure 11-33.

FORM OBJECT

```
4          Dim objSubClass As SubClass
5          Dim objBaseClass As BaseClass
6
7          objSubClass = New SubClass
8          objBaseClass = New BaseClass
9
10         MsgBox(objSubClass.RegularBaseClassFunction())
```

FIGURE 11-33a

BASE CLASS

```
3      Function RegularBaseClassFunction() As String
4          Return "Regular base class function"
5      End Function
```

FIGURE 11-33b

FIGURE 11-33c

In Figure 11-33, the procedure call statement in the Form class (line 10 in Figure 11-33a) calls a procedure that is not even in the subclass. Nonetheless, the regular base class function is executed because when a procedure is called that is not in the class specified in the call statement, Visual Basic will move up to the base class to see if the procedure is located in the base class. If so, the procedure in the base class is executed.

SUMMARY — INHERITANCE

Inheritance can be a relatively complex subject that has more ramifications that you have learned in this chapter. Nonetheless, this beginning knowledge of inheritance will serve you well as you continue your programming and developer education.

Persistence Classes

As you learned earlier in this chapter, the persistence tier in an application, sometimes called the data access tier, contains classes that are involved in saving and retrieving data that is stored on a permanent storage medium such as a hard disk, a DVD-ROM or a USB drive. A typical persistence class is the StudentCostsFile class in the Registration Costs sample program in this chapter. This class is concerned with performing all tasks required for the Student Costs File. In the sample program, this processing consists of writing the file as a text file and saving it on a USB drive. Other processing that might be required in the future for this file, and which would be carried out by this class, could be the retrieval of the text file or the transitioning of the text file into a database file. Generally, any required processing of the Student Costs File should be carried out by the StudentCostsFile class.

To define the StudentCostsFile class, comments, variables, and a constructor must be written in a manner similar to what you have seen already. The code to define the StudentCostsFile class is shown in Figure 11-34.

```
 1 ' Class:        Student Costs File
 2 ' Developer:    Corinne Hoisington
 3 ' Date:         August 29, 2012
 4 ' Purpose:      This class represents the Student Costs File. The WriteRecord
 5 '               procedure writes a comma-delimited student costs file that
 6 '               contains the Student ID, Student Name, Major,
 7 '               and Student Costs.
 8
 9 Option Strict On
10
11 Public Class StudentCostsFile
12
13
14     ' Class variables
15     Private _strStudentID As String
16     Private _strStudentName As String
17     Private _strMajor As String
18     Private _decStudentCosts As Decimal
19
20     Sub New(ByVal StudentID As String, ByVal StudentName As String, _
21             ByVal Major As String, ByVal Costs As Decimal)
22         ' This sub procedure is the constructor for the StudentCostsFile
23         ' class.
24
25         'The following code assigns the arguments to class variables
26         _strStudentID = StudentID
27         _strStudentName = StudentName
28         _strMajor = Major
29         _decStudentCosts = Costs
30
31     End Sub
```

FIGURE 11-34

In Figure 11-34, following the typical comments is the declaration of the variables used in the class. Notice that each of the variables is declared with Private access so they cannot be referenced by coding in any other class within the program.

Following the variable declarations is the constructor procedure, as identified by the keyword New. Within the constructor, the code on lines 26-29 set the values in the variables to the values passed to the StudentCostsFile class when it is instantiated.

COMMA-DELIMITED TEXT FILE

The Student Costs File is a comma-delimited text file, which means a comma separates each field in a record in the file, as shown in Figure 11-35.

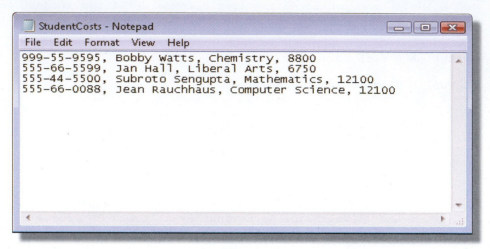

FIGURE 11-35

Notice in Figure 11-35, a comma appears at the end of each field, and no comma is displayed at the end of the record. A comma-delimited text file is common because it can be read into programs such as Microsoft Excel and Microsoft Access to import that data into the application.

In Chapter 9, you learned to use a StreamWriter to write a stream of text to a file. To create the file shown in Figure 11-35, it is required that each time new student registration costs are calculated for a student, a record that contains the Student ID, the Student Name, the Major, and the Costs should be added to the file. It is unknown how many records will be placed in the file during the registration process. Therefore, a StreamWriter must be created that can append, or add, records to the file. In addition, because a record contains four fields, the first three of which are followed by a comma, a Write statement must be used that does not create a new line in the file each time a record is written to the disk.

The coding to accomplish this processing is shown in the WriteRecord Sub procedure in Figure 11-36.

```
33      Sub WriteRecord()
34          ' This subprocedure opens the StudentCosts output text file and then
35          ' writes a record in the comma-delimited file
36
37          Dim strNameandLocationOfFile As String = "E:\StudentCosts.txt"
38
39          Try
40              Dim objWriter As IO.StreamWriter = _
41                  IO.File.AppendText(strNameandLocationOfFile)
42
43              objWriter.Write(_strStudentID & ",")
44              objWriter.Write(_strStudentName & ",")
45              objWriter.Write(_strMajor & ",")
46              objWriter.WriteLine(_decStudentCosts)
47              objWriter.Close()
48
49          Catch ex As Exception
50              MsgBox("No device available - program aborted", , "Error")
51              Application.Exit()
52
53          End Try
54
55      End Sub
```

FIGURE 11-36

In Figure 11-36, the Dim statement on line 37 declares a string that contains the name and location of the file to be written. A Try-Catch block is created on line 39 because if a USB drive is not located in drive e:, an exception will be thrown. The Catch statement on line 49 catches the exception, displays a message box containing an error message, and exits the application.

Assuming no exception occurs, the Dim statement on lines 40-41 declares the objWriter as an IO.StreamWriter. The identification of the IO.StreamWriter indicates the writer is to append text to the file. Appending the text means writing the next record in the file following the last record in the file; that is, the records accumulate in the file as it is written.

The Write procedure calls on lines 43-45 write the Student ID, the Student Name, and the Major in the record, each followed by a comma. The WriteLine procedure call on line 46 writes the Student Costs in the record and places a line return in the file, so the next record can be written. Finally, the Close procedure call on line 47 closes the file.

Program Design

As you have learned, the requirements document identifies the purpose of the program being developed, the application title, the procedures to be followed when using the program, any equations and calculations required in the program, any conditions within the program that must be tested, notes and restrictions that must be followed by the program, and any other comments that would be helpful to understanding the problem. The requirements document for the College Registration Costs application is shown in Figure 11-37.

REQUIREMENTS DOCUMENT

Date submitted: August 29, 2012

Application title: College Registration Costs

Purpose: This Windows application allows a user to enter Landelline College student registration information and then it calculates the student registration costs.

Program Procedures: In a Windows application, the user enters the Student ID, Student Name, Number of Units, selects if off-campus or on-campus resident, if on-campus resident selects housing and board, and selects the Major. The user then clicks a button. The application calculates the semester costs and records the information in a log file.

Algorithms, Processing, and Conditions:

1. The user first enters the Student ID, Student Name, and Number of Units.
2. The user selects either off-campus residence or on-campus residence. If on-campus residence is selected, the user indicates the housing/board selection (Cooper Dorm, Percey Hall, or Julian Suites). The user then selects the student's major from a list.
3. When the user clicks a button, the program calculates the semester costs and writes a log file.
4. A clear form button should be available to clear the form and place the insertion point in the Student ID text box.

FIGURE 11-37 (continues)

5. The course cost is $450.00 per unit.

6. The formula to calculate semester course costs is number of units times the cost per unit.

7. If the student is an on-campus resident, the following housing/board costs must be added to the course costs: Cooper Dorm: $2,900.00 per semester; Percey Hall: $3,400.00 per semester; Julian Suites: $4,000.00 per semester.

8. The log file is a text file that contains the Student ID, the Student Name, the Major, and the semester costs. It should be a comma-delimited file.

Notes and Restrictions:

1. The Student ID must be a completely filled-out social security number.

2. The Student Name cannot be left blank and must begin with an alphabetic character.

3. The Number of Units must be a numeric value of 1 through 24.

4. A major must be selected. The majors available are: Biology, Business, Chemistry, Computer Science, Fine Arts, Liberal Arts, Mathematics, Physics, Sociology, and Theology.

5. The housing/board selections should not be displayed in the window unless the user selects on-campus resident.

6. When the user clicks the button to calculate costs, if any errors occurred during data entry, a message box should be displayed and the user must be required to enter valid data before continuing.

7. Off-campus resident is the default selection; if a student is an on-campus resident, Cooper Dorm is the default selection.

Comments:

1. The picture (college.jpg) used in the Window is available at scsite/vb2008/ch11/images.

2. The program should use a three-tier structure with presentation, business, and persistence classes.

FIGURE 11-37 (continued)

The use case definition for the application is shown in Figure 11-38.

USE CASE DEFINITION

1. The user enters the Student ID, the Student Name and the Number of Units.
2. If necessary, the user selects off-campus or on-campus student from radio buttons. If on-campus is selected, the housing/board choices are displayed. If necessary, the user selects the housing/board choice.
3. The user selects a Major from a list.
4. The user clicks the Calculate Costs button.
5. The program calculates and displays the semester costs, including the cost of housing/board if appropriate.
6. The program writes a log of the student registration costs.
7. If necessary, the user clicks the Clear Form button to clear the form of data and place the insertion point in the Student ID text box.

FIGURE 11-38

EVENT PLANNING DOCUMENT

You will recall that the event planning document consists of a table that specifies objects in the user interface that will cause an event, the action taken by the user to trigger the event, and the event processing that must occur. In addition, an event planning document is required for each object in the program that is called from another object. The Event Planning Documents for the College Registration Costs program are shown in Figure 11-39 through Figure 11-42.

EVENT PLANNING DOCUMENT

Program Name: CollegeRegistrationCosts	Developer: Corinne Hoisington	Object: frmRegistrationCostForm	Date: August 29, 2012
OBJECT	**EVENT TRIGGER**	**EVENT PROCESSING**	

btnCalculateCosts	Click	Declare Student object
		Declare OnCampusStudent object
		Declare Boolean Input Error indicator
		If student ID mask is not full
		    Display message box with error message
		    Clear student id masked text box
		    Place focus on student id masked text box
		    Set input error indicator to true	

FIGURE 11-39 (continues)

Object	Event Trigger	Event Processing
		Else If student name text length < 1 or first character in text box less than "A"
		Display message box with error message
		Clear student name text box
		Place focus on student name text box
		Set input error indicator to true
		Else If number of units is not numeric
		Display message box with error message
		Clear number of units text box
		Place focus on number of units text box
		Set input error indicator to true
		Else If number of units is not 1-24
		Display message box with error message
		Clear number of units text box
		Place focus on number of units text box
		Set input error indicator to true
		Else If major selected index < 0
		Display message box with error message
		Place focus on major combo box
		Set input error indicator to true
		End If
		If no input error
		If off-campus radio button checked
		Instantiate student object with arguments
		Set costs label visible property to true
		Call student compute costs procedure
		Display student costs
		Else
		Instantiate on campus student object with arguments
		Set costs label visible property to true
		Call on campus student compute costs procedure
		Display student costs
		End If

FIGURE 11-39 (continues)

OBJECT	EVENT TRIGGER	EVENT PROCESSING
radOnCampus Radio Button	Selected	Make housing/board group visible
radOffCampus Radio Button	Selected	Make housing/board group not visible
btnClearForm	Click	Clear student ID masked text box Clear student name text box Clear number of units text box Set major combo box selected index to −1 Set major combo box text property to "Select a major" Set off campus radio button checked to true Set Cooper radio button checked to true Set housing/board group visible to false Set costs label visible to false Place focus on student ID masked text box

FIGURE 11-39 (continued)

EVENT PLANNING DOCUMENT

Program Name: CollegeRegistrationCosts	Developer: Corinne Hoisington	Object: objStudent (Student class)	Date: August 29, 2012
OBJECT	**EVENT TRIGGER**	**EVENT PROCESSING**	
New(student id, student name, major, units)	Class constructor	Set student id equal to passed student id Set student name equal to passed student name Set major equal passed major Convert number of units passed to integer	
ComputeCosts	Function procedure call	Cost = units * cost per unit Instantiate WriteStudentRecord object Write the student record Return the cost	

FIGURE 11-40

EVENT PLANNING DOCUMENT

Program Name: CollegeRegistrationCosts	Developer: Corinne Hoisington	Object: objOnCampusStudent (OnCampusStudent class)	Date: August 29, 2012
OBJECT	**EVENT TRIGGER**	**EVENT PROCESSING**	
New(student id, student name, major, units, Cooper Boolean, Percey Boolean, Julian Boolean)	Class constructor	Call base class constructor (student id, student name, major, units) Set Cooper Boolean to passed Cooper Boolean Set Percey Boolean to passed Percey Boolean Set Julian Boolean to passed Julian Boolean	

ComputeCosts	Function procedure call	If Cooper housing
		    Set housing cost = Cooper cost
		Else If Percey housing
		    Set housing cost = Percey costs
		Else If Julian housing
		    Set housing cost = Julian cost
		End If
		Cost = (units * cost per unit) + housing cost
		Instantiate objStudentCostsFile object
		Write the student record
		Return the cost	

FIGURE 11-41

EVENT PLANNING DOCUMENT

Program Name: CollegeRegistrationCosts	Developer: Corinne Hoisington	Object: objStudentCostsFile (StudentCostsFile class)	Date: August 4, 2012
OBJECT	**EVENT TRIGGER**	**EVENT PROCESSING**	
New(student id, student name, major, costs)	Class constructor	Set student ID equal to passed student id Set student name equal to passed student name Set major equal to passed major Set costs equal to passed costs	
WriteRecord	Function procedure call	Define stream writer for append text file Write student ID with comma Write student name with comma Write major with comma Write costs with line return Close text file	

FIGURE 11-42

DESIGN AND CODE THE PROGRAM

After identifying the objects, events, and tasks within the events, you are ready to create the program. As you have learned, creating the program means designing the user interface and then entering Visual Basic statements to accomplish the tasks specified on the event planning documents. As you enter the code, you also will implement the logic to carry out the required processing.

Guided Program Development

To design the user interface for the Student Registration Costs program and enter the code required for each class and event in the program, complete the following steps:

NOTE TO THE LEARNER

As you will recall, in the following activity, you should complete the tasks within the specified steps. Many of the tasks are accompanied by a Hint Screen. The purpose of the Hint Screen is to indicate where in the Visual Studio window you should perform the activity; it also serves as a reminder of the method you should use to create the user interface or enter code. If you need further help completing the step, refer to the figure number identified by the term ref: in the step.

Guided Program Development

1

▶ **Create a New Windows Project** Open Visual Studio using the Start button on the Windows taskbar and the All Programs submenu. Close the Start page. Click the New Project button on the Standard toolbar. Begin a Windows Application project and title the project CollegeRegistrationCosts.

▶ **Name the Form Object** Select the Form object. Change the (Name) property of the Form object to frmRegistrationCostForm.

▶ **Title the Form Object** With the frmRegistrationCostForm selected, change the Text property to College Registration Costs.

▶ **Change the Form Class Name** In the Solution Explorer window, right-click Form1.vb, select Rename on the shortcut menu, and change the class name to frmRegistrationCostForm.vb.

(continues)

Guided Program Development (continued)

▶ **Create the User Interface** Using the skills you have acquired in this course and referencing the requirements document in Figure 11-37 on page 828, create the user interface for the frmRegistrationCostForm object as shown in Figure 11-43. The heading is Tahoma font, bold, 24 pt. All other fonts are Tahoma, regular, 14 pt.

FIGURE 11-43

Guided Program Development *(continued)*

Phase 2: Code the Application

2

▶ **Open the Calculate Costs Button Event Handler** On the Windows Form object in the Design window, double-click the Calculate Costs Button object.

▶ **Enter Comments and Option Strict On** Enter the common comments for the frmRegistrationCostForm class. Include the Option Strict On statement.

HINT

```
1 ' Program:      College Registration Costs
2 ' Developer:    Corinne Hoisington
3 ' Date:         August 29, 2012
4 ' Purpose:      This program calculates the registration costs for a college
5 '               student. It also records the costs in a text file.
6
7 Option Strict On
8
9 Public Class frmRegistrationCostForm
```

▶ **Enter Comments and Define the Variables for the Calculate Costs Button Event Handler** Below the event handler intro code, write the comments and then define the variables required for the button event handler. The variables include the two object variables for the Student and OnCampusStudent objects, and the Boolean input error indicator *(ref: Figure 11-17)*.

HINT

```
11      Private Sub btnCalculateCosts_Click(ByVal sender As System.Object, ByVal e As     ↙
        System.EventArgs) Handles btnCalculateCosts.Click
12          ' This Calculate Costs button click event handler edits the
13          ' registration(costs) form to ensure it contains valid data.
14          ' Then, after passing control to the business class, it
15          ' displays the registration cost.
16
17          Dim objStudent As Student
18          Dim objOnCampusStudent As OnCampusStudent
19          Dim InputError As Boolean = False
```

(continues)

Guided Program Development (continued)

▶ **Enter the If...ElseIf Statement to Check the Input Data** Enter the code to check the input data as documented in the Program Requirements document *(ref: Figure 11-7)*.

HINT

```
21          ' Is student ID entered properly
22          If Me.txtStudentID.MaskFull = False Then
23              MsgBox("Enter your Student ID in the Student ID box", , _
24                  "Error")
25              Me.txtStudentID.Clear()
26              Me.txtStudentID.Focus()
27              InputError = True
28              ' Is student name entered properly
29          ElseIf Me.txtStudentName.TextLength < 1 Or _
30                  Me.txtStudentName.Text < "A" Then
31              MsgBox("Enter your name in the Student Name box", , "Error")
32              Me.txtStudentName.Clear()
33              Me.txtStudentName.Focus()
34              InputError = True
35              ' Is number of units entered properly
36          ElseIf Not IsNumeric(Me.txtNumberOfUnits.Text) Then
37              MsgBox("Enter the units in the Number of Units box", , _
38                  "Error")
39              Me.txtNumberOfUnits.Clear()
40              Me.txtNumberOfUnits.Focus()
41              InputError = True
42              ' Has 1-24 units been entered
43          ElseIf Convert.ToInt32(Me.txtNumberOfUnits.Text) < 1 _
44                  Or Convert.ToInt32(Me.txtNumberOfUnits.Text) > 24 Then
45              MsgBox("Units must be 1 - 24", , "Error")
46              Me.txtNumberOfUnits.Clear()
47              Me.txtNumberOfUnits.Focus()
48              InputError = True
49              ' Has a major been selected
50          ElseIf Me.cboMajor.SelectedIndex < 0 Then
51              MsgBox("Please select a major", , "Error")
52              Me.cboMajor.Focus()
53              InputError = True
54          End If
```

Guided Program Development (continued)

▶ **Enter the Code to Call the Appropriate Function Procedure in the Appropriate Object** If the input data is correct, enter the code to instantiate the Student class object or the OnCampusStudent class object and then call the ComputeCosts function in the appropriate object. Be sure to include the correct arguments for the New statement for each new object *(ref: Figure 11-20)*.

HINT

```
56              ' If no input error, process the registration costs
57          If Not InputError Then
58              If Me.radOffCampus.Checked Then
59                  objStudent = New Student(txtStudentID.Text, _
60                      txtStudentName.Text, Convert.ToString(cboMajor.SelectedItem), _
61                      txtNumberOfUnits.Text)
62                  Me.lblCosts.Visible = True
63                  Me.lblCosts.Text = "Total semester costs are: " _
64                      & (objStudent.ComputeCosts()).ToString("C2")
65              Else
66                  objOnCampusStudent = New OnCampusStudent(txtStudentID.Text, _
67                      txtStudentName.Text, Convert.ToString(cboMajor.SelectedItem), _
68                      txtNumberOfUnits.Text, radCooperDorm.Checked, _
69                      radPerceyHall.Checked, radJulianSuites.Checked)
70                  Me.lblCosts.Visible = True
71                  Me.lblCosts.Text = "Total semester costs are: " _
72                      & (objOnCampusStudent.ComputeCosts()).ToString("C2")
73
74              End If
75          End If
76
77      End Sub
```

▶ **Write the Code for the Off-Campus Radio Button CheckedChanged Event** Write the code to hide the HousingBoard Group.

HINT

```
79      Private Sub radOffCampus_CheckedChanged(ByVal sender As System.Object, ByVal e As ↙
            System.EventArgs) Handles radOffCampus.CheckedChanged
80          ' This event handler is executed when the Off Campus radio
81          ' button is selected. It hides the Housing/Board radio buttons
82
83          Me.grpHousingBoard.Visible = False
84
85      End Sub
```

(continues)

Guided Program Development (continued)

▶ **Write the Code for the On-Campus Radio Button CheckedChanged Event** Write the code to make the HousingBoard Group visible.

HINT

```
87      Private Sub radOnCampus_CheckedChanged(ByVal sender As System.Object, ByVal e As    ↙
            System.EventArgs) Handles radOnCampus.CheckedChanged
88          ' This event handler is executed when the On Campus radio button
89          ' is selected. It makes the Housing/Board radio buttons visible
90
91          Me.grpHousingBoard.Visible = True
92
93      End Sub
```

▶ **Write the Code for the Clear Form Button** Write the code to clear the form and place the focus on the Student ID text box as defined in the event planning document (Figure 11-39 on page 832).

The frmRegistrationCostForm code is completed (Figure 11-44).

RESULT OF STEP 2

```
 1 ' Program:       College Registration Costs
 2 ' Developer:     Corinne Hoisington
 3 ' Date:          August 29, 2012
 4 ' Purpose:       This program calculates the registration costs for a college
 5 '                student. It also records the costs in a text file.
 6
 7 Option Strict On
 8
 9 Public Class frmRegistrationCostForm
10
11      Private Sub btnCalculateCosts_Click(ByVal sender As System.Object, ByVal e As    ↙
            System.EventArgs) Handles btnCalculateCosts.Click
12          ' This Calculate Costs button click event handler edits the
13          ' registration(costs) form to ensure it contains valid data.
14          ' Then, after passing control to the business class, it
15          ' displays the registration cost.
16
17          Dim objStudent As Student
18          Dim objOnCampusStudent As OnCampusStudent
19          Dim InputError As Boolean = False
20
21          ' Is student ID entered properly
22          If Me.txtStudentID.MaskFull = False Then
23              MsgBox("Enter your Student ID in the Student ID box", , _
24                  "Error")
25              Me.txtStudentID.Clear()
26              Me.txtStudentID.Focus()
27              InputError = True
28              ' Is student name entered properly
29          ElseIf Me.txtStudentName.TextLength < 1 Or _
30                  Me.txtStudentName.Text < "A" Then
31              MsgBox("Enter your name in the Student Name box", , "Error")
32              Me.txtStudentName.Clear()
33              Me.txtStudentName.Focus()
```

FIGURE 11-44 (continues)

Guided Program Development *(continued)*

```
34            InputError = True
35            ' Is number of units entered properly
36        ElseIf Not IsNumeric(Me.txtNumberOfUnits.Text) Then
37            MsgBox("Enter the units in the Number of Units box", , _
38                "Error")
39            Me.txtNumberOfUnits.Clear()
40            Me.txtNumberOfUnits.Focus()
41            InputError = True
42            ' Has 1-24 units been entered
43        ElseIf Convert.ToInt32(Me.txtNumberOfUnits.Text) < 1 _
44                Or Convert.ToInt32(Me.txtNumberOfUnits.Text) > 24 Then
45            MsgBox("Units must be 1 - 24", , "Error")
46            Me.txtNumberOfUnits.Clear()
47            Me.txtNumberOfUnits.Focus()
48            InputError = True
49            ' Has a major been selected
50        ElseIf Me.cboMajor.SelectedIndex < 0 Then
51            MsgBox("Please select a major", , "Error")
52            Me.cboMajor.Focus()
53            InputError = True
54        End If
55
56        ' If no input error, process the registration costs
57        If Not InputError Then
58            If Me.radOffCampus.Checked Then
59                objStudent = New Student(txtStudentID.Text, _
60                    txtStudentName.Text, Convert.ToString(cboMajor.SelectedItem), _
61                    txtNumberOfUnits.Text)
62                Me.lblCosts.Visible = True
63                Me.lblCosts.Text = "Total semester costs are: " _
64                    & (objStudent.ComputeCosts()).ToString("C2")
65            Else
66                objOnCampusStudent = New OnCampusStudent(txtStudentID.Text, _
67                    txtStudentName.Text, Convert.ToString(cboMajor.SelectedItem), _
68                    txtNumberOfUnits.Text, radCooperDorm.Checked, _
69                    radPerceyHall.Checked, radJulianSuites.Checked)
70                Me.lblCosts.Visible = True
71                Me.lblCosts.Text = "Total semester costs are: " _
72                    & (objOnCampusStudent.ComputeCosts()).ToString("C2")
73
74            End If
75        End If
76
77    End Sub
78
79    Private Sub radOffCampus_CheckedChanged(ByVal sender As System.Object, ByVal e As ↙
System.EventArgs) Handles radOffCampus.CheckedChanged
80        ' This event handler is executed when the Off Campus radio
81        ' button is selected. It hides the Housing/Board radio buttons
82
83        Me.grpHousingBoard.Visible = False
84
85    End Sub
```

FIGURE 11-44 (continues)

(continues)

Guided Program Development (continued)

```vb
 86
 87     Private Sub radOnCampus_CheckedChanged(ByVal sender As System.Object, ByVal e As ↙
        System.EventArgs) Handles radOnCampus.CheckedChanged
 88         ' This event handler is executed when the On Campus radio button
 89         ' is selected. It makes the Housing/Board radio buttons visible
 90
 91         Me.grpHousingBoard.Visible = True
 92
 93     End Sub
 94
 95
 96     Private Sub btnClearForm_Click(ByVal sender As System.Object, ByVal e As System. ↙
        EventArgs) Handles btnClearForm.Click
 97         ' This event handler is executed when the user clicks the
 98         ' Clear Form button. It resets all objects on the user interface.
 99
100         Me.txtStudentID.Clear()
101         Me.txtStudentName.Clear()
102         Me.txtNumberOfUnits.Clear()
103         Me.cboMajor.SelectedIndex = -1
104         Me.cboMajor.Text = "Select a Major"
105         Me.radOffCampus.Checked = True
106         Me.radCooperDorm.Checked = True
107         Me.grpHousingBoard.Visible = False
108         Me.lblCosts.Visible = False
109         Me.txtStudentID.Focus()
110
111     End Sub
112 End Class
113
```

FIGURE 11-44 (continued)

Guided Program Development *(continued)*

3

▶ **Create the Classes Required for the Remainder of the Program**
Right-click the name of the project (CollegeRegistrationCosts) in the Solution Explorer, point to Add on the shortcut menu, and then click Class on the shortcut menu. Add the Student.vb class. Do the same process for the OnCampusStudent.vb class and the StudentCostsFile.vb class *(ref: Figure 11-13)*.

▶ **Enter Comments and Option Strict On for the Student Class** Display the Student class coding window. Enter the common comments for the Student class. Include the Option Strict On statement.

HINT

```
 1 ' Class:       Student
 2 ' Developer:   Corinne Hoisington
 3 ' Date:        August 29, 2012
 4 ' Purpose:     This business class for a registering college student
 5 '              calculates the semester costs for tuition. It also causes the
 6 '              student costs file to be written.
 7
 8 Option Strict On
 9
10 Public Class Student
```

(continues)

Guided Program Development *(continued)*

▶ **Define the Class Variables for the Student Class** Define the class variables for the Student class, including the declaration for the StudentCostsFile object. Remember that the variables should be declared with Protected access because they are used in the OnCampusStudent subclass.

HINT

```
12        'Class variables
13        Protected _strStudentID As String
14        Protected _strStudentName As String
15        Protected _strMajor As String
16        Protected _intUnits As Integer
17        Protected _decCost As Decimal
18        Protected _decCostPerUnit As Decimal = 450D
19
20        Dim objStudentCostsFile As StudentCostsFile
```

▶ **Write the Student Class Constructor** Write the code for the Student class constructor based on the requirements shown in the Event Planning Document *(ref: Figure 11-21)*.

HINT

```
22        Sub New(ByVal strStudentID As String, ByVal strStudentName As String, _
23              ByVal strMajor As String, ByVal intUnits As String)
24          ' This subprocedure is a constructor for the Student class. It is
25          ' called when the object is instantiated with arguments
26
27          'The following code assigns the arguments to class variables
28          _strStudentID = strStudentID
29          _strStudentName = strStudentName
30          _strMajor = strMajor
31          _intUnits = Convert.ToInt32(intUnits)
32
33        End Sub
```

Guided Program Development (continued)

▶ **Write the Code for the ComputeCosts Overridable Function Procedure** Write the code to calculate the cost, instantiate the object for the StudentCostsFile class, call the procedure to write the file, and return the cost.

HINT

```
35    Overridable Function ComputeCosts() As Decimal
36        ' This function computes the registration costs, writes a record
37        ' in the student costs file, and returns the registration costs
38
39        'Calculate cost
40        _decCost = _intUnits * _decCostPerUnit
41
42        'Write the student record
43        objStudentCostsFile = New StudentCostsFile(_strStudentID, _
44            _strStudentName, _strMajor, _decCost)
45        objStudentCostsFile.WriteRecord()
46
47        'Return the calculated cost
48        Return _decCost
49
50    End Function
```

(continues)

Guided Program Development *(continued)*

The Student class code is completed (Figure 11-45).

RESULT OF STEP 3

```
1  ' Class:        Student
2  ' Developer:    Corinne Hoisington
3  ' Date:         August 29, 2012
4  ' Purpose:      This business class for a registering college student
5  '               calculates the semester costs for tuition. It also causes the
6  '               student costs file to be written.
7
8  Option Strict On
9
10 Public Class Student
11
12     'Class variables
13     Protected _strStudentID As String
14     Protected _strStudentName As String
15     Protected _strMajor As String
16     Protected _intUnits As Integer
17     Protected _decCost As Decimal
18     Protected _decCostPerUnit As Decimal = 450D
19
20     Dim objStudentCostsFile As StudentCostsFile
21
22     Sub New(ByVal strStudentID As String, ByVal strStudentName As String, _
23             ByVal strMajor As String, ByVal intUnits As String)
24         ' This subprocedure is a constructor for the Student class. It is
25         ' called when the object is instantiated with arguments
26
27         'The following code assigns the arguments to class variables
28         _strStudentID = strStudentID
29         _strStudentName = strStudentName
30         _strMajor = strMajor
31         _intUnits = Convert.ToInt32(intUnits)
32
33     End Sub
34
35     Overridable Function ComputeCosts() As Decimal
36         ' This function computes the registration costs, writes a record
37         ' in the student costs file, and returns the registration costs
38
39         'Calculate cost
40         _decCost = _intUnits * _decCostPerUnit
41
42         'Write the student record
43         objStudentCostsFile = New StudentCostsFile(_strStudentID, _
44             _strStudentName, _strMajor, _decCost)
45         objStudentCostsFile.WriteRecord()
46
47         'Return the calculated cost
48         Return _decCost
49
50     End Function
51
52 End Class
53
```

FIGURE 11-45

Guided Program Development (continued)

4

▶ **Enter Comments and Option Strict On for the OnCampusStudent Class** Display the OnCampusStudent class coding window. Enter the common comments for the OnCampusStudent class. Include the Option Strict On statement and the Inherits statement indicating the OnCampusStudent class inherits from the Student class.

HINT

```
 1 ' Class:        OnCampusStudent
 2 ' Developer:    Corinne Hoisington
 3 ' Date:         August 29, 2012
 4 ' Purpose:      This business class for a registering an on-campus college
 5 '               student calculates the semester costs, including tuition
 6 '               and housing. It also causes the student costs file to be written.
 7
 8 Option Strict On
 9
10 Public Class OnCampusStudent
11      Inherits Student
```

▶ **Define the Class Variables for the OnCampusStudent Class** Define the class variables for the OnStudent class, including the declaration for the StudentCostsFile object. The variables should be declared with Private access.

HINT

```
13      ' Class variables
14      Private _Cooper As Boolean
15      Private _Percey As Boolean
16      Private _Julian As Boolean
17
18      Dim objStudentCostsFile As StudentCostsFile
```

▶ **Write the OnCampusStudent Class Constructor** Write the code for the OnCampusStudent class constructor based on the requirements shown in the Event Planning Document (ref: Figure 11-28).

HINT

```
20      Sub New(ByVal StudentID As String, ByVal StudentName As String, _
21           ByVal Major As String, ByVal Units As String, _
22           ByVal Cooper As Boolean, ByVal Percey As Boolean, _
23           ByVal Julian As Boolean)
24        ' This subprocedure is a constructor for the Student class. It is called when
25        ' instantiated with arguments
26
27        MyBase.New(StudentID, StudentName, Major, Units)
28
29        'The following code assigns the arguments to class variables
30        _Cooper = Cooper
31        _Percey = Percey
32        _Julian = Julian
33
34      End Sub
```

(continues)

Guided Program Development *(continued)*

▶ **Write the Code for the ComputeCosts Overriding Function Procedure** Write the code to define the variables, determine the housing/board cost, calculate the semester cost, instantiate the object for the StudentCostsFile class, call the procedure to write the file, and return the semester cost.

HINT

```
36      Overrides Function ComputeCosts() As Decimal
37          ' This function computes the registration costs, writes a record
38          ' in the student costs file, and returns the registration costs
39
40          'Define variables
41          Dim HousingCost As Decimal
42          Const cdecCooperHousingCost As Decimal = 2900D
43          Const cdecPerceyHousingCost As Decimal = 3400D
44          Const cdecJulianHousingCost As Decimal = 4000D
45
46          'Calculate the cost
47          If _Cooper Then
48              HousingCost = cdecCooperHousingCost
49          ElseIf _Percey Then
50              HousingCost = cdecPerceyHousingCost
51          ElseIf _Julian Then
52              HousingCost = cdecJulianHousingCost
53          End If
54
55          _decCost = (_intUnits * _decCostPerUnit) + HousingCost
56
57          'Write the student record
58          objStudentCostsFile = New StudentCostsFile(_strStudentID, _
59              _strStudentName, _strMajor, _decCost)
60          objStudentCostsFile.WriteRecord()
61
62          'Return the calculated cost
63          Return _decCost
64
65      End Function
```

Guided Program Development (continued)

The OnCampusStudent class code is completed (Figure 11-46).

RESULT OF STEP 4

```
 1 ' Class:         OnCampusStudent
 2 ' Developer:     Corinne Hoisington
 3 ' Date:          August 29, 2012
 4 ' Purpose:       This business class for a registering an on-campus college
 5 '                student calculates the semester costs, including tuition
 6 '                and housing. It also causes the student costs file to be written
 7
 8 Option Strict On
 9
10 Public Class OnCampusStudent
11     Inherits Student
12
13     ' Class variables
14     Private _Cooper As Boolean
15     Private _Percey As Boolean
16     Private _Julian As Boolean
17
18     Dim objStudentCostsFile As StudentCostsFile
19
20     Sub New(ByVal StudentID As String, ByVal StudentName As String, _
21            ByVal Major As String, ByVal Units As String, _
22            ByVal Cooper As Boolean, ByVal Percey As Boolean, _
23            ByVal Julian As Boolean)
24         ' This subprocedure is a constructor for the Student class. It
25         ' is called when instantiated with arguments
26
27         MyBase.New(StudentID, StudentName, Major, Units)
28
29         'The following code assigns the arguments to class variables
30         _Cooper = Cooper
31         _Percey = Percey
32         _Julian = Julian
33
34     End Sub
35
36     Overrides Function ComputeCosts() As Decimal
37         ' This function computes the registration costs, writes a record
38         ' in the student costs file, and returns the registration costs
39
40         'Define variables
41         Dim HousingCost As Decimal
42         Const cdecCooperHousingCost As Decimal = 2900D
43         Const cdecPerceyHousingCost As Decimal = 3400D
44         Const cdecJulianHousingCost As Decimal = 4000D
```

FIGURE 11-46 (continues)

(continues)

Guided Program Development (continued)

```
45
46            'Calculate the cost
47            If _Cooper Then
48                HousingCost = cdecCooperHousingCost
49            ElseIf _Percey Then
50                HousingCost = cdecPerceyHousingCost
51            ElseIf _Julian Then
52                HousingCost = cdecJulianHousingCost
53            End If
54
55            _decCost = (_intUnits * _decCostPerUnit) + HousingCost
56
57            'Write the student record
58            objStudentCostsFile = New StudentCostsFile(_strStudentID, _
59                _strStudentName, _strMajor, _decCost)
60            objStudentCostsFile.WriteRecord()
61
62            'Return the calculated cost
63            Return _decCost
64
65        End Function
66
67 End Class
```

FIGURE 11-46 (continued)

5

▶ **Enter Comments and Option Strict On for the StudentCostsFile Class** Display the StudentCostsFile class coding window. Enter the common comments for the StudentCostsFile class. Include the Option Strict On statement.

HINT

```
1 ' Class:        Create Student Costs File
2 ' Developer:    Corinne Hoisington
3 ' Date:         August 29, 2012
4 ' Purpose:      This class represents the Student Costs File. The WriteRecord
5 '               procedure writes a comma-delineated student costs file that
6 '               contains the Student ID, Student Name, Major,
7 '               and Student Costs.
8
9 Option Strict On
10
11 Public Class StudentCostsFile
```

Guided Program Development (continued)

▶ **Define the Class Variables for the StudentCostsFile Class** Define the class variables for the StudentCostsFile class. The variables should be declared with Private access.

HINT

```
14      ' Class variables
15      Private _strStudentID As String
16      Private _strStudentName As String
17      Private _strMajor As String
18      Private _decStudentCosts As Decimal
```

▶ **Write the StudentCostsFile Class Constructor** Write the code for the StudentCostsFile class constructor based on the requirements shown in the Event Planning Document.

HINT

```
20      Sub New(ByVal StudentID As String, ByVal StudentName As String, _
21              ByVal Major As String, ByVal Costs As Decimal)
22          ' This sub procedure is the constructor for the StudentCostsFile
23          ' class.
24
25          'The following code assigns the arguments to class variables
26          _strStudentID = StudentID
27          _strStudentName = StudentName
28          _strMajor = Major
29          _decStudentCosts = Costs
30
31      End Sub
```

Guided Program Development (continued)

▶ **Write the Code for the WriteRecord Sub Procedure** Write the code to define the variable; and then in a Try-Catch block, declare an IO StreamWriter, write the comma-delineated record on the file, and then close the file *(ref: Figure 11-36)*.

```
33      Sub WriteRecord()
34          ' This subprocedure opens the StudentCosts output text file and then
35          ' writes a record in the comma-delimited file
36
37          Dim strNameandLocationOfFile As String = "E:\StudentCosts.txt"
38
39          Try
40              Dim objWriter As IO.StreamWriter = _
41                  IO.File.AppendText(strNameandLocationOfFile)
42
43              objWriter.Write(_strStudentID & ",")
44              objWriter.Write(_strStudentName & ",")
45              objWriter.Write(_strMajor & ",")
46              objWriter.WriteLine(_decStudentCosts)
47              objWriter.Close()
48
49          Catch ex As Exception
50              MsgBox("No device available - program aborted", , "Error")
51              Application.Exit()
52
53          End Try
54
55      End Sub
```

The *StudentCostsFile* class code is completed (Figure 11-47).

RESULT OF STEP 5

```
1  ' Class:       Student Costs File
2  ' Developer:   Corinne Hoisington
3  ' Date:        August 29, 2012
4  ' Purpose:     This class represents the Student Costs File. The WriteRecord
5  '              procedure writes a comma-delimited student costs file that
6  '              contains the Student ID, Student Name, Major,
7  '              and Student Costs.
8
9  Option Strict On
10
11 Public Class StudentCostsFile
12
13
14     ' Class variables
15     Private _strStudentID As String
16     Private _strStudentName As String
17     Private _strMajor As String
18     Private _decStudentCosts As Decimal
```

FIGURE 11-47 (continues)

Guided Program Development (continued)

RESULT OF STEP 5

```
19
20      Sub New(ByVal StudentID As String, ByVal StudentName As String, _
21            ByVal Major As String, ByVal Costs As Decimal)
22          ' This sub procedure is the constructor for the StudentCostsFile
23          ' class.
24
25          'The following code assigns the arguments to class variables
26          _strStudentID = StudentID
27          _strStudentName = StudentName
28          _strMajor = Major
29          _decStudentCosts = Costs
30
31      End Sub
32
33      Sub WriteRecord()
34          ' This subprocedure opens the StudentCosts output text file and then
35          ' writes a record in the comma-delimited file
36
37          Dim strNameandLocationOfFile As String = "E:\StudentCosts.txt"
38
39          Try
40              Dim objWriter As IO.StreamWriter = _
41                  IO.File.AppendText(strNameandLocationOfFile)
42
43              objWriter.Write(_strStudentID & ",")
44              objWriter.Write(_strStudentName & ",")
45              objWriter.Write(_strMajor & ",")
46              objWriter.WriteLine(_decStudentCosts)
47              objWriter.Close()
48
49          Catch ex As Exception
50              MsgBox("No device available - program aborted", , "Error")
51              Application.Exit()
52
53          End Try
54
55      End Sub
56
57  End Class
58
```

FIGURE 11-47 (continued)

Summary

In this chapter you have learned to create multiple classes using the three-tier program structure and to incorporate inheritance into your program. The items listed in the table in Figure 11-48 include all the new Visual Studio and Visual Basic skills you have learned in this chapter.

Skill	Figure Number	Web Address for Video
VISUAL BASIC SKILLS		
Examine the College Registration Costs program	Figure 11-1	scsite.com/vb2008/ch11/figure11-1
Set TabIndex property	Figure 11-4	scsite.com/vb2008/ch11/figure11-4
Edit input data	Figure 11-7	
Code MaskFull property	Figure 11-8	
Code TextBox TextLength property	Figure 11-9	
Create a class	Figure 11-13	scsite.com/vb2008/ch11/figure11-13
Instantiate a class	Figure 11-17	
Code a class constructor	Figure 11-19	
Pass an argument when instantiating an object	Figure 11-20	
Call a procedure from another class	Figure 11-24	
Write code for inheritance	Figure 11-26	
Code base class and subclass constructors	Figure 11-27	
Call and code procedures for inheritance	Figure 11-29 through Figure 11-33	
Code a persistence class	Figure 11-34	
Write a comma-delimited text file	Figure 11-36	

FIGURE 11-48

Learn It Online

Start your browser and visit scsite.com/vb2008/ch11. Follow the instructions in the exercises below.

1. **Chapter Reinforcement TF, MC, SA** Click the Chapter Reinforcement link below Chapter 11. Then, at the top of the page, select the type of reinforcement you want to use (True and False, Multiple Choice, Short Answer). Answer the questions and then grade your answers. Take as many quizzes as you want.

2. **Practice Test** Click the Practice Test link below Chapter 11. Answer each question, enter your first and last name at the bottom of the page, and then click the Grade Test button. When the graded practice test is displayed on your screen, submit the graded practice test to your instructor. Continue to take the practice test until you are satisfied with your score.

3. **Crossword Puzzle Challenge** Click the Crossword Puzzle Challenge link below Chapter 11. Read the instructions, and then enter your first and last name. Click the Play button. Work the crossword puzzle. When you are finished, click the Submit button. When the crossword puzzle is redisplayed, submit it to your instructor.

Knowledge Check

1. What property can you use to specify the sequence of objects that will be selected when the user presses the TAB key?

2. What property is used to ensure the user has entered all digits in a MaskedTextBox object?

3. If the TextLength property of a TextBox object is less than 1, what does that tell you?

4. What are the names of the three tiers in a three-tier program structure? What occurs in each of the three tiers?

5. In a three-tier program structure, which tiers are allowed to communicate with each other?

6. Identify the three steps to create a new class in a Visual Basic program.

7. Write the code to instantiate the objEmployee object based on the Employee class.

8. When is a class constructor executed?

9. Write the code to instantiate the objVehicle object based on the Vehicle class and to pass the following values to the object: Color, Model, Engine. Write the New statement in the Vehicle class.

10. Write a statement to call the ComputeDiscount procedure in the objDiscountItem object.

11. Explain the benefits of using separate classes in a program.

12. Complete the following sentence: Inheritance allows one class to inherit _____ and _____ from another class.

13. Describe the difference between a base class and a subclass when using inheritance.

14. What entry must be included in the Class statement of a subclass?

(continues)

Knowledge Check

(continued)

15. What is the first statement that must be coded in a subclass constructor?

16. What is an overridable procedure? Why is it used?

17. In a class, can an attribute be referenced that is not defined in the class? How is this attribute reference resolved?

18. What is a comma-delimited text file?

19. When an IO.StreamWriter is created, what does the IO.File.AppendText entry mean?

20. What is the difference between the Write procedure and the WriteLine procedure in the IO.StreamWriter class?

Debugging Exercises

1. The code in Figure 11-49 executes when a button on a Windows Form object is clicked. Identify what will happen when a single error occurs. What happens if two errors occur at the same time? What happens if three errors occur at the same time? How can this code be repaired?

```
20          Dim InputError As Boolean = False
21
22          If Me.txtSocialSecurity.MaskFull = False Then
23              MsgBox("Enter your Student ID in the Student ID box", , _
24              "Error")
25              Me.txtSocialSecurity.Clear()
26              Me.txtSocialSecurity.Focus()
27              InputError = True
28          End If
29
30          If Me.txtLastName.TextLength < 1 Or Me.txtLastName.Text < "A" Then
31              MsgBox("Enter your name in the Student Name box", , "Error")
32              Me.txtLastName.Clear()
33              Me.txtLastName.Focus()
34              InputError = True
35          End If
36
37          If Not IsNumeric(Me.txtNumberOfDependents.Text) Then
38              MsgBox("Enter the units in the Number of Units box", , _
39               "Error")
40              Me.txtNumberOfDependents.Clear()
41              Me.txtNumberOfDependents.Focus()
42              InputError = True
43          End If
```

FIGURE 11-49

Debugging Exercises

2. Examine the following code and make any corrections required.

CALLING CLASS

```
62   Dim objSubClass As New SubClass(txtLastName, _
63          txtNumberOfDependents)
```

OBJSUBCLASS

```
4   Sub New(ByVal LastName)
```

3. Correct the following code.

```
4   Dim objStoreName As StoreName
5   StoreName = New StoreName
```

4. Referencing exercise 3 above, correct the following statement:

```
22   me.lblStoreAddress = GetAddress.objStoreName
```

Analysis Exercises

1. What is the output of the code in Figure 11-50?

```
33 Sub WriteRecord()
34     ' This subprocedure opens the StudentCosts output text file and then
35     ' writes a record in the comma-delimited file
36
37     Dim strNameandLocationOfFile As String = "E:\StudentCosts.txt"
38
39     Try
40         Dim objWriter As IO.StreamWriter = _
41             IO.File.AppendText(strNameandLocationOfFile)
42
43         objWriter.Write(_strStudentID & ",")
44         objWriter.Write(_strStudentName & ",")
45         objWriter.Write(_strMajor & ",")
46         objWriter.WriteLine(_decStudentCosts)
47         objWriter.Close()
48
49     Catch ex As Exception
50         MsgBox("No device available - program aborted", , "Error")
51         Application.Exit()
52
53     End Try
54 End Sub
```

FIGURE 11-50

(continues)

Analysis Exercises

(continued)

2. Analyze the code in Figure 11-51a, Figure 11-51b, and Figure 11-51c. What is the output of the code?

```
17          Dim objCustomer As Customer
18          Dim objInternetCustomer As InternetCustomer
19
20          objCustomer = New Customer
21          objInternetCustomer = New InternetCustomer
22
23          MsgBox.Show(objInternetCustomer.CustomerFunction())
```

FIGURE 11-51a

```
1 Public Class Customer
2
3     Function CustomerFunction() As String
4         Return "Customer function"
5     End Function
6
7     Overridable Function OverridableCustomerFunction() As String
8         Return "Overridable customer function"
9     End Function
10
11
12 End Class
13
```

FIGURE 11-51b

```
1 Public Class InternetCustomer
2     Inherits Customer
3
4     Function InternetCustomerFunction() As String
5         Return "Internet customer function"
6     End Function
7
8     Overrides Function OverridableCustomerFunction() As String
9         Return "Overrode the customer overridable function"
10     End Function
11
12 End Class
13
```

FIGURE 11-51c

Analysis Exercises

3. Analyze the code in Figure 11-52a, Figure 11-52b, and Figure 11-52c. What is the output of the code?

```
17      Dim objCustomer As Customer
18      Dim objInternetCustomer As InternetCustomer
19
20      objCustomer = New Customer
21      objInternetCustomer = New InternetCustomer
22
23      MsgBox.Show(objInternetCustomer.InternetCustomerFunction())
```

FIGURE 11-52a

```
1 Public Class Customer
2
3     Function CustomerFunction() As String
4         Return "Customer function"
5     End Function
6
7     Overridable Function OverridableCustomerFunction() As String
8         Return "Overridable customer function"
9     End Function
10
11
12 End Class
13
```

FIGURE 11-52b

```
1 Public Class InternetCustomer
2     Inherits Customer
3
4     Function InternetCustomerFunction() As String
5         Return "Internet customer function"
6     End Function
7
8     Overrides Function OverridableCustomerFunction() As String
9         Return "Overrode the customer overridable function"
10     End Function
11
12 End Class
13
```

FIGURE 11-52c

(continues)

Analysis Exercises

(continued)

4. Analyze the code in Figure 11-53a, Figure 11-53b, and Figure 11-53c. What is the output of the code?

```
17          Dim objCustomer As Customer
18          Dim objInternetCustomer As InternetCustomer
19
20          objCustomer = New Customer
21          objInternetCustomer = New InternetCustomer
22
23          MsgBox.Show(objInternetCustomer.OverridableCustomerFunction())
```

FIGURE 11-53a

```
1  Public Class Customer
2
3      Function CustomerFunction() As String
4          Return "Customer function"
5      End Function
6
7      Overridable Function OverridableCustomerFunction() As String
8          Return "Overridable customer function"
9      End Function
10
11
12 End Class
13
```

FIGURE 11-53b

```
1  Public Class InternetCustomer
2      Inherits Customer
3
4      Function InternetCustomerFunction() As String
5          Return "Internet customer function"
6      End Function
7
8      Overrides Function OverridableCustomerFunction() As String
9          Return "Overrode the customer overridable function"
10     End Function
11
12 End Class
13
```

FIGURE 11-53c

Analysis Exercises

5. Analyze the code in Figure 11-54a, Figure 11-54b, and Figure 11-54c. What is the output of the code?

```
17          Dim objCustomer As Customer
18          Dim objInternetCustomer As InternetCustomer
19
20          objCustomer = New Customer
21          objInternetCustomer = New InternetCustomer
22
23          MsgBox.Show(objCustomer.OverridableCustomerFunction())
```

FIGURE 11-54a

```
1 Public Class Customer
2
3     Function CustomerFunction() As String
4         Return "Customer function"
5     End Function
6
7     Overridable Function OverridableCustomerFunction() As String
8         Return "Overridable customer function"
9     End Function
10
11
12 End Class
13
```

FIGURE 11-54b

```
1 Public Class InternetCustomer
2     Inherits Customer
3
4     Function InternetCustomerFunction() As String
5         Return "Internet customer function"
6     End Function
7
8     Overrides Function OverridableCustomerFunction() As String
9         Return "Overrode the customer overridable function"
10     End Function
11
12 End Class
13
```

FIGURE 11-54c

Case Programming Assignments

Complete one or more of the following case programming assignments. Submit the program and materials you create to your instructor. The level of difficulty is indicated for each case programming assignment.

● = Easiest
●● = Intermediate
●●● = Challenging

1 ●

NETWORK ASSOCIATION CONFERENCE REGISTRATION

Design a Windows application and write the code that will execute according to the program requirements in Figure 11-55 and the Use Case definition in Figure 11-56. Before writing the code, create an event planning document for each event in the program. The completed Windows Form object and other objects in the user interface are shown in Figure 11-57.

REQUIREMENTS DOCUMENT

Date submitted: July 29, 2012

Application title: Network Association Conference Registration

Purpose: This Windows application allows a visitor to the Network Association conference to register for the meeting.

Program Procedures: In a Windows application, the user enters the visitor's Corporation ID, First and Last Name, the Number of Days the visitor will be attending, selects if a pre-conference course is being attended and if so, which course it is. The user then clicks a button. The application calculates the costs for attending the conference and records the information in a log file.

Algorithms, Processing, and Conditions:
1. The user first enters the visitor's Corporation ID, First and Last Name, and Number of Days attending.
2. The user selects if the visitor will attend a pre-conference course, and if so, which one (Network Security, Conquering Your WAN, or Moving Bits and Bytes.
3. When the user clicks a button, the program calculates the costs for attending the conference and writes a log file.
4. A clear form button should be available to clear the form and place the insertion point in the Corporation ID text box.
5. The conference cost is $350.00 per day. The minimum number of days is 1, and the maximum number of days is 4.
6. The formula to calculate conference costs is number of days times the cost per day.
7. If the visitor will attend one of the pre-conference courses, the cost for any pre-conference course is $675.00. This cost should be added to the conference cost.
8. The log file is a text file that contains the Corporation ID, the First Name, the Last Name, the pre-conference course taken (if no course is taken, the field should contain no data in the text file record), and the total conference costs. It should be a comma-delimited file.

FIGURE 11-55 (continues)

Case Programming Assignments

Notes and Restrictions:	1. The Corporation ID must be five numeric digits in length.
	2. The First Name and the Last Name cannot be left blank and must begin with an alphabetic character.
	3. The Number of Days must be a numeric value of 1 through 4.
	4. The pre-conference course selections should not be displayed in the window unless the user selects pre-conference course.
	5. When the user clicks the button to calculate costs, if any errors occurred during data entry, a message box should be displayed and the user must be required to enter valid data before continuing.
	6. No pre-conference course is the default value.
Comments:	1. The picture used in the Window is available at scsite/vb2008/ch11/images. Its name is conference.gif.
	2. The program should use a three-tier structure with presentation, business, and persistence classes.

FIGURE 11-55 (continued)

The use case definition for the application is shown in Figure 11-56.

USE CASE DEFINITION

1. The user enters the visitor's Corporation ID, First Name, Last Name, and the Number of Days the visitor will attend the conference.
2. If necessary, the user selects Take Pre-Conference Course and then identifies the Pre-Conference Course. If Take Pre-Conference Course is not selected, the Pre-Conference Courses are not displayed.
3. The user clicks the Calculate Costs button.
4. The program calculates and displays the conference costs, including the pre-conference course cost, if appropriate.
5. The program writes a log of the conference registration costs.
6. If necessary, the user clicks the Clear Form button to clear the form and place the insertion point in the Corporation ID text box.

FIGURE 11-56

(continues)

Case Programming Assignments

Network Association Conference Registration (continued)

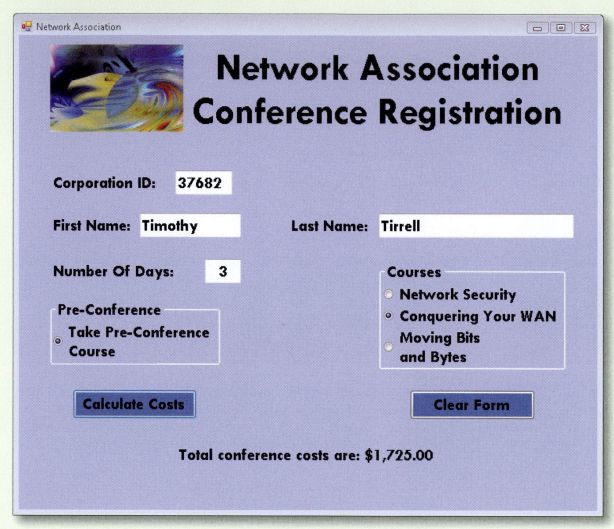

FIGURE 11-57

Case Programming Assignments

2 ● HISTORY BOOK INVENTORY

Design a Windows application and write the code that will execute according to the program requirements in Figure 11-58 and the Use Case definition in Figure 11-59. Before writing the code, create an event planning document for each event in the program. The completed Windows Form object and other objects in the user interface are shown in Figure 11-60a and Figure 11-60b.

REQUIREMENTS DOCUMENT

Date submitted: December 12, 2012

Application title: History Library Inventory

Purpose: This Windows application allows the user to enter a book into a History Library inventory. When all books have been entered, it identifies the number of books entered for each type.

Program Procedures: From a Windows application, a user enters a book ISBN number, book title, and book author(s). The user also identifies the book as a U.S. history book, a European history book, or a World history book. The program identifies the shelf area where the book will be stored, based on the type of book. A log stored on disk is kept of all inventory entries. When the user finishes entering the inventory, the program identifies the number of each type of book the user entered.

Algorithms, Processing, and Conditions:
1. The user enters the ISBN of the book, the name of the book, and the author(s) of the book.
2. The user identifies the book as a U.S. history book, an European history book, or a World history book.
3. Based on the type of book, the program displays the shelf location of the book. (U. S. history books in Section F, European history books in Section A, and World history books in Section D.)
4. When the user indicates all books have been entered, the program displays the number of each type of book that has been entered.
5. In a comma-delimited text file, the program keeps a log of all books entered. The file should contain the ISBN, the book title, and the author(s) of the book.

Notes and Restrictions:
1. Validate data the user enters using accepted standards.

Comments:
1. The picture shown in the application is available at scsite.com/vb2008/ch11/images. Its name is library.jpg.
2. The program should use a three-tier structure with presentation, business, and persistence classes.

FIGURE 11-58

(continues)

Case Programming Assignments

History Book Inventory (continued)

USE CASE DEFINITION

1. The user views the opening screen.
2. The user enters the ISBN, the book title, and the book author(s).
3. The user selects the book category.
4. The user clicks the Enter Book button to enter the book into the inventory.
5. The program displays the shelf location; it also writes a record in the inventory text file.
6. To enter another book, the user clicks the New Book button.
7. When finished, the user clicks the Inventory Entry Complete button.
8. The program displays the number of books entered by category.

FIGURE 11-59

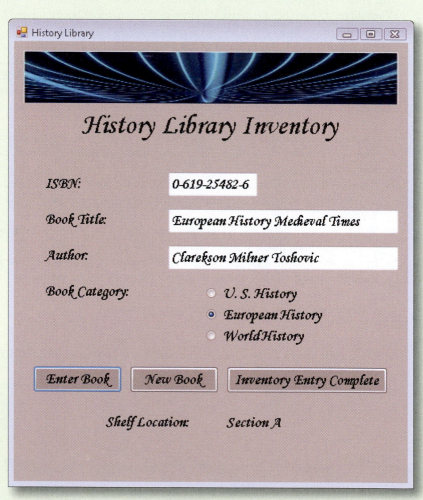

FIGURE 11-60a

Case Programming Assignments

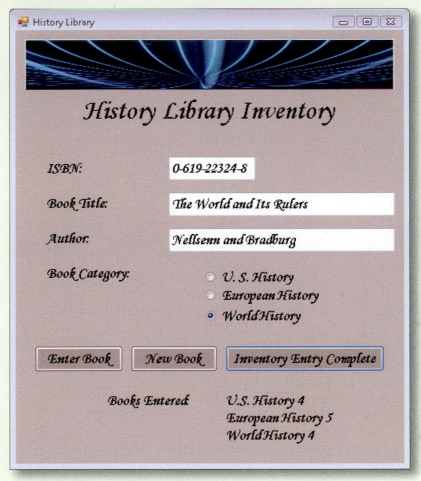

FIGURE 11-60b

Case Programming Assignments

3 ● MOBILE PHONE PURCHASE

Design a Windows application and write the code that will execute according to the program requirements in Figure 11-61 and the Use Case definition in Figure 11-62. Before writing the code, create an event planning document for each event in the program. The completed Windows Form object and other objects in the user interface are shown in Figure 11-63.

REQUIREMENTS DOCUMENT

Date submitted: September 14, 2012

Application title: Mobile Phone Purchase

Purpose: This Windows application calculates the costs for a mobile phone from the Mobile Phone Store.

Program Procedures: From a Windows application, a buyer selects a mobile telephone for purchase. The buyer also can elect to buy a charger for the particular phone. A buyer is either in the store or is buying over the Internet. The program calculates the cost of the phone and charger purchased.

Algorithms, Processing, and Conditions:
1. The consumer enters their last name, street address, and zip code. If buying over the Internet, the buyer also enters an email address.
2. The buyer selects a phone from a list of phones.
3. The user can select the type of charger from the list of chargers.
4. Based on the phone and charger selected, the program calculates the total cost.
5. The total cost for a store purchase must include 7.75% sales tax. No sales tax is included for Internet sales.
6. An Internet sale generates a shipping charge of $28.00.
7. The types of phones and their costs are: Blasstur 451: $279.81; Elecque 9801: $193.71; Gainlet 3: $328.44; Nomadic 2900: $253.72; Querta 332: $479.36.
8. Three types of chargers are available: Auto: $63.92; Mobile: $42.66; Desktop: $27.31.
9. Write a comma-delimited text file to record each sale. The text file should contain the user last name, zip code, phone choice, charger style, and total cost.

Notes and Restrictions:
1. Validate data the user enters using accepted standards.
2. In-store is the default type of buyer.
3. The Email label and text box does not display unless the user is an Internet buyer. An Internet buyer must enter an email address.

Comments:
1. The picture shown in the application is available at scsite.com/vb2008/ch11/images. Its name is cell phone.jpg.
2. The program should use a three-tier structure with presentation, business, and persistence classes.

FIGURE 11-61

Case Programming Assignments

USE CASE DEFINITION

1. The user views the opening screen.
2. The user enters their last name, street address, and zip code.
3. The user selects a phone from the phone choice list and, if desired, a charger from the charger style list.
4. The user selects either In-Store or Internet as the type of buyer. If an Internet buyer, the user must enter an email address.
5. The user clicks the Calculate Cost button.
6. The program displays the cost of the sale.
7. The program writes a record of the sale in a text file.
8. The user can click the Clear Form button to enter another sale.

FIGURE 11-62

FIGURE 11-63

Case Programming Assignments

4 ●●
BANK ACCOUNT PROJECTION

Design a Windows application and write the code that will execute according to the program requirements in Figure 11-64. Before designing the user interface, create a Use Case definition. Before writing the code, create an event planning document for each event in the program.

REQUIREMENTS DOCUMENT

Date submitted: July 10, 2012

Application title: Bank Account Projection

Purpose: This Windows application calculates and displays the expected value of different types of bank accounts one year from opening the account for current customers of the Tenth Street Regional Bank.

Program Procedures: In a Windows application, a user enters their name and current account number, selects one of five types of accounts, and then enters the amount to be placed in the account. The program calculates the value of the money one year in the future, assuming the money is not touched for a year.

Algorithms, Processing, and Conditions:
1. The user enters their name and current account number.
2. The user identifies the type of account being considered. The types of accounts are: Regular Savings, Checking, 1-year CD, 2-year CD, and 5-year CD.
3. The user enters the amount to be deposited. The minimum amount is $1,000.00.
4. The user clicks a button and the program calculates and displays the value of the account in one year.
5. The value of the account is based on the following: a) Regular Savings: 2.75% interest; b) Checking: $25.00 per month service charge; c) 1-year CD: 5.85% interest; d) 2-year CD: 7.30% interest; e) 5-year CD: 9.37% interest.
6. A comma-delimited text file is kept for each account inquiry. The text file contains the account number, the amount to be deposited, and the type of account selected.
7. The user can click a button to clear the form.

Notes and Restrictions:
1. Validate data the user enters using accepted standards.

Comments:
1. Use the Web to find an appropriate image for use in the user interface.
2. The program should use a three-tier structure with presentation, business, and persistence classes.

FIGURE 11-64

Case Programming Assignments

5 ●● SOFTWARE PACKAGE PURCHASE

Design a Windows application and write the code that will execute according to the program requirements in Figure 11-65. Before designing the user interface, create a Use Case definition. Before writing the code, create an event planning document for each event in the program.

REQUIREMENTS DOCUMENT

Date submitted: November 24, 2012

Application title: Software Purchase

Purpose: This Windows application calculates the costs for a software package from the Sync Software Store.

Program Procedures: In a Windows application, a user selects one of five software packages to purchase from a list. The user enters the buyer's credit card number, expiration date, and identifies if he or she is a student. The program calculates the cost of the software. It also keeps a log of purchases.

Algorithms, Processing, and Conditions:

1. The user enters the buyer's credit card number and expiration date.
2. The user identifies the software package the buyer is purchasing.
3. The five software packages and their prices are: Speed-Up the Internet — $334.95; A Writer's Writer — $578.90; Distance Personnel Management — $872.45; Email Photo Manager — $129.95; Keyboard SpeedLearner — $79.95.
4. For each package, a discount applies if the buyer is a student. The discounts are: Speed-Up the Internet — 26%; A Writer's Writer — 18%; Distance Personnel Management — 48%; Email Photo Manager — 65%; Keyboard SpeedLearner — 72%.
5. After entering the information, the user can click the Final Total button to determine the amount to be charged to the credit card.
6. The user can click a button to clear the form.
7. The program writes a comma-delimited text file to keep track of all software purchases. The text file contains the credit card number, the name of the software purchased, the discount amount, and the final total amount.
8. At any time, the user can click the Daily Total button and the program will calculate and display the amount of sales that have been recorded in the text file.

Notes and Restrictions:

1. Validate data the user enters using accepted standards.

Comments:

1. Use the Web to find an appropriate image for use in the user interface.
2. The program should use a three-tier structure with presentation, business, and persistence classes.

FIGURE 11-65

Case Programming Assignments

6 ●●
USED CAR INVENTORY

Design a Windows application and write the code that will execute according to the program requirements in Figure 11-66. Before designing the user interface, create a Use Case definition. Before writing the code, create an event planning document for each event in the program.

Requirements Document

Date submitted: May 19, 2012

Application title: Used Car Inventory

Purpose: This Windows application allows the user to add cars to the inventory of a used car dealer named Car Cruiser. It displays the sticker price for each car based on discounts, and also allows the user to display the entire inventory.

Program Procedures: In a Windows application, a user enters the vehicle number, make, model, year, mileage and standard price for a used car that is being placed in the inventory of the used car dealer. In addition, the user selects the color from a list of colors, and indicates if the vehicle is a convertible. The program creates the sticker price for the car and records a record for the car in the inventory text file.

Algorithms, Processing, and Conditions:

1. The user enters the vehicle number, make, model, year, mileage, and standard price for a used car being placed in inventory.
2. The user selects the car color from a list of 17 colors commonly found on cars, including black, dark gray, and red.
3. The user identifies if the car is a convertible.
4. The program calculates the sticker price for the car on the used car lot.
5. If the car is black, a 15% discount is applied to the standard price to determine the sticker price. If the car is dark gray, a 21% surcharge is added to the standard price to determine the sticker price. If the car is red, a 9% surcharge is added to the standard price to determine the sticker price. For all other cars, the standard price and the sticker price are the same.
6. If the car is a convertible, a 26% surcharge of the sticker price is added to the sticker price calculated in step 5 to determine the convertible sticker price.
7. After the user enters all the data and clicks a button, the sticker price is displayed.
8. When the button is clicked, the program also writes a comma-delimited text file that records the new entry into the inventory. The record includes the vehicle number, make, model, year, mileage, and sticker price.
9. At any time, the user can click the Inventory menu item on the Display menu on the menu bar to display the records in the inventory text file. In a separate window, the vehicle number, make, model, year, mileage, and sticker price should be displayed in a list for every car in the inventory.

Notes and Restrictions:

1. Validate data the user enters using accepted standards.

Comments:

1. Use the Web to find an appropriate image for use in the user interface.
2. The program should use a three-tier structure with presentation, business, and persistence classes.

FIGURE 11-66

Case Programming Assignments

7 ●●●
DAY SPA RESERVATIONS

Create a requirements document and a Use Case Definition document, and then design a Windows application, based on the following case project. Before writing the code, create an event planning document for each event in the program.

The RenewYourself Day Spa has asked you to create a reservation system for them. They provide a half day or full day of treatments to customers. They need to know the name of the customer and the date the customer will be attending. (Hint: For the date, consider using the DateTimePicker object or the Calendar object). If the customer is a spa member, they receive a 40% discount from the standard day price which is $675.00. A customer also can request a half-day treatment. The price for a half-day treatment is $525.00. A spa member receives a 25% discount on the half-day price. A full-day treatment begins at 9:30 a.m. A half-day treatment begins either at 9:00 a.m. or 2:00 p.m. In addition, a half-day customer must determine whether they want the massage treatment or the facial treatment. Both are the same price. The following specials are available: For Day customers: Mud Facial ($40.00); Kelp Leg Wrap ($55.00); Steaming Rocks ($39.00); Acupuncture ($219.99). For Half-Day Customers: Kelp Leg Wrap ($75.00); Acupuncture ($269.99). When the customer makes a reservation, they should be told the price they will be paying. The owners of the spa would like to view a list of their appointments at any time.

FIGURE 11-67

8 ●●●
FISH BOAT ORDERS

Create a requirements document and a Use Case Definition document, and then design a Windows application, based on the following case project. Before writing the code, create an event planning document for each event in the program.

Your friend operates a charter fishing boat. She offers both full-day and half-day excursions. When a customer catches a fish, she receives a variety of requests for handling the fish. She has narrowed these requests to the following: 1) Prepare individual filets and ship to a given address; 2) Ship the frozen fish to a given address; 3) Prepare filets and instruct a taxidermist to mount the fish. Ship to an address; 4) Prepare the fish filets and donate them to a local charity. She has determined the following prices for these services: 1) Filets are $9.25 per pound. Shipping charges are $3.89 per pound; 2) The fish is $8.75 per pound; shipping charges are $5.95 per pound; 3) The filets are the same price as number 1. The taxidermist charges a flat fee of $675.00 plus $85.00 per pound; 4) The charge for donation is $2.00 per pound. Your friend has asked you to develop an application that can help her keep track of her orders. When she enters an order, she wants to tell her customer the price at that time. She also would like to view all her orders and the dates they are due to ship.

FIGURE 11-68

Case Programming Assignments

9 ●●●
A COMMUNITY APPLICATION

Create a requirements document and a Use Case Definition document, and then design a Windows application, based on the following case project. Before writing the code, create an event planning document for each event in the program.

You have been asked to search out computer users on your campus or within your community to determine an application they need that you can write. Find an application that you can develop and then, working with your user, develop and implement the application.

FIGURE 11-69

CHAPTER TWELVE

Cell Phone Applications and Web Services

OBJECTIVES

You will have mastered the material in this chapter when you can:

- ► Create a Smartphone application
- ► Use a cell phone keypad for input
- ► Enter input using a Smartphone
- ► Enter other characters using the keypad
- ► Add Smartphone Toolbox objects
- ► Create a softkey menu
- ► Code the Smartphone application
- ► Display Message Box objects in a Smartphone environment
- ► Find Web services
- ► Create a Web service connection
- ► Call a Web service method
- ► Create a Microsoft Report
- ► Display a Report in a Web application

Introduction

In the previous chapters, you built a strong foundation to run traditional applications on various platforms such as Windows, Web, Office, and handheld devices. Besides handheld devices, Visual Basic 2008 can also work on another mobile platform for cell phones. You can program Windows-based cell phones called Smartphones using the same skills that you have already learned in Visual Basic 2008, but using a different Form object emulator designed for Smartphones. In addition, you can include Web services in your Windows applications. A Web service is software available on the Internet that uses special technology to share information. For example, local weather information displayed on a Web page uses a Web service. Web services allow developers to connect to previously coded Internet applications anywhere in the world. To explore these two technologies, this chapter offers two chapter projects. The first project is a cell phone application, and the second project introduces Web services. The chapter also covers the power of the new Microsoft Reports feature to create business reports. Microsoft Reports is a component of Visual Studio 2008 and is similar to Crystal Reports.

Chapter Projects

The first sample chapter project demonstrates how to develop a Smartphone application that computes the tip on a restaurant bill. By running the application on a cell phone, the user can calculate a tip in any restaurant without needing a separate device.

The Smartphone application allows the user to enter a restaurant bill amount and select a 10, 15, or 20 percent tip for the wait staff, as shown in the tip calculator displayed in the cell phone screen in Figure 12-1.

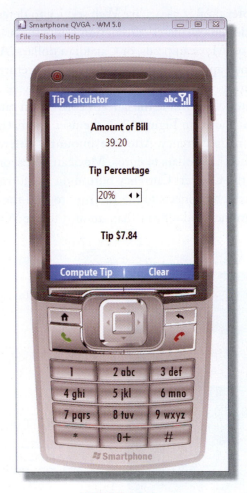

FIGURE 12-1

The user enters the bill amount by using the keypad on the cell phone. Next, the user selects the tip amount by using the navigation controls (arrow buttons) on the keypad, and then selects the Compute Tip option by pressing the left softkey, which is the upper-left button on the cell phone keypad. The user selects the Clear option to clear the tip calculator form by pressing the right softkey, which is the upper-right button on the keypad. The user enters the bill amount by using the numeric buttons on the cell phone keypad.

ONLINE REINFORCEMENT

To view a video of program execution, visit scsite.com/vb2008/ch12 and then select Figure 12-1.

The second chapter project uses a live Web service to determine up-to-date currency equivalents and then calculates currency amounts to convert U.S. dollars to European Union euros, Mexican pesos, or Canadian dollars. A Web service is a call to another programmed application via the Internet that returns information to your local application. During program execution, the Web service application makes a request to a Web site to determine the current conversion rate. In the Currency Converter application shown in Figure 12-2, the user enters the amount of U.S. dollars to convert to a foreign currency. After the amount is entered, the user can select whether to convert the U.S. dollars to euros, Mexican pesos, or Canadian dollars. After the user clicks the Convert Currency button on the form, the application contacts a Web service, which connects to the Internet to find the current conversion rate of the appropriate currency and returns that amount to the Windows application.

FIGURE 12-2

SMARTPHONE APPLICATIONS

Over a billion cell phones are now actively used across the planet. Today's cell phones can do more than provide voice communications—some can also connect to wireless data services and the Internet. Cell phones that can connect to the Internet and run mobile applications are called **Smartphones**. A Smartphone is based on a Windows mobile platform and functions like a mobile phone, but includes PDA functionality similar to the Pocket PC. Smartphones have a full-color, 240 × 320-pixel display screen, which is larger than most older cell phones yet smaller than the Pocket PC's screen. Because a Smartphone does not have a touch screen, you enter data using the number pad and various control buttons. See Figure 12-3.

FIGURE 12-3

Despite its small screen, a Smartphone can run many applications, including built-in applications similar to the ones designed for the Pocket PC but modified for the Smartphone's smaller screen and keypad input method. Correct handling of text inputs in a Smartphone application can make the difference between success and failure. Unlike the Pocket PC, the Smartphone does not have a built-in input panel. Instead, the user relies on the numeric keypad to enter both text and numbers.

Smartphones often include applications such as Outlook, which provides a calendar, task schedule, e-mail, online chat capabilities, a media player, and a mobile Internet browser. You can also install add-on software for specialized tasks including applications that display stock market quotes, language translators, alarm clocks, medical dictionaries, and cell phone games. Other programs available on the Pocket PC, such as Word, Excel, and PowerPoint, are not available on the Smartphone. To take advantage of the Pocket PC's additional capacity, some devices, called **convergence** devices, are now combining the features of a Pocket PC and a Smartphone.

All Smartphones use the **Windows CE** platform. Windows CE (sometimes abbreviated WinCE) is a variation of the Microsoft Windows operating system for handheld computers. Rather than a trimmed-down version of Windows for a PC, Windows CE is a distinctly different operating system. Windows CE is optimized for devices that have minimal storage and can run with under a megabyte of memory. Microsoft produces a standard Smartphone build of Windows CE that manufacturers and cellular providers can then enhance with branding and additional features.

HEADS UP

Although Microsoft states that the "CE" in Windows CE is not an intentional acronym, many people say CE stands for "Consumer Electronics" or "Compact Edition".

HEADS UP

When the Smartphone application is deployed to a simulation device, the resulting execution may take up to three minutes. If you want to send the application to a real Smartphone, attach the Smartphone with an interface to the computer and select the second option in the Deploy window, which selects the actual Smartphone and not the simulator.

Create a Smartphone Application

The Tip chapter project application calculates the tip amount on a cell phone mobile device. To place an application on a Smartphone, you develop the project in Visual Basic 2008 using the same commands you would use for a Windows application. Instead of creating a Windows application, however, you develop the project as a **Smart Device** application for a Smartphone. To create a Smartphone application, you can complete the following steps:

STEP 1   With Visual Studio 2008 open, click the New Project button on the Standard toolbar, click Smart Device in the Project types pane on the left side of the New Project dialog box.

The Smart Device project icon is displayed in the Templates pane (Figure 12-4).

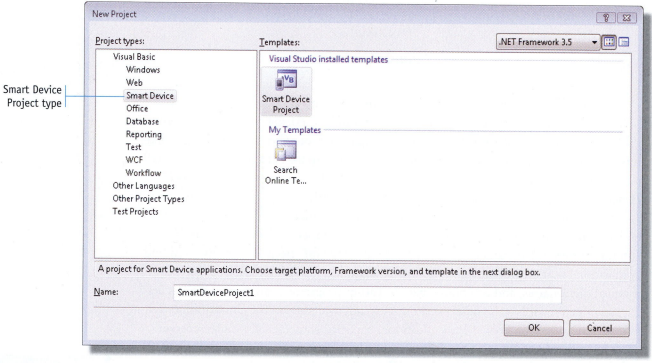

FIGURE 12-4

STEP 2   In the Name text box, change the name of the Smart Device application from SmartDeviceProject1 to Tip. Click the OK button. Select Windows Mobile 5.0 Smartphone SDK from the Target platform list button.

The Add New Smart Device Project window opens and the Target platform is selected. (Figure 12-5).

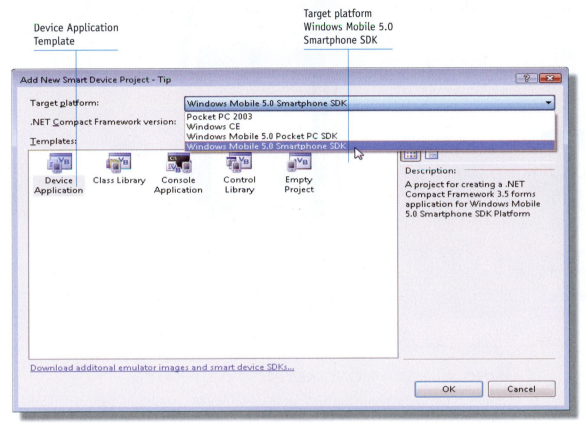

FIGURE 12-5

STEP 3   Select the Device Application Template and click the OK button.

The Smart Device application is named Tip and the Smartphone emulator form opens (Figure 12-6). As you do when working with a Windows form, you place objects from the Toolbox on the Smartphone emulator form as you design the Smartphone application.

Smartphone emulator

FIGURE 12-6

USING A CELL PHONE KEYPAD FOR INPUT

Before you begin designing the Smartphone Form object, you should understand the input interface on a cell phone keypad. In a Smartphone window, the user cannot click an object because no mouse is connected to the cell phone and the plastic screen of the cell phone is not a touch screen. The user must initiate each programmed event action using the keypad of the cell phone. You can press the number and alpha keys for data entry, and other keys such as the **softkeys** at the top of the phone keypad (directly below the screen) to select an action. A Smartphone keypad uses the two soft-keys to display menus and action options. Users interact with the Tip cell phone application mainly through the two softkeys. In other words, instead of using a stylus or pointing device in a Pocket PC or Windows application to click a Button object, the user completes actions by using the two softkeys. The user can activate a softkey by pressing the corresponding button as shown in Figure 12-7.

FIGURE 12-7

ENTERING INPUT USING A SMARTPHONE

When designing applications that require user input, be sure to minimize the number of keys the user has to press. You should understand how to enter all types of characters using the keypad when inputting text into a TextBox object on the Smartphone Form object. For example, if you want to enter the bill amount of $75.22 into the TextBox object on the Smartphone Form object using the keypad, you enter numbers and a decimal point (not the dollar symbol). To add a TextBox object and enter the amount of $75.22, you can complete the following steps:

STEP 1   With the Tip application open, name the Form object frmTip.vb. Title the Form object by changing the Text property to Tip Calculator. Add a Label object to the form named lblBillAmount. Change the Text property of the Label object to Amount of Bill. Drag a TextBox object under the Label object. Name the TextBox object txtBill. Clear the Text property. Resize the Label object to fit the text exactly. Center the Label and TextBox objects horizontally on the form.

The Label and TextBox objects are added to the Smartphone Form object (Figure 12-8).

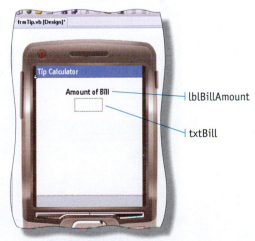

FIGURE 12-8

STEP 2   Run the Smartphone application by clicking the Start Debugging button on the Standard toolbar.

The Deploy Tip window opens (Figure 12-9).

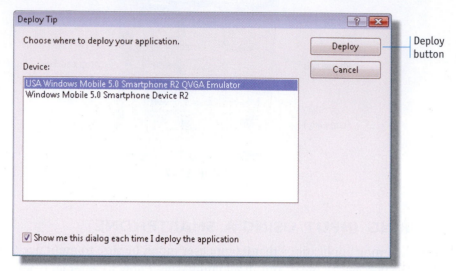

FIGURE 12-9

STEP 3   Make sure USA Windows Mobile 5.0 Smartphone R2 QVGA Emulator is selected, and then click the Deploy button.

The Smartphone Emulator first displays the Fake Network screen. Then the application loads, displaying the Label and TextBox objects (Figure 12–10).

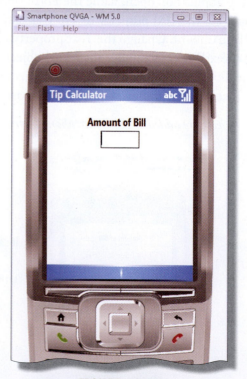

FIGURE 12-10

STEP 4   To enter the bill amount of 75.22, press the 7 key on the keypad five times quickly. The letter "p" appears first, then the letter "q," then the letter "r," then the letter "s," and lastly the number "7". Next, press the 5 key on the keypad four times quickly to enter the number 5.

The digits 7 and 5 are entered from the keypad (Figure 12-11).

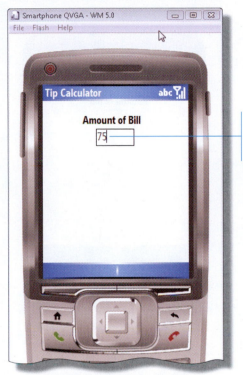

press the 7 key five times quickly, and then press the 5 key four times quickly

FIGURE 12-11

STEP 5   To enter the decimal point, press the 1 key on the cell phone. If you press the 1 key repeatedly, you can then select other symbols such as the question mark, comma, and dash.

The decimal point is placed after the number 75 (Figure 12-12).

1 key is pressed to create decimal point

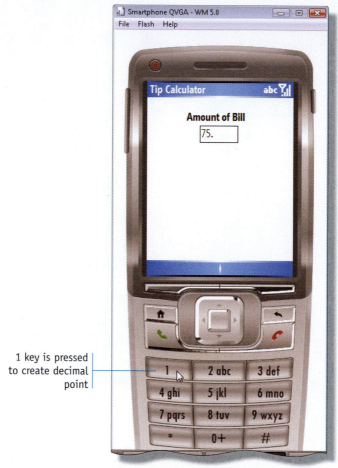

FIGURE 12-12

STEP 6   Enter the digits 22 by first pressing the 2 key four times quickly. Wait a few seconds and press the 2 key four times quickly again to display the second 2.

The bill amount of 75.22 is displayed (Figure 12-13).

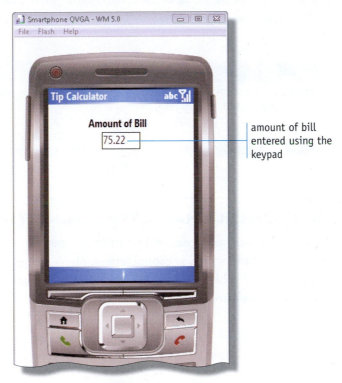

amount of bill
entered using the
keypad

FIGURE 12-13

STEP 7   To close the application, click the Close button in the upper-right corner of the program window.

The Device Emulator dialog box opens, asking if you want to save the emulator state (Figure 12-14).

click the No
button

FIGURE 12-14

STEP 8 Click the No button, and then click the OK button.

A message box opens, indicating that the remote connection to the device has been lost. Each time you deploy the application, be sure you click the No button in the Device Emulator dialog box so you do not save the emulator state. This means you can later deploy updated code to the cell phone emulator (Figure 12-15). After clicking the OK button, the form design window is displayed.

FIGURE 12-15

ENTERING OTHER CHARACTERS USING THE KEYPAD

Besides placing numbers and a decimal point in a Smartphone Form object, you can also enter other characters such as capital letters, blank spaces, deletions, and common punctuation. The table in Figure 12-16 includes instructions for entering different types of characters using a cell phone keypad.

Entries	Instructions
Uppercase letters	Press the * key and the key associated with the letter you want to enter. The first letter of a sentence is automatically capitalized.
Switch between uppercase and lowercase letters	Press the * key.
Delete a single character to the left of the insertion point	Press the Back key on the keypad.
Space character	Press the # key on the keypad.
Common punctuation such as @, !, or a comma	Press the 1 key on the keypad repeatedly.

FIGURE 12-16

ADDING SMARTPHONE TOOLBOX OBJECTS

A Smartphone application supports fewer Toolbox objects than those in a Windows application because of the limitations of the cell phone. For example, you cannot click buttons, radio buttons, or calendar objects on a cell phone screen, so these objects are not included in the Smartphone Toolbox. The 23 Toolbox objects shown in Figure 12-17 are available for the Smartphone. When designing the interface, developers must make the Smartphone form as intuitive as possible and limit the amount of input the user must enter. By default, the Text property on each object appears in a 10-point font named Segoe Condensed. Although you can change the size of the font, you should avoid doing so to maintain readability.

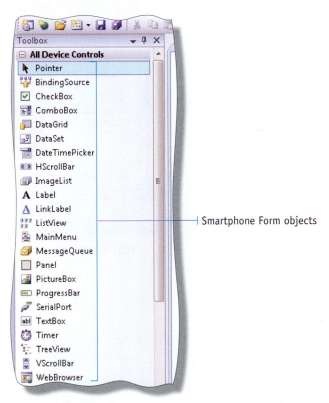

Smartphone Form objects

FIGURE 12-17

Except for the ComboBox object, the Toolbox objects work in the same manner in the Smartphone environment as they do in the Windows environment. Usually the ComboBox object displays data in a drop-down list of items, but on a Smartphone, a ComboBox object shows two arrows its right end, indicating the keys to use on the keypad. To scroll through the list of items, the user can press the left and right navigation keys on the keypad to view each item. The user can also press the Action key on the keypad to view the list of items available for selection. To add a ComboBox object to the cell phone application and select data, you can complete the following steps:

STEP 1 If necessary, open the Tip application, which includes the first Label and TextBox object on the form. Drag a second Label object named lblPercentage to the form below the TextBox object. Change the Text property to Tip Percentage. Drag the ComboBox object to the Form object below the second label. Name the ComboBox object cboTipPercent. Click the ellipsis button to the right of the Items property. Enter the three tip percentage amounts into the String Collection Editor: 10% (press ENTER), 15% (press ENTER), and 20%. Resize the objects to the exact size of the text. Center both the Label and ComboBox objects on the center of the form.

A Label and ComboBox object are added to the Smartphone Form object (Figure 12-18).

Smartphone ComboBox object

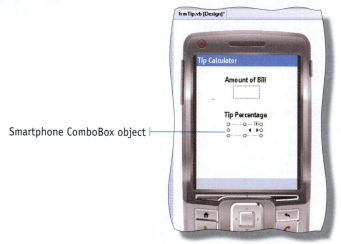

FIGURE 12-18

STEP 2 Run the Smartphone application by clicking the Start Debugging button on the Standard toolbar. In the Deploy Tip window, make sure the USA Windows Mobile 5.0 Smartphone R2 QVGA Emulator option is selected, and then click the Deploy button. When the Smartphone emulator opens and loads the application, enter 75.22 in the first TextBox object using the keypad. To move to the ComboBox object for input, click the down arrow key on the navigation keypad. To view the ComboBox items, click the right arrow on the navigation keypad; 10% is displayed in the ComboBox object. Click the right arrow again to view 15%. Select the 15% tip percentage by clicking the Action button in the center of the navigation keypad. Close the Smartphone emulator without saving the emulator state.

The bill amount is entered and the 15% tip percentage is selected (Figure 12-19).

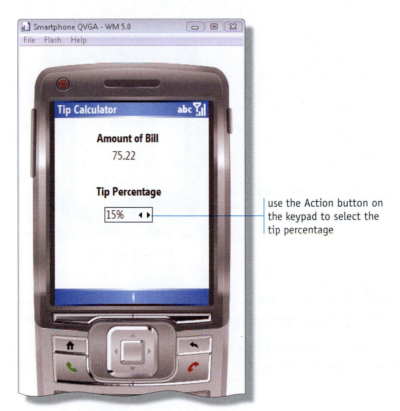

use the Action button on the keypad to select the tip percentage

FIGURE 12-19

HEADS UP

To fit the small screen size of a cell phone, use short, meaningful words and phrases for the Text property on the Form objects.

ONLINE REINFORCEMENT

To view a video of the process in the previous steps, visit scsite.com/vb2008/ch12 and then select Figure 12-18.

CREATING A SOFTKEY MENU

Softkeys are used within the Tip application instead of Button objects because cell phone users cannot select buttons using a stylus or touch screen. You can use the blue band at the bottom of the Smartphone screen, called the **Command** control area, to provide menus that are related to each softkey. When the user selects a Command control by pressing the softkey, a click event related to the Command control is executed. To create a Command control, you can complete the following steps:

STEP 1 On the frmTip Form object of the Tip application, click the left side of the Command control area.

In the Command control area, the words Type Here appear (Figure 12-20).

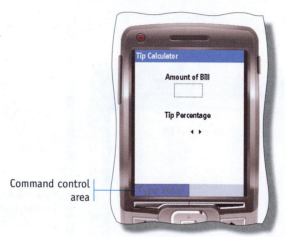

Command control
area

FIGURE 12-20

STEP 2 Type Compute Tip in the Command control area. Press ENTER. Use the (Name) property to name the Command control area mnuComputeTip.

The left Command control area displays "Compute Tip." When the application runs, the Command control area click event is executed by pressing the left softkey button on the keypad (Figure 12-21).

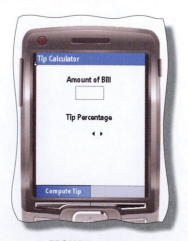

FIGURE 12-21

CODING THE SMARTPHONE APPLICATION

With the release of Visual Basic 2008, smart device developers can use the same development tools for Smartphone applications as they do for their Windows applications. The same code that works in the Windows, mobile, ASP.NET 3.5, and Office environments works in Smartphone applications. Developers who understand multiple platforms are desirable in the business world because they can develop one set of commands that works on many platforms. The first object to code in the Tip chapter project is the Command control area. To code the Command control area, you can complete the following steps:

STEP 1   In the Tip application, double-click the mnuComputeTip Command control area in the lower-left corner of the Smartphone Form object.

The code editing window opens, displaying the mnuComputeTip_Click event (Figure 12-22).

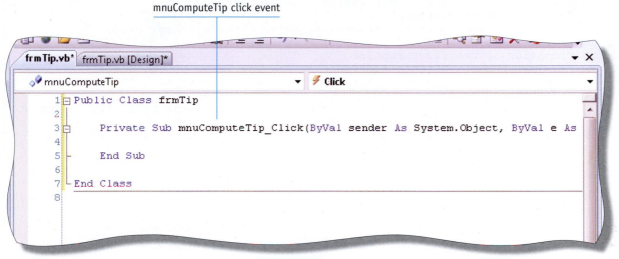

FIGURE 12-22

STEP 2 Enter the code shown in Figure 12-23 to compute the tip for the restaurant bill amount.

The mnuComputeTip_Click event code is entered, and is executed when the user clicks the Compute Tip Command control area (Figure 12-23).

```vb
12        ' The mnuComputeTip click event determines the amount of the tip
13        ' Initialize variables
14        Dim decBillAmount As Decimal
15        Dim intTipSelection As Integer
16        Dim decLowTip As Decimal = 0.1D
17        Dim decAverageTip As Decimal = 0.15D
18        Dim decGoodTip As Decimal = 0.2D
19        Dim decPercentageOfTip As Decimal
20        Dim decTipValue As Decimal
21
22        ' The Try-Catch block warns users if the bill amount is not entered properly
23        Try
24            decBillAmount = Convert.ToDecimal(Me.txtBill.Text)
25        Catch Exception As FormatException
26            ' This catch block detects letters, symbols, blank entries, etc
27            MsgBox("Please enter a U.S. Dollar amount", , "Error")
28        Catch Exception As OverflowException
29            ' This catch block detects numbers that are too large or too small
30            MsgBox("Please enter a valid U.S. Dollar amount", , "Error")
31        Catch Exception As SystemException
32            ' This catch block detects a generic exception not caught by earlier catch ↙
      blocks
33            MsgBox("Entry invalid. Please enter a valid money amount", , "Error")
34        End Try
35        ' The tip percentage is assigned
36        If Me.cboTipPercent.SelectedIndex >= 0 Then
37            intTipSelection = Convert.ToInt32(Me.cboTipPercent.SelectedIndex)
38            ' The tip percentage is set based on the user selection
39            Select Case intTipSelection
40                Case 0
41                    decPercentageOfTip = decLowTip
42                Case 1
43                    decPercentageOfTip = decAverageTip
44                Case 2
45                    decPercentageOfTip = decGoodTip
46            End Select
47            ' The amount of the tip is calculated
48            decTipValue = decBillAmount * decPercentageOfTip
49            Me.lblTipAmount.Text = "Tip " & decTipValue.ToString("C")
50        Else
51            MsgBox("Select a tip amount by using the navigation keys", , "Error")
52        End If
```

FIGURE 12-23

ONLINE REINFORCEMENT

To view a video of the process in the previous steps, visit scsite.com/vb2008/ch12 and then select Figure 12-22.

DISPLAYING MESSAGE BOX OBJECTS IN A SMARTPHONE ENVIRONMENT

The MsgBox commands on a Smartphone device are displayed differently than in the Windows environment. In the Try-Catch block in the Tip program, you can code a Message Box object to remind users to enter a valid numerical bill amount if they do not enter a valid bill amount. Instead of a small window opening to display the error message, the entire cell phone screen changes to display the reminder, as shown in Figure 12-24. The Message Box object appears on a separate screen and the user must press the left softkey to return to the application. The program resumes after the user presses the left softkey.

error message screen

FIGURE 12-24

Program Design

The requirements document for the Tip Smartphone application is shown in Figure 12-25, and the Use Case Definition document is shown in Figure 12-26.

REQUIREMENTS DOCUMENT

Date submitted:	June 4, 2011
Application title:	Tip Smartphone Application
Purpose:	This Smartphone application runs on a cell phone to compute the cost of a 10, 15, or 20 percent tip based on the amount of a restaurant bill.
Program Procedures:	In a Smartphone application, the keypad of a cell phone is used to enter the bill amount and select the tip percentage to calculate the cost of the tip for the wait staff.

Algorithms, Processing, and Conditions:

1. The user first views a Smartphone application that loads in a cell phone window. The user can use the keypad to enter the bill amount.
2. The user can click the down arrow key to move to the next entry object. A ComboBox object displays the possible tip percentage amounts of 10%, 15%, or 20%. The user can use the navigational control on the keypad to select the tip percentage.
3. The user can click the left softkey button to calculate and display the amount of the tip.
4. The user can select the right softkey button to clear the cell phone form information.

Notes and Restrictions:

Comments:

1. The user cannot click the cell phone screen.

FIGURE 12-25

USE CASE DEFINITION

1. The user views the main screen of the Smartphone tip calculator program.
2. The user uses the keypad to enter the bill amount.
3. The user clicks the down arrow key to move to the ComboBox object.
4. The user selects a tip percentage to calculate the amount of the tip.
5. The user clicks the left softkey to compute and display the tip.
6. The user clicks the right softkey to clear the form.

FIGURE 12-26

Design the Program Processing Objects

The event planning documents for the Tip Smartphone application are shown in Figure 12-27.

EVENT PLANNING DOCUMENT

Program Name: Tip Smartphone Application	Developer: Corinne Hoisington	Object: frmTip	Date: June 4, 2011

OBJECT	EVENT TRIGGER	EVENT PROCESSING
frmTip_Load	Load	Clear the Label object for the result.
mnuComputeTip	Click the left softkey	A Try-Catch block prevents exceptions in user input. Convert the bill amount to a Decimal data type. If the tip percentage is selected, assign the tip percentage to the tip value. Calculate the amount of the tip by multiplying the bill amount times the tip percentage amount. Display the total tip amount.
mnuClear	Click the right softkey	Clear the bill amount. Reset the tip percentage. Clear the tip amount.

FIGURE 12-27

Guided Program Development

To design the user interface for the Tip Smartphone application and enter the code required to process each event in the program, complete the steps in this section.

NOTE TO THE LEARNER

As you will recall, in the following activity, you should complete the tasks within the specified steps. Each of the tasks is accompanied by a Hint Screen. The purpose of the Hint Screen is to indicate where in the Visual Studio window you should perform the activity; it also serves as a reminder of the method that you should use to create the user interface or enter code. If you need further help completing the step, refer to the figure number identified by the term ref: in the step.

Guided Program Development

Phase 1: Design the Form

1

▶ **Create a New Project** Open Visual Studio using the Start button on the Windows taskbar and the All Programs sub-menu. Click the New Project button on the Standard toolbar. Select Smart Device in the Project types list; select Smart Device Project in the right (Templates) pane; name the project Tip in the Name text box; click the OK button in the New Project dialog box *(ref: Figure 12-3)*.

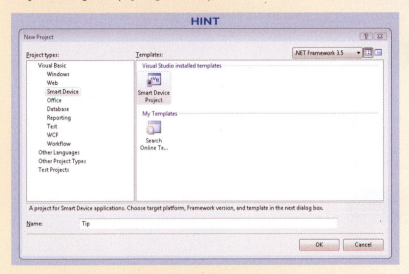

▶ **Add New Smart Device Project** Select the Target Platform of Windows Mobile 5.0 Smartphone SDK. Select the Device Application Template and click OK.

▶ **Name the Form Object** Select the Form object. Change the (Name) property of the Form object to frmTip.

▶ **Title the Form Object** Open the main Form object. Select the Form object and change the Text property to Tip Calculator.

▶ **Add the First Label and TextBox Object** Drag a label onto the Form object and name the label lblBillAmount. Enter the text for this label as Amount of Bill. Drag a TextBox object onto the Form object below the label and name the TextBox object txtBill. Delete the characters from the Text property. Resize both the Label and TextBox objects to the exact size of the text needed. Center both objects on the Form object.

▶ **Add the Second Label and a ComboBox Object** Drag another label onto the Form object and name the label lblPercentage. Enter the text for this label as Tip Percentage. Drag a ComboBox object onto the Form object below the label and name the ComboBox object cboTipPercent. Click the ellipsis button to the right of the Items property. Enter 10%, 15%, and 20% on three separate lines. Resize both the Label and ComboBox objects to the exact size of the text needed. Center both objects on the Form object *(ref: Figure 12-18)*.

▶ **Add the Result Label Object** Drag a label onto the Form object and name the label lblTipAmount. Enter the text for this label as 9 X's. Resize the Label object to the exact size of the text needed. Center the object on the Form object.

(continues)

Guided Program Development (continued)

1

▶ **Create the Command Control Area** Click the left Command control area and type Compute Tip. Name the menu Command control mnuComputeTip. Click the right Command control area and type Clear. Name the menu Command control mnuClear *(ref: Figure 12-21)*.

The Smartphone Form object is designed (Figure 12-28).

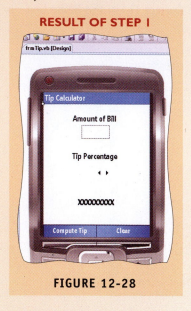

FIGURE 12-28

Phase 2: Code the Application

2

▶ **Open the Code Window for the Compute Tip Click Event** Double-click the Compute Tip Command control area on the Smartphone application screen.

▶ **Add the Comments and the Option Strict On Statement** At the top of the code window, enter the comments and Option Strict On as shown in the adjacent Hint Screen.

HINT

```
1 ' Project:   Tip Calculator Smartphone Application
2 ' Author:    Corinne Hoisington
3 ' Date:      June 4, 2011
4 ' Purpose:   This Cell Phone Application computes the cost of a restaurant tip based
5 '            on the bill amount .
6
7 Option Strict On
```

Guided Program Development (continued)

1

▶ **Initialize the Variables** Initialize the variables inside the mnuComputeTip click event as shown in the adjacent Hint Screen.

HINT

```
12          ' The mnuComputeTip click event determines the amount of the tip
13          ' Initialize variables
14          Dim decBillAmount As Decimal
15          Dim intTipSelection As Integer
16          Dim decLowTip As Decimal = 0.1D
17          Dim decAverageTip As Decimal = 0.15D
18          Dim decGoodTip As Decimal = 0.2D
19          Dim decPercentageOfTip As Decimal
20          Dim decTipValue As Decimal
```

▶ **Create a Try-Catch Block** Enter a Try-Catch block to convert the bill amount to a Decimal data type as shown in the adjacent Hint Screen.

HINT

```
22          ' The Try-Catch block warns users if the bill amount is not entered properly
23          Try
24              decBillAmount = Convert.ToDecimal(Me.txtBill.Text)
25          Catch Exception As FormatException
26              ' This catch block detects letters, symbols, blank entries, etc
27              MsgBox("Please enter a U.S. Dollar amount", , "Error")
28          Catch Exception As OverflowException
29              ' This catch block detects numbers that are too large or too small
30              MsgBox("Please enter a valid U.S. Dollar amount", , "Error")
31          Catch Exception As SystemException
32              ' This catch block detects a generic exception not caught by earlier catch ↙
        blocks
33              MsgBox("Entry invalid. Please enter a valid money amount", , "Error")
34          End Try
```

(continues)

Guided Program Development *(continued)*

▶ **Code the ComboBox Object** An If statement first determines if the user has selected the tip percentage. The selected index of the ComboBox Object is assigned to intTipSelection. A Select Case statement assigns the correct tip amount based on the user's selection of the tip percentage.

HINT

```
35          ' The tip percentage is assigned
36          If Me.cboTipPercent.SelectedIndex >= 0 Then
37              intTipSelection = Convert.ToInt32(Me.cboTipPercent.SelectedIndex)
38              ' The tip percentage is set based on the user selection
39              Select Case intTipSelection
40                  Case 0
41                      decPercentageOfTip = decLowTip
42                  Case 1
43                      decPercentageOfTip = decAverageTip
44                  Case 2
45                      decPercentageOfTip = decGoodTip
46              End Select
```

▶ **Calculate and Display the Tip Amount** To compute the final tip amount, multiply the decBillAmount and the decPercentageOfTip. Display the final result.

HINT

```
47              ' The amount of the tip is calculated
48              decTipValue = decBillAmount * decPercentageOfTip
49              Me.lblTipAmount.Text = "Tip " & decTipValue.ToString("C")
50          Else
51              MsgBox("Select a tip amount by using the navigation keys", , "Error")
52          End If
```

▶ **Code the mnuClear Click Event** Return to the design window of the Smartphone application and double-click the Clear Command control area. Enter the code in the mnuClear click event to clear the TextBox, ComboBox, and result Label objects as shown in the code in the adjacent Hint Screen.

HINT

```
57          'Clear the Tip Form
58          Me.txtBill.Text = ""
59          Me.cboTipPercent.SelectedIndex = -1
60          Me.lblTipAmount.Text = ""
```

Guided Program Development (continued)

The code is complete (Figure 12-29).

RESULT OF STEP 2

```vbnet
11      Private Sub mnuTip_Click(ByVal sender As System.Object, ByVal e As System.
        EventArgs) Handles mnuComputeTip.Click
12          ' The mnuComputeTip click event determines the amount of the tip
13          ' Initialize variables
14          Dim decBillAmount As Decimal
15          Dim intTipSelection As Integer
16          Dim decLowTip As Decimal = 0.1D
17          Dim decAverageTip As Decimal = 0.15D
18          Dim decGoodTip As Decimal = 0.2D
19          Dim decPercentageOfTip As Decimal
20          Dim decTipValue As Decimal                        ──┤ Try-Catch block
21
22          ' The Try-Catch block warns users if the bill amount is not entered properly
23          Try
24              decBillAmount = Convert.ToDecimal(Me.txtBill.Text)
25          Catch Exception As FormatException
26              ' This catch block detects letters, symbols, blank entries, etc
27              MsgBox("Please enter a U.S. Dollar amount", , "Error")
28          Catch Exception As OverflowException
29              ' This catch block detects numbers that are too large or too small
30              MsgBox("Please enter a valid U.S. Dollar amount", , "Error")
31          Catch Exception As SystemException
32              ' This catch block detects a generic exception not caught by earlier catch
        blocks
33              MsgBox("Entry invalid. Please enter a valid money amount", , "Error")
34          End Try
35          ' The tip percentage is assigned
36          If Me.cboTipPercent.SelectedIndex >= 0 Then
37              intTipSelection = Convert.ToInt32(Me.cboTipPercent.SelectedIndex)
38              ' The tip percentage is set based on the user selection
39              Select Case intTipSelection
40                  Case 0
41                      decPercentageOfTip = decLowTip
42                  Case 1
43                      decPercentageOfTip = decAverageTip
44                  Case 2
45                      decPercentageOfTip = decGoodTip
46              End Select                                    ──┤ tip amount is completed
47              ' The amount of the tip is calculated
48              decTipValue = decBillAmount * decPercentageOfTip
49              Me.lblTipAmount.Text = "Tip " & decTipValue.ToString("C")
50          Else
51              MsgBox("Select a tip amount by using the navigation keys", , "Error")
52          End If
53
54      End Sub
55
56      Private Sub mnuClear_Click(ByVal sender As System.Object, ByVal e As System.
        EventArgs) Handles mnuClear.Click
57          'Clear the Tip Form
58          Me.txtBill.Text = ""
59          Me.cboTipPercent.SelectedIndex = -1
60          Me.lblTipAmount.Text = ""
61
62      End Sub
```

FIGURE 12-29

(continues)

Guided Program Development (continued)

Phase 3: Test the Application

3

▶ **Run the Smartphone Application** Click the Start Debugging button on the Standard toolbar to begin execution of the program.

HEADS UP

If an error appears that states "Sub Main was not found" when you run the application, click Project on the menu bar, and then click Tip Properties. On the Application tab of the Tip Properties dialog box, change the Startup object to frmTip.

▶ **Deploy the Smartphone Emulator** In the Deploy Tip dialog box, select the USA Windows Mobile 5.0 Smartphone R2 QVGA Emulator device and then click the Deploy button *(ref: Figure 12-9)*.

HINT

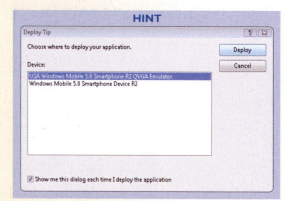

▶ **Run the Smartphone Application** The user enters all data from the keypad, using the navigation arrow keys to change the ComboBox object selections, and the softkeys to select the options from the Command control area.

▶ **Close the Smartphone Application** When the Smartphone application is executed, click the Close button in the upper-right corner of the Smartphone form.

▶ **Exit the Emulator State** A Device Emulator window opens asking if you want to save the emulator state before exiting. Click the No button *(ref: Figure 12-14)*.

HINT

The Smartphone emulator closes after execution (Figure 12-30). Click the OK button to continue.

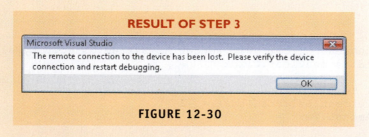

RESULT OF STEP 3

FIGURE 12-30

Web Services

You have probably used multiple Web services on the Internet without even knowing what they are. An example of a Web service is included on the city of Toledo's Web page shown in Figure 12-31. In the upper-right corner, the page shows that the weather currently in Toledo, Ohio is 26 degrees Fahrenheit. To display this up-to-date information, the developers connected the Web page to a Web service such as the National Weather Service.

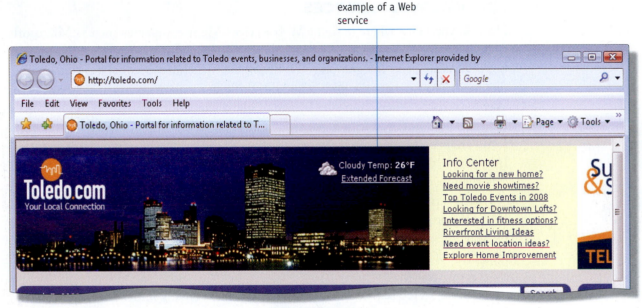

example of a Web service

FIGURE 12-31

The developers use this weather Web service to keep the user on the Toledo Web page. The longer a customer stays on a Web site, the more likely that customer will make a purchase. Web services are not limited to Web-based applications such as Web pages, but can also communicate Internet information to Windows applications and other application types. Additional examples of Web services include giving directions to a hotel or other destination, displaying a live stock quote, or providing the top news stories on a local college Web site. In short, a Web service is any piece of software available over the Internet that uses **XML** (Extensible Markup Language) to share information. More specifically, a Web service is a collection of protocols and standards used for exchanging data between applications or systems. Using a Web service typically involves three steps:

1. The Web service provider defines a format for requests for its service and the response the service will generate. Web services can cost a fixed fee per request, though some are free.
2. Next, an application makes a request for the Web services over the Internet using the predefined format.
3. When the provider receives the Web service request, the Web service performs an action, and then sends the response back to the requesting application over the Internet.

A Web service could be retrieving a stock quote, finding the best price for a particular product on the Internet, saving a new meeting to a calendar, translating text to another language, or validating a credit card number. If a developer needs to create a new feature for the company Web site, the developer can save time by first checking a Web service directory for that particular feature. Rather than possibly purchasing the data, writing the code, maintaining the data and performance of the code, the developer can use an existing Web service that suits the purpose of the site.

FINDING WEB SERVICES

How do you know where to find a Web service? Many companies such as Microsoft (*uddi.microsoft.com*) and Oasis (*www.uddi.org*) have created the Universal Description, Discovery, and Integration (UDDI) project, which has become a definitive directory of services over the Web. The UDDI directory allows companies to offer their Web services to other companies by acting like a telephone book for Web services. No costs are associated with registering your Web service in the UDDI. UDDI directories are becoming a central reference listing all the services residing across the Internet, so that developers looking for a service can use the UDDI directory to locate the most appropriate provider.

Web services use a special language called **Web Services Description Language** (**WSDL**, pronounced *wiz-dell*), which is in an XML format. WSDL provides a simple way for service providers to describe the basic format of requests to their systems regardless of the underlying protocol (such as Simple Object Access Protocol, called SOAP, or XML).

Calling a Web service is a way of sending and receiving information across the Internet. Although the Internet is the most important environment that Web services target, you can also use Web services within an application or on any other network. In particular, you can use a Web service to connect to the Internet in a Windows, Web, mobile, or VSTO application. In the Currency Conversion second chapter project, the user enters an amount of U.S. dollars to convert to one of three types of currency — European Union euros, Mexican pesos, or Canadian dollars. The Windows application calls a Web service on the Internet that keeps track of the most current exchange rates. The WSDL request gathers the current conversion rate for the selected money type and returns the rate as an argument to the line in the local application that made the Web service request. The Web service calls a class that is not within the application, but is stored somewhere on the Internet or network.

Using the UDDI directories, you can find a Web service converting currencies to other national currencies at *http://bindingpoint.com/service.aspx?skey=6113*. This site is sponsored by Binding Point, a leading Web service repository. The Binding Point Web site states that the Web service URL containing the Web service request is *http://www.webservicex.net/CurrencyConvertor.asmx?wsdl*. The WSDL request contains an XML Web page as shown in Figure 12-32.

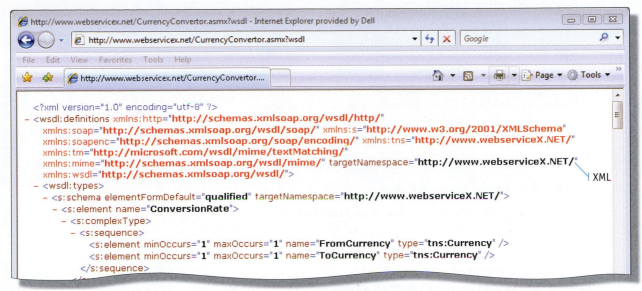

FIGURE 12-32

To create a Web service, you need a Web reference to create a hyperlink using a WSDL request as shown in Figure 12-32. To create a Web reference, you can complete the following steps:

STEP 1 With a new Windows Form object open with the project name CurrencyConverter, right-click the project name CurrencyConverter in the Solution Explorer.

A shortcut menu opens in the Solution Explorer (Figure 12-33).

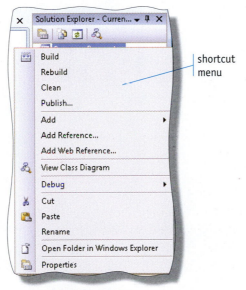

FIGURE 12-33

STEP 2   Select Add Web Reference on the shortcut menu.

The Add Web Reference window opens (Figure 12–34).

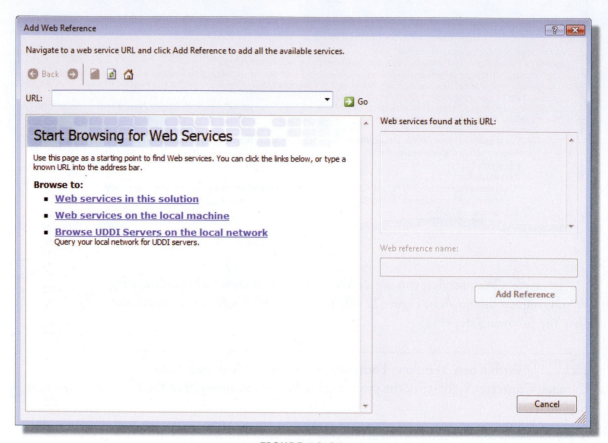

FIGURE 12-34

STEP 3   Enter the following Web service URL in the URL text box: `http://www.webservicex.net/CurrencyConvertor.asmx?wsdl`. Then click the Go button to connect to the Web service. You must be connected to the Internet to find the Web service. If the Web service is available online, a message appears stating the name of the method that will be used in the code window to call the existing Web service.

After the Web service URL is entered, the program connects to the Web service and the information about the Web service is displayed in the CurrencyConvertor Description portion of the window. The name of the method that will be called in the code window is ConversionRate (Figure 12–35).

method call

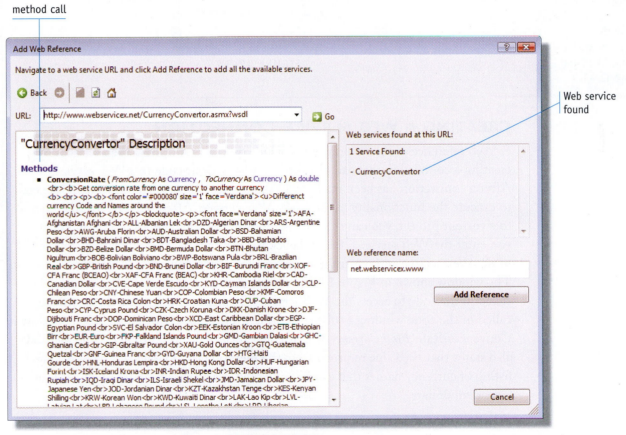

FIGURE 12-35

ONLINE REINFORCEMENT

To view a video of the process in the previous steps, visit scsite.com/vb2008/ch12 and then select Figure 12-33.

STEP 4   Click the Add Reference button in the Add Web Reference window.

A Web Reference folder containing the name of the Web service connection is displayed in the Solution Explorer. Click the plus sign next to the Web References folder if you do not see the Web service connection name (Figure 12-36).

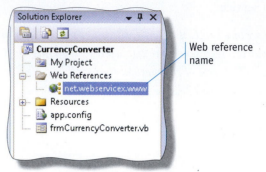

FIGURE 12-36

CREATING A WEB SERVICE CONNECTION

A Web reference enables a project to include one or more XML Web services by creating a connection that can be called by Visual Basic code to a Web service. After a connection has been made to a Web service, the next step is to write the code to execute the functionality of the XML Web service. After adding a Web reference to a current project, you can call any methods exposed by the Web service. When you enter the Web service URL and click the Go button, the application connects to the Web service and returns information about accessing that Web service. The window shown in Figure 12-37 displays the name of the method that must be called in the code to access the Web service. The name of the method that will be called in the code window as displayed in CurrencyConvertor Description window is ConversionRate(*FromCurrency* as Currency, *ToCurrency* as Currency). The method also states that the value returned from the method is a Double data type. A long listing of currency names that can be converted is also shown, including CAD for Canadian dollars.

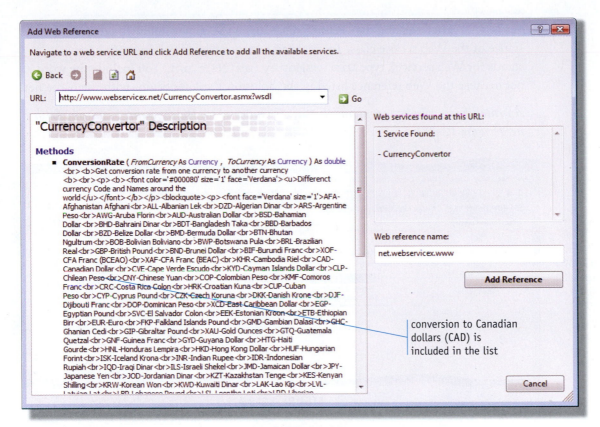

FIGURE 12-37

The Add Web Reference window also displays the Web reference name, as shown in Figure 12-37, which is net.webservicex.www. In the code window, an instance of the Web service will be written using this Web reference name. The Web services found at this URL list box also indicates that one Web service named CurrencyConvertor was found at the specified URL. The name CurrencyConvertor will also be used in the instance of the Web service.

After you add a Web reference to the XML Web service to the project, you can use the service name to create an instance of an object that allows you to call the methods in the XML Web service. In the second chapter project application, the two types of currencies are sent over the Internet to the currency conversion Web service. The XML Web service returns to the local application the present exchange rate for these types of currencies. For example, if the user wants to convert U.S. dollars to Mexican pesos, the application sends the two currency types U.S. dollars and Mexican pesos as arguments to the Web service method. The present conversion rate, such as $1.00 is equal to 11.52 pesos, is sent from the Web service to the return value in the chapter project. The return value of 11.52 is then multiplied by the number of dollars entered by the user to determine the amount of total Mexican pesos that the U.S. dollar amount is worth. Each time the Web service is called, the conversion rate could be different depending on the world currency market values.

Next, you need to write code to call the XML Web service to retrieve data that contains the currency conversion information. To create an instance of the Web service class in the code window, you can complete the following steps:

STEP 1   After creating the Web reference, open the code window to create an instance of the Web service class. To create an instance named wsMoney (where ws stands for Web service), type Dim wsMoney as New net. You include the word net because the Web reference listed in the Solution Explorer begins with the name net.

An IntelliSense window opens and displays the name of the Web reference beginning with net (Figure 12-38).

IntelliSense window for completing the net Web reference

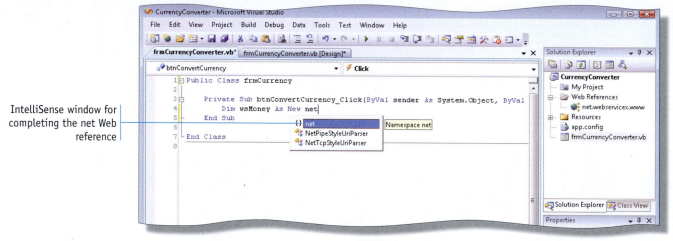

FIGURE 12-38

STEP 2   To complete the name of the Web service, type a period and webservicex appears in the IntelliSense window. Select webservicex, type a period, and www appears in the IntelliSense window. Select www and type another period.

After the Web service reference net.webservicex.www. is entered, an IntelliSense window opens requesting the method name (Figure 12-39).

IntelliSense assists in completing an instance of the Web service

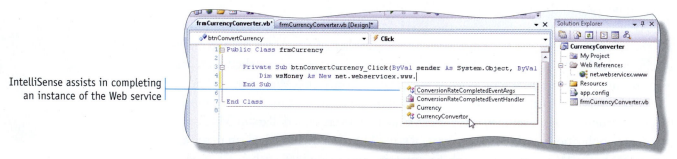

FIGURE 12-39

STEP 3   Select the Web service named CurrencyConvertor in the IntelliSense window. When the Web URL reference was entered in the Add Web Reference window shown in Figure 12-37, the Web service was displayed in the Web reference window. Press the ENTER key.

An instance of the Web service is coded (Figure 12–40).

```
1 □ Public Class frmCurrency
2
3 □     Private Sub btnConvertCurrency_Click(ByVal sender As System.Object, ByVal
4           Dim wsMoney As New net.webservicex.www.CurrencyConvertor
5           |
6       End Sub
7 └ End Class
```

FIGURE 12-40

CALLING A WEB SERVICE METHOD

After creating an instance of the Web service, you can code a method that calls the Web service. When the Web service is called, the service responds by sending the requested information to the application. A call to a Web service method involves calling the method and waiting for the computation or the process to occur on the Web service server and return a value before continuing with the rest of the code in the Windows form. Recall that the name of the Web service the Currency Converter application uses is ConversionRate. The ConversionRate method requires two arguments. The first argument represents the currency that is being converted. The second argument represents the type of currency to which the amount is converted. To call a Web service method, you can complete the following steps:

STEP 1   In the code window, assign a Double data type variable named dblConversionAmount. The data type is assigned as a Double because the Web reference stated that the return type is a Double data type.

A variable named dblConversionAmount is declared to receive the returning value from the Web service method (Figure 12–41).

```
1 □ Public Class frmCurrency
2
3 □     Private Sub btnConvertCurrency_Click(ByVal sender As System.Object, ByVal
4           Dim wsMoney As New net.webservicex.www.CurrencyConvertor
5           Dim dblConversionAmount As Double
6           |
7       End Sub
```

FIGURE 12-41

STEP 2 The variable dblConversionAmount is assigned to the returned value from the calling method ConversionRate. ConversionRate is a method of the instance of wsMoney. Type dblC and press CTRL+SPACEBAR to complete the variable dblConversionRate. Type = wsMoney. An IntelliSense list opens. Select ConversionRate, and then type a left parenthesis (.

After typing the left parenthesis, an IntelliSense listing of possible first arguments opens (Figure 12-42).

IntelliSense displays an arguments list for the ConversionRate method

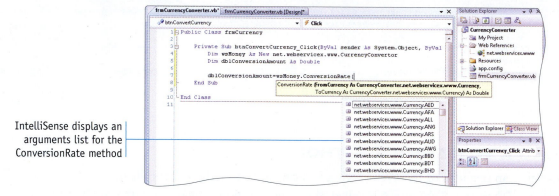

FIGURE 12-42

STEP 3 To convert U.S. dollars to euros, scroll down the list of first arguments and select net.webservicex.www.Currency.USD. Recall that the abbreviations for each country's currency were listed in Figure 12-42 when the Web reference was created earlier. Type a comma and the second list of arguments appears. Scroll down the list of second arguments and select net.webservicex.www.Currency.EUR for euros. Type a closing parenthesis.

The calling Web service method is coded (Figure 12-43).

```
20        dblConversionAmount = wsMoney.ConversionRate(net.webservicex.www.Currency.USD, ↙
          net.webservicex.www.Currency.EUR)
```

FIGURE 12-43

ONLINE REINFORCEMENT

To view a video of the process in the previous steps, visit scsite.com/vb2008/ch12 and then select Figure 12-41.

When the application is executed, the user enters the U.S. dollar amount in a TextBox object and selects the type of currency to which the U.S. dollar amount is converted (euros, pesos, or Canadian dollars) from a ComboBox object. In the code shown in Figure 12-44, the ComboBox object named cboCurrencyType uses an If statement to check if the user has selected a currency type. After the ComboBox object is assigned to the variable intSelectedCurrency, a Select Case statement determines which arguments are sent to the Web service method named ConversionRate based on the first user selection of euros, the second for Mexican pesos, and the third selection of Canadian dollars. The entire Select Case structure is placed within a Try-Catch block to catch a possible exception that could occur if the program cannot connect to the Web service. When you use a Web service, you always face the possibility that the Web server hosting that Web service may not be running.

```
34          ' Select the currency type and call the web service sending two arguments
35          If (Me.cboCurrencyType.SelectedIndex > -1) Then
36              intSelectedCurrency = Me.cboCurrencyType.SelectedIndex
37              Try
38                  Select Case intSelectedCurrency
39                      Case 0
40                          dblConversionAmount = wsMoney.ConversionRate(net.webservicex.  ↙
        www.Currency.USD, net.webservicex.www.Currency.EUR)
41                          strMoneyType = "  Euros"
42                      Case 1
43                          dblConversionAmount = wsMoney.ConversionRate(net.webservicex.  ↙
        www.Currency.USD, net.webservicex.www.Currency.MXN)
44                          strMoneyType = "  Pesos"
45                      Case 2
46                          dblConversionAmount = wsMoney.ConversionRate(net.webservicex.  ↙
        www.Currency.USD, net.webservicex.www.Currency.CAD)
47                          strMoneyType = "CA Dollars"
48                  End Select
49                  ' Calculate the conversion and display
50                  Me.lblResult.Text = (decDollarAmount * dblConversionAmount).ToString(  ↙
        "F2") & " " & strMoneyType
51              Catch Exception As SystemException
52                  MsgBox("Web Service Not Available", , "Error")
53              End Try
54          Else
55              MsgBox("Select a Conversion Currency", , "Error")
56          End If
```

FIGURE 12-44

Program Design

The requirements document for the Currency Converter Web Service application is shown in Figure 12-45, and the Use Case Definition document is shown in Figure 12-46.

REQUIREMENTS DOCUMENT

Date submitted:	August 25, 2011
Application title:	Currency Conversion Web Service Windows application
Purpose:	This Web Service Windows Application converts U.S. dollars to euros, Mexican pesos, or Canadian dollars using a Web service to determine the present conversion rate.
Program Procedures:	In a Windows application, the user enters the amount of U.S. dollars to be converted and selects the currency type to convert the dollars. The application uses a Web service to determine the present conversion rate.
Algorithms, Processing, and Conditions:	1. The user first views a Windows application that requests a U.S. dollar amount. 2. The user can select whether to convert the U.S. dollars to euros, Mexican pesos, or Canadian dollars. 3. The user can click the Convert Currency button to calculate and display the conversion amount. 4. The user can click the Clear button to reset the Form object.
Notes and Restrictions:	1. The money.jpg picture can be found at scsite/vb2008/images. 2. The Web service address is http://www.webservicex.net/CurrencyConvertor.asmx?wsdl. 3. The name of the calling method is ConversionRate. Two arguments are passed to the Web service method. U.S. dollars is represented by the argument net.webservicex.www.Currency.USD. Euros are represented by the argument net.webservicex.www.Currency.EUR. Mexican pesos are represented by the argument net.webservicex.www.Currency.MXN. Canadian dollars are represented by the argument net.webservicex.www.Currency.CAD.
Comments:	1. The user must have Internet access to connect to the Web service.

FIGURE 12-45

USE CASE DEFINITION

1. The user enters the U.S. dollar amount.
2. The user selects the conversion currency type from a ComboBox object.
3. The user clicks the Convert Currency button to display the conversion amount.
4. The user clicks the Clear button to clear the form.

FIGURE 12-46

Design the Program Processing Objects

The event planning document for the Currency Converter Web Service Windows application is shown in Figure 12-47.

EVENT PLANNING DOCUMENT

Program Name: Currency Converter Web Service Windows Application	Developer: Corinne Hoisington	Object: frmCurrencyConverter	Date: August 25, 2011

OBJECT	EVENT TRIGGER	EVENT PROCESSING
frmCurrency_Load	Load	Clear the Label object for the result.
btnConvertCurrency	Click Event	Declare an instance of the Web service. A Try-Catch block prevents exceptions in user input. Convert the U.S. dollar amount to a Decimal data type. Another Try-Catch block displays an error message if the Web service is not available over the Internet. If the conversion currency type is selected, assign the currency type to an Integer variable. Based on the conversion type selected, a case calls the ConversionRate method with two arguments representing the types of currency being converted. Calculate the amount converted by multiplying the U.S. dollar amount times the present conversion rate returned by the Web service. Display the conversion amount.
btnClear	Click Event	Clear the U.S. dollar amount. Clear the currency type. Clear the result.

FIGURE 12-47

Guided Program Development

To design the user interface for the Currency Converter Web Service Windows application and enter the code required to process each event in the program, complete the steps in this section.

NOTE TO THE LEARNER

As you will recall, in the following activity, you should complete the tasks within the specified steps. Each of the tasks is accompanied by a Hint Screen. The purpose of the Hint Screen is to indicate where in the Visual Studio window you should perform the activity; it also serves as a reminder of the method that you should use to create the user interface or enter code. If you need further help completing the step, refer to the figure number identified by the term ref: in the step.

Guided Program Development

Phase 1: Design the Form

1

▶ **Create a New Project** Open Visual Studio using the Start button on the Windows taskbar and the All Programs submenu. Click the New Project button on the Standard toolbar. Select and expand Visual Basic in the Project types list; select Windows in the left pane; select Windows Form Application in the right (Templates) pane; name the project CurrencyConverter in the Name text box; click the OK button in the New Project dialog box.

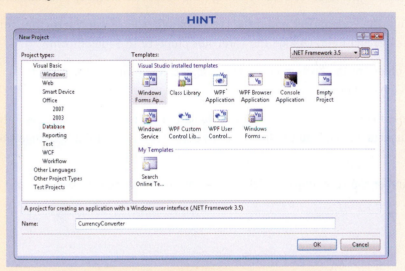

▶ **Name the Form Object** Select the Form object. Change the (Name) property of the Form object to frmCurrency.

▶ **Title the Form Object** Open the main Form object. Select the Form object and change the Text property to Web Service — Live Currency Converter.

▶ **Add a PictureBox Object** Add a PictureBox object to the left side of the form named picCalculator. Click the ellipsis button on the Image property for the PictureBox object. In the Select Resource window, click Import. On your computer, save the money.jpg picture file from scsite/vb2008/ch12/images. Import the money.jpg picture. Change the SizeMode property of the image to StretchImage.

▶ **Add the First Label and TextBox Object** Drag a label onto the Form object and name the label lblEnterAmount. Enter the text for this label as Enter U.S. Dollar Amount. Drag a TextBox object onto the Form object below the label and name the TextBox object txtDollarAmount. Delete the characters from the Text property.

Guided Program Development (continued)

▶ **Add the Second Label and a ComboBox Object** Drag another label onto the Form object and name the label lblConversion. Enter the text for this label as Conversion Currency. Drag a ComboBox object onto the Form object below the label and name the ComboBox object cboCurrencyType. Click the ellipsis button to the right of the Items property. Enter `Euro`, `Mexican Peso`, and `Canadian Dollar` on three separate lines. Select the two Label objects, TextBox object, and ComboBox object and change the font to San Serif, size 10, and Bold. Change the ForeColor property to SaddleBrown.

▶ **Add the Result Label Object** Drag a label onto the Form object and name the label lblResult. Enter the text for this label as 11 X's. Change the font to Sans Serif, size 12, and Bold. Change the ForeColor property to SaddleBrown.

▶ **Add the First Button Object** Drag a Button object to the bottom of the Form object. Name the Button object btnConvertCurrency. Enter the Text property of Convert Currency.

▶ **Add the Second Button Object** Drag a Button object below the first button. Name the Button object btnClear. Enter the Text property of Clear. Select both Button objects and change the font to Sans Serif, size 10, and Bold. Change the ForeColor property to SaddleBrown.

▶ **Create an Accept Button** Click the background of the Form object. Click to the right of the AcceptButton property of the Form object and select btnConvertCurrency.

The Windows Form object is designed (Figure 12-48).

FIGURE 12-48

Guided Program Development *(continued)*

2

▶ **Add the Web Reference** Right-click the project name CurrencyConverter in the Solution Explorer, and then click Add Web Reference on the shortcut menu. Enter the following Web service URL in the URL text box: http://www.webservicex.net/CurrencyConvertor.asmx?wsdl. Then click the Go button to connect to the Web service *(ref: Figure 12-35)*.

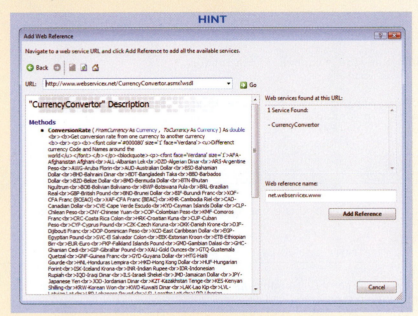

HINT

▶ **Add the Web Reference** Click the Add Reference button to connect to the Web service.

The Web Reference is created (Figure 12-49).

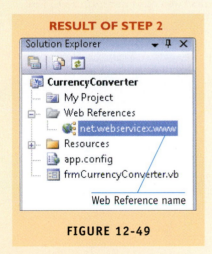

FIGURE 12-49

(continues)

Guided Program Development (continued)

Phase 2: Code the Application

3

▶ **Code the Comments** Click the View Code button to begin coding the application. Type the first four standard comments at the top of the code window. Insert the command Option Strict On at the beginning of the code to turn on strict type checking.

HINT

```
1 ' Project:   Currency Converter Web Service Windows Application
2 ' Author:    Corinne Hoisington
3 ' Date:      August 25, 2011
4 ' Purpose:   This Web Service Windows Application converts U.S. dollars
5 '            to Euros, Mexican Pesos, or Canadian Dollars using a Web service
6 '            to determine the present conversion rate.
7
8 Option Strict On
```

▶ **Code the frmCurrency Code Event** To initialize the variables of this event, type the comments and code shown in the adjacent Hint Screen.

HINT

```
11     Private Sub btnConvertCurrency_Click(ByVal sender As System.Object, ByVal e As
       System.EventArgs) Handles btnConvertCurrency.Click
12         ' Convert the Currency with a live web services to determine the present
       currency rate
13         ' Initialize the variables
14         ' Declare an instance of the web service
15       Dim wsMoney As New net.webservicex.www.CurrencyConvertor
16       Dim dblConversionAmount As Double
17       Dim intSelectedCurrency As Integer
18       Dim decDollarAmount As Decimal
19       Dim strMoneyType As String = ""
```

Guided Program Development (continued)

▶ **Code the Input of the U.S. Dollar Amount** Enter a Try-Catch block to input the TextBox object that represents the U.S. dollar amount to be converted. If an invalid value is entered, a Catch block displays an error message.

HINT

```
21          ' Input the U.S. dollar amount
22          Try
23              decDollarAmount = Convert.ToDecimal(Me.txtDollarAmount.Text)
24          Catch Exception As FormatException
25              ' This catch block detects letters, symbols, blank entries, etc
26              MsgBox("Please enter a dollar amount", , "Error")
27          Catch Exception As OverflowException
28              ' This catch block detects numbers that are too large or too small
29              MsgBox("Please enter a valid dollar amount", , "Error")
30          Catch Exception As SystemException
31              ' This catch block detects a generic exception not caught by earlier catch ↙
        blocks
32              MsgBox("Entry invalid. Please enter a valid dollar amount", , "Error")
33          End Try
```

▶ **Code the Input of the Currency Conversion Type** An If statement assigns a selected ComboBox object value to the variable intSelectedCurrency.

HINT

```
34          ' Select the currency type and call the web service sending two arguments
35          If (Me.cboCurrencyType.SelectedIndex > -1) Then
36              intSelectedCurrency = Me.cboCurrencyType.SelectedIndex
```

(continues)

Guided Program Development *(continued)*

▶ **Code the Call to the Web Service Method** Use a Try-Catch block to catch errors if the Web service is not available. Based on the user's selection in the ComboBox object, call a Case statement. The Web service method name is ConversionRate and has two arguments. The first argument represents the initial currency to convert, and the second argument is the currency type to which the initial currency is being converted. The argument net.webservicex.www .Currency.USD means that the Web service converts U.S. dollars to the second argument listed. The argument net .webservicex.www.Currency.EUR converts the first argument to euros. The argument net.webservicex.www.Currency.MXN converts the first argument to Mexican pesos. The argument net.webservicex.www.Currency.CAD converts the first argument to Canadian dollars.

HINT

```
37          Try
38              Select Case intSelectedCurrency
39                  Case 0
40                      dblConversionAmount = wsMoney.ConversionRate(net.webservicex.    ↙
    www.Currency.USD, net.webservicex.www.Currency.EUR)
41                      strMoneyType = "   Euros"
42                  Case 1
43                      dblConversionAmount = wsMoney.ConversionRate(net.webservicex.    ↙
    www.Currency.USD, net.webservicex.www.Currency.MXN)
44                      strMoneyType = "   Pesos"
45                  Case 2
46                      dblConversionAmount = wsMoney.ConversionRate(net.webservicex.    ↙
    www.Currency.USD, net.webservicex.www.Currency.CAD)
47                      strMoneyType = "CA Dollars"
48              End Select
49              ' Calculate the conversion and display
50              Me.lblResult.Text = (decDollarAmount * dblConversionAmount).ToString(    ↙
    "F2") & " " & strMoneyType
51          Catch Exception As SystemException
52              MsgBox("Web Service Not Available", , "Error")
53          End Try
54      Else
55          MsgBox("Select a Conversion Currency", , "Error")
56      End If
```

The btnConvertCurrency Click Event is coded (Figure 12-50).

RESULT OF STEP 3

```
11      Private Sub btnConvertCurrency_Click(ByVal sender As System.Object, ByVal e As    ↙
    System.EventArgs) Handles btnConvertCurrency.Click
12          ' Convert the Currency with a live web services to determine the present    ↙
    currency rate
13          ' Initialize the variables
14          ' Declare an instance of the web service
15          Dim wsMoney As New net.webservicex.www.CurrencyConvertor
16          Dim dblConversionAmount As Double
17          Dim intSelectedCurrency As Integer
18          Dim decDollarAmount As Decimal
```

FIGURE 12-50 (continues)

Guided Program Development (continued)

```
18          Dim decDollarAmount As Decimal
19          Dim strMoneyType As String = ""
20
21          ' Input the U.S. dollar amount
22          Try
23              decDollarAmount = Convert.ToDecimal(Me.txtDollarAmount.Text)
24          Catch Exception As FormatException
25              ' This catch block detects letters, symbols, blank entries, etc
26              MsgBox("Please enter a dollar amount", , "Error")
27          Catch Exception As OverflowException
28              ' This catch block detects numbers that are too large or too small
29              MsgBox("Please enter a valid dollar amount", , "Error")
30          Catch Exception As SystemException
31              ' This catch block detects a generic exception not caught by earlier catch ↙
        blocks
32              MsgBox("Entry invalid. Please enter a valid dollar amount", , "Error")
33          End Try
34          ' Select the currency type and call the web service sending two arguments
35          If (Me.cboCurrencyType.SelectedIndex > -1) Then
36              intSelectedCurrency = Me.cboCurrencyType.SelectedIndex
37              Try
38                  Select Case intSelectedCurrency
39                      Case 0
40                          dblConversionAmount = wsMoney.ConversionRate(net.webservicex. ↙
        www.Currency.USD, net.webservicex.www.Currency.EUR)
41                          strMoneyType = "  Euros"
42                      Case 1
43                          dblConversionAmount = wsMoney.ConversionRate(net.webservicex. ↙
        www.Currency.USD, net.webservicex.www.Currency.MXN)
44                          strMoneyType = "  Pesos"
45                      Case 2
46                          dblConversionAmount = wsMoney.ConversionRate(net.webservicex. ↙
        www.Currency.USD, net.webservicex.www.Currency.CAD)
47                          strMoneyType = "CA Dollars"
48                  End Select
49                  ' Calculate the conversion and display
50                  Me.lblResult.Text = (decDollarAmount * dblConversionAmount).ToString( ↙
        "F2") & " " & strMoneyType
51              Catch Exception As SystemException
52                  MsgBox("Web Service Not Available", , "Error")
53              End Try
54          Else
55              MsgBox("Select a Conversion Currency", , "Error")
56          End If
57
58      End Sub
```

FIGURE 12-50 (continued)

Guided Program Development *(continued)*

4

▶ **Code the btnClear Click Event** In the design window, double-click the Clear button, and then enter the code to clear the Form objects.

HINT

```
60      Private Sub btnClear_Click(ByVal sender As System.Object, ByVal e As System.
        EventArgs) Handles btnClear.Click
61          ' Clear the Form object
62          Me.txtDollarAmount.Clear()
63          Me.cboCurrencyType.SelectedIndex = -1
64          Me.lblResult.Text = ""
65
66      End Sub
```

▶ **Code the frmCurrency Load Event** Return to the design window and double-click the background of the Form object. Clear the placeholders in lblResult as the form loads.

HINT

```
68      Private Sub frmCurrency_Load(ByVal sender As System.Object, ByVal e As System.
        EventArgs) Handles MyBase.Load
69          ' Clear the Result Label
70          Me.lblResult.Text = ""
71
72      End Sub
```

The btnClear Click Event and frmCurrency Load Event are coded (Figure 12-51).

RESULT OF STEP 4

```
60      Private Sub btnClear_Click(ByVal sender As System.Object, ByVal e As System.
        EventArgs) Handles btnClear.Click
61          ' Clear the Form object
62          Me.txtDollarAmount.Clear()
63          Me.cboCurrencyType.SelectedIndex = -1
64          Me.lblResult.Text = ""
65
66      End Sub
67
68      Private Sub frmCurrency_Load(ByVal sender As System.Object, ByVal e As System.
        EventArgs) Handles MyBase.Load
69          ' Clear the Result Label
70          Me.lblResult.Text = ""
71
72      End Sub
```

FIGURE 12-51

Microsoft Reports

Besides offering tools to create Windows, Web, mobile, or VSTO applications, Visual Basic 2008 also provides developers a fully integrated and robust reporting solution for publishing professional reports on Windows and Web applications. The new Microsoft ReportViewer is a feature within Visual Basic that allows you to create interactive reports and forms for many types of data such as names and addresses from a database for creating and printing labels or for posting information online or for posting information on Windows forms. The Microsoft ReportViewer tool provides a fast and productive way to create and integrate presentation-quality reports without leaving the familiar Visual Basic development environment. Visual Studio 2008 introduces a Report Wizard, which guides you through the steps to create a basic report. You will select a report data source like a database, define a data set, select a report type (tabular or matrix), and apply a style to the report.

HEADS UP

Another popular report generator is called Crystal Reports, which is also part of Visual Basic 2008. The new Microsoft Report Wizard creates reports as well and it quickly gaining popularity due to its power and ease in the Visual Studio environment.

CREATING A REPORT

You can place a Microsoft Report in a Windows or Web application. For example, if you want to display the information in a database of physician referrals in the Texas area, you could create a Microsoft Report and display the report on a Web site. To create a report on a Web application, you can complete the following steps:

STEP 1   Open Visual Studio using the Start button on the Windows taskbar and the All Programs submenu. Click the New Web Site button on the Standard toolbar. In the list of Visual Studio installed templates, click ASP.NET Web Site. Name the sample report PhysicianReferral. Click the OK button.

The Web application Design window opens, displaying the Default.aspx page (Figure 12-52).

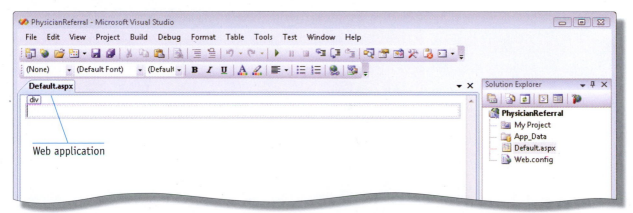

FIGURE 12-52

STEP 2   In the Toolbox, open the Reporting category by clicking the plus sign to expand the Reporting category. Drag the MicrosoftReportViewer object onto the Default.aspx page in the div control.

The MicrosoftReportViewer is placed on Web application form (Figure 12-53).

MicrosoftReportViewer object

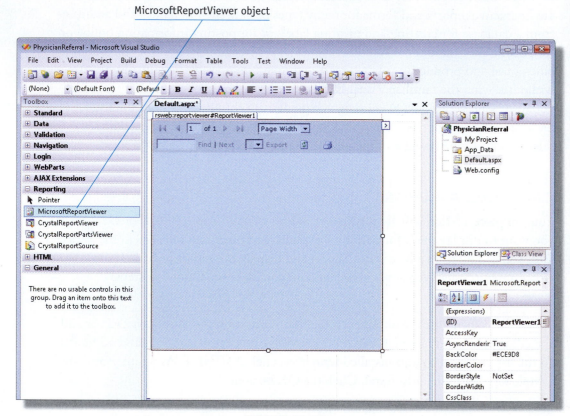

FIGURE 12-53

STEP 3   If necessary, click the action button on the MicrosoftReportViewer object, and then click the text Design a new report.

The Report Wizard opens (Figure 12–54).

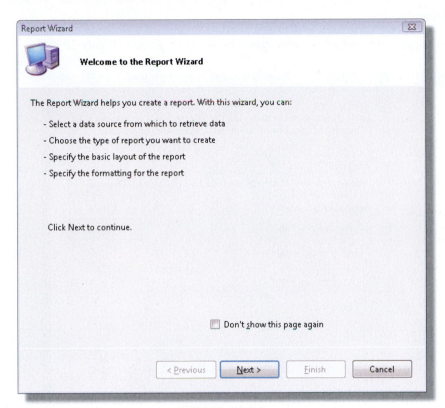

FIGURE 12-54

STEP 4 Click the Next button. Download the database named physicians.accdb from the scsite.com/vb2008/ch12 to a removable disk, such as a USB drive. Click the plus sign in front of Create New Connection to expand the options. Click the New Connection button. Browse to the physicians.accdb database and select the file. Click the Open button.

The physicians.accdb database connection is added to the project (Figure 12-55).

select the database object to display in the Microsoft Report

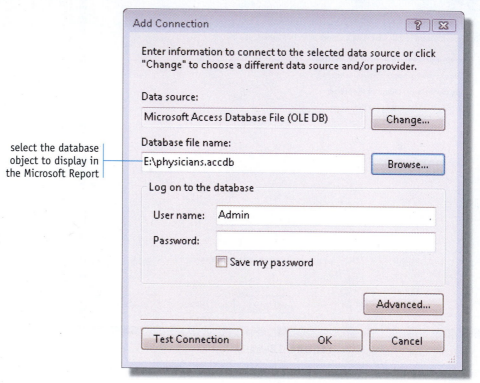

FIGURE 12-55

STEP 5   Click the OK button. Click the Next button. When asked if you want to copy the file to your current project, click the No button. Click the Next button to save the connection string. On the Choose Your Database Objects window, expand the Tables list by clicking the plus sign. Click PhysicianList to select the table.

The PhysicianList is selected (Figure 12-56).

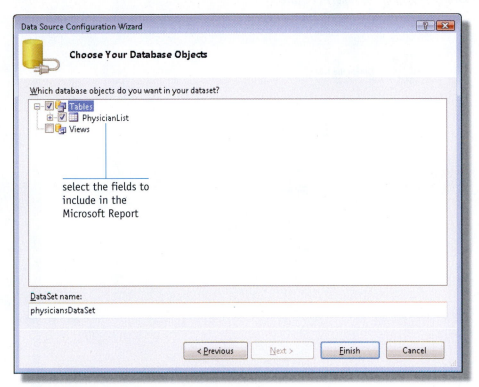

FIGURE 12-56

STEP 6   Click the Finish button. Click the Next button to select the data source. Select the Tabular report type and click the Next button. On the Design the Table window, display the first five fields of the table in the Group Section. The phone numbers will not be displayed in the report.

The Medical ID, Physician Name, City, State, and Speciality are selected to be displayed in the Group section of the report (Figure 12-57).

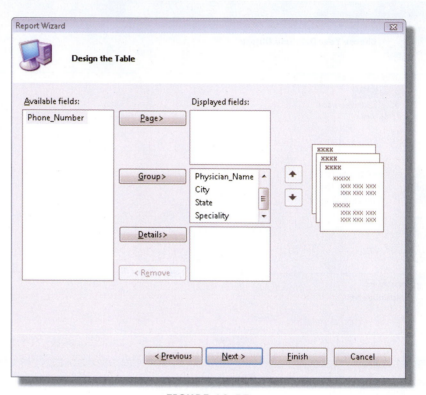

FIGURE 12-57

STEP 7 Click the Next button. Select a Block layout for the report and click the Next button again. Select the Ocean table style and click Next. Name the report Texas HMO Physicians and click the Finish button. The fields can be resized to display the entire field value in the finished Web page.

A new tab named Texas HMO Physicians.rdlc is displayed with the specified fields from the PhysicianList table (Figure 12–58).

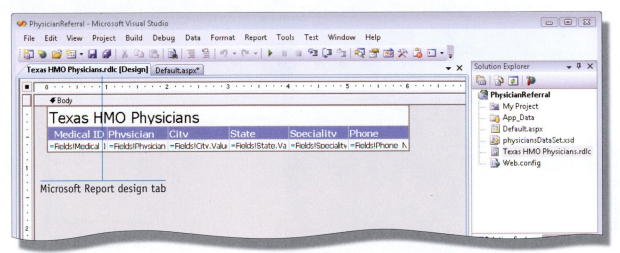

FIGURE 12-58

DISPLAYING THE REPORT

After selecting a source and style for the report, you need to select that report on the Web application form to view the report on a Web site. The Microsoft Report displays a report in a page-based layout, providing the ability to move between pages, search the data, and change the zoom ratio.

ONLINE REINFORCEMENT

To view a video of the process in the previous steps, visit scsite.com/vb2008/ch12 and then select Figure 12-52.

To display a report using the MicrosoftReportViewer object, you can complete the following steps:

STEP 1   Click the Default.aspx tab to open the Web form. Click the Smart tag to the right of the MicrosoftReportViewer object.

The ReportViewer Tasks are displayed (Figure 12-59).

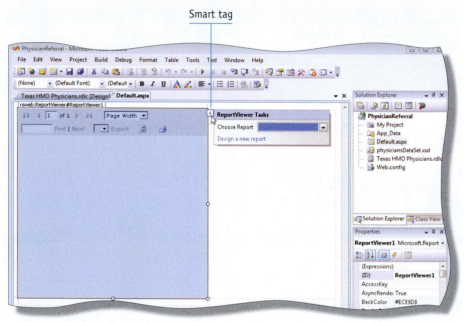

FIGURE 12-59

STEP 2   Click the Choose Report list arrow. Select Texas HMO Physicians.rdlc.

The report data source has been tied to the MicrosoftReportViewer object (Figure 12–60).

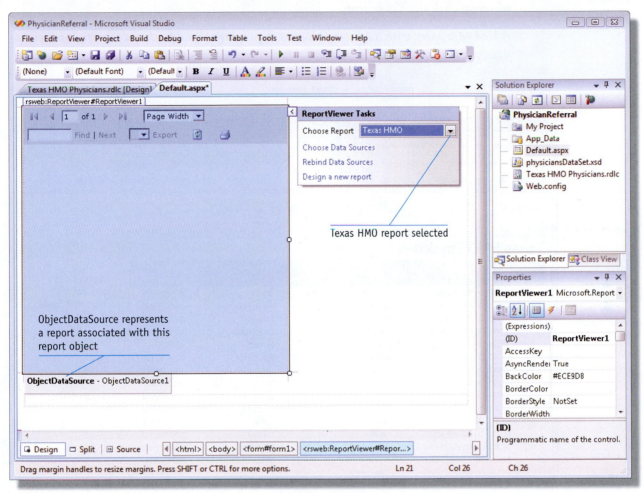

FIGURE 12-60

STEP 3 Select the MicrosoftReportViewer object and change the Height property to 500px and the Width property to 700px. Click the Start Debugging button on the Standard toolbar to execute the Web page. On the Script Debugging Displayed window, click the Yes button.

A Web page opens with a Microsoft Report displaying the fields selected from the physicians database (Figure 12-61).

zoom feature   search feature

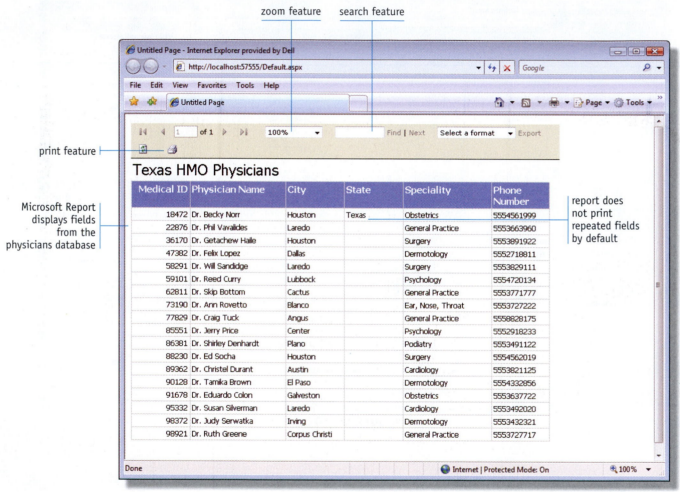

print feature

Microsoft Report displays fields from the physicians database

report does not print repeated fields by default

Texas HMO Physicians

Medical ID	Physician Name	City	State	Speciality	Phone Number
18472	Dr. Becky Norr	Houston	Texas	Obstetrics	5554561999
22876	Dr. Phil Vavalides	Laredo		General Practice	5553663960
36170	Dr. Getachew Haile	Houston		Surgery	5553891922
47382	Dr. Felix Lopez	Dallas		Dermotology	5552718811
58291	Dr. Will Sandidge	Laredo		Surgery	5553829111
59101	Dr. Reed Curry	Lubbock		Psychology	5554720134
62811	Dr. Skip Bottom	Cactus		General Practice	5553771777
73190	Dr. Ann Rovetto	Blanco		Ear, Nose, Throat	5553727222
77829	Dr. Craig Tuck	Angus		General Practice	5558828175
85551	Dr. Jerry Price	Center		Psychology	5552918233
86381	Dr. Shirley Denhardt	Plano		Podiatry	5553491122
88230	Dr. Ed Socha	Houston		Surgery	5554562019
89362	Dr. Christel Durant	Austin		Cardiology	5553821125
90128	Dr. Tamika Brown	El Paso		Dermotology	5554332856
91678	Dr. Eduardo Colon	Galveston		Obstetrics	5553637722
95332	Dr. Susan Silverman	Laredo		Cardiology	5553492020
98372	Dr. Judy Serwatka	Irving		Dermotology	5553432321
98921	Dr. Ruth Greene	Corpus Christi		General Practice	5553727717

FIGURE 12-61

Summary

In this chapter you have learned to create a Smartphone and a Web service application and use Microsoft Reports to display database reports on a Web page. The items listed in the table shown in Figure 12-62 include all the new Visual Studio and Visual Basic skills you have learned in this chapter.

	VISUAL BASIC SKILLS	
Skill	**Figure Number**	**Web Address for Video**
Examine the Tip Smartphone chapter project application	Figure 12-1	scsite.com/vb2008/ch12/figure12-1
Examine the Currency Converter Web Service chapter project application	Figure 12-2	scsite.com/vb2009/ch12/figure12-2
Create a Smartphone application	Figure 12-4	scsite.com/vb2008/ch12/figure12-4
Add a TextBox object to a Smartphone form and enter an amount	Figure 12-8	scsite.com/vb2008/ch12/figure12-8
Add a ComboBox object to the Smartphone application and select data	Figure 12-18	scsite.com/vb2008/ch12/figure12-18
Create a Command control for a Smartphone application	Figure 12-20	scsite.com/vb2008/ch12/figure12-20
Code the Command control area in a Smartphone application	Figure 12-22	scsite.com/vb2008/ch12/figure12-22
Create a Web reference	Figure 12-33	scsite.com/vb2008/ch12/figure12-33
Call a Web service method	Figure 12-38	scsite.com/vb2008/ch12/figure12-38
Create an instance of the Web service class in the code window	Figure 12-41	scsite.com/vb2008/ch12/figure12-41
Create a report on a Web application	Figure 12-52	scsite.com/vb2008/ch12/figure12-52
Display a report using the MicrosoftReportViewer object	Figure 12-59	scsite.com/vb2008/ch12/figurc12-59

FIGURE 12-62

Learn It Online

Start your browser and visit scsite.com/vb2008/ch12. Follow the instructions in the exercises below.

1. **Chapter Reinforcement TF, MC, SA** Click the Chapter Reinforcement link below Chapter 12. Then, at the top of the page, select the type of reinforcement you want to use (True and False, Multiple Choice, Short Answer). Answer the questions and then grade your answers. Take as many quizzes as you want.

2. **Practice Test** Click the Practice Test link below Chapter 12. Answer each question, enter your first and last name at the bottom of the page, and then click the Grade Test button. When the graded practice test is displayed on your screen, submit the graded practice test to your instructor. Continue to take the practice test until you are satisfied with your score.

3. **Crossword Puzzle Challenge** Click the Crossword Puzzle Challenge link below Chapter 12. Read the instructions, and then enter your first and last name. Click the Play button. Work the crossword puzzle. When you are finished, click the Submit button. When the crossword puzzle is redisplayed, submit it to your instructor.

Knowledge Check

1. All cell phones are Smartphones. True or false?

2. What size is the screen on a Smartphone?

3. Does a PDA or a Smartphone have a larger screen?

4. How does input differ between a Smartphone and a PDA?

5. What are the names of the keys on the top corners of the Smartphone?

6. Which key would you press to capitalize a letter on a Smartphone?

7. Which key creates a blank space on a Smartphone?

8. Which key would you press to insert a decimal point? How many times?

9. What is the name of the operating system on Smartphones?

10. When you combine a cell phone and a PDA, what is the name of this device?

11. What does UDDI stand for?

12. At the end of most Web services is the extension WSDL. What does WSDL stand for?

13. What does XML stand for?

14. To use a Web service in an application, the computer running the application must be connected to the Internet. True or false?

15. What is the easiest way to display a database report using Visual Basic?

Knowledge Check

16. Microsoft Reports can be used in _____ and _____ applications.

17. What Toolbox object is used to display a Microsoft Report using the Reporting category?

18. Name three options that are available for using the MicrosoftReportViewer object when the data is displayed?

19. Databases can be displayed using Microsoft Reports. True or false?

20. You must display all fields in a database when using Microsoft Reports. True or false?

Debugging Exercises

1. The following code is designed to create an instance of a Web service named wsStockQuote to access a Web reference named net.webservicex.stockquote. Correct the code in Figure 12-63.

```
20          Dim wsStockQuote As net.webservicex.stockquote
```

FIGURE 12-63

2. When you create a menu associated with the left softkey on a Smartphone application, what type of event is created?

Program Analysis

1. Explain which Smartphone keys you would press and how many times to enter R2D2 in a Smartphone TextBox object.

2. Explain which Smartphone keys you would press and how many times to enter Hula Hut in a Smartphone TextBox object.

3. Write a statement to initialize an instance with the variable name of wsFindTemp of a Web service named net.Temperature.present.

Case Programming Assignments

Complete one or more of the following case programming assignments. Submit the program and materials you create to your instructor. The level of difficulty is indicated for each case programming assignment.

● = Easiest
●● = Intermediate
●●● = Challenging

1 ●
TEMPERATURE CONVERSION

Design a Smartphone application and write the code that will execute according to the program requirements in Figure 12-64 and the Use Case definition in Figure 12-65. Before writing the code, create an event planning document for each event in the program. The completed Windows application and other objects in the user interface are shown in Figure 12-66.

REQUIREMENTS DOCUMENT

Date submitted:	August 11, 2012
Application title:	Traveler's Temperature Conversion Smartphone Application
Purpose:	This Smartphone application opens a cell phone interface that requests the user to enter a Celsius temperature, which is converted to a Fahrenheit temperature.
Program Procedures:	In a Smartphone application, a Celsius temperature entered from a cell phone numeric keypad is converted to a Fahrenheit temperature.
Algorithms, Processing, and Conditions:	1. The user first views a Smartphone application that requests the user to enter a Celsius temperature from a cell phone keypad. 2. The user can press the left softkey to compute the converted Fahrenheit temperature. 3. The user can press the right softkey to clear the Smartphone application form.
Notes and Restrictions:	The formula for converting Celsius to Fahrenheit temperatures is F = C * 1.8 + 32.
Comments:	The user cannot click the cell phone screen.

FIGURE 12-64

USE CASE DEFINITION

1. The user enters the Celsius temperature using the cell phone keypad.
2. The user presses the left softkey to display the corresponding Fahrenheit temperature.
3. The user presses the right softkey to clear the Smartphone form.

FIGURE 12-65

Case Programming Assignments

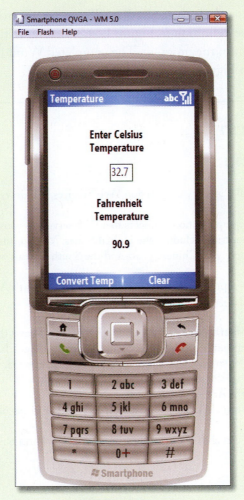

FIGURE 12-66

(continues)

Case Programming Assignments

2 MULTINATIONAL CURRENCY CONVERSION

Design a Windows application and write the code that will execute according to the program requirements in Figure 12-67 and the Use Case definition in Figure 12-68. Before writing the code, create an event planning document for each event in the program. The completed Windows application and other objects in the user interface are shown in Figure 12-69.

REQUIREMENTS DOCUMENT

Date submitted: August 31, 2011

Application title: Multinational Currency Conversion Web Services Windows Application

Purpose: This Windows application connects to a Web service to convert the currency of North American countries including the United States, Mexico, and Canada to Asian currencies such as Japanese yen, Chinese yuan, and the South Korean won.

Program Procedures: In a Windows application, a Web service converts a North American currency to an Asian currency.

Algorithms, Processing, and Conditions:
1. The user first views a Windows application that allows the user to select from the North American countries of United States, Mexico, or Canada.
2. The user enters the amount of currency to be converted.
3. The user selects the Asian country of Japan, China, or South Korea to which to convert their North American currency.
4. The user can click the Convert Currency button to calculate and display the conversion amount.
5. The user can click the Clear button to reset the Form object.

Notes and Restrictions:

Comments:
1. The cashexchange.jpg picture can be found at scsite/vb2008/images.
2. The Web service address is http://www.webservicex.net/CurrencyConvertor.asmx?wsdl.
3. The name of the calling method is ConversionRate. Two arguments are passed to the Web service method. U.S. dollar is represented by the argument net.webservicex.www.Currency.USD, Mexican pesos argument is net.webservicex.www.Currency.MXN, and the Canadian dollar argument is net.webservicesx.www.Currency.CAD. The Asian argument for the Japanese yen is represented by the argument net.webservicex.www.Currency.JPY. The Chinese yuan argument is net.webservicex.www.Currency.CNY. The South Korean won argument is net.webservicesx.www.Currency.KRW.

FIGURE 12-67

Case Programming Assignments

USE CASE DEFINITION

1. The user selects the North American country where the currency originated.
2. The user enters the amount of currency.
3. The user selects the Asian conversion currency type from a ComboBox object.
4. The user clicks the Convert Currency button to display the conversion amount.
5. The user clicks the Clear button to clear the form.

FIGURE 12-68

FIGURE 12-69

Case Programming Assignments

3 CELL PHONE WALLPAPER

Design a Windows application and write the code that will execute according to the program requirements in Figure 12-70 and the Use Case definition in Figure 12-71. Before writing the code, create an event planning document for each event in the program. The completed Windows application and other objects in the user interface are shown in Figure 12-72.

REQUIREMENTS DOCUMENT

Date submitted:	August 16, 2011
Application title:	Cell Phone Wallpaper Smartphone Application
Purpose:	This Smartphone application opens and displays a blank background. The user can select an image of a beach or mountains for a wallpaper graphic.
Program Procedures:	In a Smartphone application, the user can change the background wallpaper from a beach picture to a mountain picture by selecting the corresponding softkey.
Algorithms, Processing, and Conditions:	1. The user first views a Smartphone application that loads a Wallpaper Selection title and the following instructions: Press the Left Softkey for the Beach Wallpaper. Press the Right Softkey for the Mountain Wallpaper. 2. The user selects the left or right softkey and the wallpaper changes to the appropriate picture.
Notes and Restrictions:	Cell phones do not have a Form background property. Use the PictureBox object instead.
Comments:	The mountain.jpg and beach.jpg pictures are available for download at scsite.com/vb2008/ch12/images.

FIGURE 12-70

USE CASE DEFINITION

1. The user views directions to select a wallpaper graphic for a Smartphone.
2. The user presses the left softkey to select the beach wallpaper or the right softkey to select the mountain wallpaper.

FIGURE 12-71

Case Programming Assignments

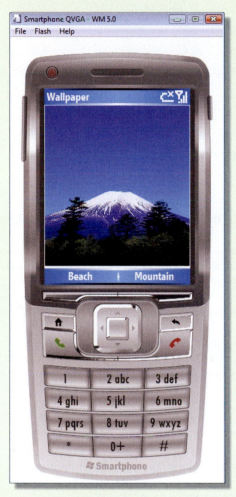

FIGURE 12-72

Case Programming Assignments

4

LITTLE LEAGUE BASEBALL TEAM MICROSOFT REPORT

Create a Web application that will execute according to the program requirements in Figure 12-73. Before designing the user interface, create a Use Case definition. Before writing the code, create an event planning document for each event in the program. This program requires the use of a database file located at scsite/vb2008/ch12.

REQUIREMENTS DOCUMENT

Date submitted: May 13, 2013

Application title: Little League Baseball National All-Stars Microsoft Reports Web Application

Purpose: This Web application opens an Access database that includes data about 23 boys and girls ages 12–14 that are playing in the national little league co-ed championship. The database can be viewed in a Web application as a report.

Program Procedures: In a Web application, the Access database file is opened and displayed in a Microsoft Report.

Algorithms, Processing, and Conditions: The user views a Web application which displays a report. The player number, player first name and last name, city, state, and age is displayed.

Notes and Restrictions: The littleleague.accdb file is located on the USB drive on F: drive.

Comments: The littleleague.accdb Access database can be downloaded from scsite.com/vb2008/ch12.

FIGURE 12-73

Case Programming Assignments

5
● ●
COLLEGE MAJORS MICROSOFT REPORT

Design a Windows application that will execute according to the program requirements in Figure 12-74. Before designing the user interface, create a Use Case definition. Before writing the code, create an event planning document for each event in the program. This program requires the use of a database file located at scsite/vb2008/ch12.

REQUIREMENTS DOCUMENT

Date submitted:	March 9, 2011
Application title:	College Majors Microsoft Reports Windows Application
Purpose:	This Windows application opens an Access database that includes data about 36 college majors in a Windows form. The database can be viewed and printed as a Microsoft Report.
Program Procedures:	In a Windows application, the Access database file is opened and viewed as a report.
Algorithms, Processing, and Conditions:	The user first views a Windows application that loads an existing Access database table which includes the department, college major, and the number of students in that major as a Microsoft Report.
Notes and Restrictions:	The college.accdb file is located on the USB drive on F: drive.
Comments:	The college.accdb Access database can be downloaded from scsite.com/vb2008/ch12.

FIGURE 12-74

Case Programming Assignments

6 ●●
MOBILE FIRST AID INFORMATION

Design a Smartphone application and write the code that will execute according to the program requirements in Figure 12-76. Before writing the code, create an event planning document for each event in the program. Use the table in Figure 12-75 in the application.

Emergency Situation	Recommended Care
Wounds	Stop the bleeding by applying pressure with a clean, absorbent cloth, or if a cloth is unavailable, use your fingers. If bleeding still does not stop, raise the wound above heart level.
Burns	Use large amounts of cool water to cool the burn. Never use ice except on small superficial burns, because it causes body heat loss. Use dry, sterile dressings or a clean cloth to help prevent infection and reduce pain.
Poison	Call the Poison Control Center immediately at 1-800-222-1222.
Choking	Stand behind a conscious choking adult, wrapping your arms around their waist. With one hand, make a fist. Place the thumb side of the fist against the victim's abdomen just above the navel. Put your other hand over the fist and give quick upward thrusts into the victim's abdomen. Continue giving thrusts until the object blocking the airway is dislodged.

FIGURE 12-75

Case Programming Assignments

REQUIREMENTS DOCUMENT

Date submitted: November 29, 2012

Application title: Mobile First Aid Smartphone Application

Purpose: This Smartphone application can be used to provide first aid information in an emergency situation.

Program Procedures: In a Smartphone application, the user can select the emergency situation and the recommended care is displayed.

Algorithms, Processing, and Conditions:
1. The user first views a Smartphone application that requests the user to enter the emergency situation from a ComboBox object.
2. The user can click the left softkey to display the recommended care for that emergency.
3. The user can click the right softkey to reset the Form object.

Notes and Restrictions:

Comments:

FIGURE 12-76

Case Programming Assignments

7 ● ● ●
MY CAR MILEAGE

Create a requirements document and a Use Case Definition document, and then design a Smartphone application, based on the description in Figure 12-77. Before writing the code, create an event planning document for each event in the program:

Create a Smartphone application to compute gas mileage each time a car is refueled. The user should first select Miles per Gallon or Kilometers per Liter. The user enters the number of miles or kilometers traveled and the number of gallons or liters of fuel needed to fill the vehicle. The application displays the miles per gallon or the kilometers per liter.

FIGURE 12-77

Case Programming Assignments

8 ● ● ●
PERSONAL PEDOMETER

Create a requirements document and a Use Case Definition document, and then design a Smartphone application, based on the description in Figure 12-78. Before writing the code, create an event planning document for each event in the program:

Create a Smartphone application that allows you to determine the calories burned during an activity. The application should ask the user how many minutes of exercise and what type of exercise was completed. Using the following table, determine the number of calories burned by the exercise activity.

Exercise Type	Calories Burned Per Hour
Aerobics	400
Cycling	440
Frisbee	215
Jogging	675
Swimming	600
Weightlifting	468

FIGURE 12-78

Case Programming Assignments

9 ●●●
EASTER SUNDAY WEB SERVICE

Create a requirements document and a Use Case Definition document, and then design a Windows application, based on the description in Figure 12-79. Before writing the code, create an event planning document for each event in the program:

Create a Windows application that calls a Web service to compute the date of the Easter holiday given the argument of the requested year (Short data type). The Web reference can be found at *www.stgregorioschurchdc.org/ wsdl/Calendar.wsdl*. The method call is named easter_date and the argument of the year is passed. The method returns the date as a string when Easter will fall during the given year. Allow the user to enter a year and display the date on which Easter will fall for that year.

FIGURE 12-79

Visual Studio Tools for Office

OBJECTIVES

You will have mastered the material in this chapter when you can:

- ► Use Visual Studio Tools in Microsoft Word
- ► Create a VSTO Word template
- ► Add a DateTimePicker object to an application
- ► Add a table to a Word document
- ► Add the Actions Pane Control
- ► Place a ComboBox object in applications
- ► Calculate payments using the Pmt Function
- ► Use Math Class methods in mathematical computations

*NOTE: VISUAL STUDIO TOOLS FOR OFFICE INSTALLATION

Visual Studio Tools for Office (VSTO) is now an integrated part of Visual Studio 2008. Both Microsoft Office 2007 and Microsoft Office 2003 are fully supported in Visual Studio 2008.

Introduction

You can use Visual Basic to create applications besides those for the Windows, mobile, and Web environments. This chapter introduces topics that allow you to develop Office applications using Microsoft Word or Microsoft Excel. In addition to the techniques you have learned thus far to program Windows applications, Smart Device applications, and Web applications, you also can use Visual Studio 2008 to develop code behind Word, Excel, PowerPoint, Visio, Outlook, Project, and InfoPath. The Visual Studio Tools for Office (VSTO) Second Edition is now packaged with Visual Studio 2008, and provides several enhancements including a new visual Ribbon designer for Microsoft Office 2007. The Ribbon designer allows a developer to design an Office Ribbon using the familiar drag-and-drop interface and to interact with the Ribbon using standard .NET code.

Chapter Project

In the sample chapter project, Microsoft Word, the word processing program in the Office suite, is used with Visual Basic 2008 to solve a problem for a car dealership. A local car dealer wants a car sales contract that allows a salesperson to enter the vehicle and buyer information to create a legal contract for the sale of a vehicle. The application will be designed using Microsoft Word to build an information form that is easy to use for the entire vehicle sales team. The Word document should have a Task Pane control on the right side of the screen that the salesperson can use to compute the monthly payment for the vehicle based on the interest rate, the length of the loan, and the amount borrowed.

When the application runs, the contract opens in a Microsoft Word 2007 template as shown in Figure EC-1.

FIGURE EC-1

The salesperson enters the year, make, model, color, and price of the vehicle, and the name of the customer. The salesperson then selects the vehicle purchase date and clicks the Create Contract button. As shown in Figure EC-2, a legal vehicle sales contract is displayed and can be printed and saved. The salesperson also can compute the monthly payments based on the total loan amount, such as $17,000, and the interest rate, such as 9.25%. To do so, the salesperson enters the values requested in the Loan Calculator in the Document Actions task pane on the right side of the window. The salesperson can enter the loan amount directly and select the length of the loan from a box that contains the choices of 12, 24, 36, 48, or 60 months.

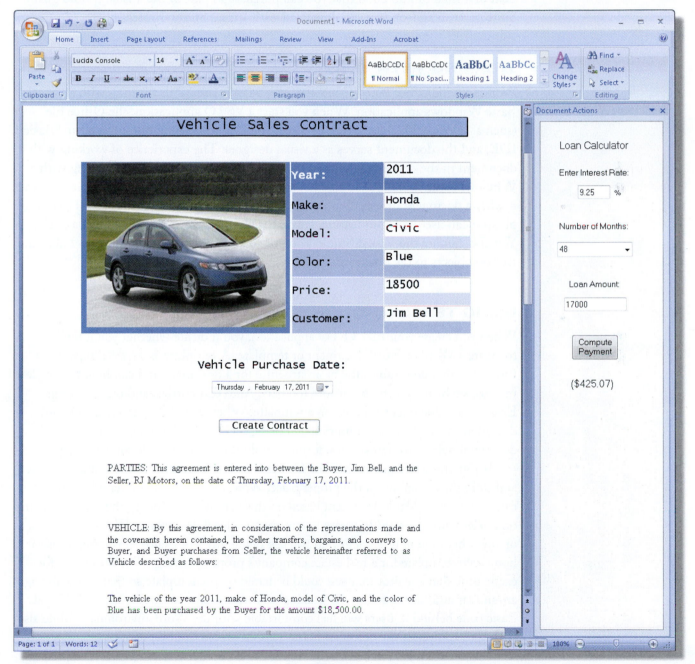

FIGURE EC-2

Programming an Office Document

Microsoft Office 2007 includes software applications that create professional documents used in the business world. Because Microsoft Office has more than a 90% market share, the robust Office environment has been joined with the power of Visual Studio's development facility. **Visual Studio Tools for Office** (VSTO, pronounced "visto") helps you build a Word document or an Excel spreadsheet that contains VB code, allowing you to create automated, customized Office documents that combine the power of Visual Basic with the familiarity of Office. VSTO is a component of Visual Studio 2008 that you can purchase as part of the Visual Studio Team Suite or as an add-on you can download with Visual Studio Professional.

WORKING WITH VSTO

Working with Office 2007 documents in VSTO is similar to working with a Visual Basic Windows application. When you start a VSTO application, the Office file (such as a Word 2007 document or Excel 2007 workbook) opens in the Visual Basic IDE, and the document serves as a visual designer. The experience of working with a document in the designer is as close as possible to the experience of working with a Windows form, making it simple to create an interactive document. You can edit and modify a document or workbook using the tools of the Office application. For example, you can use the Undo feature, create Excel formulas, and find and replace text. You also can use the Visual Studio Toolbox to add standard objects such as Label and Button objects to the document or workbook.

USING TEMPLATES

When you create your first VSTO application, you indicate whether you intend to create a Word or Excel document or template. A **template** is a special type of Office file that determines the basic structure for a document and can hold text, styles, macros, keyboard shortcuts, custom toolbars, AutoText entries, and other settings. Every Word document is based on a template. When you choose to create a Word document, you select an appropriate template, such as one for a memo or a normal document, which contains styles, formats, and other tools suitable for your purpose.

If you save a document with the file extension .dotx instead of the standard .docx and store the document in the proper place, Word recognizes it as a template. You then can create a new, blank document based on that template, including the styles, text, and other elements you need to create letters, memos, legal documents, Web pages, faxes, or any other kind of document that you use frequently. For example, you might use a home sales template for a real estate company's property listings. The document for each home that a realtor may sell could be based on the template so that all the listings are similar and easy to follow. By making a Word document or template with Visual Basic code behind it, users will feel comfortable with the Word environment while also having the power of the object and class set that Visual Studio provides.

The New Project dialog box in Visual Studio contains many project templates for creating Office 2007 and 2003 solutions such as an Excel Workbook, Word Document, Excel Template, Word Template, Outlook Add-in, PowerPoint Add-in, Visio Add-in, Project Add-in, and SharePoint template.

UNDERSTANDING VSTO TOOLBARS, MENUS, AND RIBBONS

The Office Ribbon for the selected Office application appears within the Visual Studio window and looks and acts as it does in Microsoft Office (Figure EC-6). Most Microsoft Word 2007 features are also available within Visual Basic 2008.

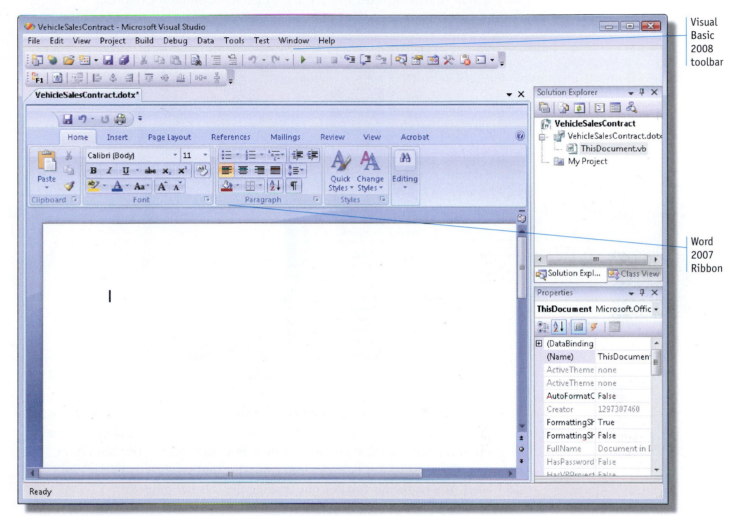

FIGURE EC-6

Using VSTO Design View

When working with Word and Excel templates in VSTO, you work in **Design view**, which enables you to customize the template by adding interactive objects. In addition, you can create Word or Excel documents and drag .NET component objects onto the document, writing Visual Basic code to control the objects.

Using the VSTO Toolbox

The VSTO Toolbox has many of the objects that have become familiar to you in Visual Basic programming. As shown in Figure EC-7, however, the VSTO Toolbox groups objects differently. Most of the objects you will use on a daily basis in VSTO are listed in alphabetic order in the category named Common Controls.

FIGURE EC-7

You can drag objects in the Common Controls category from the Visual Studio Toolbox directly into Word and Excel, as shown in Figure EC-8, and modify the object properties using the Properties window. For example, the TextBox object shown in Figure EC-8 has been dragged from the Toolbox directly to the Word document. You name the TextBox object using the (Name) property.

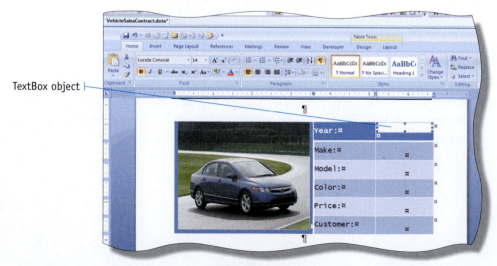

FIGURE EC-8

The GroupBox object is not available in VSTO. If you want two exclusive sets of RadioButton objects in two GroupBoxes, you must write code for the separate sets of RadioButton objects.

ADDING A DATETIMEPICKER OBJECT

The **DateTimePicker** object allows the user to select one date from a calendar of dates or times. The DateTimePicker object works in all Visual Studio applications. It appears as a drop-down list with a date or time represented in text (Figure EC-9). When you drag the .NET component onto the Windows Form object, the current date is shown. You can change this date by changing the Value property in the Properties window. The prefix used for a DateTimePicker object is dat.

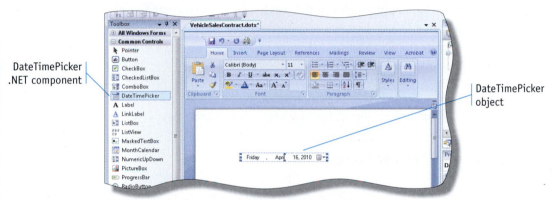

FIGURE EC-9

When you run the application, the user can click the list arrow to the right of the date to view a calendar (Figure EC-10). Using the calendar, the user can select a date and change to a different month. When the user clicks a date in the calendar, the selected date is displayed in the DateTimePicker object. In Figure EC-10, the current date is April 16 but the selected date is April 24.

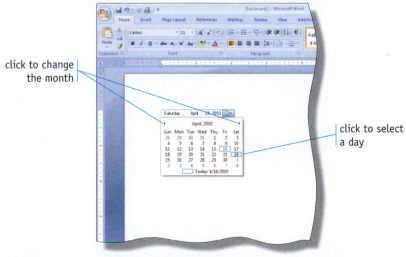

FIGURE EC-10

The selected date in the DateTimePicker can be referenced in code. For example, if the DateTimePicker object shown in Figure EC-10 is named datBirthdayMonth, the user's selected birth date can be displayed in a Label object named lblBirthday by using the code shown in Figure EC-11.

```
12    Private Sub btnBirthday_Click(ByVal sender As System.Object, ByVal e As System.    ↙
      EventArgs) Handles btnBirthday.Click
13        lblBirthday.Text = Me.datBirthdayMonth.Text.ToString()
14    End Sub
```

FIGURE EC-11

If you want to display the day of the week selected in a DateTimePicker in a MsgBox object in a Word document, enter the code shown in Figure EC-12 to display the MsgBox object shown in Figure EC-13.

```
14    MsgBox("Your birthday falls on a " &
15        Me.datBirthdayMonth.Value.DayOfWeek.ToString(), , "Birthday")
```

FIGURE EC-12

FIGURE EC-13

In Figure EC-13, the DayOfWeek procedure of the Value property returns the day. The ToString changes the returned value to a string for display in the MsgBox.

ADDING A TABLE TO A WORD DOCUMENT

Tables, which consist of rows and columns that form cells, can organize information in your document. In a VSTO Word 2007 document, click where you want to insert a table. To add a table to a Word document, you can complete the following steps:

STEP 1 On the Word 2007 Ribbon, click the Insert tab. In the Tables group, click Table.

Word displays a grid so you can select the number of rows and columns you want (Figure EC–14).

FIGURE EC-14

STEP 2 Drag to select one row and three columns in the grid.

Three cells in the first row of the table grid are selected (Figure EC–15).

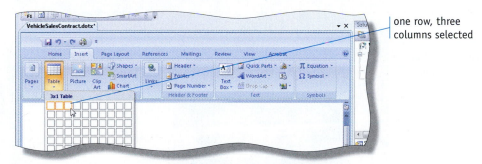

FIGURE EC-15

STEP 3 Release the mouse button to insert the table in the Word template.

A table consisting of one row and three columns appears in the Word template (Figure EC–16).

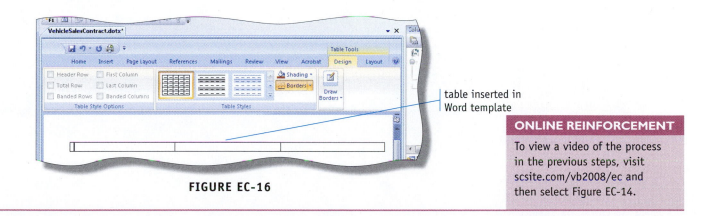

FIGURE EC-16

ONLINE REINFORCEMENT

To view a video of the process in the previous steps, visit scsite.com/vb2008/ec and then select Figure EC-14.

INSERTING A PICTURE AND ADDITIONAL CELLS IN THE TABLE

To enter text in the table, you can type directly in its cells, advancing from one cell to the next by using the TAB key. You also can place most of the Visual Basic Toolbox objects in a cell, such as a PictureBox or TextBox object. To include an image in the table, you can place a picture in a PictureBox object if you intend to change the graphic image in code, or insert a clip art image or a picture from a file directly into the table cell.

In the following example, the car.jpg image is used. You can download the image from scsite.com/vb2008/ec/images. Save it in a location you will remember. To insert the image, follow these steps:

STEP 1 Click the leftmost cell in the table. Click the Insert tab and then click Picture in the Illustrations group. In the Insert Picture dialog box, locate the car.jpg image file where you saved it. Select the car.jpg image and then click the Insert button to place the image in the table.

Word inserts the car picture in the first cell of the table (Figure EC-17).

car inserted in first cell of table

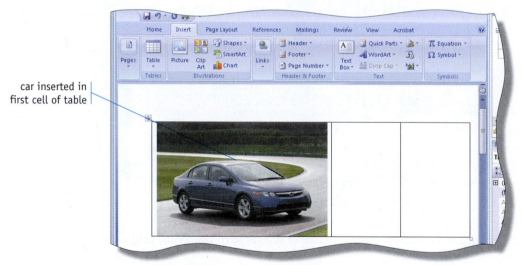

FIGURE EC-17

STEP 2   The second and third columns contain one row. To add rows to these columns, first drag across the second and third columns to select them.

The second and third columns are selected in the table (Figure EC-18).

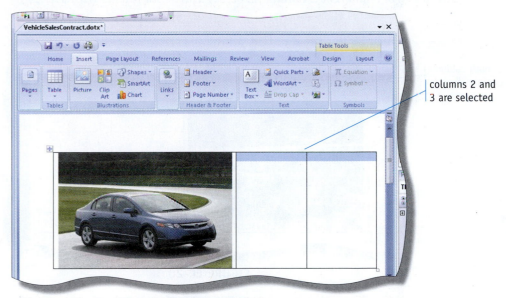

FIGURE EC-18

STEP 3   Click the Table Tools Layout tab. In the Merge group, click Split Cells.

The Split Cells dialog box is displayed (Figure EC-19).

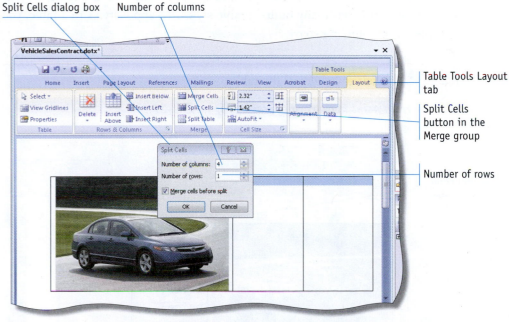

FIGURE EC-19

STEP 4 In the Split Cells dialog box, use the arrows to set the value in the Number of columns list to 2 and the value in the Number of rows list to 6. Click the OK button in the Split Cells dialog box. Click outside the table.

The two right columns now contain six evenly distributed rows (Figure EC-20).

both columns contain six rows

FIGURE EC-20

USING TABLE STYLES TO FORMAT A TABLE

You can enter data in the table by typing characters directly into the cells. In the following steps, text has been added to the table.

After creating the table by adding images and text, for example, you may want to add some finishing touches to enhance its appearance. To change the design of a table, Word 2007 has many built-in table styles. To apply styles to a table, you can complete the following steps:

STEP 1 Click anywhere in the table.

The insertion point appears in the table (Figure EC-21).

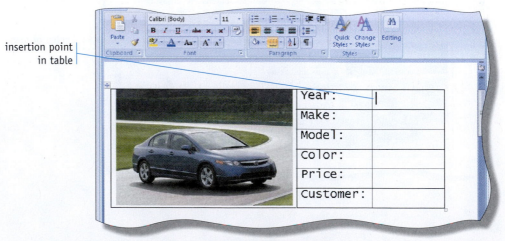

insertion point in table

FIGURE EC-21

STEP 2 Click the Table Tools Design tab. In the Table Styles group, click the More button (third arrow). In the Table Styles gallery, scroll down to find the table style named Medium Grid 3 - Accent 1.

On the Table Tools Design tab, the Tables Styles gallery is displayed. The table style Medium Grid 3 - Accent 1 is highlighted (Figure EC-22).

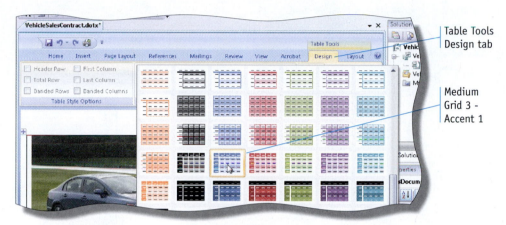

FIGURE EC-22

STEP 3 Select the Medium Grid 3 - Accent 1 table style.

The table format changes to reflect the design of the Medium Grid 3 - Accent 1 style (Figure EC-23).

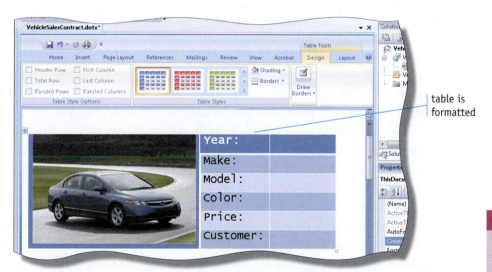

FIGURE EC-23

ADDING THE ACTIONS PANE CONTROL

The **Actions Pane Control** is a customizable task pane that appears in the Office application window. An example of a task pane is the Clip Art task pane, which is shown in Figure EC-24.

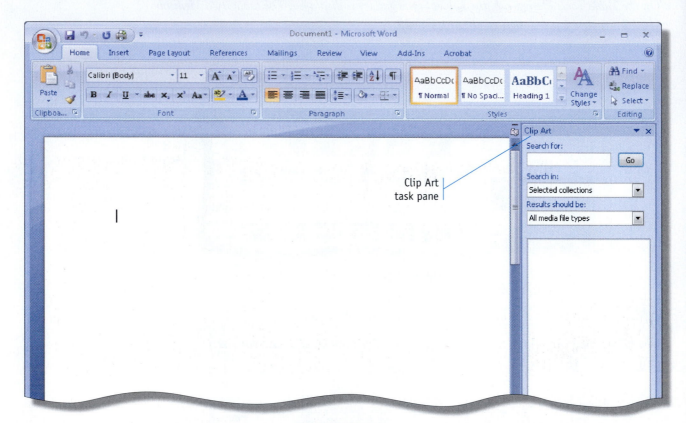

Clip Art task pane

FIGURE EC-24

Using VSTO, you can create a customized Actions Pane Control called the **Document Actions task pane**. You can include any Toolbox object in the Document Actions task pane. To do so, you use the **ActionsPane** object, which acts as a container for Visual Basic objects. Although the ActionsPane object always is available to the executed project, it does not appear until you populate it with Toolbox objects. Once the ActionsPane object is displayed, you can add or remove controls in response to the user's actions.

You can add multiple objects to the ActionsPane object and then write code to respond to events that occur from objects in the ActionsPane. You can create an ActionsPane object in two ways: by coding the ActionsPane object manually, or by dragging a Toolbox control directly onto the ActionsPane object and then coding a one-line request to display the ActionsPane object.

To manually code an ActionsPane object, you can complete the following steps:

STEP 1   Open the code window by clicking the View Code button on the Solution Explorer toolbar. Click inside the ThisDocument_Startup event.

The code window opens and the insertion point appears in the ThisDocument_Startup event (Figure EC–25).

insertion point   ThisDocument_Startup event handler

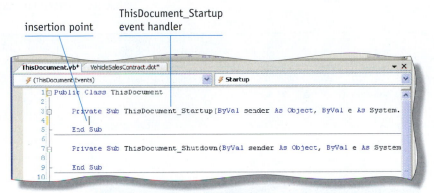

FIGURE EC-25

STEP 2   Type me.act to use IntelliSense to complete the object name ActionsPane. Using IntelliSense, add the statements .Controls.Add(New DateTimePicker). Press the ENTER key and then delete the blank line.

The code (Figure EC-26) adds a DateTimePicker object to the ActionsPane object. By adding a DateTimePicker object to the ActionsPane object, the Document Actions task pane will appear when the application is executed (see Figure EC-27). You must place at least one object inside the Add parentheses to create the ActionsPane object.

```
3     Private Sub ThisDocument_Startup(ByVal sender As Object, ByVal e As System.
      EventArgs) Handles Me.Startup
4         Me.ActionsPane.Controls.Add(New DateTimePicker)
5     End Sub
```

FIGURE EC-26

STEP 3 Test the application by clicking the Start Debugging button on the Standard toolbar. Click the calendar list arrow in the upper-right corner to open the calendar.

The Word template opens and the Document Actions task pane appears on the right side of the window (Figure EC–27).

Document Actions task pane

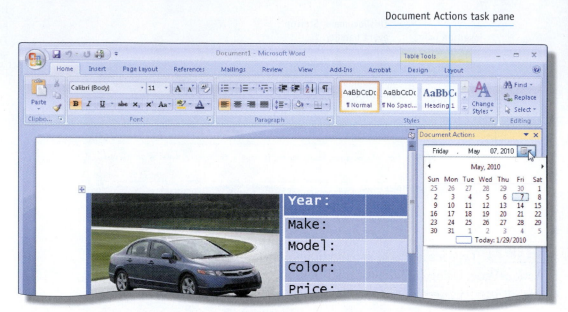

FIGURE EC-27

The second way to place an ActionsPane object on the right side of the Word window is to add an Actions Pane Control object in the Visual Studio project window by following these steps:

STEP 1 Click Project on the menu bar and then click Add New Item on the Project menu.

The Add New Item dialog box opens (Figure EC-28).

Actions Pane Control

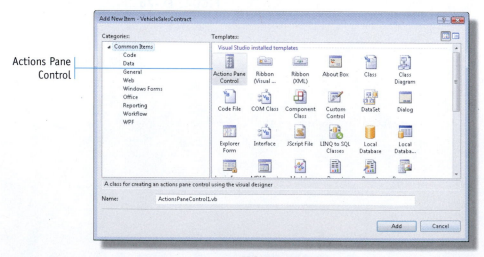

FIGURE EC-28

STEP 2   Click Actions Pane Control.

In the Add New Item dialog box, the Actions Pane Control icon is selected (Figure EC-29).

Actions Pane
Control selected

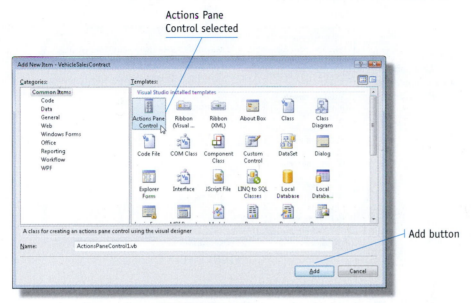

Add button

FIGURE EC-29

STEP 3   Click the Add button in the Add New Item dialog box.

The Actions Pane Control opens in a new tab (ActionsPaneControl1.vb) in Design view (Figure EC-30).

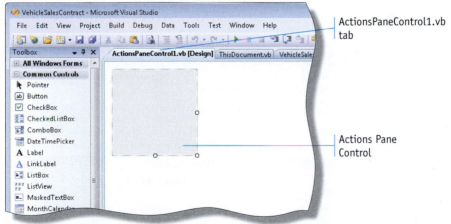

ActionsPaneControl1.vb
tab

Actions Pane
Control

FIGURE EC-30

STEP 4 Drag a Label object from the Toolbox to the Actions Pane Control. Change the (Name) property of the Label object to `lblCalculator`. Change the Text property to `Loan Calculator`, and the Font property to Sans Serif, size 12.

The Label object is placed on the Actions Pane Control (Figure EC-31).

Label object placed on Actions Pane Control

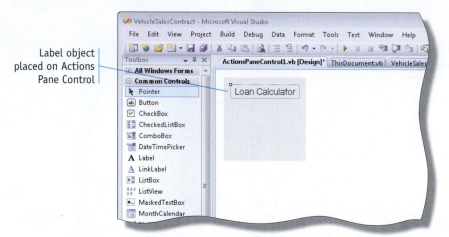

FIGURE EC-31

WATCH OUT FOR

You can resize the Actions Pane Control, but it will still be the standard size on the right side of the Office window when the application is executed.

STEP 5 To display the Actions Pane Control when the application runs, you must code a request to view the Document Actions task pane that is executed when the Word document opens. Click the ThisDocument.vb tab to open the code window for the Word template. Click in the ThisDocument_Startup event, type `me.act` and use IntelliSense to complete the rest of the line of code shown in Figure EC-32, which opens the Actions Pane Control when the application begins.

The code to open the Actions Pane Control when the document is opened is entered in the ThisDocument_Startup event (Figure EC-32).

FIGURE EC-32

STEP 6   Click the Start Debugging button on the Standard toolbar to execute the application. Microsoft Word opens with the Document Actions task pane on the right side of the window.

The Word document opens and the Actions Pane Control is displayed on the right side of the window (Figure EC-33).

Document Actions pane

Label object

FIGURE EC-33

USING A COMBOBOX OBJECT

You will recall from Chapter 8 that a ComboBox object allows the user to select an item from a list and to enter data as if using a text box. In the Document Actions task pane in the Vehicle Sales Contract chapter project, the user enters the number of months for a loan by either selecting a value from the ComboBox object items list or by entering a value in the text box portion of the ComboBox object. The code must determine that the user has either selected a value from the list or has entered a value in the text box portion.

When the user selects an item from the ComboBox object item list, the **SelectedItem** property for the ComboBox object can be assigned to a variable, as shown by the statement in Figure EC-34.

```
17          decLoanMonths = Convert.ToDecimal(Me.cboLoanMonths.SelectedItem)
```

FIGURE EC-34

In Figure EC-34, the SelectedItem property of the cboLoanMonths ComboBox object is converted to a decimal value and is placed in the decLoanMonths.

If the user enters a value in the text box portion of the ComboBox object, the SelectedItem property is assigned a null string and the value the user enters is placed in the Text property of the ComboBox object.

So, to determine if the user selected a value, the program code can check the SelectedItem property. If it is assigned a null string, then either the user entered a value in the text box portion of the ComboBox, or the user did not enter a value. This coding is shown in Figure EC-35.

```
21          If Me.cboMonths.SelectedItem = "" Then
22              If IsNumeric(Me.cboMonths.Text) Then
23                  decLoanMonths = Convert.ToDecimal(Me.cboMonths.Text)
24              Else
25                  MsgBox.Show("Please select the number of months for the loan")
26              End If
27          Else
28              decLoanMonths = Convert.ToDecimal(Me.cboMonths.SelectedItem)
29          End If
```

FIGURE EC-35

In Figure EC-35, the If statement on line 21 checks if the SelectedItem property contains a null string. If so, it next checks if the Text property for the cboMonths ComboBox object is numeric. If it is then the user entered a numeric value for months and that value is converted from a string to a decimal value and placed in the decLoanMonths variable.

If the SelectedItem property contains a null string and the user did not enter a numeric value, then a month has not been entered and the message box is displayed to remind the user to select the number of months for the loan. If the SelectedItem property is not a null string, then the user selected a value from the ComboBox list and that string value is converted to a decimal value and placed in the decLoanMonths variable.

HEADS UP

The ComboBox object also has a SelectedIndex property that returns an integer value corresponding to the selected list item.

CALCULATING LOAN PAYMENTS WITH THE PMT FUNCTION

For most people, purchasing a car requires borrowing money from a bank or from the car dealer. In the Vehicle Sales Contract Office application, coding in the Document Actions task pane calculates the monthly payments for a loan on the vehicle when the user clicks the Compute Payment button. To determine the cost of the monthly car payments, a function called **Pmt** performs the mathematical calculation. The Pmt function, which is available in Visual Basic 2008, calculates the payment for a loan based on constant payments and a constant interest rate. To use the Pmt function, you must specify the loan amount, the length of the loan, and the interest rate. The syntax of using the Pmt function in Visual Basic is shown in Figure EC-36.

General Format: Pmt function
Pmt(Rate, NPer, PV)

Rate: The interest rate for the period. For example, if a mortgage payment has an interest rate of 8.5% per year, the rate for the period based on monthly payments would be .085 / 12.

NPer: The total number of payments made over the life of the loan. For example, if a mortgage loan was for 15 years, the number of payments would be 15 * 12 = 180 payments.

PV: The present value of the loan or investment. For example, the present value of a mortgage loan amount could be $150,000. If an investment was made, the present value would be $0.

Optional Formula   Pmt(Rate, NPer, PV, FV, Due)

FV: Optional — The future value or cash balance you want after the final payment is paid. For example, the future value of a loan is $0 because that is the value after the final payment. However, if you want to save $20,000 over 18 years for your child's education, then $20,000 is the future value. If you do not include this portion, 0 is assumed.

Due: Optional — The due date can be set to either DueDate.EndOfPeriod if the payments are due at the end of the payment period, or DueDate.BegOfPeriod if payments are due at the beginning of the period. If omitted, DueDate.EndOfPeriod is assumed.

FIGURE EC-36

Consider the following two scenarios for using the Pmt function.

First Scenario: You purchase a car and need a loan for $18,500 for four years at an interest rate of 8.9%. The table shown in Figure EC-37 divides the rate by 12 because the yearly rate is divided by the 12 payments, one for each month of the year (that is, one for each payment). The NPer variable is multiplied by 12 because the four-year loan has 48 total payments.

Variable	Operation
Rate	.089 / 12
NPer	4 * 12
PV	18500

FIGURE EC-37

The code written for the first scenario is shown in Figure EC-38:

```
6          Dim decRate As Decimal
7          Dim decPeriod As Decimal
8          Dim decPrinciple As Decimal
9          Dim decMonthlyPayments As Decimal
10
11         decRate = 0.089
12         decPeriod = 4
13         decPrinciple = 18500
14
15         decMonthlyPayments = Convert.ToDecimal(Pmt(decRate / 12, decPeriod * 12, _
16             decPrinciple))
```

FIGURE EC-38

The result of the calculation, and the monthly payment amount assigned to decMonthlyPayments, is (459.50), which means you must pay $459.50 per month to pay off a car loan of $18,500 in 4 years with an interest rate of 8.9% per year.

Second Scenario: Your parents want to accumulate $25,000 in 10 years for your brother's college education. They need to know the amount of money they must place in a savings account each month to end up with $25,000 in ten years at an interest rate of 3% per year. The monthly payment is deposited in a savings account at the beginning of each month. The table shown in Figure EC-39 lists FV (Future Value) because that is the money they want to have at the end of ten years.

Variable	Operation
Rate	.03 / 12
NPer	10 * 12
PV	0
FV	25000
Due	DueDate.BegOfPeriod

FIGURE EC-39

The code written for the second scenario is shown in Figure EC-40:

```
34         decRate = 0.03
35         decPeriod = 10
36         decPresentValue = 0D
37         decPrinciple = 25000
38
39
40         decMonthlyPayments = Convert.ToDecimal(Pmt(decRate / 12, _
41             decPeriod * 12, decPresentValue, decPrinciple, DueDate.BegOfPeriod))
```

FIGURE EC-40

The monthly payment value calculated by the Pmt function and assigned to decMonthlyPayments is ($178.46), which means your parents need to place $178.46 per month for 10 years in the savings account to obtain $25,000 for your brother's college education.

CALCULATING WITH THE MATH CLASS

Visual Basic provides other math procedures to perform mathematical calculations. The procedures in the **Math** class provide you with most of the standard procedures you can use for required computations, such as find a square root, determine an absolute value, or return the larger of two values. The table in Figure EC-41 displays many of the common Math class methods. The variables x and y in this table are of type Double or Decimal.

Math Class Methods	Description	Example
Math.Abs(x)	Returns the Absolute Value of x	Math.Abs(−7.3) is 7.3
Math.Ceiling(x)	Returns the integer to the right of this number on the number line	Math.Ceiling(5.1) is 6.0
Math.Floor(x)	Returns the integer to the left of this number on the number line	Math.Floor(−4.2) is −5.0
Math.Max(x, y)	Returns the larger of the two numbers	Math.Max(2.1, 8.4) is 8.4
Math.Min(x, y)	Returns the smaller of the two numbers	Math.Min(−3.71, −6.9) is −6.9
Math.Pow(x, y)	Returns the x number raised to the power of y	Math.Pow(2.0, 3.0) is 8.0
Math.Round(x)	Returns the number rounded to the nearest integer	Math.Round(81.4) is 81.0 Math.Round(81.6) is 82.0
Math.Sqrt(x)	Returns the square root of the number	Math.Sqrt(2.0) is 1.4142135623731

FIGURE EC-41

The code shown in Figure EC-42 demonstrates how to use the Math class methods:

```
45          Dim decFirstNum As Double = 29.25
46          Dim decSecondNum As Double = -37.6
47
48          MsgBox(Math.Max(decFirstNum, decSecondNum))     ' returns 29.25
49          MsgBox(Math.Min(decFirstNum, decSecondNum))     ' returns -37.6
50          MsgBox(Math.Floor(decSecondNum))                ' returns -38
51          MsgBox(Math.Ceiling(decSecondNum))              ' returns -37
52          MsgBox(Math.Abs(decFirstNum))                   ' returns 29.25
53          MsgBox(Math.Sqrt(decFirstNum))                  ' returns 5.4083269131959
54          MsgBox(Math.Pow(decFirstNum, 2.0))              ' returns 855.5625
55
56          MsgBox(Math.PI)                                 ' returns 3.14159265358979
57          MsgBox(Math.E)                                  ' returns 2.71828182845905
```

FIGURE EC-42

In addition to common Math class methods, two constant values are defined in the Math class: PI and E. PI is the constant ratio between a circle and its diameter, and is provided for quick computations. The Math class E is the natural exponent (generally written in equations as a lowercase e) used in many mathematical operations. The code example shown in Figure EC-43 demonstrates how to invoke each constant.

```
56          MsgBox(Math.PI)                                 ' returns 3.14159265358979
57          MsgBox(Math.E)                                  ' returns 2.71828182845905
```

FIGURE EC-43

Program Design

The requirements document for the Vehicle Sales Contract Office application is shown in Figure EC-44, and the Use Case Definition document is shown in Figure EC-45.

REQUIREMENTS DOCUMENT

Date submitted: June 21, 2012

Application title: Vehicle Sales Contract Office Application

Purpose: This application uses a Microsoft Word template to allow a car salesperson to create a legal sales contract for a purchased vehicle and provides a loan calculator to calculate monthly payments for the amount financed.

Program Procedures: In a Word document, the user can enter the information about the vehicle being purchased and create a customized legal sales contract. A loan calculator in the Document Actions task pane calculates the cost of the monthly car payment.

Algorithms, Processing, and Conditions:

1. The user first views a Word document that includes a title and a table that displays a car and requests information such as year, make, model, color, price, and customer name. The date of the vehicle purchase should also be requested.
2. The Document Actions task pane should display a loan calculator requesting the interest rate, number of months, and the amount of principle being borrowed for the car.
3. When the user enters the required data and selects the date of purchase, he or she can click a button to display a legal contract including personalized information pertaining to the purchase of the car. The contract should state:

   PARTIES: This agreement is entered into between the Buyer, (Customer Name), and the Seller, RJ Motors, on the date of (Purchase Date).

   VEHICLE: By this agreement in consideration of the representations made and the covenants herein contained, the Seller transfers, bargains, and conveys to Buyer, and Buyer purchases from Seller, the vehicle hereinafter referred to as Vehicle described as follows:

   The vehicle of the year (Year), make of (Make), model of (Model), and the color of (Color) has been purchased by the Buyer for the amount (Vehicle Cost).

4. The salesperson could also enter the interest rate, the number of months in which the loan is repaid, and the amount of principle into the loan calculator to calculate the monthly payments for the car.

Notes and Restrictions:

1. The car price and the car loan may be a different amount based on a down payment.
2. The loan calculator will display the month selections of 12, 24, 36, 48, or 60 months. The user can enter the number of months other than the numbers on the list.

Comments:

1. The picture shown in the window should be selected from a picture available on the Web.

FIGURE EC-44

USE CASE DEFINITION

1. The user enters the year, make, model, color, and price of the vehicle and the customer name into the Word template.
2. The user clicks the Create Contract button to display the contract with personalized information below the Create Contract button.
3. The user enters the rate, length of the loan, and principle into the loan calculator.
4. The user clicks the Compute Payment button on the loan calculator to display loan amount.

FIGURE EC-45

Design the Program Processing Objects

The event planning document for the Vehicle Sales Contract Office application is shown in Figure EC-46.

EVENT PLANNING DOCUMENT

Program Name: Vehicle Sales Contract Office Application	Developer: Corinne Hoisington	Object:	Date: June 21, 2012
OBJECT	**EVENT TRIGGER**	**EVENT PROCESSING**	
ThisDocument_Startup	Execute the application	Documents Actions task pane opens on the right side of the Word template	
btnContract	Click	Ensure all information is entered Ensure the price is numeric Ensure a date is selected from the DateTimePicker Convert the price to a Decimal Display the Parties portion of the contract Display the Vehicle portion of the contract Display the Details portion of the contract	
btnCompute (Actions Pane Control)	Click	Ensure the number of months is selected Ensure the rate is numeric Ensure the loan amount is numeric Convert the rate to a Decimal and move the decimal place two positions to the left Convert the loan amount to a Decimal Convert the number of months to a Decimal Calculate the monthly payments with the Pmt function Display the monthly payment	

FIGURE EC-46

Guided Program Development

To design the user interface for the Vehicle Sales Contract Office application and enter the code required to process each event in the program, complete the following steps:

NOTE TO THE LEARNER

As you will recall, in the following activity, you should complete the tasks within the specified steps. Each of the tasks is accompanied by a Hint Screen. The purpose of the Hint Screen is to indicate where in the Visual Studio window you should perform the activity; it also serves as a reminder of the method that you should use to create the user interface or enter code. If you need further help completing the step, refer to the figure number identified by the term ref: in the step.

Guided Program Development

Phase 1: Design the Form

1

▶ **Create a New Office Project** Open Visual
Studio using the Start button on the Windows
taskbar and the All Programs submenu. Close
the Start Page. Click the New Project button
on the Standard toolbar. Select and expand
Visual Basic in the Project types list; select
Office in the left pane; select Word 2007
Template in the right (Templates) pane; name
the project VehicleSalesContract in the Name
text box; click the OK button in the New Project
dialog box *(ref: Figure EC-3)*.

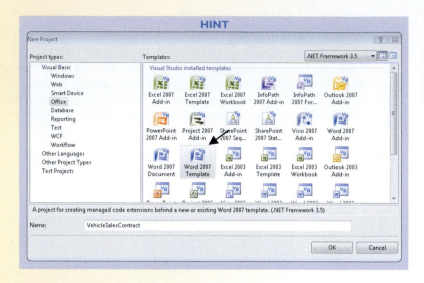

▶ **Select a Document for the Application** The
Visual Studio Tools for Office Project Wizard is
displayed. In the Wizard dialog box, select the
Create a new document radio button. Click the
OK button in the dialog box *(ref: Figure EC-4)*.

▶ **Name the Visual Basic File** The Visual
Studio Office for Tools window opens in Design
view. Notice the tab on the Windows Form object shows VehicleSalesContract.dotx, designat-
ing the document as a template. Rename the
ThisDocument.vb file in the Solution Explorer
by right-clicking the file name and then
clicking Rename in the shortcut menu. Type
`frmContractDocument.vb` and press the
ENTER key.

Guided Program Development *(continued)*

▶ **Design the Word Template** Close the Toolbox. Using the Word Home tab on the Ribbon, change the font to Lucida Console and the font size to 18. Click the Center button, and then type Vehicle Sales Contract on the first line of the document. Press the ENTER key.

HINT

Vehicle Sales Contract

▶ **Add a Border to the Title** Select the words Vehicle Sales Contract, click the Border button arrow, and then click Borders and Shading. On the Borders tabbed page of the Borders and Shading dialog box, click Shadow in the Setting list. Click the Shading tab, click the Fill list arrow, and then click Dark Blue, Text 2, Lighter 60%. Click the OK button, and then press the ENTER key to insert another blank line after the heading.

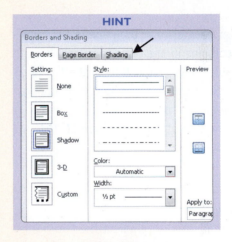

HINT

▶ **Create a Table** Click the Insert tab, click the Table button, and then drag to select a table with three columns and one row *(ref: Figure EC-14)*.

HINT

(continues)

Guided Program Development (continued)

▶ **Add a Picture** Download and save the car.jpg image file from scsite.com/vb2008/ec/images. Store it in a location you can remember. Click the first cell in the table. Click the Insert tab, and then click the Picture button in the Illustrations group. From the location where you saved the car.jpg file, insert it in the first cell of the table *(ref: Figure EC-17)*.

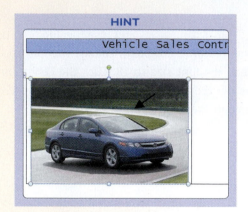

▶ **Add Rows to the Table** Drag across the two rightmost columns in the table to select them. Click the Table Tools Layout tab. In the Merge group, click Split Cells. In the Split Cells dialog box, use the arrows to select 2 columns and 6 rows. Click the OK button *(ref: Figure EC-19)*.

▶ **Enter Text in the Table** Select the two rightmost columns in the Word table. Change the font to Lucida Console, size 14. Click the top table cell in the center column. Type `Year:` and then press the DOWN ARROW key. Type `Make:` and then press the DOWN ARROW key. Enter `Model:`, `Color:`, `Price:`, and `Customer:` in the remaining center cells in the table.

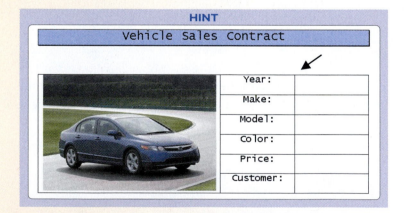

Guided Program Development (continued)

▶ **Format the Table** Click anywhere in the table except the car image, then click the Table Tools Design tab. In the Table Styles group, click the More button (the third arrow). Scroll down and click Medium Grid 3 - Accent 1 *(ref: Figure EC-22).*

▶ **Change the Text Alignment in the Table** Click the Table Tools Layout tab. Select the text in the table, click the Alignment button, and then click Align Center Left.

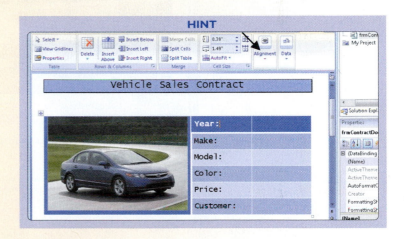

(continues)

Guided Program Development (continued)

The title and table occupy the top of the Word template (Figure EC-47).

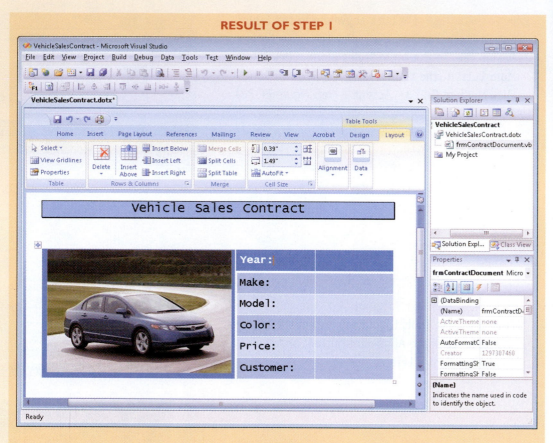

RESULT OF STEP 1

FIGURE EC-47

2

▶ **Add TextBox Objects to the Table** Open the Toolbox. If necessary, scroll so the rightmost column of the table is visible. Click the top cell in the right column to select it. Drag a TextBox .NET component from the Visual Basic Toolbox into the top cell in the third column of the table. In the Properties window for the TextBox object, name the TextBox object txtYear. Change the Font property for the TextBox object to Lucida Console, size 14. Clear the Text property for the txtYear TextBox object. Resize the txtYear TextBox object horizontally to fit in the table cell. Click the Table Tools Layout tab, click Alignment, click Cell Margins, and then change the default cell margin for the left and right to 0".

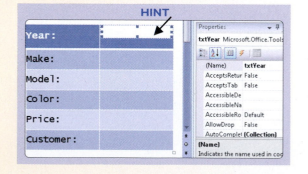

HINT

Guided Program Development *(continued)*

▶ **Use Copy and Paste to Add Five More TextBox Objects** With the TextBox in the rightmost top cell of the table selected, right-click the TextBox object and click Copy on the shortcut menu. Right-click in the next cell down in the rightmost column, and then click Paste on the shortcut menu. Repeat this process for each of the other four cells in the right column of the table. Change the (Name) property for the TextBox on the second row in the third column to `txtMake`. Change the names of the remaining TextBox objects to `txtModel`, `txtColor`, `txtPrice`, and `txtCustomer`. Note that the copied TextBox objects assume the same properties of the TextBox object that was copied. Therefore, the Font property is Lucida Console, size 14, and the alignment is Align Center Left.

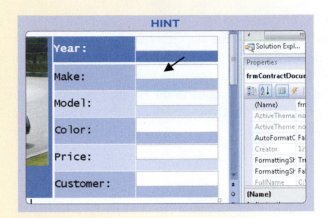

▶ **Add a DateTimePicker Object** Insert a blank line below the table, and then type `Vehicle Purchase Date:` in Lucida Console, size 14. Press the ENTER key. Click the Center button on the Formatting toolbar. Drag the DateTimePicker .NET component from the Toolbox to below the Vehicle Purchase Date title. Name the DateTimePicker object `datPurchaseDate`. Click the Center button on the Formatting toolbar to center the DateTimePicker object. Change the Font property to Times New Roman, size 10 *(ref: Figure EC-9)*.

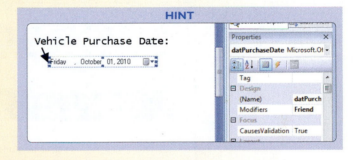

▶ **Add a Button Object** Click to the right of the DateTimePicker object and press the ENTER key. Place a Button object below the DateTimePicker object. Name the Button `btnContract`. Change the Text property of the Button object to `Create Contract`. Change the Font property to Lucida Console, bold, size 11. Resize the button to show the entire button text.

(continues)

Guided Program Development (continued)

▶ **Add Three Labels to Display the Contract** Press the ENTER key to insert a blank line after the Create Contract button. Drag three Label objects below btnContract. Name the three labels lblParties, lblVehicle, and lblDetails. Clear the Text property in each Label object. Resize each Label object to the Height property of 55 and the Width property of 400. Change the font for the three Labels to Times New Roman, size 12.

The DateTimePicker, Button, and Label objects are included in the Word template (Figure EC-48). The first Label object displayed in Figure EC-51 is selected, as shown by the outline.

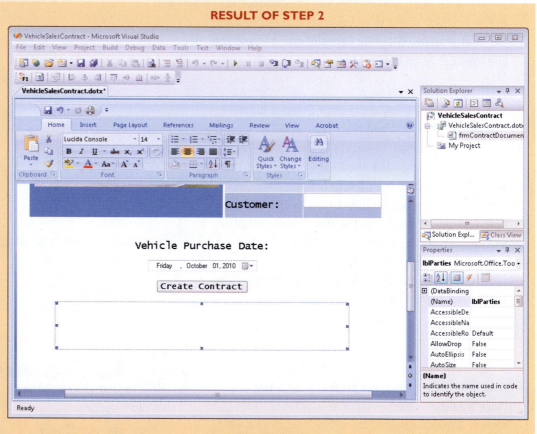

RESULT OF STEP 2

FIGURE EC-48

Guided Program Development (continued)

3

▶ **Add the Actions Pane Control** To add the
Actions Pane Control to the application, click
Project on the menu bar and then click Add New
Item on the Project menu.

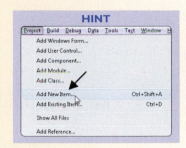

▶ **Add the Actions Pane Control** Click the
Actions Pane Control template, and then click
the Add button *(ref: Figure EC-28)*.

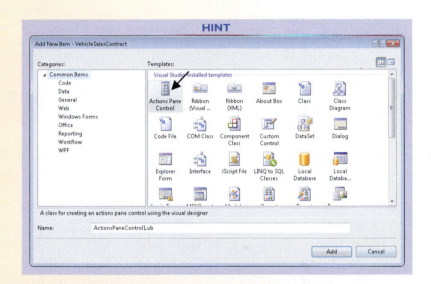

▶ **Resize the Actions Pane Control** Change the
Size property of the Actions Pane Control to
190, 500.

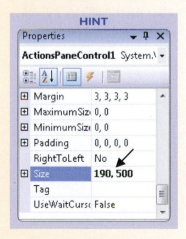

(continues)

Guided Program Development (continued)

► **Place Objects on Actions Pane Control** Place the objects shown in the adjacent hint screen on the Actions Pane Control by dragging them from the Toolbox and selecting the properties shown in the adjacent hint screen. To center all the objects, click Format on the menu bar, point to Center in Form, and click Horizontally on the submenu. Arrange the items to resemble the adjacent screen.

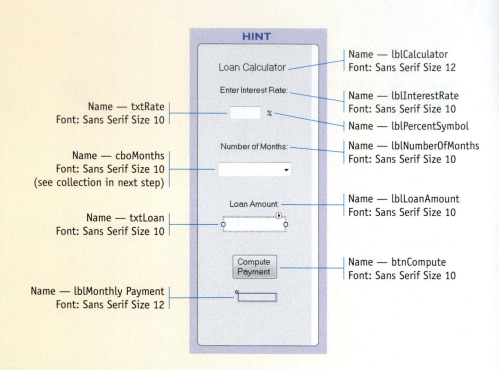

Name — txtRate
Font: Sans Serif Size 10

Name — cboMonths
Font: Sans Serif Size 10
(see collection in next step)

Name — txtLoan
Font: Sans Serif Size 10

Name — lblMonthly Payment
Font: Sans Serif Size 12

HINT

Loan Calculator

Enter Interest Rate:

%

Number of Months:

Loan Amount:

Compute Payment

Name — lblCalculator
Font: Sans Serif Size 12

Name — lblInterestRate
Font: Sans Serif Size 10

Name — lblPercentSymbol

Name — lblNumberOfMonths
Font: Sans Serif Size 10

Name — lblLoanAmount
Font: Sans Serif Size 10

Name — btnCompute
Font: Sans Serif Size 10

► **Add a Collection to the ComboBox Object** Select the cboMonths ComboBox object and click to the right of the Items property in the Properties window. Click the ellipsis button. In the String Collection Editor dialog box, type the number of months for the loan, pressing ENTER after each number: 12, 24, 36, 48, and 60. Click the OK button.

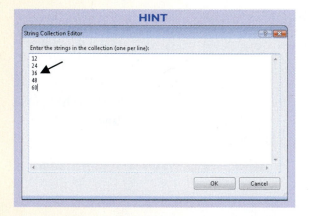

HINT

String Collection Editor

Enter the strings in the collection (one per line):

12
24
36
48
60

OK   Cancel

Guided Program Development *(continued)*

The user interface is completed (Figure EC-49).

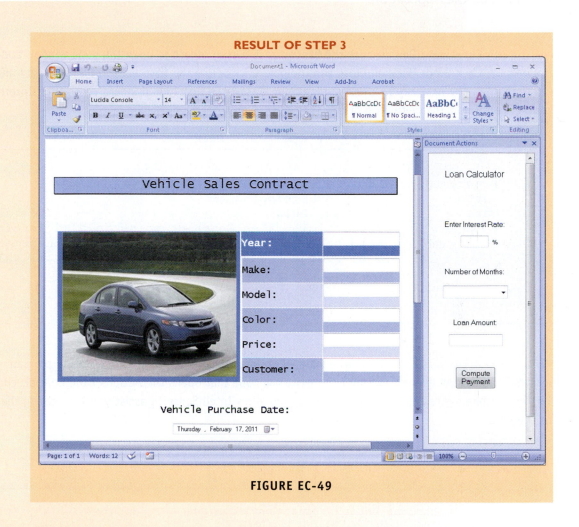

RESULT OF STEP 3

FIGURE EC-49

(continues)

Guided Program Development (continued)

Phase 2: Code the Application

4

▶ **Code the Comments** Double-click the btnContract Button object to open the code window and create the btnContract_Click Event Handler. Close the Toolbox. Click before the first word in Public Class frmContractDocument, and then press the ENTER key to create a blank line. Insert the first four standard comments. Insert the command Option Strict On at the beginning of the code to turn on strict type checking.

HINT

```
1 ' Program Name: Vehicle Sales Contract Word Application
2 ' Author:       Corinne Hoisington
3 ' Date:         June 30, 2012
4 ' Purpose:      The Vehicle Sales Contract opens in a Microsoft
5 '               Word template and requests the vehicle information of
6 '               a newly purchased vehicle to create a legal sales contract.
7
8 Option Strict On
```

▶ **Open the Actions Pane Control** When the Word document template is opened during program execution, the Actions Pane Control also should open. To write the code that opens the Actions Pane Control, click inside the ThisDocument_Startup method, type me., and allow IntelliSense to assist you in entering the rest of the code for the line.

HINT

```
12    Private Sub ThisDocument_Startup(ByVal sender As Object, ByVal e As System.
      EventArgs) Handles Me.Startup
13        'Opens the Actions Pane Control on the Word document
14
15        Me.ActionsPane.Controls.Add(New ActionsPaneControl1)
16
17    End Sub
```

Guided Program Development (continued)

▶ **Code the Document Actions Task Pane** Click the ActionsPaneControl1.vb [Design] tab and then double-click the Compute Payment button to open the code editing window and create the btnCompute_Click event handler. Code a comment to explain the purpose of the event handler. Enter the code to initialize the variables used on the Loan Calculator on the Actions Pane Control.

HINT

```
 1 Public Class ActionsPaneControl1
 2
 3     Private Sub btnCompute_Click(ByVal sender As System.Object, ByVal e As System.    ↙
       EventArgs) Handles btnCompute.Click
 4         ' The event handler opens when the user clicks the Compute Payment
 5         ' button in the Actions Pane. It calculates a monthly payment for
 6         ' a loan amount based on the length of the loan and the interest rate.
 7
 8         ' Declare variables
 9         Dim decRate As Decimal
10         Dim decPeriod As Decimal
11         Dim decPrinciple As Decimal
12         Dim decMonthlyPayments As Decimal
13         Dim decMoveDecimal As Decimal = 100D
14         Dim decTwelveMonths As Decimal = 12D
15         Dim blnPeriodIsValid As Boolean = False
```

▶ **Validate the Input from the Loan Calculator Is Numeric** Before the monthly payment is calculated, write the code to call the procedure that checks if a valid loan period has been selected or entered and then returns the loan period as a decimal value. Then, write an If statement to check if the txtRate is numeric, the txtLoan is numeric, and the loan period is valid.

HINT

```
17         CheckPeriodValidity(blnPeriodIsValid, decPeriod)
18         If IsNumeric(Me.txtRate.Text) And IsNumeric(Me.txtLoan.Text) _
19             And blnPeriodIsValid Then
```

▶ **Convert the Rate into a Decimal Amount** Inside the Then clause of the If statement, write the code to convert the value in txtRate to a Decimal data type and then divide the value by the value (100) in the decMoveDecimal variable to convert an amount such as 9.25% to .925.

HINT

```
20             decRate = Convert.ToDecimal(Me.txtRate.Text) / decMoveDecimal
```

(continues)

Guided Program Development (continued)

▶ **Convert the Loan Amount to a Decimal Value** The loan amount in the Text property of the txtLoan TextBox object must be converted from a String data type to a Decimal data type so it can be used in an arithmetic operation. Place the decimal value in the variable named decPrinciple. Write the code to accomplish this processing.

HINT

```
21          decPrinciple = Convert.ToDecimal(Me.txtLoan.Text)
```

▶ **Calculate the Monthly Payment** Write the statement to use the Pmt function to calculate the monthly car payment *(ref: Figure EC-38)*.

HINT

```
23          decMonthlyPayments = Convert.ToDecimal(Pmt(decRate / _
24              decTwelveMonths, decPeriod, decPrinciple))
```

▶ **Display the Monthly Payment** Write the statement to display the monthly loan payment in the lblMonthlyPayment Label object.

HINT

```
25          Me.lblMonthlyPayment.Text = decMonthlyPayments.ToString("C")
```

Guided Program Development (continued)

▶ **Display an Error Message Box if the Input Values Are Not Valid** If the rate, loan amount, or months selection is in error, a message box must be displayed informing the user of the error. In the Else clause of the If statement that checks these values, write the code to display a message box.

HINT

```
26          Else
27              MsgBox("The Input Entries on the Loan Calculator are Not Valid", , _
28                  "Error Message")
29          End If
```

▶ **Write the Sub Procedure to Ensure the Loan Period is Valid** To ensure the user either entered a value in the cboMonths ComboBox object or selected a value in the list, the first If statement must test if the SelectedItem property contains a null string. If so, either the user entered a value in the Text property or no selection has been made. If the Text property contains a numeric value, then the entry is valid; the value should be converted to a decimal value and the Boolean variable passed ByRef should be set to true. If the Text property is not numeric, an invalid entry was made and the Boolean variable should be set to False. If the SelectedItem property is not a null string, then a selection was made in the list, so the SelectedItem should be converted to a decimal value and the Boolean variable should be set to true. Write the code to implement this Sub procedure *(ref: Figure EC-35)*.

HINT

```
33      Private Sub CheckPeriodValidity(ByRef blnValidity As Boolean, ByRef decMonths As    ↙
        Decimal)
34          If Me.cboMonths.SelectedItem = "" Then
35              If IsNumeric(Me.cboMonths.Text) Then
36                  decMonths = Convert.ToDecimal(Me.cboMonths.Text)
37                  blnValidity = True
38              Else
39                  blnValidity = False
40              End If
41          Else
42              decMonths = Convert.ToDecimal(Me.cboMonths.SelectedItem)
43              blnValidity = True
44          End If
45      End Sub
```

(continues)

Guided Program Development (continued)

The code for the click event of the Compute Payment Button for the Actions Pane Control is completed (Figure EC-50).

RESULT OF STEP 4

```vb
1  Public Class ActionsPaneControl1
2
3      Private Sub btnCompute_Click(ByVal sender As System.Object, ByVal e As System.
   EventArgs) Handles btnCompute.Click
4          ' The event handler opens when the user clicks the Compute button
5          ' in the Actions Pane. It calculates a monthly payment for a loan
6          ' amount based on the length of the loan and the interest rate.
7
8          ' Declare variables
9          Dim decRate As Decimal
10         Dim decPeriod As Decimal
11         Dim decPrinciple As Decimal
12         Dim decMonthlyPayments As Decimal
13         Dim decMoveDecimal As Decimal = 100D
14         Dim decTwelveMonths As Decimal = 12D
15         Dim blnPeriodIsValid As Boolean = False
16
17         ' Validate that numeric values are entered on the Loan Calculator
18         CheckPeriodValidity(blnPeriodIsValid, decPeriod)
19         If IsNumeric(Me.txtRate.Text) And IsNumeric(Me.txtLoan.Text) _
20             And blnPeriodIsValid Then
21            decRate = Convert.ToDecimal(Me.txtRate.Text) / decMoveDecimal
22            decPrinciple = Convert.ToDecimal(Me.txtLoan.Text)
23            decMonthlyPayments = Convert.ToDecimal(Pmt(decRate / _
24                decTwelveMonths, decPeriod, decPrinciple))
25            Me.lblMonthlyPayment.Text = decMonthlyPayments.ToString("C")
26         Else
27            MsgBox("The Input Entries on the Loan Calculator are Not Valid", , _
28                "Error Message")
29         End If
30
31      End Sub
32
33      Private Sub CheckPeriodValidity(ByRef blnValidity As Boolean, ByRef decMonths As
   Decimal)
34         If Me.cboMonths.SelectedItem = "" Then
35            If IsNumeric(Me.cboMonths.Text) Then
36                decMonths = Convert.ToDecimal(Me.cboMonths.Text)
37                blnValidity = True
38            Else
39                blnValidity = False
40            End If
41         Else
42            decMonths = Convert.ToDecimal(Me.cboMonths.SelectedItem)
43            blnValidity = True
44         End If
45      End Sub
46  End Class
47
```

FIGURE EC-50

Guided Program Development (continued)

5

▶ **Code the Vehicle Contract** Open the VehicleSalesContract.dotx Design window and double-click the Create Contract button. In the btnContract_Click Event, write the comments that explain the processing in the event handler. Then, write the code to initialize the variable that will contain the vehicle cost.

HINT

```
22      Private Sub btnContract_Click(ByVal sender As System.Object, ByVal e As System.    ↙
        EventArgs) Handles btnContract.Click
23          ' The btnContract_Click Event displays a legal contract
24
25          ' Declare Variable
26          Dim vehicleCost As Decimal
```

▶ **Validate All Entries Are Entered** Write the If statement to test the two numeric TextBox objects, txtYear and txtPrice, to confirm their values are numeric; test the TextBox objects txtMake, txtModel, and txtColor to validate that the objects do not contain empty strings; and test the DateTimePicker object to confirm that its value is not an empty string.

HINT

```
28          If IsNumeric(Me.txtYear.Text) And Me.txtMake.Text <> "" And _
29              Me.txtModel.Text <> "" And Me.txtColor.Text <> "" And _
30              IsNumeric(Me.txtPrice.Text) And Me.txtCustomer.Text <> "" And _
31              Me.datPurchaseDate.Value.ToString() <> "" Then
```

▶ **Convert the Price to a Decimal Data Type** Write the statement to convert the price of the car to a Decimal data type. Another way to convert data types is to use the Parse command. You can use Parse in the syntax Decimal.Parse(variable name). If you are converting an Integer, the syntax is Integer.Parse(variable name).

HINT

```
32          ' Converts the txtPrice to a Decimal - Parse is supported in VSTO Word
33          vehicleCost = Decimal.Parse(Me.txtPrice.Text)
```

Guided Program Development (continued)

▶ **Display the Legal Contract** Write the code to display the legal contract in the lblParties, lblVehicle, and lblDetails Label objects.

HINT

```
34          Me.lblParties.Text = "PARTIES: This agreement is entered into " _
35              & "between the Buyer, " & Me.txtCustomer.Text _
36              & ", and the Seller, RJ Motors, on the date of " _
37              & Me.datPurchaseDate.Text & "."
38          Me.lblVehicle.Text = "VEHICLE: By this agreement, in consideration " _
39              & "of the representations made and the covenants herein " _
40              & "contained, the Seller transfers, bargains, and " _
41              & "conveys to Buyer, and Buyer purchases from Seller, " _
42              & "the vehicle hereinafter referred to as Vehicle " _
43              & "described as follows:"
44          Me.lblDetails.Text = "The vehicle of the year " & _
45              Me.txtYear.Text & ", make of " & Me.txtMake.Text _
46              & ", model of " & txtModel.Text & ", and the color of " _
47              & Me.txtColor.Text & " has been purchased by the " _
48              & "Buyer for the amount " & vehicleCost.ToString("C") & "."
```

▶ **Write the Else Portion of the If Statement** After the Then processing for the If statement is completed, you must write the Else portion of the If statement. An error message box must be displayed if any of the values are incorrect in the document text boxes. Write the code for the Else portion of the If statement.

HINT

```
49      Else
50          MsgBox("Complete the Table and Select a Date", , "Error Message")
51      End If
```

Guided Program Development (continued)

▶ **Run the Application** When a Word document opens, fill in the information and create the contract.

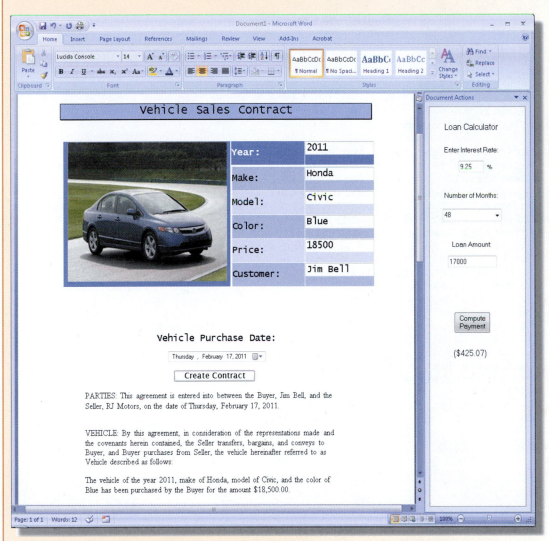

FIGURE EC-51

(continues)

Guided Program Development *(continued)*

The code for the click event of the Create Contract button for the Actions Pane Control is completed (Figure EC-52).

RESULT OF STEP 5

```
22  Private Sub btnContract_Click(ByVal sender As System.Object, ByVal e As System.
        EventArgs) Handles btnContract.Click
23          ' The btnContract_Click Event displays a legal contract
24
25          ' Declare Variable
26          Dim vehicleCost As Decimal
27
28          If IsNumeric(Me.txtYear.Text) And Me.txtMake.Text <> "" And _
29              Me.txtModel.Text <> "" And Me.txtColor.Text <> "" And _
30                IsNumeric(Me.txtPrice.Text) And Me.txtCustomer.Text <> "" And _
31                Me.datPurchaseDate.Value.ToString() <> "" Then
32            ' Converts the txtPrice to a Decimal - Parse is supported in VSTO Word
33            vehicleCost = Decimal.Parse(Me.txtPrice.Text)
34            Me.lblParties.Text = "PARTIES: This agreement is entered into " _
35                & "between the Buyer, " & Me.txtCustomer.Text _
36                & ", and the Seller, RJ Motors, on the date of " _
37                & Me.datPurchaseDate.Text & "."
38            Me.lblVehicle.Text = "VEHICLE: By this agreement, in consideration " _
39                & "of the representations made and the covenants herein " _
40                & "contained, the Seller transfers, bargains, and " _
41                & "conveys to Buyer, and Buyer purchases from Seller, " _
42                & "the vehicle hereinafter referred to as Vehicle " _
43                & "described as follows:"
44            Me.lblDetails.Text = "The vehicle of the year " & _
45                Me.txtYear.Text & ", make of " & Me.txtMake.Text _
46                & ", model of " & txtModel.Text & ", and the color of " _
47                & Me.txtColor.Text & " has been purchased by the " _
48                & "Buyer for the amount " & vehicleCost.ToString("C") & "."
49          Else
50            MsgBox("Complete the Table and Select a Date", , "Error Message")
51          End If
52
53      End Sub
```

FIGURE EC-52

Summary

In this chapter you have learned to create an Office application using Visual Studio Tools for Office. The items listed in Figure EC-53 include all the new Visual Studio and Visual Basic skills you have learned in this chapter.

VISUAL BASIC SKILLS		
Skill	**Figure Number**	**Web Address for Video**
Examine the Vehicle Sales Contract chapter project application	Figure EC-1	scsite.com/vb2008/ec/figureEC-1
Create a Visual Studio Tools for Office application	Figure EC-3	scsite.com/vb2008/ec/figureEC-3
Add a DateTimePicker object to a Form object	Figure EC-9	
Add a table to a Word document	Figure EC-14	scsite.com/vb2008/ec/figureEC-14
Add an image to a Word table	Figure EC-17	scsite.com/vb2008/ec/figureEC-17
Apply Table Styles to format a table	Figure EC-22	scsite.com/vb2008/ec/figureEC-22
Manually code an ActionsPane object	Figure EC-25	scsite.com/vb2008/ec/figureEC-25
Place an ActionsPane object in the Word window to add an Actions Pane Control item	Figure EC-28	scsite.com/vb2008/ec/figureEC-28
Code a ComboBox object on an application	Figure EC-34	
Use the Pmt Function	Figure EC-36	
Use Math Class Functions	Figure EC-41	

FIGURE EC-53

Learn It Online

Start your browser and visit scsite.com/vb2008/ec. Follow the instructions in the exercises below.

1. **Chapter Reinforcement TF, MC, SA** Click one of the Chapter Reinforcement links for Multiple Choice, True/False, or Short Answer below the Learn It Online heading. Answer each question and submit to your instructor.

2. **Practice Test** Click the Practice Test link below the Enrichment Chapter. Answer each question, enter your first and last name at the bottom of the page, and then click the Grade Test button. When the graded practice test is displayed on your screen, submit the graded practice test to your instructor. Continue to take the practice test until you are satisfied with your score.

3. **Crossword Puzzle Challenge** Click the Crossword Puzzle Challenge link below the Learn It Online heading. Read the instructions, and then click the Continue button. Work the crossword puzzle. When you are finished, click the Submit button. When the crossword puzzle is redisplayed, submit it to your instructor.

Knowledge Check

1. Which Office programs can be programmed using VSTO 2008?

2. Office 2007 no longer has menu bars and toolbars. What does Office 2007 primarily use for navigation?

3. What is the name of the VB control that can be placed in the task pane on the right side of an Office window?

4. What is the difference between a Word document and a Word template?

5. What is the file extension for a Word document?

6. What is the file extension for a Word template?

7. Write a line of code that displays the Actions Pane Control on the right side of a window.

8. What procedure should the code for question #7 use?

9. Write a line of code that displays the day of the week determined by a DateTimePicker object named datPayDay in a Label object named lblWeekDay.

10. Write a line of code that displays the date chosen by the user in a DateTimePicker object named datReservation. Print the following sentence in a Label object named lblPlaneReservation. "Your flight will depart on _____ (date chosen)".

11. Rewrite the command line shown in Figure EC-54 with the ^ symbol.

```
me.lblDisplay.Text = Math.Pow(4.0, 3.0)
```

FIGURE EC-54

12. Variables should be of the Integer data type to use the Math class methods. True or false?

13. You can place VB controls in a Word table. True or false?

14. Write the statement that assigns the square root of 81.0 to a Label object named lblSquareRoot.

Knowledge Check

15. The formula that computes the area of a circle is Pi * radius². Write a VB equation using two Math class methods to compute the area of a circle. Assign this statement to the variable decCircleArea. The radius variable is decCircleRadius.

16. Write a statement that assigns the smaller of two numbers (8.3 and 2.9) to a variable named decLessNumber.

17. Write a line of code that computes the cost of a loan payment made over 15 years for a home mortgage of $175,000 at an interest rate of 6.8%. Assign the payment amount to a variable named decPaymentAmount.

18. Write a line of code that computes the cost of a loan payment for a gaming computer system made over two years for a loan amount of $5000 at 8.9%. Assign the monthly payment amount to a variable named decGameComputer.

19. Write a line of code that computes the amount of money that you need to invest to save $10,000 for a kitchen makeover for your home. You will invest a monthly amount for the next five years at an interest rate of 4% at the beginning of each month. Assign your monthly investment amount to a variable named decKitchenRedo.

20. What is the name of the Math class that computes the absolute value of any number?

Debugging Exercises

1. Rewrite the code shown in Figure EC-55 correctly:

```
Dim firstValue As Integer = 29.25
MsgBox(Math.Round(firstValue)
```

FIGURE EC-55

2. Rewrite the code shown in Figure EC-56 correctly:

```
' The following statement computes a loan
' for 6 years, $16,000 at 12%
loanPayment = Pmt(0.12, 6, 16000)
```

FIGURE EC-56

3. Rewrite the code shown in Figure EC-57 correctly:

```
MsgBox(Math.Max(decFirstValue, decSecondValue, decThirdValue)
```

FIGURE EC-57

Program Analysis

In exercises 1 – 8, evaluate the expression to find the resulting value:

1. Math.Sqrt(16.0)

2. Math.Round(−2.45)

3. Math.Abs(−5.999)

Program Analysis

(continued)

4. Math.Ceiling(5.01)

5. Math.Floor(−2.2)

6. Math.Max(Math.PI, 3.4)

7. Math.Pow(4.0, 2.0)

8. Math.Min(1.9, Math.E)

9. Determine the output that is displayed in the ListBox object according to the code shown in Figure EC-58:

```
Dim startValue As Decimal
decStartValue = 8.0
Me.lstDisplay.Add(decStartValue)
Me.lstDisplay.Add(Math.Pow(decStartValue, 3.0))
Me.lstDisplay.Add(Math.Ceiling(decStartValue + 0.56))
Me.lstDisplay.Add(Math.Pow(Math.PI, 2.14))
Me.lstDisplay.Add(Math.Max(decStartValue, 7.99))
```

FIGURE EC-58

10. Determine the output that is displayed in the ListBox object according to the code shown in Figure EC-59:

```
Dim decMonthlyPayment As Decimal
decMonthlyPayment = Pmt(0.08 / 12, 7 * 12, 50000)
Me.lstMortgage.Add(decMonthlyPayment.ToString("C"))
```

FIGURE EC-59

11. Write lines of code for each step to determine the monthly payments for a car loan of $21,095 over 60 months at an interest rate 10.9%.

    a. Declare all the variables for the values given: decPrinciple, decMonths, decRate.

    b. Declare a variable named decLoanPayment to hold the monthly payment.

    c. Compute the payment.

    d. Display the payment in a ListBox named lstDisplayPayment.

12. Write code for each step to determine the largest of three numbers.

    a. Declare three variables named decFirstNum, decSecondNum, decThirdNum, and assign the values 5.2, 3.8, and 12.1 to them

    b. Declare a decimal data type named decTempNum.

    c. Declare a decimal data type named decLargestNum.

    d. Using a Math procedure, assign the larger of the first and second variable to decTempNum.

    e. Using a Math procedure, assign the larger of decTempNum and decThirdNum to decLargestNum.

    f. Display the largest number as a Label named lblBigNumber.

Case Programming Assignments

Complete one or more of the following case programming assignments. Submit the program and materials you create to your instructor. The level of difficulty is indicated for each case programming assignment.

● = Easiest
●● = Intermediate
●●● = Challenging

1 ● REAL ESTATE HOME PURCHASING CONTRACT

Design a VSTO application and write the code that will execute according to the program requirements in Figure EC-60 and the Use Case definition in Figure EC-61. The output is shown in Figure EC-62. Before writing the code, create an event planning document for each event in the program.

REQUIREMENTS DOCUMENT

Date submitted: January 24, 2012

Application title: Home Purchase Contract with a Mortgage Loan Calculator VSTO Application

Purpose: This application uses a Microsoft Word template to allow a real estate agent to create a legal sales contract for property sales and provide a mortgage calculator to calculate monthly payments on the Document Actions task pane.

Program Procedures: In a Word document, the realtor enters the information about the home being purchased and the application creates a home sales contract.

Algorithms, Processing, and Conditions:
1. The realtor first views a Word document that contains a title and a table displaying the home being purchased. The user must enter the home information into the table such as home address, buyer's name, purchase price, city, and state. The date of the closing of the home should also be requested.
2. The right side of the window should display a loan calculator requesting the interest rate, number of months, and the amount of principle being borrowed for the home's mortgage.
3. After entering the required data and selecting the date of closing, the user can click a button to display a legal contract that includes the personalized data of the home purchase.
4. The realtor also can enter data into the loan calculator on the task pane on the right side of the Word window to calculate the monthly payment for the home.

Notes and Restrictions:
1. The home price and the mortgage amount may be different based on the down payment.
2. The mortgage calculator should allow the loan to be paid over 10, 15, 20, or 30 years.

Comments:
1. The picture shown in the table should be selected from a graphic available on the Web.
2. The completed contract could be printed for the customer to view and keep as a legal receipt of purchase.

FIGURE EC-60

(continues)

Case Programming Assignments

Real Estate Home Purchasing Contract *(continued)*

USE CASE DEFINITION

1. User (realtor) enters the home address, buyer's name, purchase price, city, and state. A DateTimePicker object allows the user to select the date of the home closing.
2. User clicks the Create Contract button and the contract with personalized information is printed below the Create Contract button.
3. User enters values into the mortgage loan calculator. (This could also be completed before entering home information.)
4. User clicks the Compute Monthly Payments button on the loan calculator to display the loan amount.

FIGURE EC-61

FIGURE EC-62

Case Programming Assignments

2 ● BUYING A NEW COMPUTER FOR COLLEGE

Design a VSTO application and write the code that will execute according to the program requirements in Figure EC-63 and the Use Case definition in Figure EC-64. The output is shown in Figure EC-65. Before writing the code, create an event planning document for each event in the program.

REQUIREMENTS DOCUMENT

Date submitted: April 1, 2012

Application title: Computer Savings Plan VSTO Application

Purpose: This application uses a Microsoft Word template to allow the user to choose one of two computer systems needed for college. The application will calculate the cost, shipping, and tax for the computer system. The Document Actions task pane will calculate how much money the user needs to finance to purchase this system.

Program Procedures: In a Word document, the college student can select one of two computer systems to purchase.

Algorithms, Processing, and Conditions:
1. The user first views a Word template that contains a title and a table displaying two computer systems, their specifications, and cost. The two systems are based on whether you are a computer major (high-end computer) or any other major (average PC).
2. Allow the user to select one of the two systems.
3. The right side of the window should display a loan calculator requesting the interest rate, number of months, and the amount of principle being borrowed for the computer system.
4. When the user selects the computer system, a total amount is displayed. The tax rate is 6.5% and the shipping cost is $55.00.
5. The user enters the interest rate, number of payments (months), and the amount being borrowed into the loan calculator on the Document Actions task pane on the right side of the window to calculate the monthly payment for the computer.

Notes and Restrictions:
1. The user should only be able to select one of the two computer systems.

Comments:
1. The picture shown in the table should be selected from graphics available on the Web.
2. Research the current costs of computers on the Web to determine the price of the two computer systems.

FIGURE EC-63

(continues)

Case Programming Assignments

Buying a New Computer for College *(continued)*

USE CASE DEFINITION

1. Student selects which of two computer systems will be purchased based on student major.
2. Program displays total cost of the computer.
3. Student enters the interest rate, selects the number of months, and enters the principle into the loan calculator. (This could be completed before selecting the computer information.)
4. Student clicks the Payments button on the loan calculator to display the monthly payment.

FIGURE EC-64

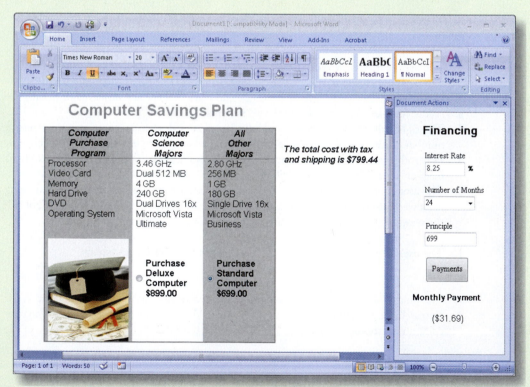

FIGURE EC-65

3 SALES COMMISSION FOR FURNITURE STORE

Design a VSTO application and write the code that will execute according to the program requirements in Figure EC-66 and the Use Case definition in Figure EC-67. The output is shown in Figure EC-68. Before writing the code, create an event planning document for each event in the program.

REQUIREMENTS DOCUMENT

Date submitted: March 4, 2012

Application title: Grand's Furniture Store Commission VSTO Application

Purpose: This application uses a Microsoft Word template to compute the commissions of six employees who work at a furniture store. The application computes the average sales commission, the total sales amount, and the total commission paid rounded to the nearest dollar.

Program Procedures: In a Word template, the store manager can enter the weekly sales amount of the sales people to compute the average sales commission, the total sales amount, and the total commission paid.

Algorithms, Processing, and Conditions:
1. The furniture store manager first views a Word document that contains a title, a table displaying a furniture store logo, and an area for six employee names and their sales amounts. Compute each salesperson's commission based on 7% of the sales amount.
2. The ending day of that week's cycle should also be recorded on the Document Actions task pane.
3. When the user enters the required data, a button can be selected to display the average sales commission, the total sales amount, and the total commission paid. All numbers should be rounded to the closest dollar amount.

Notes and Restrictions:

Comments:
1. The picture shown in the table should be selected from a graphic available on the Web.

FIGURE EC-66

(continues)

Case Programming Assignments

Sales Commission for Furniture Store (continued)

USE CASE DEFINITION

1. The furniture store manager enters the names and sales amounts for six sales people. A DateTimePicker object allows the manager to enter the ending date for this week's commissions.
2. The manager clicks the Compute Weekly Commissions Button object to print the information below the Button object.
3. The manager enters the ending date of the week. (This could be completed before entering commission information.)

FIGURE EC-67

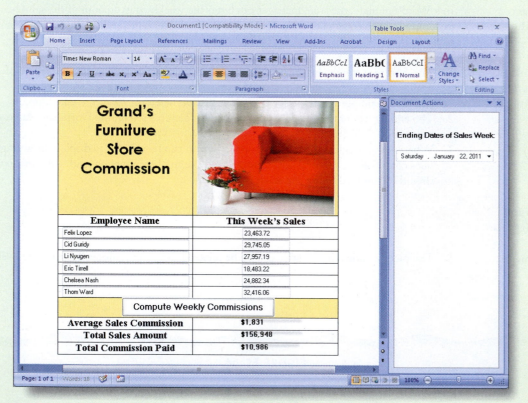

FIGURE EC-68

Case Programming Assignments

4 ●●● FUDGE RECIPE CONVERSION APPLICATION

Design a VSTO application and write the code that will execute according to the program requirements in Figure EC-69. Before designing the user interface, create a Use Case definition. Before writing the code, create an event planning document for each event in the program.

REQUIREMENTS DOCUMENT

Date submitted: June 2, 2012

Application title: Fudge Recipe Conversion VSTO Application

Purpose: This application uses a Microsoft Word document to allow the user to select one of three fudge batch sizes. The application displays a recipe based on the number of servings preferred. The Document Actions task pane displays the calculation of the U.S. measurements of cups, tablespoons, and teaspoons to grams.

Program Procedures: In a Word document, a fudge recipe displays the correct recipe based on the number of servings needed.

Algorithms, Processing, and Conditions:
1. The user first views a Word document that displays a title, a picture of chocolate fudge, and requests the user to select the serving size for 6, 12, or 18 people.
2. Display the recipe based on the amount of servings.
3. The right side of the window should display a gram conversion calculator that converts the U.S. measurements of cups, tablespoons, and teaspoons to grams.

The following recipe is based on serving six people:

INGREDIENTS:

1/4 cup butter	1 teaspoon vanilla
2 cups semisweet chocolate chips (12 ounces)	1/2 cup finely chopped pecans
1 14-oz can sweetened condensed milk	Salt to taste

PREPARATION:
Lightly grease pan. In the top of a double boiler over simmering water, melt the butter and chocolate chips, stirring until smooth. Remove from the heat. Stir in the condensed milk, pecans, vanilla, and salt, stirring until smooth or until firm. Cut into squares.

Notes and Restrictions:
1. The pictures shown in the table should be selected from graphics available on the Web.
2. The following facts are needed for the calculations in the Document Actions task pane:
   1 cup = 229.92 grams
   1 tsp = 4.745 grams
   1 tbsp = 14.235 grams

Comments:

FIGURE EC-69

Case Programming Assignments

5 ●● CAR INSURANCE COSTS

Design a VSTO application and write the code that will execute according to the program requirements in Figure EC-71. Before designing the user interface, create a Use Case definition. Before writing the code, create an event planning document for each event in the program.

Based on Edmunds.com, the table shown in Figure EC-70 displays the five best insurance rates in the industry.

Make	Model	Style	5 Year Insurance Rate	Vehicle Cost
Chrysler	PT Cruiser	4dr Wagon (2.4L 4cyl 5M)	$4,240	$17,490
GMC	Safari	SLE AWD 3dr Minivan (4.3L 6cyl 4A)	$4,298	$27,440
Dodge	Caravan	SE 4dr Minivan (2.4L 4cyl 4A)	$4,357	$21,130
Saturn	ION	1 4dr Sedan (2.2L 4cyl 5M)	$4,373	$10,430
Pontiac	Sunfire	2dr Coupe (2.2L 4cyl 5M)	$4,389	$14,930

FIGURE EC-70

(continues)

Case Programming Assignments

Car Insurance Costs (continued)

REQUIREMENTS DOCUMENT

Date submitted: May 11, 2012

Application title: Finding the Best Insurance Rates VSTO Application

Purpose: This application uses a Microsoft Word template to determine which cars have the best insurance rates. Customers often call the insurance company requesting the best insurance rates on new vehicles. The Document Actions task pane displays a loan calculator to determine the monthly payments for a car payment.

Program Procedures: In a Word template, the insurance agent can find which cars have the lowest insurance rates based on safety tests.

Algorithms, Processing, and Conditions:
1. When a customer calls the insurance agent, a Word template can be opened that displays a ComboBox object containing the make and model of five vehicles with the best insurance rates this year. When a car is selected, a table displays a picture of a car, make, model, style, five-year insurance costs, and purchase price.
2. A Find Lowest button also compares all the insurance costs and displays the result in the table.
3. The Document Actions task pane displays five radio buttons with the names of these five vehicles. Allow the user to select the model and make of the car, the interest rate, and a 2, 3, 4, or 5-year loan. The user enters the number of years instead of selecting the number of years from the list. Display an error message if the user enters more than six years or a negative number. The principle to be financed is also entered. Display the monthly payment.

Notes and Restrictions:
1. The picture shown in the table should be selected from a graphic available on the Web.
2. The information is this year's five best insurance rates from *www.edmunds.com*.

Comments:

FIGURE EC-71

Case Programming Assignments

6 •• 401K MATCHING CONTRIBUTION INVESTMENT

Design a VSTO application and write the code that will execute according to the program requirements in Figure EC-72. Before designing the user interface, create a Use Case definition. Before writing the code, create an event planning document for each event in the program.

REQUIREMENTS DOCUMENT

Date submitted:	January 4, 2012
Application title:	401K Employer Matching Contribution Investment VSTO Application
Purpose:	This application uses a Microsoft Word template to allow an employee to see how much their 401K will gain.
Program Procedures:	In a Word template, an employee enters their monthly contribution into a company 401K investment program. The result displays the amount that will be in their account at retirement.

Algorithms, Processing, and Conditions:

1. The employee first views a Word template that displays a title, company logo, a table that requests the employee to enter their name and the monthly amount they want to contribute. When an employer offers 401k matching, they are guaranteeing that they will match a certain percentage of the employee's contributions. The local company common match is 50 cents on the dollar, meaning that if an employee invests one dollar in a 401k plan, the employer will match the contribution by contributing 50 cents. The company is currently giving 6% for an investment interest rate. The table in the Word template also requests the number of years until retirement.
2. After entering the requested information, the employee clicks the Compute 401K Value button. The value of the 401K will be displayed with the employer's matching contribution calculated.
3. The Document Actions task pane should display a loan calculator requesting the interest rate, number of months, and the amount of money invested if you were to invest the same amount without having the matching employer contribution.

Notes and Restrictions:

Comments: The logo shown in the table should be selected from pictures available on the Web.

FIGURE EC-72

Case Programming Assignments

7 ●●●
AZTEC RENTAL AGENCY

Create a requirements document and a Use Case Definition document, and then design a VSTO application based on the following case project. Before writing the code, create an event planning document for each event in the program:

A home project equipment rental store requests a Word application that allows a sales associate to record customer information, the item(s) rented, and the rental duration (full or half day). The table below shows typical rental items. The document will compute the total rental cost. A picture of the item that is being rented will be displayed. The Document Actions task pane will display a calendar allowing the sales associate to select the beginning date of rental.

Items Rented	Half-Day Cost	Full-Day Cost
Sander	$18.00	$30.00
Wallpaper steamer	$15.00	$24.00
Power washer	$21.00	$36.00
Garden tiller	$27.00	$47.00

FIGURE EC-73

(continues)

Case Programming Assignments

8 ●●●
GEOMETRY REVIEW

Create a requirements document and a Use Case Definition document, and then design a VSTO application based on the following case project. Before writing the code, create an event planning document for each event in the program:

A local teacher wants you to create a practice Word template for students to review calculating the circumference of a circle and the hypotenuse of a right triangle. Allow the student to enter the radius of a circle in the Word template and the two sides of a triangle in the Document Actions task pane. Display the results. Research both formulas needed. Use a Math Class Method in each formula.

FIGURE EC-74

9 ●●●
ECONOMIC COST OF LIVING

Create a requirements document and a Use Case Definition document, and then design a VSTO application based on the following case project. Before writing the code, create an event planning document for each event in the program:

A local economist is studying the national problem of the cost of living increase. The current average pay in the United States is $17.77 an hour (U.S. Department of Labor) and has been increasing at 1.9% per year. The cost of living has been increasing at 2.5%. Create a Word template to allow a user to enter a number of years between 5 and 20. Display a ListBox object starting with the present year, average yearly salary (based on 52 weeks a year), and how much you would need to earn per year to keep up with the cost of living increase using the initial average yearly salary as the baseline. Create a Document Actions task pane to allow the user to see the amount they would have in savings if $50 a month were saved over the same period at a four percent interest rate.

FIGURE EC-75

APPENDIX A Unicode

The 256 characters and symbols that are represented by ASCII and EBCDIC codes are sufficient for English and western European languages (see Figure A-1), but do not provide enough characters for Asian and other languages that use different alphabets. Further compounding the problem is that many of these languages use symbols, called ideograms, to represent multiple words and ideas. One solution to the problem of accommodating universal alphabets is Unicode. Unicode is a 16-bit coding scheme that can represent all the world's current, classic, and historical languages in more than 65,000 characters and symbols. In Unicode, 30,000 codes are reserved for future use, such as ancient languages, and 6,000 codes are reserved for private use. Existing ASCII coded data is fully compatible with Unicode because the first 256 codes are the same. Unicode is implemented in several operating systems, including Windows Vista, Windows XP, Mac OS X, and Linux. To view a complete Unicode chart, see *www.unicode.org*.

UNICODE KEYBOARD CHARACTERS				
Decimal	Hexadecimal	Octal	Binary	Character
32	20	040	00100000	
33	21	041	00100001	!
34	22	042	00100010	"
35	23	043	00100010	#
36	24	044	00100100	$
37	25	045	00100101	%
38	26	046	00100110	&
39	27	047	00100111	'
40	28	050	00101000	(
41	29	051	00101001	)

FIGURE A-1 (continues)

Decimal	Hexadecimal	Octal	Binary	Character
42	2A	052	00101010	*
43	2B	053	00101011	+
44	2C	054	00101100	,
45	2D	055	00101101	–
46	2E	056	00101110	.
47	2F	057	00101111	/
48	30	060	00110000	0
49	31	061	00110001	1
50	32	062	00110010	2
51	33	063	00110011	3
52	34	064	00110100	4
53	35	065	00110101	5
54	36	066	00110110	6
55	37	067	00110111	7
56	38	070	00111000	8
57	39	071	00111001	9
58	3A	072	00111010	:
59	3B	073	00111011	;
60	3C	074	00111100	<
61	3D	075	00111101	=
62	3E	076	00111110	>
63	3F	077	00111111	?
64	40	100	01000000	@
65	41	101	01000001	A
66	42	102	01000010	B
67	43	103	01000011	C
68	44	104	01000100	D
69	45	105	01000101	E
70	46	106	01000110	F

FIGURE A-1 (continued)

Decimal	Hexadecimal	Octal	Binary	Character
71	47	107	01000111	G
72	48	110	01001000	H
73	49	111	01001001	I
74	4A	112	01001010	J
75	4B	113	01001011	K
76	4C	114	01001100	L
77	4D	115	01001101	M
78	4E	116	01001110	N
79	4F	117	01001111	O
80	50	120	01010000	P
81	51	121	01010001	Q
82	52	122	01010010	R
83	53	123	01010011	S
84	54	124	01010100	T
85	55	125	01010101	U
86	56	126	01010110	V
87	57	127	01010111	W
88	58	130	01011000	X
89	59	131	01011001	Y
90	5A	132	01011010	Z
91	5B	133	01011011	[
92	5C	134	01011100	\
93	5D	135	01011101	]
94	5E	136	01011110	^
95	5F	137	01011111	]
96	60	140	01100000	,
97	61	141	01100001	a
98	62	142	01100010	b

FIGURE A-1 (continued)

Decimal	Hexadecimal	Octal	Binary	Character
99	63	143	01100011	c
100	64	144	01100100	d
101	65	145	01100101	e
102	66	146	01100110	f
103	67	147	01100111	g
104	68	150	01101000	h
105	69	151	01101001	i
106	6A	152	01101010	j
107	6B	153	01101011	k
108	6C	154	01101100	l
109	6D	155	01101101	m
110	6E	156	01101110	n
111	6F	157	01101111	o
112	70	160	01110000	p
113	71	161	01110001	q
114	72	162	01110010	r
115	73	163	01110011	s
116	74	164	01110100	t
117	75	165	01110101	u
118	76	166	01110110	v
119	77	167	01110111	w
120	78	170	01111000	x
121	79	171	01111001	y
122	7A	172	01111010	z
123	7B	173	01111011	{
124	7C	174	01111100		
125	7D	175	01111101	}
126	7E	176	01111110	~

FIGURE A-1 (continued)

The My Namespace

Rapid application development (RAD) uses a number of tools to help build graphical user interfaces that would normally take a large development effort. One of the Visual Basic RAD tool innovations introduced in the 2005 version and continued with the 2008 version is the **My** namespace. The My namespace provides a shortcut to several categories of information and functionality and is organized so that you can use IntelliSense to find code elements you use often. Microsoft created the My namespace to make it easier to execute common code patterns that you use when developing .NET applications. By providing a shortcut to the most commonly used .NET Framework Class Library classes and methods, the My namespace helps you retrieve settings and resources that your application requires.

The My namespace feature provides rapid access to the classes and methods through the My classes shown in the table in Figure B-1.

Object	Allows Access to
My.Application	The application information and its services such as name, version, log, and current directory.
My.Computer	The host computer and its resources, and services. My.Computer provides access to a number of very important resources including My.Computer.Network, My.Computer.FileSystem, and My.Computer.Printers.
My.Forms	All the forms in the current project.
My.Request	The current Web request.
My.Resources	The resource elements.
My.Response	The current Web response.
My.Settings	The configuration settings of the user and application level. This object enables great personalization without writing many lines of code.

FIGURE B-1 (continues)

Object	Allows Access to
My.User	The security context of the current authenticated user. The My.User object analyzes the user at runtime, which assists security issues.
My.WebServices	The XML Web services referenced by the current project. Consuming Web services is a necessary ability for modern Web applications.

FIGURE B-1 (continued)

Coding Examples

My is an object like Me, but instead of being a self-referencing object, it is a wrapper that makes accessing the advanced features of .NET easier. For example, you can use the class **My.Application** to determine the version of the current application by using the line of code shown in Figure B-2. Figure B-3 shows the dialog box that displays the version number. You often need to know the latest version of the application to determine whether the application is in final form.

```
MsgBox(My.Application.Info.Version.ToString())
```

FIGURE B-2

FIGURE B-3

The **My.Application** class can also be used to display the current setting of the culture of a computer. Figure B-4 shows the code you can use to display the culture, which is the language that the computer has been assigned in the language settings. In Figure B-5, the culture is set to English – United States.

```
MsgBox(My.Application.Culture.ToString())
```

FIGURE B-4

FIGURE B-5

Another class called **My.Computer** can return information about the computer on which the application is deployed, as determined at run time. The My.Computer class provides properties for manipulating computer components such as audio, the clock, the keyboard, and the file system. The My.Computer Class can play .wav files and system sounds using the Audio object. You can use the My.Computer.Audio.Play and My.Computer.Audio.PlaySystemSound methods to play .wav sound files and system sounds. The code shown in Figure B-6 plays a .wav file named beachmusic.wav.

```
My.Computer.Audio.Play("C:\beachmusic.wav")
```

FIGURE B-6

A .wav file can also be played in the background when AudioPlayMode .Background is specified, as shown in Figure B-7.

```
My.Computer.Audio.Play("C:\blues.wav", _
            AudioPlayMode.Background)
```

FIGURE B-7

The My.Computer Class can access the Clipboard and show what is temporarily stored in the system buffer. For example, if you copied the phrase "Examples of the My.Computer Class", the phrase would be stored in the Clipboard system buffer of the computer. Use the code shown in Figure B-8 to display the contents of the Clipboard in a dialog box as shown in Figure B-9.

```
MsgBox(My.Computer.Clipboard.GetText())
```

FIGURE B-8

FIGURE B-9

The My.Computer Class can access an object that provides properties for displaying the current local date and time according to the system clock by entering the code shown in B-10. Figure B-11 shows the dialog box that displays the system date and time.

```
MsgBox(My.Computer.Clock.LocalTime.ToString())
```

FIGURE B-10

FIGURE B-11

Another My.Computer class determines the current state of the keyboard, such as which keys are pressed, including the CAPS LOCK or NUM LOCK key. The code shown in Figure B-12 provides a true result if the CAPS LOCK key has been pressed. Figure B-13 shows the dialog box that displays the result.

```
MsgBox(My.Computer.Keyboard.CapsLock.ToString())
```

FIGURE B-12

FIGURE B-13

The My.Computer.Mouse class allows you to determine the state and hardware characteristics of the attached mouse, such as the number of buttons or whether the mouse has a wheel. The code shown in Figure B-14 determines if the mouse has a wheel, and Figure B-15 shows the dialog box that displays the result.

```
MsgBox(My.Computer.Mouse.WheelExists.ToString())
```

FIGURE B-14

FIGURE B-15

The My.Computer.Network class interacts with the network to which the computer is connected. For example, if the code in Figure B-16 is entered in the code window, the result would be true, as shown in Figure B-17, if the computer is connected to an intranet or Internet network.

```
MsgBox(My.Computer.Network.IsAvailable.ToString())
```

FIGURE B-16

FIGURE B-17

You can use the My.Computer.Network class to ping another computer. Ping is a basic network function that allows you to verify a particular IP address exists and can accept requests. Ping is used diagnostically to ensure that a host computer you are trying to reach is operating. The code shown in Figure B-18 determines if the IP address is active, and the dialog box shown in Figure B-19 displays the result.

```
MsgBox(My.Computer.Network.Ping("71.2.41.1"))
```

FIGURE B-18

FIGURE B-19

The My.Computer.Screen object can be used to determine many properties of the screen connected to the computer system. You can determine the properties of each monitor attached to the computer system, including the name, the brightness of the screen, and the working area size. The number of bits per pixel can be determined by the code shown in Figure B-20. In a digitized image, the number of bits used to represent the brightness contained in each pixel is called bits per pixel. Bits per pixel is a term that represents the brightness of the screen resolution. Figure B-21 shows the result of the code.

```
MsgBox(My.Computer.Screen.BitsPerPixel.ToString())
```

FIGURE B-20

FIGURE B-21

The My.Computer.Screen class can also display the current resolution size of the user screen, as shown in Figures B-22 and B-23.

```
MsgBox(My.Computer.Screen.Bounds.Size.ToString())
```

FIGURE B-22

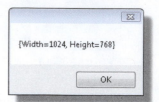

FIGURE B-23

Another class called **My.User** allows you to gather information about the current user. The code example in Figure B-24 shows how to use the **My.User.Name** property to view the user's login name. An application uses Windows authentication by default, so **My.User** returns the Windows information about the user who started the application, as shown in Figure B-25.

```
MsgBox(My.User.Name)
```

FIGURE B-24

FIGURE B-25

The My namespace also provides a simpler way of opening multiple forms in the same project by using the My.Forms object. If the project includes more than one form, the code shown in Figure B-26 opens a second form named Form2.

```
My.Forms.Form2.Show()
```

FIGURE B-26

Using Help in Microsoft Visual Basic 2008

Using the Help features in Visual Basic 2008 can assist you in creating productive code. Help topics are stored in Help collections, which were selected during installation. Be sure you install the MSDN library help files after installing Visual Studio to use the following elements of Help.

Using Dynamic Help

The Help feature in Visual Basic is fully integrated into the integrated development environment (IDE), complete with a Dynamic Help feature that lists relevant topics in a docked window you can display as you work. The Dynamic Help window reacts to what you are coding, so that it provides context-sensitive help. As you are writing a line of code, you can view the Help topics for the current command or object. To open the Dynamic Help window, click Help on the menu bar, and then click Dynamic Help, as shown in Figure C-1.

Dynamic Help on Help menu

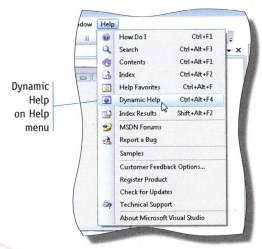

FIGURE C-1

The Dynamic Help window opens on the Properties window in the lower-left corner of the Visual Basic IDE, as shown in Figure C-2.

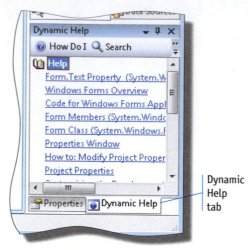

FIGURE C-2

When you first open the Dynamic Help window, it displays generic help about topics such as Visual Basic Language Keywords and How to: Treat Forms as Objects. The Dynamic Help window can also display a list of links to topics related to the current code. The topics can contain procedures for completing a task, a walkthrough designed to introduce new technologies, or programming practices for completing portions of a development effort. Other categories of Dynamic Help include coding samples and related training topics with both local Help files and online assistance. For example, if you were writing the code shown in Figure C-3 in the code window, the contents of the Dynamic Help window change as you type the command My.Computer.Screen, as shown in Figure C-4.

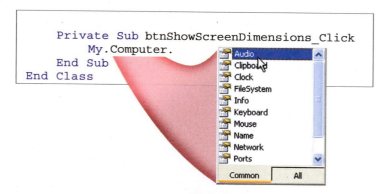

FIGURE C-3

Dynamic Help window

FIGURE C-4

When you click the first Help option in the Dynamic Help window, detailed information about the My.Computer.Screen Property is displayed, as shown in Figure C-5. The information includes Visual Basic coding samples, information on return values, coding requirements, and links to other related Help features.

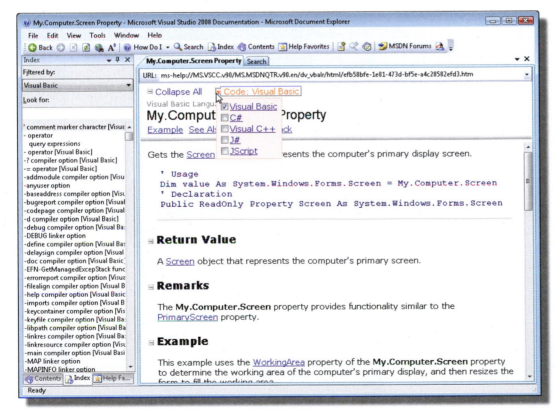

FIGURE C-5

Using the F1 Key to Access Help

The Dynamic Help feature works as you enter commands, but you can also press the
F1 function key to view a Help topic on the command that has the focus in the code
window. For example, when entering a Do Until loop, you could click the Do Until
line in the code window, as shown in Figure C-6, and then press the F1 key.

```
Private  Sub
         Do  Until

         Loop
End  Sub
```

press F1

FIGURE C-6

The Help window opens as shown in Figure C-7, providing detailed information
about the Do Loop statement in Visual Basic.

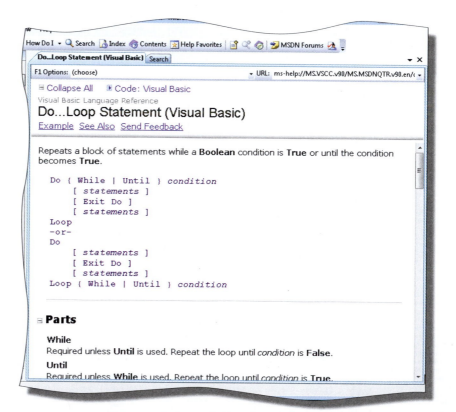

FIGURE C-7

When the Dynamic Help window and F1 Help do not meet your needs, you can use the keyword index, How Do I page, full-text search, and Help contents provided with **Microsoft Document Explorer**. Using the MSDN Library, you can also re-search new technologies. The library includes periodicals and technical articles. In addition, you can choose to search online Help sources, such as the Codezone Community and MSDN Online.

Using the Microsoft Document Explorer

Microsoft Document Explorer provides a way of interacting with the Help topics that are written for Visual Studio 2005. With Microsoft Document Explorer, you can perform the following tasks:

▶ Browse for topics by category using **How Do I**

▶ Search the full text of topics using the **Search** page

▶ Browse coding topic titles using the **Contents** window

▶ Search for topics by keyword using the **Index** window

▶ Bookmark a useful topic in the **Help Favorites** window

Accessing the How Do I Help Topics

When you are using Microsoft Document Explorer, you can open a subject listing of Help topics by using the **How Do I** command. Visual Studio displays Help in the Microsoft Document Explorer How Do I pages with information that contains a static list of detailed information about all four programming languages and all the deployment environments including Windows applications, Smart Device application, ASP.NET 3.5, ADO.NET 3.5, and Visual Studio Tools for Office applications. Depending on the products you have installed, multiple How Do I pages might be available. For example, if you wanted to know how to develop a Web site using Visual Studio, you can click Help on the menu bar, click How Do I on the How Do I in Visual Basic page, and then click a main category such as Web Applications, as shown in Figure C-8.

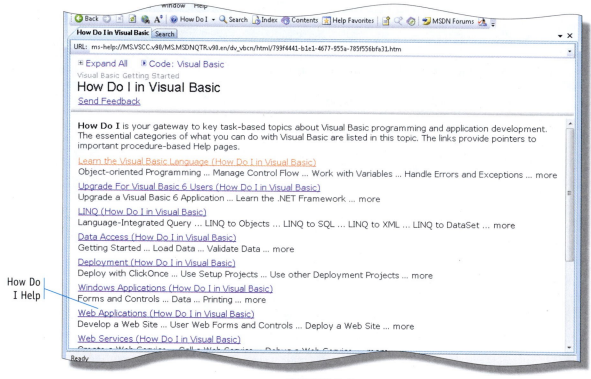

FIGURE C-8

The next Help window displays topics on items that have been updated since the last version, walkthroughs that give step-by-step instructions for common scenarios, and how-to instructions that provide detailed steps to complete a particular process. The How Do I pages are a good place to start learning about a particular feature, as shown in Figure C-9.

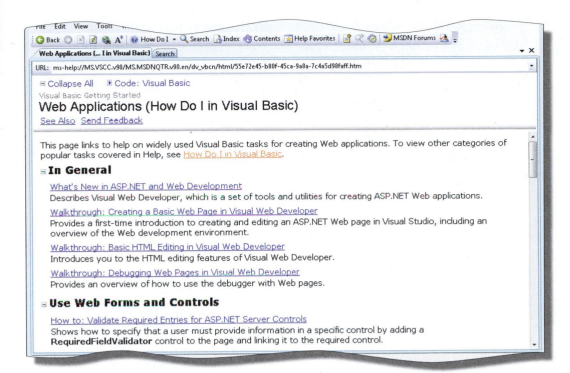

FIGURE C-9

Searching Help Topics

The Microsoft Document Explorer allows you to use the **Search** feature to locate all Help topics that contain a particular word or phrase. You can also refine and customize a search using filters, wildcard expressions using an asterisk (*), nested expressions, and logical operators. To access the Search feature, select Help on the menu bar, and then click Search. In the Search box shown in Figure C-10, type the word or phrase you want to find such as ListBox. In the filter area, specify which filters you want to search such as .NET Compact Framework, ASP.NET, or Office Development. A filter selection specifies that the information being searched is within that category.

FIGURE C-10

After you click the Search button, a results window displays links about the ListBox object to 500 local Help topics, 100 MSDN online Help topics, 100 Codezone Community topics, and Questions answered about the topics on blogs, as shown in Figure C-11. The Codezone Community consists of content from the Web sites posted by experts around the world. These independent experts on the Microsoft .NET Framework and Microsoft Visual Studio provide a wealth of knowledge to you and other developers. The Codezone Community provides a connection to individual contributors, user groups, community sites, experts, and speakers.

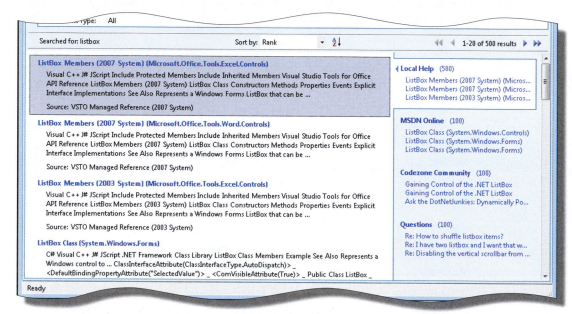

FIGURE C-11

Using the Help Table of Contents

In the **Contents** window in the Microsoft Document Explorer, you can browse an organized list of the Help articles installed on your computer and navigate to specific topics in those collections. To open the Contents window, click Help on the menu bar, and then click Contents. The left side of the Contents Help window opens with a tree view of Visual Studio topics, as shown in Figure C-12.

FIGURE C-12

To view the Contents Help article, expand a topic by clicking the plus sign next to the topic. Continue to expand topics until you reach the article of interest. After clicking the article title, the article opens in the right side of the window, as show in Figure C-13.

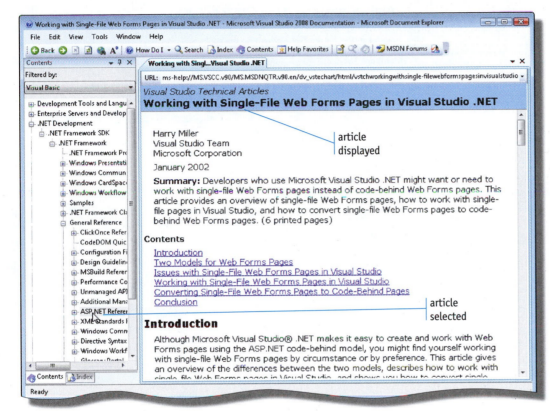

FIGURE C-13

Accessing the Help Index

The Microsoft Document Explorer also includes an **Index** Help window to assist in searching for information about coding and tools. To open the Index Help window, click Help on the menu bar, and then click Index. The left side of the window consists of the language that the help should be filtered by and a Look for box to enter the search keyword. Press ENTER to display the topic that corresponds to the keyword. In Figure C-14 on the next page, the keyword Label is entered in the Look for box.

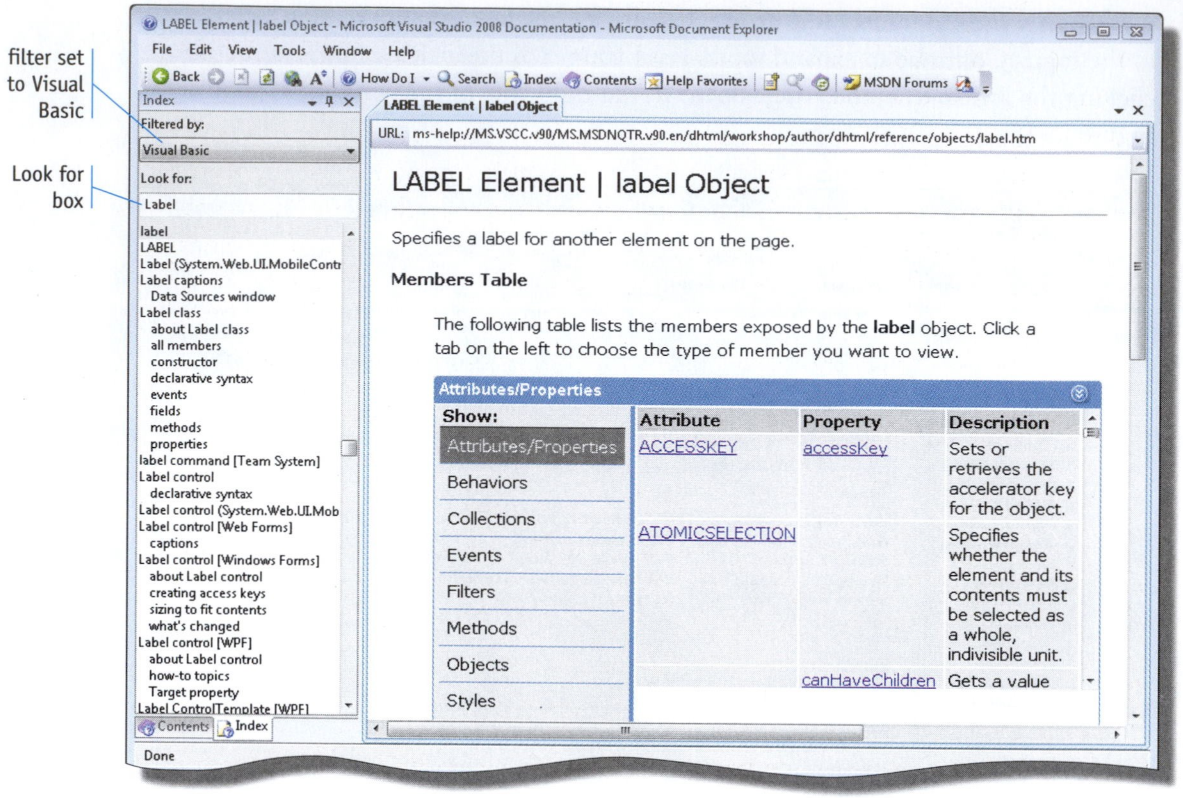

filter set
to Visual
Basic

Look for
box

FIGURE C-14

Follow these general guidelines when entering search entries:

▶ Scroll through the index entries. Not all topics are indexed the same way, and the one that could most help you might be higher or lower in the list than you expected.

▶ Omit articles such as "an" or "the" because the Index window ignores them.

▶ Reverse the order of the words you enter if you do not find the entries you expect.

▶ Use filters to decrease the number of topics in the Index Results window.

▶ Index keywords are case-sensitive. Lowercase entries appear before uppercase entries in alphabetical order.

Using the Help Favorites Window

The **Help Favorites** window in the Microsoft Document Explorer allows you to bookmark the Help topics of your choice. Use the Help Favorites window to display links to items, such as Help topics and Web pages, which contain important information you might want to read again. This window also saves search queries so you can save complex searches for future use. To access this dialog box, use the Help Favorites command on the Help menu. To create a bookmark in the Help Favorites window:

1. Open the topic or Web site that you want to add to your list of favorites.
2. On the Standard toolbar, click the Add to Help Favorites button.
3. Use the Up and Down arrow buttons to move the bookmarked topic higher or lower in the list.

For example, if you wanted to create a bookmark to the Label object topic that was found by using the Index Help window in Figure C-14, click the Add to Help Favorites button, as shown in Figure C-15.

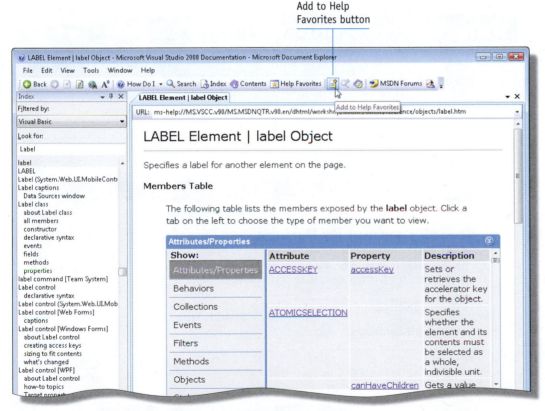

FIGURE C-15

After adding the information to the Help Favorites list, you can view the topics you saved by clicking the Help Favorites button, as shown in Figure C-16. The Help Favorites list opens on the left side of the window, displaying the Label topic that you saved as a bookmark. Creating bookmarks assists you in quickly viewing the topics needed for a particular application.

FIGURE C-16

Using MSDN Forums

Another way to access the Help topics you need is to click the **MSDN Forums** button on the Standard toolbar, as shown in Figure C-17.

FIGURE C-17

The MSDN forum displays responses to previously answered questions and also allows you to sign up to post your own question. The questions are answered by the Microsoft Community, which is a public forum where you can ask questions and get answers from other people using Microsoft products. An e-mail will be sent to you when a response is posted to your question.

Naming Conventions

The table in Figure D-1 displays the common data types used in Visual Basic 2005 with the recommended naming convention for the three-character prefix preceding variable names of the data type.

Data Type	Sample Value	Memory	Range of Values	Prefix
Integer	48	4 bytes	−2,147,483,648 to 2,147,483,647	int
Double	5.3452307	8 bytes	from negative 1.79769313486232e308 to positive 1.79769313486232e308	dbl
Decimal	3.14519	16 bytes	Decimal values that may have up to 29 significant digits	dec
Char	'?' or 'C'	2 bytes	Single character	chr
String	"The Dow is up .03%"	Depends on number of character	Letters, numbers, symbols	str
Boolean	True or False	2 bytes	True or False	bln

FIGURE D-1

The table in Figure D-2 displays the less common data types used in Visual Basic 2005 with the recommended naming convention for the three-character prefix preceding variable names of the data type

Data Type	Sample Value	Memory	Range of Values	Prefix
Byte	7	1 byte	0 to 255	byt
Date	April 22, 2008	8 bytes	Dates and times	dtm
Long	345,234,567	8 bytes	$-9,223,372,036,854,775,808$ through $+9,223,372,036,854,775,807$	lng
Object	Holds a reference	4 bytes	A memory address	obj
Short	16,567	2 bytes	$-32,786$ through 32,767	shr
Single	234,654.1246	4 bytes	$-3.4028235E+38$ through $-1.401298E-45$ for negative values and from $1.401298E-45$ through $3.4028235E+38$ for positive values	sng

FIGURE D-2

Form Object Naming Conventions

The table in Figure D-3 displays the prefix naming conventions for Form objects. The three-letter prefixes used before variables names are especially helpful when you use IntelliSense.

Object Type	Prefix	Object Type	Prefix
Button	btn	ListBox	lst
Calendar	cld	MenuStrip	mnu
CheckBox	chk	NumericUpDown	nud
ComboBox	cbo	PictureBox	pic
CompareValidator	cmv	RadioButton	rad
DataGrid	dgd	RangeValidator	rgv
DateTimePicker	dtp	RegularExpressionValidator	rev
DropDownList	ddl	RequiredFieldValidator	rfv
Form	frm	TextBox	txt
GroupBox	grp	ValidationSummary	vsm
Label	lbl		

FIGURE D-3

APPENDIX E

Using LINQ with Visual Basic 2008

Introducing Language Integrated Query (LINQ)

LINQ (Language Integrated Query, pronounced "link") is a new feature provided with Visual Basic 2008 and .NET Framework 3.5. LINQ allows you to query data with easily accessible SQL (Structured Query Language) commands within the Visual Basic code window. The addition of LINQ within Visual Studio allows database administrators to use the familiar SQL syntax within the Visual Basic programming environment. Many SQL database developers can feel comfortable using their querying skills in the Visual Studio environment. ADO.NET 3.5 supports LINQ queries to manipulate any object associated with database tables using SQL.

The example used in this appendix is the Northwind database, which is provided with the Visual Studio 2008 standard installation. The file is named Northwind.mdf. (Note that this is not the same database as the one included with Microsoft Office Access.) If you cannot find this file on your local machine or USB drive, you can download it at *http://microsoft.com/downloads*. Search for "Northwind" and download the Northwind.mdf file from the Microsoft site. The Windows application featured in this appendix uses the Northwind SQL database to display the new LINQ to SQL object features. The Northwind database contains a table named Customers, as shown in Figure E-1.

Customers table in the SQL Northwind sample database

CustomerID	CompanyName	ContactName	ContactTitle	Address	City	Region	PostalCode	Country
ALFKI	Alfreds Futterki...	Maria Anders	Sales Represent...	Obere Str. 57	Berlin		12209	Germany
ANATR	Ana Trujillo Em...	Ana Trujillo	Owner	Avda. de la Con...	México D.F.		05021	Mexico
ANTON	Antonio Moren...	Antonio Moreno	Owner	Mataderos 2312	México D.F.		05023	Mexico
AROUT	Around the Horn	Thomas Hardy	Sales Represent...	120 Hanover Sq.	London		WA1 1DP	UK
BERGS	Berglunds snab...	Christina Bergl...	Order Administ...	Berguvsvägen 8	Luleå		S-958 22	Sweden
BLAUS	Blauer See Delik...	Hanna Moos	Sales Represent...	Forsterstr. 57	Mannheim		68306	Germany
BLONP	Blondesddsl pè...	Frédérique Cite...	Marketing Man...	24, place Kléber	Strasbourg		67000	France
BOLID	Bólido Comida...	Martín Sommer	Owner	C/ Araquil, 67	Madrid		28023	Spain
BONAP	Bon app'	Laurence Lebih...	Owner	12, rue des Bou...	Marseille		13008	France
BOTTM	Bottom-Dollar ...	Elizabeth Lincoln	Accounting Ma...	23 Tsawassen B...	Tsawassen	BC	T2F 8M4	Canada
BSBEV	B's Beverages	Victoria Ashwor...	Sales Represent...	Fauntleroy Circus	London		EC2 5NT	UK
CACTU	Cactus Comida...	Patricio Simpson	Sales Agent	Cerrito 333	Buenos Aires		1010	Argentina
CENTC	Centro comerci...	Francisco Chang	Marketing Man...	Sierras de Gran...	México D.F.		05022	Mexico
CHOPS	Chop-suey Chi...	Yang Wang	Owner	Hauptstr. 29	Bern		3012	Switzerland

the Customers table has 91 rows; not all rows are displayed in this figure

FIGURE E-1

Creating a SQL query expression involves three major steps: accessing a connection to the data source, creating a query using LINQ, and executing the query displaying the requested data. You use a query to define which data you want to retrieve from a data source. In addition, you can manipulate the data by sorting, grouping, and filtering it.

When you create a query, you store it in a query variable and initialize it with a query expression. A SQL query expression has three clauses: From, Where, and Select. The "From" clause defines the data source; the "Select" clause defines what is returned; and the "Where" clause (which is optional) lets you refine a search to include only data that meets certain criteria. The general format of a SQL statement is shown in Figure E-2. This example searches the Customers table in the Northwind database for records that contain "Seattle" in the City field.

General Format: SQL Statement

```
From match In db.Customers _
Where match.City = "Seattle" _
Select match
Customers is the name of a table in the Northwind SQL database.
City is the name of a field within the Customers table.
```

FIGURE E-2

This appendix uses the LINQ commands to access data in the Northwind SQL database. Using the Customers table within Northwind, the application will determine which customers are living in the city entered by the user.

Establishing a Connection to a Database

The first step in accessing database information is to establish a connection with the database source, which is named Northwind in this example. You can create a connection by specifying a path from the Windows application to the database source. To connect to the database using the Data Source Configuration Wizard, you can complete the following steps:

STEP 1   With Visual Studio 2008 open, click the New Project button on the Standard toolbar, and then click Windows under Visual Basic in the Project types pane in the New Project dialog box. Name the project `LinqExample`, and then click the OK button. When the Windows Form object opens, name it `frmCustomer.vb`. Change the Text property to Find Customers by City. Resize the form to a size of 310,342. At the top of the form, place a Label object named `lblCity`. Change the Text property to Enter City Name:. Under the Label object, place a TextBox object named `txtCity`. Place the ListBox object named `lstNames` under the TextBox object. To complete the design of the form, place a Button object named `btnFind` under the ListBox object. Change the Text property to Find Customer(s). Center all objects horizontally on the form. Select all the objects on the form and change the Font property to Arial, size 12. Change any of the other objects on the form to match Figure E-3. Close the Toolbox. Click Data on the menu bar.

The Windows form is created and the Data menu is opened (Figure E–3).

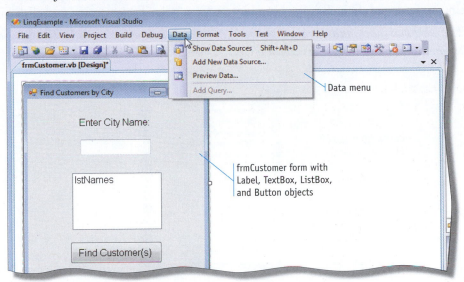

FIGURE E-3

STEP 2   Click Add New Data Source on the Data menu. In the Choose a Data
Source Type dialog box, click Database, and then click Next. Click the New Connection
button. In the Choose Data Source dialog box, under Data source, select Microsoft SQL
Server Database File, and then click the Continue button. On the Add Connection dialog box, click the Browse button, and then select the Northwind database saved on your
local machine or USB drive. Click the Open button. The Add Connection dialog box
reopens. Click the OK button in the Add Connection dialog box.

The Choose Your Data Connection dialog box reopens (Figure E–4).

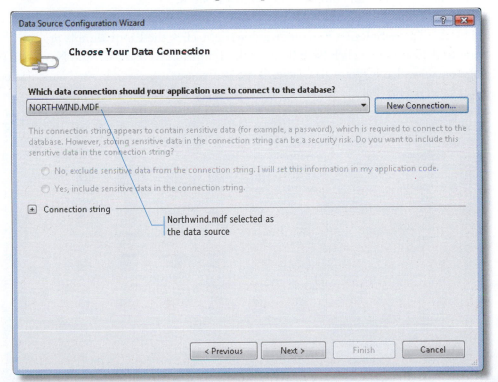

FIGURE E-4

STEP 3   Click the Next button. Click the No button to prevent a copy of the database being created, and then click the Next button. Check the Tables option and click Finish.

The dialog box closes, and a connection to the Northwind database is made. The Solution Explorer displays the DataSet named NORTHWINDDataSet.xsd (Figure E-5).

NORTHWIND Dataset is added to the program

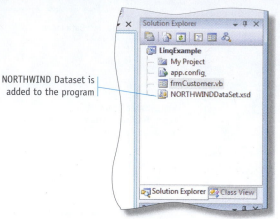

FIGURE E-5

Working with LINQ to SQL

By using LINQ to SQL, you can use the LINQ technology to access SQL databases. Using Visual Basic, you can query, insert, update, and delete information from tables. A LINQ to SQL object needs to be mapped to the database tables. The LINQ to SQL object automatically generates classes for each of the tables, which allows a developer to perform LINQ queries in the code window. To create a LINQ to SQL business object, you can complete the following steps:

STEP 1   In the Solution Explorer window, right-click the LinqExample project. Point to Add and then click New Item. In the Templates pane of the Add New Item dialog box, select LINQ to SQL Classes. Type Northwind.dbml in the Name text box.

The LINQ to SQL Classes item is selected and named Northwind.dbml (Figure E-6).

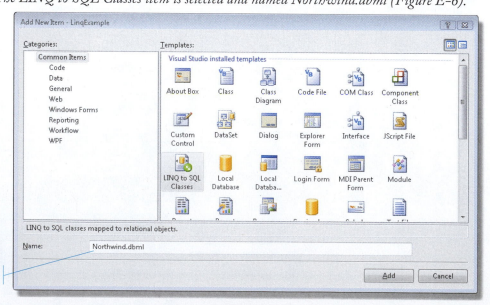

LINQ to SQL Classes item is named Northwind.dbml

FIGURE E-6

STEP 2   Click the Add button.

The Northwind.dbml LINQ to SQL classes object is added to the project (Figure E-7).

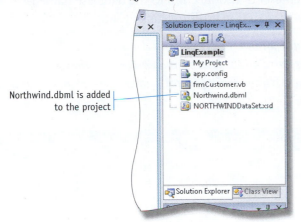

Northwind.dbml is added to the project

FIGURE E-7

STEP 3   Double-click the Northwind.dbml connection in the Solution Explorer window. The Method Pane is displayed with the tab name Northwind.dbml. Click View on the menu bar, and then click Server Explorer. In the Server Explorer pane on the left side of the window, click the plus sign to expand the Northwind database. Click the plus sign to expand Tables folder. Drag the Customers table to the Method Pane in the center of the screen.

The Customers table is placed on the Method Pane (Figure E-8).

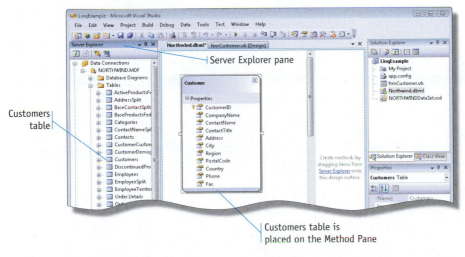

Server Explorer pane

Customers table

Customers table is placed on the Method Pane

FIGURE E-8

Coding SQL Commands Using LINQ

The purpose of the sample application is to open the Customers table in the Northwind database and to search for the city requested by the user. The name(s) of those customers residing in the matching city will be displayed in the ListBox object called lstNames. Using LINQ, you can use SQL-like commands to query the SQL database. To code using LINQ, you can complete the following steps:

STEP 1   Click the frmCustomer.vb tab. Double-click the btnFind Button object. To create a new method that represents a connection to the database named Northwind, type `Dim db as nor` in the btnFind click event.

The variable db can access any table within the Northwind database. The NorthwindDataContext object is based on the Northwind.dbml connection. IntelliSense appends the Northwind file name with the ending DataContext to create an object named NorthwindDataContext (Figure E-9).

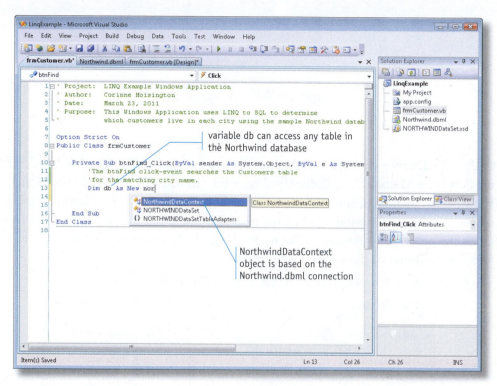

FIGURE E-9

STEP 2   Select NorthwindDataContext in the IntelliSense window and press ENTER. Type in the code shown in Figure E-10.

The LINQ code is added to the application (Figure E-10).

```
14          Dim strCity As String
15
16          strCity = Me.txtCity.Text
17          'LINQ code
18          Dim matchingCustomers = From match In db.Customers _
19                  Where match.City = strCity _
20                  Select match
```

FIGURE E-10

After the user has entered the name of the city, the text entered in the TextBox object txtCity is assigned to the variable strCity. Line 18 in Figure E-10 initializes a variable named matchingCustomers, which will be assigned to the retrieved records that match the city search string. The From statement determines which database to search. In this case, the variable db connects to the Northwind database, and db.Customers represents the connection to the Customers table within that database. The Where statement is searching for the condition where the city specified in strCity (the city name entered by the user) is equal to the City field in the Customers table. In other words, the Where statement is filtering for records that contain the city name entered by the user. The Select statement assigns the filtered rows that match the entered city name to a variable named match for retrieval later in the code.

The last section of code shown in Figure E-11 displays the names of the customers who live in the requested city. The field that is assigned to the customer name in the Customers database is called ContactName. The For Each loop displays each of the filtered rows with the matching city and displays the ContactName field. The SQL statement might match none of the records in the database, one of the records, or many of the records. In the last case, multiple customer names are displayed in the ListBox object named lstNames. The For Each loop repeats until all ContactName fields are displayed within the ListBox object.

```
21          'Display matching customers to Listbox object
22          For Each customer In matchingCustomers
23              lstNames.Items.Add(customer.ContactName)
24          Next
25
26      End Sub
27 End Class
```

FIGURE E-11

Executing the Query

As the application is executed, the user enters a city name in the TextBox object. In the example shown in Figure E-12, the user enters the city name of Sao Paulo. The user then clicks the Find Customer(s) button, and the query is executed. The LINQ code connects to the Customers table within the Northwind database and searches for records that have a City field value matching Sao Paulo. The For Each loop then displays each of the customer names found in the matching records in the ListBox object. The application displays the names of four customers who live in Sao Paulo.

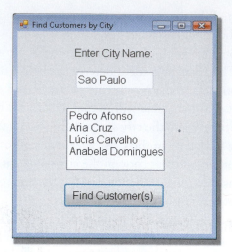

FIGURE E-12

LINQ is a significant addition to the Visual Basic 2008 environment. LINQ provides consistency by defining a set of standard query operators that work across data sources. The deep integration of LINQ into Visual Basic allows developers to be more productive, using the same commands in both the SQL and Visual Basic environments.

INDEX

PHOTO CREDITS